LANDMARKS
OF
TWENTIETH-CENTURY
DESIGN

AN ILLUSTRATED HANDBOOK

By Kathryn B. Hiesinger and George H. Marcus

Abbeville Press Publishers

New York   London   Paris

FRONT COVER: George Nelson, *Marshmallow* sofa, 1956, (no. 247);
Walter Dorwin Teague, Radio, 1934 (no. 156)
SPINE: Marco Zanini, *Alpha Centauri* vase, 1982 (no. 365)
BACK COVER: Frank Lloyd Wright, Desk and chair, 1937 (no. 163)
FRONTISPIECE: Alberto Fraser, *Nastro* Table Lamp, 1983–84 (no. 368)
PAGE 6: Gerhard Marcks, *Sintrax* coffee maker, 1925 (no. 93)

EDITOR: Constance Herndon
DESIGNER: Nai Chang
PICTURE EDITORS: Margot Clark-Junkins, Lori Hogan, Maya Kaimal, Lisa Rosen
PRODUCTION EDITORS: Robin James and Abigail Asher
PRODUCTION MANAGER: Simone René

Library of Congress Cataloging-in-Publication Data
Hiesinger, Kathryn B., 1943–
Landmarks of twentieth-century design/Kathryn B. Hiesinger; George H. Marcus.
p.   cm.
ISBN 1-55859-279-2
1. Design—history—20th century—Themes, motives. 2. Design, industrial—
history—20th century—Themes, motives. I. Marcus, George H. II. Title.
NK1390.H44 1993
745.4'442—dc20   93-180

LANDMARKS
OF
TWENTIETH-CENTURY
DESIGN

Don Gresswell Ltd., L   DG 02242/71

CONTENTS

FOREWORD

This book identifies four hundred objects as landmarks of twentieth-century design, some selected for their innovative form, material, or manufacturing technique, others for their place in the history of style, culture, or technology. The boundaries defined by these works embrace a pluralistic and sometimes chaotic culture in which competing styles have each claimed validity as "modern," some impelled by idealism and pure theory, others by commercialism and competition, and still others by nationalism. The most consistent polarities of design in the century, however, have set manifestations of technical progress against traditional craft-oriented approaches.

The visual vocabulary that characterized technology and progress for most of the century was ascetic and purist, based on clean, simple forms with bare surfaces. It flourished during the 1920s in Germany, where progressive designers developed what they considered to be the appropriate aesthetic response to industrial production, a style based on principles of economy and efficiency. In 1927 seventeen leading European architects and fifty-five interior designers created an experimental housing development and exhibition for the Deutscher Werkbund association in Stuttgart that was intended to demonstrate these new principles and techniques in domestic design. Held in the suburb of Weissenhof, this exhibition, *Die Wohnung (The Home),* was advertised by three posters: two, canceled out with thick red crosses, showed dark, ornate interiors crowded with elaborately carved furniture; the third, a photomontage of models and photographs of the new development, showed bare interiors with smooth white walls and built-in storage units. While the posters were criticized as propagandistic and misleading, they successfully distanced the new, sparse, modern spaces from the superfluity of the stuffy old-fashioned interiors; at the same time they gave stable identity to the formal austerities that came to define one of the most enduring expressions of modern design in the twentieth century.

The process of stripping away, so characteristic of this form of modernism, had begun early in the century, advanced by pioneers such as CHARLES RENNIE MACKINTOSH and JOSEF HOFFMANN, who dematerialized surfaces by painting them white and reduced furniture to simple, mathematical shapes; in the process, they legitimized abstraction as a source of new form. But Mackintosh's vision was more purely artistic and visual, while the Stuttgart program was overlaid with the utopian functionalist ambition of trying to make the home a more efficient place for domestic work.

The chief theorist of the rationalized, efficient modern interior was LE CORBUSIER, most famous of the Weissenhof architects, who in his work and writings during the 1920s promoted the "minimum dwelling," mass-produced both in its exterior fabric and interior fittings and economical in space and cost. In 1921 Le Corbusier wrote that the "house was a machine for living in,"[1] a statement often quoted and misinterpreted but intended to suggest an ideal form suitable for standardized industrial methods and clean, efficient living. As an interior designer Le Corbusier advocated open, uncluttered spaces with furnishings that resembled industrial equipment.

At the Bauhaus art and design school, WALTER GROPIUS pioneered similar ideas about standardization and rationalization, and the spare interiors he created for the cubic houses of the Bauhaus masters in Dessau (1925–26), with metal furniture by MARCEL BREUER, prefigured the houses he designed for the Weissenhof development. In *The New Architecture and the Bauhaus* (1935), Gropius wrote that standard products and buildings necessitated "the elimination of the personal content of their designers and all otherwise ungeneric or non-essential features."[2] The view of the home as a uniform mass-produced object (even though in practice these new houses had little to do with the realities of mass production) together with the aesthetic of austerity symbolized modern machine-age culture in the 1920s. The problem was that the "machine for living in" reflected an attitude toward the home that was simply too uncompromising for its inhabitants, who added their own personalizing curtains and printed wallpapers to the bare interiors. Yet it has remained powerfully influential as a measure of modernity in this century, and many of the most innovative industrial and interior designs were conceived with its aesthetic standards in mind. The opposition, which was quite vocal at the time, complained about the impersonality, the "robot modernism," of these designs from which all vestiges of the past, of locality, and of personal expression were banished. There was, moreover, considerable discussion about the failure of the new design to solve the problem of cheap housing and furnishings for the lower classes. At Weissenhof, for example, which was expensive to build, a maid's room was included in nearly every house.

Against the ambitions of the machine style to be universal and prototypical, technocratic and antihistorical, and completely of its time, other designers working in northern Europe and France stressed regional variety and individuality. In Finland, the architect ALVAR AALTO used processed wood (a modern "traditional" material) and organic rather than rectilinear forms, and made symbolic references to nature in his work. Aalto was also inspired by a strong sense of cultural and social responsibility, and he actually succeeded in designing new furniture forms for low-cost machine production. Beginning in the 1930s, Aalto and other Scandinavian designers developed a truly popularist program of design, manufacture, and marketing of quality middle-class furnishings seldom achieved by modern designers everywhere.

With no pretense to egalitarianism or interest in mass production, French luxury design in the 1920s reasserted the traditional national values of skilled handcraft for a small, privileged clientele. Designers made formal references variously to earlier French styles and to contemporary painting, producing furniture and metalwork that elegantly combined fine materials with decorative craft techniques. Displayed and publicized as showpieces in ornate interiors at the Paris *Exposition Internationale des Arts Décoratifs et Industriels Modernes* in 1925, these objects promoted surface decoration of various kinds (about which Le Corbusier complained). The taste for complex, decorated surfaces ran its course within a decade, just before the Depression and World War II halted the trade in such luxury domestic furnishings. It reappeared in Italy in the late 1970s and 1980s among the postmodern design groups Alchimia and Memphis, which used brightly colored, dense designs (some based on African textile patterns) for printed fabrics and plastic laminates. Like the French luxury goods of the 1920s, these Italian objects were largely handmade and expensive, but in diluted forms they were widely diffused through department stores.

Thus when Italian postmodernism announced itself as an antidote to the formal and theoretical austerities of rational modernism, it could hardly be said to have lacked precedents. Favoring eclecticism; historical, symbolic, and associative reference; and decoration, postmodernism allied itself long after the fact with French design of the 1920s. But it also echoed other episodes that ran counter to and concurrent with the rigorous and visually limited standards by which modern design had been defined at Weissenhof and elsewhere, in styles ranging from the floral naturalism of art nouveau at the turn of the century to Pop objects of the 1960s, which drew on popular culture as sources for their novel shapes and expressive design features.

Another "machine" style was invented in the United States in the 1920s and 1930s by the new industrial design professionals—including HENRY DREYFUSS, NORMAN BEL GEDDES, RAYMOND LOEWY, and WALTER DORWIN TEAGUE—for the unprecedented number of household appliances that entered the consumer market. Neither ascetic nor purist, these products were given the look of technology by styling that imitated the smooth windswept forms of automobiles and streamlined aircraft, a symbolic pretense that projected a forceful, popular modern image of speed and efficiency on household work. In the same way, the styling of audio equipment in the 1970s and 1980s as military or professional hardware suggested the values of quality and precision.

Alternative images of technological progress also appeared in the United States in the 1940s and 1950s, created by the architects Richard Buckminster Fuller and CHARLES EAMES, both of whom deliberately sacrificed formal purity for pragmatic, do-it-yourself approaches, Eames creating a family of quirky metal-legged chairs with plastic or plywood bodies. These rivaled the furniture designs of Le Corbusier, Breuer, and others for their wide influence and for the fact that they could be mass-produced at reasonable cost. Similarly undermining the symbolic equation between simple, precise forms and technology, Italian designers in the 1960s and 1970s combined a variety of advanced plastic materials with manual, craftlike production methods to develop elegantly novel shapes and design features for objects and furnished environments. To certain critics, however, these form-givers seemed preoccupied with style and appearance, populating the world with superfluous consumer objects. "Anti-design" groups alternatively postulated domestic environments without objects, carrying the modernist process of stripping away to its most radical conclusion.

By the late twentieth century, technology had progressed beyond any of its contemporary stylistic equations, with miniaturization, for example, rendering obsolete the traditional association of function and form in household appliances and consumer electronics. Many designers accordingly shifted their emphasis from aesthetics to technology and, in a burst of innovation, entered the "information age," where a corresponding new language of forms has yet to be defined.

ACKNOWLEDGMENTS

The initial concept of this book, along with the selection of objects for illustration, was thoughtfully reviewed by our editorial board: John Heskett, Richard Martin, Joseph Rykwert, and Kerstin Wickman. We are also grateful to our many colleagues who have offered their advice, among them Susan Brown.

No book with the encyclopaedic focus of *Landmarks of Twentieth-Century Design* could be written today without access to the United States Interlibrary Loan system and its on-line computer access. We extend our gratitude to the many librarians throughout the country who have supplied us with books and journal articles to further our study, and especially to Lilah J. Mittelstaedt at the Philadelphia Museum of Art, who has been our conduit to the riches of these libraries.

We owe a great debt to the many designers and manufacturers whose products are shown here for providing information and assistance with photographs. Particular help has been given by the following colleagues, designers, scholars, manufacturers, archivists, and publishers who have helped us in rooting out specific sources and information:

Ateliers Jean Perzel, Paris; Peter Backhausen, Joh. Backhausen & Söhne, Vienna; Andrea-Maria Barchfeld, Vereinigte Werkstätten, Munich; Judith Berman, University Museum, University of Pennsylvania, Philadelphia; Chantal Bizot, Musée des Arts Décoratifs, Paris; Robert Blaich, Philips, Eindhoven, the Netherlands; Dilys Blum, Philadelphia Museum of Art; Torsten Bröhan, Düsseldorf; Axel Bruchhäuser, Tecta, Lauenförde, Germany; François Burkhardt, Centre de Création Industrielle CCI, Centre Georges Pompidou, Paris; Ann Carter, National Museum of Science & Industry, Science Museum, London; Giulio Castelli, Kartell SpA, Noviglio, Italy; Craig Clark, April Greiman Inc., Los Angeles; Michelle L. Cotton, Corning Glass Works, Corning, New York; Michael A. Cousins, Cousins Design, New York; G. DeConinck-Van Gerwen, Koninklijke Musea voor Kunst en Geschiedenis, Brussels; Lauren C. DeAngelis, Cook and Shanosky Associates, Princeton, New Jersey; Guillemette Delaporte, Musée des Arts Décoratifs, Paris; Luc d'Iberville-Moreau, Musée des Arts Décoratifs de Montreal; Ulysses G. Dietz, Newark Museum, Newark, New Jersey; Andrea Dirscherl, Internationales Design Zentrum, Berlin; Eda Diskant, Philadelphia Museum of Art; Attilia Dorigato, Museo Vetrario di Murano, Civici Musei Veneziani d'Arte e di Storia, Venice; Leah Douglas, University of the Arts, Philadelphia; Yoshiko Ebihara, Gallery 91, New York; Marianne Ertberg, Danske Kunstindustrimuseum, Copenhagen; Claudio Fait, Ideal Standard, Milan; Ignazia Favata, Studio Joe Colombo, Milan; Linda Folland, Herman Miller Inc., Zeeland, Michigan; Saburō Funakoshi, Hoya Corporation, Tokyo; Mary Godwin, Design Museum, London; Joan Gosnell, J.C. Penney Co., Dallas; Torgeir Mjør Grimsrud, Håg, Oslo; Satu Grönstrand, Iittala Glass Museum, Iittala, Finland; David Hanks, New York; Susan M. Hare, Goldsmiths' Hall, London; Jürgen Häusser; Susan Hay, Museum of Art, Rhode Island School of Design, Providence; Christine Hopfengart, Kunstgewerbe-museum, Berlin; Nigel Hopwood, Jacob Jensen Design, Hojslev, Denmark; Terrance Keenan, Syracuse University Library, Syracuse, New York; David Kelley, Palo Alto, California; André Koch, Rijksuniversiteit Te Leiden, Leiden; Reyer Kras, Stedelijk Museum, Amsterdam; Annelies Krekel-Aalberse, Van Kempens Begeer Museum, Zoetermeer, the Netherlands; Hanna Kunz, West Chester, Pennsylvania; Yasuo Kuroki, Sony Corporation, Tokyo; Jack Lenor Larsen, New York; Esa Leskinen, Iittala Glass Museum, Iittala, Finland; Gilles Lombard-Platet, Bianchini Férier, Lyon; E. Maggini, Museo delle Porcellane di Doccia, Sesto Fiorentino, Italy; David R. McFadden, Cooper-Hewitt Museum, New York; Andreas Mikkelsen, Royal Copenhagen A/S, Copenhagen; R. Craig Miller, Denver Art Museum; Nason & Moretti s.r.l, Murano, Italy; Barbara Morris, Brighton, England; Barbara Mundt, Kunstgewerbe-museum, Berlin; Waltraud Neuwirth, Vienna; Larry Paul, Baltimore Gas & Electric Company, Baltimore; Diane Pilgrim, Cooper-Hewitt Museum, New York; Evelyne Possémé, Musée des Arts Décoratifs, Paris; Tamara Préaud, Manufacture Nationale de Sèvres, Sèvres, France; Laurent Prevost-Marcilhacy, Christie's France, Paris; Arthur Pulos, Syracuse, New York; Marja Pystynen, Artek Oy, Helsinki; Barbara Radice, Milan; Margot Raissac, Musée Bouilhet Christofle, Saint-Denis, France; Jens Risom, New Canaan, Connecticut; Wolfgang Ritschka, Galerie Metropol, New York; T. Dawn Roads, Aga-Rayburn, Ketley Telford, , England; H. Sakurai, Tendo Mokko, Tokyo; Astrid Sampe, Stockholm; Fred Sandstedt, National-museum, Stockholm; Timo Sarpaneva, Helsinki; Ella Schaap, Philadelphia Museum of Art; Mary Schoeser, London; Paul Schreckengost, Cerritos, California; Aivi Gallen-Kallela Siren; Elliot Sivowitch, National Museum of American History, Washington, D.C.; Nicky Smith, Anglepoise Lighting Limited, Redditch, England; Christien F. W. Smits, Haags Gemeentemuseum, The Hague; Jack Solomon, Circle Fine Art Corporation, Chicago; Milton Sonday, Cooper-Hewitt Museum, New York; Larry Stapleton, Technology Design, Bellevue, Washington; Hartmut Stroth, Braun AG, Kronberg im Taunus, Germany; Reiko Sudo, Nuno, Tokyo; Emilia Terragni, Studio Terragni, Como, Italy; Suzanne Tise, Paris; G. E. Viola, Istituto della Enciclopedia Italiana, Rome; Sigrid W. Weltge, Philadelphia; Bunny White, AT&T Archives, Warren, New Jersey; Hans Wichmann, Neue Sammlung, Munich; Armin Zweite, Gabriele Münter-und Johannes Eichner-Stiftung, Munich.

Chapter One
Toward Industrialization 1895–1910

No phenomenon had greater impact on the history of design than industrialization. From the mid-nineteenth century, artists, designers, and critics called for reform in the design of domestic products to counteract what they viewed as the declining aesthetic quality caused by the proliferation of machine production and commercialism. The French art critic Philippe Burty blamed the "tyranny of public taste" for the fact that machine production had to a great extent supplanted traditional hand labor and craftsmanship: "The perfection of the chisel and foundry are conditions of the craft, which have fought, often unequally, against the introduction of the machine and chemical processes,"[1] he asserted in 1866. Machine production was confronted in a number of different ways. In Great Britain, where the Industrial Revolution began, lines were drawn between reformers, like the critic John Ruskin and the Arts and Crafts Movement leader William Morris, and defenders of mechanized production, particularly within industry itself. Ruskin and his followers sweepingly condemned industry and its products while advocating the revival of the handcraft techniques, aesthetics, guild system, and even social values of a preindustrial way of life, while their opponents attempted to improve quality by capitalizing on changes in production technology and by employing trained artists as product designers.

By the late nineteenth century, even the domestic "art" industries such as furniture or glass manufacture had already become highly mechanized and their products were valued by the public and the popular press for the technical perfection that better tools and new techniques could command. Industry could and did provide furnishings in a variety of earlier stylistic forms, bringing the most refined and luxurious products of the past within reach of those with a taste for richness and ornament. The furniture trade vaunted the revival pieces as superior to original models because of the absolute precision of cabinetry that machine manufacture could achieve. Electroforming and electroplating processes developed by George Richards Elkington in England in 1840 and popularized in France by the firm of Charles Christofle similarly allowed perfect regularity in the duplication of elaborate tablewares, which were admired, not despised, as substitutes for solid silver. "In our day, art has been obliged to become industrialized," wrote one journalist in an 1868 review of Christofle's work. "Consequently, taste and luxury are now the patrimony of the classes that are the least well to do. Art loses nothing by popularizing itself in this way—it can even gain immeasurably, as it already has, by putting science to work for it."[2]

The Crystal Palace Exhibition, held in London in 1851, was the first of the "great exhibitions," which brought the arts and industries of all nations into competition with each other.

Manufacturers vied for fame and markets beginning in 1851 at a series of great international exhibitions in London (1851, 1862), Paris (1855, 1867, 1878, 1889, 1900), New York (1853), Vienna (1873), Philadelphia (1876), Chicago (1893), Turin (1902), and Saint Louis (1904), exhibitions that were critically judged and reviewed. Fired by international competition, critics advanced new principles of design aimed at improving national standards, awakening manufacturers to the importance of applying art to industry and countering threats offered to the home trades by cheaper products from abroad. Among the most forward-looking were members of the circle around Queen Victoria's consort, Prince Albert, who was responsible for the first "Great Exhibition" at London's Crystal Palace in 1851. Principal among the participants were the painter, designer, and educator Richard Redgrave as well as Henry Cole, a life-long civil servant and the first director of the South Kensington Museum, later the Victoria and Albert Museum. In the reports of the *Crystal Palace Exhibition* and in the *Journal of Design and Manufacture* (1849–52), Redgrave preached that function or use was design's primary consideration and that ornament was secondary to the object constructed: "It is impossible to examine the works of the Great Exhibition, without seeing how often utility and construction are made secondary to decoration . . . which is apt to sicken us of decoration and leads us to admire those objects of absolute utility (the machines and utensils of various kinds) where use is so paramount that ornament is repudiated, and fitness of purpose being the end sought, a noble simplicity is the result."[3] Cole put theory to practice, launching the short-lived Summerly's Art Manufactures (1847–49) in which like-minded artists of his choice, including Redgrave, designed useful wares modestly and "appropriately" decorated, which were produced by several cooperative manufacturers; the ceramics firm of Herbert Minton was among the first to be involved. Later, such progressive retail firms as Liberty's in London and Wertheim's in Berlin similarly employed artists and architects as designers to create new ranges of merchandise. Liberty's promoted the Cymric and Tudric lines of silver and pewter (no. 30), and Wertheim's sponsored a series of "modern home furnishings," which were exhibited in their stores to a broad public at the turn of the century.

While the "art" industries were aimed at a prosperous middle-class market, William Morris wanted to create well-designed and well-made products for the masses, calling for an "art of the people, by the people, and for the people."[4] A founder of English socialism, Morris intended not only to create well-designed products but to make possible a better life for the lower classes through handcraft, which he viewed as satisfying, morally uplifting, teachable, and income-producing. However, as early as 1902, even while Morris's programs were at the height of their popularity, the influential German architect and critic Hermann Muthesius attacked Morris's results. Then attached to his country's embassy in London, Muthesius pointed out that "in the end, Morris and the English artist-socialists produce such expensive things that at the very most only the upper [classes] can consider buying them."[5] This was true not only of Morris's company, which sold furniture, textiles, wallpapers, and other goods, but also of the Arts and Crafts groups and collaborative workshops that similarly focused on handcraft and proliferated in Morris's wake. In England these included the Century Guild (established by A. H. Mackmurdo in 1882) and the Guild and School of Handicraft (established by CHARLES ROBERT ASHBEE in 1888); in Austria the Wiener Werkstätte (established in 1903 by JOSEF HOFFMANN, KOLOMAN MOSER, and Fritz Wärndorfer); and in the United States the Roycroft community (established by Elbert Hubbard in 1894).

The ideas of Morris and the Arts and Crafts guildsmen as well as their style of simply expressed forms and good craftsmanship were well known to American and European craftsmen through such publications as *The Studio*, which was inaugurated in 1893, and through personal contact and exhibitions of British work abroad. Muthesius described how influential this journal was in Germany: "One day a tastefully laid-out periodical, *The Studio*, appeared, which through its reasonable price was accessible to everyone and which opened up to the Continental world the horizon onto a new art. . . . The situation changed at a stroke. No visitor to Germany can enter a store without English merchandise being praised above everything else."[6] British designers like Ashbee traveled to the United States and were also employed by important European clients. The architect M. H. Baillie Scott, for example, was commissioned in 1897 by Ernst Ludwig, grand duke of Hesse, to decorate a drawing room and a dining room in his palace in Darmstadt, for which the furnishings were executed by Ashbee's Guild of Handicraft. In 1901, Richard Graul, director of the Kunstgewerbemuseum in Leipzig, spoke of Germany's "artistic Anglomania," evident in "lighter and plainer shapes in furniture; the English style has pleaded for simplicity in the name of common sense."[7]

Not all organizations inspired by British examples adopted the Arts and Crafts principle of handwork to the letter. Munich's Vereinigte Werkstätten für Kunst im Handwerk (United Workshops for Art in Handicraft, established 1897) successfully produced popular "middle-class" designs by both handcraft and machine techniques and made no particular distinction between them. GUSTAV STICKLEY, founder of the United Crafts (later Craftsman) Workshops in Eastwood, New York, in 1900, similarly depended on mechanization to turn out his products in large numbers, noting in 1906 that "in this day of well-nigh perfect machinery [to say] that anything to be good must be done entirely by hand is going rather far. There are certain purely mechanical processes that can be accomplished much better and more economically by machinery."[8] Even such an early pioneer of the English Arts and Crafts Movement as Ashbee gradually lost faith in the need to emulate traditional techniques and in handcraft per se, writing in 1911 that "modern civilization rests on machinery and no system for the endowment, or the encouragement, or the teaching of art can be sound that does not recognize this."[9] Two vociferously influential designers on opposite

Cabinet by Philip Webb, with painted decoration by Sir Edward Burne-Jones, 1861. Made by Morris, Marshall, Faulkner and Company. Painted wood and leather. Height: 73" (185.4 cm). (Metropolitan Museum of Art, New York, Rogers Fund.) William Morris turned to the medieval period for its sturdy forms, structural honesty, and decorative details

sides of the Atlantic also proclaimed the importance of the machine, although neither put theory into practice to any particular extent. In an article in *Pan* in 1897, the Belgian designer HENRY VAN DE VELDE declared his ambition of "systematically avoiding designing anything that cannot be mass-produced. My ideal would be to have my projects executed a thousand times."[10] The American architect FRANK LLOYD WRIGHT in his manifesto "The Art and Craft of the Machine" (1901) demonstrated that Morris's desire for simple forms could best be achieved by a machine if it were properly "instructed" by a sympathetic designer:

> The tyros are taught in the name of John Ruskin and William Morris to shun and despise the essential tool of their age as a matter commercial and antagonistic to Art. . . . But, I say, usurped by Greed and deserted by its natural interpreter, the Artist, the Machine is only the creature, not the creator of this iniquity! I say the Machine has noble possibilities unwillingly forced to this degradation, degraded by the Arts themselves. . . . I will show you . . . that the Machine is, to begin with, a marvellous simplifier in no merely negative sense.[11]

The aesthetic of design reform had been defined by Redgrave and others since the mid-nineteenth century as one of "simplicity." What gave the neo-Gothic style of William Morris and the rural vernacular of the Arts and Crafts Movement so much moral weight was its use of plain sturdy forms, its claim to structural honesty, and its austere application of the color and ornament that the mid-nineteenth century had discovered in other historical styles. However, by the turn of the century, historicism of almost any kind was being discredited by design reformers in Europe and America, who called for a new style that expressed their own time. From Vienna, where the architect OTTO WAGNER proclaimed that architecture should orient itself to "modern life," to Paris, where the art dealer Siegfried Bing opened the international gallery L'Art Nouveau in 1895 and showed innovative

Casa Mila by Antoní Gaudí, Barcelona, 1910–1912.

designs unhampered by imitation and tradition, to Brussels, where van de Velde sought "to work out the foundations on which to build a new style,"[12] reformist designers endeavored to break with the past and create an original language of forms that would have validity in the modern world. It was this attitude, almost more than the specific responses to it, that defined modern design around the turn of the century and differed so radically with what had preceded it.

The most characteristic and influential of the new styles was known as art nouveau in France, from the name of Bing's shop and the progressive work shown there. This included interiors and furniture by van de Velde, glass by the American LOUIS COMFORT TIFFANY, glass and furniture by EMILE GALLÉ, and jewelry by RENÉ LALIQUE, all created with highly ornate and curvilinear forms largely derived from nature. The ornamental use of curving lines in the "new art" was further distinguished by the critic Julius Meier-Graefe into "floral" and "linear" idioms, with Gallé identified as chief protagonist of those designers who found inspiration in nature, specifically in plants, and van de Velde as protagonist of a decorative vocabulary based on "abstract line."[13] In Germany, the style was referred to as Jugendstil from the magazine *Jugend* (*Youth*), which was founded in Munich in 1896; in Italy it was known as Stile Liberty, or Floreale, after the firm Liberty's, which marketed fabrics and other objects in this floral style (no. 3). Art nouveau was an international style shown in its richest array at the *Exposition Universelle* in Paris in 1900, and popularized by the illustrations and typography in art and literary magazines, which sprang up everywhere in the 1890s, including *La Revue Blanche* in Paris (founded in 1891), *Van Nu en Straks* in Brussels (1892), *The Chap-Book* (no. 6) in Chicago (1894), *Dekorative Kunst* in Munich (1897), and *Mir Iskusstva* in Saint Petersburg (1899).

In Austria, the new style of reform was called Secession (Sezessionstil) after the radical exhibition society founded in Vienna in 1897 by Hoffmann, Moser, JOSEPH MARIA OLBRICH, and others; unlike art nouveau it abandoned curves for simple abstract geometric shapes and ornament, and frequently reduced color to white and black or gray. This style developed partly under the influence of a small group of artists working in Glasgow led by CHARLES RENNIE MACKINTOSH and known widely in Europe through publication of their work and their appearance at the Secession exhibition in Vienna in 1900. The Wiener Werkstätte popularized the Secession style in the furniture, metalwork (nos. 31, 36), graphics (no. 33), bookbinding, textiles, and glass it produced with the cooperation of such progressive Viennese manufacturers as Jacob & Josef Kohn (no. 43), Gebrüder Thonet, E. Bakolowitz, and Johann Backhausen. Both art nouveau and Secession designers conceived of total artistic environments in which architecture, interior design, and furnishings would be united in their decorative treatment: the most typical forum was residential, whether an apartment building like HECTOR GUIMARD's Castel Béranger in Paris of 1894–98 (nos. 7, 8) or Hoffmann's Palais Stoclet, a large villa outside Brussels begun in 1905 and entirely furnished with objects by

Siegfried Bing's Paris shop, L'Art Nouveau, shown here in 1900, gave its name to the art nouveau movement.

Palais Stoclet, by Joseph Hoffmann, Brussels, 1905–11. This influential house was furnished completely by the Wiener Werkstätte..

the Wiener Werkstätte. There were parallels between the work of the Secession designers and Frank Lloyd Wright, who shared their penchant for rectilinearity and calculated simplicity as well as for interrelating the fittings of a building with its structure (nos. 13, 26).

Associated with the domestic interior and its furnishings and embracing both fine art and design, examples of art nouveau and Secession began to appear in exhibitions usually reserved for painting and sculpture: in France, the Société Nationale des Beaux-Arts admitted applied arts for the first time in 1891 as did the international art exhibition held in Munich's Glaspalast in 1897. The exhibitions of the Société des Artistes-Décorateurs (founded 1901) and the Société du Salon d'Automne (founded 1903) provided important sources of information about new French designs after the turn of the century. By 1910, however, art nouveau had largely run its course, victimized, according to many contemporary critics, by its own immense popularity and by the large numbers of poorly crafted products made in its name. The willful artfulness and ornamentalism of art nouveau were also faulted by those who continued to seek virtue in simplicity. The clean forms and geometric aspects of the Secession style, however, insured its survival into the next decades.

While a number of the less expensive objects made for the Wiener Werkstätte involved machine processes, the designers associated with the workshops made no real attempts to come to grips with industrial production. Like others inspired by Morris, Ruskin, and the Arts and Crafts Movement in England, they continued to associate quality with hand labor and craftsmanship. In Germany, however, then the world's fastest-growing industrial nation, design reform became inextricably linked after the turn of the century with machine production. The chief theorist of this movement was Hermann Muthesius,[14] and the designers largely responsible for its success were RICHARD RIEMERSCHMID and PETER BEHRENS. Between 1904 and 1906 for the Dresdner Werkstätten für Handwerkskunst (Dresden Workshops for

Handicraft Art, established 1898), Riemerschmid developed a pioneering program of machine-made furniture (*Maschinenmöbel*) available in ready-made suites at reasonable prices (no. 38), which one contemporary critic described as "artistic machine furniture."[15] In 1908 the designer Bruno Paul introduced a similar program, *Typenmöbel*, or standard furniture, for the Vereinigte Werkstätten in Munich. Subscribing to the reform virtues of plainness, practicality, and comfort, these furniture series married the two opposing viewpoints of the nineteenth century—those of art and industry. Using standardized and simplified wooden shapes, serially made but assembled and finished by hand, they could be manufactured relatively cheaply by machine in large quantities while maintaining a certain individuality for the consumer. Even more revolutionary was Peter Behrens's total program for the Allgemeine Elektricitäts-Gesellschaft (AEG) from 1907, which imposed one aesthetic on all aspects of the activities of the German electric company, creating a broad range of architecture, graphic (no. 45), and product designs. The company's electrical appliances were mass-produced, truly the products of industry although sometimes, as in his series of electric kettles (no. 46), Behrens used mechanical means to imitate handcraft techniques; he also pioneered a system of standardization and interchangeability of parts that would later serve Germany's efforts to regulate technical measurements on a national basis.

In 1907 both Behrens and Riemerschmid became founding members of the Deutscher Werkbund, an organization of designers and manufacturers dedicated to improving the design and quality of German consumer goods. Muthesius, often cited as the father of the Werkbund, introduced many of the themes that were subsequently incorporated into the Werkbund program: the aesthetic ideals of "honesty, integrity and simplicity"; the virtues of quality and good taste; the idea of appealing to "manufacturers to adopt the so-called new manner instead of continuing to make reproductions"; and, finally, the patriotic goal of enhancing Germany's reputation on the world market.[16] Between 1908 and World War I, the Werkbund developed a national organization with both individual and corporate members and a broad public relations program aimed at consumer education and the reform of product design. In an effort to win over consumers, producers, and artists to simply designed high-quality goods and to the possibilities of machine production, the Werkbund sponsored such projects as the founding of an applied arts museum in Hagen (1909); competitions and a school for display art in Berlin (1910); several exhibitions; and, most importantly, the restructuring of art schools and the revision of professional standards for architects. For Muthesius, the Werkbund gave proof that Germany, capable of tapping its remarkable strength and energy, had gained a leading position in the field of design, even supplanting England "where the foundations for a thorough reorganization of the industrial arts had been laid."[17]

1
HENRY VAN DE VELDE
Chair, c. 1895

This chair was originally designed for the dining room of Bloemenwerf, the house Henry van de Velde built for himself at Uccle, near Brussels, and furnished entirely with objects after his own designs (1894–95). Van de Velde credited the influence of John Ruskin and William Morris for his conversion from painting to decorative arts and architecture, and like Morris's own Red House in Kent, Bloemenwerf was the artist's first important exercise in these fields. Inspired as well by the work of other English craftsmen such as Ernest Gimson and C.F.A. VOYSEY, the house included chaste interiors with white walls and clean-lined "cottage" furniture that, like this chair, echoed English rustic designs of the eighteenth century. Published immediately and widely, Bloemenwerf was also visited in 1895 by the art dealer Siegfried Bing, who commissioned van de Velde to design model rooms and to provide versions of the Bloemenwerf furniture, including this chair, for Bing's new shop, L'Art Nouveau, which was to open in Paris in December of that year. While the style of the chair had recognizable roots in the rural vernacular, its boldly springing curves announced van de Velde's modern ideas of a "new art," which the exhibition in Bing's gallery did much to publicize. It was later put into commercial production by the Société Van de Velde, a decorating firm and factory founded by the artist in 1898.

Oak and rush. 37 1/16 x 17 7/16 x 15 1/2" (94.1 x 44.3 x 39.4 cm). (Museum of Modern Art, New York, purchase.)

2
HERMANN OBRIST
Cyclamen wall hanging, c. 1895

One of the earliest expressions of Jugendstil, this celebrated silk embroidery was first exhibited in Munich in April 1896 and afterward in Berlin and London along with some thirty-five others designed by Hermann Obrist. Titled *Cyclamen*, it soon became known as the *Whiplash* after a contemporary description by the poet and critic Georg Fuchs, who recognized in its stylized plant form Obrist's expressive power as well as the source of a new German style. "This racing movement seems to us like the abrupt, powerful convolution of the whiplash," he wrote. "Here we find for the first time the surfaces of a utilitarian object adorned with artistic creations that were neither copied from old forms nor influenced by the English, French, or Japanese."[18] *The Studio* reviewed Obrist's London exhibition and described the embroideries as not only startingly original but also "things to live with . . . to hang on our walls, to lay on our floors, to cover our chairs and tables with, things which can never tyrannise and never become indifferent. The power and movement of the lines cannot but stimulate our energies in a thousand ways."[19]

Made by Berthe Ruchet. Wool and silk. 47 x 72 1/4" (119 x 183 cm). (Stadtmuseum, Munich.)

3
C.F.A. VOYSEY
Fabric, c. 1897

Around 1883, while awaiting building commissions, the young English architect C.F.A. Voysey began to create ornamental designs, selling them first to the wallpaper manufacturer Jeffrey and Company and then to other wallpaper, textile, and carpet firms as well. Voysey's earliest work was inspired by the dense naturalism of William Morris, but the originality of his own approach lay in his translation of such natural forms into flat surface patterns executed in brighter colors than Morris normally used. "To go to Nature is, of course, to approach the fountain-head," he explained, "but a literal transcript will not result in good ornament; before a living plant a man must go through an elaborate process of selection and analysis, and think of the balance, repetition, and many other qualities of his design, thereby calling his individual taste into play and adding a human interest to his work."[20] Voysey's recasting of nature is seen in this fabric, in which three types of tulips and three kinds of leaves sprout from one serpentine stem in a calculated rhythmical arrangement set against a dark red ground. Voysey's designs were often produced virtually unchanged in different mediums by different companies. This pattern, here a roller-printed velveteen made by Baker for Liberty's, was repeated by Baker in cotton and linen; by Essex &

Company as a wallpaper called *The Nure* (1899); and by Alexander Morton & Company as a leno weave.

Made by G. P. and J. Baker, London, for Liberty & Company, London. Printed velveteen. Width: 33¹/₁₆" (84 cm). (Württembergisches Landesmuseum, Stuttgart.)

4
EMILE BERLINER
Model B **gramophone, c. 1896**

Using flat discs instead of the cylinders that Thomas Alva Edison's phonograph required for sound reproduction, the German-born Emile Berliner introduced the first version of his gramophone in Philadelphia in 1888. Because the discs produced better sound and could be economically duplicated commercially (but, unlike cylinders, could not be recorded at home), Berliner's firm opened its own sound studios to manufacture discs for his machines, recording performances of the most popular musicians of his day and initiating a highly successful recording industry. With its shiny brass horn and its plain wooden box, which encloses a clockwork motor turned by a vertical crank, Berliner's *Model B* gramophone subscribes to no particular decorative style but is simply a wondrous instrument that brought music into the home. Gramophone technology hardly changed over the next decade, although the designs became decidedly more baroque, sporting colored horns in flower forms and cases carved in a variety of ornamental styles. None, however, can surpass the fame of this early model, designed about 1896. It is this instrument that enthralled the little dog Nipper with his master's voice on the trademark of Berliner's successor, the Victor Talking Machine Company, founded by Eldridge Johnson about 1900, which continued to manufacture and market this model internationally.

Made by Eldridge Johnson, Camden, New Jersey. Oak, brass, and metal. Height: 15¹/₂" (39.4 cm). (Daniel Marty, Agora d'Evry, France.)

5
LOUIS COMFORT TIFFANY
Peacock vase, 1893–96

The spectacular glass of Louis Comfort Tiffany, with its
fluid shapes, brilliant coloring, and sinuous ornamentation, became America's great contribution to the international art nouveau style. It was lavishly praised in
1898 by Siegfried Bing, proprietor of the Paris shop
L'Art Nouveau, especially for its decoration, which was
not applied to the finished form but integrated into the
molten glass during the manufacturing process itself.
Bing, who was Tiffany's distributor abroad, considered
his peacock-feather decorations to be his most impressive accomplishment, a tour de force of the glassblow-
er's skill. He described Tiffany's success in learning to
achieve these effects after a year of "feverish activity":

> Never, perhaps, has any man carried to greater per-
> fection the art of faithfully rendering Nature in her
> most seductive aspects. . . . This power which the
> artist possesses of assigning in advance to each
> morsel of glass, whatever its colour or chemical
> composition, the exact place which it is to occupy
> when the article leaves the glassblower's hands—
> this truly unique art is combined in these peacocks'
> feathers with the charm of iridescence which bathes
> the subtle and velvety ornamentation with an
> almost supernatural light.[21]

*Made by Tiffany Glass and Decorating Company, New York.
Colored glass. Height: 14 1/8" (35.9 cm). (Metropolitan
Museum of Art, New York, gift of H. O. Havemeyer,
1896.)*

6
WILL H. BRADLEY
Poster for *The Chap-Book*, 1895

Reverberations of European art nouveau were quickly
felt in America as designers responded to the stylized
illustrations they found in the latest magazines from
abroad. America's foremost interpreter of this new
graphic mode was Will H. Bradley, a self-taught designer and illustrator, who was inspired particularly by the
tortuous lines, dense ornament, and flat patterns of the
English artist Aubrey Beardsley. The covers and posters
he created in 1894–95 for *The Inland Printer, Harper's
Bazar*, and the Chicago literary magazine *The Chap-
Book*, and from 1896 for his own magazine *Bradley: His
Book*, married bold and expressive calligraphic images
with original hand-drawn letterforms (several of which
were acquired by type founders for use as metal type).
He treated his lettering in unconventional ways, overlapped by the illustration, as it is here, or rigorously
organized into blocks without regard for standard
typographic rules. Fostered primarily by commissions
from publishers, modern posters such as Bradley's proliferated during the mid-1890s in America and were
collected and exhibited as a distinct art form. Shown in
Chicago the month it was published, this advertisement
for the Thanksgiving 1895 issue of *The Chap-Book* was
exhibited the next year in Richmond and Philadelphia,
and in a retrospective of posters in the French city of
Reims.

*Published by Stone and Kimball, Chicago. Lithograph. 20 3/4 x
18 7/8" (52.8 x 35.2 cm). (Newberry Library, Chicago.)*

7
HECTOR GUIMARD
Wallpaper, c. 1898

This wallpaper was designed for the vestibule of
Hector Guimard's first major building in Paris, the
Castel Béranger on the rue La Fontaine (1894–98).
The young and practically unknown architect was given
carte blanche to design not only the structure of the
apartment house but also its interior fittings, from furniture and hardware to stained-glass windows, carpets,
and wallpapers. It was Guimard's commitment to total
interior design, based on the example set by the
Belgian architect Victor Horta, that impressed contemporary critics. The main entrance gate in wrought iron
and copper was shaped as an ogival arch bent back on
itself like a hairpin, and these lines were repeated
throughout the building—in this wallpaper pattern and
the carpet that matched it, as well as the iron banisters
and papier-mâché ceiling decorations. This ornament
was the first sign of the innovative art nouveau style for
which Guimard would later be known and which one
confounded critic was forced to recognize as having
"the elements of a new aesthetic" even as he protest-
ed its "bizarre combinations of lines and colors."[22]

Made by Le Mardelé, Paris. Printed paper. 11 1/8 x 19 5/8"
(102 x 50 cm). (Bibliothèque Fomey, Paris.)

8
HECTOR GUIMARD
Desk, c. 1898

As the first manifestation of his mature style, the Castel
Béranger apartment house in Paris clearly meant a
great deal to Hector Guimard. Here he located his
own studio, furnished with such pieces as this desk
with an asymmetrical top and irregularly shaped framed
panels that announced the abstract idiom of Guimard's

art nouveau. While one critic questioned Guimard's "obvious horror of simplicity and the straight line" and ridiculed his promotion of what he called the "Style Guimard,"[23] the architect maintained that his style met the needs of a new age and that it had been uniquely derived from science and nature. Claiming "logic, harmony, and sentiment" as the principles upon which his style was based,[24] Guimard demonstrated the rationalism of his theories here by combining the desk's opulent art nouveau curves with a clean unencumbered silhouette.

Olive and ash. 28 3/4 x 101 x 47 3/4" (73 x 256.5 x 121.3 cm). (Museum of Modern Art, New York, gift of Mme. Guimard.)

9
CHARLES RENNIE MACKINTOSH
Poster for *The Scottish Musical Review*, 1896

Illustrated in 1897 in the widely circulated art magazine *The Studio*, this poster and the other works published there first achieved an international reputation for a group of Glasgow artists led by Charles Rennie

Mackintosh. Still at the beginning of the architectural career for which he was later known, Mackintosh here displays the tendency toward abstraction and tense linear pattern that came to define his work around the turn of the century. The mannered graphic style of overelongated figures, stylized gestures, symbols, and self-conscious Celtic rhythms employed by Mackintosh and his circle so annoyed their English contemporaries that they were dubbed "the spook school" when they exhibited at the London Arts and Crafts exhibition in 1896. *The Studio* came to their defense. "It must never be forgotten," wrote Gleeson White, the magazine's editor,

> that the purpose of a poster is to attract notice, and the mildest eccentricity would not be out of place provided it aroused curiosity and so riveted the attention of passers-by. Mr. Mackintosh's posters may be somewhat trying to the average person. . . . But there is so much decorative method in his perversion of humanity, that despite all the ridicule and abuse it has excited, after long intimacy it is possible to defend his treatment . . .

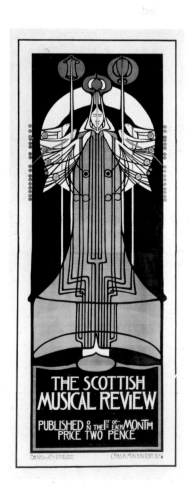

for when a man has something to say and knows how to say it the conversion of others is usually but a question of time.[25]

Printed by Banks & Company, Edinburgh and Glasgow. Lithograph. 97 x 40" (246 x 101.5 cm). (Museum of Modern Art, New York, acquired by exchange.)

10
CHARLES RENNIE MACKINTOSH
Chair, 1896–97

The first in a series of highly individual high-back chairs designed by Charles Rennie Mackintosh, this piece was created for the Argyle Street Tea Rooms in Glasgow, where it was used in the Luncheon Room. The Tea Rooms, designed by Mackintosh in 1896–97, were the largest and most important of his early commissions and combined both architectural and furniture design. All of the Argyle Street furniture was made of broad oak planks and distinguished by rectilinear, boxy shapes and bold, simple outlines. This chair, however, with its exaggeratedly high back and oval back rail, is unlike the other furniture there; its height served no practical function but became an architectural element emphasizing the long narrow space in which it stood. In 1900 Mackintosh used the chair in his own apartment at 120 Mains Street, Glasgow, and in an interior presented in Vienna at the eighth exhibition of the Secession. While Mackintosh's work was already known internationally from articles in *The Studio* (1897) and *Dekorative Kunst* (1898), it was this exhibition that introduced him to the group of young Viennese designers, including JOSEF

HOFFMANN and KOLOMAN MOSER, who would adapt his ideas to the geometric idiom they developed in the years that followed.

Oak with horsehair upholstery over rush. 53⅞ x 19⅞ x 18¼" (136.8 x 50.5 x 46.2 cm). (Philadelphia Museum of Art, purchased: Fiske Kimball Fund and Thomas Skelton Harrison Fund.)

11
PETER BEHRENS
Glass service, 1898

Devoid of any decorative elements, these gracefully curved glasses were designed for inexpensive mass manufacture. They were among the first examples of applied art designed by Peter Behrens and prophetic of his standardized product designs for the giant electric concern AEG, where he served as artistic adviser from 1907 to 1914. The glasses were first displayed as part of the artist's dining-room ensemble in the Munich Glaspalast exhibition of 1899, where they stood in the greatest conceivable contrast to the elaborately ornamented table glasses then in common use. In reviewing the exhibition, the critic Julius Meier-Graefe recognized the innovative aspects of Behrens's display as a "new way" in design: "Striking is the moderate use of decoration, just enough to be complete. . . . The glasses as well as the china are calm and simple in shape, a happy idea that one increasingly comes to appreciate."[26]

Made by Benedikt von Poschinger, Oberzwieselau, Germany. Clear blown glass. Height of champagne glass: 8¼" (21 cm). (Prof. Dr. Tilmann Buddensieg, Sinzig, Germany.)

12
JURRIAAN JURRIAAN KOK
Tea service, 1900

One of the most original and exotic manifestations of the art nouveau style was created at the Rozenburg porcelain factory in the Netherlands, where Theodorus A. C. Colenbrander, Rozenburg's first artistic director, applied the abstract ornamental style of Javanese batik-printed textiles to ceramics. While commercial relations had existed between Holland and Indonesia since the seventeenth century, it was in the later nineteenth century that Dutch interest in the arts and crafts of the colony peaked: museums were founded, societies organized, and exhibitions and lectures held to educate the Dutch public. One of Java's oldest art forms, batik typically displayed flat, complicated, outlined designs that Colenbrander freely translated into ceramic decorations. When Jurriaan Jurriaan Kok began to direct the factory in 1894 he introduced more recognizable naturalistic motifs into the Rozenburg repertory. But the influence of the batik designs persisted, as can be seen in the decoration of this tea service, which sets a parrot against a finely painted jungle of textilelike geometric and floral patterns. Under Kok's direction in 1899, the factory started production of the extremely thin and translucent "egg shell" porcelain. This ceramic body was particularly suited to the sharp, angular profiles and attenuated handles and finials of services such as this, which became a specialty of the firm. The following year, Rozenburg showed "egg shell" porcelains like this at the *Exposition Universelle* in Paris, where critics unanimously acclaimed the firm's remarkable achievement.

Made by Koninklijke Porselein-en Aardewerkfabriek
Rozenburg, The Hague. Soft-paste porcelain with enamel

decoration. Height of teapot: 7 1/2" (19 cm). (Philadelphia Museum of Art, purchased: Fiske and Marie Kimball Fund.)

13
FRANK LLOYD WRIGHT
Dining table and chairs, 1899–1900

With his dining room for the Joseph W. Husser house in Chicago, Frank Lloyd Wright established the pattern of high-back slatted chairs and large tables with thick, overhanging tops and massive legs that he continued to use in furnishing his Prairie houses throughout the

ensuing decade. The tall, slightly curved Tusser chairs, with gently flaring legs and square spindles that extend almost to the floor, are exaggerated in scale like those of CHARLES RENNIE MACKINTOSH (no. 10). They were not designed as individual components but as part of a total unit: the twenty-four chairs and three tables formed a regular, rhythmical pattern of geometrical shapes, with the slatted bases on the table ends completing the composition. The furniture also related to the interior decoration of the paneled room, the thin molding around the legs of the tables and chairs lining up with the baseboard and the checkerboard carving on the edges of the tables repeating the ornament of the woodwork.

Probably made by John W. Ayers, Chicago. Oak with leather upholstery. Table: 28 x 54 x 60" (71.2 x 137.2 x 152.4 cm); chairs: 51⅛ x 17¼ x 17¼" (131.8 x 43.8 x 43.8 cm). (Domino Center for Architecture and Design, Ann Arbor, Michigan.)

14
LOUIS MAJORELLE
Dressing table, c. 1900

By 1900 Louis Majorelle had become the main producer of art nouveau furniture in France, and his display at the Paris *Exposition Universelle* that year, where this dressing table was shown, was considered the very best of his work. His bedroom, dining room, and library furniture earned him the warm admiration of critics, who described the cabinetmaker as "a prodigiously imaginative artist and perhaps the most extraordinary virtuoso of our time in his chosen field."[27] Although Majorelle had been designing furniture in art nouveau styles for less than a decade, one critic in 1900 already spoke of the phenomenon of "*majorelisme*, an industry offering for sale furniture in which everything is taken from M. Majorelle, except his talent."[28] Like those of EMILE GALLÉ and the other artists who worked in Nancy, Majorelle's forms and their decorations were inspired by nature. The entire suite of bedroom furniture was designed around the theme of orchids, from the structural members, modeled naturalistically as orchid leaves dividing and as flowers bursting from their stalks, to the inlays in the figurative marquetry panels, spangled with mother-of-pearl and edged with tendrils of pewter, to the drawer handles cast in gilded bronze. This realistic interpretation of nature distinguished artists in Nancy from their counterparts in Paris and elsewhere, who, avoiding floral marquetries and such literal decorative themes, created a version of art nouveau that was more abstract.

Walnut inlaid with amaranth and thuya, pewter, and mother-of-pearl, and gilded bronze. Length 96" (243.8 cm). (Benedict Silverman Collection, New York.)

15
RICHARD RIEMERSCHMID
Chair, 1898–99

In 1898 the Vereinigte Werkstätten für Kunst im Handwerk was commissioned by J. Mayer & Company, a Munich piano manufacturer, to provide a music room "in plain but modern shape" for the Dresden and Paris international exhibitions of 1899 and 1900. Richard Riemerschmid, a cofounder of the Vereinigte Werkstätten, designed the interior and its furnishings for the firm, including a musicians' platform and an alcove with seating. With its striking diagonal side strut connecting front feet to back rail, which functioned as both a structural and decorative element, this musician's chair remains Riemerschmid's most celebrated work. Its combination of utilitarian simplicity and gracefully curved forms was also a characteristic example of Jugendstil design. Originally produced as model number 4059 by the Vereinigte Werkstätten, it became widely known through the edition made by Liberty and Company in London shortly after 1900, and continues in production today.

Made by Vereinigte Werkstätten für Kunst im Handwerk, Munich. Oak with leather upholstery. 30³/₄ x 18⁷/₈ x 22¹/₂" (78 x 48 x 57.2 cm). (Philadelphia Museum of Art, purchased: Fiske Kimball Fund.)

16
RICHARD RIEMERSCHMID
Cutlery, 1899–1900

Richard Riemerschmid's distinctive silver table service was shown at the Munich Secession exhibition of 1899 where it was praised as the "first attempt to reform cutlery" with new shapes "as practical as they are original."[29] Slightly revised for the Paris *Exposition Universelle* of 1900, the cutlery had little of the fluid elegance typical of tablewares at the turn of the century. With the exception of the knife handle, which is strengthened at back by a deep round curve, the forms of the twelve-piece service are simple in profile, their handles shaped into nearly straight lines and ninety-degree angles. The aggressively pointed edges of the scimitar-like blades and the tines particularly impressed contemporary critics, one remarking that Riemerschmid had "at last reintroduced cutlery of character"[30] into modern tablewares.

Made by Vereinigte Werkstätten für Kunst im Handwerk, Munich. Silver. Length of knife: 9³/₈" (23.8 cm). (Württembergisches Landesmuseum, Stuttgart.)

18
ANTONÍ GAUDÍ
Armchair, 1898–1900

This armchair was one of a group of furnishings designed by Antoní Gaudí for the Casa Calvet, a large apartment house with offices located on the Calle Caspe in Barcelona. The building was commissioned by the widow and sons of the Catalan textile magnate Pedro Mártir Calvet. The textile business's offices and its fabric warehouse occupied the ground and basement floors while apartments were situated on the upper floors. Gaudí's earlier furniture for the Calvet family apartments was, like his architecture, highly personal yet historical in style. But the furniture he created for the Calvet offices, such as this armchair, broke radically with traditional concepts, boldly defying symmetry and introducing a new sculptural quality into turn-of-the-century design. The brutal bonelike elements and grasping scrolls at the ends of this chair's arms convey an expressive force quite beyond the more conventionally organic designs of Gaudí's contemporaries and extend the boundaries of art nouveau toward expressionism.

Oak. Height: 37³/₄" (96 cm). (Location unknown.)

17
HENRY VAN DE VELDE
Candelabrum, c. 1899

Unlike many art nouveau designers, particularly those in France, Henry van de Velde reached beyond the direct imitation of nature to exploit the dynamic and abstract possibilities of line, which he saw as nature's essence, arguing in one of his many essays on design that "a line is a force" and as such should be the basis of the "new" ornament.[31] This candelabrum was first shown in Munich in 1899 and the next year in Brussels at the seventh Salon de la Libre Esthétique. One reviewer described it as a splendid composition, recognizing the artist's "rational and ingenious theory about the direction of lines": "M. van de Velde translates into knowingly arranged curves the rhythms he has captured in the lines of the branches," wrote Octave Maus, "constantly simplifying his design in order to further concentrate its expression."[32]

Silver-plated bronze. Height: 23" (58.7 cm); diameter: 20" (51.2 cm). (Musées Royaux d'Art et d'Histoire, Brussels.)

19

LOUIS COMFORT TIFFANY
Screen, 1900

Created for the *Exposition Universelle* in Paris in 1900, where it stood at the entrance to the United States pavilion, Louis Comfort Tiffany's freestanding dining-room screen echoed the spectacular leaded-glass windows his firm had installed throughout America during the previous two decades. The vivid composition creates the illusion of a view over a trellised parapet at sunset. The bronze frame forms the architectural elements and the lead not only outlines the climbing vines luxuriant with wisteria, gourds, and grapes, but also becomes the sinuous stems of the vines themselves. In a studio booklet from 1896, Tiffany described the leaded "favrile" glass used here and elsewhere: "In range, depth and brilliancy of color it has never been equaled, and when we employ it in window work the greatest care is exercised in selecting the piece in order that we may attain the desired effect both in color and texture. . . . All our windows are built in accordance

with the mosaic theory, without the intervention of paint, stains, or enamels."[33] "Favrile," Tiffany's trademark, was concocted from "fabrile," a word referring to the handwork of a craftsman.

Made by Tiffany Studios, New York. Leaded opalescent glass and bronze. 70 3/8 x 88 3/4" (178.7 x 225.6 cm). (Lillian Nassau Ltd., New York.)

20

GRUEBY FAIENCE COMPANY
Vase, c. 1900

Boston's Grueby pottery was introduced abroad in 1900 at the *Exposition Universelle* in Paris, where medals were awarded to the firm's presentation, its "enamel" (the term then used for opaque glaze), and its designer George Prentice Kendrick. Grueby was one of the few American potteries to receive international recognition, and its products were collected, as was this vase, by foreign museums. The factory's founder, William H. Grueby, developed the novel dense, tactile, matte green glaze that became synonymous with his

that never repeats itself, that has in each vase some new message of beauty."[35] This insistence on individuality—the company's campaign to distinguish itself from ordinary commercial industries—belies the fact that by 1900, when this large vase was shown in Paris at the *Exposition Universelle*, Rookwood was turning out over 10,000 pieces annually. While each was hand painted and thus unique, their shapes were established and the decoration fell into eight specific types—this vase belonging to the Standard line, which according to the catalog was "noted for its low tones, usually yellow, red and brown in color, with flower decoration, characterized by a luxuriant painting in warm colors under a brilliant glaze."[36] However, the many painters who worked in the decorating studio created distinct images and styles that reappeared on their products in a series of themes and variations. The beautifully painted, tactile yellow-pink roses on the front of this vase and the thorny stems and leaves on the back reveal the freely naturalistic style of its Japanese decorator, Kataro Shirayamadani, one of Rookwood's finest painters who, except for a period of ten years, worked for the factory from 1887 until his death in 1948.

Earthenware with underglaze decoration. Height: 17 3/8"
(44.1 cm); diameter: 11 1/2" (29.2 cm). (Philadelphia
Museum of Art, gift of John T. Morris.)

name, while Kendrick, a director of the company from its incorporation in 1897 to about 1901, was generally responsible for the design of vases during the period. The subtle patterns in low relief that decorate Grueby wares, here a measured leaf-and-bud design highlighted with touches of intense yellow glaze, were fashioned of thin clay ropes—hand applied by the young women the factory employed as decorators—and flattened into the body of the hand-thrown forms. Purchased in 1900 from Siegfried Bing's Paris shop, L'Art Nouveau, this understated vase subscribes more to the Arts and Crafts precept of simplicity than to the florid style now associated with the shop's name although this distinction was not made at the time. In fact Bing's wares represented a variety of styles intended to express "the refinement of taste and a charm of simple beauty"[34] in even the most modest object.

Glazed stoneware. Height: 11 1/4" (28.6 cm); diameter: 5 1/4"
(13.3 cm). (Danske Kunstindustrimuseum, Copenhagen.)

21
ROOKWOOD POTTERY
Vase, 1900

"Whatever of artistic satisfaction lies in Rookwood," claimed the Cincinnati pottery's 1904 catalog, "is due first to the individuality of its artists, to their freedom of expression in the ever-changing language of an art

22
AKSELI GALLEN-KALLELA
Flame rug, 1900

A strong movement toward cultural nationalism emerged in Finnish literature, history, and art in the late nineteenth century, a fascination that stressed a romantic involvement with nature and the historic past. This movement was led among others by the painter and designer Akseli Gallen-Kallela, who built himself a log studio in the wilderness and looked to his country's folk art for artistic inspiration. His frescoes depicting the national epic, the *Kalevala*, adorned the Finnish pavilion which ELIEL SAARINEN's firm designed at the *Exposition Universelle* in Paris in 1900, and his *Flame* rug, a revival of the *ryijy*, or pile, technique, was exhibited there also. Woven by Suomen Käsityön Ystävät (Friends of Finnish Handicraft), which itself had been organized in 1879 for the purpose of keeping the textile traditions of Finland alive, the rug transformed flat, angular folk patterns into a more fluid, asymmetrical flame design in red, blue, and natural white, later woven in other variations. *Ryijy* rugs were typically used as bed or bench covers; in Paris the *Flame* rug was shown covering a bench and extending onto the floor under a table. It was one of sixteen pieces of furniture, rugs, and textiles designed by Gallen-Kallela for the display of the progressive Iris factory in Porvoo, founded with his encouragement in 1897 by his Swedish friend Louis Sparre to manufacture well-designed domestic furnishings.

Made by Suomen Käsityön Ystävät, Helsinki. Wool. 120 x 67³/4" (305 x 172 cm). (Gallen-Kallela Museum, Espoo, Finland.)

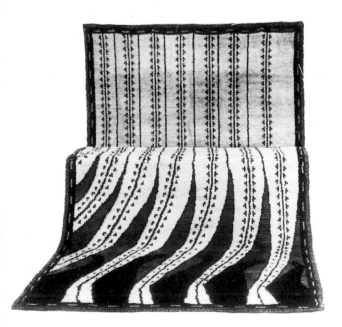

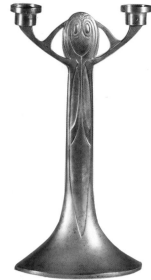

23
JOSEPH MARIA OLBRICH
Candelabrum, c. 1901

With its rigorous symmetry and redoubled linear ornament, this curiously anthropomorphic candelabrum typifies the avant-garde Secession style of geometric forms and decoration that Joseph Maria Olbrich brought from Vienna to Darmstadt when he was called as an architect to the artists' colony established there in 1899 by Grand Duke Ernst Ludwig of Hesse. His work at the colony included the design of most of the buildings as well as such furnishings as this candelabrum, which was also sold among other "modern decorative arts" by the Darmstadt store of Karl Rittershaus. Olbrich designed several different candelabra, produced in silver and decorated with colorful semiprecious stones that further embellished the metal surfaces. His work at Darmstadt, from the stenciled squares of his interior decorations to his ornamental metalwares, was highly influential, finding a widely imitative audience in Germany through the portfolios published in 1904 on his architecture and design, which included this candelabrum.

Made by Edvard Hueck, Lüdenscheid, Germany. Silvered pewter. Height: 14" (36.4 cm). (Badisches Landesmuseum, Karlsruhe, Germany.)

24
CARLO BUGATTI
Chair, 1902

The most eclectic and eccentric of turn-of-the-century designers, Carlo Bugatti showed a large quantity of his furniture at the *Esposizione Internazionale* in Turin in 1902, both individual pieces in an exotic, vaguely Moorish style and those in room settings, which were distinctly original and organic in conception. One room was described as reminiscent, within and without, of a snail: entering through a low arched door, visitors followed a spiral ramp to a circular sitting room hung with great ornamented discs and furnished with banquettes, a couch that ended in a large snail head, and several of these chairs. Reflecting the dominant spiral motif in its curved structure and circular seat and back, the sand-colored chair also reflects Bugatti's preference for unusual materials: here, wood covered with painted parchment (held in place by a glue of his own invention), which masks structural joints and creates a smooth flowing surface. Faced by the "doubt and uncertainty" of visitors to this presentation, the critic Vittorio Pica offered this rejoinder:

> Let the Philistines say what they want! This furniture of Bugatti is beautiful and imposing. It is neither connected with nor inspired by any precedent, but is the immediate reward of the truth that is to be found in nature. The room is transformed into the interior of a house touched by the fairies, or that of a king of the Orient or the Sun. . . . It has a beautiful atmosphere that is both superhuman and paradoxical.[37]

Wood covered with painted parchment, and copper. 35 × 16 1/2 × 21" (88.9 × 41.8 × 53.3 cm). (Virginia Museum of Fine Arts, Richmond, purchased, the Sydney and Frances Lewis Art Nouveau Fund.)

25
THORVALD BINDESBØLL
Dish, 1901

Thorvald Bindesbøll's work expressed a completely independent vision from that of other turn-of-the-century designers. While at first he looked to nature and the ornamental designs of the East for inspiration like others of his generation, many of the pieces he completed toward the end of his career anticipated the freely conceived abstraction of later periods. Abruptly cropped patterns, insistent calligraphy, and bold contrasts establish the individuality of this large black-and-white plate, its motifs painted in slip and then outlined in sgraffito technique. In this forceful design there is little indication of the plant forms with which he had decorated ceramics for the same factory in previous decades. Bindesbøll was equally creative in other mediums, especially silver and textiles; indeed when various aspects of his work were shown in Paris at the *Exposition Universelle* in 1900, Julius Meier-Graefe, owner of the shop La Maison Moderne, compared him to Henry van de Velde in his taste for abstraction and individualism.[38]

Made by Københavns Lervarefabrik, Copenhagen. Glazed earthenware. Diameter: 17 3/4" (45 cm). (Danske Kunstindustrimuseum, Copenhagen.)

26
FRANK LLOYD WRIGHT
Table lamp, 1903

In his essay "In the Cause of Architecture," Frank Lloyd Wright laid out his concept of "organic integrity," explaining how "the formal elements of design" of each of his buildings were derived from "one basic idea." The "grammar" of the design, he said, "may be deduced from some plant form that has appealed to me, as certain properties in line and form of the sumach were used in the Lawrence house at Springfield [Illinois]; but in every case the motif is adhered to throughout so that it is not too much to say that each building aesthetically is cut from one piece of goods and consistently hangs together with an integrity impossible otherwise."[39] The house Wright built between 1902 and 1904 for Susan Lawrence Dana was in fact one of the first in which he was able to express a complete programmatic concept. The theme of sumac and other fall flowers was followed on several levels: naturalistically, in a painted frieze decorating the dining room; conventionally, in the ornamental glass windows and lamps; and implicitly, in the autumnal colors of the rugs, textiles, and warm oak furniture that completed the interior. In this massive bronze and leaded-glass table lamp, the sumac has been abstracted into the simple, chevroned motif that appears on the ends of the shade, echoing versions in varying complexity that appear in leaded glass throughout the house. Art glass for the Dana house was provided by Chicago's Linden Glass Company, which proudly advertised, in the issue of *The Architectural Record* where Wright's essay was published, that it had made the glass for this residence.

Made by Linden Glass Company, Chicago. Bronze and leaded glass. 23¹/₄ x 32 x 19" (59 x 81.3 x 48.3 cm). (Dana-Thomas House Foundation, Springfield, Illinois.)

27
CHARLES RENNIE MACKINTOSH
Cabinet, 1902

One of the most spectacular of Charles Rennie Mackintosh's designs, this cabinet combines the white paint and colored glass that the artist had used in the furnishings of the white-painted rooms of his own Glasgow apartment at 120 Mains Street in 1900. While the designers M. H. Baillie Scott and George Walton had both advocated the use of white for painted furniture, Mackintosh's examples and his designs for a competition sponsored by the German magazine *Zeitschrift für Innendekoration* (1901) received particular publicity in art periodicals and contributed much to his fame as a designer as well as to the vogue for white interiors. This cabinet was one of a pair designed for a Mrs. Rowat at 14 Kingsborough Gardens in Glasgow. The silvered inner doors are decorated in inlaid colored glass, each door with the flat, attenuated, apparently weightless, curved figure of a girl. These mannered figures recall the symbolist style of Mackintosh's earliest graphic designs (no. 9), a style also practiced by the painter Margaret Macdonald, who married Mackintosh in 1900 and who is thought to have contributed to his use of such "spiritual" images during this period.

Painted oak, silver leaf, and colored glass. 60⁵/₈ x 39 x 15⁵/₈" (154.3 x 99.3 x 39.7 cm). (Hunterian Art Gallery, University of Glasgow.)

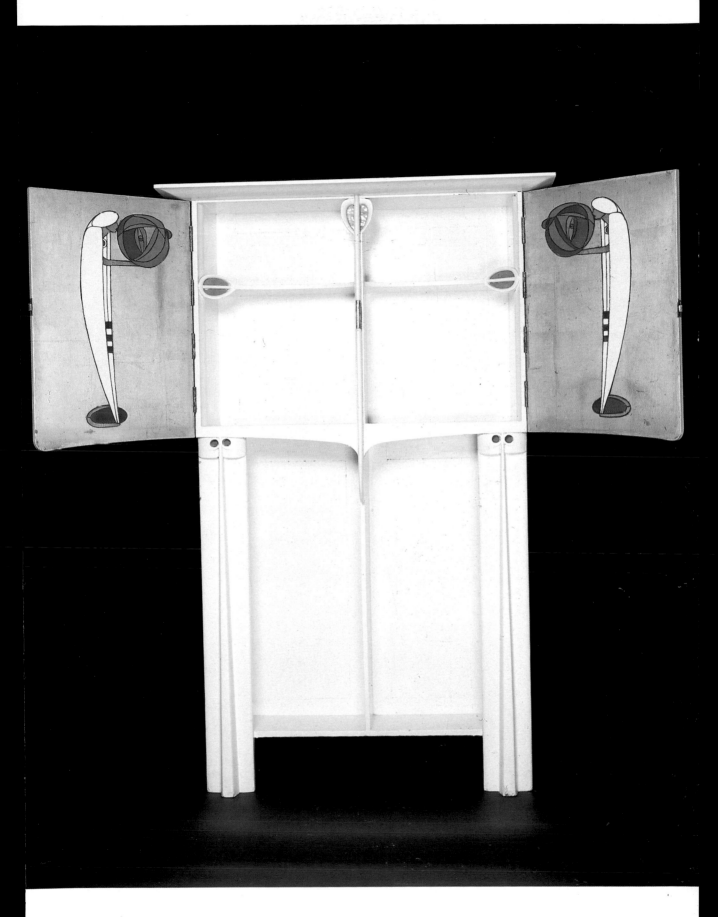

28
CHARLES ROBERT ASHBEE
Jam or butter dish, 1901

This jam or butter dish was one of the most elaborate of several loop-handled dishes designed by Charles Robert Ashbee around the turn of the century. The silver dishes were made by hand with single and double handles, sometimes with covers, and were variously decorated with enamels and colored gemstones. More than any other product of the Guild of Handicraft, which Ashbee founded in London in 1888, Ashbee's metalwork brought him international recognition and was widely imitated. From the Wiener Werkstätte in Vienna to Chicago's Kalo Shops (founded in 1900), the city's largest producer of Arts and Crafts silver, Ashbee's emphasis on the metal itself and on traditional methods of working the material in simple shapes with plain surfaces inspired new "English" standards of craftsmanship. At the same time, these expensively produced craft works were forced to compete—often unsuccessfully—with those made by large industrial firms whose products imitated qualities of handcraftsmanship by mechanical means.

Made by Guild of Handicraft, London. Silver and chrysoprase. Height: 2³/₈" (6 cm); diameter: 4¹/₂" (11.5 cm); width: 12" (30.5 cm). (Kurland/Zabar, New York.)

29
GUSTAV STICKLEY
Sideboard, 1902

Save for his use of machinery, Gustav Stickley was devoted in his application of English Arts and Crafts principles to the furniture he designed and manufactured in the immensely popular Craftsman or Mission style. Following William Morris, Stickley expounded simplicity and utility while eschewing any ornamentation that did not derive from the structure or materials of his furniture, and insisted on the highest standards for the products made at his Craftsman Workshops. This monumental sideboard, which was designed for Stickley's own dining room, is simple in profile and straightforward in construction: the natural graining of the light quartersawn oak, Stickley's favorite wood, is its only surface decoration, and the hardware of hammered wrought iron is the only applied element. The sideboard was illustrated by Samuel Howe in *The Craftsman* along with his expressive appreciation of Stickley's house: "When I enter I note a rich grandeur in the passion for size, scale and sense of bigness. How soothing—wistful—simple, is this house. The quiet sense of humanity pervades it. The soul of the workman is manifest in his work."[40]

Made by Craftsman Workshops, Eastwood (Syracuse), New York. Oak and iron. 44¹/₂ x 120³/₄ x 24³/₄" (113 x 306.7 x 62.9 cm). (Private collection.)

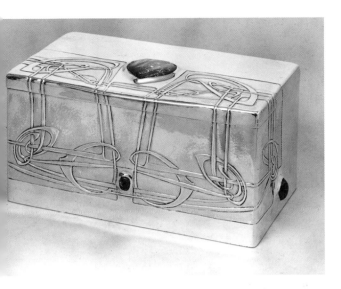

30
ARCHIBALD KNOX
Casket, 1903–4

This casket belongs to the remarkable range of original silverwork and jewelry sponsored by Arthur Lasenby Liberty, founder of the Regent Street firm that bears his name, which grew into one of Britain's great department stores. Unlike most other merchants, Liberty aimed "to educate public taste, not follow ephemeral fashions,"[41] introducing Japanese, Indian, Aesthetic Movement, and art nouveau designs by such progressive artists as Archibald Knox, C.F.A. VOYSEY, and Arthur Silver. Although his firm was from its foundation more closely associated with fabrics than with any other product, Liberty turned his attention to metalwork in 1899, commissioning silverwares exhibited under the title Cymric, or Welsh, and forging an association with the Birmingham firm of W. H. Haseler, which was to make the Liberty Cymric wares as well as a line of Tudric pewter. Around this same time Knox began to work for Liberty's, becoming the firm's most prolific designer of silver and jewelry, although he also designed carpets and textiles. The nationalistic Celtic theme of Liberty's silver was particularly suited to Knox, a native of the Isle of Man. The intricate interlacing ornament in the Celtic manner that he designed for this box and other Cymric wares was intended to rival the swirling forms associated with continental art nouveau. The Cymric line was designed for mass production, despite the use of semiprecious stones, such as the opal matrix here, which had to be inserted individually in the silver. One of the Cymric stock designs, this casket was originally owned by Liberty himself.

Made by W. H. Haseler, Birmingham, for Liberty and Company, London. Silver, wood, and opal matrix. Length: 8 1/2" (21.6 cm). (Victoria and Albert Museum, London.)

31
JOSEF HOFFMANN
Cutlery, c. 1903–4

This cutlery was the first designed by Josef Hoffmann for the Wiener Werkstätte and all three founding members of the Werkstätte—Hoffmann, KOLOMAN MOSER, and Fritz Wärndorfer—ordered it for their personal use. Available in silver, plated silver, and gilded silver, the cutlery was first publicly displayed in Vienna at the *Gedeckte Tisch* (*Dining Table*) exhibition of the Wiener Werkstätte in 1906, where critics found its smooth, broad surfaces and regular geometric shapes, devoid of ornament save for the row of round beads at the end of the handles, a sacrifice of utility to style. The newspaper *Hamburger Fremdenblatt* described the service as "uncomfortable" and "suggestive of anatomical instruments"[42] while the *Deutsche Zeitung* complained that Hoffmann made "geometry, not art" and prophesied that his geometric style was doomed to popular failure "for practical considerations."[43] While this model, listed as the *Flaches Modell* (*Flat Model*) and numbering thirty-three different pieces, did in fact enjoy only a limited production run (it was largely produced between 1904 and 1908), the style it advanced survived in many other forms.

Made by Wiener Werkstätte, Vienna. Silver. Length of fish fork: 7" (19.2 cm). (Virginia Museum of Fine Arts, Richmond.)

initially with figurative arts and architecture and later with applied arts and interior design, members of the Secession created an original new Viennese "modern" style of abstract, decorative forms that broke with the past. The Secession's journal, *Ver Sacrum*, and its commercial graphics, including calendars, postcards, and posters, publicized the group's aesthetic ideas and themes. This, the last and most advanced of five posters Alfred Roller designed for the Secession, demonstrates the stylized linearity that preoccupied most of the Secession artists. Here the subject of the poster is the lettering itself, with the *S* letterforms of the title arbitrarily distorted vertically into long curves and set against a small repeated geometric pattern resembling a printed textile or wallpaper. The letters at the bottom of the poster, different in shape from the title, are set within rigid rectangles and contribute to the overall sense of decorative geometricity that was the most influential aspect of Viennese design at the turn of the century.

32
TIFFANY AND COMPANY
Vase, c. 1900

In the 1890s the New York silversmith Tiffany and Company turned from its earlier romanticized decorations based on Native American subjects to a more ethnographic approach, creating a number of metal vessels inspired by Native American basketry, which was among the Indian artifacts then being acquired by museums and collectors; serious interest was heightened by the landmark study *Indian Basketry* (1901) by G. W. James. Several vases, including this copper piece, were exhibited at the *Exposition Universelle* in Paris in 1900, and it was shown again at the *Pan-American Exhibition* in Buffalo the following year. The vase suggests the form of a Native American basket, possibly from northern California, while the silver and turquoise decoration borrows familiar Indian motifs but combines them in new arrangements.

Copper, silver, and turquoise. Height: 7 1/2" (19 cm). (High Museum of Art, Atlanta, Virginia Carroll Crawford Collection.)

33
ALFRED ROLLER
Poster for Sixteenth Vienna Secession Exhibition, 1903

In 1897 a group of artists in Vienna led by the painter Gustav Klimt seceded from the conservative Wiener Künstlerhaus (Vienna House of Artists) and established a new exhibition society, the Vereinigung Bildender Künstler Österreichs (Association of Austrian Artists), known generally as the Vienna Secession. Concerned

Printed by Albert Berger, Vienna. Lithograph. 62³/₈ x 25"
(188.9 x 63.5 cm). (Merrill C. Berman, New York.)

34
HECTOR GUIMARD
Jardiniere, 1902–3

This vase, created by Hector Guimard for the French national porcelain manufactory, reflects Sèvres's efforts to modernize its production by using progressive artists. The ancient factory, restructured in 1891, enlisted not only Guimard but also the sculptors Joseph Chéret and Agathon Léonard to design new models in art nouveau styles. The jardiniere was the last, largest, and most spectacular of Guimard's three designs for the company. The surfaces of all three vases are richly decorated with delicate iridescent crystals—an effect well known at Sèvres before 1900 but first deliberately exploited around the turn of the century on the new stoneware body (*grès cérame*) out of which this jar-

diniere is made. The forms and decorations of Sèvres's art nouveau ceramics were widely imitated, particularly in the United States by such designers as Artus van Briggle and Taxile Doat, the latter a Sèvres decorator who founded a pottery in University City, Missouri, in 1910, which specialized in crystalline glazes.

Made by Manufacture Nationale de Sèvres, Sèvres, France. Glazed stoneware. Height: 51⁵/₈" (131 cm); diameter: 17³/₄" (45 cm). (Manufacture Nationale de Sèvres, Sèvres, France.)

35
GEORG JENSEN
***Blossom* teapot, c. 1904–5**

The *Blossom* teapot, which Georg Jensen designed about 1904–5, was the first silver hollowware he created for sale alongside his art nouveau jewelry in the shop he opened in Copenhagen in 1904. The teapot was raised by hand into its distinctive bulbous shape, with the cast feet and soldered seed balls applied separately along with the hand-wrought naturalistic squash-blossom finials from which the service takes its name. To achieve the particular matte finish that became identified with Jensen silver, the surface was coated with a film of platinum and then polished with pumice. The coffeepot, creamer, and sugar bowl that completed the service were probably added in 1906, while the matching cutlery did not enter production until 1919. In 1905 this *Blossom* teapot was acquired by the Kunstindustrimuseum in Copenhagen, and it was among the first of Jensen's silver to be exhibited abroad, at the Folkwang Museum in Hagen, Germany, the same year.

Made by Georg Jensen Sølvsmedie, Copenhagen. Silver and ivory. Height: 5³/₄" (14.6 cm). (Danske Kunstindustrimuseum, Copenhagen.)

36
KOLOMAN MOSER OR JOSEF HOFFMANN
Plant stand, 1903–4

With the visionary appearance of a miniature sky-scraper, this tall metal plant stand furnished the first reception-showroom of the Wiener Werkstätte in Vienna, which opened its new quarters on Neu-stiftgasse in October 1903. The stand is the most imposing of a large series of metalwares with similar perforated decoration made by the workshop and numbered among its first products. Both Koloman Moser and Josef Hoffmann provided designs for these semi-industrial wares, which were intended for modest households and marketed alongside the Werkstätte's handcrafted objects, although more expensive versions of certain designs were also produced in silver. These perforated wares were made from prefabricated metal sheets, which the young company purchased from out-side distributors and then formed into shape and fin-ished in their own workshops; after about 1910 most of the perforated articles were actually produced on consignment outside the Wiener Werkstätte.

Made by the Wiener Werkstätte, Vienna. Painted metal. 62 1/2 x 22 x 22" (158.8 x 55.9 x 55.9 cm). (Catherine Woodard and Nelson Blitz, Jr., New York.)

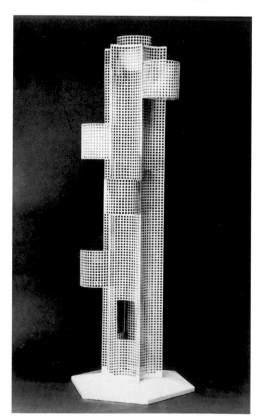

37
OTTO WAGNER
Armchair, 1905–6

This chair was designed for the boardroom of the Österreichische Postsparkasse (Imperial Austrian Postal Savings Bank) in Vienna, one of Otto Wagner's most important buildings (1904–6; 1910–12). It was pro-duced commercially afterward in several variations by Jacob & Josef Kohn and the rival firm of Gebrüder Thonet, which had also manufactured furnishings for the savings bank. Widely considered the father of Viennese art reform, Wagner was a highly influential architect, designer, and teacher, advocating the rational use of new materials and methods of construction to create an original "modern" style. Although the general form of this chair is borrowed from an armchair of about 1900 by the head of Kohn's design department, Gustav Siegel, Wagner reframed it in a more rectilinear fashion, adding horizontal splats between the back stiles and a squared-off ring stretcher for stability as well as ornamentation. In addition, Wagner fitted the feet of the chair with large aluminum sabots or shoes and applied aluminum strips to the armrests to further protect and decorate it, thereby making the first use of aluminum as a furniture component in Austria. Wagner used aluminum throughout the Postsparkasse, most notably on the facade where large aluminum bolts visi-bly secured the sheets of marble cladding to the rein-forced concrete frame.

Made by Jacob & Josef Kohn, Vienna. Beechwood, laminated wood, and aluminum. 30⅝ x 21¾ x 22" (78 x 55.5 x 56 cm). (Victoria and Albert Museum, London.)

38
RICHARD RIEMERSCHMID
Desk, 1905

This desk belongs to an extensive program of machine-made furniture (*Maschinenmöbel*) designed by Richard Riemerschmid for the Dresdner Werkstätten für Handwerkskunst (Dresden Workshops for Handicraft Art) and first exhibited in Dresden in 1906. The program was considered revolutionary by contemporary critics, who admired the unexpected "artistry" and "noble simplicity" of the furniture. Made serially by machine and finished by hand, it was characterized by well-proportioned forms, clear structure, bare ornament, and modest prices.[44] The program was developed in three price ranges, each consisting of living room, bedroom, and kitchen furniture, with the most expensive also including furniture for a dining room and a gentleman's study. This desk was designed to furnish the gentleman's room, together with a desk chair, two side chairs, a bookcase, and a sofa. While the complete upper range sold for 2,600 marks and was aimed at an upper-middle-class market, the most affordable line in the *Maschinenmöbel* program was easily within reach of the ordinary German buyer at 570 marks. Affordable and well designed, Riemerschmid's ready-made furniture had a decisive influence on German design in the period before World War I. Its popular success, which evaded Riemerschmid's contemporaries in Britain, heralded the rise of modern mass-produced furniture.

Made by Dresdner Werkstätten für Handwerkskunst, Dresden. Oak and iron. 30 x 55 x 27½" (76 x 140 x 70 cm). (K. Barlow and A. Widmann, London.)

39

EMILE GALLÉ
Dawn and Dusk bed, 1904

Most celebrated of all Emile Gallé's furniture, his *Dawn and Dusk (Aube et Crépuscule)* bed was one of four pieces commissioned by the magistrate Henri Hirsch, who was an equally important collector of Gallé's glasswares. Described by Gallé as the "furniture with sleeping butterflies" and the "miraculous bed," it was first shown at the *Exposition d'Art Décoratif* in Nancy in October 1904, three weeks after Gallé's death. Like the glass for which he had long been renowned (no. 40), Gallé's furniture was invariably decorated with natural motifs, the marquetry veneers and incrustations carefully chosen, as he described in an article in 1900,[45] to suggest the forms and textures of the plants and animals depicted. Here, the opulently applied glass and mother-of-pearl in the bodies and wings of the insects suggest the thin shell-like skin of the exoskeletons, and the alternating pattern of light and dark woods invokes the distinctive markings of the wings. A self-proclaimed symbolist who often inscribed the verses of symbolist poets on his works, Gallé almost certainly intended the butterfly as an allegorical reference to Pysche, the mythical mortal united in perpetual and blissful marriage to the god Cupid, whose name in Greek denotes both a butterfly and the soul. The bed was, in fact, part of the furniture made for Hirsch's 1903 marriage. Gallé gave Hirsch as a wedding present a footed glass similarly decorated with cicadas and the words "their hearts beat in unison."

Rosewood inlaid with ebony, mother-of-pearl, and glass.
Height: 56¼" (143 cm); length: 85¾" (218 cm).
(Musée de l'Ecole de Nancy, Nancy, France.)

40
EMILE GALLÉ
Dragonfly coupe, 1903

Emile Gallé was the most important and original artist-glassmaker of his time and his works were eagerly bought by collectors and public institutions. No other glassmaker commanded Gallé's sheer technical virtuosity: he employed a wide variety of decorative techniques—flashing and clouding colors; exploiting air bubbles, crazing, and other "imperfections" in the glass; acid etching; wheel engraving; and enamel painting. In 1898 he patented two processes, both of which are employed in this *Dragonfly* (*Libellule*) coupe. In the first process, patina, Gallé utilized wood or coal ashes to create coloristic and textural effects on and under the vessel surfaces, as in the mottled wings of the dragonfly; in the second process, marquetry, he inserted shaped and sometimes previously decorated color glass fragments into and onto the hot glass body. Gallé wrote eloquently of his technical achievements, explaining that "had [I] limited myself to the application of ready-made decorations conceived for other materials, [I would never have succeeded in] opening up to modern French crystal the doors of the museums and those of the no-less-lofty private collections. . . . Insofar as I can, from the start I impose upon the changeable and changing material at my disposal the qualities I should like it to have . . . in order to incarnate my dream, my design."[46]

Colored glass, blown, cut, and engraved, interior marquetry and metal foil, patina, and applied marquetry decoration. Height: 7³/₁₆" (18.3 cm); diameter: 7³/₄" (19.7 cm). (Corning Museum of Glass, Corning, New York, and private collection.)

41
TIFFANY STUDIOS
Cobweb lamp, c. 1904

Louis Comfort Tiffany's glowing leaded-glass lamps, introduced in 1899, were practical adaptations of his famous decorative windows, scaled-down works that put to economical use the smaller remnants of colored glass that remained from window production. Because its shade was combined with a glass mosaic base rather than a standard bronze one, the *Cobweb* lamp was the most expensive of the more than 100 oil lamps that appeared in the Tiffany Studios price list of 1906, where it sold for $500. The lamp is conceived as a completely unified, thematic composition, its irregular shade of clear- and colored-glass segments sitting perfectly on the outstretched bronze branches that form its support. It represents a miniature, self-contained landscape, a field of narcissus blooming within a grove of trees whose branches are dotted with apple blossoms and interlaced with cobwebs.

Glass, lead, and bronze. Height: 30" (76.2 cm); diameter: 20¹/₂" (52.1 cm). (Charles Homer Morse Museum of American Art, Winter Park, Florida.)

42
FRANK LLOYD WRIGHT
Chair, 1904

While Frank Lloyd Wright often recommended Mission furniture (no. 29) when his own designs were not to be used throughout an interior, he later discredited these commercially available pieces, explaining in his *Autobiography* the difference he perceived between their undecorated forms and his own concept of simplicity. "Plainness was not necessarily simplicity. That was evident. Crude furniture of the Roycroft-Stickley-Mission style . . . was offensively plain, plain as a barndoor—but never simple in any true sense. Nor, I found, were merely machine-made things in themselves necessarily simple. . . . I believe that no one thing in itself is ever so, but must achieve simplicity . . . as a perfectly realized part of some organic whole."[47] Designed in 1904 as an integral part of his studio in Oak Park, Illinois (and used in a somewhat varied form in the offices and restaurant of the Larkin Company Administration Building in Buffalo, which Wright completed in 1905), this chair is intended to have the inspired simplicity that Wright's comments invoke. Made of basic rectilinear elements but with an angled back held in place by exposed pegs, the chair was per-

fectly adapted to elementary machine construction, as Wright himself noted; "Furniture," he explained, "takes the clean cut, straight-line forms that the machine can render far better than would be possible by hand."[48]

Oak with leather upholstery. 40¼ x 15 x 18¾" (102.2 x 38.1 x 47.6 cm). (Virginia Museum of Fine Arts, Richmond, gift of Sydney and Frances Lewis.)

43
JOSEF HOFFMANN
Chair, 1904–6

Created as part of the Wiener Werkstätte furnishings for the first-floor dining room of the sanatorium in Purkersdorf that Josef Hoffmann built in 1904–6, this severely rectilinear bentwood chair reflected the interior design of the room it originally furnished—a long rectangular hall framed and outlined by straight ceiling beams. The chair, widely illustrated and praised, became a paradigm of the geometric Secession style and one of Hoffmann's best-known designs. The critic Ludwig Hevesi remarked that the wooden spheres placed at the joints were an example of Hoffmann's "bubbling inventiveness" relieving the nearly cubic outline of the chair frame.[49] These spheres were not purely decorative, however, they served to reinforce the joints and replaced the then-standard stretchers and brackets on other bentwood chairs. The chair was put into commercial production by Jacob & Josef Kohn in Vienna and appeared in the firm's 1906 catalog with an accompanying table, settee, and armchair.

Made by Jacob & Josef Kohn, Vienna. Beechwood with leather upholstery. 38⁵/₈ x 17 x 17¹/₂" (98.5 x 43 x 44.5 cm). (Philadelphia Museum of Art, purchased: Bloomfield Moore Fund.)

rigorous formalism—exercised in the interplay of curvilinear and rectilinear elements—utterly transforms the generic neo-Georgian easy chair popularized by Morris into one of the paradigmatic examples of the geometric style so closely associated with Viennese art reform after the turn of the century.

Made by Jacob & Josef Kohn, Vienna. Beechwood and metal. 22¹/₈ x 26¹/₄ x 44" (56 x 66 x 112 cm). (Victoria and Albert Museum, London.)

44
JOSEF HOFFMANN
Armchair, c. 1908

One of a number of models designed by Josef Hoffmann and produced by the Jacob & Josef Kohn bentwood furniture company in the years before World War I, this chair was first exhibited at the *Kunstschau* in Vienna in 1908. It was shown there upholstered with tufted cushions in the hall of a well publicized model country house that Hoffmann had designed for the display of Kohn products. With its adjustable back and loose cushions, Hoffmann's much-imitated chair itself must have been inspired by the famous morris chair sold by the English firm of Morris and Company from the 1860s. However, Hoffmann's

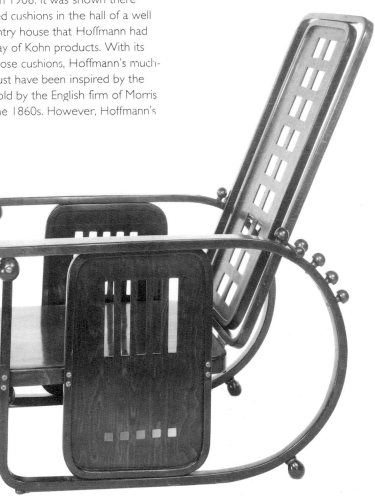

45

PETER BEHRENS
Poster for AEG metal-filament lamps, 1907

Already well known as a book designer and typographer, Peter Behrens created this, his first poster for AEG, in the same year he was appointed the firm's artistic director and was given responsibility for the design of its publicity material and products. Distancing himself

from the sinuous lines and forms of his own earlier Jugendstil designs, Behrens developed a new graphic program based on abstract geometrical forms. The metal-filament lamp illustrated here is inscribed within a triangle and other geometric shapes composed of dots. Dots contained within the triangle radiate out from the lamp like stars against a dark sky, suggesting the power of the light source. At the same time, Behrens's symmetrical layout and use of precise, mathematical elements invested the image of the lamp and the company that produced it with associations of technical rationality, functional efficiency, and economy. For Behrens, this rationalized design derived from the same formal principles as those that governed industrial production. "From now on," he wrote, outlining his design policy for AEG, "the tendency of our age should be followed and a manner of design established appropriate to machine production. . . . In the logical application of these intentions, the company also attaches great importance to the artistic and typographic design of all its publications."[50]

Printed by Hollerbaum & Schmidt, Berlin. Lithograph. 26 x 20½" (67 x 52 cm). (Merrill C. Berman, New York.)

46

PETER BEHRENS
Kettles, 1909

These electric kettles are part of a large and innovative series based on standardized elements that Peter Behrens designed for AEG, the German electrical appli-

ance company. Available in three different shapes, materials, surface finishes, and sizes, and two each of lids, handles, and bases, the kettle components could be combined to give over eighty designs, although only thirty were actually offered for sale by the manufacturer. In one, the combination of a wound cane handle and hammered finish suggests hand techniques; other combinations with smooth undecorated surfaces adopt more obviously industrial appearances. The issue of standardization was central to design theory in the first decade of this century, and although Behrens spoke moderately about it, his work, including the kettle series, set an important design precedent for broad ranges of products. During World War I Behrens advised the German government committee on industrial standards, which in 1916 began an extensive program of standardizing technical measurements to ensure interchangeability of elements on a national basis.

Made by Allgemeine Elektricitäts-Gesellschaft, Berlin. Brass, chromium-plated metal, Bakelite, and cane. Heights: 8 1/4" (21.1 cm); diameters: 6 3/8" (16.2 cm). (Private collection.)

47
GREENE & GREENE
Writing table, 1907

The Arts and Crafts Movement had its fullest expression in America in the "bungalows" that the brothers Charles Sumner Greene and Henry Mather Greene built in California between 1907 and 1909. These highly refined houses were integrated compositions of architecture, landscape, interior woodwork, stained glass, decorative objects, and the furniture that the English architect CHARLES ROBERT ASHBEE described as "without exception the best and most characteristic" he had seen in America. At the workshop of the Greenes' craftsmen, Peter and John Hall, he admired their "beautiful cabinets and chairs of walnut and lignum-vitae, exquisite dowelling and pegging, and in all a supreme feeling for the material, quite up to the best of our English craftsmanship."[51] But the Greenes owed a substantial debt to the traditional Chinese and Japanese elements in the California cultural landscape, and this desk from the living room of their Blacker house in Pasadena (1907), hand made of mahogany oiled and polished to a high finish, bespeaks a dual

inspiration. The influence is felt not only in the overall form, the curved brackets, and the low carving of the legs, which evoke Ming furniture, but also in many of the details: the use of ebony for pegs; the richly inlaid tree limbs on the plank front and the sides; and the stylized Japanese cloud symbols forming the backplates of the drawer handles.

Made by Peter Hall Manufacturing Company, Pasadena, California. Mahogany, ebony, and laminated wood inlaid with fruitwood, copper, and silver. 47 1/8 x 50 1/2 x 26 1/2" (119.6 x 128.2 x 67.3 cm). (Richard Anderson and Richard Anderson II.)

48
JAN EISENLOEFFEL
Tea service, c. 1908

Between about 1908 and 1911, the Dutch designer Jan Eisenloeffel worked in Munich for the Vereinigte Werkstätten für Kunst im Handwerk, designing, among other products, this tea service for which he became best known. Characterized by broad, undecorated surfaces and a geometricized silhouette, the service drew on elements in services the artist had created earlier for Amstelhoek in Amsterdam and Begeer in Utrecht. The Vereinigte Werkstätten, which regularly employed machinery in the production of modern decorative designs, found a sympathetic collaborator in Eisenloeffel, a passionate socialist committed to mass

production and to designs that expressed the technology of the machine. The Munich magazine *Dekorative Kunst* praised the "industrial character" of his work as its most meaningful aspect.[52] Like RICHARD RIEMERSCHMID and PETER BEHRENS, Eisenloeffel was one of several designers working in Germany who formulated a new modern aesthetic with industrial associations.

Made by Vereinigte Werkstätten für Kunst im Handwerk, Munich. Brass. Height of teapot: 6 3/4" (17 cm); coffeepot: 8 7/8" (22.5 cm); sugarbowl: 3" (9.2 cm); creamer: 1 1/2" (4 cm). (Badisches Landesmuseum, Karlsruhe, Germany.)

49
CAMILLO OLIVETTI
Typewriter, 1908–10

Conceived and developed between 1908 and 1910 and introduced at the *Esposizione Universale* in Turin in 1911, Camillo Olivetti's *M1* typewriter was the first to be manufactured in Italy. Drawing on the successive models produced abroad since the earliest Remington entered industrial production in America in 1873, the typewriter incorporates most of the features of what would have been considered a standard machine. Unlike other typewriters then in production, however, Olivetti's model exhibits a well-thought-out and restrained form in keeping with the designer's philoso-

phy that "a typewriter should not be a gewgaw for the drawing room, ornate or in questionable taste. It should have an appearance that is serious and elegant at the same time."[53] Olivetti's belief that he should convey the functional meaning of a machine through its design elements and his use of strong graphics promi-

nently on the typewriter itself to emphasize company identification became the basis of the Olivetti company's design policy, which continues to this day.

Made by Ing. C. Olivetti & C., Ivrea, Italy. Metal. Height: 14 15/16" (38 cm). (Ing. C. Olivetti & C., Ivrea, Italy.)

Chapter Two
Movements for Change 1910–1920

The Deutscher Werkbund, an association of artists and manufacturers, was the world's most influential design organization in the second decade of this century. Founded to strengthen Germany's competitive position in world markets by improving the quality and design of its consumer goods, the Werkbund produced exhibitions and illustrated yearbooks that impressed international audiences with displays of simple, well-designed products conceived for mass distribution; likewise the talent and organizational skills of such designers as PETER BEHRENS highlighted the progressive role of industry. Even in the years around and during World War I, the Werkbund found imitators abroad, determined to secure for their countries the advantages the Werkbund provided Germany.

The Werkbund inspired equivalent associations in other European countries, including Austria (1910) and Switzerland (1913), while the nineteenth century Svenska Slöjdföreningen (Swedish Society of Industrial Design) was also reorganized based on Werkbund precepts at this time. In 1917 its impressive *Hemutställningen* (*Home Exhibition*) in Stockholm reflected the Werkbund's social concerns for quality in the production of objects for everyday use (no. 66). Werkbund influence was also felt beyond the continent. An exhibition of some 1,300 German and Austrian objects designed largely by Werkbund members from "every branch of art activity" circulated through the United States in 1912 (and again, in a different form, in 1922). The display inspired American critics to urge that manufacturers follow the "modern and untraditional" example of their progressive European counterparts, whose active role in improving the design and quality of their products was widely reported.[1] The *Exhibition of German and Austrian Articles Typifying Successful Design* held in London in 1915 led to the establishment of Britain's Design and Industries Association (DIA) in the same year. Emulating the Werkbund, this association of designers, craftsmen, manufacturers, and retailers (the latter including AMBROSE HEAL) was founded to promote public awareness of design in industry, the value of "many machine processes," and an "Efficiency Style."[2] Like the Werkbund, the DIA held exhibitions, lectures, tours, and published pamphlets and yearbooks illustrating a wide range of architecture and industrial design.

In 1910 at the Salon d'Automne in Paris, an exhibition by a group of Munich designers, mostly members of the Werkbund including RICHARD RIEMERSCHMID and Adelbert Niemeyer, provoked a crisis in French design. Installed in eighteen rooms in the Grand Palais, the exhi-

opposite:
Lucian Bernhard, Poster for Bosch spark plugs, 1911 (no. 70)

"Reception Room" by Theodore Veil at the Salon d'Automne, Paris, 1910. This is one of eighteen "harmonious" interiors by German designers shown at the Salon; several were illustrated in *L'Art Décoratif,* October 1910.

bition was organized as a series of furnished interiors by different designers, "a conspicuous success," observed one German reporter, "to judge by the multitudes which visited the exhibition. So great was the throng that the aid of the police was necessary to regulate the crowd for hours together—an experience quite new in the history of the Salon."[3] The German products were also distinctly competitive in the French home market, grossing an unexpected number of sales in the six weeks the exhibition was open. What further impressed French critics was the novel use of materials, the high quality and economy of manufacture, and the unity of interior design: "The ruling principle that inspires the young German school is to create harmonious ensembles through a collaboration of sculpture, painting, and architecture," wrote the critic Louis Vauxcelles, "and the group has endeavored to realize this first by reforming the aesthetics of the home to make the modern house a combined work of art, a practical construction of simple and dignified beauty. . . . Thanks to the simplicity which they intentionally seek, they have succeeded in creating furniture designs of good quality and irreproachable form that may be executed entirely by machine, so that they are within the reach of modest budgets."[4]

The effects of the exhibition and the foreign competition it posed were extensive. *The Studio* yearbook reported in 1912 that a government-sponsored international exhibition of decorative arts, first proposed in 1906 and scheduled to take place in Paris in 1915, "had been postponed till 1920 because of the fears entertained in France regarding Germany's ascendancy to France's erstwhile unassailable lead among the nations in this field. In the meantime, there would, it was hoped, be an opportunity of making good the lost ground."[5] While the report was not entirely accurate (the project was actually ratified later in 1912 by the French Chamber of Deputies), the exhibition was indeed postponed for a few years, and then, because of the war, postponed again until 1925. Calls were also made for a competitive and identifiable modern movement in French design. The German ability to create "harmonious ensembles" inspired French *ensembliers* such as PAUL IRIBE and André Groult to design completely furnished interiors and to select, assemble, and coordinate the work of other designers in unified schemes. From 1912, FRANCIS JOURDAIN designed simple, well-made, commercial furniture that he sold to a middle-class market from his studio, Les Ateliers Modernes (no. 59). Unlike anything being produced in France at the time, Jourdain's plain furniture, stripped of ornament, was accused of being severe, Protestant, German, and socialist when it was first shown at the Salon d'Automne in 1913.[6] Most French designers, however, elected not to compete with Werkbund designers on the same ground, but to return to the past and adapt French traditions of style and handcraft to the twentieth century. The chief theorist of this nationalist revival was the landscape architect and critic André Vera, who published a manifesto in the magazine *L'Art Décoratif* in 1912:

> It is simultaneously because of the new demands of our tastes and in reaction to [foreign] influences that we should submit ourselves to the discipline of French traditions. Let us continue the French tradition in such a way that the new style will pick up where the last genuine traditional style left off, that is to say the style of Louis Philippe. . . . We will seek those qualities of order, clarity, and harmony that can be seen to characterize the seventeenth century and, at the same time, we will take up the tradition abandoned around 1848. The motifs of the new style will be the flower basket and swags of fruit and flowers, just as in the eighteenth century the torch, bow, quiver and arrows were the hallmarks of that style.[7]

Among those designers who followed Vera in the "discipline" of French tradition and craftsmanship, using such techniques as veneering and decorative carving to create the prescribed floral ornament in their furniture, were Louis Süe and André Mare (see SÜE ET MARE), EMILE-JACQUES RUHLMANN (no. 69), and PAUL FOLLOT (no. 74). These artists were not, however, specifically imitative, and developed personal styles that shared qualities of formal simplicity and geometry with modern styles elsewhere. The couturier PAUL POIRET independently sought inspiration for a new French aesthetic in simple peasant and children's art (as he had seen adopted in Germany and Austria), in 1911 establishing his ATELIER MARTINE, a Parisian school for young girls and a decorating business that sold printed fabrics, rugs, wallpapers, ceramics, and glass based on the designs of the students (no. 55). With their fresh motifs, unfamiliar forms, and bright, clear colors, Martine products set new fashions in French design.

The most important source of new design ideas came from the avant-garde artists who worked in Paris as well as Italy, the Netherlands, and Russia in the years around World War I. Of these, the cubist painters Pablo Picasso and Georges Braque were most influential, pro-

The *Maison Cubiste (Cubist House)* by André Mare, Raymond Duchamp-Villon, and Jacques Villon (shown here as a model) was exhibited at the Salon d'Automne in Paris in 1912.

viding an analytical, abstract pictorial language of broken surfaces and faceted forms that was appropriated by designers, particularly after the well-publicized exhibition of cubist art at the Salon des Indépendents in Paris in 1911. In 1912 at the Salon d'Automne, André Mare, in collaboration with the artists Raymond Duchamp-Villon and Jacques Villon, exhibited their *Maison Cubiste (Cubist House)* with broken, angular, sculpted decoration around the entrance. A group of architects and designers in Prague led by Pavel Janák and JOSEF GOČÁR successfully applied the lessons of cubism to architecture, furniture, and other objects from before the war well into the 1920s (no. 52). In England, the Omega Workshops, founded in 1913 by ROGER FRY, an admirer first of French postimpressionist painting and subsequently of cubism, produced furniture, textiles, and ceramics with surface decorations in flat, abstract patterns (nos. 56, 57), while EDWARD McKNIGHT KAUFFER adapted cubistic forms to his graphic art (no. 71).

Partly fueled by their own emphasis on industrial production, designers identified with the mechanical imagery and romantic theories of the machine developed by other avant-garde artists. The Italian futurists challenged the idea of venerating the cultural past, advocating instead the forms of modern technology, from engineering structures to the automobile: "A roaring car that seems to ride on grapeshot is more beautiful than the *Victory of Samothrace*," wrote the poet Filippo Tommaso Marinetti in the futurists' 1909 manifesto. "We want to hymn the man at the wheel, who hurls the lance of his spirit across the Earth. . . . We will sing of . . . greedy railway stations . . . factories . . . deep-chested locomotives . . . and the sleek flight of planes."[8] Seeking new forms to express revolution and movement, Marinetti radicalized typographic design with dynamic, nonlinear, pictorial compositions animated by typefaces in different styles, sizes, and colors. To convey kinetic dynamics in interior design, Giacomo Balla began in 1918 to refurbish his house in Rome according to a futurist "reconstruction" and complemented it with colorful furniture sporting irregular silhouettes.

Drawing on sources in both cubism and futurism, a group of artists in Russia, including KAZIMIR MALEVICH and EL LISSITZKY, developed successive abstract styles of elementary forms and colors known as suprematism and constructivism. In his paintings and drawings, Malevich arranged a minimal number of geometric elements in dynamic compositions to express the "supremacy of feeling in art." By 1920, however, most progressive Russian artists were under pressure to turn their attention to more practical ends in the service of the new Russian revolutionary society. In 1921 Aleksandr Rodchenko, a founder of the First Working Group of Constructivists, declared art for art's sake redundant and advocated instead "production art" by Marxist-educated designers. The most characteristic constructivist activities were in the area of typography and graphic design, perhaps best realized by Lissitzky, who used geometric elements and letterforms constructed on dynamic axes to create propaganda posters (no. 82) along with magazine and book designs.

In the Netherlands in 1917 a loose association of artists and architects called De Stijl was organized. The group took their name from the magazine De Stijl (no. 73) established by the painter Theo van Doesburg and first published in October 1917. Following a cubist analytical approach, these artists shared an interest in pure abstraction and in reducing their visual expression to rectangular shapes, horizontal and vertical lines, and the three primary colors—red, yellow, and blue along with black, white, and gray. De Stijl artists intended this formal language of strict geometrical elements to express universal values and absolute harmony. Unlike members of other avant-garde movements of the war years, De Stijl artists were able to realize their theories in practical achievements, most notably in the work of the cabinetmaker GERRIT RIETVELD, whose celebrated Red/Blue chair of 1918 radically separated and reduced the constituent parts of a chair to abstract lines and planes (no. 81).

Toward the end of the decade Charles-Edouard Jeanneret (who called himself LE CORBUSIER from 1920) and Amédée Ozenfant in Paris also developed from cubism a pictorial language of pure geometrical shapes with universal, general qualities, a style they called "purism." Unlike the total abstractions of De Stijl, purist paintings remained representational, portraying man-made objects with a mathematical precision that came to symbolize for Le Corbusier (and for the many influenced by his theories) the economy and efficiency of machine production. The simple, exact, geometric elements in his paintings provided Le Corbusier with a source of forms he considered appropriate for the modern machine age, and which he applied to his architecture and furniture designs of the 1920s and 1930s (nos. 125, 131).

The title page of Filippo Tommaso Marinetti's *Zang Tumb Tumb*, published in 1914, combines disparate typefaces, styles, and sizes into a dynamic futurist composition.

Many parallels can be found between the ideas and styles of these avant-garde movements, among them the search for objectivity, logic, order, and clarity. Although they shared similar utopian goals for society, they stood in opposition to expressionist artists, who worked from an internal universe of poetic and spiritual values (no. 72). The expressionists championed the right to absolute individuality and created subjects, sometimes roughly stylized in the fashion of folk or children's art, that, while recognizable, were not always easily identifiable. In the years around the war, these ideas fueled a controversy over the role of the designer as creative artist or as anonymous form-giver, a debate that had also arisen between defenders of Arts and Crafts values and those committed to mass production and modern technology. The controversy divided the Deutscher Werkbund, most visibly at the congress held in conjunction with the large Werkbund exhibition in Cologne in 1914. There, Hermann Muthesius advanced ten propositions defining the Werkbund's aims as he saw them, beginning with standardization to achieve "universal significance" and "good taste" as well as broader markets for German products. But the standard industrial type was understood by others, among them HENRY VAN DE VELDE, as a threat to artistic freedom and to individuality in design. Van de Velde and his allies offered their own counter-propositions, which endorsed the "gifts of individual manual skill" and a "belief in the beauty of highly differentiated execution."[9]

The issues of art, craft, and industry as well as many of the international avant-garde aesthetic theories surfaced at the Staatliches Bauhaus in Weimar, the most important art and design school of the twentieth century. The Bauhaus was founded in 1919 from a restructuring and combining of the old Weimar Grossherzogliche Sächsische Kunstgewerbeschule (Grand-Ducal Saxon School of Arts and Crafts), lately directed by van de Velde, with the Grossherzogliche Sächsische Hochschule für Bildende Kunst (Grand-Ducal Saxon School for the Fine Arts). WALTER GROPIUS, the first director of the school, sought to

Machine Hall by Walter Gropius and Adolf Meyer at the Werkbund Exhibition, Cologne, 1914. With its unornamented glass and steel surfaces, the Machine Hall was itself an example of the Werkbund's espousal of technology and standardization.

unite opposing views, but at first remained committed to the necessity of handcraft for design training. "Architects, sculptors, painters, we all must return to the crafts!" he wrote in the first Bauhaus program of April 1919. "The Bauhaus strives to bring together all creative effort into one whole, to reunify all the disciplines of practical art—sculpture, painting, handicrafts, and the crafts. . . . hence, a thorough training in the crafts, acquired in workshops and in experimental and practical sites, is required of all students as the indispensable basis for all artistic production."[10] Initially the Bauhaus included workshops for stone sculpture, woodcarving, cabinetmaking, metal, pottery, stained glass, wall-painting, weaving, bookbinding, printing, and stagecraft.

The school's preliminary course (*Vorkurs*), required of all students, was created by the Swiss painter Johannes Itten, who taught abstract theories of form, color, and line and encouraged free experimentation in the workshops without too much regard for the practical outcome. But the program came under attack from local government and craft organizations for its impracticality. Influenced by Theo van Doesburg (who came to Weimar in 1921–22) and the Hungarian constructivist LÁSZLÓ MOHOLY-NAGY (who took over the preliminary course from Itten in 1923), Gropius began to shift the emphasis of the Bauhaus from individualist handcraft training toward designing for machine production. In *The Theory and Organization of the Bauhaus* (1923) he wrote that "the teaching of a craft is meant to prepare for designing for mass production. . . . It follows that the Bauhaus does not pretend to be a crafts school. Contact with industry is consciously sought, for the old trades are no longer very vital and a turning back to them would therefore be an atavistic mistake."[11] Shedding the last vestiges of the Arts and Crafts Movement from his program, Gropius cast the Bauhaus as a true offspring of the Werkbund as he sought closer links between art and industry.

50
RICHARD RIEMERSCHMID
Floor covering, 1910

Like his compatriot PETER BEHRENS, Richard Riemerschmid must be counted among this century's first modern industrial designers. His belief in the necessity of mass production and of a modern style suited to it made him a model for the progressive designers in the Deutscher Werkbund who sought to raise the standards of German industry. A practicing architect, Riemerschmid created furniture, ceramics, glass, metalwares, carpets, textiles, and linoleum for companies throughout Germany. Countering the contemporary trend for floral patterns on ordinary printed linoleums, the limited, repetitive geometry of Riemerschmid's floor covering, which makes it seem so precociously modern, was actually designed to simplify the production, which was made by dyeing and shaping each part of the pattern separately, and then pressing it onto the burlap backing in squares of different colors, like tiles. The pattern was produced in several color variations.

Made by Deutsche Linoleum-Werke, Delmenhorst, Germany. Linoleum. 19 1/2 x 19 1/4" (49.5 x 49 cm). (Architektur Museum, Technischen Universität, Munich.)

51
RICHARD RIEMERSCHMID
Tea service, 1912

This pewter tea service stands as a paradigmatic example of the simple, serially made wares identified with progressive German design in the years around World War I. Richard Riemerschmid, a founding member of the Deutscher Werkbund, had designed for the Deutsche Werkstätten in Dresden from the time it

was established in 1898 by his brother-in-law, Karl Schmidt. Committed to producing a full range of inexpensive and well-designed interior furnishings, Schmidt began manufacturing pewter wares in Hellerau in 1912, using designs by Riemerschmid and Wolfgang von Wersin. By the following year Schmidt and the Werkstätten were already being credited with reviving the "almost forgotten" production of pewter in Saxony; likewise Riemerschmid and Wersin, "two modern artists in the best sense," were praised for designs placing these pewter wares "among the happiest achievements of German decorative art."[12] This tea service was illustrated in contemporary periodicals and exhibited at the large Werkbund exhibition in Cologne in 1914. Its production, in eight design variations, continued until 1936.

Made by Deutsche Werkstätten, Dresden. Pewter and cane. Height of teapot: 4 3/4" (12 cm); sugar box: 3" (7.5 cm); creamer: 2 3/8" (6 cm). (Neue Sammlung, Munich.)

52
JOSEF GOČÁR
Sofa, 1913

Cubism found fertile expression in Prague after 1911, when an organization called Skupina Výtvarných Umělců (Group of Avant-Garde Artists) was established there. Through direct contacts with Paris, exhibitions in Prague (which in 1913 and 1914 included works by Braque and Picasso), and the cubist collection of the Prague art historian Vincenc Kramář (the foremost in Europe before World War I), members of the group came in touch with the theories and developments at the heart of this movement. Cubism was adopted not just by painters and sculptors but by

architects as well, notably Josef Gočár, Pavel Janák, and Vlastislav Hofman. In a remarkable plastic transformation, they applied the angularities and analytical dissections of cubist forms to construct the outlines and volumes of their buildings and furnishings. This sofa belonged to one of the most complete of cubist interiors, the bedroom and study Gočár designed in 1913 for the actor Otto Boleška. The furnishings included a large suite of black-stained oak furniture and two extraordinary metal accessories, a hanging lamp and a clock, all with faceted, geometric surfaces and angular silhouettes. The furniture was manufactured by Pražské Umělecké Dílny (Prague Artistic Workshops), founded by the Skupina in 1912 for the production of their designs.

Made by Pražské Umělecké Dílny, Prague. Stained oak with cotton upholstery. 46¹/₂ x 90¹/₂ x 29¹/₂" (118.1 x 229.9 x 74.9 cm). (Museum of Decorative Arts, Prague.)

53
GUSTAV STICKLEY
Rug, c. 1910

Textiles were an important part of Gustav Stickley's concept of the integrated Craftsman interior and articles about their use in the home appeared regularly in his *Craftsman* magazine. Intended to add color, texture, and decoration to the Craftsman room, rugs, curtains, pillows, portieres, table scarves, and covers were provided by the Craftsman Workshops from about 1903. A version of this rug was advertised in 1910 in Stickley's catalog alongside the *Donegal* rug and the *Drugget* rug made "especially" for the Craftsman. With the exception of the *Donegal* model, the rugs were

designed in the Craftsman studios in patterns ranging from conventionalized floral motifs to modified Native American designs. A good Craftsman rug, the catalog decreed, "should be apparently, as well as actually, sturdy and durable; it should be unobtrusive in design, so that it helps to give a quiet and harmonious background to the furnishings of the room, and its coloring should be soft and subdued, repeating the tones that prevail throughout the general decorative scheme."[13]

Made by Craftsman Workshops, Eastwood (Syracuse), New York. Wool. 73 x 76" (185.4 x 193 cm) (High Museum of Art, Atlanta, Virginia Carroll Crawford Collection.)

54
FULPER POTTERY COMPANY
Table lamp, c. 1910–12

Introduced in 1910 and patented in 1912,[14] the Fulper Pottery Company's electrified ceramic lamps were exhibited in 1915 at the *Panama-Pacific International Exposition* in San Francisco, where the firm was awarded a medal of honor. The affinity of the simple lamps with Mission-style furniture (no. 29) was underscored there by the decision of GUSTAV STICKLEY and Fulper to exhibit together. Praised for the "artistic unity" of their materials,[15] the lamps in Fulper's Vase Kraft line employed glazed stoneware inset with colored opalescent glass for both base and shade. Operated by an unobtrusive "Fulper pin switch" and with sockets, bulbs, and wiring hidden by the overhanging shade and in the base, there was little to detract from the unusual coloristic and textural effects of Fulper's glazes and the aura of the glowing glass. Although the lamps were generally production models made in a mold, because of the unique effects resulting from the individual firing of each form they were advertised like studio pottery— "no two alike, each piece distinctive and an exact duplicate can never be produced."[16] Glazes ranged from dark, smooth, mirrorlike finishes to crackled surfaces or the mottled *verte antique* glaze on this mushroom-shaped lamp.

Glazed stoneware, colored glass, and lead. Height: 18" (45.7 cm); diameter: 13" (33 cm). (Virginia Museum of Fine Arts, Richmond, gift of Sydney and Frances Lewis.)

55
ATELIER MARTINE
Poppies wallpaper, c. 1912.

The Atelier Martine, the design school and workshop established in Paris by the couturier PAUL POIRET in 1911, introduced a new fashion in French interior decoration. Basing his ideas on the naive designs of its students, Martine created rooms decorated with bright floral cushions, fabrics, rugs, wallpapers, and furnished "ensembles" in a fresh style that endured for over a decade. Poiret emphasized personal creativity among the students in his workshop, unlike the strictly disciplined approach and the "geometricizing of nature" he observed at design schools he visited in Vienna and Berlin, after which his own atelier was modeled. "My rôle," he wrote in his autobiography, "consisted in stimulating their activity and their taste, without ever influencing them or criticising, so that the source of their inspiration should be kept pure and intact." He encouraged his students to draw from nature on trips to the country, from which they "used to bring back the most charming things. There would be fields of ripe corn, starred with marguerites, poppies, and cornflowers; there were baskets of begonias, masses of hortensias . . . all done with an untamed naturalness . . . which sometimes approach the prettiest pictures of the douanier Rousseau."[17] From these drawings and watercolors Poiret selected designs for brilliant and large-scale floral patterns, such as the poppies on this roller-printed wallpaper, which typified the products made for sale in the Martine shops.

Printed paper. 36⅝ x 31⅛" (93 x 79 cm). (Bibliothèque Fornay, Paris.)

56
DUNCAN GRANT
Lilypond screen, 1913

In 1912 ROGER FRY announced that postimpressionism "has brought the artist back to the problems of design so that he is once more in a position to grasp sympathetically the conditions of applied art."[18] In fact, Fry looked to the day when such distinctions would not be relevant. In the interior decoration of the Omega Workshops and in its painted furniture—chairs, tables, bedsteads, cupboards, chests, and screens—fine and applied art readily came together. Like many other

Omega works, Duncan Grant's *Lilypond* design relates to figurative images, in this case an oil study of water lilies and goldfish in a pond at Fry's country house. Abstracted into a flat, vividly colored pattern by Grant, the design was applied to tabletops as well as screens by various members of the workshops, impersonalizing the art of painting and using it as but one of the group's methods of serial production. *Lilypond* is said to have been one of the most popular designs that Omega produced.

Made by Omega Workshops, London. Oil on wood. Four panels, each 68 3/4 x 23 3/4" (175 x 60.5 cm). (Courtauld Institute Galleries, London, Fry Collection.)

57
ROGER FRY
Amenophis fabric, 1913

Through his artists' design studio, the Omega Work-shops, Roger Fry hoped to introduce postimpressionism (which he had brought to London in exhibitions in 1910 and 1912) into the applied arts and interior dec-oration. Indeed this fabric design was derived from one of his earlier still lifes in a style imitative of Cézanne: from it he borrowed the outlines of a book, jug, and two eggs (still recognizable in the small oval shapes), which he rearranged to create a decorative composi-tion. Each of the five other printed linens produced like this one for the opening of the workshops in 1913—created anonymously according to the Omega philoso-phy, but variously attributed to VANESSA BELL, Frederick Etchells, Fry, and DUNCAN GRANT—was also distinctly nonfigurative, a flat pattern spread across the surface of the material, and available in several different color schemes. Fry would never reveal which French firm printed these textiles, apparently because he feared competition, but he did explain in the first Omega cata-log that they "employed a number of special technical processes in order to preserve as far as possible the freedom and spontaneity of the original drawing."[19]

Probably made by Maromme, Rouen, France, for Omega Workshops, London. Printed linen. Width: 31" (78.7 cm). (Victoria and Albert Museum, London.)

58
WALTER GROPIUS
Chair, 1914

This chair belongs to a suite of furniture designed by Walter Gropius for the Fagus shoe-last factory in Alfeld, the first important commission the architect received after establishing his practice with Adolf Meyer in Berlin in 1910. Built between 1910 and 1911, with additions in 1913–14 that included the vestibule for which the furniture was created, the factory is considered the first in this century to define the ele-ments of modern architecture, with glass curtain walls, unrelieved cubic blocks, and corners left free of visible supports. Using a steel-frame construction and ferro-concrete ceilings and pillars, Gropius developed a new architectural language out of contemporary industrial construction forms. If not equally radical in its state-ment of new principles, the Fagus furniture—compris-ing a sofa, bench, table, and chairs—exemplified the uncompromisingly spare, rational style then being pro-moted by progressive designers within the Deutscher Werkbund. Simpler and more geometric than any fur-niture Gropius had previously designed, it anticipated the furnishings developed from squares and cubes that the architect would create for his own director's office at the Bauhaus in Weimar in the early 1920s.

Wood with upholstery. Height: 32¹¹/₁₆" (83 cm). (Fagus Werke, Alfeld an der Leine, Germany.)

59
FRANCIS JOURDAIN
Armchair, 1913

Strongly influenced by the anti-ornament polemic "Ornament and Crime" by the Viennese architect Adolf Loos, Francis Jourdain was among the first designers in France to espouse a spare, undecorated, rationalist style. He created economical, standardized furniture that could be adapted to machine manufac-ture and made available to a broad public. His interiors were rectilinear and geometrically ordered; likewise his furniture, such as this mahogany armchair with its straight lines and flat surfaces enlivened only by the woven pattern of the cane seat, was constructed sim-ply. This was one of a set of chairs made for Jourdain's own apartment in Paris, which was totally utilitarian in conception and outfitted with his "interchangeable fur-niture," tables, cabinets, and seating created for multi-ple uses. Jourdain exhibited the entire furnishings of his living-dining room at the Salon d'Automne in 1913, where one critic, complaining of its austerity, lamented that "not a curve, not a molding, not an ornament comes forth to break the implacable rigidity of the lines."[20]

Made by Les Ateliers Modernes, Esbly, France. Mahogany and cane. 31½ x 21⁷/₈ x 19⁵/₈" (80 x 55.6 x 49.8 cm). (Metropolitan Museum of Art, New York.)

60
GERTRAUD VON SCHNELLENBÜHEL
Candelabrum, c. 1913

The masterwork of a little-known artist, this twenty-four-light candelabrum is the triumphant culmination of Jugendstil in Munich and testimony to its longevity, combining in its spiraling silvery form the abstract ornament, rationalized structure, and smooth bare surfaces of the movement's best products. Recorded in Gertraud von Schnellenbühel's studio in 1913 by the artist Wolfgang von Wersin, who gave it the title *Flowering Tree*,[21] the candelabrum was first shown at the Cologne Werkbund exhibition of 1914. There the critic for *Die Kunst* described it as "at first glance capricious with its singularly branching lines . . . but when seriously considered the shapes appear full of measure and rhythm, drawn from the artist's inner treasury of forms."[22] The candelabrum was acquired for his own use by HERMANN OBRIST, Schnellenbühel's teacher and founder of the school in Munich where she first took up metalwork design.

Made by Steinicken & Lohr, Munich. Silver-plated brass.
Height: 19 1/16" (48.5 cm). (Stadtmuseum, Munich.)

61
PAUL IRIBE
Armchair, 1913

The graphic artist Paul Iribe had been creating modish furniture and interiors in his satiric drawings, advertisements, and fashion plates for over a decade when in 1912 he opened a decorating shop in Paris. There he sold furniture and accessories of his own design. The same year the couturier Jacques Doucet, whose discovery of modern art and decoration had prompted him to disperse his renowned collection of eighteenth-century furnishings, engaged Iribe to outfit his apartment in Paris with the work of contemporary designers. Iribe, assisted by PIERRE LEGRAIN, provided Doucet with many pieces of his own, including a suite of low-back chairs with spirals similar to those seen here, as well as lacquerwork by EILEEN GRAY and glass and lighting by RENÉ LALIQUE. Like EMILE-JACQUES RUHLMANN, Iribe invoked the traditional forms and craftsmanship of Parisian furniture making without being specifically imitative. The extravagant proportions of this chair and its extraordinary large spiral arms encircled with strands of carved pearls are, however, distinctly original, and anticipate the bold geometries of the 1920s.

Rosewood with upholstery. 42 1/2 x 29 1/2 x 23 5/8"
(108 x 75 x 60 cm). (Félix Marcilhac, Paris.)

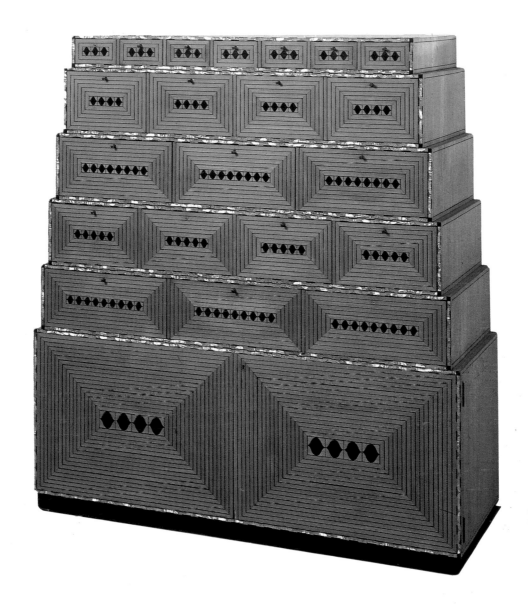

62
EDUARD JOSEF WIMMER
Cupboard, 1913

With its decoration of multiple framed rows of ebony lozenges and its outline of repeated steps, Eduard Josef Wimmer's cupboard is one of the most elaborate pieces of furniture produced in Vienna in the years just before World War I. Both its staggered profile and its geometric decoration are typical of works produced in the circle of JOSEF HOFFMANN and the Wiener Werkstätte, but the insistent use of these basic design ideas as a pattern repeat is the contribution of

Wimmer, a gifted ornamental designer and head of the Wiener Werkstätte's fashion department after 1910. In his textiles, clothing, carpets, interiors, bookbindings, and graphics for the Wiener Werkstätte and other firms, Wimmer produced richly complex designs, which resemble this cupboard's closely patterned light beech and dark ebony veneer.

Made by W. Niedermoser, Vienna. Beech inlaid with ebony and mother-of-pearl, and brass. 56³/₄ x 51¹/₈ x 20⁷/₈" (144 x 130 x 53 cm). (Österreichisches Museum für Angewandte Kunst, Vienna.)

63
BELL TELEPHONE COMPANY
Telephone, 1914

In 1881, five years after he was granted a patent for his "improvement in telegraphy"—the telephone—Alexander Graham Bell acquired control of the manufacturing company of his rival, Elisha Gray. Renamed the Western Electric Manufacturing Company, it became the exclusive supplier of equipment for Bell's fledgling telephone industry. Bell Telephone and Western Electric worked together on the design of new equipment and in 1907 their engineering departments were centralized, becoming the forerunner of the Bell Telephone Laboratories, created in 1925. Telephone instruments for Bell's subscribers evolved slowly, with changes based primarily on performance improvements and economics. This telephone from 1914 capped the evolution of the "desk stand" model introduced in 1892, which was composed of a transmitter on a pedestal and a hand-held receiver with the ringer and calling function in a separately mounted box. This model remained the standard subscriber telephone until the first handset with transmitter and receiver in one unit was made available in 1927. With its black enamel finish and straight pedestal—and without the sharp edges and visible wire connections of its predecessors—the instrument summarizes the unobtrusive and unassuming look that characterized American telephone imagery for the next half century.

Made by Western Electric Company, New York. Enameled and nickel-plated brass. Height: 12" (30.5 cm). (AT&T Archives, Warren, New Jersey.)

64
CORNING GLASS WORKS
Cookware, 1915

Tradition at the Corning Glass Works attributes the development of its heat-resistant Pyrex cookware to the enthusiasm of a company scientist, J. T. Littleton, who in 1913 demonstrated the thermal properties of glass by cutting off the bottom of a laboratory battery jar and asking his wife to bake a cake in it. Company records, however, indicate that research on glass cookware was underway by 1912, and a 1913 report concluded that "there seems to be a future for these glass utensils when used as casseroles, as baking dishes or as combination baking dishes and serving dishes." But it was not until late 1914 or early 1915 that a suitable and reasonable low-expansion glass was developed. Patent applications for the borosilicate glass as well as heat-resistant glass baking dishes were made in 1915 by two company chemists, Eugene C. Sullivan and William C. Taylor, with patents being granted in 1919. The earliest Pyrex pieces introduced in 1915 included baking dishes, pie plates, and bread pans—except for their lack of handles, virtually identical in their smooth undecorated form to those in production today, although the glass was thicker and heavier and had minor visual imperfections. An October 1915 advertisement in *Good Housekeeping* exhorted housewives to "Bake in Glass!" describing its many benefits: "With Pyrex you bake faster and better; these glass dishes cook at a higher temperature than earthenware or metal. You bake and serve in the same dishes. You clean Pyrex dishes with the utmost ease—polish them to a brilliant sheen. You save work, time, fuel (money) pantry space."

Pressed glass. Height of covered casserole: 9" (22.9 cm). (Corning, Inc., Archives, Corning, New York.)

65
CHARLES RENNIE MACKINTOSH
Clock, 1917

One of the most advanced of Charles Rennie Mackintosh's late designs, this mantle clock belongs to a series of furnishings created for W. J. Bassett-Lowke, an engineering modelmaker in Northampton, England, who was Mackintosh's major client during World War I. (The case was actually made by German craftsmen interned on the Isle of Man.) An early member of the Design and Industries Association, Bassett-Lowke was committed to raising standards of British design and, like his association colleague AMBROSE HEAL, he defined those standards through the creations of Mackintosh and the other designers of the Arts and Crafts Movement who had worked in Britain around the turn of the century. The overall form of the clock is developed from one that Mackintosh had made in

1905, but its emphasis on spare geometrical forms, even to the use of domino spots instead of numerals, and its decoration with inlays of colored Erinoid, a milk-derived plastic that was used liberally during the war, anticipate designs of the 1920s.

Ebonized wood inlaid with Erinoid. 10 x 5 1/8 x 5" (25.5 x 13 x 12.8 cm). (Private collection.)

66
WILHELM KÅGE
Blue Lily table service, 1917

At the *Hemutställningen* (*Home Exhibition*) in Stockholm in 1917 manufacturers and designers presented objects intended to bring rationality and beauty into the homes of the ordinary Swedish citizen by means of simple, economical wares. Highly regarded by the press but not by the public, who continued to prefer housewares in more traditional, decorated forms, the exhibition did not immediately achieve its social goal. However, it did encourage further experimentation as the public became more accustomed to this new aesthetic. With his *Blue Lily* (*Liljeblå*) tableware, known as the "Workers" service after it was introduced at the Stockholm exhibition, Wilhelm Kåge renounced Gustavsberg's earlier more elaborate wares for a white service economically decorated with a simple folklike pattern.

Made by Gustavsberg, Gustavsberg, Sweden. Glazed earthenware with transfer-printed underglaze decoration. Diameter of plate: 11 3/4" (29.8 cm). (Victoria and Albert Museum, London.)

67
DAGOBERT PECHE
Jewelry box, c. 1918

Dagobert Peche's jewelry box was first displayed in the
Wiener Werkstätte showroom in Zurich, where he
had been sent from Vienna to open and manage the
new display space in 1917. Peche designed many of
the products sold at the showroom, his boxes, decorative objects, and tulle embroideries distinguished by
fanciful and delicately executed plant and animal motifs.
Like his contemporaries in France, Peche sought inspiration for new forms of expression in the past, creating
luxury objects in sumptuous materials that reasserted
the values of traditional handcraft. With its foliage-
spouting gazelle poised on the lid, this box is reminiscent in its frivolity and spirited exuberance of the rococo designs admired and studied by Peche. Such exclusive, elegantly humorous objects are said to have been
produced by the Wiener Werkstätte in reaction to the
effects and privations of World War I, and appeared in
wartime exhibitions of Austrian arts and crafts in Berlin,
Stockholm, and Zurich.

Made by Wiener Werkstätte, Vienna. Silver. Height: 15 1/2"
(39.5 cm). (Metropolitan Museum of Art, New York.)

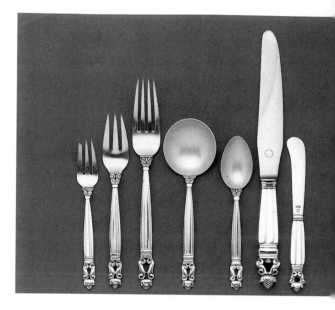

68
JOHAN ROHDE
Acorn cutlery, 1915

From its introduction in 1915, Johan Rohde's *Acorn* cutlery—known as the *King's* pattern (*Kongemønsteret*) in
Denmark—was Georg Jensen's best-selling flatware
pattern; indeed, with the numerous pieces added over
the years, it became the most extensive silver service
anywhere in production, numbering over two hundred
separate items. Its classical vocabulary of fluted shaft
and stylized acorn finial broke with the naturalistic decorations and curvilinear forms that the firm had used
earlier to rival the continental art nouveau (no. 35) and
reflects the neoclassical sources that Rohde freely combined in other of his silverware designs of this period.
Rohde's taste for the regularity, proportions, and decorative details of classicism was shared by many of his
European contemporaries, from painters such as
Picasso to decorative artists and architects such as
JOSEF HOFFMANN.

*Made by Georg Jensen Sølvsmedie, Copenhagen. Silver and
steel. Length of knife: 9" (23 cm). (Private collection.)*

69
EMILE-JACQUES RUHLMANN
Corner cabinet, 1916

"The genius of Ruhlmann," noted a review of the
Exposition Internationale des Arts Décoratifs in Paris in

1925, "endows us with furniture of the most refined forms, great grand nephews of the most delightful Louis XVI pieces."[23] Many of the elements that would suggest Emile-Jacques Ruhlmann's debt to the past throughout the Twenties are already present in this work: its references to eighteenth-century forms; its measured, balanced proportions; the rare and costly materials exquisitely combined and finished; and the round and fluted or faceted "spindle" (*en fuseau*) leg he himself introduced, with an ivory volute at the top and a shoe (*sabot*) at the bottom, which attaches to the side of the cabinet.

But while his work was often compared to that of the celebrated eighteenth-century cabinetmakers, it was distinguished by extreme simplification and stylization of floral ornament and by its larger scale—an adaptation of traditional forms to modern tastes.

Lacquered rosewood inlaid with rare woods and ivory.
50 1/2 x 33 1/2 x 23 3/4" (128.3 x 85 x 60.3 cm).
(Virginia Museum of Fine Arts, Richmond, gift of Sydney and Frances Lewis.)

70
LUCIAN BERNHARD
Poster for Bosch spark plugs, 1914

The influential, modern pictorial poster style that Lucian Bernhard devised around 1905 served him well for more than two decades in Germany. His most successful posters were those reduced to only three elements: a bold image of a product, sometimes almost a caricature, set against a flat color and identified by the briefest version of the manufacturer's name in distinctive, rounded letterforms. In this poster advertising spark plugs for the Bosch automotive firm, Bernhard added a dynamic fillip to his simple imagery with a comic-book burst of light and jarring color contrasts that suggest the power of the product itself. Bernhard and a group of similarly imaginative colleagues attached to the Hollerbaum & Schmidt printing company established this Berlin firm as one of the pioneers of progressive advertising design in the first two decades of the century.

Printed by Hollerbaum & Schmidt, Berlin. Lithograph. 18 x 25 1/4" (45.6 x 64.2 cm). (Merrill C. Berman, New York.)

71
EDWARD McKNIGHT
Poster for the *Daily Herald*, 1918

Described by Edward McKnight Kauffer as the "first and only cubist poster design in England,"[24] this large billboard advertisement for the *Daily Herald* was one of the earliest graphic works of this American expatriate designer, a central figure in the world of commercial design in England for almost three decades. Kauffer introduced modernist ideas into English advertising art, and his extensive series of posters for the London Underground helped to establish the extremely high design standard for which the city's transport system became world renowned. With this poster's angular,

cubist pattern of overlapping birds soaring in a vast yellow sky, Kauffer suggested the dynamics of modern life, and although the layout was not all his (it was changed after he sold the design to an advertising agency), the expansive composition works as a particularly apt expression of its message.

Printed for Her Majesty's Stationery Office by UDO (Litho), London. Lithograph. 117 3/16 x 59 15/16" (297.7 x 152.2 cm). (Victoria and Albert Museum, London.)

72
EGON SCHIELE
Poster for Forty-ninth Vienna Secession Exhibition, 1918

Exhibition posters played an important role in the spread of expressionist ideas in Germany and Austria, with the powerful graphic statements of such artists as Egon Schiele, Alfred Kubin, and Oskar Kokoschka proclaiming the values of the spirit over those of pure form. Distorting recognizable elements often to the point of abstraction, the expressionists pursued their inner visions with brutal directness and conveyed them with great immediacy through an equally bold attitude toward type. Here, rudely simplified faceless figures inspired by vernacular woodcuts sit around a table that

slopes eerily out of normal perspective, their red-brown and ocher clothing and chairs luridly illuminated against a blank, blacked-out background. The large, irregular text letters, a hallmark of expressionist graphics, suggest crudely cut type although they are drawn with a brush; they list out of alignment, accenting the spatial disarticulation of the figures above. This poster, based on a self-portrait of Schiele seated at the head of a table with his artist friends in the manner of a Last Supper, advertised a Secession exhibition that was, in effect, a Schiele retrospective, although it included the work of many of the artist's colleagues.

Printed by Albert Berger, Vienna. Lithograph. 26³/4 x 21" (68 x 53.2 cm). (Museum of Modern Art, New York, gift of Dr. and Mrs. Otto Kallir.)

73
VILMOS HUSZAR
Cover of *De Stijl,* 1917

Vilmos Huszar was a founding member of the avant-garde association of Dutch artists whose monthly magazine, *De Stijl,* gave its name to the style they practiced. Led by the painter Theo van Doesburg, who edited the magazine, the artists of De Stijl were committed to the principle of abstraction, which they realized with strictly determined geometrical elements and, initially, with an equally strict palette of black, white, gray, and primary colors. Striving for a precise, pure visual lan-guage and the harmony and balance it achieved, De Stijl aesthetics were derived from the work of the cubists, who, as van Doesburg wrote, subtract "mathematical form from natural form, achieving a pure art form. This art form is the inner one, the spiritual one."[25] For this first cover of *De Stijl,* Huszar designed title letters constructed from small horizontal and vertical rectangles with white interspaces, the type set over an abstract composition similarly but solidly composed of rectangular shapes within a rectangular frame whose dimensions correspond exactly to the letters above. Van Doesburg wrote a special caption for the cover design, which remained in use until 1921, stating that the abstract composition was applied "in order to create an aesthetic harmony and unity with the printing."[26] For Huszar, the typography and composition presented a study of fragmented, positive and negative figure-ground relationships in which he tried "to give white and black equal value, without ground."[27] Huszar's experiments with geometrical letter shapes and combinations as well as typographic composition in tight rectangular blocks proved influential in the 1920s, through the wide circulation of *De Stijl.*

Printed by X. Harms Tiepen, Delft. Letterpress. 10¹/4 x 7¹/2" (26 x 19 cm). (Gemeentemuseum, The Hague.)

74
PAUL FOLLOT
Dressing table and chair, c. 1919

Calling on the forms and craft traditions of French cabinetry in this broad interpretation of Louis XVI sources, Paul Follot's luxuriantly modeled and gilded dressing table and chair reflect his early study of sculpture, his taste for dense ornament, and the new motifs that became popular in France during the Teens. The ensemble, with its fluted legs and carved floral cornucopias, was first exhibited in 1920 at the Salon des Artistes Décorateurs. But it may have been conceived around 1912–14 when Follot was building his house in Paris, in collaboration with the architect Pierre Selmersheim, and embellishing it with unified carved-and-gilded decoration. When it was shown at the 1920 exhibition, the critic for *Art et Décoration* expressed admiration for its "harmonious design" but reproached Follot for its gilded excess—"One would hope for a moment of rest," he wrote, "a respite in this furniture, which is very well conceived in all its parts, but too rich."[28]

Lacquered and gilded wood, marble, and glass. Table: 52 x 47 1/4 x 18 7/8" (132 x 120 x 48 cm); chair: 33 1/8 x 18 5/16 x 22 1/16" (85 x 46.5 x 56 cm). (Musée d'Art Moderne de la Ville de Paris.)

75
EMILE-JACQUES RUHLMANN
Chariot sideboard, 1919

The *Chariot* sideboard, based on a sketch made in 1917, was the first important work Emile-Jacques Ruhlmann exhibited in Paris after World War I, at the 1919 Salon d'Automne. Reviewing the exhibition in the journal *Art et Décoration*, the critic Jean-Louis Vaudoyer described it as "probably the masterpiece of cabinetry at the Salon"; its reputation was later enhanced when versions were acquired for the collections of the city of Paris and the Louvre. "The material employed," Vaudoyer continued, "is macassar ebony, which in some ways resembles marble. It has balanced proportions, elegance, and majesty; one can only lament the inlaid motif, which mars its center, this chariot of Apollo drawn by horses that resemble screech owls."[29] Vaudoyer's negative reaction notwithstanding, the ivory decoration with its modish female charioteer confirms Ruhlmann's early commitment to the progressive formal vocabulary expressed in luxury materials that would culminate in 1925 at the *Exposition Internationale des Arts Décoratifs* in Paris.

Made by Ruhlmann & Laurent, Paris. Macassar ebony inlaid with mahogany and ivory. Length: 89 3/4" (228 cm). (Musée d'Art Moderne de la Ville de Paris.)

76
RAOUL DUFY
Hibiscus fabric, 1917

In 1911 the painter Raoul Dufy began to create textiles in a small workshop established for him in Paris by the couturier PAUL POIRET, whose fashions were soon enlivened by the freshness and simplicity of Dufy's designs and the inventiveness of his techniques and materials. Within a year Dufy had been offered a contract with the Lyons silk manufacturer Bianchini-Férier, forming an association that lasted until 1928 and left Dufy free to create independently; this period saw the conception of thousands of original designs for printed and woven fabrics—florals, exotic and mythological animals, figures from Parisian life, colorful geometrics, and, around 1920, bold, flat, black-and-white configurations—not all of which, however, were put into production. The *Hibiscus* fabric is a sophisticated example of Dufy's creations, combining the free, lyrical drawing of his paintings with broad areas of flat, bright colors.

Made by Bianchini-Férier, Lyons. Printed silk and cotton. Width: 51 3/16" (130 cm). (Musée Historique des Tissus, Lyon.)

77
AMBROSE HEAL
Cupboard chest, c. 1919

Beginning about 1900 the prosperous, long-established London furniture firm of Heal and Son took up the innovations of the Arts and Crafts Movement. Into the next decade they produced solid "honest" furniture made of English woods with frame-and-panel construction and in simple cubic shapes. In so doing, Heal's proved that this kind of furniture could be successfully designed, made, and sold commercially. Advertised as part of a bedroom ensemble in Heal's *Cottage Furniture* catalog (1919), this cupboard chest was offered in mahogany or painted white; oak was also possible for manufacture although it was in short supply because of

the war. While technically the furniture was highly traditional, the square shapes, flush surfaces, and exact angles developed by Heal's in pieces such as this cupboard were as original and "modern" in their utilitarian simplicity as any furniture being produced on the continent. Published in the yearbooks of the Design and Industries Association, of which Ambrose Heal was a founder, and in catalogs of what the company called "Cottage" and "Reasonable" furniture, Heal's products set standards for rational design in Britain with their uncompromising, no-frills appearance and their references to the Arts and Crafts tradition.

Made by Heal and Son, London. Pine with ebonized bands. Height: 57" (144.8 cm). (Design Museum, London, Heal Archive.)

79
JOHAN ROHDE
Pitcher, 1920

With its simple form and continuous sweep of handle and lip, this elegant pitcher is unlike any other household silver then designed by Johan Rohde or manufactured by Georg Jensen, for it is restrained in its outline and almost entirely without applied decoration. The small ornament that masks the joining of the handle at its base is the only hint of the stylish classical vocabulary used by the designer and the firm at this time (no. 68), while its shimmering surface comes from the thousands of individual hammerstrokes that built up its shape. This unornamented style became more prevalent during the 1920s, most notably in the Werkbund's famous 1924 exhibition in Stuttgart, *Form ohne Ornament* (*Unornamented Form*), where extremely simplified objects were displayed as types suitable for mass production and as aesthetic paradigms. While Rohde first conceived this vessel in a drawing of 1920, it was not exhibited until 1925 at the *Exposition Internationale des Arts Décoratifs* in Paris.

Made by Georg Jensen Sølvsmedie, Copenhagen. Silver. Height: 8³/4" (22.4 cm). (Danske Kunstindustrimuseum, Copenhagen.)

78
EDWARD HALD
Women Playing with a Ball bowl, 1920

The engraved glass Edward Hald created as the second artist-designer employed by Orrefors (having come to the Swedish glassmaker a year after the painter Simon Gate) depicted not only classical and allegorical nudes but also contemporary subjects including circuses, masquerades, and other scenes with figures dressed in a modern fashion. Contemporary, too, is the flat, graphic style of this lyrical composition of young women playing ball, an image unique among Hald's work. Designed in 1920 and exhibited in the *Exposition Internationale des Arts Décoratifs* in Paris in 1925, it reflects in its joyful movement the celebrated canvases of dancers painted by Henri Matisse in the previous decade, about the time Hald was studying with him in Paris.

Made by Orrefors Glasbruk, Orrefors, Sweden. Clear glass with engraved decoration. Height: 9³/4" (23.5 cm). (Nationalmuseum, Stockholm.)

all 'part of the structure.''[30] To integrate all aspects of his building Wright employed geometric figures—in this chair he combined hexagon, square, and triangle, repeating the shapes found in the structure itself and in its lavish surface ornamentation as well as in the other furnishings and tableware he provided.

Oak with upholstery. 33 x 16 x 17" (96.5 x 40.6 x 43.2 cm). (Philadelphia Museum of Art, gift of the Imperial Hotel, Tokyo.)

81
GERRIT RIETVELD
Red/Blue armchair, 1918

One of the most original and important pieces of furniture designed in the twentieth century, Gerrit Rietveld's *Red/Blue* chair challenged the traditional shapes of useful objects by redefining the structure of their forms and internal spaces. Inspired in part by the simple wooden plank-and-rail furniture of FRANK LLOYD WRIGHT and using the strictest vocabulary of

80
FRANK LLOYD WRIGHT
Chair, c. 1918–22

The genius of Frank Lloyd Wright, which he himself promoted relentlessly, was startlingly affirmed when his Imperial Hotel in Tokyo withstood a devastating earthquake in 1923, just after it was completed and just as he predicted it would. Wright created the hotel (1916–22, now demolished) as a unified entity, intricately engineered for safety, richly ornamented, and fully furnished with woodwork, furniture, carpets, lamps, silver, and china of his own design, almost all manufactured in Japan. In his autobiography, Wright described how he "had brought examples of good furniture from home and took them apart to teach the Japanese workmen how to make them according to the new designs which made them

boards and listels, Rietveld approached this design like a sculptor, creating an open construction through complex combinations of standard units in modular lengths. Although born to and trained as a cabinetmaker, Rietveld rejected traditional ideals of hand craftsmanship, asserting in this and in the more than seventy-five other objects he created during his lifetime the new "modern" values of objectivity and anonymity. Recognized from its creation as a revolutionary invention, the chair became the standard of the Dutch De Stijl group, which Rietveld joined in 1919. After its publication in the *De Stijl* magazine that year, where it was described as a "new form . . . the (abstract-real) image of our future interior,"[31] the chair also had an almost immediate influence on comparable experiments abroad among the Russian constructivists and German designers at the Bauhaus (no. 89). The first model was unpainted and included side panels below the arms. This version, with elements painted in red, black, and blue and edged in yellow, reflects the use of flat primary colors by the De Stijl painters Piet Mondrian, VILMOS HUSZAR, and Theo van Doesburg, and similarly serves to reinforce the visual independence of its parts.

Painted wood. 33⁷/₈ x 25¹/₈ x 26³/₄" (86 x 63.8 x 67.9 cm).
(Stedelijk Museum, Amsterdam.)

82
EL LISSITZKY
Poster for the Soviet Political Administration of the Western Front, 1920

In this extraordinary propaganda poster designed to hearten the Bolshevik troops during the Russo-Polish war of 1920, El Lissitzky used the new language of abstraction to communicate a message so directly that it would be understood even by those who could not read its fighting words: "Beat the Whites with the Red Wedge." With two colors and the three primal shapes of the suprematist artists (circle, triangle, and rectangle), he symbolically depicted the anticipated victory of the Bolsheviks (Reds) over the counterrevolutionaries (Whites)—the red triangles break through the white circle, the forces of light vanquish those in darkness—and he added typography to support the action, both visually and verbally. Lissitzky's revolutionary use of abstract graphic forms in the service of narration anticipated his well-known suprematist storybook for children, *Of Two Squares*, published in 1922, in which a black and a red square work together to bring order to a world in chaos.

Lithograph. 20⁷/₈ x 27⁹/₁₆" (53 x 70 cm). (Stedelijk Van Abbemuseum, Eindhoven, The Netherlands.)

Chapter Three
Styles of Modernism 1920–1930

Just as the *Exposition Universelle* in Paris in 1900 represented the apogee of the art nouveau style and progressive tendencies in design at the turn of the century, so the long-delayed *Exposition Internationale des Arts Décoratifs et Industriels Modernes*, held in Paris in 1925, epitomized the style that later gave art deco its name. Twenty-one countries in addition to France and its colonies participated, but Germany and the United States were notably absent—Germany for political and economic reasons boycotted a belated invitation[1] and the United States declined "one of the best sites"[2] because "American manufacturers and craftsmen had almost nothing to exhibit in the modern spirit."[3] Despite the diversity of exhibitors, however, journalists unanimously identified a pervasive new "modern" style of decoration that used abstract, geometric, cubist-inspired forms, albeit often in romantic or traditional ways. The results of the exposition were summarized by Waldemar George, writing in *L'Amour de l'Art*:

> We have observed that the distinctive feature of the exposition is the adoption of the geometric style by the best of the exhibitors. This style, which has been abused, even risks becoming trite. . . . [although] one must recognize that the taste for pure forms, which excludes anything figurative, constitutes progress. Even ten years ago, the few cubist painters who spoke of the specific virtues of lines and colors were considered crazy, if not charlatans, by the press. . . . [Now] architects, furniture makers, and decorative designers uniformly apply the principles of composition introduced by Pablo Picasso, Georges Braque, and Juan Gris. . . . Stained glass, perfume bottles, embroideries, carpets, wallpapers, table services, wrought iron, in a word, the whole modern production in the field of decorative arts evolves under the sign of cubism.[4]

Like the curvilinear forms of art nouveau, the new geometric vocabulary championed by the French at the exposition was broadly commercialized and spread rapidly as an international style. In Paris during the early 1920s the large department stores opened decorating departments and commissioned original lines of furnishings from their art directors to popularize the modern style, and each of these stores had individual pavilions bearing the names of their studio lines at the 1925 exposition. PAUL FOLLOT directed the Pomone studio at Le Bon Marché; Maurice Dufrène, La Maîtrise at the Galeries Lafayette; Etienne Kohlmann and Maurice Matet, Studium at the Grands Magasins du

Primavera, the pavilion of Le Printemps department store, by Henri Sauvage and Georges Wybo for the *Exposition Internationale des Arts Décoratifs,* Paris, 1925. The Paris department stores were represented at the exhibition with separate pavilions displaying their own lines.

"House of a Collector" by Emile-Jacques Ruhlmann for the *Exposition Internationale des Arts Décoratifs,* Paris, 1925.

Louvre; and René Guilleré with Charlotte Chauchet-Guilleré, Primavera at Le Printemps.

Selected objects from the Paris exposition, which had been widely publicized, traveled abroad, and in 1926, under the auspices of the American Association of Museums, they toured the United States (the exhibition catalog noting that "the great department stores of Paris have contributed a very important element to the modern movement . . . [bringing] examples of the new manner within reach of the ordinary purse"[5]). In 1928 they even went to Japan, where objects by EMILE-JACQUES RUHLMANN, Jules Leleu, and others were shown in Tokyo. American stores followed their French counterparts in promoting the modern style, with R. H. Macy and Company and Lord and Taylor in New York holding highly successful exhibitions of largely French designs in 1927 and 1928. The 1927 exhibition at Macy's was organized with the advice of the Metropolitan Museum of Art "in the cause of the furtherance of good taste and art in modern life."[6] The museum, which had held annual exhibitions of American design since 1917, purchased objects from the *Exposition Internationale des Arts Décoratifs* and displayed them early in 1926 (no. 106). The style was popularized in the United States by DONALD DESKEY, who had visited the exposition in Paris, and by the Austrian emigré PAUL T. FRANKL, who created an idiomatic range of cubistic "skyscraper" furniture (no. 130), which he promoted in his books *New Dimensions* (1928) and *Form and Re-Form* (1930). Retailers and manufacturers elsewhere also adopted the French idea of the studio line; in England, the Paris-trained Serge Chermayeff directed Waring & Gillow's Modern Art Studio, creating furniture and interior design of decidedly Continental persuasion between 1928 and 1931, and even Heal's, a bastion of the English Arts and Crafts survival, produced cubist-inspired furniture for its Signed Edition Series during the same period.

Like art nouveau, this style, which ran to bold color schemes and patterns of zig-zags, circles, lightning bolts, and pyramids, outraged purist designers, not least because the abstracted symbols and basic geometric forms favored by the cubist, futurist, De Stijl, and constructivist movements had been borrowed seemingly without understanding and used solely for decorative purposes. At one level the issue revolved around the concept of decoration, as it had so often in the past. In his book *L'Art décoratif d'aujourd'hui* (*The Decorative Art of Today*, 1925), LE CORBUSIER noted:

> Eloquent showmen have flooded us with "decorative" schemes and here we are, ready to take our place at the great international presentation of decoration. Behind the decoration we shall find, where expected, the real elements of the tension. . . . Previously, decorative objects were rare and costly. Today they are commonplace and cheap. Previously, plain objects were commonplace and cheap; today they are rare and expensive. Previously, decorative objects were items for special display. . . . Today decorative objects flood the shelves of the Department Stores. . . . If they sell cheaply, it is because they are badly made and because decoration hides faults in their manufacture and the poor quality of their materials: decoration is disguise.[7]

The journalist Gabriel Mourey complained that the exhibition of 1925 was immoral and antisocial, criticizing the vast amounts of money spent there in a period of economic crisis. The exhibition objects were conservative and retrograde, he declared, produced apparently for a popular market but actually made for the rich, as Ruhlmann's pavilion (the "House of a Collector") and the "French Embassy" theme chosen for the Société des Artistes Décorateurs pavilion so cynically seemed to affirm.[8] Among the most popular pavilions at the exhibition, these were furnished with luxury objects that depended largely on traditional forms and techniques of production updated by a simplified geometry (no. 107). Representing the grand tradition of French eighteenth-century cabinetmaking, Ruhlmann designed most of the furniture, carpets, and fabrics displayed in his pavilion but also included opulent silverwares, ironwork, ceramics, and glass by, respectively, JEAN PUIFORCAT, Edgar Brandt, Emile Lenoble, and François-Emile Décorchement, works that were as rich in materials and decoration and as self-consciously crafted as Ruhlmann's own.

Considered by Le Corbusier to be "works of art" rather than functional household "equipment,"[9] these traditional luxury objects as well as their less costly derivatives were despised by progressive designers, who argued that the only rational response to modern conditions was industrial production and that the creation of entirely new forms, by new methods, with new materials, was the designer's charge. The only presentations at the exposition of 1925 that fulfilled their strictest critical expectations were the Russian pavilion, a simple glass-and-wood building in the shape of a parallelogram by Konstantin Melnikov, and Le Corbusier's flat-surfaced, concrete-framed Pavillon de l'Esprit Nouveau. The Soviet structure housed an experimental constructivist environment in the form of a Workers' Club by Aleksandr Rodchenko, fur-

"Workers Club" by Aleksandr Rodchenko, displayed in the U.S.S.R. pavilion at the *Exposition Internationale des Arts Décoratifs*, Paris, 1925.

Pavillon de l'Esprit Nouveau by Le Corbusier and Pierre Jeanneret, at the *Exposition Internationale des Arts Décoratifs*, Paris, 1925.

nished with wooden furniture painted in De Stijl fashion in four colors, and designed for "simplicity of use, standardization, and the necessity of being able to expand or contract the numbers of its parts."[10] Using standardized wooden units in simple geometrical forms, Rodchenko created such multifunctional furniture to serve the general requirements of the new Soviet state, requirements he defined as "social usefulness, consumer-efficiency, technical simplicity, functional efficacity and economy."[11] Le Corbusier's Pavillon de l'Esprit Nouveau, a prototypical standardized dwelling, was furnished, as the architect described, with "standard furniture, industrially fabricated, commercially traded, and having no *artistic* character provided by decorations full of pretentions. We wanted to furnish our pavilion with industrial products where the law of economy, commercial selection, would confer on these objects what one might call a style."[12] Le Corbusier placed in the pavilion the "humble" but "noble" bentwood Thonet armchair, designed in the nineteenth century and sold "by the millions," as well as his own version of a commercial leather armchair made by Maples & Company in England.[13] Hitherto used chiefly in hotels and other commercial interiors, these chairs were shown to be suitable also for domestic use.

The most radical experimentation in design for industrial production, however, took place not in France but in Russia and Germany. At the Bauhaus design school, first in Weimar and then Dessau, where it moved in 1925, WALTER GROPIUS threw off the craft bias of his original curriculum and declared the Bauhaus workshops

> essentially laboratories in which prototypes of products suitable for mass production and typical of our time are carefully developed and constantly improved. In these laboratories the Bauhaus wants to train a new kind of collaborator for industry and handcraft who has an equal command of both technology and form. . . . The finished products produced from Bauhaus prototypes can be offered at a reasonable price through the utilization of all the modern economical means of standardization (industrial mass production) and wide marketing.[14]

Among the first Bauhaus prototypes were models designed by THEODOR BOGLER in the school's pottery workshop, models that were manufactured by the Staatliche Porzellanmanufaktur in Berlin and the Steingutfabrik at Velten-Vordamm in 1923 (no. 96). At the metal workshop LÁSZLÓ MOHOLY-NAGY, its head from 1923 to 1928, described the transition from craft to production design:

> When Gropius appointed me to take over the metal workshop, he asked me to reorganize it as a workshop for industrial design. Until my arrival, the metal workshop had been a gold and silver workshop where wine jugs, samovars, elaborate jewelry, coffee services, etc. were made. Changing the policy of this workshop involved a revolution . . . for in their pride the gold and silversmiths avoided the use of ferrous metals, nickel and chromium plating and abhorred the idea of making models for electrical household appliances or lighting fixtures. It took quite a while to

The Bauhaus building at Dessau by Walter Gropius, 1925–26.

get under way the kind of work which later made the Bauhaus a leader in designing for the lighting fixture industry.[15]

The international faculty at the Bauhaus included the most avant-garde of European artists and designers, among them the American Lyonel Feininger, the Hungarians Moholy-Nagy and MARCEL BREUER, the Swiss Johannes Itten and Paul Klee, and the Russian Wassily Kandinsky. While not officially a Bauhaus member, the Dutch painter and theorist Theo van Doesburg visited Weimar in 1921 and 1922 and published his magazine *De Stijl* there; Kandinsky had taught at the new Soviet Vkhutemas (a contraction of Vysshie gosudarstvennye khudozh-estvenno-teknicheskie masterskie, the Higher State Artistic and Technical Workshops) in Moscow before his Bauhaus stay and the links between the two design schools continued through the later Bauhaus director Hannes Meyer, who eventually quit Germany for practice in Russia between 1930 and 1936.

Like the Bauhaus, the Vkhutemas aimed to train artists for industry, although in Russia the emphasis was on practical, functional formulas rather than the aesthetics or theory of design as it was initially at the Bauhaus. Constructivist designers including EL LISSITZKY, Rodchenko, Lyubov Popova, and VARVARA STEPANOVA were among the most progressive of the heterogeneous Vkhutemas faculty. Unlike the Bauhaus weaving workshop, the textile faculty, for example, retained a variety of attitudes toward the construction and decoration of fabrics, displaying at the *Exposition Internationale des Arts Décoratifs* of 1925 an eclectic collection of printed fabrics that ranged from peasant floral patterns and depictions of modern machinery to abstract constructivist designs. The early products of both the Bauhaus and the Vkhutemas shared an emphasis on geometric shapes, from KAZIMIR MALEVICH's cubistic porcelains (no. 95) to Marcel Breuer's wooden furniture made in the Bauhaus in the manner of GERRIT RIETVELD (no. 89).

This geometric constructivist/De Stijl approach to form was also influenced at the Bauhaus by the purist theories of Le Corbusier, who employed basic Euclidean figures to give his "type-objects" the assurance and beauty of mathematics as well as reduce them to their most concise "anonymous" form for mass production. Although Gropius rejected the idea of a "Bauhaus style," the spare and controlled attitude toward form that existed at the school was based on principles of simple efficiency and economy that he outlined as a doctrine of functionalism: "In order to create something that functions properly—a container, a chair, a house . . . it should serve its purpose to perfection, i.e., it should fulfil its function practically and should be durable, inexpensive, and 'beautiful.'"[16] Among the most visible faculties at both schools were those of furniture and metalwork, which were eventually merged at the Vkhutemas in 1926 under Rodchenko and at the Bauhaus in 1928 under Josef Albers. Both schools produced prototypes, the Vkhutemas attempting to help alleviate the Soviet housing shortage by experimenting with space-saving, multifunctional, collapsible wooden furniture such as the modular units designed by Lissitzky in 1928. However, as far as is known, few of the Vkhutemas prototypes were actually adopted for mass production whereas from about 1927 Marcel Breuer's tubular steel furniture was produced by Standard-Möbel in Berlin while lighting fixtures by MARIANNE BRANDT (no. 118) and WILHELM WAGENFELD were manufactured in large quantities by Körting & Matthieson in Leipzig and Schwintzer & Gräff in Berlin.

Among the first to exploit the possibilities of tubular steel for mass-produced furniture, Breuer, who headed the Bauhaus cabinetmaking workshop from 1925 to 1928, sought a material that expressed its modern industrial origins in a way that processed wood, also a modern material, did not. For Breuer, standardized steel tubing was light, manageable, and durable—qualities that he did not expect critics of metal furniture to appreciate. As he explained, "When I saw the finished version of my first steel club armchair, I thought that this out of all my work would bring me the most criticism. It is my most extreme work both in its outward appearance and in the use of materials; it is the least artistic, the most logical, the least 'cosy' and the most mechanical."[17] Two other architects later affiliated with the Bauhaus, LUDWIG MIES VAN DER ROHE and Mart Stam, were also pioneers in metal furniture design, developing cantilevered steel chairs without back legs almost simultaneously about 1927 (no. 123). The chairs were both shown that year in the celebrated Werkbund-sponsored exhibition *Die Wohnung* (*The Home*), devoted to the theme of contemporary living and held in the Stuttgart suburb of Weissenhof. The permanent housing development built there by sixteen leading European architects, including Mies and Stam, Gropius, Le Corbusier, Bruno Taut, J.J.P. Oud, Hans Poelzig, and PETER BEHRENS, was intended to reform living standards by making the home a more efficient place for domestic work, showcasing the latest in technical and aesthetic developments, and utilizing new materials and cost-cutting construction techniques. Spare and functional, the steel-and-glass houses, with their flat roofs and horizontal strip windows, built-in storage units, and bare interiors sparsely furnished with standard wooden and metal furniture, epitomized the ambition of progressive designers in the 1920s to create new forms for a clean, efficient new world through modern technology.

Opposition to the Weissenhof housing within and without Germany was drawn along political as well as socio-cultural and aesthetic lines, critics deploring to varying degrees the loss of traditional values—in Germany, National Socialists viewed the "international" objective (*sachlich*) style of the exhibition and the Deutscher Werkbund that sponsored it as a betrayal of the German popular heritage. The machine aesthetic of the new international style deeply incensed those who defended the humanizing principles of the Arts and Crafts Movement. In England, John Gloag, a designer and sometime editor of the Design and Industries Association yearbook, identified the "new art" movement as foreign in origin and described it as "Robot modernism". "Although metal equipment may be satisfying to the standards of commercial life, and may adequately resist the wear and tear of an office, there does not appear to be any case for substituting metal for wood in furniture that is designed to give convenience and harmony to a home. A desire for novelty for its own sake may be the excuse for dramatic experiments in mechanistic design . . . [but] metal is cold and brutally hard, and . . . it gives no comfort to the eye."[18] A group of French artists, including those who had been considered most "modern" at the 1925 exposition—FRANCIS JOURDAIN, PIERRE CHAREAU, CHARLOTTE PERRIAND, RENÉ HERBST, Hélène Henry, and ROBERT MALLET-STEVENS—broke away from the conservative Société des Artistes Décorateurs in 1929 to found the Union des Artistes Modernes (UAM), defending "the modern spirit" against those who accused it of being "foreign in inspiration, a slave to the machine, and destructive of art trades and the tradition of craftsmanship."[19] These designers commonly used new technological materials, from artificial fibers in the furnishing fabrics of Henry to steel tubes and aluminum in the furniture of Herbst and Perriand (nos. 125, 126, 131).

These advanced designs and their critics notwithstanding, metal and other new materials were not widely accepted for domestic use in the years before World War II except for household appliances and equipment. While domestic electric equipment and lighting had been available since the turn of the century, technical improvements and more economical means of production in the years following the war brought greater demands for these products, which included electric refrigerators, stoves, washing machines, dishwashers, vacuum cleaners, irons, toasters, hot plates, and clocks. Progressive designers like Le Corbusier admired the geometric forms, economy of means and materials, and anonymity of the best vernacular products and machines and called for a new aesthetic of "purity" and "precision" derived from them.[20] Tubular lamps and simple lighting fixtures with bare bulbs designed at the Bauhaus and by Rietveld in Holland (no. 88) deliberately exposed the mechanical function of these fixtures, and as Le Corbusier prescribed, created from it a new machine aesthetic for the home.

83
ARMAND-ALBERT RATEAU
Chaise longue, c. 1920–22

A unique amalgam of refined classical and exotic forms, this bronze chaise longue was created for the French couturiere Jeanne Lanvin, who in 1920 entrusted the furnishing of her house in Paris to the decorator and bronzeworker Armand Rateau. Supported on the arched bodies of four greyhounds, the bed is a blanket of stylized bronze daisies (or marguerites, a motif alluding to the name of Lanvin's daughter that is repeated throughout the house) stretched like a spring from the sides and ends of the frame. The elegant shape of the day bed is based on the form of a Roman couch with high curved back, inspired by the works of antiquity that Rateau had seen on his travels to Pompeii and Naples in 1914. But the specific plant and animal imagery of the chased and sculpted decoration is personal to Rateau, adding a lush, unconventional, oriental aspect to this design. Versions of the chaise longue and other bronzework created for Lanvin were exhibited in the Pavillon de l'Elégance at the *Exposition Internationale des Arts Décoratifs* in Paris in 1925.

Patinated bronze. 25³/₁₆ x 60¹/₄ x 23³/₈" (64 x 153 x 60 cm). (Musée des Arts Décoratifs, Paris.)

84
EILEEN GRAY
Screen, 1922

The idea for this screen, built up of movable, lacquered-wood blocks, was borrowed from the Paris apartment that Eileen Gray designed for the milliner Mme. Mathieu-Lévy between 1919 and 1924, a luxurious but sparsely decorated interior virtually covered in lacquer and directly inspired by the angularity of cubism. The entrance hall was sheathed with similar lacquer blocks, some 450 pieces in gray, gold, and silver, and it was this configuration that she transformed

into the freestanding screen. Two such screens in white lacquer were also included among the cubistic lamps, rugs, furniture, and lacquerwork in the "Bedroom-Boudoir for Monte Carlo" that Gray showed at the Salon des Artistes Décorateurs in Paris in 1923. While her presentation was seen by some as an interesting curiosity distinct from most of the other work at the exhibition, its architectonic conception brought her to the attention of the De Stijl group—she became the subject of several articles in Dutch journals, with an entire issue of *Wendingen* in 1924 being devoted to her work. Screens of this design in black and in white lacquer were made for sale at Galerie Jean Désert, the shop Gray opened in Paris in 1922.

*Lacquered wood and aluminum. 71⁵/₈ x 70¹/₄ x 3/4" (181.9
    x 178.6 x 1.9 cm). (Virginia Museum of Fine Arts,
    Richmond, gift of Sydney and Frances Lewis.)*

85
PIERRE CHAREAU
The Nun lamp, 1923

One of the most advanced French designers of the 1920s, Pierre Chareau introduced such modern materials as metal and glass into his interiors and treated furniture and lighting as part of his architectural spaces. As in many of his product designs that made decorative use of the elements of which they were constructed, this floor lamp boldly reveals the wrought-metal fittings that secure the triangular slices of its alabaster shade. Chareau exploited the translucency of the alabaster to conceal the light source and provide a gentle, diffused illumination, an effect he developed into the glowing ambience of his glass-and-steel Maison de Verre (House of Glass) built in Paris between 1928 and 1933. Dubbed *The Nun (La Religieuse)* because its baroque outline suggested the coifs of French sisters and its conical standard their severe silhouettes, the lamp was first exhibited at the Salon des Artistes Décorateurs in Paris in 1924. That year it was included along with a number of Chareau's other lamps in the futuristic movie *L'Inhumaine* by Marcel l'Herbier, with settings, furnishings, and costumes by the circle of progressive artists with whom Chareau associated, including the painter Fernand Léger and the designers PAUL POIRET, ROBERT MALLET-STEVENS, JEAN PUIFORCAT, and RENÉ LALIQUE.

*Metal and alabaster. Height: 72¹/₂" (184.1 cm). (DeLorenzo
    Gallery, New York.)*

86
PIERRE LEGRAIN
Stool, 1922–26

No one had greater impact on the vogue for "African" furnishings in the early 1920s than the couturier and art patron Jacques Doucet, who used this style to create a suitable ambience for his own collection of African sculpture and his astounding fauve and cubist paintings—he owned, for example, Picasso's *Demoiselles d'Avignon*. Pierre Legrain was one of a number of artists Doucet commissioned to design furnishings for his Paris apartment and then his studio in Neuilly (built between 1926 and 1929). Of Legrain's designs in the African mode, some were anthropological, copying the forms of actual objects, while others, like this rosewood stool with latticed carving and pegged block feet, had less specific sources. These designs evoked the strength of African furniture, transposed into another dimension by the fine materials and craftsmanship of French cabinetmakers. Even before World War I, French avant-garde artists had been inspired by the traditional arts of Africa and other non-Western cultures, which were considered expressive in their naive stylizations of deep spiritual and symbolic ideals.

Rosewood. 12 x 29 x 9³/4" (30.5 x 73.6 x 24.8 cm).
   (Metropolitan Museum of Art, New York.)

87
GREGORY BROWN
Fabric, 1922

Gregory Brown's printed-linen fabric for the firm of William Foxton was one of the most advanced British exhibits at the *Exposition Internationale des Arts Décoratifs* in Paris in 1925. There he won a gold medal as an associate of Foxton, while the firm itself was awarded a diploma of honor for its textile display. The unselfconscious acceptance of slight irregularities in the drawing and printing of the black-and-gray design (other less sophisticated color combinations were also produced) owes much to the liberating experiments of the Omega Workshops a decade earlier (no. 57), while its cubistic, overlapping forms reflect progressive continental tendencies. Brown was one of a number of free-lance designers, including CHARLES RENNIE MACKINTOSH and the graphic artist Claud Lovat Fraser, to supply textile patterns for Foxton's, which during the 1920s and 1930s became known for its inexpensive printed fabrics in modern styles. Both Brown and William Foxton were founding members of the Design and Industries Association in 1915, and this fabric was one of the exemplary products published in 1922 in the association's yearbook, *Design in Modern Industry*.

Made by William Foxton, London. Printed linen. 44 x 37"
   (111.8 x 94 cm). (Victoria and Albert Museum, London.)

88
GERRIT RIETVELD
Hanging lamp, 1920–24

A four-bulb version of this hanging lamp was designed in 1920 by Gerrit Rietveld for the consulting room of Dr. A. M. Hartog's clinic at Maarssen in the Netherlands, one of Rietveld's earliest interiors and one of the first interior designs associated with the De Stijl movement, to which he belonged. The doctor's chair, file drawers, and lamp were all similarly conceived as an open construction of separate parts in compositions restricted to straight lines and right angles. Put together from standard tubular light bulbs and suspended from the ceiling by stock electrical wiring, this lamp exemplified the functionalist precept that advocated the use of undisguised materials, here brilliantly arranged as a series of mathematical coordinates in space. The fixture was modified by Rietveld to its present design for use in the Schröder house, which he designed and built in 1924–25, and was closely imitated by WALTER GROPIUS for his office at the Bauhaus in Weimar (1923), another clear influence of De Stijl on the German design school.

Glass and wood. 55 1/8 x 15 3/4 x 15 3/4" (140 x 40 x 40 cm). (Stedelijk Museum, Amsterdam.)

89
MARCEL BREUER
Armchair, 1922

Contact with other progressive design groups—the constructivists in the Soviet Union, for example, or the De Stijl group in the Netherlands—was a source of fertile inspiration for the Bauhaus in Weimar. The importance of these influences on the German design school (felt directly through visits by such artists as the Dutchman Theo van Doesburg and indirectly through publications) was firmly disputed at the time by its director, WALTER GROPIUS, but comparison of Marcel Breuer's armchair of 1922 with the furniture of GERRIT RIETVELD leaves little doubt of the debt that this Bauhaus student owed to the Netherlands. With its rigid open construction of intersecting horizontal and vertical elements and its cantilevered arms, the armchair relates to Rietveld's famous *Red/Blue* chair of 1918 (no. 81) and even more closely to his similarly constructed child's chair of 1920–21. Conceived with an eye to its abstract composition, the armchair was nevertheless recommended in the catalog of new Bauhaus work in 1925 not for its intellectual or artistic achievement but for the comfort and support that its sloping seat and fabric bands could provide to the body.

Made at Bauhaus cabinetmaking workshop, Weimar. Oak with canvas upholstery. 37 5/16 x 22 1/16 x 22 1/2" (94.8 x 56 x 57.1 cm). (Art Institute of Chicago.)

90
**HERBERT BAYER AND
LÁSZLÓ MOHOLY-NAGY**
Cover and title page of *Staatliches Bauhaus,
Weimar, 1919–1923,* 1923

This book cataloged the first public exhibition of the
Bauhaus and established the principles of the school's
new typography, if not its final resolution. The title
page and layout were designed by László Moholy-
Nagy, the youngest master at the Bauhaus and head of
both its foundation course and metal workshop. He
also contributed essays to the book, among them "The
New Typography," in which he emphasized the importance of typography for communication. "It must be
communication in its most intense form," he wrote.
"The emphasis must be on absolute clarity . . .
unequivocal clarity in all typographical compositions. . . . The essence and the purpose of printing
demand an uninhibited use of all linear directions . . .
all typefaces, type sizes, geometric forms, colors, etc.
We want to create a new language of typography
whose elasticity, variability, and freshness of typographical composition is exclusively dictated by the inner law
of expression and the optical effect."[21] This book's
interior design demonstrates Moholy's drive toward
clarity using a rich new vocabulary partly inspired by EL
LISSITZKY and other constructivist designers. The cover,
the work of Herbert Bayer, then an advanced student
of Moholy and Wassily Kandinsky, uses rough, hand-
drawn lettering, dividing words into blocks of red and
blue while condensing some letters and spacing others
more widely to make the lines equal in length. Like the
exhibition as a whole, the book caused much public
debate and was criticized for its "shopwindow" effects,
"brutal" color, and lack of "refinement in form."[22]

*Printed book. 10 x 9 1/4" (25.4 x 23.6 cm). (Philadelphia
Museum of Art.)*

91
MARIANNE BRANDT
Teapot, 1924

Many students at the Weimar Bauhaus took up the
challenge of creating new forms from geometric constructions pioneered elsewhere in Europe by cubist,
De Stijl, purist, and constructivist artists. Applying these
chiefly pictorial lessons to the design of household
objects, often for the first time, Bauhaus designers
experimented with three-dimensional figures in various
combinations. Conceived as sections of circles and
spheres, the body, lid, and handle of Marianne Brandt's
teapot are each clearly defined, each executed with
the mathematical discipline and exactitude considered
necessary to the new aesthetic. Such early products of
the Bauhaus metal workshop, made and finished by
hand and including decanters, samovars, and jewelry,
reflected the craft bias of the school, a bias that gradually gave way to the demands of industrial production
for more utilitarian, less complicated shapes. The pot
was also made with a swing handle as part of a larger
tea service.

*Made at Bauhaus metal workshop, Weimar. Brass, ebony,
and silver. Height: 2 15/16" (7.5 cm); diameter: 6 1/8" (15.5
cm). (Bauhaus-Archiv, Berlin.)*

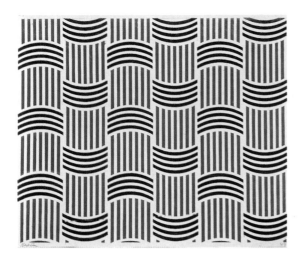

92
VARVARA STEPANOVA
Fabric, 1924

The role of art in the new society established by the Revolution of 1917 became a topic of intense discussion in the Soviet Union, with some theorists proposing that art should function as propaganda and others insisting that the ideal socialist order be expressed through abstraction. For their part, the constructivists declared that pure art was dead and demanded that artists become directly involved in production. With industry totally in disrepair and materials in short supply, little headway was made in bringing artists into factories until the early 1920s. In 1923 Varvara Stepanova and Lyubov Popova were invited to work in the large First State Textile Printing Factory (Pervaya Gosudarstvennaya Sittsenabivnaya Fabrika) in Moscow where for about a year they designed fabrics and worked on organizing the factory's production. Stepanova wanted to replace the traditional floral patterns with geometry, and so with compass and ruler alone she created rigorous, geometrically based designs of amazing complexity. With a restricted, economical palette, usually just one or two colors, she conceived a series of projects for fabrics whose optical illusionism suggested depth and movement. Stepanova created some 150 such designs, 20 to 30 of which ultimately entered production.

Made by First State Textile Printing Factory, Moscow.
Printed cotton. 30 1/2 x 19 11/16" (77.5 x 48.5 cm).
(Centre Georges Pompidou, Paris.)

93
GERHARD MARCKS
Sintrax **coffee maker, 1925**

Patented in the United States before the turn of the century, glass coffee makers of this type grew in popularity in several countries in spite of their fragility because they were considered sanitary, novel, and better for making coffee than metal ones, which oxidized and were said to spoil the flavor. Gerhard Marcks's version, the *Sintrax* coffee maker, was praised for its particular beauty of form, its shapes "clearly arranged for specific tasks."[23] Head of the Bauhaus pottery workshop at the time, Marcks rationalized the shapes of the glass vessels used in this coffee maker, creating several models whose simplicity and sleekness paralleled other Bauhaus products. The instructions that accompanied the *Sintrax* explained that the coffee maker, which came with stand and spirit lamp, was not a kitchen utensil but "meant especially for the living room to make Mokka. It is particularly suited for the coffee table."

Made by Jenaer Glaswerk, Schott & Gen., Jena, Germany.
Glass, cork, wood, and metal. Height: 12 5/8" (32 cm).
(Galerie Torsten Bröhan, Düsseldorf.)

94
**KARL J. JUCKER AND
WILHELM WAGENFELD**
Table lamp, 1923–24

Sleek and unobtrusively wired through a metal tube within the glass stem, this lamp was one of the most successful designs of the early years of the Bauhaus metal workshop, a time when complicated forms and experimental mechanisms distinguished other lighting fixtures created there. LÁSZLÓ MOHOLY-NAGY. director of the metal workshop, described these early lamps:

> I remember the first lighting fixture by K. Jucker, done before 1923, with devices for pushing and pulling, heavy strips and rods of iron and brass, looking more like a dinosaur than a functional object. But even this was a great victory, for it meant a new beginning. After this we developed lighting fixtures introducing such useful ideas as: the close-fitting ceiling cap; combinations of opaque and frosted glass in simple forms technically determined by the action of the light; securing the globe to the metal chassis; the use of aluminum, particularly for reflectors, etc. All of these were adopted for industrial production.[24]

A version of this lamp with a metal base, attributed to Wagenfeld alone, appeared in the Bauhaus catalog of 1925, the year in which he patented the socket that joined the lamp parts together "in a simple and safe manner."

Made at Bauhaus metal workshop, Weimar. Clear glass, opalescent glass, nickel-plated brass, and steel. Height: 15 3/8" (38 cm). (Bauhaus-Archiv, Berlin.)

95
KAZIMIR MALEVICH AND ILIA CHASHNIK
Cup, 1923

Described as "a cup cut halfway across and impractical for drinking" when it was shown in an exhibition of Soviet porcelain in 1926, this work was designed by Kazimir Malevich, the inventor of suprematism. A nonobjective style that employed abstract symbols—square, triangle, and circle—suprematism sought to convey feelings through the creation of primordial rhythms. Choosing the opposing elements of a straight line and a half circle, Malevich used this cup and a cubistic teapot, which the reviewer called "strange" and "reminiscent of a steam engine,"[25] to explore his ideas about resolving the "dissonances" between shapes, creating utilitarian objects that in their insistence on abstract form seem more concerned with geometry than with function. The painted decoration is the work of Ilia Chashnik, a student of Malevich and one of a number of suprematist artists who began to work at the State Porcelain Factory in Petrograd in 1923.

Made by State Porcelain Factory, Petrograd. Glazed porcelain with enamel decoration. Height: 2 3/8" (6 cm). (Cooper-Hewitt Museum, New York, Henry and Ludmilla Shapiro Collection.)

96
THEODOR BOGLER
Teapot, 1923

One of the first designs for industry to be made at the Bauhaus pottery workshop and illustrated in the school's catalog of 1925, this teapot was produced in four variations with the individual parts—handles, spouts, and lids—differently positioned. The idea of interchanging parts in a series production (pioneered by PETER BEHRENS; no. 46) was one Theodor Bogler pursued during his career at the Bauhaus pottery workshop; these designs, the first from the Bauhaus actually mass-produced, included containers for kitchen supplies made by the Steingutfabrik at Velten-Vordamm and a take-apart mocha machine made by the Staatliche Porzellanmanufaktur in Berlin (1923). Bogler's use of elementary shapes, as in this teapot, with each part clearly defined and set off in simple contrast from the next, was designed to facilitate serial production. The strength, simplicity, and clarity of form that this teapot and other Bogler designs conveyed were features widely adopted by the German ceramics industry during the 1920s and 1930s—even though the Bauhaus pottery workshop was effectively dissolved after the school moved to Dessau in 1925.

Made at Bauhaus pottery workshop, Dornburg an der Saale, Germany. Glazed earthenware. Height: 4 15/16" (12.5 cm). (Bauhaus-Archiv, Berlin.)

97
ANNI ALBERS
Wall hanging, 1925

One of the early products of the Bauhaus weaving workshop after its move to Dessau in 1925, this hanging represented an evolution in theory and practice from the first textiles made in the weaving workshop at Weimar. These Anni Albers recalled as amateurishly experimental, "unburdened by any practical considerations." Later, when the students "became concerned with a practical purpose . . . a shift took place from free play with forms to logical composition. As a result, more systematic training in the mechanics of weaving was introduced, as well as a course in the dyeing of yarns."[26] As the workshop at Dessau became increasingly concerned with designing for industry, the transition from handwork to machine work became necessary. Although design ideas for machine production continued to be worked out on hand looms, the workshop acquired the Jacquard power looms on which this hanging was created. The looms simplified the process of figure weaving through a mechanized warp selection, increased the speed of production, and ultimately reduced the price of the finished fabric. Albers's grid designs like this, incorporating man-made materials that could be produced on commercial machines, stressed the fundamental construction of woven fabrics as the intersection at right angles of two separate systems of thread. Such simple constructions were also best suited to a manufacture aiming at quantity, speed, and low cost, and to the aesthetic quality of "simplicity—clarified vision," which Anni Albers claimed as her goal.[27]

Made at Bauhaus weaving workshop, Dessau, Germany. Silk, cotton, and acetate. 50 x 38" (145 x 92 cm). (Neue Sammlung, Munich.)

98
EL LISSITZKY
Advertisement for Pelikan ink, 1924

The posters, letterheads, advertisements, packaging, and brochures that El Lissitzky undertook in 1924 and 1925 for the firm of Günther Wagner, manufacturer of Pelikan art supplies and stationery products, introduced a new approach to commercial graphics. Rejecting simplicity of representation and clarity of product identification, they brought complex structural compositions and enigmatic imagery to the world of advertising. Lissitzky's designs focused on typography arranged in bold and unorthodox ways and created imaginative effects through the experimental use of photography. For this advertisement, he employed the photogram, an imprecise process for capturing images directly without the intervention of a camera lens, which was also being explored by Christian Schad, MAN RAY, and LÁSZLÓ MOHOLY-NAGY. He obtained the shadowy composition of fountain pen, ink bottle, and the Pelikan mark by exposing light-sensitive paper to light flashed on objects in a darkroom, and set it off with the product message—flat, white letters of the word *Tinte* (ink) that seem to be stenciled on the picture surface.

Photomontage. 5³/4 x 4" (14.6 x 10.1 cm). (Museum für Gestaltung, Basel.)

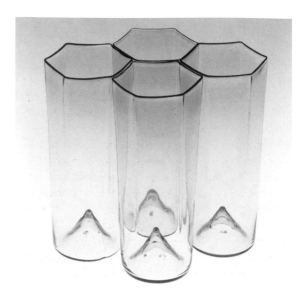

99
CAPPELLIN-VENINI & C.
Glasses, 1921–25

The reports of the Paris exhibition of 1925, at which Venini & C. (recent successor to Cappellin-Venini & C.) was awarded a grand prize, credited the firm with "having effected in only a few years, a magnificent recovery"[28] in the art of glassmaking in Murano. Rejecting the ornamentalism and the furnace-formed decorations of the Venetian island's traditional products, "Venini & its associates have decided that such a formula no longer corresponds to modern taste. They have refined the designs and forms, striving for simple compositions, for frank and logical resolutions. The great purity of logically studied lines appears in their glass tablewares, in the forms of their vases, in the curve of the handles, in the airy branches of a candelabrum."[29] The sharp angularity of these simple, pure hexagonal glasses gives an unexpectedly modern appearance to tableware and clearly distinguishes it from the usual rounded, utilitarian forms of blown glass. The glasses with their accompanying bottle are illustrated as model 213 in the earliest known Venini catalog, where they are dated to 1921–25, the period when PAOLO VENINI was a partner in Cappellin-Venini & C. The glasses are still being made by the Venini glass factory in Murano, although in the recent production the indented base is less pronounced.

Blown glass with colored decoration. Height: 6³/16" (15.7 cm). (Philadelphia Museum of Art, gift of Maude de Schauensee and Maxine Lewis.)

100
MAURICE MARINOT
Covered jar, 1924

One of the most celebrated glassmakers of the twentieth century, Maurice Marinot, a painter, took up glassmaking about 1911 and reached artistic maturity in the mid-1920s with works such as this. In 1925 Marinot served as a jury member for the glass section of the Paris international exposition. His own work of the period often shared the preoccupation with abstract, cubist-inspired forms that many of the exhibitors displayed and that informs the geometric shapes of this jar and its cover. Marinot's glasses evolved, in his words, from "within the material,"[30] which had to be worked hot in a malleable state. His unsurpassed technical mastery of glass as a material and of the methods of working it resulted in such highly original textural effects as the ascending air bubbles embedded in the thick walls of this jar, acid etching and wheel cutting employed in novel ways, and "crackled" coatings of colored metallic oxides. Marinot defended his preoccupation with the craft of glassmaking and wrote in 1924 that only those artists whose works expressed their medium in such a direct and personal way should have a "special place" at the exhibition of 1925; at the same time he criticized the teaching of applied arts in France in which "technique occupied only a small place" resulting in "decorative compositions" lacking the "lucidity and balance" of true craft.[31]

Gray bubbled glass. Height: 10 3/4" (27.3 cm). (Philadelphia Museum of Art, gift of Mlle. Florence Marinot.)

101
SONIA DELAUNAY
Fabric, 1924

With the words "Atelier Simultané" printed on the selvedge of the fabrics Sonia Delaunay produced for her shop in Paris, the painter-turned-designer showed her continuing allegiance to "simultaneity," or orphism, the avant-garde style of painting with geometrical shapes in pure color oppositions that she pioneered with her husband Robert. In painterly fashion, Delaunay prepared her patterns of squares, triangles, diamonds, and stripes as gouache sketches, using very harsh color contrasts—deep blue, bright red, black, white, and yellow or green. She then recast them into a number of different tonal combinations for printing. Affirming that she had undertaken "a total revision in the values of textile art," Robert Delaunay paid homage to the modernity of his wife's designs: "They are responsive to the painting, to the architecture of modern life, to the bodies of cars, to the beautiful and original forms of airplanes—in short, to the aspirations of this active, modern age, which has forged a style intimately related to its incredibly fast and intense life."[32]

Printed chiffon. Length: 21 1/4" (54 cm). (Musée de l'Impression sur Etoffes, Mulhouse, France.)

102
JEAN PROUVÉ
Chair, 1924

Made of bent, welded, and lacquered sheet steel, Jean Prouvé's innovative metal furniture was aligned more with the automotive and aeronautical industries than with the manufacture and aesthetics of traditional French decorative arts. "I used to think of furniture as being on a par with the seating of heavy-duty machinery," he later recounted. "I therefore took the same care over construction and applied the same tensile standards to the materials, indeed using the very same materials. I found curved steel tubing unsatisfactory, while sheet steel inspired me to fold, joint, score and then weld it. This produced areas of uniform strength and strict outlines which were set off by the attention paid to detail and by the quality of the finish."[33] Despite its industrial conception, Prouvé's early furniture was produced in small batches and made to order, a process that accommodated variations as the designs continued to be produced. This chair, with its adjustable folding seat, is closely related to a model Prouvé made for the wedding of his sister in 1928; both were shown in 1930 in his installation at the first exhibition of the Union des Artistes Modernes.

Made by Ateliers Jean Prouvé, Nancy. Steel with canvas upholstery. Height: 40¹/2" (103 cm). (Location unknown.)

103
ROBERT MALLET-STEVENS
Armchair, c. 1924

Constructed of thick tubular metal lacquered in green, this chair represents an early domestic application of tubular metal furniture. It comes from the villa that Robert Mallet-Stevens designed in 1923–24 for the Vicomte de Noailles, a noted patron and collector of avant-garde art. One of the earliest modern structures built in France, the low country house set in the hillside of Hyères in Provence was furnished with the work of the architect's friends PIERRE CHAREAU, FRANCIS JOURDAIN, and EILEEN GRAY, his student Edouard-Joseph Djo-Bourgeois, along with that of MARCEL BREUER and other Bauhaus designers. The stylish squared frame of this chair is neither upholstered nor ornamented but remains open with a canvas seat loosely slung from the top to the front rail. Like Breuer, whose iconic tubular-steel armchair (no. 104) parallels it in date and in the simplicity of its open geometric form, Mallet-Stevens worked toward creating "an aesthetic corresponding to modern life," as he wrote in 1924. "The machine triumphs. The eye understands the accuracy, the simplicity of machines. We are accustomed to the lines of motor cars, locomotives, aeroplanes, telephones, electric radiators, radio aerials, and we like them. Smooth surfaces, crisp articulation, clean curves, polished materials, right angles; clarity, order. This is the logical and geometrical house of tomorrow."[34]

Lacquered metal with canvas upholstery. 357/16 x 337/8 x 2413/16" (90 x 86 x 63 cm). (Galerie Maria de Beyrie, Paris.)

104
MARCEL BREUER
Armchair, 1925

One of the first examples of modern tubular-steel furniture, this armchair has become inextricably associated with the Bauhaus. Marcel Breuer created it independently of his work there, however, and, to the displeasure of Bauhaus director WALTER GROPIUS, produced it outside the school's workshops. He manufactured it first in his own studio, then through Standard-Möbel, the firm founded for this purpose by

Breuer and the Hungarian architect Kalman Lengyel, and later through other licensed manufacturers, including the large international bentwood furniture maker Thonet. As the story goes, a bicycle Breuer purchased after his return to teach at the Dessau Bauhaus in 1925 inspired him to experiment with tubular steel, hiring a plumber to weld the tubes together for his prototypes. These progressed from a version with four separate legs to the definitive design with runners shown here, which gives the impression that the chair is constructed from a single piece of gleaming bent tubing, fluidly outlining a cube in space and containing the resilient, tautly stretched canvas seat and back. Listed in the 1927 Standard-Möbel catalog as Model *B3*, the chair received the name *Wassily* (after the painter Kandinsky, whose early praise reassured Breuer in his new effort) only when it was brought back into production by the firm of Gavina in 1962.

Probably made by Gebrüder Thonet, Frankenberg, Germany. Chrome-plated tubular steel with canvas upholstery. 281/8 x 301/4 x 273/4" (71.4 x 76.8 x 70.5 cm). (Museum of Modern Art, New York, gift of Herbert Bayer.)

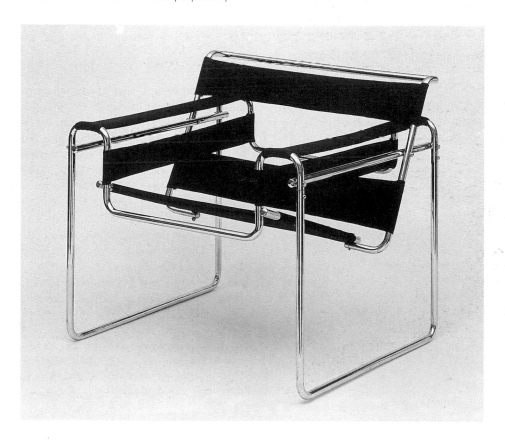

105
CLÉMENT ROUSSEAU
Chairs, 1925

Clément Rousseau was the master of color in French luxury furniture design during the 1920s, using precious materials—most spectacularly and characteristically, natural and dyed shagreen or sharkskin—almost as pigments to create pictorial effects. In these chairs, which borrow a late eighteenth-century silhouette, he combined mother-of-pearl with sharkskin to create floral patterns on the backs and a sunray motif on the sides of the seats, taking advantage of the grain of the skin

to add a richly textured overall surface pattern. Rousseau had learned to prepare and apply sharkskin as an assistant to PAUL IRIBE, who reintroduced this eighteenth-century technique around 1910. But it was Rousseau who expanded its decorative and pictorial use and applied it most lavishly to furniture and accessories throughout the next two decades.

Rosewood, sharkskin, and mother-of-pearl, with upholstery. Each: 36 1/2 x 17 x 20 1/2" (92.7 x 43.2 x 52.1 cm). (Virginia Museum of Fine Arts, Richmond, gift of Sydney and Frances Lewis.)

106
SÜE ET MARE
Desk, c. 1924

The *Exposition Internationale des Arts Décoratifs et Industriels Modernes* in 1925 was conceived to reinvigorate the French decorative arts and to thwart the incursion of mass-produced, standardized furnishings from abroad. While the exhibition allowed only works in a new style—reproductions were forbidden—the majority of French exhibitors continued to mine nationalist traditions without being specifically imitative. They relied on both the know-how of French hand craftsmanship and on luxury materials, as well as the stylistic creations of their past; the latter they studied, according to one reviewer, "with gifts of remarkable invention, which have permitted them to renew their forms, distill their spirit, and accentuate their charm, conferring on them a rhythm and a harmony that makes them totally creations of our time."[35] Such was the case with this desk and the other furnishings shown in the "Museum of Contemporary Art," the exhibit of the firm established by Louis Süe and André

Mare (known also as the Compagnie des Arts Français). Süe et Mare's characteristic bulbous forms and the stark contrast of ebony surface with gilded over-ample palmettes distinguish the desk completely from the type of Louis XV writing table with cabriole legs and rococo ornament on which it is ultimately based.

Ebony and gilded bronze. 30 1/4 x 61 7/8 x 32 1/2" (76.8 x 157.2 x 82.5 cm). (Metropolitan Museum of Art, New York, purchase, Edward C Moore, Jr., Gift Fund, 1925.)

107
PIERRE CHAREAU
Desk, 1925

The Société des Artistes Décorateurs, founded in 1901, was represented in 1925 at the *Exposition Internationale des Arts Décoratifs* with a separate pavilion conceived as "A French Embassy." The building was designed and coordinated by Pierre Selmersheim and Henri Rapin and its rooms furnished by members of the society representing a sharply divided range of decorative and theoretical persuasions—from the "colorist-decorator" PAUL FOLLOT to the advanced "engineer-builders" ROBERT MALLET-STEVENS and Pierre Chareau. The library-study in the private apartments of the "embassy" was assigned to Chareau, who created a nearly bare, paneled circular room encased in bookshelves. Above was a cupola lit by artificial light with an ingenious revolving shutter system designed to control its intensity. Below as the focus of the room stood this polished wood desk, abstract in shape with angled surfaces, fitted compartments, and U-shaped

steel handles. The piece was described in a review as "a perfect example of cabinetwork, designed like a piece of architecture, with sloping planes to prevent books and papers from piling up, conveying the orderliness and discipline which characterizes modern life."[36]

Brazilian rosewood, mahogany, oak, and steel. 30 x 55 1/8 x 30 1/4" (76 x 140 x 77 cm). (Musée des Arts Décoratifs, Paris.)

108
JEAN DUNAND
Vase, c. 1925

Jean Dunand, the best-known and most successful artist to work in lacquer in this period, transformed the traditional craft technique into a modern idiom. He applied lacquer first to metalware and then to the wooden screens and furniture for which he is also known. Lacquer initially enhanced the subtle coloristic effects he had previously achieved in metalwork through acid-derived patinas and inlays of softer metals, including gold, silver, and nickel. Later he typically coated his base-metal forms with a thick, richly colored lacquer into which he carved or incised geometric designs. By the mid-1920s, he had begun to explore a new, formally advanced cubist vocabulary, breaking through the pure outlines of his vessels with intersecting ribs and eccentric collars such as this.

Lacquered brass. Height: 8" (21 cm). (DeLorenzo Gallery, New York.)

109
EILEEN GRAY
Transat armchair, c. 1927

While Eileen Gray chose modern materials for the progressive furnishings she designed during the later 1920s, she was decidedly opposed to the aesthetic formalism of many of her contemporaries:

> To consider the construction of a table or a chair as the realization of a sculpture, undertaking it only from the point of view of the harmony of form, necessarily results in excess and absurdity, which misleads public taste and makes those who have not lost the notion of practical utility appear backward. Tubular steel as it is conceived and used by avant-garde architects is expensive, unstable, and cold. The need to call attention to oneself, to be original at any price, results in suppressing the most elementary concern for practical comfort.[37]

Gray's *Transat* chair was designed with comfort and flexibility in mind for a small vacation house called *E.1027*, which she built for the architectural critic and publisher Jean Badovici at Roquebrune in the south of France. Initially sketched about 1924 and patented in 1930, the chair has a disassemblable rectangular frame constructed of lacquered wood rods joined with chromed-steel connectors and an adjustable leather headrest and a pliable seat. Following the nautical theme of a house at the edge of the sea, it is based on the idea of a deck chair (*transatlantique* in French, from

which the name *Transat* is derived). Black lacquer and leather were used on the *Transat* chairs for *E.1027*, but versions in other colors, like this one, were also sold at Gray's shop in Paris, Galerie Jean Désert.

Lacquered wood and chromed steel with leather upholstery. Height: 31 1/2" (80 cm). (Victoria and Albert Museum, London.)

110
GIO PONTI
My Women vase, c. 1925

Borrowing the seventeenth-century idea of a portrait-filled "gallery of beauties," with "his women" decorating not the walls of a room but the surface of this ceramic vase, Gio Ponti demonstrated his adherence to the traditional values of Italian classicism, both in the subject of his design and his pictorial style. Hired in 1923 to renovate the production of the Richard-Ginori firm, Ponti was one of a number of progressive young Italian designers who sought to synthesize a nationalistic vocabulary with the exigencies of modern mass production, creating a new rationalized form of neo-classicism that became identified with Italian architecture and design in the 1920s and 30s. The voluptuous Renaissance beauties on the *My Women (Le Mie Donne)* vase were reduced to contour lines against a fantastic architectural background that Ponti referred to as "Palladian"[38] after the sixteenth-century Italian architect. These decorations were applied not only to

vases but also to a series of large dishes. Ponti's ceramics for Ginori were first exhibited at the *Esposizione Internazionale delle Arti Decorative* (the Biennale) in Monza in 1923, where the firm was awarded a grand prize; later at the Paris exposition of 1925 Ponti and the firm were awarded individual grand prizes.

Made by Richard-Ginori, Sesto Fiorentino, Italy. Glazed earthenware. Height: 18³/₄" (47.5 cm); diameter: 16¹⁵/₁₆" (43 cm). (Museo delle Porcellane di Doccia, Sesto Fiorentino, Italy.)

111
RENÉ LALIQUE
Tourbillons vase, 1926

The technique of creating pressed glass, a machine-manufacturing process used from the early nineteenth century for popular imitations of cut and engraved glass, was taken up by René Lalique for luxury mass production—first for the perfume bottles he designed and manufactured for Coty beginning about 1908 and then for a variety of his other wares, including vases, bowls, and his renowned automobile mascots. By using a different kind of glass body, a malleable "demi-crystal" with a composition low enough in lead to be unaffected by high temperatures, Lalique was able to adapt the technique to create perfect glasswares with sharp edges and deep bold forms, unlike the soft imprecise decoration of earlier pressed glass. Lalique's *Tourbillons* or *Whirlwinds* vase is perhaps the most powerful of these designs; its abstract decoration has deep beveled indentations and swirling lines in varying thicknesses of opalescent glass defined here in shiny black enamel quite unlike the naturalistic low-relief compositions of figures, plants, and animals that predominate in his other work. Versions in colored glass were also produced.

Made by René Lalique & Cie, Wingen-sur-Moder, France. Molded colorless glass with enamel decoration. Height: 7⁷/₈" (20 cm). (Philadelphia Museum of Art, the Henry P. McIlhenny Collection.)

112
JEAN PERZEL
Wall lamp, 1927–28

During the 1920s and 30s, when a keen interest developed in the science of lighting and its aesthetic, physiological, and psychological effects, designers and engineers began to emphasize the even illumination of diffused and indirect lighting. While PIERRE CHAREAU sought to diffuse light with sheets of translucent alabaster (no. 85), Jean Perzel used a type of semi-opaque glass he himself had developed. "It would be pretentious to say," he wrote, "that I would like to treat electricity in the way that the old stained glass artists treated the sun, but that is what I tried to do. I wanted to mask entirely the luminous source in using its rays; from which came my research into the relative opacity of nacreous and frosted glass."[39] His glass was sandblasted on the inside to give subtle uniform illumination and then enameled without in white or with a light tint of color—this wall lamp, for example, has concentric circles of milky white and yellow. The geometric forms of Perzel's fixtures could be very simple, designed, according to *Mobilier & Décoration*, "with an astonishing ingenuity and a strict logic."[40]

Chromed brass and enameled glass. Diameter: 13 3/8" (34 cm). (Musée des Arts Décoratifs, Paris.)

113
S. STRUSEVICH
Electric Light Bulbs fabric, c. 1928–30

The geometric textile designs introduced by the constructivists (no. 92) fell out of favor in the later 1920s along with traditional Soviet floral patterns, when the more practical agitational and propagandistic uses of art were emphasized again as they had been after the Revolution of 1917. "Textile design," the introduction to the Moscow exhibition of Soviet domestic textiles in 1928 stated, "has an enormous part to play in changing old tastes, in breaking old aesthetic traditions and habits (along with the ideological ones that are so bound up in them); it is a vehicle for the new culture and the new ideology."[41] Themes such as industrialization, construction, transportation, communication, sports, and the new Russian pioneer were depicted in Soviet textiles, some of which had been shown in Paris in 1925 alongside those by the constructivists. Airplanes, steamships, tractors, and machinery were represented literally (often interspersed with Soviet emblems), sometimes in traditional decorative formats, sometimes in angular, stylized repetitions that reinforced the dynamism of the new society. The emblematic light bulbs on this cotton print created for the Soviet Republics of Central Asia make graphically clear the energy involved in the process of electrification, which was taking place during the time of the first Five Year Plan (1928–32) when this fabric was produced.

Made by Sosnevsk Amalgamated Mills, Ivanovo, Russia. Printed cotton. (Location unknown.)

114
A. M. CASSANDRE
Poster for the *Etoile du Nord*, 1927

The French government of the 1920s and 30s gave renewed support to the nation's traditional decorating industry and the reputation of its designers and craftsmen through commissions for furnishing new steamships and railway cars. They were outfitted in a range of modern styles by such designers as the ATELIER MARTINE, FRANCIS JOURDAIN, RENÉ LALIQUE, EMILE-JACQUES RUHLMANN, and JEAN DUNAND. As transport became more commodious, the means and activity of travel took on new importance, and these rather than the destination began to be emphasized in advertisements commissioned from progressive designers. A. M. Cassandre drew on cubism and futurism for the mechanistic image of speeding trains in several posters he designed for the French national railways beginning in 1927; in other instances, however, he took a more expressive approach. Here, with stencils and airbrush, he created a deep, mysterious landscape in which four railway tracks lead to a distant horizon and converge on a gleaming star symbolizing the name of the train, the *Etoile du Nord* (*North Star*), printed at the bottom of the image in overlapping block letters.

Printed by Hachard & Cie, Paris. Lithograph. 41 3/8 x 29 3/4"
(106 x 75.5 cm). (Reinhold-Brown Gallery, New York.)

115
PAUL POIRET
Vanity, 1928

Explaining that "the unity of the whole room is more important than is the beauty of any individual piece,"[42] Contempora exhibited eight "Harmonized Rooms" in New York in 1929, soon after the group was formed to bring modern design to American homes. These ensembles were mass-produced for sale at moderate prices and each was available in six different color ranges; they were to be bought as complete units, including furniture, floor and wall coverings, draperies, and lighting (with hangings, paintings, or reliefs to serve as their decoration), all designed by the group's members, Bruno Paul, LUCIAN BERNHARD, Rockwell Kent, and Paul Poiret, as well as three associated artists. Integrated within the sweeping lines of Poiret's vanity and matching bed were seating and storage units, tables, and lighted shelving, the whole covered with washable DuPont Fabrikoid. This gilded and silvered dressing table, lacquered in chartreuse—a "hue now so fashionable" said the *New York Times*[43]—captures the flamboyant stylishness that had been the hallmark of Poiret's ATELIER MARTINE and anticipates both the streamlined designs and the unit-furnishing concepts of the 1930s.

Made for Contempora, New York. Lacquered, gilded, and silvered Fabrikoid over plywood, glass, and bronze. Height: 52" (132 cm). (DeLorenzo Collection.)

116
POUL HENNINGSEN
Hanging lamp, 1926

Using his studies on the dispersion of light, the architect Poul Henningsen conceived a series of table and hanging lamps that won all six prizes in a 1924 lighting competition for the Danish pavilion at the upcoming *Exposition Internationale des Arts Décoratifs* in Paris. The designs then won a gold medal when the models were shown at the exhibition the next year and formed the basis of the series of PH lamps manufactured by Louis Poulsen. Instead of diffusing light through translucent materials to minimize the harshness of the incandescent bulbs (nos. 85, 112), Henningsen cast the light where he wanted it by altering the shape and position of the shades; he was able to direct it downward from one shade while providing ambient lighting from another, at the same time controlling the intensity of the light reflected off the shades and masking the bulb itself. The first production model, this hanging lamp with tiered opal-glass shade, was introduced in 1926 as part of the furnishings for the new Forum exhibition hall in Copenhagen. By 1927 PH lamps were well-enough known abroad to be included among the furnishings of Stuttgart's Weissenhof experimental housing development. In 1928 they were illustrated among the progressive lighting in the Deutscher Werkbund architects' reference book on lighting, *Licht und Beleuchtung*.

Made by Louis Poulsen & Company, Copenhagen. Opal glass and brass. Diameter: 195/8" (50 cm). (Louis Poulsen & Company, Copenhagen.)

117
EDOUARD-WILFRID BUQUET
Lamp, 1927

Patented in France in 1927,[44] Edouard-Wilfrid Buquet's rationalized lamp has a base that can also be easily mounted to a wall or angled surface and jointed, counterweighted arms that can be adjusted and rotated at any angle to bring light within a large radius. According to the patent, the lamp "is movable with the slightest possible effort, and its stability does not vary at all with its extension, nor the size or lightness of its base. It can thus occupy all positions and orientations in space without exception, for the arms can describe complete circles around each of their joints. To achieve this, each of the jointed arms is balanced in such a way that its center of gravity coincides with its point of articulation." The lamp was extremely popular among architects and decorators during the later 1920s for its unornamented usefulness and was frequently reproduced in art and architecture magazines as part of their ensembles. One version was used in the office of the French designer Lucien Rollin who exhibited another at the Salon of the Société des Artistes Décorateurs in Paris on his maple *Desk of a Technician* in 1929. Rollin and his French colleagues who remained with the society and opposed the use of metal furniture, favoring severe designs in wood instead, nonetheless willingly accepted metal accessories in their interiors.

Made by W. W. Buquet. Nickel-plated brass, aluminum, and lacquered wood. Height (extended): 36" (91.4 cm). (Museum of Modern Art, New York, D. S. and R. H. Gottesman Foundation.)

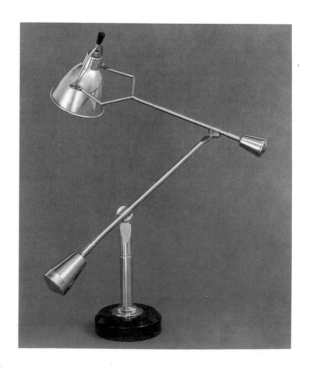

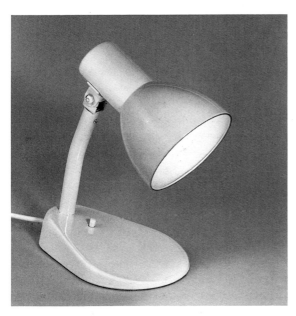

**118
MARIANNE BRANDT**
Kandem table lamp, c. 1927

The metal workshop of the Bauhaus most successfully realized the ambition of WALTER GROPIUS to create prototypes for industry and to make the Bauhaus a "laboratory for mass production" where products "typical of our time are carefully developed and constantly improved."[45] The workshop was oriented toward the development and manufacture of articles for everyday use to serve "present-day housing, from the simplest household appliances to the finished dwelling."[46] Marianne Brandt was among the most gifted of the metal workshop's apprentices and journeymen, designing a series of simple, efficient lamps with clear, geometrical forms that were widely produced by metal firms in Berlin, Leipzig, and Stuttgart. The most commercially successful and popular of Brandt's designs, this small, sturdy table lamp with an adjustable shade is an example of the products developed by the Bauhaus that could be offered, as Gropius conceived, "at a reasonable price through the utilization of all the modern economical means of standardization (industrial mass production) and wide marketing."[47]

Made by Körting & Matthieson, Leipzig. Lacquered steel. Height: 9⁷/₈" (25 cm). (Bauhaus-Archiv, Berlin.)

**119
HERBERT BAYER**
Cover of *bauhaus*, 1928

In 1925 with the move of the Bauhaus from Weimar to Dessau, Herbert Bayer was appointed master and director of the school's newly founded printing and advertising workshops. He was responsible for the design and production of all Bauhaus printed materials as well as for commissions from the industrial community. Applying to typography the call of director WALTER GROPIUS for functional, universal design, Bayer abolished the use of capital letters and imposed sans-serif typefaces in all Bauhaus printed matter and correspondence. He argued that using a single lowercase alphabet was more economical because it was faster and more efficient for typesetting and because it more accurately represented the spoken language. He rejected calligraphic letterforms as historicizing, insisting on a simple typeface without serifs because he considered its clear forms more legible and more in line with the image of modern times. Like LÁSZLÓ MOHOLY-NAGY, Bayer extended the range of his design technique by integrating photographic elements with typography, employing it nowhere more originally than in the cover of the first issue of *bauhaus* magazine. In this photocollage he incorporated a partially folded copy of the magazine itself, part of its lowercase, sans-serif title clearly visible, and arranged upon it a sharpened pencil, transparent triangle, and white cone, sphere, cube, and rectangle. Borrowing these three-dimensional geometric shapes and designer's tools from the Bauhaus workshops and foundation course, Bayer visually communicated the aesthetics and ideology of the school's educational program without written text.

Letterpress. 10¹/₁₆ x 10¹/₄" (25.5 x 26 cm). (Bauhaus-Archiv, Berlin.)

120
LUDWIG MIES VAN DER ROHE
Chair, 1929

Ludwig Mies van der Rohe designed this chrome chair in 1929 for the German national pavilion at the Barcelona world's fair, from which the piece, now known as the Barcelona chair, later took its name. Two of these chairs were installed side by side to receive the king and queen of Spain on their official visit to the building, which was built principally for such ceremonial purposes. Set on a black carpet beside a golden onyx wall within the austere glass-and-marble pavilion—the only modernist structure at the fair (and now reconstructed)—the broad, white, tufted-leather chairs were no less than luxurious modern thrones. Mies based his design on early symbols of authority, the X-frame stools and folding chairs used by those in positions of power in antiquity. He employed a structure of two flat steel bars, the back and front leg composed of one bar in a single curve and the seat support and back leg created by another, curved twice. In this highly visible international context the chairs served to legitimize the use of metal for luxury furnishings. Produced commercially by a succession of manufacturers in Europe before World War II, the chair was revived by Knoll in

America in 1948, when it was modified under Mies's direction. The original chrome-plated steel construction was replaced with stainless steel and the thickened area where the bars intersect was modified with a more refined joining, while tighter, regular tufting on the upholstery added a precise, technological appearance to this still mostly handmade chair.

Made by Bamberg Metallwerkstätten, Berlin-Neukölln.
   Chrome-plated steel with leather upholstery. Height:
   29³/4" (75.5 cm). (Art Institute of Chicago, gift of Mr. and
   Mrs. George B. Young.)

121
ELIEL SAARINEN AND LOJA SAARINEN
Carpet, 1928–29

Eliel Saarinen, chief architect at the Cranbrook Academy of Art (and later its president), and his wife, Loja, immigrated to the United States in 1923, bringing with them from Finland the taste for neoclassical and nationalistic folk styles shared by many of their European contemporaries during the years before and after World War I. This collaboratively designed carpet was made in the weaving studio created for Loja in 1928 to provide furnishing textiles for Cranbrook's

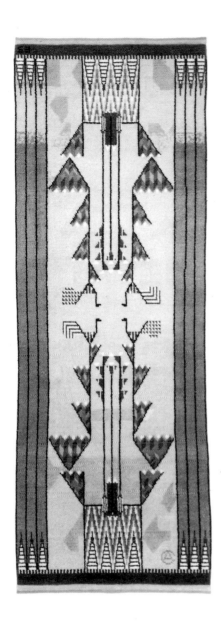

122
GUNTA STÖLZL
Wall hanging, 1927–28

The influence of the Bauhaus master Paul Klee is evident in this boldly colored masterwork of Gunta Stölzl, who took complete charge of the school's weaving workshop at Dessau in 1927. Klee investigated the relationships and expressive values of colors, particularly colors arranged in grids or checkerboard patterns; here Stölzl has followed that cue, building a refined mosaic of largely red and green geometric fields arranged tightly against each other, with wavy forms set next to rectilinear ones in a complex, dynamic composition that she had developed in a number of watercolor sketches. Elements of this composition can be found in Stölzl's earliest Bauhaus designs. This piece, a study of contrasting materials, weaves, colors, and textures, accurately reflects her highly rational approach to textile design as well as her aim of experimenting with materials and textures for industrial weaves. "Weaving," she later wrote, "is an old craft which developed its own principles upon which present-day mechanical weaving must still build. . . . A very natural result of the work [at the Bauhaus] with the flat-loom was economy in the use of materials, moderation of color range, and relating the form to the process of weaving."[48]

Made at Bauhaus weaving workshop, Dessau, Germany. Cotton, wool, silk, and linen. 59 x 43" (150 x 110 cm). (Bauhaus-Archiv, Berlin.)

new buildings. Using bright clear colors and affecting a simplicity in materials, craftsmanship, and design borrowed from peasant arts and crafts, Loja Saarinen designed and produced carpets, table runners, curtain materials, and wall hangings with the assistance of a staff of Swedish designers and weavers. Typical of the early Cranbrook production, which inspired a generation of American textile artists, this rug with peacock motifs is in a traditional Scandinavian flatwoven format with simplified outlined forms, blocks of deep color, and geometric ornamentation.

Made by Studio Loja Saarinen, Bloomfield Hills, Michigan. Cotton and wool. 110 1/2 x 39" (280.7 x 99 cm). (Cranbrook Academy of Art/Museum, Bloomfield Hills, Michigan.)

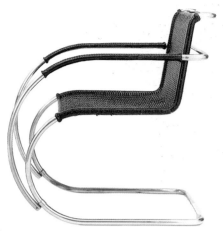

123
LUDWIG MIES VAN DER ROHE
Armchair, 1927

The later 1920s saw the creation of a number of bent-steel cantilevered chairs, and along with them disputes over design credits and royalties. Although Ludwig Mies van der Rohe did not invent the cantilevered chair—credit for that seems to belong to a prototype made out of gas pipes and fittings by the Dutch architect Mart Stam—he claimed that he was "the first to have exploited consistently the spring quality of steel tubes"[49] and applied for a patent covering the principle in 1927. Mies's first application of his resilient cantilever was in this chair design, which, like MARCEL BREUER's chair from 1925 (no. 104), was made to appear as if constructed of continuous metal tubing. With the frame and attached arms curving out in front and the back left open, this new design must have been disconcerting for those accustomed to chairs with four legs. Fitted with leather sling backs and seats, these chairs, matching chairs without arms, stools, and glass coffee tables were used to furnish the apartment house Mies designed for the Weissenhof housing exhibition in Stuttgart in the summer of 1927; other versions appeared later with colored enameled steel and with woven cane seats like this example.

Made by Berliner Metallgewerbe Joseph Müller, Berlin. Chrome-plated steel and lacquered cane. 31 x 18 1/2 x 28 5/16" (79 x 47 x 72 cm). (Philadelphia Museum of Art, gift of COLLAB.)

124
MARCEL BREUER
Chair, c. 1928

Marcel Breuer's version of the cantilevered chair, designed about 1928, had the most widespread influence of any designed by his contemporaries and remains the best-known tubular-steel chair on the market today. According to Breuer, he developed this model from his own U-shaped stool of 1925–26 turned on its side, and this early date was the basis for his claim of precedence in what became a tangled dispute over the origin of the cantilever concept. The bent steel he used, which is held rigid by the bentwood frame of seat and back, is sufficiently strong to support the chair without rear legs, and it has an elasticity that "makes a light, completely self-sprung seat which is as comfortable as an upholstered chair, but is many times lighter, handier and more hygienic, and therefore many times more practical in use."[50] Like Breuer's earlier armchair (no. 104), this model did not receive its now familiar designation *Cesca* (a diminutive of Francesca, the name of Breuer's daughter) until it was returned to production by Gavina in 1962.

Made by Gebrüder Thonet, Frankenberg, Germany. Chrome-plated steel and wood, and cane. 32 x 18 1/4 x 22 1/2" (81.5 x 46.5 x 57 cm). (Museum of Modern Art, New York, Edgar J. Kaufmann, Jr., Fund.)

125
LE CORBUSIER, PIERRE JEANNERET, AND CHARLOTTE PERRIAND
Chaise longue, 1928

While Le Corbusier was already recognized as the most advanced architect and theorist practicing in France, not until 1927, when Charlotte Perriand joined the office he shared with his cousin Pierre Jeanneret, did the firm begin to design furniture that was as radical as his buildings in its statement of new principles. In Paris at the Salon d'Automne of 1927, Perriand had

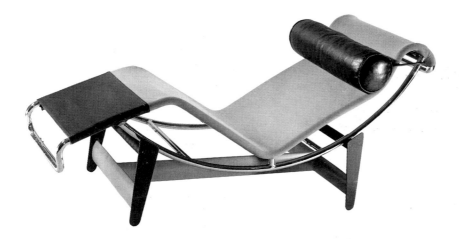

exhibited a group of furniture in chromed steel and anodized aluminum. After she joined Le Corbusier and Jeanneret the three architects turned to metal as the furniture medium most expressive of modern industrial technology. A version of this curved tubular-steel chaise resting on the same H-shaped stretcher, which allowed it to be variously positioned, appeared along with their *Grand Confort* armchair (no. 131) in the interior they realized together for the Salon d'Automne of 1929. According to the writer for *Les Echos d'Art* who reviewed the Salon display:

> With more boldness and intrepidity than it is possible to credit, and with an absolute scorn for historicizing forms, their sole consideration being logic, the architects Le Corbusier and Jeanneret, in collaboration with Madame Charlotte Perriand, have presented what they call the interior equipment of a dwelling, signaling by that, that they are the enemies of all decorative refinements and that with their intelligence alone they place themselves purely and simply before a problem to be solved.[51]

Made by Thonet Frères, Paris. Chromed and painted steel with leather and fabric upholstery. 24 x 62⁵/₁₆ x 19⁹/₁₆" (60.9 x 158.3 x 49.7 cm). (Museum of Modern Art, New York, gift of Thonet Industries.)

126
RENÉ HERBST
Chair, 1930

René Herbst was among the progressive designers who left the Société des Artistes Décorateurs in 1929 to found the Union des Artistes Modernes, the organization that became the principal forum for the presentation of advanced design in France during the 1930s. "Every year we go with pleasure to the exposition of the U.A.M.," wrote a reviewer for *Architecture d'Aujourd'hui* in 1933. "The works are never very

numerous, but are well chosen and nicely presented; they endeavor to express the new aesthetic. . . . In short, the prices are affordable, the works practical, simple, logical, and often charming. One can thus do right and at a good price in the spirit of our time."[52] In the group's annual salons, to which Herbst contributed regularly from 1930, he showed a range of his chrome chairs with seating made not of traditional upholstery but of bungees, or pliable rubber tubing, which the reviewer in 1933 called both an "ingenious solution" and "amusing." Made by his own firm using intricate hand procedures to bend, weld, and finish, these chairs came in models with separated or continuous backs and seats, and with or without arms; like his other furniture, they avoid a strict rationalism for a more decorative approach, even while employing prefabricated elements of industrial production.

Chrome-plated steel and rubber. 32¹/₄ x 16¹⁵/₁₆ x 17⁵/₁₆" (82 x 43 x 44 cm). (Musée des Arts Décoratifs, Paris.)

127
EDWARD STEICHEN
Mothballs and Sugar Cubes fabric, c. 1927

One of many artists commissioned by the Stehli Silk Corporation to supply modern, unconventional fabric designs for its Americana Print series introduced in 1925, Edward Steichen found fresh inspiration in common objects. Matches and matchboxes, cigarettes, carpet tacks, buttons and thread, sugar cubes, mothballs, beans, rice, and coffee were arranged by Steichen and lit to create dramatic allover patterns that could be photographed and translated into colorful textile prints. In his biography of Steichen, Carl Sandburg describes how the photographer's technique as a "master workman" carried over into these commercial designs:

> They are justifications of the Machine Age. They mean that for once "that charlatan, Light" is met with, controlled, and guided into magical and pleasing behavior. Matches, we learn, have different existences and souls under different arrangements of their corporate unities; . . . And we ask, "What kind of phantoms are these?" on seeing sugar lumps set forth as cubes of destiny, odd phalanxes of little individuals endowed with personal characters of time, place and name."[53]

Steichen's designs as well as the photographs from which they were made were shown with other Stehli silks at the *Exposition of Art in Trade* at R. H. Macy's in New York in 1927, where the firm's display was described as one of the "exhibits which showed direct relationship between creative art and large-scale production."[54]

Made by the Stehli Silk Corporation, New York. Printed silk. Width: 40" (101.6 cm). (Newark Museum, New Jersey.)

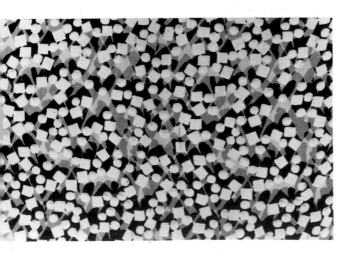

128
ERIK MAGNUSSEN
Cubic coffee service, 1927

With its triangular facets and close-keyed gold, silver, and brown-toned palette, Erik Magnussen's *Cubic* coffee service could be a literal translation of a cubist still life. Designed and executed by Magnussen for the Gorham Manufacturing Company in Providence, Rhode Island, where he worked between 1925 and 1929, this was the Danish silversmith's most daring service and an even more daring design for Gorham: its modernist, colored forms broke completely with Gorham's historicizing wares and with the restrained, classically derived shapes and motifs of Magnussen's own earlier hammered-silver pieces. Magnussen called on contemporary imagery for several other works at this time—a matching salad-serving fork and spoon and, most notably, his *Manhattan* serving pieces with handles shaped like skyscrapers. But only with this coffee service did he so thoroughly employ the formal elements of a new style. It could have been none other than this spectacular service that provoked the derision of a tradition-minded commentator for *The New Republic*. Fed up with the proliferation of cubist-inspired designs in America, he recounted how he "came upon a display of Modern American silverware on Fifth Avenue . . . which was both painful and funny," and continued:

> It was funny because the manufacturer had obviously gritted his teeth and said to the designer: "Go as far as you like." It was painful because the designer had applied a cubistic technique to surfaces that, in the sheer nature of things, cannot be treated cubistically; and because, instead of deriving his design from the actual function of a tea set and a

salad set, he had sought to derive it, the advertisement placard said, from the skyscrapers of New York! Our skyscraper worship has produced some pretty sad results; but I think this cubistic claptrap in silver is about the worst I have seen.[55]

Made by Gorham Manufacturing Company, Providence, Rhode Island. Silver, gilded silver, and oxidized silver. Height of coffeepot: 9 1/2" (24.1 cm); length of tray: 21 1/2" (54.6 cm). (Gorham Manufacturing Company Collection, Providence, Rhode Island.)

129
JEAN GOULDEN
Table lamp, c. 1929

Jean Goulden adopted cubist and constructivist ideas for the small decorative luxury furnishings in which he specialized during the 1920s. Using overlapping and fragmented geometric shapes, he built up such objects as this lamp into playful, decorative forms (this one reminiscent of a skyscraper) whose function was secondary to their design. As a student and then a colleague of JEAN DUNAND, Goulden mastered the craft of enameling, which he had first admired in the Byzantine metalwork he had seen in Greece after World War I; like Dunand, Goulden also created brilliant, small-scale, handmade objects in highly experimental forms, but decorated them by traditional means.

Silver, enamel, and glass. Height: 12 1/2" (31.8 cm). (Private collection.)

130
PAUL T. FRANKL
Combination desk and bookcase, c. 1927

As early as 1925 Paul T. Frankl designed for sale in his New York gallery the first of his "skyscraper" furniture—wooden cabinetry with flat surfaces, sharp angles, and stepped silhouettes inspired by the buildings constructed in Manhattan after the recent open-air ordinance mandated terracing and setbacks of the upper stories. His work was considered thoroughly modern and purely American—"as New Yorkish as Fifth Avenue itself."[56] But it was not completely independent of European precedents, particularly the ornamental style of his native Vienna where he trained as an architect and worked until 1914. While his book, *New Dimensions* (1928), in which this desk was illustrated, extolled the skyscraper as a "distinctive and noble creation . . . , a monument of towering engineering and business enterprise," Frankl was not a partisan of the industrialized methods that had given birth to it. He rejected the idea that modern furniture should be standardized and mass-produced, "just another factory-made machine product,"[57] instead promoting individual craftsmanship and spelling out the same ideals of honesty, simplicity, and beauty in natural materials found in the writings of the Arts and Crafts Movement and of FRANK LLOYD WRIGHT, to whom *New Dimensions* was dedicated.

Made by Frankl Galleries, New York. Lacquered redwood. 86 1/2 x 64 1/2 x 33 1/2" (219.7 x 163.8 x 85 cm). (Grand Rapids Art Museum, Michigan.)

131
LE CORBUSIER, PIERRE JEANNERET, AND CHARLOTTE PERRIAND
Grand Confort armchair, 1928

Designed by Le Corbusier, Pierre Jeanneret, and Charlotte Perriand, this armchair was exhibited as part of the architects' "interior equipment of a dwelling" at the Salon d'Automne of 1929 and appeared again, along with the chaise longue from the exhibition (no. 125), among the furnishings of Corbusier's villa for the Church family at Ville d'Avray the same year. A paradoxical combination of slender and massive components—enormous leather cushions, which provide "maximum comfort," supported by a thin framework of tubular steel—the chair is a rationalized version of the nineteenth century's solid and ubiquitous upholstered armchair. Le Corbusier had copied just such an upholstered armchair after those made by the London firm of Maples & Company in his Pavillon de l'Esprit Nouveau in Paris at the exhibition of 1925, defending it in his *L'Art décoratif d'aujourd'hui* as a chair that "is attuned to our movements and quick to respond to them." This, for Le Corbusier, distinguished what he referred to as the functional "type-object" or "tool-object," discrete and responsive to human needs like an "artificial limb," from the "sentiment-object" or self-determined "work of art." Strictly regularizing the profile of the chair into a cube with space carved out for the human body, the architects derived the form of the chair from the geometrical vocabulary Le Corbusier considered central to his mechanical and standardized new aesthetic of "purity and precision."[58] The armchair was made in two sizes and, like the chaise longue, was produced initially by Thonet and later reissued by the firms of Heidi Weber (1959) and Cassina (1965).

Chromed steel with leather upholstery. 24 1/8 x 38 3/8 x 28 3/4" (61.3 x 97.5 x 73 cm). (Atelier International, Long Island City, New York.)

132
DONALD DESKEY
Table lamp, 1927

October 1928 saw the first exhibition of the American Designers' Gallery in New York, which earlier that year had been established as a showplace for contemporary furnishings by fifteen designers, including Donald Deskey, RUTH REEVES, and Joseph Urban. According to *House Beautiful*, the gallery was "one of the first decided steps on the part of both manufacturer and artist to cooperate to the mutual advantage of both, in producing fine modern art and making it generally available."[59] The work of these designers was presented in ten complete room settings and in separate exhibits of textiles, furniture, and decorative objects. Deskey's contribution was a sleek "Man's (Smoking) Room" with an aluminum ceiling, cork walls, and linoleum floor. His furnishings were made of aluminum, chrome-plated steel, plastic, and leather, and included an aluminum-edged wooden desk on which this saw-tooth lamp was placed. A review commented on "the artistic use of industrial materials"[60] to be found among the objects exhibited, and for Deskey considerations of manufacture—his furniture and lamps were designed for mass production by his firm, Deskey-Vollmer—as well as modernity influenced his choice of materials.

Made by Deskey-Vollmer, New York. Chrome-plated steel and glass. 12 1/4 x 4 1/4 x 5 1/8" (31.1 x 10.8 x 13 cm). (Fifty/50, New York.)

133
IVAN DA SILVA BRUHNS
Carpet, c. 1930

During the 1920s Ivan da Silva Bruhns established the fashion for bold, abstract, centralized carpet designs. "Little by little," *Mobilier & Décoration* noted in 1929, the modern home "has shown itself intolerant of all decoration. We reject from our walls, our ceilings, floors, and furniture any ornament that appears to us unnecessary and encumbering. . . . For this reason also, certain objects have taken on a singular importance in the arrangement of the ensemble, to the extent that they acquire an architectural value of the first rank. Such are carpets. And Da Silva Bruhns is among those who have best understood this."[61] Using traditional knotting techniques and closely harmonized colors, he created monumental contemporary designs such as this, with large overlapping geometric shapes isolated against a flat background, inspired by the forms of cubist painting.

Made by Manufacture de Tapis de Savigny, France. Wool. 115 3/8 x 76 3/4" (293 x 195 cm). (Museum für Angewandte Kunst, Cologne.)

Chapter Four
The Machine Age 1930–1940

Around 1930, a new industrial design idiom emerged in the United States that was widely successful in influencing industry and public taste, and in symbolizing the "machine age." While many avant-garde European design theories of the 1920s were based on utopian ideals of the machine and industrial production, these ideals had only limited impact on the design of everyday objects and affected only a tiny segment of the general public, "the professional class mainly, and a small minority of wealthy merchants and industrialists who uphold the modern style."[1] In the United States in the wake of the Paris exposition of 1925, a call for a new, popular American design aesthetic emerged, which the critic Lewis Mumford said should be based on "honest" machine production. Like LE CORBUSIER, Mumford found the conceptual and aesthetic bases of modern design in engineering, although unlike the Swiss architect he did not require that his machine age style be expressed in pure geometric forms:

> During the last thirty years we have become more conscious of the esthetic possibilities of the exact arts; and it is no accident that our newest instruments, the automobile and the aeroplane, are not the weakest but the best of our machine products, a distinction which they share with American kitchen equipment and bathroom fixtures. Under our very eyes, an improvement in design has taken place, transforming the awkward mass and the broken lines of the primitive auto into the unified mass and the slick stream-lines of the modern car; or, by an even greater revolution in design, turning the imperfectly related planes of the push-power aeroplane into the more buoyant, gull-like tractor plane of to-day, with body and wing both gaining in beauty as they were adapted more carefully to the mechanical requirements of flight.[2]

Mumford's "stream-lines" referred to a scientific principle in the fields of hydrodynamics and aerodynamics in which a body is shaped so that it meets the least resistance as it travels through a fluid (liquid or gas)—blunt, rounded, smoothly finished, often in the form of a teardrop. Applied first in the late nineteenth century to steamships designed to move efficiently at high speeds, streamlining was essential to new technologies of transportation as they developed in the early twentieth century—to submarines, ocean liners, dirigibles, airplanes, and automobiles.[3] In the 1930s streamlining was also applied to a broad variety of static consumer products to make them appear modern and commercially appealing; in many instances "streamlined"

Hudson J–3a by Henry Dreyfuss for the New York Central Railroad, 1938. Streamlining was applied to all aspects of transportation during the 1930s.

opposite:
Walter Dorwin Teague, Radio, 1934 (no. 156)

household appliances became the vehicle for introducing modern design to the American mass consumer.

The simultaneous spread of electricity and the rapid growth of the household appliances industry in the United States as well as Europe during the 1920s and 1930s caused domestic environments to become increasingly mechanized and subject to design considerations, as the "Electric House," built for display at the *IV Triennale* of 1930 in Monza, Italy, demonstrated.[4] Concern for hygiene and household efficiency prompted those who could afford to buy labor-saving appliances to select any that aided cleanliness or could be cleaned effectively. In the design of stoves, the major technological advance was the slow-combustion Swedish range called the AGA, restyled for the British market about 1934 (no. 153): among its virtues were its low fuel consumption, creation of little or no dirt, and all-over enamel surface with rounded corners, which could be easily cleaned. The form of the American gas stove was standardized first by NORMAN BEL GEDDES for the Standard Gas Equipment Corporation in 1931, its simple, enameled form conceived in modular units to allow a range of models to be produced (no. 151). With regard to food storage, electric refrigerators were first made for the domestic market in the 1920s and American models, which led the world market, were both exported and made abroad in the 1930s under foreign license. In the mid-1930s, streamlined by the American designer RAYMOND LOEWY, the refrigerator's appearance was changed from a square box perched on high legs to a sleek, smooth-surfaced, single body that reached almost to the floor (no. 152).

In addition to equipment that made the home cleaner and housework more efficient, electricity brought entertainment in the form of the radio, an instrument that had no precedent before the 1920s and that by 1939 was available in such quantity that nearly everyone had access to a set (no. 144). In the 1930s, American and European designers were commissioned by manufacturers to find appropriate modern forms for the radio: while R. D. RUSSELL, an English furniture designer, created radios and later televisions in the shape of well-designed modern cabinetry (no. 181), WELLS COATES in England (no. 145) and WALTER DORWIN TEAGUE in the United States (no. 156) designed sleek machine-age sets, the former using curved Bakelite, the latter, mirrored glass and shiny chrome fittings. At the *VII Triennale* exhibition of 1940 in Milan, a separate display of radio sets affirmed the principle that they should not look like pieces of furniture. According to the progressive magazine *Domus*, "The radio set must be above all a piece of 'equipment,' a machine, or if you will, an instrument . . . where all the component parts, including the

Chrysler's *Airflow Imperial*, 1934.

housing, respond only to their adequate function and in which the word 'furniture' never has occasion to appear."[5] A group of Italian designers, among them Franco Albini and LIVIO CASTIGLIONI, PIER GIACOMO CASTIGLIONI, and LUIGI CACCIA DOMINIONI, exhibited advanced designs for radios there (no. 180) that expressed the nature of the medium as technical equipment.

In the United States, streamlining gave aesthetic character to such electrical equipment. Considered both a scientific concept and a symbol of modernity, streamlining was accepted as the American "machine" style. Advocates of streamlining in the United States praised its technical advantages (it facilitated production of pressed metal), its ready assimilation into production processes, and its suitability for plastic materials like Bakelite, which flowed evenly in curved molds. Other materials associated with streamlining were chromium, aluminum, glass, plywood, cork, and synthetic fibers; they were used for their novelty and for their suitability to particular purposes, by both European and American designers.

Streamlined products saturated the American market through the Depression, World War II, and into the 1950s. In 1940 the designer Harold van Doren noted:

> Streamlining has taken the modern world by storm. We live in a maelstrom of streamlined trains, refrigerators, and furnaces; streamlined bathing beauties, soda crackers, and facial massages. . . . The manufacturer who wants his laundry tubs, his typewriters, or his furnaces streamlined is in reality asking you to modernize them, to find the means for substituting curvilinear forms for rectilinear forms. He wants you to make cast iron and die-cast zinc and plastics and sheet metal conform to the current taste, or fad if you will, for cylinders and spheres or the soft flowing curves of the modern automobile in place of the harsh angles and ungainly shapes of a decade ago.[6]

The association of the power and speed of transportation with streamlining was reinforced many times over in the 1930s with the introduction in the United States and Europe of automobiles, locomotives, airplanes, and ocean liners of advanced design. Aeronautical images and names were applied to a wide range of products during the 1930s, from KEM WEBER's *Airline* chair, made in California (no. 142), and Robert Heller's *Airflow* fan to MARION DORN's *Aircraft* fabric (no. 171), used to furnish the British ocean liner *Orcades* in 1937.

The designers most responsible for creating the new American idiom, HENRY DREYFUSS, Norman Bel Geddes, Raymond Loewy, and Walter Dorwin Teague, achieved highly diversified practices encompassing industrial, interior, and graphic design for both engineering and consumer products—their commercial pragmatism far removed from the utopian ideals and formal determinism that informed most progressive European design. Defining broad standards for industrial design in the United States, these men were depicted by their admirers as heroic pioneers whose stature could be attributed to their simultaneous mas-

"Industrial Designer's Office" by Raymond Loewy and Lee Simonson, for the *Contemporary American Industrial Art* exhibition at the Metropolitan Museum of Art, New York, 1934.

tery of aesthetics, technology, administration, and salesmanship,[7] and to the breadth of their undertakings, from the design of the smallest object to that of a model industrial community. What these designers had in common in the early years of the Depression was the charge by their clientele to stimulate consumer interest and multiply sales. Certain well-publicized successes firmly linked their practices with the advance of economic recovery. For instance, Loewy's series of redesigns of the Sears *Coldspot* refrigerator caused sales to increase from 15,000 units to 275,000 units within five years. In their prolific writings these designers often spoke the language of European functionalism, Teague describing universal "aesthetic laws" and a constant "standard of rightness . . . fitness to function, materials, techniques; unity and simplicity";[8] he also identified with its early protagonists: Le Corbusier and WALTER GROPIUS.[9] Nevertheless, in their practices and in expressive visionary designs such as those published by Geddes in his book *Horizons* (1932), Dreyfuss, Geddes, Loewy, and Teague endorsed a new relativist aesthetic in which designs could be valid at a given time for a given purpose. The *Coldspot* refrigerator, introduced in 1935, was redesigned by Loewy three times in three successive years (1936–38),[10] each model touted as progressively better than the model it replaced. The practice of annual style changes had been conceived in the automobile industry in 1927 by Alfred P. Sloan, Jr., president of General Motors, his policy of planned obsolescence intended to stimulate the market for new cars and to satisfy the public taste for change. The household appliance industry followed the automobile industry in creating obsolescence to increase demand, changing the appearance of new products to make the old look inadequate even if they were not so mechanically.

Fueled by advertising and the skills of designers, and in spite of the Depression, the United States became a center of its own modern design idiom in the 1930s, with streamlined products visually glorifying American industry at the *Century of Progress Exposition* in Chicago in 1933–34 and the *New York World's Fair* in 1939–40. Against the background of this American design movement came a wave of European immigration that brought many of Europe's most advanced functionalist designers to the United States. In the years after Hitler came to power

New York World's Fair, 1939.

in Germany in 1933, LÁSZLÓ MOHOLY-NAGY, Gropius, LUDWIG MIES VAN DER ROHE, Josef Albers, ANNI ALBERS, MARCEL BREUER, and HERBERT BAYER, all at one time members of the Bauhaus staff, immigrated to America. Moholy-Nagy and Mies van der Rohe went to Chicago where the former served as director of the New Bauhaus (1937–38) and the School of Design (later the Institute of Design; 1939–46), and in 1938 Mies became head of the architecture department of the Armour Institute (after 1940, the Illinois Institute of Technology). Both of the Alberses joined the faculty of Black Mountain College in North Carolina (1933–49); Gropius and Breuer went to Harvard University in Cambridge, Gropius as chairman of the architecture department (1938–52) and Breuer as associate professor of architecture (1937–46); while Bayer practiced independently in New York. Their work exerted enormous influence on American design although it was often conflated with the other "modern" style associated with industry—streamlining—so popular at the time and from which it differed substantially.

The most ardent promoters of the emigrés' International Style were American streamlining's severest critics; they spoke out largely on ideological grounds, but at least partly their stance was meant to distance one set of modern design principles from the other. Just as cubistic design was criticized by theorists in the 1920s as an ephemeral, eclectic, deviant style, which distorted true modernity and gave primacy to decoration over function, so too was streamlining attacked in the 1930s for its superficiality and facile mannerisms, and held accountable to the standards and example of the Bauhaus. Planned obsolescence ran directly counter to Gropius's ambition of realizing "standards of excellence, not creating transient novelties,"[11] and of designing standard types as a social necessity.

This criticism originated at the Museum of Modern Art in New York with a series of exhibitions in the 1930s, including *Modern Architecture: International Exhibition* (1932), *Machine Art* (1934), and *Bauhaus 1919–1928* (1938). *Machine Art* followed the Werkbund-Bauhaus path, with industrial components, kitchenware, scientific instruments, and laboratory glass and porcelain occupying two-thirds of the exhibition. The catalog condemned as a "problem" in American design the desire for "'styling' objects for advertising. Styling a commercial object gives it more 'eye-appeal' and therefore helps sales. Principles such as 'streamlining' often receive homage out of all proportion to their applicability."[12]

An alternative to the extremes of European functionalism and American streamlining appeared during the 1930s in Scandinavia, where industrialization arrived late and where much of the consumer products industry was still based in traditional craft shops well endowed with skilled artisans. Even large mechanized industries retained craft traditions and values, including Arabia, Finland's leading industrial pottery, which in 1932 established an art studio where artists could work within the factory, independently designing unique works as well as lines for mass production. In contrast to France, which supported a skilled craft trade in expensive furnishings and interior designs, in Scandinavia the best-known designers and craftsmen sought to provide popular and practical consumer goods. Although similarly historicist, Scandinavian designers preserved vernacular traditions that expressed the unpretentious simplicity and asceticism of village life. The kind of simplicity valued as a Nordic characteristic was often conflated with ideas of rationalization and standardization imported from Germany and the Bauhaus in the late 1920s. In the Scandinavian potteries, the best-selling tablewares of the 1930s were typically decorated with traditional vernacular floral motifs, albeit applied sparingly in functionalist fashion. Similarly simplified historical forms also persisted, notably in such smaller craft shops as those belonging to members of the Copenhagen Cabinetmakers Guild, where the rationalized storage units of its most advanced designer, KAARE KLINT, were derived from such sources as English Georgian cabinets (no. 137). It was this curious amalgam of stripped historical, particularly classicist, forms and vernacular ornament that the Finnish architect ELIEL SAARINEN brought so successfully to the Cranbrook Academy of Art in Michigan as its first president and chief architect (nos. 121, 154). Scandinavian artists who taught at Cranbrook in the 1930s followed Saarinen's lead, among them the ceramicist Maija Grotell, the weavers Lillian Holm, Marianne Strengell, and Maja Andersson Wirde, and the sculptor Carl Milles.

German ideas about rational design and production made their first important Scandinavian appearance in 1930 at the *Stockholmsutställningen* (*Stockholm Exhibition*), which, with some reference to the celebrated Werkbund exhibition at Weissenhof in 1927, displayed residential architecture and furnishings that, even by Scandinavian standards, were spare, practical, and hygienic in design. While foreign critics like P. Morton Shand, writing in *Architectural Review*, regarded the exhibition as a triumph of International Style functionalism ("For the 1930 Stockholm Exhibition has at least taught us that the future of the machine as an integral organ of modern culture is assured; and that its technical perfection as an art-form is only a matter of time"[13]), it appeared to the Finnish architect and designer ALVAR AALTO in retrospect as a kind of Scandinavian version of Chicago's popular *Century of Progress Exposition*, showcasing broad possibilities for industrial design and including as it did "motorboats, railway carriages, refrigerators, and gramophones" as "part of life."[14]

For foreign observers, the democratic element in Scandinavian design was its low cost. The arrival of the Depression in Scandinavia had forced its consumer industries to expand production of useful wares that could be made and sold at reasonable prices. The Finnish glasshouses Riihimäki and Karhula-Iittala held competitions to encourage practical low-cost designs; AINO MARSIO AALTO won a prize from Karhula-Iittala in 1932 for pressed glasswares with molded rings devised to hide imperfections in the lower quality material (no. 148).

Alvar Aalto, Scandinavia's most influential and articulate designer of the period, evolved a personal, democratic version of the International Style in Finland during the early 1930s. Although he was committed to the virtues and economic necessity of rationalizing and

Finnish Pavilion by Alvar Aalto, at the New York World's Fair, 1939. Aalto's pavilion popularized Scandinavian organic design in the United States.

standardizing designs for production, Aalto's language of curvilinear and organic forms based in nature, as well as his use of natural materials, expressed both a personal and a regional identity quite different from the values of universality and anonymity sought by modern designers elsewhere. The need to give modern design a human face was a recurring theme in Aalto's work and writings, notably in his pioneering furniture designs in laminated birchwood and birch plywood (nos. 140, 141). "Objects that properly can be given the label rational often suffer from a noticeable lack of human qualities," he wrote. "Originally rationalism meant something connected with the method of production. . . . But a chair has an endless series of requirements that it should when finished, fulfill . . . [including] psychological needs."[15] Aalto's ingeniously simple wooden furniture, standardized for mass production and sold at low prices, was shown internationally for the first time in London at the Fortnum and Mason department store and at the *V Triennale* exhibition in Milan in 1933. So immediately successful was the furniture that an English company, Finmar, was founded to import it, and a Swiss firm, Wohnbedarf, made arrangements that year to do the same. His furniture also inspired designers working in England, among them Marcel Breuer (who practiced in London from 1935 to 1937 before immigrating to the United States; no. 158), as well as BRUNO MATHSSON in Sweden (no. 159).

As forums for progressive ideas, the international exhibitions of the 1930s were particularly important for Scandinavian designers, who were much premiated there, at the *Triennale* exhibitions in Milan (which had evolved from the *Biennale* in Monza) in 1933, 1936, and 1940, in Paris at the *Exposition Internationale des Arts et Techniques dans la Vie Moderne* in 1937, and in New York at the *World's Fair* in 1939. Aalto's work on the Finnish pavilions in Paris and New York, for example, made him a popular world figure.

The word most often used to describe Aalto's form of modernism, and Scandinavian design in general, was "organic," which seemed to refer to his use of natural materials and soft curving forms. However rationally conceived or functional his designs might have been, these features imbued them with the imagery and comforts of tradi-

Exhibition of radios at the *VII Triennale* in Milan, 1940.

tional domestic furnishings. For many Europeans, Scandinavian design represented a more palatable modern style than avant-garde industrial designs from Germany or those produced in France by members of the Union des Artistes Modernes, who were criticized in Paris at the exposition of 1937 as "adherents of functionalism, voluntarily imprisoned in a misguided system because the needs of men cannot be satisfied by uniquely rational solutions."[16] The Dutch designer Paul Bromberg wrote in 1936 that functionalism was no longer valid, "having achieved its objective," and that organic, decorative, but simple Scandinavian forms offered an alternative: "Here we find an application of ornament which is acceptable to modern ideas . . . a genuine simplicity achieved through genuine control."[17]

"Organic" was a term also used elsewhere referring to an integrated design approach like Aalto's, based on human factors. In 1934 Lewis Mumford described a post–machine age aesthetic as "organic" in this sense: "Our capacity to go beyond the machine rests in our power to assimilate the machine. Until we have absorbed the lessons of . . . the mechanical realm, we cannot go further in our development toward the more richly organic, the more profoundly human. . . . The economic: the objective: the collective: and finally the integration of these principles in a new conception of the organic—these are the marks, already discernible, of our assimilation of the machine not merely as an instrument of practical action but as a valuable mode of life."[18] In 1940 the Museum of Modern Art in New York organized an "inter-American" competition for "Organic Design in Home Furnishings," defining organic design as "an harmonious organization of the parts within the whole, according to structure, material, and purpose. Within this definition, there can be no vain ornamentation or superfluity."[19]

Technical-rational functionalism as conceived at the Bauhaus continued to be practiced among German industrial designers during the 1930s, both despite and because of the conservative policies of the Third Reich. The turbulent political and social forces unleashed in Germany discouraged radical experiments in design that focused on modernity per se. The Bauhaus was closed in 1933, while the Werkbund, incorporated into the Reichskammer der Bildenden Künste (Reich Chamber of the Visual Arts) in 1934, ceased to exist as a private association. The official arbiters of taste in Germany promoted the values of Germanic neoclassicism alongside other native styles with a strongly nationalistic flavor. At the same time, however, because the Depression had produced a rapid deterioration in the quality of German manufactures, the National Socialists adopted the old Werkbund (and Arts and Crafts) goal of quality work (Wertarbeit) at a reasonable price, and created the Schönheit der Arbeit (Beauty in Work) bureau, which actually recruited former Werkbund designers to carry out its programs. Other Werkbund members, including Hermann Gretsch and the Bauhaus-trained WILHELM WAGENFELD (nos. 147, 178), produced superior designs for private industry in the 1930s. They thus carried on the ideals of simplicity, clarity, and unornamented forms in industrial design despite the politicization and destruction of the institutions that had pioneered them.

134
JEAN HEIBERG
Telephone, 1930

During the 1920s L M ERICSSON, Sweden's telephone company, developed plans through its Norwegian affiliate, Norsk Elektrisk Bureau, for a molded-plastic desk telephone to replace the model then in use, an updated metal version of a telephone from 1892 with a movable cradle holding the handset. Concerned with both visual appeal and technology, the company decided to bring in an artist to collaborate on the design of the instrument, a task that fell to the painter Jean Heiberg. He gave it a strong, modern, sensitively sculpted form with both handset and instrument case conceived as one coherent unit. While this telephone was not the earliest to be produced in plastic—the *Neophone* by Siemens, for example, appeared in 1929—it was the first to be rationally designed in regard to the use of the plastic material and the arrangement of the internal mechanism, which was worked out with the Norwegian engineer Johan Christian Bjerknes. Produced by Ericsson, the new model was introduced in Sweden in 1931, and through international manufacturing licenses it became the standard desk telephone in Scandinavia, Great Britain, and many other countries. It also inspired the well-known American molded-phenolic-plastic instrument designed by HENRY DREYFUSS for Bell Laboratories in 1937.

Made by L M Ericsson, Stockholm. Bakelite. 5 7/8 x 9 1/4 x 7 1/8" (15 x 23.5 x 18 cm). (L M Ericsson, Stockholm.)

135
RUTH REEVES
Manhattan fabric, 1930

In 1930 W. & J. Sloane, the New York decorating firm, commissioned Ruth Reeves to design a new line of fabrics for the *International Exhibition of Decorative Metalwork and Cotton Textiles*, which was being organized by the American Federation of Arts. Twelve of her fabrics were first exhibited at the Sloane store on

Fifth Avenue in December 1930 and eight, including this dynamic view of Manhattan, were selected for the 1930–31 touring exhibition, the most from any of the hundreds of designers represented. As an exploration of the uses of cotton and techniques of textile printing, Reeves's work was outstanding: she chose several different color schemes for each design and printed them on a variety of cotton fabrics, including voile, velvet, billiard cloth, muslin, airplane cloth, homespun, Turkish toweling, monk's cloth, percale, chintz, and osnaburg cloth. With their overlapping planes, flattened figurative motifs, and abstract compositions, Reeves's designs drew on aspects of the avant-garde cubist painting she had seen in Paris, where she had studied with Fernand Léger, but in its subject and linearity, *Manhattan* seems to be allied more with the graphics of such American avant-garde artists as John Marin and Louis Lozowick.

Made by W. & J. Sloane, New York. Printed cotton. Width: 37" (94 cm). (Victoria and Albert Museum, London.)

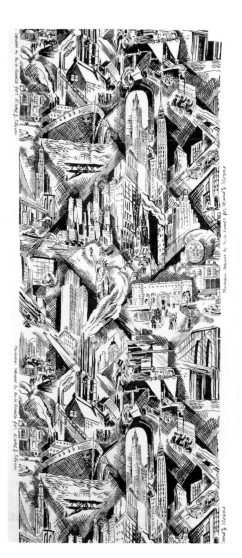

136
TRUDE PETRI
Urbino table service, 1931

With the establishment of the Weimar republic in 1918, the old royal porcelain manufactory in Berlin (founded in 1763 as the Königliche Porzellan-manufaktur) became the Berlin state porcelain factory. By 1925 the Prussian parliament had called for the factory to take a new direction and produce anti-inflationary, economical, standardized, popular wares instead of the luxury goods for which it had been tra-ditionally known. In 1929, Günther von Pechmann was made artistic and commercial director to implement that policy, and when Trude Petri joined the firm as designer that same year, her first work involved mod-ernizing the nineteenth-century *Rheinisches* table ser-vice, which she accomplished by stripping away the modeled relief decoration that ornamented its forms. Petri's most famous design, the *Urbino* table service, was inspired by the strong, clean contours of the Italian Renaissance dishes with narrow rims that gave the ser-

vice its name; the refined shapes of early Chinese porcelains, which apart from occasional molded or incised features tended to be bare of further orna-ment, also informed Petri's design. *Urbino* set standards for high-quality commercial porcelain tablewares in the 1930s that, like Hermann Gretsch's *1382* service for Arzberg, subscribed to Werkbund and Bauhaus princi-ples of economy of means and design. Both a critical and commercial success, *Urbino* was awarded a grand prize at the exposition of 1937 in Paris. Best known in white, *Urbino* was also produced with banded and flo-ral decorations.

Made by the Staatliche Porzellanmanufaktur, Berlin. Porcelain. Diameter of covered dish: 10³/₈" (26.5 cm); height: 4¹/₂" (11.5 cm). (Neue Sammlung, Munich.)

137
KAARE KLINT
Sideboard, 1930

Emphasizing comfort and function over inventiveness of form, Kaare Klint used studies of human proportions and the measurements of household objects as the basis of his work, pioneering even before World War I the modern study of ergonomics and anticipating the standardized and modular storage "pigeon-holes" LE CORBUSIER published in 1920. For this wonderfully neat mahogany sideboard Klint and his students at the Kongelige Danske Kunstakademi (Royal Danish Academy of Fine Arts) in Copenhagen measured the contents of typical Danish cupboards, providing tight efficient spaces for their utensils, tableware, and linens, and quantifying the items that could fit into each of the standardized drawers or shelves. These measurements then determined the overall size of the cabinet and the other modular components designed in series with it.

The form, however, like many of Klint's other designs, depends upon traditional styles, favored for what he considered their timeless qualities; here, he took inspiration from eighteenth-century English cabinets-on-stands, but added the two pullout shelves below the sliding doors for convenience.

Made by Rudolf Rasmussens Snedkerier, Copenhagen. Mahogany. 37 9/16 x 59 13/16 x 24 1/2" (95.5 x 152 x 62 cm). (Danske Kunstindustrimuseum, Copenhagen, gift of the New Carlsberg Foundation.)

138
EMILE LETTRÉ
Cutlery, c. 1931

With its complete lack of ornament and flattened geometric shapes, this cutlery designed by Emile Lettré reflects the influence of German avant-garde theories of form in the 1930s—its reductive geometry considered functionally to be most suitable for mass production and theoretically to best communicate the objective assurance and beauty of mathematics. Under the direction of Peter Bruckmann, Jr., the nineteenth-century family firm that manufactured this cutlery had allied itself with progressive design since the turn of the century. Bruckmann's ambition "to fashion everyday cutlery according to modern ideas and give the mass-produced article an artistic signature"[20] resulted in commissions to such distinguished designers as Friedrich Adler, PETER BEHRENS, and Paul Haustein. Bruckmann, a founding member of the Deutscher Werkbund and one of the organization's principal figures, acted as president or vice-president almost continuously from 1909 until 1932. Representing the interests of manufacturers in the Werkbund, he continued

to defend quality craftsmanship, good design, and the creation of a national modern style, as his collaboration with Emile Lettré, an independent gold- and silversmith in Berlin, demonstrates here.

Made by P. Bruckmann & Söhne, Heilbronn, Germany. Silver. Length of knife: 8 3/4" (22.3 cm). (Neue Sammlung, Munich.)

139
WILHELM KÅGE
Praktika table service, 1933

Wilhelm Kåge's *Praktika* dinner service marked a new direction for Scandinavian ceramic tablewares, which had been largely tied to the forms and decorations of vernacular pottery (no. 66). In this service Kåge followed a functionalist approach, conceiving standardized round and oval shapes with no surface articulation and only very sparse hand-painted decoration. This service was designed for ease of cleaning, handling, and storage: its sturdy pieces, which stack and nest, were given multiple uses, such as dishes that also serve as lids. For the first time, too, Gustavsberg dinnerware was offered in open stock: instead of having to buy a complete, predetermined service, the consumer was now allowed to choose from a wide range of components and sizes to create exactly the ensemble required. Flexibility, durability, and critical praise notwithstanding, *Praktika* did not find a wide market in the mid-1930s ready to invest in this cleanly beautiful, modern service.

Made by Gustavsberg, Gustavsberg, Sweden. Glazed earthenware with enamel decoration. Diameter of dish: 8 5/8" (21.8 cm). (Gustavsberg, Gustavsberg, Sweden.)

140
ALVAR AALTO
Armchair, c. 1931–32

Built as a free cantilever, a principle previously applied
only to metal furniture (nos. 123, 124), this standard
armchair designed for mass production by Alvar Aalto
carried the use of curved plywood beyond the closed
frame of his Paimio model (no. 141). First shown at
the Nordic building exhibition in Helsinki in 1932 and
in all subsequent exhibitions of Aalto's furniture in the
1930s, it has a seat and back formed from one long
curving panel of springy molded plywood suspended
between two U-shaped loops of thicker laminated
strips. This chair and other examples of Aalto's furniture became such immediate successes that efforts

were made to make them widely available: an English
company, Finmar, was founded to import Aalto furniture on a regular basis; a similar import arrangement
was developed with Wohnbedarf in Zurich; and in
1935 a company called Artek was established in
Helsinki by Aalto himself, his wife, AINO MARSIO
AALTO, and others to produce and market all of
Aalto's designs. Exhibited in New York at the Museum
of Modern Art in 1938, Aalto's furniture was praised
for its aesthetic distinction, human engineering, mass
production, and low pricing, which put it within popular
reach. "Any one of the chairs is the result not only of a
painstaking study of posture, the properties of laminated wood and esthetic considerations, but also of the
study of efficient (and consequently economical)
mechanical methods of mass-production," wrote John
McAndrew, the exhibition organizer. "In fact, a major
distinction of the furniture is its cheapness. Low-cost
housing of good modern design has been produced for
the last fifteen years; now probably for the first time, a
whole line of good modern furniture is approaching an
inexpensive price level."[21]

*Made by Huonekalu-ja Rakennustyötendas, Turku, Finland.
Laminated birch and birch plywood. 26⁵/₈ x 24⁵/₁₆ x
29¹⁵/₁₆" (67.6 x 61.7 x 76 cm). (Philadelphia Museum
of Art, gift of COLLAB.)*

141
ALVAR AALTO
Armchair, c. 1931–32

Alvar Aalto's best known piece of furniture, this armchair was one of several designed by the architect
during the period in which he was building the tuber-

culosis sanatorium at Paimio, Finland (1929–33). Aalto wanted to supply the sanatorium with furniture that was more comfortable than the newly introduced metal furniture, which was considered suitable for institutional use. As he later explained, "tubular and chromium surfaces are good solutions technically, but psychophysically these materials are not good for the human being. The sanatorium needed furniture that should be light, flexible, easy to clean, and so on. After extensive experimentation in wood, the flexible system was discovered and a method and material combined to produce furniture that was better for the human touch and more suitable as the general material for the long and painful life in a sanatorium."[22] From the late 1920s, Aalto experimented with laminated wood, working with Otto Korhonen, technical director of Huonekalu-ja Rakennustyötendas, a furniture company in Turku near Paimio; over a period of several years he resolved the technical problems inherent in producing a form as revolutionary as the closed, ribbonlike frame of this chair. The seat and back are formed from a single piece of laminated wood bent and rolled at each end in curved scrolls that provide both decoration and support. Challenging the new metal furniture with designs such as this, Aalto's technical virtuosity revealed processed wood as an obviously modern material.

Made by Huonekalu-ja Rakennustyötendas, Turku, Finland. Laminated birch and birch plywood. 26 x 23³/₄ x 34⁷/₈" (66 x 60.3 x 88.6 cm). (Museum of Modern Art, New York, gift of Edgar Kaufmann, Jr.)

142
KEM WEBER
Airline armchair, 1934

Designed for strength, lightness, and portability, Kem Weber's *Airline* chair was an advanced cantilever construction in wood, which paralleled experiments being made in European furniture. Independent of his counterparts abroad, he resolved the problem of achieving resiliency and comfort by using a spring principle similar to that introduced by LUDWIG MIES VAN DER ROHE in metal (no. 123) and ALVAR AALTO in wood (no. 140). Here, the molded seat and back, made of two pieces of plywood hinged together, hang from the frame and attach at the front. As a person sits down the seat yields; the pressure also brings movement in the frame rails, which are not solidly joined, giving it a strength far out of proportion to the lightness of its elements. Composed of a back, a seat, two wooden side pieces, and two cross members that slip into self-tightening joints, the *Airline* chair was designed to be sold knocked down in a carton and was provided with instructions for easy assembly at home.

Made by Airline Chair Company, Los Angeles. Wood, plywood, and metal, with leather upholstery. 30¹/₂ x 25 x 34" (80 x 63.5 x 86.3 cm). (University Art Museum, University of California, Santa Barbara.)

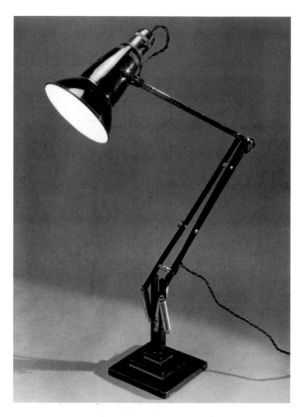

144
WALTER MARIA KERSTING
VE 301 People's Radio, 1928–33

Designed independently but co-opted by the Nazi regime, Walter Maria Kersting's *VE 301 People's Radio* (*VE 301 Volksempfänger*) was put into subsidized mass production in 1933 with the goal of making it available and affordable to every household in Germany. By 1939, twelve and a half million of this model or others closely related had been sold, a scale of production that in the 1930s was rivaled only in the United States. A political and propaganda success (its model number *VE 301* commemorated the date of January 30, 1933, when Adolf Hitler became chancellor of Germany), the set had just enough range to receive local stations but was not powerful enough to bring in disruptive transmissions from abroad. Housed in dark-brown plastic, the unornamented radio is rectangular in shape and close in form to its prototype of 1928, following the philosophy of reductive design that had been promoted in Germany during the previous decades.

Made by Hagenuh, Kiel, Germany. Bakelite. 15³/₈ x 11 x 6³/₄" (39 x 28 x 17 cm). (Neue Sammlung, Munich.)

143
GEORGE CARWARDINE
Anglepoise lamp, 1932

Following the idea of the articulated work lamp made in France by EDOUARD-WILFRID BUQUET (no. 117), but using springs instead of counterweights to hold the arm poised at the desired angle, George Carwardine modeled the structure of his *Anglepoise* lamp on the way the human arm bends. Although this piece was originally designed for the Herbert Terry company in England, where it has sold in great numbers for over half a century, it also became the prototype for an internationally better-known lamp, the *Luxo* light. Having acquired rights to the *Anglepoise* patent in 1937, the Danish manufacturer Jacob Jacobsen redesigned it slightly and began to produce and distribute it in Scandinavia under the *Luxo* name. The lamp was virtually identical in the way it functioned, and its revisions were limited to the shape of the shade and the elimination of the square stepped base.

Made by Herbert Terry & Sons, Redditch, England. Lacquered metal and Bakelite. Height: 35⁷/₁₆" (90 cm). (National Museum of Science and Industry, London.)

145
WELLS COATES
Ekco radio, 1932–34

Wells Coates's round *Ekco* radio—conceived specifically for its modern material, plastic—clearly projected
the image of a radio as an object of modern technology at a time when most production models could
hardly be distinguished from other pieces of wooden
furniture. Designed to fit the shape of a circular loudspeaker, the radio won first prize in a limited competition organized by the manufacturer E. K. Cole in 1932.
Since the round design was less complicated and thus
less expensive to mold than plastic radios with angular

shapes, it could be sold at a lower price, and after
entering production in 1934, it became one of the
best-selling receivers in Britain. With the Ekco line,
E. K. Cole successfully turned away from the manufacture of wooden cabinets by tooling up for plastic
molding and by seeking out such designers as Coates,
Serge Chermayeff, and Misha Black to create progressive forms for their products.

Made by E. K. Cole, Southend, England. Bakelite and chrome.
Height 14" (35.5 cm). (Design Museum, London.)

146
ERNEST PAILLARD & CIE
Hermes Baby typewriter, 1932–35

Identified with the Greek god of travel and commerce,
the *Hermes Baby* was the first truly portable typewriter
to be put on the market. Engineered by Giuseppe
Prezioso for the Swiss firm of Ernest Paillard, it was
small, very light, and inexpensive, conceived to fit into
a briefcase. The overall size of the typewriter was
greatly reduced thanks to its economical construction
in which the case itself strengthened the frame of the
machine and the parts were regularized. Its new
method of printing capitals by raising the carriage and
roller instead of the typebars also avoided the necessity for extra space within the housing, yet its keyboard
and operation were exactly like those of a standard
machine. The clean angular housing, which describes
the irregular configuration of the keys and space bar
and fits around the spools and rollers, combined with
the cool color scheme—gray metal casing, the red
wings of the trademark, and black plastic keys—gave it
the requisite functionalist look of a product connected
with the modern age.

Lacquered steel housing. 2³/₈ x 11 x 11" (6 x 28 x 28 cm).
(Design Collection, Museum für Gestaltung, Zurich.)

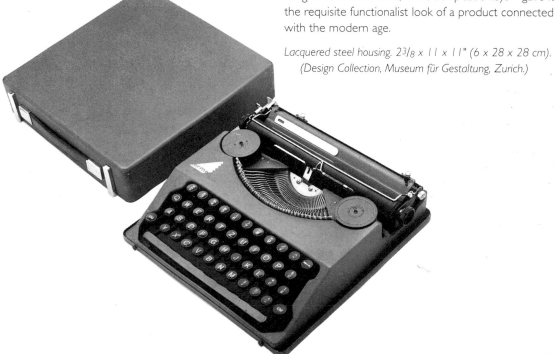

147
WILHELM WAGENFELD
Tea service, 1931

One of the few former members of the Bauhaus faculty to practice successfully in Germany during the Third Reich, Wilhelm Wagenfeld became the country's leading industrial designer during the 1930s. Brought to the Jenaer Glaswerk by its principal, Erich Schott, Wagenfeld was commissioned to design heat-resistant glass products that could function both in the kitchen and at the table. The tea service was Wagenfeld's first design for Schott and included a teapot made in three different sizes with a central diffuser to strain the tea; a creamer; a sugar bowl; tea cups and saucers in two sizes; plates; and a tray, all in simple geometric shapes. The service brought immediate recognition to its designer and Schott wanted to promote it under his name. "In my opinion," Wagenfeld later explained, "practical and rational considerations spoke against this idea. I recommended eliminating even the family name of the enterprise in a new trademark design. The consumer should remember merely the name of the place where the glass came from. This would increase his appreciation of the product itself."[23] Advertised simply as Jenaer glass, Wagenfeld's tablewares were promoted as economical and multipurpose. For Wagenfeld, as he had been taught at the Bauhaus, product design meant the creation of anonymous standard types that transcended any individual aspect of external style or personality "This is perhaps the main difference between handcraft and industry," he wrote: "the former is still bound to the individual . . . whereas the industrial product is the expression of collective work and collective execution. Only through the joint efforts of designer, techni-

cian, and craftsman does the [industrial] product arrive at its final form."[24]

Made by Jenaer Glaswerk, Schott & Gen., Jena, Germany. Clear glass. Height of teapot: 4 1/2" (11.5 cm); height of cup: 1 1/2" (4 cm); diameter of saucer: 6" (16.2 cm). (Museum of Modern Art, New York.)

148
AINO MARSIO AALTO
Glass service, 1932

Inexpensive and sturdy, this pressed glass service was designed by the architect Aino Marsio Aalto in simple, disciplined, ribbed forms to hide imperfections in the lower quality material. Intended as standard everyday ware for the domestic market and praised by critics for its aesthetic simplicity, this service, along with the series of vases designed by her husband, ALVAR AALTO (no. 177), brought international attention to Finnish modern glass. At the same time it answered the social concerns of functional practicality and appropriate cost that Aalto shared with other progressive designers in the Depression years of the 1930s. Aalto's service won second prize in the pressed-glass section of a competition sponsored by the Karhula-Iittala glassworks in 1932, one of several the firm held to promote modern design for decorative and utility glasswares. The line, which entered production in 1934, included jug, tumbler, sugar bowl, creamer, shallow dishes, and bowls in different sizes. It was awarded a gold medal when it was shown at the *VI Triennale* in Milan in 1936.

Made by Karhula-Iittala, Karhula, Finland. Colored pressed glass. Height of jug: 6 1/2" (16.7 cm). (Iittala, Inc., Elmsford, New York.)

149
GIUSEPPE TERRAGNI
Armchair, 1932–36

One of the most advanced designs produced in Italy in the years before World War II, this armchair by Giuseppe Terragni reflected the established idiom of cantilevered tubular-steel furniture that had been created in France, Germany (nos. 123, 124), the Netherlands, and other countries in the 1920s. With its spidery, skeletal, continuous, curving frame, Terragni's chair belonged to the experimental fringe of this international style, which was derisively labeled "steel macaroni." The chair was designed for the Fascist party headquarters, the Casa del Fascio (now the Casa del Popolo), in Como, which Terragni built between 1932 and 1936. Unlike the anti-modern approach taken in Nazi Germany, buildings and furnishings designed to symbolize Italian Fascism sought to incorporate new industrial forms, processes, and materials in a harmonious, rationalized environment that blended architecture, decoration, and industrial design. The main meeting room of the Casa del Fascio, where chairs of this design were used, was decorated with a cubistic photomontage wall relief by Mario Radice that included a portrait of Mussolini; thus the political purpose of the structure was linked with a style that its architect offered as an alternative to traditional Italian forms.

Steel with leather upholstery. 31 x 21 x 26" (79 x 55 x 68 cm). (Terragni Foundation, Como, Italy.)

150
GERALD SUMMERS
Armchair, c. 1934

Cut from a single sheet of plywood and given its final form without joinery of any kind, Gerald Summers's armchair is audaciously simple in construction. After parallel cuts in the plywood separated legs from seat and arms, these elements were bent in opposite directions into their fluid shapes. Although Summers must have been aware of the modern plywood furniture of Alvar Aalto (shown in London in 1933), the immediate impetus for this design was apparently a commission for furniture to be used in tropical climates: by eliminating joinery and upholstery Summers avoided the problems of weakened joints and rotting caused by extreme humidity. The chair was manufactured by Summers's own firm, Makers of Simple Furniture. An early example of a chair made of single-piece construction, it would not be equaled again in this regard for several decades as this goal continued to elude designers working in metal and plastics.

Made by Makers of Simple Furniture, London. Plywood. 30 x 24 x 37" (76.2 x 61 x 94 cm). (Mitchell Wolfson, Jr., Collection, courtesy the Wolfsonian Foundation, Miami, Florida.)

151
NORMAN BEL GEDDES
Oriole stove, 1931–36

The form of today's kitchen stove was essentially established when the all-white enameled gas range was designed by Norman Bel Geddes for the Standard Gas Equipment Corporation and published in idealized prototypes in his book *Horizons* in 1932. With "immaculateness . . . a major consideration in the design,"[25] as he explained, Geddes sought to avoid anything that might catch food particles or dirt—shunning surface articulation or projections, rounding corners, making doors flush, covering unused burners with hinged metal panels, and eliminating legs and open space below by setting units on recessed bases. Cleaning was simplified, too, by the innovative white vitreous-enamel surface. To avoid the damage to the enamel surfaces that earlier models had sustained when shipped intact, Geddes devised the structure of his stove by borrowing one of the principles of skyscraper construction. He projected a steel-frame chassis to which a skin of enameled panels would be clipped only when the stove was installed. Geddes conceived his design as a modular system allowing a wide range of configurations: this model ordered by Baltimore's gas company in 1936 approximates those in sketches of 1931 that Geddes showed in his book. The influence of the *Oriole* stove was immediate; not only was it copied by other stove manufacturers but, with sales of the stove doubling after Geddes's redesign, it also made corporations aware of the commercial benefits of good design, bringing a rash of commissions to Geddes and his colleagues for

refrigerators (no. 152), washers, and other appliances (no. 165).

Made for Standard Gas Equipment Corporation, Baltimore. Enameled steel and iron, brass, and Bakelite. 36 x 37 x 25³/4" (91.5 x 94 x 65.4 cm). (Baltimore Gas & Electric Company, Baltimore, Maryland, on loan to Henry Ford Museum, Dearborn, Michigan.)

152
RAYMOND LOEWY
Coldspot Super Six refrigerator, 1934

The classic example of a household appliance whose enormous sales success could be directly attributed to the attentions of the industrial designer, Raymond Loewy's *Coldspot Super Six* refrigerator for Sears, Roebuck was advertised for its "lovely modern design" as well as its quality and value when it was introduced in 1935. Primarily an exterior remake of the previous flat, angular model, which was divided into two rectangular panels, the *Coldspot* was conceived as a unified, streamlined sculptural form cinctured down the center by three molded bands—the only conspicuous feature

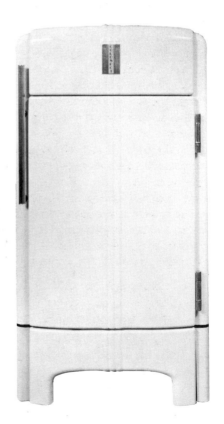

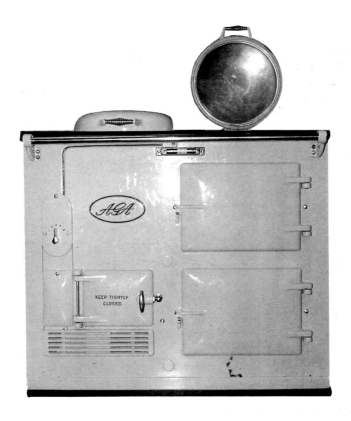

aside from its outline specifically indicated on the design patent issued in 1937.[26] The jewel-like nameplate with blue lettering, hinges, and extended "feather touch" handle (which responded to even light pressure) significantly upgraded the quality of the hardware over the previous model while the vertical linear articulation added a prominent decorative emphasis. In a further effort to increase sales, the refrigerator was newly restyled in each of the three years after its introduction and marketed for its design improvements. In creating the *Coldspot*, Loewy used full-scale clay prototypes to assess the viability of his proposed designs, a sculptural approach that would later become the standard technique in the automotive industry and that he had pioneered in 1929 in reformatting the Gestetner mimeograph machine, generally considered the first industrial redesign.

Made by Sears, Roebuck and Company, Chicago. Porcelain on steel and aluminum. 58³/₁₆ x 30 x 26" (148 x 76.2 x 66 cm). (Whirlpool Corporation, Benton Harbor, Michigan.)

153
AGA HEAT LIMITED
New Standard stove, c. 1934–41

This type of fully controllable and clean-cooking solid-fuel stove was invented in 1922 by the Swede Gustaf Dalen, a Nobel prize laureate in physics (1912) and president of an acetylene company, Aktiebolaget Gasaccumulator (AGA). It was not put into large-scale production, however, until about 1931, when it was first licensed for manufacture in Britain. The cast-iron AGA stove works on the principle of heat storage; a very hot, heavily insulated furnace maintains constant, separate, preset temperatures for the cooking areas—a boiling and simmering plate above (topped by hinged insulated covers when not in use) and the several ovens below. AGA stoves are noted for their fuel efficiency, economical operation, and the quality of their cooking, much of it done in the ovens, which can also hold cooked food for a long time without it drying out. The *New Standard* model was introduced about 1934 when AGA Heat Limited was formed, and since then the design has been altered somewhat—in 1941, when manufacturing with standardized and interchangeable parts began; and again in the 1950s and 1960s when the forms were refined, oil and gas fuels introduced, and colors, most popularly dark blue, added to supplement the standard cream-enamel finish. Nevertheless the basic feature, its heat-storage cooking, remains true to the 1922 concept.

Enameled cast iron and chromium alloy. 30⁵/₈ x 38¹/₄ x 26⁵/₈" (85.5 x 98 x 68.5 cm). (National Museum of Science and Industry, London.)

154
ELIEL SAARINEN
Tea urn and tray, 1934

Like WALTER GROPIUS at the Bauhaus in the 1920s, Eliel Saarinen conceived the Cranbrook Academy of Art in Bloomfield Hills, Michigan, both as a school of art and design founded on the premise of handicraft training and as a laboratory for industry. Its craft workshops supplied prototypes for commercial manufacture as a source of income and promoted high-quality modern design in series production. Chief architect (and later president) of Cranbrook from the mid-1920s, Saarinen himself created designs for mass-produced metalwares, although Cranbrook's silver workshop under the conservative direction of Arthur Nevill Kirk did not. Most spectacular of any of Saarinen's silverwares, this urn, which borrows its spherical shape from late eighteenth-century tea machines, displays the abstract geometric and architectural forms then identified with progressive design. During the early 1930s Saarinen designed silver for several firms including the International Silver Company, which made this urn; Reed and Barton; and R. Wallace and Sons. International Silver was Saarinen's most important client, producing silverwares after Saarinen's designs that were shown in a series of well-publicized interior and industrial design exhibitions at the Metropolitan Museum of Art in New York. This urn appeared in Saarinen's "Room for a Lady" in the Metropolitan's *Contemporary American Industrial Art* exhibition of 1934.

Made by International Silver Company, Meriden, Connecticut. Silver. Height of urn: 14 1/4" (36.2 cm); diameter of tray: 18" (45.7 cm). (Cranbrook Academy of Art/Museum, Bloomfield Hills, Michigan.)

155
PETER MÜLLER-MUNK
Normandie **pitcher, c. 1937**

Peter Müller-Munk came to industrial design with a background as a silversmith, and his first work in America after his arrival from Germany in 1926 was as a designer of handmade silver for TIFFANY AND COMPANY. But he early considered the problems of production metalwork and in an article entitled "Machine—Hand" (1929) complained about the lack of designs suitable for machine manufacture. "Why does nobody ever try to define the process of the machine in action and to deduct the forms and decorations most closely related to it?" he wrote. "Why, in other words, do not our manufacturers try to improve upon their merchandise by adapting it to their machines, instead of doing the contrary? . . . If we could have designers who knew the machines which were to turn out their designs, and if these men would give the machine what it most longs for, we would really have achieved a new art resulting from the harmony of technique and object."[27] When later he had the opportunity to design metalwork for production, he clearly considered the capabilities of the machine, emphasizing the precise curves and polished surfaces that could be attained mechanically. Taking its name from the French luxury liner, his *Normandie* pitcher for the Revere Copper and Brass Company was conceived as a similarly streamlined form, an uninterrupted aerodynamic shape then considered as readily adapted to the efficiency of manufacture as it was to the ease of movement.

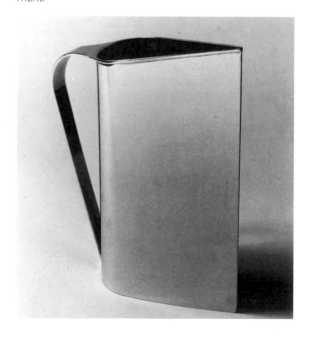

Made by Revere Copper and Brass Company, Rome, New York. Chrome-plated metal. 12 x 9 1/2 x 3 1/4" (30.5 x 24.1 x 8.2 cm). (Baltimore Museum of Art..)

156
WALTER DORWIN TEAGUE
Radio, 1934

Of the leading industrial designers of the 1930s, Walter Dorwin Teague was most concerned with formal values. In his search for perfection in the relationship of forms he followed LE CORBUSIER, deriving a new aesthetic of geometry and economy from machines. For Teague, "the art of our newly masterful machine age" was "more closely allied to the art of the great age in Greece than to any art before or between. The Greeks invented their geometry, it is true, but we have acquired ours from our machines. . . . We are recovering a realization that line and proportion . . . are the basic elements in all design on which all other factors are superimposed."[28] Like contemporary designers elsewhere (no. 157), Teague employed basic Euclidean figures. This radio, one of several different circular and rectangular cabinets he designed for the Sparton Corporation between 1934 and 1936 and noted as a special model on Teague's drawings for it, is composed of a perfect blue-mirrored circle and a precise chromed-metal arc with its controls and dials symmetrically organized in a grid of straight lines. Teague created this radio as a monumental mirrored facade almost totally unrelated to the design of the instrument itself—the receiver and speaker are merely attachments in a rectangular black-lacquered sheet-metal box

screwed to the back. The standard printed dial is of an archaic design quite out of step with Teague's overall modernistic conception.

Made by Sparton Corporation, Jackson, Michigan. Colored mirrored glass and chrome-plated and lacquered metal. 45 1/2 x 43 1/2 x 15 1/2" (115.6 x 110.5 x 39.4 cm). (Mitchell Wolfson, Jr., Collection, courtesy the Wolfsonian Foundation, Miami, Florida.)

157
JEAN PUIFORCAT
Tureen, 1937

This silver tureen was designed by Jean Puiforcat for display in 1937 at the *Exposition Internationale des Arts et Techniques dans la Vie Moderne* where it demonstrated the continuing strong affection progressive French designers maintained for pure geometric shapes. Using the ratio of the golden section as his guide and the sphere, cone, and cylinder as his forms, Puiforcat attempted to achieve pure volumes and perfect proportions here and in his other silverware designs during the 1930s. In his drawings or "harmonic traces," as he called them, he worked out their intricate harmonious relationships on paper before translating them into metal. A beautifully conceived, full-scale study for this tureen in the Puiforcat archives in Paris shows how the angles, arcs, and ratios were generated by mathematics and how they are fully interconnected, but their mathematical origin neither diminishes the sensuality of the globe's shiny surface nor lessens the brilliance of the blue hematite balls, which transform this silver tureen into a visionary, astral sphere.

Silver and hematite. Diameter: 11 3/4" (30 cm). (Philadelphia Museum of Art, purchase.)

158
MARCEL BREUER
Lounge chair, 1935–36

Marcel Breuer's lounge chair translated into plywood a commercially unsuccessful design that had been award-ed both first prizes in 1934 at an international compe-tition for the best aluminum chair. The wooden parts were made broader by necessity and also more fluid, paralleling simultaneous plywood designs of ALVAR AALTO (nos. 140, 141) and BRUNO MATHSSON (no. 159), but otherwise the chair faithfully followed the stamped-aluminum prototype in its overall form and in many details. Breuer even mimicked the continuous aluminum-bar frame by constructing each side of the base with what appears to be a single piece of split wood, one part bending upward to form the undulating arms and the other continuing forward to support the seat. Recognizing popular resistance to metal furniture, especially in Britain where Breuer went to live in 1935, his mentor, WALTER GROPIUS, asked Breuer to design the wooden version for the Isokon Furniture Company. This was the first chair contracted for Isokon, which had been established that year with Gropius's help to pro-duce comfortable modern furniture using primarily ply-wood. Unlike Breuer's aluminum model, which required expensive factory tooling, the plywood chair could be adapted to the small workshop production methods that Isokon came to rely on.

Made by Isokon Furniture Company, London. Laminated birch and plywood with upholstery. 32 x 58 x 24" (81.3 x 147.3 x 61 cm). (Museum of Modern Art, New York, purchase.)

159
BRUNO MATHSSON
Armchair, 1934

Like ALVAR AALTO in Finland and MARCEL BREUER in England, Bruno Mathsson designed organic wooden fur-niture during the 1930s and 1940s, creating a series of chairs whose sinuous lines are now unmistakably identi-fied as his work. Following an ergonomic approach like that of KAARE KLINT, Mathsson determined the forms of his furniture after extensive studies of human propor-tions; indeed all of his chairs were designed specifically for what he concluded were the optimum positions for sitting, working, or lounging. Each chair is constructed in two parts, a curved seating frame of solid light-colored wood in complexly joined sections, which is cradled on a base of bent plywood. It is completed with webbed upholstery of leather or hemp, the system he consid-ered most suited to the physiology of seating. Mathsson himself worked out many of the manufacturing pro-cesses by experimenting with methods of lamination and bending. All of his wooden furniture was manufac-tured in limited numbers in his father's workshop and sold directly to consumers.

Made by Karl Mathsson, Värnamo, Sweden. Beech and birch ply-wood with hemp upholstery. 32³/4 x 19¹/4 x 29¹/8" (83.5 x 49 x 74 cm). (Mathsson International, Värnamo, Sweden.)

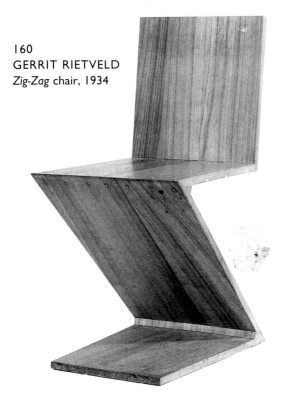

160
GERRIT RIETVELD
Zig-Zag chair, 1934

After World War I, Joseph de Leeuw, owner and director of Metz & Co., sponsored an original range of products for his store in Amsterdam, engaging both Dutch designers like Paul Bromberg and foreign artists like SONIA DELAUNAY to design furniture and textiles for its collections. Among the most remarkable of the Metz products was the furniture of Gerrit Rietveld, whose association with the firm can be dated to 1932 when he made a drawing for a tubular-steel version of this chair. Finally executed of four simple wooden rectangles joined together in a single closed-Z form and reinforced with triangular blocks at seat and foot, the chair followed the series of freestanding steel cantilevered chairs developed in Germany by MARCEL BREUER and LUDWIG MIES VAN DER ROHE in the late 1920s, and the one-piece plywood seat shells of ALVAR AALTO in Finland in the early 1930s. Eschewing the mix of materials and independence of seat from frame that characterized these earlier designs, Rietveld's *Zig-Zag* chair was far more visually cohesive, anticipating the single-piece continuous constructions of the 1960s when the wide availability of plastic materials made that goal technologically and commercially possible (no. 288). Experimental, austere, and economical in form, the *Zig-Zag* chair was designed for mass production and, like Rietveld's other furniture for Metz, was actually produced in several variations (with high backs and perforated backs and arms) in fairly large numbers through the 1950s. Rietveld's compatriot J.J.P. Oud noted the willingness of de Leeuw and Metz to support designs of

such startling originality, and "the freedom we were given in every way . . . to strive for that which architecture had already achieved."[29]

Made by Metz & Co., Amsterdam. Wood and brass. 29 x 14 x 17" (73.7 x 35.6 x 43.2 cm). (Stedelijk Museum, Amsterdam.)

161
GILBERT ROHDE
Armchair, c. 1933

When Gilbert Rohde was hired as a consultant designer for the Herman Miller Furniture Company about 1930, the firm made a commitment to the modern style that put it in the forefront of progressive furniture manufacturing in America. Rohde, like DONALD DESKEY, created tubular-steel furniture based on the stylish forms he had seen on a European trip in 1927, but he also introduced simple wooden furniture including bentwood chairs, storage components, and sectional seating, which were made by large-scale manufacturing techniques and sold at relatively inexpensive prices. This modest armchair with a bentwood frame was factory made by what Rohde called an "automobile type of assembly";[30] it was sold disassembled and the armless model was illustrated that way in the Herman Miller literature to show that only eight bolts and a wrench were needed to put it together. Rohde designed two other versions of this chair, one of which, a more elegant model with a sinuous single-piece upholstered seat and back and straight front legs, sold over 250,000 pieces in the decade after its introduction by the Heywood-Wakefield Company about 1931.

Made by Herman Miller Furniture Company, Zeeland, Michigan. Wood, with upholstery. 31 x 23 x 22" (78.7 x 58.4 x 56 cm). (Herman Miller, Zeeland, Michigan.)

162
VANESSA BELL
Fabric, 1934–36

The textile manufacturer Allan Walton, himself a painter and decorator, looked to his artistic colleagues to bring a fresh approach to the English textile industry. Between 1931 and 1939 he commissioned designs for printed fabrics from a number of the country's most progressive artists, among them Vanessa Bell, DUNCAN GRANT, and the sculptor Frank Dobson. The still life, floral, and classical subjects these artists produced were colorful loosely drawn designs suited to the imprecision of screen printing, a relatively inexpensive process that allowed Walton to introduce experimental designs economically in short runs. Bell's unusual design of a vase of flowers illuminated by a table lamp is compressed into a dense, flattened, allover composition by the tight half-drop repeat, the stippled swath of

light continuing diagonally across the width of the fabric. It is printed in six pastel colors on a satin-finish that Walton particularly admired for the intensity it gave to the colors.

Made by Allan Walton Textiles, London. Screen-printed cotton and rayon. Width: 48" (121.9 cm). (Victoria and Albert Museum, London.)

163
FRANK LLOYD WRIGHT
Desk and chair, 1937

Designed like virtually all of his furniture for a specific interior space (nos. 13, 26, 80), Frank Lloyd Wright's strikingly original desk and chair reflect the circular shapes and brick color of his S. C. Johnson Administration Building in Racine, Wisconsin (1936–39). Wright specified a frame of cast-aluminum piping painted in warm tones to harmonize with the prairie surroundings, along with oiled wooden tops and comfortable seats. He focused on the engineering details of the desk, which came in several models, designing multilevel cantilevered work surfaces, swinging rather than sliding drawers, removable wastebaskets, and built-in lighting tubes. These ingenious aspects are clearly indicated in the drawings submitted for a design patent; another was also granted to the unusual three-legged armchair, which was made in versions with four legs and without arms as well.[31]

Made by Metal Office Furniture Company, Grand Rapids, Michigan. Painted metal and walnut with upholstery. Desk: 33³/4 x 84 x 32" (85.7 x 173.4 x 81.3 cm); chair: 36 x 17³/4 x 20" (91.4 x 45.1 x 50.8 cm). (Steelcase, Inc.)

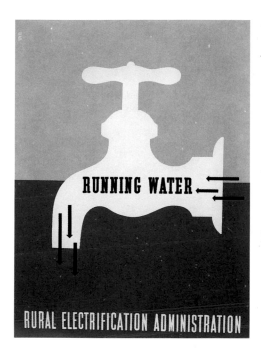

RUNNING WATER ←

RURAL ELECTRIFICATION ADMINISTRATION

164
LESTER BEALL
Poster for the Rural Electrification Administration, 1937

The 1938 annual report of the Rural Electrification Administration boasted that electricity "has changed profoundly the modes and standards of living in hundreds of farm communities over wide areas of the United States. . . . [It] is supplanting the oil lamp, and providing power to run . . . farm machinery. It is pumping water more cheaply than this can be done by hand, and making modern plumbing available, in most regions for the first time."[32] Much of this progress was achieved through cooperative projects funded by loans from the agency; Lester Beall's series of posters extolling the virtues of electricity encouraged farmers to bring power to their communities by joining together in cooperatives. Beall dealt with the immediate needs of the farm family, showing light bulbs, washing machines, plumbing, and radios in large, flat, silkscreened images and relying on primary colors. When his posters were exhibited at the Museum of Modern Art in New York in 1937, the *New York Times* admired the fact that they "reduce to the simplest graphic terms the few symbols necessary. Thus, the artist respects what should always be a poster's first attribute: uncluttered clarity, established at a single quick glance in the spectator's mind."[33]

Silkscreen. 40 x 30" (101.6 x 76.2 cm). (Rochester Institute of Technology.)

165
HENRY DREYFUSS
One Fifty vacuum cleaner, 1933–36

With his customary concern to fit the forms of his products to the people who used them, Henry Dreyfuss developed the *One Fifty* vacuum cleaner in close association with the Hoover Company's engineers. This was not a superficial redesign but a complete rethinking of all aspects of the product—"an excellent example of successfully combining good form and function," wrote the designer. "New in mechanism, form, color, materials, and even merchandising, it marks another step forward in the movement toward appearance improvement of strictly utilitarian products." By replacing much of the aluminum in Hoover's earlier vacuums with new materials—Bakelite and magnesium—this model was made considerably lighter. Because the molding of Bakelite allowed for a greater complexity of shapes than the stamping of metal, the move also gave Dreyfuss more freedom in the design of the housings. "No detail was considered too small for thorough research and design attention—each was considered a major problem in itself," he wrote. "The handle grip was considered from the standpoint of comfort—the clip-on plug to the cord was designed so as to be able to pull out easily from the socket—the bail, the lettering and the bag as well as the bolts and minor parts were all carefully designed." The attention to detail extended even to the colors, Hoover's traditional black and silver being replaced with what Dreyfuss called "stratosphere" gray and blue. By harmonizing even the specially woven plaid fabric on the hose and the packaging, Dreyfuss succeeded in creating "one complete and harmonious unit,"[34] bringing a new sophistication and a refreshed marketing image to the product.

Made by the Hoover Company, North Canton, Ohio. Bakelite, aluminum, and magnesium alloys. 40 x 12 1/2 x 14" (101.6 x 31.8 x 35.6 cm). (Hoover Historical Center, North Canton, Ohio.)

166
HERBERT MATTER
Poster for Swiss National Tourist Office, 1935

Herbert Matter developed photomontage, explored earlier by such designers as EL LISSITZKY, HERBERT BAYER, and LÁSZLÓ MOHOLY-NAGY, as an effective, expressive communication technique, most notably in the posters he created for the Swiss National Tourist Office from 1934 to 1936. This design, announcing in the nine languages in which it was printed that all roads lead to Switzerland, conjoins three separate photographs, two of them famous tourist views of the Alps. The images are cropped, compressed, and recomposed surrealistically into one spacious, dizzying landscape. To confound the viewer further, the monochromatic scene is topped with a toned blue sky and overprinted with a bold message in red, set at an angle that both mirrors the cobblestone road and echoes the dynamic arrangement of sans-serif lettering that had become a convention of the new typography codified by Jan Tschichold in the 1920s.

Printed by Gebrüder Fretz, Zurich. Photogravure. 39⁷/₈ x 25¹/₂" (101.3 x 64.1 cm). (Museum of Modern Art, New York, gift of Bernard Davis.)

167
KAY BOJESEN
Cutlery, 1938

This plain silver cutlery was Kay Bojesen's statement of liberation from the hand-hammered surfaces and naturalistic ornamentation of the tradition of GEORG JENSEN in which he had been trained. In contemplating a complete break with tradition, he based his design on a rethinking of the proportions of traditional formal services, using shorter handles, a more rounded knife blade, and shorter and stronger prongs for the fork. With its rounded silhouette and total lack of decoration, this service was considered an example of progressive design although it did not subscribe to the hard-edge machine imagery of Bauhaus-inspired flatwear. The cutlery, which later was also produced in stainless steel, became known as the *Grand Prix* service when, after a wartime interruption, it won a grand prize at Milan's *IX Triennale* in 1951.

Silver. Length of knife: 7⁷/₈" (19.9 cm). (Danske Kunst-industrimuseum, Copenhagen.)

168
HANS CORAY
Landi chair, 1938

The "national" chair of the *Schweizerische Landesausstellung (Swiss National Exhibition)* in Zurich in 1939, Hans Coray's design of a molded and perforated aluminum shell supported by a thin splayed-leg frame anticipates the work of CHARLES EAMES and EERO SAARINEN in the 1940s. More costly than steel, aluminum was little used in furniture production in the 1930s except when its high strength-to-weight ratio assumed particular importance, notably in the furnishings of Germany's zeppelins. But as a major Swiss export (in 1938 accounting for 34 million kilograms and 73 million francs in revenue), aluminum seemed a good choice to represent modern Swiss industry at the exhibition. Overriding initial opposition from furniture manufacturers who judged the chair too complex and too costly to produce, Coray succeeded in creating a single shell form molded in complex curves that could be entirely shaped by machine. Engineered by the designer and the Blattmann metalwares firm, the chair was made of aluminum sheet metal cut, pressed into shape, and perforated; the legs were similarly pressed and later screwed to the seat shell. This chair was sold in its original silver finish or with its seat dyed red, green, yellow, or black, and with white or black rubber feet. Designed as outdoor exhibition furniture, the *Landi* chair was quickly promoted and produced for domestic use; it has been in continuous production since 1939 with only slight modifications in 1962.

Made by Blattmann Metallwarenfabrik, Wädenswil, Switzerland. Aluminum alloy and rubber. 30⁵/₁₆ x 20⁷/₈ x 24⁹/₁₆" (77 x 53 x 63 cm). (Blattmann Metallwaren-fabric, Wädenswil, Switzerland.)

169
VICKE LINDSTRAND
Pearl Diver vase, 1935

The sculptor Vicke Lindstrand, the third artist-designer employed by Sweden's Orrefors glassworks (following the painters Simon Gate and EDWARD HALD), brought powerful streamlined forms and simple, bold engraving to ornamental glass in the 1930s. Where once the emphasis had been on allover surface decoration, now it focused on isolated figures and the refractive qualities of the glass itself. Lindstrand's footed *Pearl Diver* vase, one of the factory's most popular designs during this period and produced from 1935 to about 1963, has an imaginative underwater scene of a suspended diver cut within the walls of the thick body. The depth of the wheel engraving varies greatly to define the broad forms of the stylized muscular figure and the delicate detail of its outline. Lindstrand exploited the undulating interior of the vessel to create a sense of aquatic movement, and appropriated bubbles—used decoratively by such earlier designers as MAURICE MARINOT (no. 100)—for narrative ends.

Made by Orrefors Glasbruk, Orrefors, Sweden. Clear glass with wheel-engraved decoration. Height: 11 1/8" (28.4 cm). (Philadelphia Museum of Art, gift of Mrs. Henry W. Breyer.)

170
FREDERICK HURTEN RHEAD
Fiesta table service, from 1935

Low in price, sold at five and dimes, and promoted with the gimmick of mixing and matching its five original colors (orange-red, blue, green, egg yellow, and ivory), *Fiesta* dinnerware signaled the democratization of the modern style in America. Introduced in 1936, it achieved annual production figures in the tens of millions of pieces and continued to be manufactured until 1973. Its designer, Frederick Hurten Rhead, was asked for a dinnerware line with brilliantly colored glazes, and he explained how he was able to open up the broad low end of the market to *Fiesta*'s sleek, more sophisticated, undecorated forms:

> It was our feeling that while a modernistic interpretation of a formal table service—however attractive—might be met with some reservation by the every day housewife, an easy going informal series of articles, smart enough to fit in any house and obvious enough to furnish spots of emphasis, might get by. . . . We wanted a suggestion of a stream line shape, but one which would be subordinate to texture and color. . . . The color must be the chief decorative note, but in order that the shape be not too severely plain we broke the edges with varying concentric bands.[35]

Like RUSSEL WRIGHT, Rhead achieved success by promoting informality at the table, even for entertaining,

and offering a variety of colorful individualized forms for food preparation, service, and table decoration, from mixing bowls, vases, and footed compotes to large chop plates, compartmented dinner plates, tumblers, and demitasse cups.

Made by Homer Laughlin China Company, East Liverpool, Ohio. Glazed earthenware. Diameter of largest plate: 12 1/4" (31.1 cm). (Collector Books, Paducah, Kentucky.)

171
MARION DORN
Aircraft fabric, 1936

Marion Dorn's lyrical *Aircraft* fabric has an extreme figurative simplicity singular in British textiles in this period. Screen-printed as green, yellow, navy, and turquoise solids without shading or modulation, the pattern comprises four birds and their overlapped "shadows." It parallels the design of pairs of opposing birds in *Cyprus*, a woven fabric that Dorn created about the same time for Donald Brothers, although there the birds are stiffly arranged in regular bands. *Aircraft* was printed on linen woven with rayon, a lustrous synthetic material used to give added interest to furnishing fabrics during the 1930s. This pattern was chosen for use in the decoration of the British ocean liner *Orcades*, which entered service in 1937.

Made by Old Bleach Linen Company, Randalstown, England. Screen-printed linen and rayon. Width: 50" (127 cm). (Victoria and Albert Museum, London.)

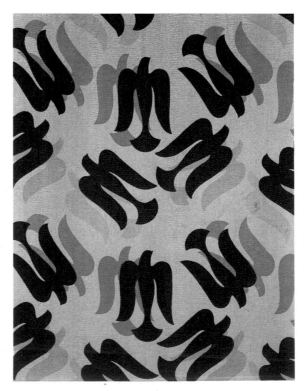

172
PAUL SCHRECKENGOST
Pitcher, 1938

Aerodynamically styled and ornamented with horizontal lines suggesting speed, Paul Schreckengost's glazed ceramic pitcher reworks on its modest domestic scale the stylistic vocabulary of 1930s streamlined design. The centrifugal design, an expression of pure sculptural form like the Perisphere at the *New York World's Fair*, arises from a simple white sphere—or rather it appears to, for in fact the pitcher is exceedingly flattened with its spherical section only half as wide as it is high. Like so much of streamlining, from trains to vacuum cleaners, the conception is meant to work from one viewpoint—profile. Indeed streamlined designs often seemed to be conceived as much for their impact on the advertising page as on the sales floor or in the showcase.

Made by Gem Clay Forming Company, Sebring, Ohio. Glazed
earthenware. 7¹/₂ x 11¹/₂ x 4" (19 x 29.2 x 10.2 cm).
(Paul R. Schreckengost, Cerritos, California.)

173
RUSSEL WRIGHT
American Modern table service, 1937

With its flowing, organic forms, both ample and comfortable, Russel Wright's *American Modern* dinnerware was unlike anything designed for the American market at the time, and it took him two years to convince a manufacturer to produce the service. The design of the dinnerware, which included several idiosyncratic serving pieces, notably the tapered water pitcher and the celery dish with folded rim, expressed Wright's philosophy of relaxed, informal entertaining; it was

designed to be used in interchangeable combinations of six low-key, mottled colors—Seafoam Blue, Granite Grey, Chartreuse Curry, Coral, Bean Brown, and a warm white. Wright promoted the service directly through full-page newspaper advertising, spurring sales by creating the "starter set," which encouraged consumers to buy place settings at a low price with the hopes that they would complete their services from open stock. His confidence in his design proved justified: from 1939 to 1959 *American Modern* sold over 80 million pieces, making it the most popular ceramic pattern ever created and proving that good design could truly be for everyone—including children, who were able to play with miniature plastic replicas produced by the Ideal Toy company in the mid-1950s.

Made by Steubenville Pottery, East Liverpool, Ohio. Glazed
earthenware. Height of pitcher: 10³/₄" (27.3 cm);
diameter: 8³/₄" (22.2 cm). (Metropolitan Museum of Art,
New York.)

174
MAN RAY
Poster for London Transport, 1939

Celebrated for the quality of design he maintained for
the London Underground over two decades, Frank
Pick extended these standards to the city's centralized
bus, trolley, subway, and rail network when he became
chief executive of the New London Passenger
Transport Board in 1933. Posters were his principal
advertising medium, and his policy for commissioning
them followed a very broad approach: "There is room
in posters for all styles. They are the most eclectic
form of art. It is possible to move from the most literal
representation to the wildest impressionism as long as
the subject remains understandable to the man in the
street."[36] Visually understandable but conceptually enigmatic, this design by the American surrealist artist Man
Ray was probably commissioned on the recommendation of his friend and supporter in England, EDWARD
MCKNIGHT KAUFFER, the Underground's most prolific
designer. In making a clever analogy between Saturn
and the transport symbol of circle and bar, Man Ray
exploited the fantasy and abrupt juxtapositions of
surrealism to imply that the transport system was as

steady, dependable, and long lived as the planets. Its
legend, "London Transport—Keeps London Going,"
was also disjunctive, for it was spread across a pair of
posters meant to be read sequentially as the traveler
moved through the system.

*Lithograph. 40 x 25" (101.6 x 63.5 cm). (Museum of
Modern Art, New York, gift of Bernard Davis.)*

175
GRUPO AUSTRAL
B.K.F. chair, 1938

One of the most imitated chairs of the twentieth
century, the *B.K.F.* chair (named after the last initials of
its three designers, Antonio Bonet, Juan Kurchan, and
Jorge Ferrari-Hardoy) was itself imitative of a much
earlier design, having been adapted from a wooden
folding chair with a similar frame and canvas seat
patented by an Englishman, Joseph Beverley Fenby, in
1877. The manufacturing rights had been sold in several countries and the Fenby chair had become widely
known in Europe both as an army officer's chair and as
a beach chair, while in America a version had been
produced continuously since 1895. Taking this earlier
chair as their model, the three designers in Buenos
Aires created their own version using an interlocking
tubular-steel frame and a quatrefoil-shaped canvas-
lined leather seat that fit over the edges. When the
chair was published in America in 1940 after it won an
Argentinian design prize, Clifford Pascoe, the New
York importer of the Artek line of furniture by ALVAR
AALTO, arranged for its production. Relatively few of
the chairs were made before wartime metal shortages
interrupted production, but the distinctive design had
begun to catch on. When manufacture resumed after
the war, and after the rights had passed to Hans Knoll,

-KEEPS LONDON GOING

142

its popularity and simplicity spawned numerous copies in large quantities, and it became known as the *Hardoy*, *Butterfly*, or *Sling* chair. Knoll instituted a design infringement suit in 1950, but because of the derivative origin of his own model the suit proved unsuccessful and paved the way for even greater numbers of copies, both by commercial manufacturers and do-it-yourselfers.

Made by Artek-Pascoe, New York. Iron with leather upholstery. Height: 34³/4" (88.2 cm). (Museum of Modern Art, New York, gift of Edgar Kaufmann Jr. Fund.)

176
FREDERICK KIESLER
Nested tables, 1935–38

Opposed to European functionalism, which he discredited as abstract and static, Frederick Kiesler believed in an endless organic flux of cyclical interrelationships with function "as a process of continuous transmutation."[37] This organic conception of design was given physical form in the flowing outlines of his nesting tables. Here the joining of the separate parts visually demonstrates their "correlation," a term Kiesler often used and equated with the design process itself. Sharing the continuous biomorphic contours of the sculpture of his friend Jean Arp, the table is a precursor of the free-form and kidney shapes that proliferated in the design vocabulary of the 1940s and 50s. Based on designs from as early as 1935 and made during the period that Kiesler directed his Laboratory for Design Correlation at Columbia University from 1937 to 1942, this table reflects his experiments with a variety of processes and materials, in this instance with cast aluminum, the fluidity of which accommodates this organic form.

Cast aluminum. 9³/4 x 34¹/2 x 22¹/4" (24.8 x 87.6 x 56.5 cm). (Isobel Grossman, New York.)

177
ALVAR AALTO
Vase, 1936

Entirely plain but shaped with free organic curves to provide decorative interest, this vase was one of a series by Alvar Aalto that introduced a new abstract vocabulary into glass design, a development that critics have attributed both to the designer's fondness for natural forms and to the influence of such surrealist artists as Jean Arp. Sometimes known as the *Savoy vase* from its use in the Savoy restaurant in Helsinki, which Aalto built in 1937, this piece and others in the series took first prize in a competition sponsored by the Finnish manufacturer Karhula-Iittala in 1936. The competition aimed to find new tableware and art-glass designs for the international exhibition in Paris in 1937, where these pieces were first exhibited. They ranged from a shallow dish 3 inches (8 centimeters) high to a tall vase about 39 inches (a meter) high. This model was originally produced in clear, brown, azure blue, green, and smoke-colored glass.

Made by Karhula-Iittala, Karhula, Finland. Colored mold-blown glass. Height: 5¹/2" (14 cm). (Iittala Glass Museum, Iittala, Finland.)

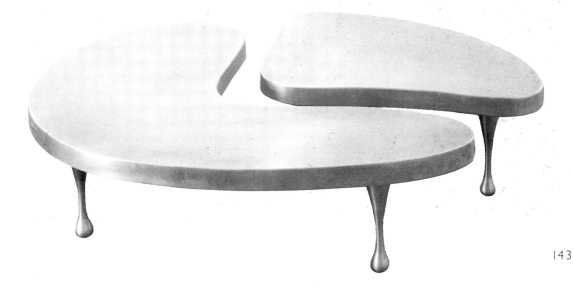

178
WILHELM WAGENFELD
Kubus food storage containers, 1938

In 1935 Wilhelm Wagenfeld was appointed artistic director of the Vereinigte Lausitzer Glaswerke and for the thirteen years he was associated with the firm was responsible both for their high-quality goods and the development of inexpensive pressed glass. Creating a comprehensive program of new types and forms, Wagenfeld designed hundreds of glasses for commercial and domestic use. Of these, the best known are his *Kubus* containers, seven household storage dishes in different sizes, three with lids, based on a module of 4.5 by 9 by 9 centimeters. For economy of space, these mass-produced pressed-glass containers were made to nest tightly against one another in simple square shapes. Visibly demonstrating the Bauhaus idea that form in design is a product of arithmetic, Wagenfeld also practiced the Bauhaus philosophy of developing standardized objects as a social necessity. Advertised as "ready for the table from the larder and refrigerator," the *Kubus* series continued the program that Wagenfeld had initiated for Jenaer Glaswerk (no. 147) of promoting inexpensive multipurpose household products that could function both in the kitchen and dining room.

Made by Vereinigte Lausitzer Glaswerke, Weisswasser, Germany. Clear pressed glass. Large dish: 3 1/8 x 7 1/8 x 7 1/8" (9 x 18 x 18 x cm). (Neue Sammlung, Munich.)

179
W. ARCHIBALD WELDEN
Revere Ware cooking utensils, 1938

Simplification and streamlining revamped many cooking sets and small appliances during the 1930s, but few redesigns were as carefully considered and thoroughly engineered as that of the *Revere Ware* cooking utensils, introduced in 1938 and in production today virtually unchanged. The work of the company's consultant designer, W. Archibald Welden, the line was created to take advantage of a new process that Revere's engineers had developed to combine a copper exterior, which provides maximum heating efficiency, with a noncorrosive and easily cleaned stainless-steel interior. This combination called for coating the exterior of the bottom surface and lower part of the side of a stainless steel pot with electrolytically deposited copper.[38] Welden's approach was to launch a thorough design study taking into account his own consumer research into the handling of cookware; he focused on the convenience of carrying and use, and made cleaning easier by enlarging the radius of the curve at the bottom and avoiding crevices around the beading at the rim. The elegantly curved shape of the plastic handle, following an early American form, gave *Revere Ware* a hint of Colonial design that suggested a connection with the high-quality silverwork of the company's namesake, Paul Revere.

Made by Revere Copper and Brass Company, Rome, New York. Stainless steel and copper with plastic. Length: 13" (33.3 cm). (Revere Ware Corporation, Clinton, Illinois.)

180
LIVIO CASTIGLIONI, PIER GIACOMO CASTIGLIONI, AND LUIGI CACCIA DOMINIONI
Radio, 1939

Turning their backs on the wooden cabinetry that had characterized radio design in Italy for the previous

decade, Livio and Pier Giacomo Castiglioni and Luigi Caccia Dominioni organized an exhibition of rationally conceived radios for the *VII Triennale* in Milan in 1940. Among the instruments they themselves created was this model, 547, for Phonola, a plastic radio tied not to an ideal form but to the configuration of the components within. Taking the path telephone and typewriter design had followed earlier, they sheathed the tubes and electrical parts—by then reduced in number and greatly simplified—with a molded-plastic case to produce an organically determined radio. By locating the speaker, dial, and push-button controls on an angle, they also created an instrument that could function equally well sitting on a table or hanging on a wall.

Made by Phonola, Milan. Plastic. 7⁷/₈ x 9¹³/₁₆ x 10¹/₄" (20 x 25 x 26 cm). (Dr. Achille Castiglioni, Milan.)

181
R. D. RUSSELL
Television, 1937

During the 1920s Gordon Russell followed AMBROSE HEAL and Ernest Gimson in their continuation of the Arts and Crafts tradition of furniture design and manufacture, but he also broadened his firm's production to include simple angular furniture suitable for machine manufacture, with flush doors and little ornamental detailing. On seeing Russell's "modern" forms, which reflected continental styles then being subtly assimilated in England, Frank Murphy, a manufacturer of radios, commissioned wooden cabinets from the firm in 1930. Although the first modern designs were provided by Russell himself, it was his younger brother, R. D. Russell, an architect and designer trained in London at the school of the Architectural Association, who created the Murphy line beginning in 1931. So successful did

this collaboration prove that the firm had to supplement its workshop in the Cotswolds with a factory built for this purpose in London. Russell established a system of unified design and mass production new to radio manufacture, a system that included working with mechanical and electrical engineers to fully integrate technology and cabinetry. Leaving the simple rectangular cabinets undecorated and emphasizing the graining of the plywood or wood veneers of which they were made, Russell created the finest mass-produced cabinetry ever used on radio equipment and set a new style for the entire British furniture industry. The same approach was taken for this television designed by R. D. Russell in the later 1930s, in which only the speaker interrupted the broad, unadorned expanse of handsome veneer. As in many early televisions, the tube is installed vertically in the cabinet with the picture reflected from a mirror on the underside of the raised lacquered cover.

Made by Gordon Russell, London, for Murphy Radio Company, Welwyn Garden City, England. Rosewood, figured mahogany, and sycamore with lacquer and metal 34 x 31¹/₂ x 18" (87.5 x 80 x 45.8 cm). (Steelcase Strafor.)

Chapter Five
Austerity 1940–1950

World War II had epic and lasting repercussions on the manufacture and design of consumer products. Combatant countries restricted use of strategic materials, labor, and factories; the latter were converted from consumer trade to war production, causing shortages in virtually every industry. No country, including Germany, exercised greater control over consumer products than Great Britain. Two days after the declaration of war, in September 1939, the British Ministry of Supply imposed timber-control regulations under the Defence of the Realm Acts, and by July 1940 all timber supplies to the furniture industry had ceased.[1] Controls were also levied on other materials, including silk, rayon, leather, wool, cotton, iron and steel, aluminum, non-ferrous metals, flax, hemp, and jute. Quotas for the manufacture of many consumer products were introduced in late 1940 in Britain and the supply of certain items, notably aluminum hollowware, was completely withdrawn. In 1941 the rationing of furnishing fabrics and carpets was introduced. From 1942 the prices of domestic pottery were controlled, and although there was no rationing of pottery, the manufacture of decorated and "inessential" ware for the home was prohibited.

In 1942 a tightly controlled program of standardized furniture that subscribed to wartime exigencies was created. Restricted to newlyweds and people whose homes had been destroyed by bombing, the Utility furniture program as defined by the British Board of Trade specified not only who could buy the furniture but who could make it, as well as the actual designs and retail prices (no. 187). The ADVISORY COMMITTEE ON UTILITY FURNITURE, which included the designer Gordon Russell, was appointed "to produce specifications for furniture of good, sound construction in simple but agreeable designs for sale at reasonable prices, and ensuring the maximum economy of raw materials and labour."[2] In just over three months, in October 1942, the Utility lines of living-room, dining-room, bedroom, kitchen, and nursery furniture, as well as other miscellaneous pieces, were designed and exhibited to the public in prototype in London. A catalog was published in January 1943 and by the end of February 25,000 units of furniture had been sold. A team of designers provided drawings for the furniture, which was required to be strong, serviceable, and sparing in its use of raw material. Economical in design and production, Utility furniture recalled both traditional Arts and Crafts forms and, in the enthusiasm of the committee to influence popular taste, the socialist ideals of the Arts and Crafts Movement. According to Russell, who in 1943 had become chairman of a separate Utility design panel, "to raise the whole

opposite:
Charles Eames, Chair, 1946
(no. 194)

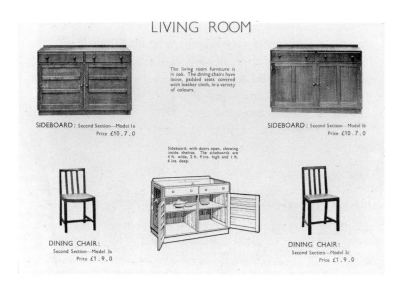

LIVING ROOM

The living room furniture is in oak. The dining chairs have loose, padded seats covered with leather cloth, in a variety of colours.

SIDEBOARD: Second Section—Model 1a
Price £10.7.0

SIDEBOARD: Second Section—Model 1b
Price £10.7.0

Sideboard, with doors open, showing inside shelves. The sideboards are 4 ft. wide, 2 ft. 9 ins. high and 1 ft. 6 ins. deep.

DINING CHAIR:
Second Section—Model 3a
Price £1.9.0

DINING CHAIR:
Second Section—Model 3c
Price £1.9.0

Page from the first *Utility Furniture* catalog, 1943, showing the program's living room furniture, which was available to newlyweds and those who had lost their possessions during the bombing of Great Britain.

standard of furniture for the mass of the people was not a bad war job, and it has always seemed sound to me, when in doubt as to people's requirements, to aim at giving them something better than they might be expected to demand."[3]

The furniture industry never reconciled itself to the complete control the Board of Trade exercised over its activities, and it remained fundamentally opposed to price controls and the concentration of production in some 150 designated factories. Furnishing fabrics were added to the Utility program in 1944, largely designed by ENID MARX (no. 188). Like the Utility furniture, the fabrics were restricted by materials shortages, with limitations imposed on the types and amounts of yarn and even the colors allowed. While the austere style of the Utility furnishings could be attributed to necessity—materials and labor were in short supply—its efficiency and economy were directly in line both with the straightforward, common-sense forms of the Arts and Crafts Movement and with modern ideas of functional simplicity promoted by advanced European designers. "It was an acid test," observed Russell in his autobiography, and "must have been a bit of a shock that a type of design which had been pioneered for years by a small minority—whilst the trade looked on and laughed—should prove its mettle in a national emergency, but so it was, to the amusement of some and to the amazement of others."[4]

Arts and Crafts traditions and functionalist values were similarly reestablished in Germany during the Third Reich under the official sponsorship of the Deutsche Arbeitsfront (German Labor Front) and its Schönheit der Arbeit (Beauty in Work) program of 1934. The program was intended to improve the aesthetic environment of plants and factories throughout Germany in an effort to win the support of German labor. As Albert Speer, Hitler's architect and armaments minister who then headed the program, recalled:

> The name had provoked a good deal of mockery. . . . The project turned out to be an extremely gratifying one, at least for me personally. First, we persuaded factory owners to modernize

their offices and to have some flowers about. . . . What was more, we designed the necessary artifacts for these reforms, from simple, well-shaped flatware to sturdy furniture, all of which we had manufactured in large quantities. We provided educational movies and a counseling service to help businessmen on questions of illumination and ventilation. . . . One and all devoted themselves to the cause of making some improvements in the workers' living conditions.[5]

Under contract from 1934 to the Schönheit der Arbeit office, Heinrich Löffelhardt designed ceramic tablewares with simple banded borders, which were produced by various manufacturers for use in plants, canteens, and recreation centers and later in military facilities. Furniture in rustic forms and native woods emphasized the ethnic and traditional side of the program. In the manner of the British return to Arts and Crafts as a patriotic style during the national emergency, the National Socialists promoted such popular or *volkish* designs. Unlike Britain's later Utility program, Schönheit der Arbeit was never regulated by law; no industries were nationalized and compliance was optional. In fact, even after the outbreak of war Germany never approached the absolute control over consumer industries that Great Britain exercised. Wide guidelines and restrictions were introduced for various aspects of daily life, from the delivery of furniture to suitable household effects in small dwellings, but as Speer wrote in his memoirs:

> It remains one of the oddities of this war, that Hitler demanded far less from his people than Churchill and Roosevelt did from their respective nations. The discrepancy between the total mobilization of labor forces in democratic England and the casual treatment of this question in authoritarian Germany is proof of the regime's anxiety not to risk any shift in the popular mood. The German leaders were not disposed to make sacrifices

Interior designed for Germany's Schönheit der Arbeit (Beauty of Work) program, c. 1935, based on Arts and Crafts values.

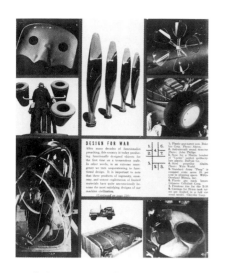

In 1943 *Architectural Forum* claimed that in times of extreme emergency, one turns "unquestioningly to functional design" and that "these products of ingenuity, economy, and utmost exploitation of limited materials have unconsciously become the most satisfying designs of our machine civilization."

themselves or to ask sacrifices of the people. . . . In order to anticipate any discontent, more effort and money were expended on supplies of consumer goods, on military pensions, or compensation to women for the loss of earnings by their men in the services, than in the countries with democratic governments.[6]

In 1942, in order to produce what he thought was needed for the war industries as well as for basic necessities, Speer attempted unsuccessfully to effect a sizable cut in the German consumer industries, which were then producing goods at a rate only three percent below their peacetime level.[7]

Elsewhere, the war necessitated drastic cutbacks in consumer industries. In the United States in 1942, the Office of Price Administration was created to establish price ceilings on such consumer goods as refrigerators, stoves, radios, and typewriters. Materials essential to the war effort were rationed and controlled, from timber to steel, chromium, aluminum, and copper. Glass products were commonly substituted for metal, while plywood along with corrugated and solid-fiber board replaced timber. The country's best known industrial designers were involved in war work. HENRY DREYFUSS, NORMAN BEL GEDDES, RAYMOND LOEWY, and WALTER DORWIN TEAGUE were commissioned by the government to design everything from military weapons and a mobile field hospital to photographic recognition training programs. Some manufacturers that had been able to maintain limited commercial production during World War I were totally converted to war production after Pearl Harbor. In March 1942 all manufacture of silverware was stopped by government order because silver, a substitute for copper in military applications, was needed for the war effort. Oneida, a large metal- and silverwares firm with plants in New York State and Canada, retooled and from 1942 to 1945 produced only military supplies. Because of quotas on and shortages of wool as well as increased manufacturing costs and war production, the Bigelow-Sanford Carpet Company produced just a third of the carpeting it had marketed before the war, and its entire list was reduced to a single wool-rayon-blend line.

In Japan, where rationing began in 1939 and the use of certain materials was controlled, copper could not be used for household utensils and the supply of cotton for domestic consumption was withdrawn. In July 1940, civilian consumption was curtailed further by ministerial order: the production and sale of luxury goods was prohibited and the prices of other items were controlled.[8] Although consumer furnishings and utensils were traditionally fewer than in the West because of the greater simplicity of the Japanese house and life style, shortages arose nonetheless as manufacturers converted from civilian to military production. Paper products, based largely on imported pulp and used in Japanese interiors for sliding doors, screens, translucent panels, and lamps, were produced in 1944 at only thirty-five percent of their 1940 level.[9]

Material shortages and a lack of labor, production facilities, and capital continued to plague consumer industries in the United States and Western Europe through the postwar period of the 1940s and early 1950s. Austerity restrictions persisted, such as those in the Netherlands, where Dutch potteries were obliged to produce a stipulated amount of household wares until they were deregulated in 1949. Scrap war materials, from aircraft aluminum and surplus parachute cloth to packing materials, were also used for consumer goods immediately after the war by such manufacturers as the new British furniture firm of ERNEST RACE (no. 189) and the Dutch weaving mill and wholesaler De Ploeg.

Designers everywhere faced the necessity of providing low-cost mass-produced objects in virtually every industry. They were universally sparing in their use of materials and frequently ingenious in capitalizing on developments and discoveries made for the war effort. Advances in polymer chemistry gave rise to new synthetic fibers and families of plastic materials. Nylon, invented at DuPont in 1939 and remarkable for its unusual flexibility and strength, replaced silk for American-made parachutes during the war and as surplus was sold commercially during the 1940s as upholstery and furnishing fabric (no. 185). Polyethylene, a new lightweight flexible plastic, was used first by the Tupper Corporation after the war in the manufacture of food and liquid containers (no. 204). By the late 1940s several firms in Western Europe were even specializing in plastic housewares, among them Rosti in Denmark, founded in 1944, and Gustavsberg in Sweden, beginning in 1945. Rosti used melamine, which resists heat and is easily colored, for its popular housewares, some of which were designed by Denmark's first industrial design firm, BERNADOTTE & BJØRN (no. 216).

Using fiberglass, a glass-reinforced plastic developed for aircraft radar domes in 1942, and plastic resin materials, which he had found in war-surplus stores, the American CHARLES EAMES, with his wife, Ray Eames, adapted a stamped-metal chair design of 1948 to the new technology.[10] Produced in 1950 by Zenith Plastics for Herman Miller, the inexpensive and subsequently much imitated molded fiberglass-shell armchair visibly exposed this material (no. 210). At the same time EERO SAARINEN, who had collaborated with Eames on molded-chair prototypes for the "Organic Design in Home Furnishings" competition at the Museum of Modern Art in New York (1940), designed a similar, molded, reinforced-plastic chair that was produced by Knoll in 1948. Saarinen, however, elected to cover the shell with foam-rubber padding and upholstery for comfort rather than leaving the fiberglass exposed (no. 201). The "Organic Design" prototypes that Eames and Saarinen created in 1940 involved experimenting with molding shells in compound curves, and with electronic cycle-welding borrowed from the automotive industry. Eames applied these techniques to molded-plywood chair seats as well as to the splints, stretchers, aircraft parts, and glider shells that he developed for the department of the navy during the war. In 1946, Eames exhibited the first of his later famous chairs composed of plywood shells, including some mounted on steel rod legs by means of a rubber-weld joint attached with a new synthetic resin developed for war use (no. 194). The plywood and fiberglass chairs achieved Eames's goal of designing low-cost, high-quality furniture for mass production; widely published, they also provided an example to other designers of how new materials and technologies could be used to achieve that goal.

In an effort to stimulate postwar sales of consumer goods, and to demonstrate to the public the importance that design could have in improving living standards, designers, manufacturers, and museums in the United States and Europe, sometimes with the support of their governments, addressed the problems of postwar consumer production in a number of exhibitions. These provided a widely influential forum for design ideas. At a time when materials and manufacturing were limited, they gave designers the opportunity to experiment freely with new forms and technology and to show their advanced work, generally as prototypes. In 1946 the Riunione Italiana Mostre Arredamento (Italian Association for Exhibitions of Furnishings) held an exhibition in Milan of interior design and furniture that stressed the need for flexible, inexpensive furnishings, as did the *VIII Triennale* in Milan in 1947, which focused on housing and the home. The bold freedom of form and heterogeneous variety of materials displayed by Italian designers at the exhibitions, and publicized in such magazines as *Domus*, surprised one foreign critic, who later wrote, "Italy, freed successively from a Fascist regime, a German occupation, and an allied one, defeated, apparently ruined, and with all the essential ingredients of a first-rate revolution, has instead staged a design revolution that puts her ahead of almost all others."[11] Some of the new Italian ideas, including chairs with steel-wire-strut bases by Guido Gai, a steel-rod and canvas sling chair by MARCO ZANUSO, and storage units on poles by Franco Albini and Gino Colombini, appeared again in 1948 when the Museum of Modern Art in New York held the "International Competition for Low-Cost Furniture Design." The competition acknowledged the importance of low-cost housing and home furnishings "to the national economy and the general welfare of the peoples of all countries. . . . To serve the needs of the vast majority of people we must have furniture that is adaptable to small apartments and houses, furniture that is well-designed yet moderate in price, that is comfortable but not bulky, and that can be easily moved, stored, and cared for; in other words, mass-produced furniture that is planned and executed to fit the needs of modern living, production and merchandising."[12] Competition entries from North and South America, Europe, and Japan included furniture that could be "knocked down," or shipped flat in cartons and easily assembled by the consumer; furniture that exploited new synthetic materials, including Eames's reinforced-plastic chair; flexible storage units by the British designers Robin Day and Clive Latimer; and chairs that ganged and stacked by Ilmari Tapiovaara of Finland. Other even more experimental designs were also included, one by an American team for "a comfortable one-piece chair in molded plastic designed to issue from its mold fully finished with integral coloring and a perfect sur-

The role of the industrial designer was highlighted in Misha Black's *Birth of an Egg Cup* display in the *Britain Can Make It* exhibition at the Victoria and Albert Museum, London, 1946.

face."[13] Some such ideas for low-cost furnishings were put into commercial production in the late 1940s, particularly in the United States, including universal glasswares by Freda Diamond and modular furniture components that could be combined to form room dividers by PAUL MCCOBB (no. 213). Lamps by the American GILBERT A. WATROUS (no. 212) and the Italian ROBERTO MENGHI (no. 205) differed in appearance but addressed the same issue of providing a flexible and readily available light source that could be used anywhere.

One of the most important exhibitions of industrial design, called *Britain Can Make It*, opened in London in September 1946 and was seen by nearly half a million visitors; it showed a large array of new consumer goods (largely still unavailable) and set out to explain what was involved in the design process along with industry's need for the special skills the designer could provide. A similar exhibition, *Enterprise Scotland*, was held in Edinburgh in 1947, followed the next year by *Design at Work* in London. Similarly, in Paris in late 1949, the Union des Artistes Modernes (UAM), headed by RENÉ HERBST, launched the first in a series of public exhibitions of *Formes Utiles* (*Useful Forms*); these were designed to dispel the prewar image of French modern goods as exclusively luxurious and to show that "there exist contemporary, everyday, affordable objects of quality, produced both by craftsmen and by industry, so designed that they can contribute to the harmony, health, and joy of life."[14] During a period of privation, this exhibition and others offered consumers a tantalizing glimpse of what the future—as shaped by the designer—could be.

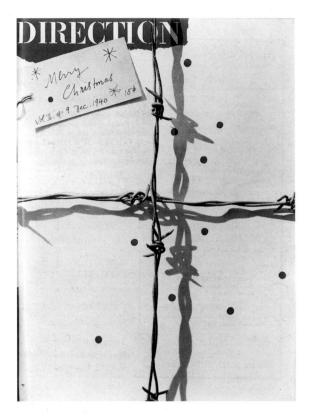

182
PAUL RAND
Cover of *Direction*, 1940

With the world torn by war, American graphic designer Paul Rand offered an ironic present for Christmas
1940 in the form of a photocollage cover of *Direction*
magazine, seemingly tied with barbed wire and identified with a handwritten gift tag. The strong shadows
that throw the cruciform wire and tag into bold relief
bring ominous reality to the black-and-white photograph, but this realism is confounded by the artifice of
the flat red color applied over the image, defining the
torn paper on which *Direction* is stenciled, the string of
the gift tag, and the "festive" dots. Consciously imitat-
ing the sophisticated techniques of European avant-
garde painters such as Picasso, Léger, and van
Doesburg, Rand used abstract shapes for their expressive and symbolic content, building up layers of meaning from a series of collaged elements. According to
Rand, the designer can "contribute to the effectiveness
of the basic meaning of the symbol, by interpretation,
addition, subtraction, juxtaposition, alteration, adjustment, association, intensification, and clarification,"[15]
most of which come into play in this grim composition.

*Published by M. Tjader Harris, Darien, Connecticut. Printed
magazine. 10 1/2 x 8" (26.7 x 20.3 cm). (Library of
Congress, Washington, D.C.)*

183
PETER SCHLUMBOHM
Chemex coffee maker, 1941

Extolling the benefits of coffee made by filtration
rather than boiling (which, according to Peter
Schlumbohm's instructional brochure, releases coffee
fats that are "disgusting even before turning rancid"),
the chemist-inventor offered a coffee maker that repli-
cated the filtration process of the laboratory and aped
its glass equipment as well. It was in fact as a "filtering
device," not a coffee maker, that he first sought to
protect his invention when he applied for a patent in
Germany in 1938 and in America, after his arrival, in
1939.[16] But it was his methods of promotion along
with his product that convinced millions of Americans
to switch to the hourglass-shaped *Chemex*, and the
coffee maker has continued to sell in great numbers
for over fifty years. Assembled in his own factory from
a Pyrex decanter supplied by the CORNING GLASS
WORKS, to which his workers added a varnished wood
handle tied with a leather thong, this was the first of the
line of "products for the Chemist's Kitchen" that he
developed over the next two decades (no. 203).

*Made by Chemex Corporation, New York. Glass, wood, and
leather. Height: 9 1/2" (24.1 cm). (Museum of Modern Art,
New York, gift of Lewis and Conger.)*

184
RAYMOND LOEWY
Package for Lucky Strike cigarettes, 1940–42

Wartime shortages affected many areas of design, including packaging and graphics, as Raymond Loewy's Lucky Strike target pack illustrates. The package received its white color in 1942 when the ink used to print the earlier green version was discontinued because of its metal content. Actually, this was a second redesign, the first having occurred in 1940 when Loewy was asked to improve the green and red package to increase sales, as he had done for many other products (no. 152). His first solution was to put more emphasis on the red target trademark, adding a ring to the two that surrounded it, strengthening the red bars at top and bottom, and replacing a large version of the word *cigarettes* with discreet, reduced type. He also put the trademark on both sides of the package, thereby doubling its advertising exposure at no extra cost to the company. Although these alterations were low-key, Loewy was aware that any "change in the appearance of an accepted product thoroughly identifiable by the public is a risky thing. If done correctly, it usually brings results immediate and lasting. It conveys the feeling of liveliness, of freshness." Two years later when Loewy had to respond to the ink restrictions, the package gained more than just a new color, as he explained: "Owing to its impeccable whiteness, the Lucky pack looks, and is, clean. It automatically connotes freshness of content and immaculate manufacturing."[17]

Made by the American Tobacco Company. Printed package. (Location unknown).

JENS RISOM
Chair, 1941–42

Jens Risom's angled and canted chair introduced a new look to American furniture in the 1940s. It combined standardized components with wood in the spare, simple style associated with design in Scandinavia (where Risom had studied). Its webbing, too, had a specific precedent in the upholstery used by the Swede Bruno Mathsson (no. 159). Designed for low-cost production, the chair was easily assembled from a few simple parts. At first cedar was used since hardwood was restricted by wartime controls, and the nylon webbing was cheaply bought from army surplus. (This slightly modified version, made around 1946 just as wartime restrictions were relaxed, is created of birch and plastic webbing.) Risom's chair, for which he received a design patent in 1945,[18] was the first created for Hans Knoll, whose newly established firm would become a leader in the production and distribution of contemporary furniture. When Knoll issued his first catalog in April 1942, fifteen of the twenty-five pieces illustrated were Risom's designs.

Made by Hans G. Knoll Furniture, New York. Birch with plastic upholstery. 30 5/16 x 17 1/2 x 20 1/4" (77 x 44.5 x 51.5 cm). (Musée des Arts Décoratifs de Montreal.)

29⁷/₈ x 39⁵/₈" (75.9 x 100.7 cm). (Museum of Modern Art, New York, gift of the Office for Emergency Management.)

186
JEAN CARLU
Poster for the United States Division of Information, Office for Emergency Management, 1941

Jean Carlu's *America's Answer—Production* was the first poster commissioned by the United States government for the American and Allied war efforts and was published six months before Pearl Harbor at the start of the lend-lease program. In March 1941, Franklin Roosevelt had called upon the country to be the great arsenal of democracy, supplying war materials to the Allies through sale, loan, or lease. To encourage the factory workers who would be producing these materials, Carlu and five other graphic artists were asked to submit designs to the Division of Information for posters that could be hung in factories across the country. His terse answer was expressed as a visual symbol of machine assembly, a single gloved hand forcefully grasping a wrench and turning the first O in the title word *production* as if it were a metal nut. This single angular gesture conveyed in a few economical strokes all the tenseness and alertness of the war effort, visually bolting together word and image into a message of great power. Awarded the New York Art Directors Club prize as the best poster of 1941, it was printed in 100,000 copies. Carlu, who had come to the United States from France in 1940, quickly became an important propagandist in wartime America, creating posters and publicity materials for such organizations as the Committee to Defend America by Aiding the Allies, the Free French Movement in America, and the American-French War Relief.

Printed by the U.S. Government Printing Office, Washington, D.C. Lithograph.

187
ADVISORY COMMITTEE ON UTILITY FURNITURE
Table, c. 1945

This table belonged to the Cotswold line of domestic furniture produced under the Utility system of civilian wartime manufacture "to provide for those who really need it, furniture which is sound in construction, agreeable in design and reasonable in price."[19] "Those who really need it" were defined as newlyweds setting up a home or citizens who had lost their furniture through bombings. For reasons of equity, efficiency, and economy in wartime, every piece of furniture manufactured in Britain after January 1943 was required to follow the same design patterns, using the same hardwood materials and prescribed methods of construction. The furniture depended on nineteenth-century Arts and Crafts principles and the example of such twentieth-century manufacturers as Heal's (no. 77), Gordon Russell, and Betty Joel; created collaboratively, the pieces looked back to the stolid, reassuring tradition of British vernacular furniture. Trim, strong, plain, economical, and well made, Utility furniture as it evolved over the next few years provided an example of design and manufacturing quality in the postwar period.

Mahogany. Height: 30" (76.2 cm). (Geffrye Museum, London.)

188
ENID MARX
Star and Stripe fabric, 1945

As a member of the design panel of the ADVISORY COMMITTEE ON UTILITY FURNITURE, the body charged with overseeing the design of civilian furnishings in wartime Britain, Enid Marx was responsible for most of the cotton fabrics produced under its auspices. With materials in short supply, she had numerous restrictions to consider. Designs had to be small to avoid waste in piecing upholstery together (repeats did not exceed four inches), and both the types of yarn and amounts available were also strictly limited. Until 1946, when the rules began to become less stringent, only four colors could be used—rust, blue, green, and natural—and the colors themselves were muted because of the shortage of dyes. Despite the limited range open to her, Marx created a rich variety of designs, choosing geometric patterns of diamonds, chevrons, stars, stripes, dots, rings, and plaids for the ease of the small repeats; in a fabric such as *Star and Stripe* she imaginatively exploited a number of weaving and coloristic possibilities to create within its narrow scope a design with four differently patterned stars and four different stripes.

Cotton. Width: 16 1/4" (41.2 cm). (Philadelphia Museum of Art.)

189
ERNEST RACE
BA chair, 1945

Rationing and restrictions on the use of raw materials continued in Great Britain well beyond the end of World War II, and with furniture manufacture strictly controlled by the ADVISORY COMMITTEE ON UTILITY FURNITURE, a young firm such as Ernest Race's, founded in 1945, had virtually no access to the limited supplies of wood and furnishing fabrics then available. To get permission to start manufacturing furniture, Race had to settle for whatever materials were at hand; thus scrap aluminum from airplanes and surplus parachute cloth were used to produce his *BA* dining chair. Race constructed the chair out of five sand-cast (later die-cast) aluminum elements—four tapering uprights and a seat frame—and added an upholstered seat and back. Although made from an unconventional furniture material, the lightweight, eminently serviceable, aluminum *BA* chair had enormous success, and over a quarter of a million units had been sold for domestic and commercial use by the time it was withdrawn from production in 1969. The chair was first shown at the *Britain Can Make It* exhibition in London in 1946 and won a gold medal at the *X Triennale* in Milan in 1954.

Made by Race Furniture Limited, Sheerness, England. Aluminum alloy and plywood with upholstery. 31 1/4 x 23 13/16 x 18 7/8" (79.5 x 60.5 x 48 cm). (Victoria and Albert Museum, London.)

190
ANGELO TESTA
Filo fabric, 1942

As the first graduate of Chicago's Institute of Design—founded in 1937 as the New Bauhaus—Angelo Testa became a self-styled spokesperson for the Bauhaus program as it was implemented there under the directorship of LÁSZLÓ MOHOLY-NAGY. Testa introduced abstract printed textiles such as this within the Bauhaus functionalist aesthetic, which had originally rejected such decorative designs in favor of structural patterns and textural effects. "Texture," he wrote, "should be emphasized where the decorative function of the fabric is minimized, and color and form where the function is purely decorative,"[20] a remark that gave ornament a functional justification in itself. A fabric such as *Filo*, designed while he was still a student and printed in his own workshop, embodies his advocacy of abstract,

small-scale, linear patterns; continuous lines in two different colors create a design of horizontal bands that was considered small enough to allow the fabric to be used either as upholstery or drapery material. His work, illustrated in numerous international design publications, was instrumental in introducing printed fabrics into contemporary architectural interiors.

Screen-printed cotton. Repeat: 19 1/2 x 23 3/8" (49.5 x 59.4 cm). (Art Institute of Chicago.)

191
KAARE KLINT
Fruit hanging lamp, 1944

Kaare Klint's folded-paper *Fruit* lamp was the first production model of a craft and cottage industry that developed around the turn of the century when Klint's father began to experiment with paper shades for a ceramic lamp he had made. Family and friends helped him to perfect construction techniques and created additional designs for manufacture; when demand became too great, a family firm called Le Klint was established in the early 1940s to produce the lamp shades commercially, starting with this design. The inexpensive paper lamps quickly achieved substantial success in a market short of consumer goods. Well designed, economical, and festive in spirit, Le Klint lamps have remained in continuous production since the war. The firm now produces over 100,000 shades annually, most assembled by hand using paper (or plastic for some other models) that has been mechanically scored with the intricate pleating and folding lines of each design.

Made by Le Klint, Odense, Denmark. Paper. Height: 20 7/8" (53 cm). (Le Klint, Odense, Denmark.)

192
EVA ZEISEL
Museum table service, 1946

In the early 1940s Castleton China began to seek a designer "to evolve a fine modern shape for formal dinnerware of high quality,"[21] a position for which the Museum of Modern Art in New York recommended the European-trained Eva Zeisel in 1942. The results, this *Museum* service, were exhibited in a collection of twenty-five pieces at the museum in 1946, where they were hailed as "the first fine china of modern design to be manufactured in this country."[22] Originally produced in ivory and bare of ornament, the service departed from the simple geometric forms of circles and spheres popularized by functionalist ceramics designers in the 1930s. Organic in design, the softly curving shapes were conceived as a form of personal expression, not with compass and ruler. "We must register a new trend in modern design," wrote Zeisel. "Lines and forms have become communicative once more. They express the designer's moods and his sense of humor . . . whether changes in production processes induced the designing of softer and more modeled shapes— I do not know. Non-objective art, abstract sculpture particularly, which is now being taught in all art and design schools, may have been one of the influences."[23]

Made by Shenango Company, New Castle, Pennsylvania, for Castleton China, Inc., New Castle, Pennsylvania. Height of coffeepot: 10 1/2" (26.9 cm). (Musée des Arts Décoratifs, Montreal.)

193
ISAMU NOGUCHI
Coffee table, c. 1947

Rationally conceived and engineered like any functionalist piece of furniture, Isamu Noguchi's freely organic coffee table is nonetheless as abstract as his sculpture. Composed of two identical pieces of walnut locked together with a pin and socket coupling, this sleek table is held rigid by the weight of its "free-form" plate-glass top. The assembly was so simple that the manufacturer Herman Miller successfully promoted the table for sale in substantial numbers as knock-down furniture. By his own admission Noguchi was propelled into the creation of this table by revenge, claiming that a similar custom design he had done for the designer T. H. Robsjohn-Gibbings was being manufactured and advertised without his authorization. Both tables go back to Noguchi's earlier version of the design, a glass-topped coffee table with a base of two sculpted pieces of rosewood joined by a sphere, which was made in 1939 for the then-president of the Museum of Modern Art, A. Conger Goodyear. Faced with someone else's commercial adaptation of his own design, Noguchi decided to make "my own variant of my own table, articulated as in the Goodyear Table, but reduced to rudiments."[24]

Made by Herman Miller Furniture Company, Zeeland, Michigan. Ebonized birch and glass. 15 5/8 x 50 x 36" (39.7 x 127 x 91.5 cm). (Museum of Modern Art, New York, gift of Robert Gruen.)

194
CHARLES EAMES
Chair, 1946

The most influential piece of furniture of the immediate post-war period, this chair grew out of experiments Charles Eames made with EERO SAARINEN around 1940 in molding chair shells with compound curves. After their prototype had won first prize in the "Organic Design in Home Furnishings" competition in 1940, organized by the Museum of Modern Art in New York, Eames continued his research in developing low-cost techniques for wood lamination and plywood molding, work he pursued during the war under contract to the department of the navy. A version of this chair with three legs was shown in the exhibition *New Furniture Designed by Charles Eames* at the Museum of Modern Art in 1946, but could not be mass-produced due to problems of stability. The present four-legged version replaced the three-legged model and was first put into production in the summer of 1946 by the Evans Products Company. It was marketed and distributed by the Herman Miller Furniture Company, who took over the manufacturing rights in 1949. Using synthetic resins developed during the war to bond the plywood and to join the steel-rod legs to the plywood seat with rubber shock mounts, Eames succeeded in creating a simple plywood and metal chair that could be inexpensively manufactured by machine. With its thin steel support and separate shells for seat and back, this spidery chair seemed a model of economy and rational design in a period of material shortages and cost restrictions; not surprisingly, it was widely copied.

Made by Evans Products Company, Venice, California. Plywood, steel, and rubber. 29 1/4 x 20 1/4 x 21 1/2" (74.5 x 51.5 x 54.5 cm). (Museum of Fine Arts, Boston, gift of Edward J. Wormley.)

195
GEORGE NELSON
Basic Cabinet Series components, 1946

George Nelson's *Basic Cabinet Series* of freestanding, standardized storage components followed the idea of the built-in *Storagewall* that he and Henry Wright, associate editors at *Architectural Forum*, had presented in 1944 as a way to provide efficient, architecturally integrated storage for postwar American households; the *Storagewall* received popular attention the following year in *Life* magazine. The modular *Basic Cabinet Series* was conceived to "look as 'architectural' as possible," Nelson later explained. "The great virtue of modular cases . . . was their very neutrality, their built-in appearance."[25] The modular system used platform benches (or legs) to support cabinets of different dimensions and functions (shelves, drawers, or more

specialized units such as writing tables and radio, television, and speaker installations). It could be set against a wall or function as a room divider, offering wide options for combining components to satisfy specific storage needs in different spaces. Nelson gave variety to the line by offering its elements with different wood or colored-lacquer finishes and several "families" of hardware.

Made by Herman Miller Furniture Company, Zeeland, Michigan. Birch and plywood. 86¹/₂ x 92¹/₄ x 18¹/₂" (219.7 x 234 x 47 cm). (Musée des Arts Décoratifs de Montreal.)

196
WELLS COATES
Princess-Handbag radio, 1947

A precursor of the miniature personal radio, Wells Coates's *Princess-Handbag* radio was likewise designed for portability at a time when the miniaturization of audio equipment was just at the beginning stages. But it was also designed with its market in mind, specifically targeting a female audience. Conceived like a woman's shoulder bag, the light green plastic portable could be carried either by a plastic strap or by its clear diagonal handle. The radio itself, with the controls on top, formed a complete unit that fit into a frame onto which the identical front and back panels were snapped; it also used standardized parts, which simplified the manufacturing process. This radio was shown at the London exhibition *Design at Work* in 1948.

Made by E. K. Cole, Southend, England. Plastic housing. Width: 8" (20.3 cm). (Central Museum, Southend-on-Sea, Essex, England.)

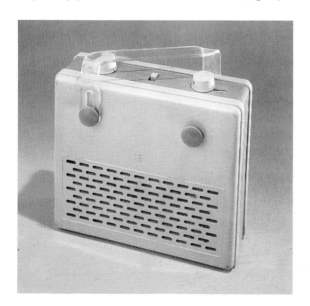

197
RAYMOND LOEWY ASSOCIATES
Television, 1948

In an attempt to broaden its specialized, prewar market in electrical equipment for the postwar era, the Hallicrafters Company hired the Chicago office of Raymond Loewy Associates to help reexamine the premises of its products. Rather than redesign completely, the Loewy design team headed by Richard Latham advised Hallicrafters to update their homemade "ham" radio look in favor of the sleek appearance of precision instruments in metal housings. Working with Hallicrafters' engineers, they examined and remodeled each element, simplifying the operating system and emphasizing the basic controls—on–off switch, tuner, and volume control—while minimizing the less important ones by reducing their size and organizing them into groups. With the experience and commercial success gained from their work on radios, the Loewy team then tackled the design of the firm's television receivers. Retaining the successfully rationalized radio format, they inserted the screen in place of the radio dial and continued to suggest by the scale and position of the pretuned push-button controls their relative importance and function. With its formal organization and legible graphics, the television recalled the high-quality professional instrumentation and tonal quality for which Hallicrafters had become known, thus instilling a sense of confidence in the broader audience then approaching the considerable investment of their first television purchase.

Made by the Hallicrafters Company, Chicago. Metal and plastic. 9³/₄ x 20 x 16" (24.7 x 50.8 x 40.6 cm). (E. Buk, New York.)

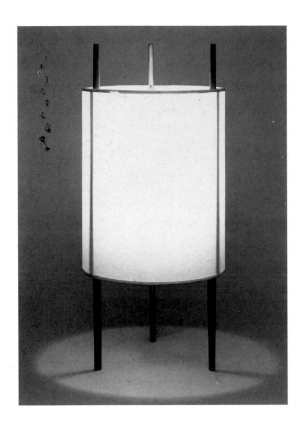

fact that his Lunars were restricted to wealthy clients and initially attracted no commercial interest. But then, as he recalled, "I made a lamp for my sister, three legs through an aluminum cylinder. I made some variations for friends with plastic or paper instead of the metal, and a year later the firm of Knoll undertook to manufacture a small version. Soon imitations were all over the place, and I had neglected to patent it"[26]—a constant complaint with Noguchi, whose work was so original and so successful when it was produced that it was widely pirated.

Made by Knoll Associates, New York. Plastic and wood.
Height: 153/4" (40 cm). (Philadelphia Museum of Art,
gift of Mr. and Mrs. James Dermody.)

198
ISAMU NOGUCHI
Table lamp, 1945

Isamu Noguchi's spare lighting designs were conceived as both functional fixtures and works of art. This rigid cylindrical table lamp and his soft glowing Akari lamps (no. 314) relate to a series of illuminated wall sculptures, or Lunars, he made in the early 1940s. Noguchi later wrote that he "thought of a luminous object as a source of delight in itself—like fire it attracts and protects us from the beasts of the night," lamenting the

199
BARTOLUCCI & WALDHEIM
Barwa lounge chair, 1947

Assessed in 1947 as "the most satisfactory solution to the sitting-lounging chair problem since the Morris chair,"[27] traditional symbol of nineteenth-century comfort, Bartolucci & Waldheim's *Barwa* lounge chair was also easy to move about the casual living spaces of American postwar houses and outdoors onto terraces and patios. Its design, in which "the shape of the back, seat and leg rest conform to the countour of the spinal column and skeletal frame of the occupant," was strikingly comfortable for the sitter, who could easily switch to a reclining position with the legs elevated above the head. "The center of gravity of the chair, either with or without an occupant, is so located that it will rest in stable equilibrium [in either position]," explained John J. Waldheim's patent application of 1944 for a tilting chair, "and is also so located that only a slight shift in weight is required to move the chair from one position to the other."[28] Made of lightweight aluminum tubing with colorful canvas stretched over it, the *Barwa* lounge chair was based on this patent but its design was more resolved than that illustrated in the patent drawings.

Made by Barwa Associates, Chicago. Aluminum and canvas.
38 x 201/4 x 52" (96.5 x 51.4 x 132.1 cm). (Musée des
Arts Décoratifs, Montreal, gift of Mr. Edgar Bartolucci.)

200
GEORGE NELSON
Atomic wall clock, 1949

Borrowing rods and spheres from familiar models of atomic structure, George Nelson introduced a modern scientific reference to industrial design and with it prefigured the symbolic, even jocular, associations that postmodern objects would bring to the field in the 1980s and 90s. The *Atomic* clock belongs to the Chronopak series of electric wall and table clocks that Nelson designed for the Howard Miller Clock Company beginning in 1949 and to which he added regularly over the next decades. His wall clocks generally took either star or spokelike forms such as this or had an outer ring to mark the hours; his characteristic arrow-shape hour hand and metronome-like minute hand were attached to a central brass cylinder that housed the works. Considering his designs in relation to architecture (no. 195), Nelson gave his clocks unusual silhouettes, using them as accent pieces in the design of an entire wall.

Made by Howard Miller Clock Company, Zeeland, Michigan. Brass, steel, and painted wood. Diameter: 13 3/8" (34 cm). (Philadelphia Museum of Art, purchased with funds contributed by COLLAB.)

201
EERO SAARINEN
Womb armchair, 1948

The first fiberglass chair to be mass-produced, Eero Saarinen's armchair was hailed as revolutionary when it appeared on the American market in 1948. According to *Life* magazine, the industrial materials Saarinen used "produce strange and unfamiliar shapes which are nonetheless comfortable and which, if more widely accepted, could lead to a whole new kind of really cheap, handsome furniture."[29] This chair was derived from experiments Saarinen had conducted with CHARLES EAMES on molded-plywood seat shells, which had been awarded first prize in the Museum of Modern Art's "Organic Design" competition of 1940; like the original prototype shown in 1940, this production model was fitted with foam-rubber padding and a fabric cover to secure continuous comfortable support using a minimum of material. Available commercially only after the war, the glass-reinforced plastic out of which Saarinen made the molded shell gave the chair added resiliency. As LE CORBUSIER had done in the *Grand Confort* armchair (no. 131), Saarinen conceived of this chair as a contemporary version of the traditional overstuffed club armchair. "In arriving at the design," Saarinen later wrote, "there were many problems which had to be recognized. First, there is the fact that people sit differently today than in the Victorian era. They want to sit lower and they like to slouch. . . . I attempted to shape the slouch in an organized way by giving support for the back as well as the seat, shoulders and head. The 'Womb' chair also has three planes of support . . . [and] also attempts to achieve a psychological comfort by providing a great big cup-like shell into which you can curl up and pull up your legs."[30]

Made by Knoll Associates, New York. Glass-reinforced plastic and chromium-plated steel with fabric-covered latex-foam upholstery. Height: 36 1/2" (93 cm); width: 40" (101.6 cm). (Museum of Modern Art, New York, gift of Knoll International, New York.)

ed additional no-nonsense products for what he conceived of as the "Chemist's Kitchen," all similarly based on functionally determined laboratory equipment and employing such materials as heat-resistant glass, insulating cork, and filter paper. The configuration of this efficient vessel, modeled on a lab flask, allowed water to be brought rapidly to a boil, while the cork-ball device vented steam through the glass tube and protected the top from heat so that it could be held for pouring, as Schlumbohm explained in his patent application of 1947.[31] *Chemex* products were singled out by critics in the 1950s for their consistency of design and praised for setting a standard of excellence for consumer products.

Made by Chemex Corporation, New York. Blown glass and cork. Height: 12⁵/₁₆" (31.3 cm). (Philadelphia Museum of Art, gift of the manufacturer.)

202
EKCO PRODUCTS COMPANY
Flint 1900 kitchen tools, 1946

With its Flint 1900 line, the Ekco Products Company established design and production standards for kitchen tools that have yet to be superseded. While previous cooking utensils had been cheaply made of stamped metal (which rusted) and turned wooden handles (which split with repeated washing), these implements were fabricated from stainless steel and molded plastic. Without rethinking the basic utensil forms, the Ekco staff improved their construction by using a single piece of metal for tool and shank, which was inserted fully into the handle and solidly riveted. The sense of strength and durability that the rivets and polished steel convey associated these tools with fine cutlery, a connection Ekco encouraged by adopting the Flint trademark from their own line of well-made knives. Sold as a set along with a rack from which to hang them, *Flint 1900* tools were considerably more expensive than other utensils, but this did not seem to have discouraged buyers, who appreciated the quality of a product that had not formerly been given such design consideration.

Stainless steel and plastic. Length of spatula: 10¹¹/₁₆" (27.8 cm). (Philadelphia Museum of Art.)

203
PETER SCHLUMBOHM
Water kettle, 1947

Following the success of his *Chemex* coffee maker designed in 1941 (no. 183), Peter Schlumbohm creat-

204
EARL S. TUPPER
Tupperware pitcher and food storage containers, c. 1945

Calling Earl S. Tupper's storage bowls "objects of great beauty," *House Beautiful* in 1947 rhapsodized over the wondrous new material of which they were molded: "If you have never touched polyethylene we need to

tell you that it has the appearance of great fragility and delicacy—yet has great strength. It has the fingering qualities of jade, but at the same time it reminds you of alabaster and mother of pearl. Held up to the light it becomes opalescent and translucent and has an interesting, new ability to transfer light. So these bowls look like art objects—even before you know what they do."[32] The bowls were among twenty-five different pastel-colored items—refrigerator containers, tumblers, and even poker chips—that made up the line of polyethylene products Tupper introduced at the end of the war. Tupper's improved manufacturing process produced a plastic that did not crack (which he called "Poly-T"), and his flexible containers could be squeezed to form a spout for pouring, while their patented airtight lids[33] formed partial vacuums when slight pressure was exerted on them.

Made by Tupper Corporation, Farnumsville, Massachusetts. Polyethylene. Height of pitcher: 9 1/2" (21.8 cm). (Museum of Modern Art, New York, gift of the manufacturer.)

205
ROBERTO MENGHI
Libra Lux lamp, 1948

Advertised as a "universal lamp," Roberto Menghi's *Libra Lux* ingeniously provided a flexible and readily available light source using the simple principle of the counterweight. It was promoted for use anywhere—on a desk, a piano, a slanted drawing board, the arm of an upholstered chair, or a table. Instead of including arms that extend and adjust to throw light where it is required as in the earlier *Anglepoise* lamp (no. 143), Menghi made the entire fixture portable. Because of the balance given by the weight, the lamp remains in place without adjustment, and the height and angle of the shade can be altered if desired.

Made by P. Lamperti & C., Milan. Brass and enameled aluminum. Height: 34" (86.3 cm). (Roberto Menghi, Milan.)

206
TAPIO WIRKKALA
Kantarelli vase, 1946

This blown-glass vase belongs to the Kantarelli (Chanterelle) series, which first brought international recognition to the Finnish craftsman and designer Tapio Wirkkala. Mimicking in paper-thin glass the natural structure and surface of the frail ribboned mushroom that gave the series its name, Wirkkala's simple and elegant form captures the spirit of organic growth in its swelling shape and the vertical lines of its cut decoration. Wirkkala himself later explained that the craft aesthetic in postwar Finland, ornamental, romantic, and based on natural forms and materials, "survives principally under the patronage of the large industrial firms. Industry has secured the services of craftsmen who can avail themselves of the technical facilities of the factory without, however, forfeiting their own artistic

individuality."[34] Wirkkala's irregular shapes and surface decorations, particularly the decorative lines he cut in different depths to produce an elaborate relief effect, initially proved difficult for the glassblowers at the Iittala factory to make. Wirkkala, however, collaborated with the glass craftsmen and helped them succeed in producing these and a number of similarly textured vases. Exhibited at the *IX* and *X Triennale* exhibitions in Milan in 1951 and 1954, where the designer won six grand prizes, the Kantarelli series was produced between 1947 and 1960.

Made by Karhula-Iittala, Iittala, Finland. Clear blown glass. Height: 8 1/2" (21.6 cm). (Metropolitan Museum of Art, gift of Aarne Simenon, 1956.)

207
GEORGE NAKASHIMA
Coffee table, c. 1948

George Nakashima was at once craftsman, manufacturer, and distributor, designing furniture and fabricating it in high-quality series production in his own workshop, which was also his salesroom. In the 1940s and 1950s his method was frequently cited as an alternative to the increasingly popular large-scale mass production of furniture in the United States. "Our approach," he explained, "is to realize a synthesis between the hand and the machine working as a small unit. It is a return to the business methods of the early American craftsman who made chairs, tables and cabinets, and put them in carts for transporting and selling directly to the customers who wanted them."[35] This approach allowed him to exploit the organic expressiveness and chance effects of the individual piece of wood, which could not easily be accommodated in repetitive factory production—its grain, its knots or burls, and its "free edge," that is, the natural form of a plank left untrimmed as it is cut from the log (such as the irregular side of this

coffee table). Nakashima explored a personal design style, drawing on vernacular American and Japanese craft forms and construction techniques as well as the rational approach of International Style architecture, the latter of which is introduced in the strong architectonic base of this low slab coffee table.

American black walnut. 12¼ x 56 x 17" (31.1 x 142.2 x 43.2 cm). (Kevin Nakashima.)

208
CARLO MOLLINO
Tea table, 1950

Paralleling such examples as the one-piece plywood chair of GERALD SUMMERS (no. 150), the seating experiments of CHARLES EAMES (no. 194), and the plywood sculpture of Ray Eames, and probably influenced as well by the sculpture of Henry Moore, with this table Carlo Mollino staked his own claim to the single, continuous piece of plywood as a furniture medium. During the 1950s he produced a fantastic series of tables, some with bases cut and bent in scroll shapes like this tea table and dining tables supported by one-piece bases with fingerlike interlockings. This example was made especially for the *Italy at Work* exhibition that toured America in 1950. In an effort to fit Mollino's exuberant creations into a modernist mold and to provide a context for his unusual designs, the accompanying publication suggested that he represented "a peculiarly Italian type of functionalism in which contemporary engineering devices are used with a sense of line and form which in spite of its daring has still an echo of tradition."³⁶

Made by Apelli, Varesio, & C., Turin. Maple plywood and glass. 21 x 44 x 17" (53.3 x 111.7 x 43.2 cm). (Brooklyn Museum, New York, gift of the Italian Government.)

209
PAOLO VENINI
Handkerchief vase, 1949

In 1949 Paolo Venini, along with one of his firm's designers, Fulvio Bianconi, created the series of Handkerchief (Fazzoletto) vases manufactured by his firm from squares of free-blown glass "folded" into an irregular form. These vases were produced in various sizes, some in strong opaque colors (solid or with a different color inside and out), others with internal decorations embedded in clear glass as in this example. Reviving earlier methods of Venetian glassmaking, Venini introduced expressive ornamentalism into postwar design through color, texture, and the individual effects of hand craftsmanship. Using the nineteenth-century *zanfirico* technique of encased twisted filigree, here Venini created a pattern of three repeating bands, one with fine pink strands forming an allover linen effect, the others with spirals in pink and white.

Made by Venini, Murano, Italy. Clear and colored blown glass. Diameter: 10⅝" (27 cm). (Philadelphia Museum of Art, gift of the manufacturer.)

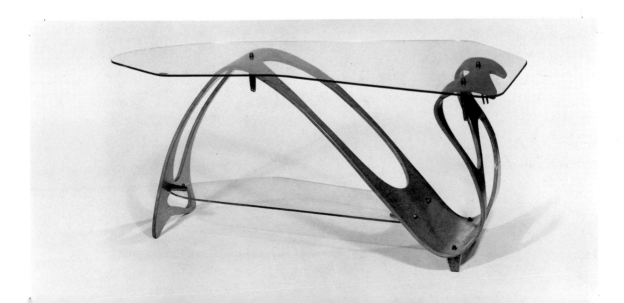

210
CHARLES EAMES
Chair, 1948–50

While EERO SAARINEN's *Womb* armchair was the first fiberglass chair in production (no. 201), this chair by Charles Eames was the first to leave the new glass-reinforced plastic material exposed. The two designers had collaborated on molded chair prototypes for the "Organic Design in Home Furnishings" competition at the Museum of Modern Art in New York in 1940, but it was only as a result of the development of fiberglass during the war that the one-piece seat shell they conceived could actually be produced. Based on a metal chair design of 1948 that Eames created for the "International Competition for Low-Cost Furniture Design," again at the Museum of Modern Art, this plastic adaptation was three years in development. When the chair was finally produced by Zenith Plastics for Herman Miller in 1950, it was highly acclaimed by Edgar Kaufmann, Jr., at the museum. "Perhaps the greatest advantage of this chair is the extraordinary lustre and soft, smooth surface of the plastic which, strengthened by the silky threads of glass imbedded within it, quickly absorbs room temperatures," he wrote. "Never before used in furniture, this airplane plastic is virtually indestructible and withstands stains and mars. Both to the eye and to the touch this plastic is a most desirable addition to the gamut of materials available for modern rooms."[37]

Made by Zenith Plastics, Gardena, California, for Herman Miller Furniture Company, Zeeland, Michigan. Fiberglass, rubber, and steel. Height: 31 1/4" (79.4 cm). (Museum of Modern Art, New York.)

211
MAX BILL
Sun lamp, 1950

Max Bill was the foremost practitioner and theorist of neofunctionalism in the postwar period, carrying on Werkbund and Bauhaus ideas about the need for well-designed domestic articles based on universally valid forms, good materials, fine workmanship, and bare ornament. Like his predecessors, Bill found visual solutions in pure geometry and developed a personal style based on the reduction and perfection of form. This elegant sun lamp consists of two identically shaped metal cones, one housing the light bulb, the other—its mirror image—an adaptor for different voltages; the two are connected by a flexible tube that not only allows the light to be adjusted but serves as a handle for carrying. Following a Werkbund tradition from the 1920s of publishing "good" design in magazines like *Die Form*, Bill illustrated a group of exemplary products including this lamp in his book *Form*, which appeared in 1952. Many of the objects in *Form* had already appeared in the traveling exhibition *Die Gute Form* (*Good Design*), which Bill had organized for the Schweizer Werkbund in 1949.

Made by Novelectric, Zurich. Enameled metal. Height (extended): 22 1/2" (57.1 cm). (Museum of Modern Art, New York.)

212
GILBERT A. WATROUS
Floor lamp, 1950

area than the earlier adjustable desk lamps to which it might be compared, it has a four-foot-long counterbalanced arm that may be poised at virtually any height and rotated to virtually any position. The polished brass arm, set on a tripod stand, is held tight in its spherical socket by a magnetic swivel.

Made by Heifetz Manufacturing Company, New York. Brass, steel and fiberglass. Height (extended): 55" (139.7 cm). (Museum of Modern Art, New York, gift of the manufacturer.)

213
PAUL McCOBB
Planner Group components, 1949

Paul McCobb's *Planner Group* was the first system of modular furniture components to be brought within the reach of the majority of Americans, and the first such series to succeed commercially. From the start it was conceived for economy, being constructed of low-cost materials and manufactured with volume production techniques. The basic, multipurpose units were made to be combined into "living walls" or room dividers, concepts associated popularly with McCobb but developed earlier. The storage components—drawer units and cabinets with interchangeable interiors—could also be set on platforms or benches with splayed legs. The *Planner Group* found a ready market in department stores across the country when it was introduced in 1950, and its success was immediate; the line was soon expanded to include some fifty pieces, sold in a variety of finishes, and it became the best selling line of contemporary furniture in America during the next decade.

Made by Wichendon Furniture Company, Wichendon, Massachusetts. Maple. Length: 48" (122 cm). (Philadelphia Museum of Art, gift of COLLAB.)

Apparently on the suggestion of MARCEL BREUER, who felt that well-designed modern lamps were not available on the American market, in 1950 the Museum of Modern Art in New York announced a design competition for portable table and floor lamps. Some three thousand submissions were received and the jury, which included Breuer, gave awards to fifteen entries; ten of these were put into production by the cosponsor of the competition, the Heifetz Manufacturing Company, and shown at the museum in the spring of 1951. A special prize for floor lamps was given to Gilbert A. Watrous's entry,[38] which addressed the need for flexible furnishings engendered by the small scale of postwar housing. Able to extend over a much larger

214
MARCELLO NIZZOLI
Lettera 22 typewriter, 1950

With a nod to the compact presentation as well as the success of the *Hermes Baby* typewriter, introduced by ERNEST PAILLARD & CIE in 1935 (no. 146) and refined in 1940, Marcello Nizzoli designed his light and efficient *Lettera 22* portable model for Olivetti in 1950, which was awarded a Compasso d'Oro prize in 1954. As he did with the office equipment he had already developed for the firm, notably the *Lexikon 80* typewriter of 1948, Nizzoli presented the machine as an organic sculptural form, not predetermined by the rigid internal mechanical structure but bound to it by a close study of its requirements. His subtle sensitivity to form is apparent in the fluid profile he gave to the housing and the modeled carriage handle, which opens at an acute angle for use and folds back to fit tightly for travel in the smart, form-fitting case. In a stunning demonstration of the impact of color on design and product identity, he set off the muted tones that distinguished Olivetti's products and the black keys with one accent, the deep red tabulator key.

Made by Ing. C. Olivetti & C., Milan. Enameled-metal housing. Width: 11 3/8" (28.9 cm). (Museum of Modern Art, New York, gift of Olivetti Corporation of America.)

215
GIOVANNI PINTORI
Poster for Olivetti, 1949

Adriano Olivetti, president of the family firm from 1938 until his death in 1960, established an integrated design program that encompassed all its endeavors—products, graphics, advertising, shops, and architecture. To achieve this he relied on two imaginative designers, both of whom worked for the firm for three decades—MARCELLO NIZZOLI was responsible for product design and Giovanni Pintori for advertising and graphics. This poster is one example of Pintori's innovative approach: instead of advertising a specific product it conveys a broader message about the company. The poster promotes Olivetti's technological achievement in the field of calculating, which it had recently entered with a line of adding machines (the most impressive of these was Nizzoli's revolutionary *Divisumma 14* mechanical calculator of 1948). Symbolizing the ease with which its new products could bring control and order to the world of numbers, a diminutive company logotype sits at dead center of the chaotic composition of numerals in many different sizes, type styles, and colors. The logo, with its lowercase, letter-spaced, sans-serif letters, was also a design of Pintori, which in 1947 replaced the Olivetti logo in typewriter type designed in 1934.

Lithograph. 37 3/8 x 26 1/4" (94.9 x 66.7 cm). (Museum of Modern Art, New York, gift of the designer.)

Henning Koppel's silver wine pitcher clearly demonstrates the individual expressive qualities he introduced to the Georg Jensen line, qualities that were quite different from the direct naturalism of the firm's early wares and the more severe geometric functionalism that appeared in Jensen's products during the 1930s. Trained as a sculptor, Koppel transformed utilitarian objects into abstract sculptural shapes. From hollowware serving pieces to flatware, his tableware reflected this approach, both in the spirited silhouettes of his sinuous forms and in the patterns of light that reflect from the smooth silver surfaces. Koppel conceived this pitcher, one of a series with low-bellied bowls that he began to design in 1947, in ink sketches on paper, translating his fluid forms into three-dimensional models and working drawings for the silversmith to use when he raised it from a thin sheet of silver.

Made by Georg Jensen Sølvsmedie, Copenhagen. Silver. Height: 13⅞" (35.3 cm). (Musée des Arts Décoratifs de Montreal.)

216
BERNADOTTE & BJØRN
Margrethe bowls, 1950

One of the early examples of plastic kitchenwares produced in Scandinavia and one still in production today, Bernadotte & Bjørn's *Margrethe* bowls are particularly well suited for mixing and preparing food; they were totally engineered, as perhaps no simple kitchen vessels had been, with material and function in mind as well as the requirements of manufacture. Commissioned from Scandinavia's first industrial design firm, the nesting bowls were meant to expand a line of melamine products already being produced by Rosti, a manufacturer of plastic products founded in 1944. The designers used a comparative analysis of bowls in all shapes, sizes, and materials from around the world to develop the requirements for their product. The bowls, which have handles for gripping, lips for pouring, and rubber rings to keep them steady, are rigid and light, impact and temperature resistant, and colorful as well—a complement of characteristics not easily achieved by bowls made by natural materials that these melamine versions were meant to challenge.

Made by Rosti, Ballerup, Denmark. Melamine and rubber. Height (stacked): 7½" (19 cm). (Philadelphia Museum of Art, gift of Rosti.)

218
HANS J. WEGNER
Armchair, 1949

In the design of this armchair Hans J. Wegner maintained the delicate balance between, on the one hand, rational ideas of production, which had been pursued by designers since the 1920s, and craft values and traditions on the other. Combining an expressive form that draws on Chinese precedents with natural materials and a rationally conceived design destined for the most exacting factory manufacture, he simplified the chair's structure so that the sculpted backrest and arms form one continuous element; likewise, the turned legs rigidly support the deep seat rail and top piece without the need for stretchers. Shown in 1949 at the Copenhagen Cabinetmakers Guild exhibition, the round-backed armchair received great acclaim almost immediately and became the chair consistently cited as the paradigm of contemporary Scandinavian design. Wegner, however, had released the design before he was fully satisfied with it: the butt joints that connected the three elements forming the back and arms did not satisfy him, and thus in the earliest models the back, like the seat, was wrapped with caning. Later, when he had devised a broader sawtooth joining, the chair was sold without a covered back.

Made by Johannes Hansen, Copenhagen. Beech and cane. Height: 30" (76.2 cm). (Philadelphia Museum of Art, gift of Carl L. Steele.)

219
HANS J. WEGNER
Peacock armchair, 1947

Hans J. Wegner attributed the emergence of a new style in Danish furniture to the initiative of a group of young cabinetmakers who, in the later 1920s, began to invite architects to submit designs for annual competitions of modern furniture. "From an artistic point of view," he wrote,

> the architects built on and were inspired by the experiences and traditions of the past; they did not want to copy specific styles, but on the other hand, they thought it would be absurd not to learn from what had existed for generations. Many younger architects were especially attracted to the simple rusticity of Danish furniture, to the structural elegance of Windsor chairs, to the honest and restrained expression of Shaker chairs, and to the brilliance of Thonet's bentwood chairs.[39]

Wegner, himself a cabinetmaker as well as an architect, contributed numerous designs to the Copenhagen Cabinetmakers Guild competitions, many derived from

traditional sources. His *Peacock* chair, while dependent on the English Windsor form, is a modern adaptation, distinctive in its exaggerated proportions, the flattened oval segments of the tapered spindles, and the laminated wood used for the rounded back, all designed for factory production.

Made by Johannes Hansen, Copenhagen. Ash and teak with cord upholstery. Height: 41" (104.1cm). (Philadelphia Museum of Art, gift of the estate of George Patton.)

220
FINN JUHL
Chieftain armchair, 1949

The furniture of Finn Juhl—as much a tribute to its maker, Niels Vodder, as to its designer—was among the best-known examples of the "Danish modern" style, which became fashionable in Europe and America in the early postwar era. Organic in aesthetic effect, Juhl's work is quite different from the rationalist designs of his compatriots KAARE KLINT and ARNE JACOBSEN; rather, like the freely curving furniture forms of ALVAR AALTO in Finland, it draws its inspiration from abstract sculpture. The frame itself is visually separated from the deeply curved back and seat as well as the baroque armrests, which in Juhl's characteristic fashion appear to float away, unsupported. The precision and care of the joinery is highlighted by the natural finish of the lacquered-and-oiled teak. While this chair exemplifies the Danish tradition of high-quality hand craftsmanship epitomized by Niels Vodder, many of Juhl's designs were also successfully adapted for manufacture to the designer's standards by factory methods at the Baker Furniture Company in Grand Rapids, Michigan, in the early 1950s.

Made by Niels Vodder, Allerød, Denmark. Walnut with leather upholstery. 36³/₈ x 41 x 28⁵/₈" (93.3 x 105.4 x 73.7 cm). (Art Institute of Chicago.)

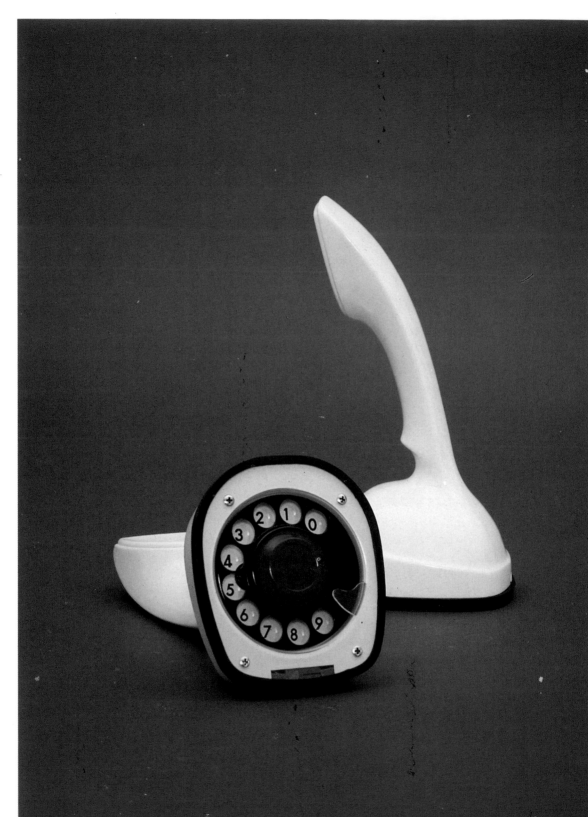

Chapter Six
Good Design 1950–1960

The United States emerged from World War II as the richest, most advanced, and most powerful nation in the world, and American business took the credit—for its superior industrial performance during the war and for the extraordinary revival of the consumer market afterwards. Industrial design, which had been developed professionally in the United States in the previous decades, was widely mythologized as the agent of American success, and Europeans "looked enviously at the technological marvels that were coming out of American factories, or were being presented in exhibitions as a way of life which was only just around the corner. . . . Cars became longer and sleeker, and created a new symbology of status and power. It was a world in which happiness could be found in possessions and the possessions were smarter, bigger, and more modern in America than anywhere else."[1] To promote their own country's competitiveness abroad and in domestic markets as well, many foreign governments created national design organizations and design centers. The first of these, Britain's Council of Industrial Design, had been founded in London in 1944 to play a "vital part after the War in stimulating the sale, at home and overseas, of a wide range of goods of which we can all be justly proud."[2] At the inaugural meeting of the Council, Hugh Dalton, president of the Board of Trade, observed, "Something like an industrial revolution has taken place in the United States—a revolution in industrial design. It has made many of our exports old fashioned and less acceptable."[3]

A fundamental aim of the Council and its European counterparts was to promote higher standards of design in industry and to further this by providing information about the industrial design profession and the design process. In 1953 the Council began to plan for a permanent exhibition in London of what it considered to be well-designed products and in 1956 opened the Design Centre, supported in part by the government and in part by a group of British manufacturers. Since 1957 the Design Centre has annually given awards to exemplary British products,[4] a policy also followed in other countries. In 1949 the Netherlands became the second country to sponsor a national design organization, now known as the Instituut voor Industriële Vormgeving (Institute of Industrial Design);[5] its industrial design center (Centrum voor Industriële Vormgeving) was opened in 1962. The Dutch were also directly inspired by the American example: in 1952 and 1953 the Institute brought HENRY DREYFUSS to the Netherlands for a series of lectures, translated *Design This Day* by WALTER DORWIN TEAGUE, and sent a group of designers to the United States for first-hand study. The

opposite:
L M Ericsson, *Ericofon* telephone, 1949–54 (no. 239)

Good Design exhibition at the Museum of Modern Art, New York, 1951.

Cover of the Dutch design magazine *Goed Wonen*, May 1952.

5 vijfde jaargang no. 5 Mei 1952

goed wonen

keuze
en
keur

recovery of West German industry aided by the Marshall Plan was signaled by the founding of the Rat für Formgebung (Design Council) in 1951, with its Internationales Design Zentrum (International Design Center) in Berlin and Gute Form prize established in 1969. The Japanese Ministry of International Trade and Industry (MITI) created the Japanese Design Promotion Council and introduced its G-Mark (good) design awards in 1957. In 1951 RAYMOND LOEWY was invited to Japan, and his autobiography, *Never Leave Well Enough Alone*, was translated into Japanese. Like the Dutch, the Japanese also sent designers to study in the United States, particularly to the Art Center College of Design in Pasadena, California, from 1957, where the program sponsored under the Japanese External Trade Recovery Act continues to this day.

The standard of industrial design used by these government organizations was defined as "good"—in a moral as well as an aesthetic sense. The term appeared everywhere in the 1950s, from the *Good Design* exhibitions held annually at the Museum of Modern Art in New York and the Merchandise Mart in Chicago from 1950 to 1955 to the Council of Industrial Design's catch phrase, "Good Design and Good Business." To provide good low-cost housing and furnishings, the Stichting Goed Wonen or Good Living Foundation was established in the Netherlands after the war—as well as a magazine, *Goed Wonen,* and a seal of approval—by Mart Stam with other designers, manufacturers, and retailers. Renamed the Good Design Committee in 1959, the Japan International Design Committee was established in 1953 by a group of designers and architects including SORI YANAGI, Isamu Kenmochi, Riki Watanabe, and Kenzo Tange to promote "international good design" as well as Japanese participation in international conferences and exhibitions.[6] In the 1930s good design meant good sales, as NORMAN BEL GEDDES, who was much admired in the 1950s for his commercial successes, had outlined in *Horizons*: "Far-sighted manufacturers are eager to incorporate good design in their products: Good design offers new advertising opportunities. Good design increases sales appeal in any object. Good design instills a pride of ownership which increases the value of the piece. . . . Good design adds length of life to an object because it takes longer to tire of it. Good design tends towards further simplification of manufacturing processes and hence to economies in production. Good design improves the merit of the product."[7]

In the 1950s, however, high-minded good design theorists publicly disdained the commercial approach of designers like Geddes, claiming that good design was instead a matter of universally valid qualities that could be discerned by unbiased aesthetic judgment. As particularly befitted an art museum, good design was defined at the Museum of Modern Art in New York as "a thorough merging of form and function . . . revealing a practical, uncomplicated, sensible beauty."[8] Under the direction of Edgar Kaufmann, Jr., objects were selected for the *Good Design* exhibitions on the basis of their "eye-appeal, function, construction and price, with emphasis on the first"; in 1953 the exhibition included some two hundred items chosen from around eight thousand entries in the fields of furniture, floor coverings, fabrics, lamps, accessories, tablewares, kitchen and cleaning equipment, and household appliances.[9] Retailers, too, promoted good design aesthetics, most notably the Milanese department store La Rinascente through its sponsorship beginning in 1954 of the Compasso d'Oro (Golden Compass) awards, which since 1967 have been under the auspices of the Italian Associazione per il Disegno Industriale (Industrial Design Association). The first Compasso d'Oro prizes were given "for the aesthetics of the product"; one of the winners, the glass of FLAVIO POLI (no. 271), was described as being "united in form and material," a virtue that fulfilled the "aesthetic requirements" to which the Compasso d'Oro was dedicated.[10] In 1955 the Matsuya department store in Tokyo set up a "Good Design Corner" with exemplary products selected by Yanagi, Watanabe, and other members of the International Design Committee. Aesthetics was a prime consideration at the decade's most important design school, the Hochschule für Gestaltung (Institute of Design), which opened in Ulm, West Germany, in 1955. Its cofounder and director, MAX BILL, proclaimed: "The founders of the Ulm School believe art to be the highest expression of human life and their aim is therefore to help in turning itself into a work of art. In the words of that memorable challenge thrown down by Henry van de Velde over 50 years ago, we mean 'to wage war on ugliness'; and ugliness can only be combatted with what is intrinsically good—'good' because at once seemly and practical."[11]

While each organization could and did identify good design in simple aesthetic terms, its seals of approval were fixed to a wide and complex variety of domestic objects that represented very different artistic values, although lack of ornament was a common theme. This was particularly evident at the international *Triennale* exhibitions in Milan in 1951, 1954, and 1957, where prizes were awarded both to technological displays of laminates, alloys, and micromechanics and to craft-based works that were inherently decorative and expressive.

The most ascetic style of the 1950s was a continuation or revival of the International Style, now centered at the Hochschule für Gestaltung. The school had, in fact, been founded to promote the principles of the Bauhaus, "the direct heir to van de Velde's own school at Weimar, the Dessau Bauhaus [which] had set itself precisely the same objects. If we intend to go rather further at Ulm than they did at Dessau," wrote Bill, who had himself been trained at the Bauhaus, "this is because post-war requirements clearly postulate the necessity for certain additions to the original curriculum. For instance, we mean to give still greater prominence to the design of ordinary things in everyday use."[12] Like the Bauhaus, the Hochschule für Gestaltung was intended to be financed by earnings from industrial commissions, and like WALTER GROPIUS, Bill gathered around him a brilliant international teaching staff, including Tomás Maldonado, an Argentine painter, writer, and educator; HANS GUGELOT, a Dutch industrial designer trained in Switzerland; and Otl Aicher, a German graphic designer. The neofunctionalist stylistic idiom of the school first appeared in 1955 in an exhibition of radios and phonographs designed for the firm of Max Braun by Gugelot and Aicher in collaboration with the Braun management, Artur Braun and Fritz Eichler. One of the first commissions the school received from industry, this project established the formal characteristics of Braun design, which have remained to the present: austerely simple, "essential," undecorated, clean-lined forms with clearly ordered operating elements and functions that are comprehensible at a glance. Perhaps nowhere was this exemplified more clearly than in the *Phonosuper* combination radio and phonograph of 1956 (no. 242), designed by Gugelot and DIETER RAMS with a clear plastic lid, which displayed the operating panel and record player even when it was closed. This rational, objective approach was reinforced by the use of white surface finishes with gray and black details.

Around this time Gugelot also pioneered the development of product systems. At Braun this took the form of families of interconnected and related products—for example, a loudspeaker by Rams that matched the *Phonosuper* unit in dimensions and formal elements and that could be used to supplement its integrated speaker. Outside his work for Braun, Gugelot also developed modular knock-down furniture, the *M125* cabinet system, based on a 125 mm module that could be customized by every consumer into shelving and storage wall units (no. 244)—a system that, thanks to more efficient production techniques, realized the Bauhaus dream of standardization to a degree impossible before the war. These neofunctionalist products designed by the Ulm faculty, including some pieces by Bill himself (no. 257), seemed to many critics to embody modern design's most lofty social task—the creation of enduring standard types based, as Gropius had prescribed, on "intrinsic laws" and "clear reflection," not on the "personal" or "accidental." The International Style revival was given weight in America through the work of Bauhaus teachers and students who had immigrated there, as well as through the re-editions and reproductions of their furnishings issued beginning in the late 1940s. Ulm was also one center of what came to be called the international typographic style, which represented an equally universal approach to graphic design. Rooted in De Stijl and Bauhaus ideas, it was based on the use of sans-serif typefaces and clear, legible texts and images. This style was also developed in Basel and Zurich by Emil Ruder and other designers who used mathematically constructed grid layouts to achieve clarity of graphic organization (no. 245).

Handcraft, whose proponents defended the use of traditional materials as well as accidents of manufacture and the personality of craftsmen, appeared as an alternative to neofunctionalism in the 1950s. The use of vernacular forms and materials appealed to nationalist tastes and ran counter to the anonymity of International Style functionalism. Certain designers updated traditional forms that relied on natural materials. The Italian architect GIO PONTI, for example, designed his *Superleggera* chair (no. 265) after nineteenth-century popular models in light woods with caned seats made in the vicinity of Chiavari. Other designers created apparently traditional forms out of modern materials, as Yanagi demonstrated in his plywood *Butterfly* stool (no. 255) or TIMO SARPANEVA in his enameled cookware (no. 272). This craft idiom was immensely popular worldwide, although as the American designer GEORGE NELSON pointed out in 1953, the effects that made it so successful were seldom, if ever, created entirely by hand, and had "little to do with either the function or the actual manufacturing technique."[13]

The International Style principles of standardization and rationalization, introduced in craft-based industries in the 1930s with only limited success, returned in the 1950s supported by the increasing economic prosperity of the West and its vast export market, which the Scandinavian countries in particular sought to exploit. Designing for export as well as for a needy domestic market, Scandinavian craftsmen adapted their materials and methods to the exigencies of large-scale production, with knock-down furniture and stacking tablewares designed for ease of packing and shipping and processed plywood ending the supremacy of solid wood. Market economics introduced a new level of product research and development that now often involved the designer. At Finland's Nuutajärvi glassworks and the Arabia ceramic factory (both part of the Wärtsilä group), "our system was to hold design conferences with technical and sales personnel," recalled Saara Hopea-Untracht, then a glass designer for Nuutajärvi, "and together, we made decisions about what to design and produce."[14] Developing within industry, traditionally craft-based products began to take on certain formal functionalist characteristics associated with mass production such as smooth surfaces and lack of applied ornament, while at the same time industrial materials—chromium-plated steel, plate glass, plastics, and synthetic lacquers—found their way with increasing frequency into domestic use. Yet the high value the handcraft market placed on individualism and on recognizable personal qualities persisted, often in a boldly expressive freedom of outline. This was notably demonstrated by the Danish sculptor HENNING KOPPEL in his handraised silverwares for Georg Jensen, with their low, bulging curves (no. 217); by the Finnish designer KAJ FRANCK in his *Kremlin Bells* (no. 261), a series of eccentric double decanters; and by the Danish architect ARNE JACOBSEN in his *Ant, Swan,* and *Egg* chairs (nos. 228, 252), which stand as organic symbols, expressed respectively by forms suggestive of a bird with outswept wings, an enveloping oval shell, and the cutout shape of an insect on slender metal legs. To introduce further individuality in his mass-produced glasswares, Franck colored the stoppers of his decanters individually, a decision that created multiple color combinations and gave him the opportunity to make each inexpensive decanter unique.

The most characteristic stylistic idiom of the decade, however, and one with the greatest impact, might be called the pragmatic engineering aesthetic. Originally an American movement pioneered in the 1920s and 1930s by the architect-inventor R. Buckminster Fuller, this aesthetic was exemplified by the work of CHARLES EAMES and EERO SAARINEN, whose influential experiments with molded seat shells during the previous decade continued to provide an entirely original if sometimes ungainly repertory of shapes and design features for a world of eager imitators. The catalog of the X *Triennale* in Milan in 1954 described the phenomenon as "the interpolation of the concept of 'form' into the industrial process, or into the formal aspect of technology."[15] While its forms were no more or less derived from industrial processes than those of the International Style, they differed vastly from its austere geometries in their novelty and their attitude toward modern materials and construction techniques. Eames made mechanical details like the rubber shock mounts and bolts in his chairs plainly visible, and he designed the first storage furniture that used steel angles for an exposed structural frame, adapting an industrial vocabulary to domestic use. Eames was personally involved in the technology of all his designs and rejected the primacy of aesthetics. "Thinking of how a chair looks comes pretty far down on the list of things I worry about when designing," he admitted. "I only think about how they look in relation to how they are doing their job. They must be comfortable—comfortable for the kind of use they're going to get." Saarinen invented a one-legged pedestal-based chair (no. 243), intending to make it "all one thing . . . a structural total"[16] cast in one piece of one material—plastic. After a two-year period of extensive experimentation, however, the durability and load-bearing capabilities of the glass-reinforced plastic could not be assured and the weightlessly elegant chair was instead produced with an aluminum stem and a reinforced-plastic shell.

The quirkier side of this technical approach appeared at the *Festival of Britain* in 1951, which was conceived to mark the centenary of the *Crystal Palace Exhibition* along with the midpoint of the twentieth century and celebrated the nation's recovery from the deprivations of war. Britain's Council of Industrial Design was responsible for coordinating design throughout the festival, which focused on the areas of art, science, technology, and industrial design, as well as for all the some ten

thousand manufactured products included in it, from street signs to cafe chairs. The festival celebrated technical progress: the *Antelope* chair by ERNEST RACE (no. 226), for instance, borrowed the new combination of plywood and steel rods from Eames, although the light, springy frame and ball feet that gave the chair its name injected a fresh note of whimsy into the design. A series of decorative designs called the "Festival Pattern" was also developed based on the structure of crystals and applied by twenty-six manufacturers to such products as textiles (no. 225), light fittings, and tablewares; these were created to promote British industry, and were showcased at the exhibition, most notably in the Regatta Restaurant on London's South Bank. The *Architectural Review* saw the use of the pattern as a "drawing together of art and science" well in line with the festival's emphasis on technology.[17]

Italian designers followed the American lead (Eames was published in *Domus* in 1947) and because of postwar shortages and cost considerations adopted similar economies in the use of light, man-made materials that appeared in equally novel forms. Pursuing rationalism as their principal goal, they attempted to solve the problems of cheap industrial production for the domestic working-class or middle-class market—although as at the Bauhaus many of their designs were barely industrial and certainly not cheap. Most outstanding and characteristic of the rationalist designers was MARCO ZANUSO, who worked to find new uses for foam rubber and nylon cord and later even turned to

Design at the 1951 *Festival of Britain,* from the exhibition buildings to furniture and graphics, was totally coordinated by Britain's Council of Industrial Design.

"Point-contact" transistor (greatly enlarged), invented at Bell Laboratories by John Bardeen, Walter Brattain, and William Shockley, 1947.

stamped, welded, and spray-painted sheet metal borrowed from automobile technology to create new furniture systems—like Eames, involving himself fundamentally in production processes. Commissioned by the Pirelli company to investigate possibilities for the applications of their new material, foam rubber, Zanuso discovered its implications for the field of upholstered furniture. "It would revolutionize not only padding systems," he later wrote, "but also structural, manufacturing, and formal possibilities. As prototypes began to take exciting new formal definitions, a company was established to put these models, such as the *Lady* armchair (no. 230). into production on an industrial scale never before imagined."[18] The brothers ACHILLE and PIER GIACOMO CASTIGLIONI also worked according to strict rationalist methods and pursued the possibilities of new technologies (no. 221), yet their interests were different from those of Zanuso. More cerebral, the Castiglionis also made forms that communicated social ideas, sometimes ironically—a tractor seat, for example, was converted to domestic use (no. 266).

The most significant engineering advances of the decade were made by designers in the consumer electronics industry. This field was born in 1947 when the transistor was invented at Bell Telephone Laboratories; it was opened to commercial development in 1952 when Bell held a symposium on transistors and offered patent licenses at $25,000 each through Western Electric. Among the first licensees was one of the future industry leaders, the TOKYO TELECOMMUNICATIONS ENGINEERING CORPORATION, later known as the SONY CORPORATION, which was sponsored by Japan's MITI. Replacing bulky vacuum tubes, transistors were initially difficult to produce, and also required engineers to design completely new electronic circuitry, which likewise occupied much smaller spaces. Like the products of many other firms, Sony's first efforts, tape recorders and transistor radios, were designed inside and out by the firm's engineers. Sony's first full-time industrial designer was hired in 1954 and by 1961 the company had a design staff of seventeen. By the end of the decade, with the world's first fully transistorized television, the Sony staff had created a form as novel as the technology it housed, a compact unit reflecting the company's technical aptitude for miniaturization with a projecting hood overhanging the screen like a traditional Japanese roof (no. 273).

Critics who viewed with admiration the brilliant handling of novel forms and technical solutions in designs of the 1950s reacted with dismay to the introduction of historicizing elements by certain designers at the end of the decade.[19] The controversy ostensibly revolved around neo-Liberty, the revival in Italian architecture and design of art nouveau forms and decorations, and called generally into question the validity of eclecticism in modern design. The dogma of the International Style was fundamentally opposed to such historicism. It insisted that design reflect the conditions and demands of modern industrial life and that its forms reflect the technology they incorporate, although how that was to be done was always open to interpretation. While these principles continued to be followed by neofunctionalists, other designers regarded the

Torre Velasca, by Ernesto Rogers and Enrico Peressutti, Milan, 1958. This controversial building was one of the earliest postwar multistory structures to disregard the American skyscraper style and call on historical precedents, drawing on medieval towers and the neighboring Cathedral of Milan.

past as the source of a suitable repertoire of forms and details, expressed interest in traditional handcraft, and devised pragmatic and unconventional solutions to engineering problems, making it plain that no one modern "good" design idiom had hegemony in the 1950s.

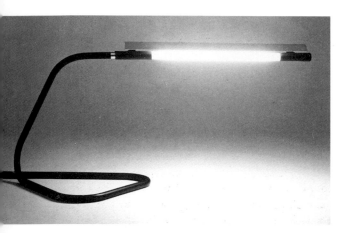

221
ACHILLE CASTIGLIONI AND PIER GIACOMO CASTIGLIONI
Tubino desk or wall lamp, 1951

First developed in the 1930s, fluorescent lamps offered economic advantages for the postwar household, requiring less electricity and generating less heat than incandescent bulbs and proving more cost effective by producing bright lighting that could be distributed by small sources. Seeking out new technology as they responded to the challenge of producing much-needed goods for the Italian consumer, Achille and Pier Giacomo Castiglioni transformed a very small fluorescent tube that had just been made available from the United States into their *Tubino* lamp. The thin, reduced dimensions of the glass tube inspired the linearity of the lamp and its minimal design—a bold graphic form made even more apparent when the lamp is suspended from a wall. Using such industrial materials as metal tubing and aluminum in undisguised form, the designers sought to provide an alternative to the period imitations then dominating the Italian market. *Tubino* was one of some thirty lamps of all types that were presented in the light-

ing section of the *IX Triennale* in Milan in 1951, for which Achille Castiglioni served on the organizing and installation committee.

Made by Flos, Brescia, Italy. Enameled metal and aluminum. Height: 11 13/16" (30 cm); length: 29 1/2" (75 cm). (Dr. Achille Castiglioni, Milan.)

222
HARRY BERTOIA
Diamond lounge chair, 1951–52

Harry Bertoia's enormously influential bent-wire furniture grew out of an enlightened arrangement with its manufacturer. Bertoia was offered a salary and a studio by his former Cranbrook Academy colleague Florence Knoll and her husband Hans, principals of the firm of Knoll Associates, and given the freedom to create without any particular demands from his employers. Moving to the studio, in Pennsylvania not far from the Knoll factory, he first worked on metal sculpture but within two years, as the Knolls had hoped, conceived a line of furniture that could be put into production. Developed with the collaboration of Knoll technicians, the lounge and side chairs he designed were fabricated of wire mesh formed into seating shells (sometimes with cushions or upholstery added), and set into metal stands. Bertoia saw his furniture as parallel to his sculpture, which, as he explained, was "concerned primarily with space, form, and the characteristics of metal. In the chairs many functional problems have to be satisfied first . . . but when you get right down to it the chairs are studies in space, form, and metal too. . . . If you will look at these chairs, you will find that they are mostly made of air, just like sculpture. Space passes right through them."[20]

Made by Knoll Associates, New York. Steel with upholstery. 30 1/2 x 33 3/4 x 28" (77.5 x 85.7 x 71.1 cm). (Knoll International, New York.)

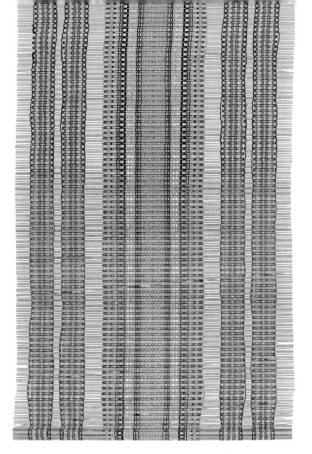

223
DOROTHY LIEBES
Window blinds, c. 1952

The weaving of Dorothy Liebes was distinguished for its "varied and completely unorthodox yarns," noted *Interiors* magazine, adding the disclaimer "if they can be called yarns," for, the article continued, "warp or woof may be ribbon, bamboo, chenille, lucite, fiberglas, extruded plastics, grass, strings of beads and brilliants, and metallic threads, not to mention such commonplace things as silk, wool, aralac, rayon, mohair, jute, cotton, nylon, and linen."[21] The article went on to point out that her fabrics might not even be regarded as fabrics but rather a more unusual sort of woven product such as the "roller cloth" shown here. Flexible and brightly colored, both useful and decorative, roller cloth employed such rigid materials as wood and reeds, used horizontally for window blinds and vertically for lampshades. Liebes's studios in San Francisco and New York manufactured large amounts of handwoven furnishing fabrics and roller cloths on special order, and she was one of the first craftspeople in America to adapt handweaves for series production; while her window blinds could not be made by machinery, a production version with aluminum slats was manufactured by the Bridgeport Brass Company in the 1960s using a large-scale hand assembly method.

Wood, lurex, and chenille. Length: 72" (182.9 cm). (Philadelphia Museum of Art, gift of Jeanette Epstein.)

224
DON WALLANCE
Design 1 cutlery, 1954

With the market for contemporary design expanding in the United States during the 1950s, the American Company H. E. Lauffer commissioned Don Wallance to create a cutlery service to accompany the all-white German china dinnerware the firm was importing from the Arzberg factory and promoting for modern interiors. Wallance approached his task thoughtfully with regard to function, developing his designs through extensive studies of practical comfort and efficiency worked out through three-dimensional models. He altered the features of standard utensils, shortening the tines of the fork and the blade of the knife (which he set at an angle) and deepening the soup spoon into a ladle-like bowl. But he also gave great thought to style, responding with highly sculptural, organic forms to the request for an innovative design. While Lauffer did not specify that stainless steel be used for the *Design 1* service, it had by then become the medium of modernity, used in nearly one out of three American homes. Strong, hard, corrosion-resistant, and easy to clean, stainless steel appealed to the American consumer for its economy and serviceability as well as its contemporaneity.

Made by Pott, Solingen, Germany, for H. E. Lauffer, New York. Stainless steel. Length of knife: 7 15/16" (20.1 cm). (Philadelphia Museum of Art, gift of C. Hugo Pott.)

225
MARIANNE STRAUB
Helmsley fabric, 1951

The Festival Pattern, a decorative program created under the auspices of the Council of Industrial Design and based on the structure of submicroscopic crystals, was introduced at the *Festival of Britain* in 1951. Participating designers from some twenty-six manufacturing concerns, among them British Celanese, Old Bleach Linen, Warner, and Wedgwood, used scientific diagrams based on X-rays of the repeating, symmetrical patterns of crystals as their inspiration for both organic and geometrical ornament. Marianne Straub's *Helmsley* fabric, for example, followed the structural diagram of the nylon crystal, and was produced for Warner in cotton and rayon damask at two different scales and in several color schemes. Crystal-structure diagrams were most applicable to flat patterning and the program was most heavily centered on textiles, but glass, silverware, lighting, wallpaper, and plastics were also similarly decorated. While it was initiated to build up the "modern" image of postwar British design and to encourage exports, the Festival Pattern was also heralded as a prime example of the melding of science and art, and for suggesting a fresh source of subject matter for design.

Made by Warner & Sons, London. Cotton and rayon damask. Width: 48" (122 cm). (Victoria and Albert Museum, London.)

226
ERNEST RACE
Antelope chair, 1951

Design at the *Festival of Britain* in 1951 was the province of the Council of Industrial Design, which had been founded in 1944 to improve the quality of British manufactured goods. Architecture, street furniture, graphics, even souvenirs required the approval of the Council, which exercised unprecedented control over the design of the public environment; this project set the stage for its future involvement exhibiting, publicizing, and commissioning industrial design. Two chairs by Ernest Race, both made of thin enameled-steel rods, were chosen from the proposals submitted for seating at the festival—the *Antelope*, with a plywood seat and back, and the *Springbok*, with plastic-covered springs for its seating surface. Race had earlier used welded-steel-rod frames for the integral structure of upholstered furniture, but he also drew his inspiration from the by then well-published bent-plywood and steel-rod chair of CHARLES EAMES (no. 194). With its fluid open structure, splayed legs, and ball feet, his *Antelope* chair came to symbolize the spirit of the festival itself and, along with the distinctive architecture and the decorative crystal-structure patterns introduced there (no. 225), it became an important component of what is loosely known as the "Festival" style.

Enameled steel and painted plywood. Height: 31 1/8" (79 cm). (Victoria and Albert Museum, London.)

227
LUCIENNE DAY
Calyx fabric, 1951

Created for the *Festival of Britain* in 1951, Lucienne Day's screen-printed *Calyx* fabric is often credited with giving rise to the colorful, abstract designs that proliferated in the following decade. The use of screen printing, fully mechanized in Britain only in the 1950s, also offered the industry new economy and the flexibility to respond quickly to such changes in style. Mimicking the relationships if not the exact forms of plant life, *Calyx* celebrated a new, more analytical interest in botanical subjects among designers and greater freedom for the British textile industry, which was no longer subject to the shortages and restrictive rules of the Utility era (no. 188). The pattern is an entanglement of reserved, or unprinted, shapes fixed to stems on a brown ground, some filled in with orange, yellow, or darker brown, others enhanced with a variety of textural effects. *Calyx* won a gold medal at Milan's *IX Triennale* in 1951, and in 1952 it was designated the year's best textile on the American market by the American Institute of Decorators.

Made by Heal Fabrics, London. Screen-printed linen. Width: 48" (122 cm). (Victoria and Albert Museum, London.)

228
ARNE JACOBSEN
Chair, 1951

Arne Jacobsen's model 3,100 chair (more familiarly known as the *Ant*) owes much to the technology of the molded-plywood and metal chair that CHARLES EAMES designed in 1946 (no. 194), sharing its materials and its emphasis on elasticity. Both chairs similarly cushion the junctures between support and seating shell with thick rubber disks, which yield with body pressure and give a sense of resilience. The three legs of Jacobsen's structure also mimic the first version of Eames's chair, which was shown in the Eames exhibition at the Museum of Modern Art in New York in 1946, but Jacobsen's was better balanced and could be successfully manufactured. Jacobsen's also has its own distinctive features, notably its markedly organic profile, the minimal construction of its three thin projecting legs, and its light, oddly scrolled plywood shell, which allows it to be moved about easily and to be stacked. Originally produced in a black finish, the chair has since been offered in a range of bright colors and wood veneers as well as with colored-epoxy legs. The first Danish chair designed for large-scale factory production and the most commercially successful of Jacobsen's designs, it became the mainstay of Fritz Hansen's line when it was put on the market in 1952. At the *XI Triennale* in Milan in 1957 Jacobsen was awarded a grand prize for the entire range of his furniture produced in collaboration with Hansen.

Made by Fritz Hansen, Allerød, Denmark. Plywood and chromed steel. Height: 30⅝" (77.7 cm). (Philadelphia Museum of Art, gift of Fritz Hansen.)

229
TADEUSZ TREPKOWSKI
Antiwar Poster, 1952

As the Iron Curtain fell on Eastern Europe and the Cold War intensified, Poland again felt the precariousness of its position as the corridor between Russia and the West. The country had been devastated during World War II, and Tadeusz Trepkowski's antiwar poster presented a simple but powerful plea that it should never happen again: the word *No!* shrieks against the form of a falling bomb whose shape reveals that its target is the center of a city. The directness of Trepkowski's pictorial poster style, which set a few large, symbolic elements against flat color grounds, was applied during the postwar decade to many different types of messages—to commemorate such events as the liberation of Poland and the glory of May Day as well as to advertise theatrical productions and films. His work was an important inspiration for his compa-

triot graphic designers, among them Henryk Tomaszewski and Jan Lenica, who in the 1950s firmly established Poland's international reputation as a center for the creation of lively and inventive theater, movie, and circus posters.

Published by Wydawnictwo Artystyczno-Graficzne, Warsaw.
Silkscreen. 39³/₈ x 27⁹/₁₆" (100 x 70 cm). (Neue
Sammlung, Munich.)

230
MARCO ZANUSO
Lady **armchair, 1951**

Seeking applications for foam rubber, a material that had been introduced in the 1930s but was not yet widely used, in the immediate postwar period the Pirelli rubber company began experimenting with it as an upholstery material, particularly for automobile seats. Initial success led Pirelli to ask Marco Zanuso to design foam-upholstered furniture that could be mass-produced, the first in Italy to be developed in conjunction with factory technicians specifically for industrial rather than traditional craft-based production methods. "The implications for the field of upholstered furniture were enormous," Zanuso later wrote. "It would revolutionize not only padding systems but also structural, manufacturing, and formal possibilities." In fact a new company called Arflex was established in 1950 just to produce this furniture "on an industrial scale never before imagined."[22] Its first products, Zanuso's chairs and sofas, were introduced in 1951 at the *IX Triennale* in Milan, where his *Lady* armchair won a gold medal. The chair, with its wooden frame (later pressed sheet metal) set on metal legs and its elastic webbing support, was adapted to factory upholstering by being divided into separate elements—arms, seat, and back. Each was stuffed with foam rubber of a different firmness according to the support needed and covered with fabric before being assembled into a complete

chair, which, however, retained the unified appearance of having been custom upholstered.

Made by Arflex, Milan. Wood, metal, and elastic webbing, with fabric-covered foam-rubber upholstery. Height: 32 1/4" (82 cm). (Arflex, Milan.)

231
ROBERTO SAMBONET
Fish cooker/server, 1954

In the series of stainless-steel cookware and tableware that he began to create for his family's company in 1954, Roberto Sambonet demonstrated his underlying interest in aesthetic formalism and its application to industrial products, concerns one might expect from a designer who is also a successful painter. One of his earliest designs, this fish cooker/server was produced the year he began to work for the firm; its long, unbroken outline of polished metal recast traditional forms for cooking and serving fish. With a grooved hinge that allows the top to be kept open at two different positions, the dish was rationally conceived to accommodate a range of cooking methods. It was also intended to be brought to the table for serving, thereby introducing stainless steel metalwares of uncommon elegance to Italian dining. Sambonet worked on the aesthetic integration of his products on many levels, and his early pieces would later become part of a comprehensive packaging and marketing program (no. 290).

Made by Sambonet, Vercelli, Italy. Stainless steel. Length: 20" (50.8 cm). (Philadelphia Museum of Art, gift of Sambonet.)

232
GINO SARFATTI
Table lamp, 1954

Gino Sarfatti, the most inventive creator of lighting in the early postwar period, designed and manufactured his own lamps under the name of Arteluce and sold them as well in his shop in Milan. With the attitude of a craftsman, he made lamps in small quantities; thus he was easily able to put experimental designs into production, allowing new bulbs and lighting technology rather than abstract formal ideas to direct the path of his design. Shortly before he died in 1985, he described how the long bulb of this lamp determined its configuration and how the reflecting screen was attached by simple means and could be rotated to variable positions: "It is a good example of rationalism. It includes a tubular bulb about 30 cm (11 3/4") in length inserted within a component in the form of a cylinder, which houses it and diffuses its light. The black screen that you see in the photo was simply supported at the end of the bulb itself, and could easily make a rotation around the cylinder."[23]

Made by Arteluce, Brescia, Italy. Plastic. (Arteluce, Brescia, Italy.)

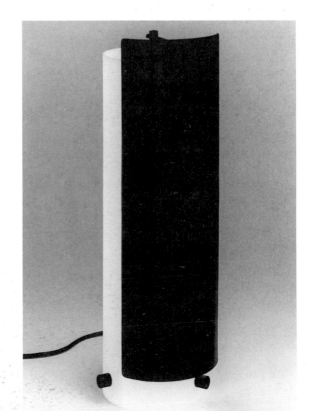

233
TAPIO WIRKKALA
Bowl, 1951

In 1951 Tapio Wirkkala's international reputation continued to develop: he won three grand prizes at his first Milan *Triennale* exhibition, where he also served as interior architect for the entire Finnish section, and was named artistic director of Helsinki's Taideteollinen oppilaitos (School for Industrial Arts). Characteristic of the aesthetic approach that brought Wirkkala recognition is the link between nature and man made objects seen in this bowl, which was displayed at the *IX Triennale* and called "the most beautiful object of 1951" by the American magazine *House Beautiful.*[24] While wood was a traditional medium for Finnish arts and crafts because of the country's abundant birch forests, Wirkkala, like many of his compatriots, also experimented with plywood, a natural material recomposed by man. Wirkkala's sympathetic approach to the material was described at the time by the American critic Edgar Kaufmann, Jr.:

> What others have discovered in today's plastic materials, he has discovered in laminated wood—a fabricated substance which he, man and artist, is

qualified to create. He composes his own wood, layer upon layer, with the craftsman-like care of a textile designer weaving his own fabric. This technique makes possible the careful balance of dark and light streaks, and the placing of cheerful veins of colored wood which shine here and there like peacock feathers. Then, by his own mysterious method of kniving and scooping, Wirkkala urges the laminated blocks into swirling forms, emulating that world of natural things which he firmly controls.[25]

Birch plywood. Length: 13 3/4" (35 cm). (Finnish Society of Crafts and Design, Helsinki.)

234
KAJ FRANCK
Kilta table service, 1952

Kaj Franck's aim in creating his line of *Kilta* tableware was to simplify the formal services of the past, discarding the many traditional pieces devoted to specific separate uses for more generalized forms with multiple functions, including food preparation, serving, and storage. Considered modern and revolutionary when it was introduced in 1953, this inexpensive earthenware line brought together concepts that had already been

developed abroad for ceramic and glass services during the decades before the war: multiple uses and interchangeable elements (no. 139); oven-to-table and storage functions (no. 64); mix-and-match colors (no. 173); and open-stock purchasing (no. 139). The coordinated sizes facilitated stacking and storage in the tighter spaces of postwar housing for which they were designed. The circular and rectangular shapes were originally available in white, yellow, black, brown, and green. Of all the products Franck designed as artistic director for utilitarian wares at Arabia between 1945 and 1960, this was the most popular with a wide range of his countrymen, a success much in line with the broad social aims he projected for industrial design. *Kilta* was awarded a grand prize at the *XI Triennale* in Milan in 1957.

Made by Wärtsilä, Arabia, Helsinki. Glazed earthenware. Diameter of largest plate: 9 1/8" (23.5 cm). (Hackman Arabia Oy, Helsinki.)

235
RUSSEL WRIGHT
Residential table service, 1953

Sold door-to-door as well as in stores, with a ten-year guarantee against breakage calculated to combat public perception that plastics were not durable, Russel Wright's *Residential* dinnerware was the first plastic service to be marketed successfully on a large scale for home use in the United States. Like his *American Modern* ceramic dinnerware (no. 173), this melamine set came in rich distinctive colors—originally Sea Mist, Grey, Lemon Ice, Black Velvet, and Copper Penny—and had a slightly mottled finish achieved after much experimentation by overlapping two colors during manufacture. Its forms underscore Wright's penchant for organic curves such as that of the cup handle, which flows out of the rim and turns back to join the side, forms that were well suited to the capabilities of compression molding.

Made by Northern Industrial Chemical Company, Boston. Melamine. (Robert Shaw, New York.)

236
KAREL APPEL
Fabric, 1953

During the 1950s avant-garde painting inspired European and American textile manufacturers seeking to update their traditional patterns with contemporary designs. This pattern of flat, overlapping color was one of several abstract designs commissioned by Amsterdam's Bijenkorf department store from Karel Appel, a well-known member of the Cobra group of painters. It was translated into hand-printed linen curtain material by the textile firm 't Paapje and produced in several different color combinations. The fabric was exhibited in the store in 1953 along with the work of other Dutch designers, many of whom had also been commissioned to create products especially for this presentation. Bijenkorf had begun in 1948 to present the latest of exemplary modern furnishings in an annual series called Ons Huis Ons Thuis (The House Is a Home). The store became the country's commercial center for the dissemination of international modern design, but when Appel's fabric was shown there, the series for the first time focused exclusively on the work of Dutch designers.

Made by 't Paapje, Voorschoten, the Netherlands. Printed linen. (Stedelijk Museum, Amsterdam.)

237
GIO PONTI
Sink and toilet, 1953

Gio Ponti's sink and toilet revolutionized the design of sanitary fittings and were often compared to contemporary sculpture for their formal beauty. Ponti sought to reshape the fittings not according to the requisites of pure engineering or abstract geometry but by allowing their "true" forms to emerge naturally from their functions and materials. As the designer later recounted:

> I began by rejecting the architectural concept of the "column" for the wash basin, as that so-called column is only a casing and does not support the basin, which is attached to the wall by brackets. I substituted for the false column the true form of the casing. I also refused to use a rim around the wash basin, and, in keeping with previous insights, avoided giving the basin a geometrical or architectural shape (oval, rectangular, or the like) but rather a shape corresponding to the movement of the forearms of a man who is washing himself—a true

form. I also left the largest possible area free to lay things on—a useful feature and therefore a true form. In the other pieces of equipment I similarly discarded every architectural and geometrical vestige. . . . I went back to the shape these pieces would have had if those who first built them had not labored under stylistic preconceptions of form.[26]

Made by Ideal Standard, Milan. Porcelain. Height of sink: 31 1/2" (80 cm); height of toilet: 15" (38.1 cm). (Philadelphia Museum of Art, gift of Ideal Standard.)

238
MARCELLO NIZZOLI
Mirella **sewing machine, 1956**

With expressive sculptural contours related to his designs for Olivetti (no. 214), Marcello Nizzoli's *Mirella* sewing machine presented a new aesthetic interpretation of the product. While he worked closely with the company's engineers and technicians on its form, the fluid exterior lines are not determined by the interior

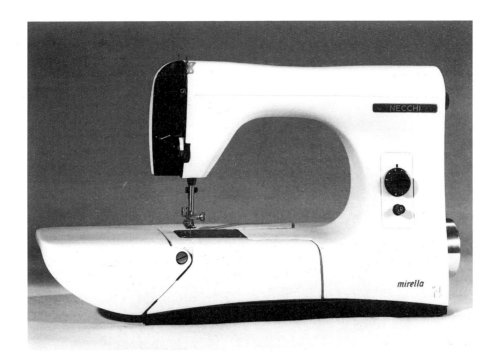

mechanism but conceived with what Nizzoli termed a "freedom of fantasy."[27] As appraised by the Compasso d'Oro jury:

> The sewing machine is distinguished for its unprecedented conception of the relationship between the product's technical form and the aesthetic quality of its housing. This is realized with Nizzoli's well-known sensibility and sobriety in a plasticity inspired by contemporary nonfigurative sculpture and is completely justified with respect to the internal workings. . . . The rejection of established formal canons in "machines" for domestic use indicates the importance of this great example of collaboration between industry and the designer.[28]

The *Mirella* was awarded the Compasso d'Oro prize in 1957, his earlier *Supernova BU*, also for Necchi, having been similarly recognized in 1954.

Made by Necchi, Pavia, Italy. Enameled-aluminum housing. Length: 19¹/₁₆" (48.5 cm). (Museum of Modern Art, New York, gift of Vittorio Necchi.)

239
L M ERICSSON
Ericofon telephone, 1949–54

Taking advantage of new, lighter materials and of miniaturization technology, L M Ericsson developed a compact plastic telephone that included all user-related components (earpiece, mouthpiece, dial, and switch) in one unit. Working over a fifteen-year period begin-

ning in 1940, but most assiduously between 1949 and 1954, the Ericsson design team made a deliberate attempt to give a dynamic form to this new concept. They evolved a large series of models with expressive, organic forms, but the most efficient arrangement of the elements and their weight, which was not supposed to exceed that of the standard two-piece unit's handset, was their practical concern. For stability and convenience, the dial and circuitry were placed at the bottom, the dial being recessed and enclosed by a rubber gasket; a large red nylon ball switch was added in the center, to be activated by the weight of the unit itself. When introduced in four pastel and two saturated colors in 1956, *Ericofon* telephones were hailed by the Swedish design journal *Form* as "technical sculptures," which "more clearly than anything else, depict the art of our age."[29]

Made by Telefonaktiebolaget L M Ericsson, Stockholm. Plastic, rubber, and nylon housing. Height: 9¹/₁₆" (23 cm); base: 4⁷/₁₆ x 3⁷/₈" (11.3 x 9.9 cm). (L M Ericsson, Stockholm.)

240
UMBERTO NASON
Cocktail pitcher and glasses, 1954

Unlike the majority of Muranese glassworks, Nason & Moretti had specialized since its establishment in 1923 in the production of utilitarian table glass rather than in the manufacture of expensive, unique decorative pieces. Among the varied products the firm issued in the postwar period was this set of undecorated bicolored tableware—cocktail glasses, pitcher, and bowls in several sizes—designed by one of its founders, Umberto Nason, and awarded a Compasso d'Oro prize in 1955. The mold-blown cased glasses join a layer of milk glass with one of color used either as the inner layer, as seen here, or as the outer. The prize jury commended Nason & Moretti for its "pure and chaste forms," based on hemispheres, cylinders, and cones, and its "note of freshness and elegance."[30]

Made by Nason & Moretti, Murano, Italy. Mold-blown colored glass. Height of pitcher: 8 1/4" (21 cm). (Museum of Modern Art, New York, Phyllis B. Lambert Fund.)

241
DORA JUNG
Line Play fabric, 1956

A weaver as well as textile designer, Dora Jung devoted her craft to exploring the possibilities of the compound reversible damask weave, greatly expanding its use for decorative hangings and bringing a new sophistication to the production of table linens in linear, abstract, and stylized floral designs. Jung followed the functionalist approach of her schooling during the late 1920s and early 1930s, which for a textile designer meant using natural materials and colors, and depending on the structure of the weave to create its decorative interest. Here, the play of lines in the woven pattern creates a cool, highly refined design in dark on light (which appears as light on dark in reverse), achieved through a precise and economical use of its manufacturing process. Awarded a grand prize at the *XI Triennale* in Milan in 1957, Jung's *Line Play* fabric remained in production from 1956 to 1973.

Made by Tampella, Tampere, Finland. Damask linen. Width: 50 3/8 (129 cm). (Taideteollisuusmuseo, Helsinki.)

242
HANS GUGELOT AND DIETER RAMS
Phonosuper phonograph and radio, 1956

While the firm of Max Braun had produced radio–record player combinations under the title *Phonosuper* since the 1930s, the cabinet designed in 1956 by Hans Gugelot and Dieter Rams revolutionized the series and introduced the concept of the transparent plexiglass cover, which gained worldwide acceptance in the hi-fi industry. A loudspeaker in a separate cabinet that matched the radio-phonograph unit in dimensions and design was created the following year. Characterized by the same wooden sides and slotted

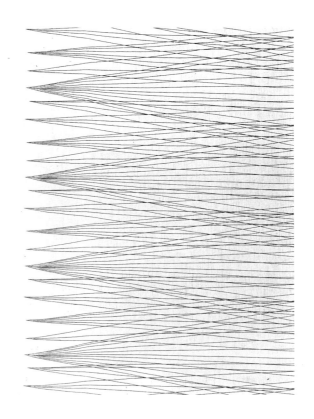

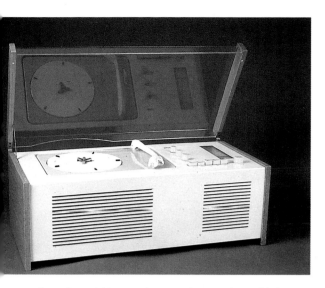

front, it could be used to supplement the unit's integrated loudspeaker; this additional element introduced the component product family now common in stereophonic equipment. With its refined detailing, white front, and transparent lid, the *Phonosuper* cabinet epitomized Braun's new minimalist aesthetic in which all superfluous embellishments were removed and function was visibly displayed—here the record player and operating panel can be seen even when the lid is closed. Following the functionalist principle, which separated the "essential" standard form from any accidental details, the designers intended to make the radio–record player look and function as simply as possible. The original model was made out of sheet metal with wooden ends; the cover was also to be made of metal, but because of its highly vibratory nature plexiglass was substituted. The *Phonosuper* was exhibited at the *XI Triennale* in Milan in 1957, when the firm of Max Braun was awarded a grand prize for its entire production.

Made by Max Braun, Frankfurt. Metal, wood, and plexiglass. 9 1/2 x 22 7/8 x 1 1 1/2" (24 x 58 x 29 cm). (Braun, Kronberg im Taunus, Germany.)

243
EERO SAARINEN
Armchair, 1957

Eero Saarinen's last furniture design, this armchair belongs to the series of chairs, stools, and tables supported on a single cast aluminum stem or pedestal that he developed over a period of about five years. Assisted by a research team from the Knoll firm headed by Donald Petit, Saarinen faced the problem of trying to treat the leg structurally and visually as part of the reinforced-plastic molded seat shell, an issue that had challenged him since he and CHARLES EAMES con-

ducted their first experiments with molded seat shells about 1940. Saarinen's elegant solution, a revolutionary one-leg design, satisfied the architect's aesthetic criteria if not his technological goal of a continuous single-piece construction; the load-bearing capability of reinforced plastic, which he would have liked to use for the pedestal as well as the seat, was then still untested and he had to use aluminum lacquered to match the plastic finish instead. Saarinen discussed both aspects in a historical review of his own furniture:

> The undercarriage of chairs and tables in a typical interior makes an ugly, confusing, unrestful world. I wanted to clear up the slum of legs. I wanted to make the chair all one thing again. All the great furniture of the past from Tutankhamun's chair to Thomas Chippendale's have always been a structural total. With our excitement over plastic and plywood shells, we grew away from this structural total. As now manufactured, the pedestal furniture is half-plastic, half-metal. I look forward to the day when the plastic industry has advanced to the point where the chair will be one material, as designed.[31]

Made by Knoll Associates, New York. Fiberglass-reinforced plastic and lacquered aluminum with upholstery. 31 1/2 x 25 1/2 x 23 1/2" (80 x 65 x 60 5 cm). (Knoll International, New York.)

244
HANS GUGELOT
M125 cabinet system, 1950–56

A system based on standardized elements that could be completely knocked down, Hans Gugelot's *M125* cabinet system followed a long tradition of industrially produced standardized furniture in Germany, from Bruno Paul's *Typenmöbel* and RICHARD RIEMERSCHMID'S *Maschinenmöbel* (no. 38) before World War I to furniture designed by Adolf Schneck for the Deutsche Werkstätten in the 1920s. Although sharing the standardization of parts, ease of transportation, lightness, and low cost of earlier systems, Gugelot's *M125* was conceived not as a program of ready-made suites nor even as individual pieces of furniture but as a wall system. "The cupboard is no longer a piece of furniture," the designer explained, "but part of the wall, with the same multiple relationships to man as a wall. . . . To build the wall, the elements are measured so they can be rationally made and so the space they occupy for storage and shipping is primarily two-dimensional. . . . The length and width of the different parts are multiples of the module 125 mm ($4^7/_8$"), chosen to coordinate with smaller and larger elements."[32] The ascetic white finish and wood-and-black trim of the panels give visible expression to Gugelot's concerns for clarity of design and for mathematical order, concerns he fostered at the Hochschule für Gestaltung in Ulm, where he taught during the 1950s and 1960s and where many of the mechanical drawings were executed for this system.

Made by Wilhelm Bofinger, Stuttgart. PVC-foil-covered chipboard with metal. Height: 64" (162.5 cm). (Philadelphia Museum of Art, gift of Wilhelm Bofinger & Co.)

245
JOSEF MÜLLER-BROCKMANN
Poster for Tonhalle-Gesellschaft Zurich, 1955

The concert posters that Josef Müller-Brockmann designed for the Tonhalle in Zurich beginning in 1951 shared a grid system of organization that was developed in Switzerland in the postwar period and has since become one of the basic tools used internationally for the structuring of graphic design. Depending on mathematics to create a series of divisions and subdivisions, which provides an unseen armature for the placement of typography and illustrations, the grid principle fosters an order and economy that its adherents claim can better convey the content, or what they see as informational systems. The grid of this poster

beethoven

tonhalle grosser saal
dienstag, den 22. februar 1955,
20.15 uhr.
4. extrakonzert
der tonhalle-gesellschaft
leitung carl schuricht
solist wolfgang schneiderhan
beethoven ouverture zu «coriolan», op. 62
violinkonzert in d-dur, op. 61
siebente sinfonie in a-dur, op. 92
vorverkauf tonhalle-kasse, hug, jecklin,
kuoni
karten zu fr. 3.50 bis 9.50

cal arrangements or stresses to enliven the grid; geo-metrical figures; and ample blank space—all prominent components of this poster.

Lithograph. 50¹/₄ x 35¹/₂" (128.7 x 91 cm). (Reinhold-Brown Gallery, New York.)

246
GERD ALFRED MÜLLER
Kitchen Machine food processor, 1957

In 1957 Braun introduced Gerd Alfred Müller's sleek food processor, a powerful, multipurpose unit with several accessories including a blender, shredder/slicer, meat chopper, and coffee mill. Unlike other processors then on the market, the clean-lined *Kitchen Machine* was composed as a simple mass with the joints in the casing treated as an orderly series of parallel lines. Finished in white plastic with black type, Braun's processor presented the same austere appearance as the firm's other products (nos. 242, 259). After just three years of collaboration with the Hochschule für Gestaltung at Ulm, Braun had created a recognizable corporate image to which all the company's products conformed and which was extended into every aspect of the company's activities, including its logo, advertising, and packaging. At the *XI Triennale* in Milan in 1957, where the *Kitchen Machine* was first displayed, Braun's stand was designed by the same Ulm professors, HANS GUGELOT and OTL AICHER, who were responsible for the firm's promotional material. A system of show-window displays also designed by Gugelot and Aicher for this and other Braun products included the elements of a complete display wall, promoting with clear, legible type and images the identity of Braun as an orderly and efficient company.

Made by Max Braun, Frankfurt. Polystyrol housing. 10¹/₄ x 15 x 9¹/₂" (26 x 38 x 24 cm). (Braun, Kronberg im Taunus, Germany.)

divides the sheet into four equal vertical columns, indicated by the type forming two columns at lower left (flush right on the left column and flush left on the right). But the system of horizontal grid lines on which the type is positioned is not so easily extrapolated. The circular segments also play off the grid, with the one horizontal and two vertical edges likewise marking the underlying structure, while their graduated widths suggest tonal intervals and the laws of music that Müller-Brockmann saw as analogous to the compositions of his posters. Müller-Brockmann and his Swiss colleagues, among them Armin Hofmann in Basel, favored sans-serif type for its clean lines and modernity; asymmetri-

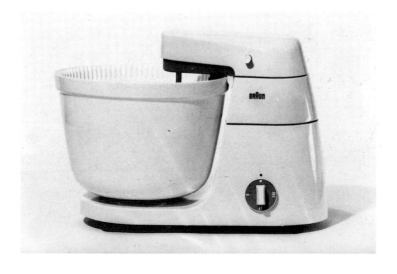

247
GEORGE NELSON
Marshmallow sofa, 1956

As design director for the Herman Miller Furniture Company, a position he held for twenty years after succeeding GILBERT ROHDE in 1946, George Nelson followed his predecessor in helping to bring the company into the forefront of progressive American manufacturers. His own designs as well as those of such talented designers as CHARLES EAMES, whom he brought to the firm, created a distinctive identity for Herman Miller products, which in the 1950s had an ad hoc quality as the firm sought new and unconventional solutions to low-cost furniture production. Nelson was always cognizant of manufacturing techniques; his *Marshmallow* sofa offered an idiosyncratic but pragmatic solution for the factory production of upholstered seating, customarily a time-consuming hand operation. The separate cushions are standard mass-produced barstool seats—vinyl-covered foam cushions in bright colors (sometimes several mixed in one sofa). These are mounted individually on metal disks and set into rods attached to the thin, curved metal armature. With this additive system of ready-made units, the sofa could be manufactured in any length, and examples with as many as ten cushions side by side were made.

Made by Herman Miller Furniture Company, Zeeland, Michigan. Painted steel and chrome-plated metal with vinyl and foam-rubber upholstery. 31 x 51 x 31" (78.7 x 129.5 x 78.7 cm). (Bernard and Sandra Featherman.)

248
MAIJA ISOLA
Stones fabric, 1956

The fabrics that Maia Isola designed for Printex, the Finnish company that produced Marimekko textiles, introduced oversize geometric patterns that can be seen in their full repeat only when displayed as curtains or wall hangings; when used as upholstery or clothing material, the patterns break down into large, flat, indecipherable, abstract areas of color. The bold popular patterns such as *Stones* (*Kivet*) were sometimes printed in black or only a single saturated color on white, at other times in a combination of more subtle close-valued tones. They were promoted also for their appearance of craftsmanship created by the slight irregularities of the screen-printing process. Marimekko (which means "Mary's Little Dresses") was founded under the name of Printex in 1951 by Armi Ratia, and changed its name when it began to market clothing made from these fabrics; it became a highly visible international fashion and furnishing fabric company during the 1960s.

Made by Printex, Helsinki, for Marimekko. Screen-printed cotton. Width: 54" (137.2 cm). (Philadelphia Museum of Art, gift of the manufacturer.)

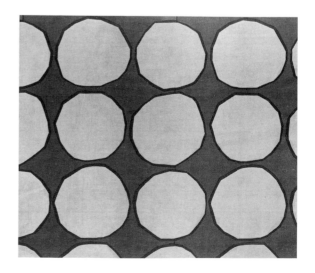

249

MONTAGNI, BERIZZI, BUTTÈ, ARCHITETTI
Television, 1956

"This, by God, is no longer a piece of furniture," wrote GIO PONTI, editor of *Domus*, about Phonola's television, "it is an appliance, with an expressive form that is right, true to itself, and genuine. Below is the mechanism, above the visual trumpet (a little like the auditory trumpet of the great old gramophones)."[33] Expressive indeed is the swivel-screen television designed for Phonola by the young architectural firm of Montagni, Berizzi, Buttè, with its elongated curved form tightly sheathing the picture tube and screen. In the Milanese rationalist tradition, the appliance is separated according to function into distinct parts—viewing screen, chassis with clearly organized controls and speaker, and optional stand. The stand has crisscrossed struts, which keep the legs rigid as it is pushed about on wheels and are clearly revealed, and the set is removable to allow its alternative use here as a table model or within shelving or component units.

Made by Phonola, Milan. Metal housing. (Photographic Archives, Triennale, Milan.)

250
SAUL BASS
Poster for *The Man with the Golden Arm*, 1955

The image on this poster was developed by Saul Bass for the first visual identity program ever created for a motion picture. Breaking with the photographs of actors and actresses and the texts traditionally used to promote films, the producer-director Otto Preminger commissioned a comprehensive graphic program for

The Man with the Golden Arm that included printed logos, theater posters, and newspaper advertisements as well as the animated titles in the film itself. These worked equally well in simple bold colors or black-and-white. Reducing the design to a single dominant symbol, Bass identified this film about drug addiction with a jagged arm thrusting sharply downward, suggesting in a powerful pictograph the torment of an addict's existence. While this symbol revolutionized film graphics and led to Bass's subsequent programs for Preminger's *Anatomy of a Murder* (1959) and *Exodus* (1960), the designer later recalled that its use initially inspired much dissent: "I know that almost everybody hated those ads. They broke all the rules of what a campaign should do, because they only told one thing—they didn't provide the normal stew, with potatoes, meat, and carrots. My ads were so reductive they became metaphors. The trick, of course, with that approach was how do you get the essence of the film and yet present it in a sufficiently provocative way to excite the audience to go to the film?"[34] Denied the Production Code's seal of approval for its sensational content, the film was released independently to great commercial success.

Bass/Yager and Associates, Los Angeles. Silkscreen. 36 x 25" (91.4 x 63.5 cm). (Bass/Yager and Associates, Los Angeles.)

251
POUL KJAERHOLM
Chair, 1955

Although he was schooled as a cabinetmaker in the Danish methods of hand craftsmanship, Poul Kjaerholm spent most of his career designing for mass production and employing materials not typically associated with traditional crafts. Like ARNE JACOBSEN, one of Scandinavia's principal practitioners of the late International Style, Kjaerholm used stylistic idioms and materials introduced for home furnishings in the 1920s, employing tempered spring steel here instead of Danish oiled wood. Indeed the minimal design of this chair, reduced essentially to three elements—legs, connecting clamps, and seat—embodied Kjaerholm's neofunctionalist idiom with perfect precision and clarity. Because welding would not work with the spring steel, Kjaerholm assembled the chair with clamps and Allen screws and was successful in stabilizing the structure even with its cantilevered seat. The chair was first sold with leather upholstery offered in four colors or a canvas seat and back in six (caning was introduced as an alternative in 1957); the chair was exhibited in leather at the *XI Triennale* in Milan in 1957, where it was awarded a grand prize.

Made by E. Kold Christensen, Copenhagen. Chrome plated steel and cane. Height: 28" (71.1 cm). (Danske Kunstindustrimuseum, Copenhagen.)

252
ARNE JACOBSEN
Egg chair and ottoman, 1957

Arne Jacobsen was the leading exponent of the late International Style in Scandinavia, although he often adopted organic, symbolic forms that earlier modernists would have considered subjective and idiosyncratic. His most influential commission was the Scandinavian Airlines System Royal Hotel and Air Terminal in Copenhagen, which he built between 1956 and 1960 and for which he designed all furnishings as well: rugs, curtains, beds, chairs, lighting fixtures, glassware, cutlery (no. 253)—everything down to its ceramic ashtrays. These furnishings were produced by various manufacturers and concurrently offered for sale to the public, with the hotel interior providing an extraordinary showcase of Danish industrial design. Manufactured by Fritz Hansen and used throughout the hotel, Jacobsen's *Egg* (Aegget) chair is a personal interpretation of a wing chair in an enveloping oval shape that suggested its name. It swivels and tilts on a chromed-steel base and has a molded fiberglass and foam-rubber shell designed for comfortable seating.

The innovative forms and materials in this and Jacobsen's equally well known winged *Swan* (Svanen) chair, also designed for the hotel and manufactured by Hansen, required new production methods and a precision of execution in order to fit the leather or fabric upholstery to their unusual shapes.

Made by Fritz Hansen, Allerød, Denmark. Fiberglass and chromed steel with leather-covered foam rubber upholstery. Height of chair: 41 7/8" (106.4 cm). (Fritz Hansen, Allerød, Denmark.)

253
ARNE JACOBSEN
Cutlery, 1957

Designed in conjunction with his commission for the SAS Royal Hotel in Copenhagen (no. 252), Arne Jacobsen's stainless steel cutlery was not successfully used there but did develop an international commercial market during the 1960s. Manufactured by the long-established Danish silversmith A. Michelsen, jeweler to the crown, it was the firm's first tableware fabricated in the "modern" medium of stainless steel. Unlike the many cutlery services then being created with forms dependent on the results of anatomical and ergonomic studies, this design was a formal exercise in utter simplicity. The implements have only a minimal sense of specificity: from the tiny coffee spoon to the long salad servers, they share the same flat, rudimentary handles, which continue uninterrupted to the end of the utensils. Slight depressions form the bowls of the spoons, short prongs denote the forks, and flat uniform blades signify the knives, the uses of which are otherwise almost unrecognizable.

Made by A. Michelsen, Copenhagen. Stainless steel. Length of knife: 7 7/8" (20 cm). (Neue Sammlung, Munich.)

254
LINO SABATTINI
Como tea and coffee service, 1955–56

The expressive, abstract styles that characterized useful objects in the 1930s and 1940s continued to offer an alternative to the strong rationalist bias of European architecture and design in the 1950s. HENNING KOPPEL, DON WALLANCE, and Lino Sabattini were among the designers who revived this approach through their use of exaggerated and asymmetrical forms such as those of Sabattini's *Como* tea and coffee service. Designed for his own studio in Milan, the entire service was produced by the Parisian silversmith Christofle from 1957 to about 1962, during the period when Sabattini was director of Christofle's design department; it continues to be made in Italy by the small production workshop the designer established in 1964 in Bregnano, near Lake Como, his childhood home. The vessels are hand fabricated from sheets of plated silver, cut and bent into their individualistic shapes, and the handles covered in cane for heat insulation.

Made by Christofle, Paris. Plated silver and cane. Height of coffeepot: 8⁷/₁₆" (21.5 cm). (Musée Bouilhet-Christofle, Saint-Denis, France.)

255
SORI YANAGI
Butterfly stool, 1956

The *Butterfly* stool is the most celebrated work of Sori Yanagi, Japan's pioneering industrial designer and a founding member in the 1950s of Japan's most important design organizations. Although he had been an assistant to CHARLOTTE PERRIAND in Japan during World War II, Yanagi never adopted the International Style idiom that Perriand practiced or that continued to exert such a strong influence in the years that followed.

Instead, seeking a new national style for a modern industrialized Japan, Yanagi opened a dialogue with tradition that became widely influential, employing modern materials and manufacturing processes—his use of bent plywood here, for example—while exploiting vernacular forms and traditional styles. The *Butterfly* stool blurred the strict distinctions between Western and Japanese furnishings that existed in well-to-do Japanese houses before the war: while the stool as a type belonged to the Western interior, Yanagi's form suggests the exuberant curves of Japanese architecture—the buoyant upward sweep of the legs and the overhang of the seat—giving it the appearance of floating free like the butterfly that inspired its name. Non-Western, too, is the stool's particular calligraphic outline, which de-emphasizes its structure and three-dimensional form. The *Butterfly* stool was shown at the *XI Triennale* in Milan in 1957, where Yanagi won a gold medal for his work.

Made by Tendo Company, Tokyo. Plywood and metal. Height: 15¹¹/₁₆" (39.9 cm). (Philadelphia Museum of Art, gift of Tendo Company, Ltd.)

256
CHARLES EAMES
Lounge chair and ottoman, 1956

The last in Charles Eames's series of plywood-shell chairs and the most complicated, expensive, as well as the most comfortable of his designs, this lounge chair consists of three doubly curved rosewood shells padded with leather cushions. Headrest, back, and seat shells are joined by cast-aluminum connectors; both the ottoman and the chair are supported on star bases machined to receive a pivot assembly. With its headrest articulated like a barber's chair and a pedestal that swivels, Eames's lounge chair was more flexible than most other chairs designed to rival the traditional nineteenth-century solid armchair, allowing the user to control the chair's angle and position. Despite its apparent complexity, the chair was designed so it could be assembled or knocked down by one person with a screwdriver, a process demonstrated in a whimsical film made by the designer with his wife and partner, Ray Eames, in 1956. In the film, the assembly takes place in fast motion in a matter of seconds, allowing the technician additional time to daydream comfortably in the luxurious lounge. The lounge chair and ottoman were awarded a gold medal at the *XII Triennale* in Milan in 1960.

Made by Herman Miller Furniture Company, Zeeland, Michigan. Rosewood plywood, aluminum, and rubber, with leather upholstery. Chair: 33 x 33³/₄ x 32" (83.8 x 85.7 x 81.3 cm); ottoman: 24³/₄ x 17 x 21¹/₄" (61 x 43.2 x 54 cm). (Philadelphia Museum of Art, purchased with funds contributed by Mr. and Mrs. Adolph G. Rosengarten, Jr., in memory of Calvin S. Hathaway.)

257
MAX BILL
Wall clock, 1957

With its emphasis on simple shapes and clean-lined, comprehensible graphic display, this wall clock is a paradigm of the influential neofunctionalist aesthetic that its designer Max Bill taught at the Hochschule für Gestaltung in Ulm between 1950 and 1956 and practiced consistently in his designs for industry. The clear, graphic impact of the clock was an effect Bill had admired even as a child. His grandfather was a clock-maker, and of the many clocks at home, he

> particularly liked a wall clock, a sleek Empire model, because the face with its numbers and indicators was delicate and its weights and pendulum were simple. This wall clock had some of that precision measure that one finds in factory time clocks. . . . By chance through a misunderstanding, I happened to design clocks. A man associated with a clock manufacturer came one day to ask me to design decorative clocks for his firm. . . . I didn't like this idea at all, but since I already had a drawing of my ideal clock . . . I explained to my visitor that I would make clocks of a different kind, no decorative clocks, no temporary "annual" models. On the contrary, I would make clocks that were as far from that as possible, so timeless that they would just go accurately on their own.[35]

Made by Gebrüder Junghans, Schramberg, Germany. Stainless
steel and aluminum housing. Diameter: 11" (30.2 cm).
(Museum of Modern Art, New York; Philip Johnson Fund.)

258
TOKYO TELECOMMUNICATIONS ENGINEERING CORPORATION
Sony radio, 1958

Marketed by the Tokyo Telecommunications Engineering Corporation under the name *Sony* (a combination of the Latin *sonus*, meaning "sound," and the English *sonny*, suggesting a lively boy), this pocket transistor radio had a success that was so exceptional that the name was adopted for the firm as a whole the same year. The pocket transistor radio program, introduced in 1957 and developed with this *TR-610* model the following year, was responsible for establishing the SONY CORPORATION's international reputation and creating an export market that brought the Japanese firm to the head of a competitive field previously dominated by European and American companies. The *Sony* radio was thinner and smaller than the firm's earlier *TR-63* pocket radio, with rounded corners; all operating elements were also located at the top so that it could fit more comfortably into a pocket and be manipulated with one hand. The addition of a small handle that could also be used as a stand made the radio easier to carry. The Japanese magazine *Kogei News* later commented on the popular appeal of this model, not only "for all age groups in many countries" but in Japan, too, where it ranked second only to an electric rice cooker in the magazine's 1959 survey of the best Japanese products made since the war.[36] The Japanese Ministry of International Trade and Industry conferred a G-Mark award on it in 1958 for its good design.

Plastic housing. 4⅜ x 2⅝ x 1¼" (11.2 x 7.1 x 3.2 cm.) (Sony
Corporation, Park Ridge, New Jersey.)

Made by Max Braun, Frankfurt. Plastic and metal housing. 6 x 9 1/2 x 2" (15.3 x 23.5 x 5 cm). (Braun, Kronberg im Taunus, Germany.)

260
HANS ROERICHT
Table service, 1959

This compact dinnerware service, Hans Roericht's diploma project at the Hochschule für Gestaltung in Ulm, Germany, in 1959, was put into production almost immediately by Rosenthal through its affiliate, Thomas. Aesthetically satisfying according to the school's philosophy because of its well-researched functions and sound manufacture, the service exemplifies the rational design precepts and procedures taught at Ulm under Tomás Maldonado. Roericht derived his specifications from extensive measurements of existing forms and from surveys of the requirements for dinnerware designed specifically for institutions (although this was sold also for domestic use). Disregarding conventional tableware forms, Roericht conceived his standardized set with two modular norms—a vertical stepped cylinder for cups and pitchers and a constant angle for the sides of bowls and plates—and he coordinated the shapes and sizes so that all pieces of the same diameter regardless of type could function as interchangeable components and be stacked or nested.

Made by Thomas Porzellan-Werke, Waldershot, Germany. Porcelain. Height of cup: 2 3/4" (7 cm). (Museum of Modern Art, New York, gift of Rosenthal China.)

259
DIETER RAMS
Combination phonograph and radio, 1959

This combination phonograph and radio was one of a highly innovative series of austerely simple portable units that marked Dieter Rams's debut as an independent product designer for Braun. While portable radios had been produced by Braun since the 1930s, the new postwar technology of the transistor, which made miniaturization possible, revolutionized the industry and rendered the bulky vacuum tubes and lead rechargers of the earlier sets obsolete. Rams's small but powerful pocket radio, which forms part of this unit, was one of the first of its kind anywhere; its size and light weight made it ideal for combinations with other small products such as loudspeakers and clocks, although this radio and record player, connected by a bracket, were the only such combination to be produced successfully. Within a few years Braun's pocket radio program was discontinued because it could not compete with lower priced Japanese imports.

261
KAJ FRANCK
Kremlin Bells double decanter, 1957

Known as *Kremlin Bells* and suggestive of the circular forms of Russian onion domes, Kaj Franck's double decanter combines the elegant simplicity of his multi-purpose utilitarian designs for the Nuutajärvi glass-works with the lively inventiveness of his decorative art glass. Blown of thin clear glass, the decanter is a composite of very simple shapes and was made in various color combinations. It is composed of two parts—a small elaborate decanter above formed of a cylindrical base and circular body with a spherical stopper, and a larger rounded decanter below for which the small decanter serves as the stopper. In 1957, the year this piece was designed, Franck won the Compasso d'Oro grand international prize for the high aesthetic quality of his production. Several examples were also exhibited in the Finnish section of Milan's *XI Triennale* that year.

Made by Wärtsilä, Nuutajärvi Glassworks, Nuutajärvi, Finland. Clear and colored blown glass. Height: 13 3/4" (35 cm). (Philadelphia Museum of Art, purchased with funds contributed by COLLAB.)

262
TIMO SARPANEVA
Bottles, 1959

In competition with the Nuutajärvi glassworks, in 1956 Finland's Iittala glassworks introduced its i-line of thin, delicately colored glassware. Created by the master glass designer Timo Sarpaneva, the line conveyed a sense of the individuality and expressiveness of art glass, although it was manufactured in a large production run intended for wide distribution. The i-line offered a broad range of tablewares in clear and colored glass with muted and compatible tonalities, as seen in these small, elegantly formed concave bottles, which were designed to be stacked. Like other designers of the period, Sarpaneva also designed the logo and packaging for the line, from the by-now familiar trademark of an i in a red circle to boxes whose colors were coordinated with the glassware they contained.

Made by Ahlström Iittala, Iittala, Finland. Blown colored and clear glass. Height: 6" (15.2 cm). (Iittala Glass Museum, Iittala, Finland.)

263
POUL HENNINGSEN
PH Artichoke hanging lamp, 1958

Poul Henningsen's *Artichoke* lamp follows the principles of his earlier widely influential *PH* designs, which used several shades to direct the light and mask its glare (no. 116). This version's fragmented, overlapping flaps set at different angles, however, give it a spectacular and decorative impact unmatched in Henningsen's production. The lamp also washes the room with a distinctively colored tone, the copper of the shades adding its warmth to the reflected light; this feature gives a stronger, more deliberate effect than the other *PH* fixtures for which Henningsen engineered subtle tonal changes by adjusting the position of the bulb or coloring the interior of the shades. Designed for the Langelinie Pavilion restaurant in Copenhagen, the *Artichoke* lamp was also produced in reduced form for domestic use.

Made by Louis Poulsen & Company, Copenhagen. Copper. Height: 27 1/8" (69 cm); diameter: 33 1/8" (84 cm). (Louis Poulsen & Company, Copenhagen.)

264
BEN SHAHN
Poster for *Ballets U.S.A.* exhibition, 1959

Ben Shahn brought the techniques of an artist to his occasional work as a graphic designer over a period of several decades. His work ranged from angular, figurative pen-and-ink drawings with calligraphic script to this abstract collage of hand-colored rectangular shapes and superimposed letters he produced for an exhibition of Jerome Robbins's ballet photographs in London. (In 1958, Shahn had designed stage sets for Robbins's ballet "New York Export Opus Jazz.") The painterly techniques Shahn adopted here were particularly appropriate to his client's program, the brightly colored irregular rectangles and letters becoming a metaphor for the invention and modernism of the American ballet scene. Shahn first used the idea of colored rectangles in his painting *Paterson* of 1950 and a related poster of 1953, inspired by the dyed fabrics he saw hung in the factory windows of Paterson, New Jersey. For Shahn, abstract forms could be used effectively to communicate ideas: "An artist may abstract the essential form of an object by freeing it from details. He may, for instance interpret Jazz—an idea, a content—by abstracting out of a confusion of figures and instruments just the staccato rhythms and the blare . . . blaring sound becomes blaring color; rhythm of timing becomes rhythm of forms . . . a highly intellectual content [becomes] formulated into a single immediate impression."[37]

Silkscreen and lithograph. 31 3/8 x 21 1/4" (79.7 x 54 cm). (Museum of Modern Art, New York, anonymous gift.)

EXHIBIT-JEROME ROBBINS "BALLETS U.S.A."-U.S.I.S. GALLERY 41 GROSVENOR SQ. LONDON W.I. SEPT. 15-OCT. 23. 1959

207

265
GIO PONTI
Superleggera chair, 1957

Pursuing a personal tradition of exploring the past
(no. 110), Gio Ponti borrowed the form and materials
of his *Superleggera* (*Super Light*) chair from a series
of nineteenth-century vernacular chairs made in the
vicinity of the Ligurian town of Chiavari. Like its antecedents, this chair is tinted and upholstered with cane.
Rejecting modernist catch phrases like "rational" to
describe the first of several versions of the chair, Ponti
attributed the success of the chair to its simplicity and
appeal to tradition, writing about it in *Domus*, the
design magazine he had founded in 1928:

> This is the kind of chair that one should really tend
> to: a chair which would be light and strong at the
> same time, its design smooth, its price moderate. A
> chair-chair, modestly, without adjectives. . . . It
> must be light, slim, and convenient. If one wants to
> go in the right direction, as I always repeat, one has
> to shift from heavy to light, from opaque to trans-
> parent, from costly to convenient. . . . Our chair-
> chair, which had grown up alone as an anonymous,
> innocent virgin, has been progressively admitted as a
> revelation, as the true "traditional chair."[38]

Made by Figli di Amedeo Cassina, Meda, Italy. Tinted ash
and cane. Height: 323/4" (83.2 cm). (Philadelphia
Museum of Art, gift of Atelier International.)

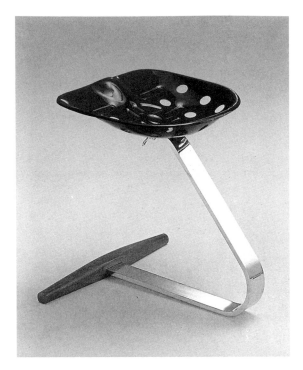

266
ACHILLE CASTIGLIONI AND PIER GIACOMO CASTIGLIONI
Mezzadro stool, 1957–71

With the name *Mezzadro*, the term for an Italian ten-
ant farmer, this stool ironically suggests the introduction of both the tractor seat and the driver into the
contemporary interior. Achille and Pier Giacomo
Castiglioni were not the first twentieth-century designers to consider the tractor seat in relation to sophisticated furniture production: LUDWIG MIES VAN DER
ROHE used it for the *Conchoidal* chairs he conceived
during the early 1940s, while *Architectural Record* published a four-legged garden stool with tractor seat by
Design Unit New York in 1949. The first version of the
Mezzadro stool, with an unpierced molded seat and an
integrated dark metal base, was shown in Milan at the
X Triennale in 1954; it was revised into its present form
when it was included in the Castiglionis' experimental
eclectic interior at the exhibition *Colori e Forme nella
Casa d'Oggi* (*Colors and Shapes in the House of Today*),
held in Como, Italy, in 1957. As finally produced in
1971, the stool is composed of a brilliantly colored
metal seat cantilevered on a resilient bent-steel support
with a wooden crosspiece for stability, and held together by a large wing nut—an elegant, additive construction of four disparate mechanical elements.

*Made by Zanotta, Nova Milanese, Italy. Chromed steel,
enameled metal, and wood. Height: 20¹¹/₁₆" (51 cm).
(Zanotta, Nova Milanese, Italy.)*

267
PHILCO CORPORATION
Predicta television, 1958

Advertised as the "world's first swivel screen television," Philco's *Predicta* was the first American model to break away from the standard cabinet format of a box with a window in it—a daring step for such a corporation although a similar idea had already been put into production in Italy by Phonola (no. 249) and in France by Téléavia. The viewing screen and tube were completely encased in a two-toned plastic capsule supported on a brass base. It was made to swivel on the top of a table- or pedestal-model chassis for viewing from any direction; a third version with the screen totally separated from the chassis and speaker could be placed anywhere, connected only by a flat, twenty-five-foot-long cable. Philco's design depended on a recently introduced flattened picture tube, which the company's engineers adapted further by shortening the neck, thereby reducing the protrusion at the back of the separated tube and minimizing its bulk as much as possible. The limited flexibility this design promised was soon made obsolete by the introduction of small, portable models (no. 273).

*Plastic and brass housing with wooden cabinet. Height: 24"
(61 cm). (Arnold L. Chase, Hartford, Connecticut.)*

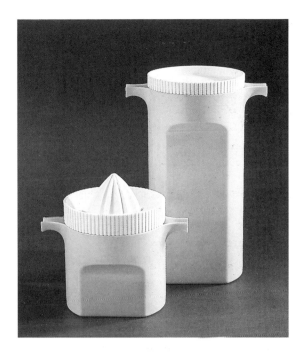

268
CARL-ARNE BREGER
Juicer-pitcher, 1959

The nineteenth-century Swedish ceramic factory at Gustavsberg, which had aligned itself with progressive design earlier in the century when it hired WILHELM KÅGE as art director, took another step forward in 1945 when it began to manufacture plastics. This step proved economically prophetic since plastic products for homes, institutions, and industry would later comprise the greater part of its activity. As designer for Gustavsberg from 1953, Carl-Arne Breger used a number of different plastic materials to make forms that would have been difficult to achieve in commercial ceramics. Propene plastic gives this juicer-pitcher its rigid shape and its thin, light, hard, and smooth body. The molded cylindrical design has flattened sides that form a natural grip and sharp, overhanging, futuristic lips; the thinness, lightness, and strength of the plastic make it durable and easy to use. The orange-colored pitcher was made in several heights but only one diameter, with the same interchangeable tops for juicing and storage.

*Made by Gustavsberg, Gustavsberg, Sweden. Propene plastic.
Height of larger pitcher: 8¹/₄" (21 cm). (Gustavsberg
Fabrike, Gustavsberg, Sweden.)*

269
YUSAKU KAMEKURA
Poster for Nikon, 1957

Using glowing optical patterns and strong, white letter-forms against an intensely dark background, Yusaku Kamekura's poster suggests the brilliance and the clarity achieved with the Nikon lens as well as the technical perfection of his client's camera. Kamekura designed his first poster for Nikon in 1954, the beginning of a long and successful association in which he established the firm's corporate image through a complete graphic program of posters, packaging, signage, and logos. While the association of graphic designers and corporate clients, such as GIOVANNI PINTORI with Olivetti (no. 215) and PAUL RAND with IBM (no. 381), were already producing coherent programs of visual identification in the West, Kamekura and Nikon were the first to develop this kind of sympathetic relationship in postwar Japan. Nikon gave Kamekura the opportunity to create a fresh and modern public image, one the designer later credited with first establishing his own artistic identity. Published in *Graphis Annual* in 1957, this poster brought Kamekura and Japanese graphic design to international attention, followed by the program Kamekura designed only a few years later for the Tokyo Olympics.

Offset lithograph. 40 1/2 x 28 11/16" (103 x 72.8 cm). (Yusaku Kamekura, Japan.)

270
BRUNO MUNARI
Cube ashtray, 1957

Staking a claim to an area that had not been the focus of recent progressive design activity—small domestic objects such as ashtrays, desk accessories, waste baskets, umbrella holders, and permanent calendars, as well as vases, bowls, serving dishes, and lamps—the

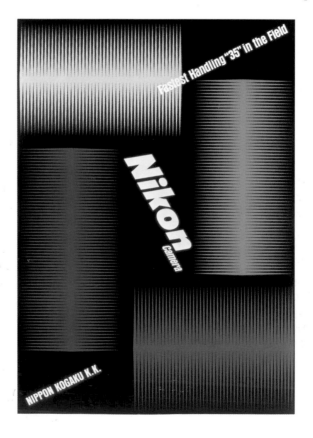

Danese firm's products shared a coherent minimalist aesthetic and a level of manufacture that aspired to perfection. To achieve this Danese called on a limited number of designers, among them Bruno Munari, ENZO MARI, and Angelo Mangiarotti; the firm also relied on craft-based production methods, although some of its products were eventually made in considerable numbers. Munari's *Cube (Cubo)* ashtray was one of the products introduced in 1957, the year Danese was established. Made in two sizes, it is formed of a melamine cube in black, white, orange, or red, with a bent strip of aluminum within, which serves as the cigarette rest and for collecting and removing ashes. The design formula that Munari outlined in his book *Design as Art* could stand equally as well for the philosophy of the entire Danese production: "Subtract rather than add: this rule must be understood in the sense of reaching simplicity, getting at the essence of the object by eliminating anything superfluous until no further simplification is possible. . . . By designing without any stylistic or formal preconceived notions, and tending towards the natural formation of things, one gets the essence of a product."[39]

Made by Danese, Milan. Melamine and aluminum. 3¹/₈ x 3¹/₈ x 3¹/₈" (8 x 8 x 8 cm). (Danese, Milan.)

271
FLAVIO POLI
Vase, 1960

Pure in outline, thick in body, and densely colored, the glass Flavio Poli designed for Seguso Vetri d'Arte has a vitality that expressed a new outlook for the age-old glass industry in Murano, which had relied for centuries on furnace-wrought decoration. Like this blown-glass vase of boldly contrasting colors, his work generally eschewed extraneous ornament; indeed he was praised by the jury that awarded him a Compasso d'Oro prize in 1954 for "pursuing essential expressions, a valiant example in a field suffering from trifling decorativism."[40] At each of the four *Triennale* exhibitions held in Milan between 1950 and 1960, Poli won a grand prize for his Seguso glass.

Made by Seguso Vetri d'Arte, Murano, Italy. Blown cased glass. Height: 10⁵/₈" (27 cm). (Corning Museum of Glass, Corning, New York, gift of Flavio Poli.)

272
TIMO SARPANEVA
Saucepan, 1959

Timo Sarpaneva's brightly colored, enameled cast-iron cookware for the Finnish manufacturer Rosenlew was both well suited for cooking and decorative enough for the table. The saucepan, with its sensitively curved teak handle, suggests traditional Scandinavian metal cookware (cast-iron pots had been used in Finland since the seventeenth century) and implies the joining of hand craftsmanship with industrial production. The pan shares with a casserole and roasting pan in the same line the continuous undulating raised rim with openings for grasping the vessels, but only this small piece has a detachable notched handle, which can be used to lift the cover during cooking and to pick up the pot itself. Sarpaneva's cast-iron cookware for Rosenlew won a silver medal at the *XII Triennale* in Milan in 1960.

Made by W. Rosenlew, Pori, Finland. Enameled cast iron and teak. Height: 7 1/16" (18 cm). (Taideteollisuusmuseo, Helsinki.)

273
SONY CORPORATION
Television, 1959

The world's first all-transistor television, Sony's small model with an eight-inch screen capitalized on the experience the firm's technical staff had already had in engineering circuitry for very small spaces and designing and producing miniaturized parts, particularly for its pocket radios (no. 258). The television operated on either household current or batteries and weighed only 13 1/4 pounds—light enough to be easily portable. One of a series of technological "firsts" introduced by Sony, it signaled Japan's fast-growing leadership in high-quality consumer electronics requiring precision manufacture. At the same time Sony, along with a number of other Japanese firms, began to focus more attention on design. Unlike elaborate American televisions or the cool, clean, uncluttered products designed in Germany, this model was distinctively Japanese in style—with a projecting hood overhanging the screen like a traditional Japanese roof and knobs and grill slots disposed as randomly as the room sequence in a traditional Japanese house. Compact in its tightly sheathed metal housing, it offered quality performance with appealing, unconventional styling and established Sony's reputation for originality in design as well as engineering.

Metal housing. Width: 8 1/4" (21 cm). (Sony Corporation, Park Ridge, New Jersey.)

274

GREGOTTI, MENEGHETTI, STOPPINO, ARCHITETTI
Cavour armchair, 1959

In the later 1950s a challenge to the hegemony of the modernist, rationalist tradition arose in Italy in the form of a group of historicizing buildings and objects, a development that was viewed at the time as the worrisome admission of a growing lack of faith in the direction of modern design. Grouped under the rubric "neo-Liberty"—and indeed reflecting some influences of the art nouveau or Liberty style in works by such designers as Gae Aulenti—the movement was nonetheless broader than a stylistic revival, and also included formal allusions to other historical and traditional styles. As inspiration for their highbacked armchair of curved, laminated wood, the Piedmontese

architectural firm of Gregotti, Meneghetti, Stoppino called on early Risorgimento furniture design, an antecedent clearly signaled by naming the chair *Cavour* after the nineteenth-century Italian statesman. Neo-Liberty designs, including this chair, were shown in Milan in 1960 at the exhibition *Nuovi Disegni per il Mobile Italiano (New Designs for Italian Furniture)*. Criticizing its backward-looking premise in *Domus*, one reviewer noted: "Nonetheless, this exhibition has had its value: that of stirring up the stagnant waters of the art of furniture, of putting the finger on the plague of the by-now slavish imitations of Danish and Finnish modules, and moreover, of showing us an unquestionable sympathy for an 'ornamental component.'"[41]

Made by SIM. Laminated wood with upholstery.
  (Vittorio Gregotti.)

Chapter Seven
Alternatives 1960–1970

The 1960s witnessed the polemical rejection of International Style functionalism as an aesthetic and as an idea—an aesthetic based on the myth that pure mathematical shapes were the intrinsic expression of industrial production and an idea that such shapes communicated utopian values of permanence and universality. The first broadside came from Reyner Banham, editor of Britain's *Architectural Review*, who suggested the inappropriateness of a universal aesthetic with eternal validity in an age of accelerating technology and expendable mass products. WALTER GROPIUS and LE CORBUSIER, Banham wrote, postulated "a common dependence on laws of form that were objective, absolute, universal and eternally valid. The illusion of a common 'objectivity' residing in the concept of function, and in the laws of Platonic esthetics, has been a stumbling block to product-criticism ever since." "We live in a throw-away economy," he added, "a culture in which the most fundamental classification of our ideas and worldly possessions is in terms of their relative expendability. . . . It is clearly absurd to demand that objects designed for a short useful life should exhibit qualities signifying eternal validity."[1] As an alternative, Banham proposed that the aesthetics of consumer products should be derived from popular culture and based on symbols that could be commonly recognized and understood. Challenging functionalist critical theory, Banham found his preferred source of symbols in automotive styling, which he legitimized as a kind of popular folk art. The Buick *V-8* of 1955 embodied the qualities he deemed necessary for design, displaying "glitter, a sense of bulk, a sense of three-dimensionality, [and] deliberate exposure of technical means, all building up to signify power and make an immediate impact on whoever sees it."[2]

Other critics shared Banham's view that functionalism was no longer valid and sought a new design aesthetic of fresh forms and symbols.[3] Having denied functionalism's claims on the eternal, the only possibility seemed to involve endorsing Banham's relativist aesthetic, if not his specific form-language of "popular" art, and finding virtue in a world of disordered complexity. The American architect Philip Johnson, once a primary promoter of the International Style through his own buildings and in his capacity as director of the department of architecture and design at the Museum of Modern Art in New York, wrote in response to Banham, "The International Style is dying and *The Architectural Review* is looking for 'a new, compelling, unifying slogan.' But if we live in an age when we do not like 'compelling slogans' or styles or disciplines or even

The 1955 Buick provided a readily understood symbol of popular culture.

opposite:
Verner Panton, Chair, 1960–67
(no. 288).

Supergraphics by Barbara Stauffacher Solomon for the Sea Ranch Swim Club, Sonoma, California, 1966. Like Pop objects, supergraphics gave a decorative and humanizing character to architectural spaces during the 1960s.

capital letters, can't we just wander around aimlessly? . . . We are going through a foggy chaos. Let us enjoy the multiplicity of it all."[4]

In an article entitled "The Challenge of Pop," Paul Reilly, head of Britain's Design Council, observed, "We are shifting perhaps from attachment to permanent, universal values to acceptance that a design may be valid at a given time for a given purpose. . . . All that means is that a product must be good of its kind for the set of circumstances for which it has been designed. For example, in this age of accelerating technology, to refuse to take notice of the transitory or to reject the ephemeral per se is to ignore a fact of life. . . . For consumer goods, though form may have followed function in the good old days, in this electric age they are neck and neck."[5] At the Hochschule für Gestaltung in Ulm, the "crisis of functionalism" was discussed by one of the faculty members, Abraham Moles, who described in Marxist terms an over-supply of consumer products polarized between the popular "neokitsch of the supermarket on the one side and ascetic fulfillment of function on the other."[6]

The chief theorist for complexity and against what appeared to be the antiseptic and dehumanizing qualities of functionalism was the American architect ROBERT VENTURI, who, in *Complexity and Contradiction in Architecture*, wrote "of a complex and contradictory architecture based on the richness and ambiguity of modern experi-ence."[7] Many industrial designers voiced the difficulties of defining new standards for design in a changing society and through a variety of eco-nomic conditions. The International Design Conference in 1964 at Aspen, Colorado, designated "Design '64: Directions and Dilemmas" by program chairman ELIOT NOYES, was planned to explore "the free-doms and restraints within which the designer must work and the ways in which the serious designer may reconcile his standards with the out-side forces which affect design today."[8] At the conference "Design in America" held at Princeton University the same year, CHARLES EAMES announced that there were no simple solutions. "The whole idea of choice in terms of aesthetics or form seems to be really foreign. . . . The fact that, at this point, we have the opportunity to choose puts us in a pretty precarious position, because we are in fact not equipped to choose."[9] Throughout the decade, political, economic, and social events—economic recession and inflation, the Vietnam War, and the widespread student revolts that occurred internationally in 1967–68—all engendered a period of uncertainty and unrest that contributed to the crisis of identity and purpose many designers felt. However even as the continuing process of technological change demonstrated the futility of seeking permanent values, technology itself offered designers new freedom to develop creatively.

The change from aesthetic to technological and methodological imperatives was forecast at Ulm when MAX BILL left the school in 1957 and the curriculum was radically changed. Otl Aicher, one of the tri-umvirate of directors who replaced Bill, later described the develop-ment of a new program for engineering science by HANS GUGELOT and Walter Zeischegg, and instruction plans for information theory by

Tomás Maldonado: "the ulm model was born: a model for design education based on science and technology. the designer was no longer the lofty artist . . . the last remaining relics of the werkbund arts and crafts were abandoned."[10] In 1964 Maldonado, also a director, and faculty member Gui Bonsiepe characterized the school as a "citadel" of design methodology based on the relationship between science and design.[11] Seeking to integrate the physical sciences, behavioral sciences, and technology in the design process, Maldonado intended industrial design to encompass the entire social, cultural, and physical environment:

> During these last years one of the illusions most obstinately cherished by the Design Establishment has entered into a crisis: there now arises a doubt as to whether the sum of good design objects must necessarily result in a good design environment. . . . Ecologists have [now] given a much subtler and better differentiated version of the structure of human environment. Our habitat is an open system, whose components are not merely "man-made things" or simply "things." . . . Human environment is composed both of things and persons, and also by events. It is not simply a static collection of things and persons.[12]

Maldonado's ideas were extremely influential, particularly in Italy where designers were beginning to conceive of objects and their users as environmental ensembles in constantly changing patterns of relationship. This philosophy was manifest in the design of furniture and objects that were flexible in function and permitted multiple modes of use and arrangement. Their designs nearly always depended on the use of synthetic materials, which were largely lightweight and easily molded or formed in new and unconventional colors and shapes. As their international patents expired many of these materials, such as polyethylene, which had been introduced before World War II, were suddenly less costly and more widely available. Challenging the user's experience of the relationship between the weight and size of objects as well as expectations of color and transparency, and having the ability to be molded into almost any shape, they sabotaged the conventional look of efficiency associated with functionalism—its self-effacing standardized finishes and regular forms.

JOE COLOMBO experimented with synthetic materials during the 1960s, creating flexible furniture systems and units that combined a variety of domestic services into a single assembly. Using slabs of polyurethane foam in different heights (no. 309) and cylinders of polyvinyl chloride (PVC) in different diameters, Colombo created two furniture systems that allowed the user to combine these segments in a variety of forms and infinitely extendable lengths. Among Colombo's other innovative designs were his mobile *Mini Kitchen* (no. 283) and a sectional storage system, both first shown and awarded prizes at the *XIII Triennale* in Milan in 1964. The *Mini Kitchen* contained a stove, refrigerator, drawers, and a cupboard, compacting the "essential" kitchen within about a cubic yard for use in small living spaces.

Colombo also developed large experimental environmental units that were similarly self-contained, including a completely furnished living center divided into four service areas: kitchen, bath, and spaces for day and night time use. The living center was displayed at the international furniture fair in Cologne in 1969 in the "Visiona 69" installation, sponsored by the German plastics firm of Bayer. In an effort to promote domestic applications of plastic materials, Bayer commissioned environments from several designers for the "Visiona" exhibitions, among them the Danish designer VERNER PANTON, who created a soft polyurethane seating system for "Visiona 2" in 1970, and the French designer OLIVIER MOURGUE, who developed modular furniture and moveable room dividers for "Visiona 3" in 1972. "Man has always built a shell around himself for protection and collected in it the objects he needed," Colombo wrote. "Thus the container has always influenced the contents. Now, if the elements and objects man needs to live with could be designed considering only the possibility of moving, flexing, and folding them to the utmost, we would build living quarters adaptable to any sort of situation regarding space and time. . . . Once we have created contents suiting perfectly their aims, we shall be able to begin thinking about more rational methods for the designing of the container."[13]

Other designers also investigated the idea of maximum user flexibility—for example with the *Sacco* seating by GATTI, PAOLINI, TEODORO (no. 308), a soft leather sack filled with polystyrene pellets that adapts itself to any body shape or size. Similar ideas were explored with the unstructured *Malitte* seating system by the painter ROBERTO SEBASTIAN MATTA (no. 310) and the first commercially produced inflatable chair, created by DE PAS, D'URBINO, LOMAZZI (no. 306). With the introduction of high-frequency PVC welding in the mid-1960s, inflatable chairs were also manufactured by a number of British and French designers. Paradigmatic of Banham's relativist and transient aesthetic, these bulging air-supported seats could be made to collapse and disappear in about the same time it took the user to inflate them.

The challenge to engage the consumer at a sociocultural as well as physical level was taken up by a number of designers who borrowed features from popular culture or used ready-made industrial elements. Among the best known of their works was the *Joe* sofa in the form of a gargantuan baseball glove, made of polyurethane and covered in leather (no. 322), designed by De Pas, D'Urbino, Lomazzi; and the Up series of furniture by GAETANO PESCE (no. 307), which included a *Lady* armchair with rounded breasts and a deep lap. Made of molded, flexible polyurethane foam, the Up series was compressed or "deflated" for easy transport in airtight plastic envelopes, solving one of the most persistent problems of the furniture industry. Even household appliances were rethought from the user's point of view—among them a small hinged-unit telephone by MARCO ZANUSO and RICHARD SAPPER that could be held conveniently in one hand (no. 299) and a cheerful, portable bright red typewriter by ETTORE SOTTSASS, JR., with PERRY A. KING (no. 319). Irony and humor were devices also used with great formal elegance by the brothers ACHILLE and PIER GIACOMO

Armchair by Gunnar Aagaard Andersen, 1964. Polyurethane. Height: 29 1/2" (75 cm). Museum of Modern Art, New York, gift of the designer. Demonstrating the structural properties of the plastic material, this rigid chair was made without a mold by pouring buckets of polyurethane.

CASTIGLIONI, who borrowed and adaptively reused industrial elements; having earlier recycled a tractor seat for their *Mezzadro* stool (no. 266), now they employed an automobile headlight in the *Toio* floor lamp (no. 302).

In some cases the new materials and processes were left to speak for themselves. An experimental armchair by the Danish sculptor Gunnar Aagaard Andersen of 1964, for example, was built up without a mold by pouring bucketfuls of resin by hand, demonstrating that rigid polyurethane could be a structural material in itself. As upholstery for a range of aluminum furniture (no. 300), the French architect ROGER TALLON chose the profile-cut flexible polyurethane foam "egg box" sheeting normally used for packaging; and LIVIO CASTIGLIONI and GIANFRANCO FRATTINI fitted transparent PVC tubing with wiring and bulbs to make their snakelike *Boalum* lamp (no. 316).

Whether or not they were visibly demonstrating new processes and materials in unconventional forms, designers everywhere were affected by the aesthetic properties these materials presented—lightness, transparency, bright color, and sculptural, organic shape. As a result, the designers of certain consumer goods appeared to turn away deliberately from solid mass and form to an aesthetic of reflection and luminosity, of literal transparency. Joe Colombo's C-shaped diffuser, for example, used clear acrylic to conduct light from a fluorescent element in its base (no. 282); the same medium was employed in furniture and lighting designed by the American Neal Small and in the *Plia* folding and stacking chairs by the Italian Giancarlo Piretti. The American textile designer JACK LENOR LARSEN used Saran (polyvinylidene chloride), a glassy synthetic in filament form, to weave his *Interplay* fabric (no. 275), which he loosely constructed with noticeable air spaces as a casement to screen large expanses of glass. While some new furniture forms were still supported from within by tubular-steel frames, as in the *Ribbon* chair by PIERRE PAULIN (no. 295) and Olivier Mourgue's Djinn series (no. 296), others often appeared to float and mimic the flowing behavior of resins in molds. The rocking chair without conventional arms and legs by LEONARDI-STAGI, ARCHITETTI (no. 311), appeared to demonstrate the tensile strength of the molded material, as did the first single-piece molded chair in commercial production, the cantilevered stacking chair designed by Verner Panton (no. 288).

These furnishings, which demonstrated a new dynamic aesthetic, were made of what were considered throw-away synthetic materials, widely viewed as anonymous, popular, and cheap. Actually they were no cheaper than any other material; indeed the research and development involved in producing what were often highly experimental, novel forms was often quite costly. Italy was, in fact, one of the few countries in the world where the combination of new shapes, new materials, and new processes could successfully result in some form of commercial production. As an outgrowth of traditional family-owned craft shops employing skilled craftsmen and artisans, the small Italian furniture industry was able to take risks in developing new products that were discouraged elsewhere by high engineering costs. A small group of skilled craftsmen gave furniture manufacturers the freedom to experiment and to change models, minimizing investment in research and development through their ability to create not only prototypes but also molds and tools for manufacture.

In Italy this technical capability also resulted in mass-marketed household objects as well as limited series, some of the most interesting of which were based on the methodology of product design taught at Ulm. There, Maldonado considered products to be mathematical systems composed of subsystems, which in turn consist of components, all of which interact at various levels.[14] Carefully analyzing the possible mathematical relationships in his *Center Line* cookware—eight concentric stainless-steel containers for cooking, serving, and storing food—ROBERTO SAMBONET designed four graduated pots and four shallow pans of corresponding diameters, pieces that can be used as lids or trays and nest within one another to form a single unit for economical storage (no. 290). Another rationalized tableware series was the *Cylinda* line designed by the Danish architect ARNE JACOBSEN (no. 293). The progressive firm of Kartell also developed modular systematic approaches to a variety of products. A wall-mounted dish rack by Gino Colombini is composed of individual structural-plastic elements threaded onto six small steel poles, which can be extended at will, allowing maximum flexibility of use; similarly, the modular storage units in acryonitrile butadiene styrene (ABS) designed by ANNA CASTELLI FERRIERI can be assembled in different combinations without tools merely by setting them atop one another (no. 318). Like many Kartell designs, these were and have remained popular best-sellers.

From the idea of product systems developed mathematically, Maldonado went on to define *ergonomics* as "man-machine-systems," insisting that the engineering of objects and tools for human use should

Day of the Heroic Guerrilla by Elena Serrano, 1968. Offset lithograph. 19 1/2 × 13 1/8" (49.5 × 33.3 cm). Museum of Modern Art, New York, gift of OSPAAAL. In the 1960s, posters were a readily accessible means for challenging authority, fighting oppression, and rallying popular support for revolutionary causes.

also consider all forms of relationships between man and equipment.[15] At about the same time in the United States, one of the pioneers of ergonomics, HENRY DREYFUSS, published the first of his graphic representations of median measurements of American males and females in *The Measure of Man*. For the *Trimline* telephone (no. 298) Dreyfuss's firm made thousands of studies based on these measurements to assure that the most efficient and comfortable design was achieved.

Even when objects such as these were distinguished by their rational production techniques and by systems analyses that looked back to the functionalist method, they most characteristically expressed a symbolic and formalist approach to design that remained counter to it. Discrete and self-effacing no longer, objects of the 1960s could be as brash and assertive in their appearance as they were bold in their planning, technology, and use of materials. Reyner Banham identified the roots of such an approach in his *Theory and Design in the First Machine Age* (1960), where he traced a straight line of technological advancement from the futurist Filippo Tommaso Marinetti to Buckminster Fuller and onward as an alternative mainstream of functionalist modernism. His reverence for the technological glitter of the Buick *V-8* and for the symbols of popular culture in the 1960s follows from futurism in its celebration of modern technology. Even such a staunch apologist for functionalism as Siegfried Giedion recognized the limitations of universal functionalist solutions when he added a chapter on the architect JØRN UTZON to his *Space, Time, and Architecture* (1967).[16] Giedion demonstrated that since the 1920s, design had developed with a more conscious regard for the client and had grown more interactive with the environment, that planning had become open-ended to incorporate the possibilities of changing conditions, and that expressive, sculptural tendencies like those of Utzon (no. 312) had become more evident. Giedion, a close friend and advocate of Le Corbusier and of many International Style architects and an admirer of expressionism, suggested that these differences actually represented part of a continuum, a carrying forward of earlier ideas to the present generation, thereby, like Banham, finding his explanation of the 1960s in the past.

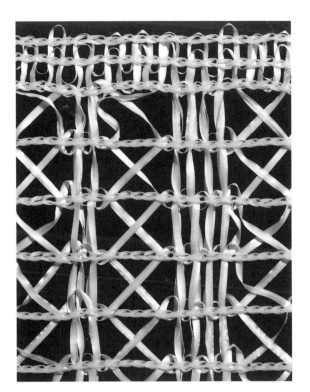

275
JACK LENOR LARSEN
Interplay fabric, 1960

One of the century's most innovative fabric designers, Jack Lenor Larsen came to international prominence in the 1960s for the technical and formal ingenuity of his designs. For the United States pavilion at the *XIII Triennale* in Milan in 1964, Larsen created a light quiet interior of white synthetic fabrics, including an undulating canopy of stretched nylon; he received a gold medal as design director and commissioner of the pavilion. Among the advanced designs he showed there was his warp-knit *Interplay*. Using an extruded filament made of Saran (polyvinylidene chloride)—an artificial, chemical-resistant, nonflammable, and nontoxic material—Larsen created this open casement fabric, its warp yarns separated by noticeable air spaces and reinforced by diagonals. While such loosely constructed fabrics normally sag and lose their shape in high humidity, this one is stable and unyielding because of the heat-setting properties of the Saran. Larsen's casement fabrics are intended for use in the domestic environment: they provide acoustical insulation, reduce glare without blocking light, and serve as interior screen walls.

Saran. Width: 48" (122 cm). (Philadelphia Museum of Art, gift of Jack Lenor Larsen, Incorporated.)

276
ACHILLE CASTIGLIONI AND PIER GIACOMO CASTIGLIONI
Arco floor lamp, 1962

Designed in response to a particular lighting problem—how to illuminate a dining table without relying on a permanently placed fixture suspended from the ceiling—Achille and Pier Giacomo Castiglioni's *Arco* lamp has been frequently misunderstood as an exercise in pure form. The lamp has been shown as a sleek silvery arc thrust into an open living area, and it was this fantastic sculptural image that made it the Castiglionis' best-known and most imitated product as well as one of the most potent design symbols of the 1960s. The stainless steel arc, which is high and broad enough to allow circulation around the table, is composed of three telescoping pieces, which can be adjusted to three positions so that the height and the angle of the lamp can be regulated. The arc is supported by a vertical post set into a marble base that acts as a counterweight.

Made by Flos, Brescia, Italy. Marble, stainless steel, and aluminum. Height: 95" (241.3 cm). (Museum of Modern Art, New York.)

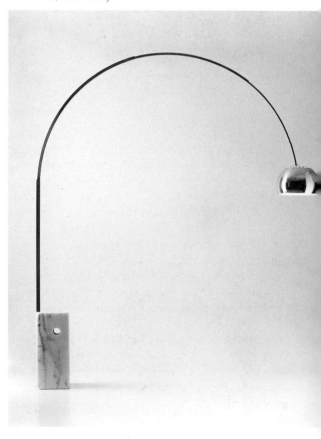

Made by General Fireproofing Company, Youngstown, Ohio.
Chromed and vinyl-coated steel. Height: 30" (76.2 cm).
(Philadelphia Museum of Art, gift of the designer.)

278
SABURŌ FUNAKOSHI
Oil and vinegar bottles, 1960

Saburō Funakoshi was one of the first professional designers to enter the Japanese tablewares industry after the war, joining the Hoya glass company in 1957. These sleek architectural oil and vinegar bottles, which Funakoshi derived from a set of crystal sake containers he designed in 1958, elevated Hoya to the first rank of modern utilitarian glass producers. Spare, elegant, and without applied ornament, they appealed to a popular conception of a technological or industrial society; their design expressed a pure geometric aesthetic that was international in character, one transcending locality. Against the backdrop of Japan's increasingly powerful economy and its dominance in certain high-technology products, Funakoshi exploited the purity, clarity, and brilliance of Hoya's lead glass and brought modern industrial design to the Japanese table. The bottles were awarded MITI's G-Mark in 1964 and Long-Life Design Award in 1980.

Made by Hoya Glassworks, Tokyo. Blown glass. Heights:
8⅝" (22 cm); 7¼" (18.5 cm). (Hoya Corporation,
Tokyo.)

277
DAVID ROWLAND
40 in 4 **chair, 1963**

Comfortable and compact, David Rowland's *40 in 4* chair was designed with such close engineering tolerances that, as its name implies, forty could be stacked in a four-foot-high space (at a 45-degree angle on a special trolley). Conceived to provide flexible seating for public spaces and compact storage, the slender, lightweight, wire-rod chair won a grand prize as the best single object at the *XIII Triennale* in Milan in 1964, the year it was first produced. It has since become extensively adapted for domestic as well as institutional use. The subtle and confident fluidity of its tubular-chrome structure reflects Rowland's practice of developing his products with small-scale wire models, which allows him to translate his first sketches on paper into three dimensions while retaining the freshness of a graphic conception.

279
KENJI FUJIMORI
Chair, 1961

Designed to be used at floor level in a tatami mat room according to traditional Japanese dining customs, these stacking chairs by Kenji Fujimori contributed a new furniture form to the modern Japanese interior. Fujimori's legless seats were the first of their kind and enjoyed considerable commercial success, inspiring numerous variations and imitations. Like CHARLES EAMES (no. 194) and SORI YANAGI (no. 255), Fujimori used molded-plywood shells for the contruction of his seats, which can be mass-produced inexpensively. This light seat shell is also designed for economical storage.

In continuous production since 1961, the chair was awarded MITI's Long-Life Design Award in 1982.

Made by Tendo Mokko, Tokyo. Rosewood plywood. 15³/₄ x 13 x 19¹/₄" (40 x 33 x 49 cm). (Tendo Mokko, Tokyo.)

280
ELIOT NOYES
Selectric typewriter, 1961

Following the example set by Olivetti in Italy and using the design talents of Eliot Noyes, the IBM Corporation developed one of the first integrated corporate design programs in America. Noyes brought an intelligence to the company's design image that reinforced and promoted the quality of its products. Through his own work and that of the highly regarded designers he recommended, especially PAUL RAND for graphics and CHARLES EAMES for films, he ensured that a high level of design would be maintained in all areas of corporate activity. In designing the *Selectric* typewriter, Noyes employed a completely new operating system with an interchangeable moving type-ball and a stationary carriage, a technological advance that allowed the model to be more compact. For its rounded forms he looked to the sculpturally conceived products that MARCELLO NIZZOLI had created in the previous decades for Olivetti (no. 214) and Necchi (no. 238), introducing organic shapes as well as sophisticated colors to America's most visible communications equipment.

Made by International Business Machine Corporation, Armonk, New York. Aluminum housing. Length: 15¹/₄" (38.7 cm). (IBM Corporation, Armonk, New York.)

281
ACHILLE CASTIGLIONI AND PIER GIACOMO CASTIGLIONI
Taccia table lamp, 1962

Anticipating the postmodern vocabulary of the 1980s in its use of a classical, fluted, columnar form and the irony of its industrial application, Achille and Pier Giacomo Castiglioni's *Taccia* lamp was ingeniously conceived as a source of diffused light, which could be directed by a simple built-in means. The lamp is assembled of three independent stacked elements: its fluted aluminum housing, which holds a flood lamp and masks two series of ventilation openings; a clear parabolic glass bowl; and an aluminum reflector, which fits into the bowl. The light shines upward and reflects off the concave opaque white reflector, which can be easily rotated to direct light in any direction or from any angle and remains in position without any mechanical means. Achille Castiglioni was to tackle a similar lighting problem in his *Gibigiana* lamp of 1980 (no. 374), but there he relied on an intricately designed mechanical device to control the direction of the light.

Made by Flos, Brescia, Italy. Aluminum and glass. Height: 21"
(53.3 cm). (Flos, Brescia, Italy.)

282
JOE COLOMBO
Table lamp, 1962

This lamp was one of Joe Colombo's first designs for industry; created with the assistance of his brother Gianni, it already demonstrated the bold use of plastics for which the designer would become known. Awarded a gold medal at the *XIII Triennale* in Milan in 1964, the lamp exploited the optical and thermoplastic properties of acrylic. With developments in extrusion and vacuum forming making it possible to produce the material in larger units, and with its thermal properties improved to mold at higher temperatures, acrylic was growing popular for domestic furnishings. Easily molded under heat and pressure into a curved shape that exploits the material's tensile strength, this C-shaped piece of transparent acrylic conducts light from a fluorescent element in the metal base, visibly demonstrating the way acrylic carries light even around bends. While the light collects principally at the forward edge, the entire surface of the lamp is luminous, casting a soft, even, and very clear light.

Made by O-Luce, Milan. Acrylic and brass. Height: 9⁷/₁₆" (24 cm). (Philadelphia Museum of Art, gift of O-Luce.)

283
JOE COLOMBO
Mini Kitchen, 1963

Joe Colombo's *Mini Kitchen* was the first and most famous of his series of innovative products that combined aspects of space planning with furniture design. A mobile kitchen on wheels, which could be used at any electrical outlet, it contained a range with two electric burners, a refrigerator, drawers and a cupboard that stored a table service for six, a cutting board, a can opener, a knife box, and a stove cover that could double as a serving tray—in short, a synthesis of the "essential" kitchen compacted within about one cubic yard. Colombo conceived of this as a minimal unit for small living spaces but one that could also serve for larger residences as a supplementary kitchen that could be pulled up beside the dining-room table or moved outdoors to terrace or garden. The *Mini Kitchen* was shown at the *XIII Triennale* in Milan in 1964 where it won a silver medal, as did another mobile unit by Colombo, the *Combi Center*—a sectional storage system that could be constructed in tower form to the buyer's specifications from various components. Like other designers of his generation backed by strong developments in technology, Colombo sought to define new space-saving forms for an ever-expanding population.

Made by Boffi, Cesano Mademo, Italy. Wood and stainless steel. Height: 37" (94.9 cm). (Museum of Modern Art, New York, gift of the manufacturer)

284
LIGHTOLIER
Track lighting system, 1963

Lightolier's track lighting system offered the increased flexibility that had been the objective of numerous individual lighting fixtures in the previous decades. Providing electricity at any point along the length of four- and eight-foot-long extruded aluminum tracks, which could be flush or surface-mounted on ceilings or walls, the system achieved maximum flexibility of location and light intensity with its variety of spotlights, floodlights, and special fixtures that could be snapped into place and adjusted by dimmers and individual switches. The system was first explored in 1957 by two of the firm's staff members, Anthony Donato, designer, and Manfred Neumann, engineer; the two designed easily moveable lighting mounts for pole lamps that, according to the patent, "may readily be positioned at any location . . . and securely yet releasably locked at such location with a relatively simple manipulation without any need for tools."[17] This was refined by their subsequent developments of a recessed lighting mount and a method for distributing

electrical power into a modular track system that could supply lighting throughout an entire room.

Aluminum. Length of right fixture: 8¹/₄" (21 cm); diameter: 6¹/₈" (15.6 cm). (Lightolier/The Genlyte Group.)

Made by Gavina, Foligno, Italy. Enameled steel. Height: 30¹¹/₁₆" (78 cm). (Philadelphia Museum of Art, gift of the designer.)

285
MARCO ZANUSO
Lambda chair, 1962–64

Consistently innovative with technological processes, Marco Zanuso traced the development of his *Lambda* chair in enameled steel to 1959, when he was commissioned to design a kitchen chair for mass production. He was asked to use a plastic laminate for the seat and back, but to devise his own system to connect and support them. The designs and prototypes he put together took him from plastic to metal. He also moved beyond the design of the kitchen chair (which was manufactured by conventional means) to begin an independent research project on structural continuity, which extended over the next five years. Through scores of prototypes (including one accorded a silver medal at the *XII Triennale* in Milan in 1960), he developed a method of fabricating the chair with shell construction to form a continuous system of structural members and seating surfaces. As put into production in 1964, the *Lambda* chair is composed of three elements—a double-surfaced seat and back unit, four legs, and four connective parts— all stamped out of sheet metal borrowing automobile technology. Following automobile-production methods, too, the pieces were joined by spot welding and the chair was spray-painted to produce its dense colored-enamel finish. Zanuso's approach allowed him to manufacture large numbers of inexpensive chairs with a fully integrated structure and a satisfying formal composition.

chair—from wooden prototypes to metal versions related to Marco Zanuso's *Lambda* chair (no. 285) to explorations of fiberglass—came to an end with the decision to rethink the project entirely. A new material, polyethylene, had suddenly become economically feasible after the expiration of international patents in the early 1960s and Zanuso, with his collaborator Richard Sapper, decided to explore its potential. Having made this decision, the two were then forced to work within its technical requirements, principally the need to make the molded-plastic structure quite thick. But it was the requirement for stacking that gave the designers greater concern, for much of the seat would have had to be cut away for one chair to fit over the other. When they came up with the idea of using the thick cylindrical legs as the means of stacking (by setting them into the chair's back), the unanticipated solution extended the design's potential into the area of play. "The final result . . . surprised even us," Zanuso wrote; "we had created a chair that was also a toy, which would stimulate a child's fantasy in his construction of castles, towers, trains, and slides. At the same time it was indestructible, and soft enough that it could not harm anyone yet too heavy to be thrown."[18]

Made by Kartell, Milan. Polyethylene. Height: 19 1/2" (49.5 cm). (Kartell, Milan.)

286
PETER MURDOCH
Spotty child's chair, 1963

Peter Murdoch's *Spotty* child's chair was the first piece of commercial furniture made of paper. Inexpensive and durable, the chair was sold as flat, brightly ornamented, laminated sheets in supermarkets and department stores to be assembled at home simply by folding along prescored lines and inserting the tabs to make a solid form. Designed when Murdoch was a student at the Royal College of Art in London in 1963 and brought to production the following year when he was in New York, *Spotty* was produced in limited numbers between 1964 and 1965 by the International Paper Corporation. Murdoch developed a second line of fiberboard furniture in 1967, which was marketed by Perspective Designs in London under the name *Those Things* and sold over seventy thousand pieces within the first six months.

Made by International Paper Corporation, New York. Screen-printed, polyethylene-coated, laminated kraft paper. Height: 20 1/4" (51.4 cm). (Victoria and Albert Museum, London.)

287
MARCO ZANUSO AND RICHARD SAPPER
Child's chair, 1964

The long period of gestation that preceded the design of this boldly sculptured and brilliantly colored child's

Made by Herman Miller, Basel. Fiberglass-reinforced poly-
ester. Height: 32 1/2" (82.5 cm). (Philadelphia Museum of
Art, puchased with funds contributed by Mr. and Mrs.
John W. Drayton.)

289
EERO AARNIO
Ball chair, 1965

Designers responded independently and personally to
a new environmental awareness in the 1960s and
1970s, some reaching out to make their work interact
with their surroundings and others creating complete
microcosms set apart from the world at large. Eero
Aarnio's *Ball* chair isolates its user within a large, low,
shiny sphere, blocking out both sight and sound from
all but a frontal direction (although full accessibility is
achieved as the fiberglass shell swivels on its steel
base). Its fully upholstered interior creates a hushed,
self-contained environment, calm and relaxing, an
escape from sensory overload; but it is not difficult to
understand why many owners had other plans for
their *Ball* chairs, fitting them out with audio equipment
to create stereo listening booths or, as the designer
himself did, with telephones.

Made by Asko, Lahti, Finland. Molded fiberglass and steel,
with fabric-covered foam upholstery. Height: 49" (124.5
cm); width of shell: 43 1/4" (109.8 cm). (Asko, Lahti,
Finland.)

288
VERNER PANTON
Chair, 1960–67

Borrowing a cantilever shape dating back to GERRIT
RIETVELD's *Zig-Zag* design of 1934 (no. 160) and
fulfilling EERO SAARINEN's goal of making furniture
completely of plastic (no. 243), Verner Panton's stacking chair was the first single-piece continuously constructed chair to enter large-scale production. Panton
conceived it in 1960 for fabrication in rigid polyurethane foam, but technical difficulties prevented its
successful manufacture in this material. The chair was
not adapted for commercial production until 1967,
when an injection-molded fiberglass-reinforced polyester version was marketed in six colors—white, black,
red, blue, yellow, and green. Saarinen's goal of eliminating legs was not the basis of Panton's innovative furniture forms. "I try to forget existing examples even
though they may be good, and concern myself above
all with the material," he remarked. "The result then
rarely has four legs, not because I do not wish to make
such a chair, but because the processing of materials
like wire or polyester calls for new shapes."[19]

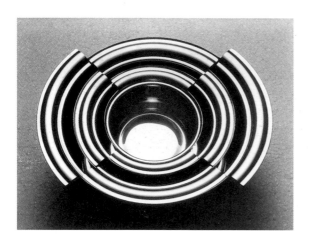

290
ROBERTO SAMBONET
Center Line cookware, 1964

In 1970 Roberto Sambonet was awarded the
Compasso d'Oro for the metal cookware he had been
designing for his family firm since 1954 (no. 231).
"These reveal technical ability, sensitivity of design, and
a capacity to see objects as a series," declared the jury.
"They also demonstrate a rational utilisation of space
and an appropriate use of the material employed.
Moreover, the artistic coherence which characterises
the packaging of the objects, and the way in which this
contributes to the creation of a unified image, has
been judged worthy of special mention."[20] This sum-
mation of Sambonet's achievement alludes both to the
overall consistency of his creative program and to his
organization of objects in systems, best seen in his
most integrated work, the concentric *Center Line* cookware. Composed of four deep pots and four shallow
ones of corresponding diameters, which can be used
either as lids or as separate pans or casseroles, the set

of graduated stainless-steel vessels was designed for
stovetop or oven cooking as well as storage and table
use. The pots are without handles so that they can
nest (the entire series takes up no more space than
the largest pot and lid) but are fitted with flaring seg-
mental flanges that can be used to lift and move the
pots and that add a formal complexity to the otherwise strictly logical design.

*Made by Sambonet, Vercelli, Italy. Stainless steel. Height of
largest pot (covered): 7 1/16" (18 cm). (Philadelphia
Museum of Art, gift of Sambonet.)*

291
BRUNO MATHSSON AND PIET HEIN
Superellipse table, 1964

The "superellipse" or flattened oval shape that the
Danish scientist Piet Hein derived mathematically in
1959 for the form of an urban plaza in Stockholm
inspired applications in other fields including household
objects and furniture. Bruno Mathsson sought Hein's
collaboration to use this newly created harmonious figure with the idea of arriving at a more compact table
design. Like the plaza, the superellipse table top offers
more surface area than a standard ellipse while avoiding right angles, so it is able to seat more people comfortably. Supporting the table is a second of Hein's
inventions refined in collaboration with Mathsson, a
self-clamping leg under tension in a slim V-shaped
form, which is inserted into the underside of the table
without tools and is easy to remove for shipping or
storage.

*Made by Karl Mathsson, Värnamo, Sweden. Birch and
chromed steel. Diameter: 35 7/16" (90 cm). (Mathsson
International AB.)*

292
GEORGE NELSON
Sling sofa, 1964

Like his *Marshmallow* sofa (no. 247), George Nelson's *Sling* sofa was designed to simplify the industrial manufacture of upholstered furniture by creatively using technology borrowed from other industries. Its modular rectangular structure of straight (front) and curved (side) tubular-steel sections was assembled into sofas of three- or four-seat lengths that give the impression of a light, continuously flowing frame— a conception derived from tubular-steel chairs of the 1920s. This was achieved by inserting chrome T-bar connections between the modular elements where the legs meet the frame and joining them almost invisibly with epoxy glue, a substance then not widely used in furniture manufacture but common in the airplane industry. The upholstery method was also new: the rounded leather-covered cushions were supported by a stretched-rubber (neoprene) platform bonded to metal hooks and attached to metal bars that screwed into the chrome frame. Because the back cushions rest against rubber straps within the angled frame the sofa has the appearance of a sling form, but with its firm platform construction the sling is actually a misnomer.

Made by Herman Miller Furniture Company, Zeeland, Michigan. Chromed steel and neoprene with leather-covered urethane-foam upholstery. Width: 87" (221 cm). (Herman Miller Inc., Zeeland, Michigan.)

293
ARNE JACOBSEN
Cylinda Line teapot, 1964–67

Arne Jacobsen's *Cylinda Line* represents the broadest and most commercially successful application of formalist principles for home consumption, a triumph of neofunctionalism for the mass market. The series based on the form of the cylinder included an extensive range of table- and cookware—from saucepans and coffeepots to tea strainers and ice tongs. Developed over a three-year period by the International Style architect Jacobsen in conjunction with its manufacturer, Stelton, the Cylinda Line featured a close design correlation among all elements and a consistency of details throughout, including logo and packaging. The semiautomated equipment and modern welding techniques used to create the pieces gave a rigorous precision to their production, the extremely high machine tolerances yielding sleek surfaces and crisp forms. Machine tooling also allowed the geometrical regularity of the thin-bodied stainless-steel wares to be maintained regardless of size. The set-off black nylon handles were likewise formally conceived, their dark rectangular outlines and interior arcs serving as foils for the shimmering cylindrical vessels.

Made by Stelton, Copenhagen. Stainless steel and nylon. Height: 4 3/8" (11 cm). (Philadelphia Museum of Art, gift of Stelton.)

of molded-plastic furniture made later in the decade (nos. 288, 311). Created for the Dutch manufacturer Artifort for whom Paulin had been working since 1958, his furniture had a tubular-metal frame over which rubber sheeting was tightly stretched and then covered with foam rubber. A completely presewn slipcover made of stretch fabric was then fitted over the form and attached at the base. The availability of natural and synthetic double-knit fabrics made Paulin's designs possible. Developed in Eastern Europe and first distributed commercially in the late 1950s, these stretch fabrics hugged his unusual forms tightly without any slack, achieving form-fitting upholstery even on his most daring of pieces, the *Ribbon* chair.

Made by Artifort, Maastricht, The Netherlands. Metal, rubber, and lacquered wood, with fabric-covered foam upholstery. 27⁹/₁₆ x 39³/₈ x 29¹/₈" (70 x 100 x 74 cm). (Artifort, Maastricht.)

294
JOE COLOMBO
Armchair, 1963–65

The simplest and most elegant of Joe Colombo's designs for mass production, this chair consists of three curved plywood elements slotted together, which can be easily assembled and disassembled by the user. Although the form of the chair presents a visual tour de force of continuous curves and countercurves, Colombo's objectives with this chair and in his other product designs were social and technological as well as stylistic. Here he strove to create an inexpensive, knockdown, "modern" chair for the middle-class market using up-to-date production methods. "The situation now is the exact opposite of the past when design was only sold in a few deluxe shops," he said. "Clients do not exist any more. Instead there are consumers, and we have to think in terms of mass producion."[21] Originally designed in 1963, the chair was in technical development for two years and produced by Kartell only in 1965.

Made by Kartell, Milan. Lacquered plywood. 23¹/₈ x 27³/₄ x 24³/₄" (58.7 x 70.5 x 62.9 cm). (Museum of Modern Art, New York.)

295
PIERRE PAULIN
Ribbon chair, 1965

In the early 1960s the French designer Pierre Paulin devised a method for constructing upholstered furniture with which he was able to create innovative sculptural shapes that could be fabricated completely by factory means; his designs anticipated the freer forms

296
OLIVIER MOURGUE
Djinn chaise longue, 1964–65

Olivier Mourgue's Djinn series of expressive, fully upholstered furniture followed a structural formula that had been used by PIERRE PAULIN: a steel skeleton webbed with rubber and tightly covered with nylon stretch jersey over polyester foam (no. 295). However, Mourgue's softly rounded sculptural shapes, which form the uninterrupted undulating span that animates this chaise longue, were more suggestive of a new attitude toward furniture design. "The good object," Mourgue wrote, "is very movable and displaceable; inventions and creations are light. It was in this spirit that I constructed my 'Djinn' seats. In these models . . . I was looking for several things: the use of new covering materials . . . but also lightness, so that one could carry it under one's arm."[22] This series was considered suffi-

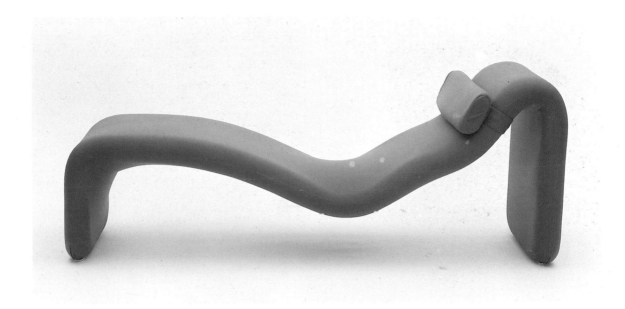

ciently futuristic to be used for the space-station interior in Stanley Kubrick's science fiction film *2001: A Space Odyssey* (1968), providing coloristic and curvilinear relief to an otherwise geometric and sterile vision of the future.

Made by Airborne, Tournus, France. Steel and rubber with nylon-covered polyester-foam upholstery. 25⁵/₈ x 68¹/₈ x 23⁵/₈" (65 x 173 x 60 cm). (Museum of Modern Art, New York, gift of George Tanier, Inc.)

297
WES WILSON
Poster for the Fillmore Auditorium, 1966

Wes Wilson's brilliant concert posters for the Fillmore Auditorium in San Francisco came at the beginning of a poster craze rivaled only by that of the art nouveau period. Print runs for individual posters rose from only a few hundred copies in 1966 to the tens of thousands by 1967; they were created not just for advertising but also for sale in newly opened "hippie" shops to a new breed of collector, and it was said that these concerts were actually financed by profits from the psychedelic posters. Wilson's compact, sinuous, freely drawn, and virtually indecipherable lettering recalls the art nouveau style and its typographic liberties. Made even more illegible by his use of intense, clashing, complementary colors, the red, flamelike letters in this poster suggest the liberated freneticism of the Fillmore's acid-rock concerts, this one by several almost-forgotten groups, including the Association, Along Comes Mary, and Quicksilver Messenger Service. Wilson drew inspiration for his Fillmore posters specifically from the Viennese artists ALFRED ROLLER, KOLOMAN MOSER,

and Gustav Klimt, whose work had been shown in a large art nouveau exhibition at the University Art Gallery in Berkeley in 1965. Following his lead, other California designers also borrowed from this aesthetic for the design of their own figurative and typographic posters.

Lithograph. 19¹¹/₁₆ x 13³/₄" (50 x 34.9 cm). (Museum of Modern Art, New York, gift of the designer.)

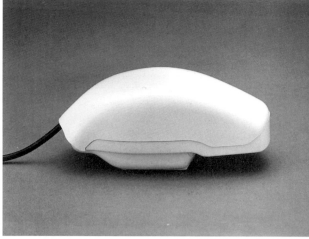

298
HENRY DREYFUSS ASSOCIATES
Trimline telephone, 1965

Until the battle over divestiture broke BELL TELEPHONE COMPANY's monopoly in 1984, American telephones were designed like no other consumer product, with a guaranteed sale and without concern for competition. Western Electric, a company owned by Bell Telephone, built the units to last and leased them to subscribers. New models were introduced very slowly, every ten to fifteen years, incorporating the results of research into sound transmission, circuitry, and user preference. At first purely an engineering concern, design was turned over in 1930 to an independent consultant, Henry Dreyfuss, who collaborated with Bell Laboratories on its successive standard telephones, including the *300* (1937), *500* (1950), and *Trimline* (1965) models. Small and more sculptural than the *500* model then in use, the *Trimline* was the first Bell telephone to incorporate a dial into the handset. The design was derived from extensive human-factors studies and field trials: five different models were tested between 1958 and 1963 using hundreds of Bell employees and then thousands of customers, whose reactions and preferences were considered in determining the form of each subsequent model. Weight emerged as a major consideration and the solution, which took the form of miniaturization, affected every aspect of the design: the dial was made smaller by eliminating the space between 1 and 0, lighter materials were used, and for the first time printed circuitry was introduced.

Made by Western Electric, New York, for Bell Telephone Company, New York. Plastic housing. Length: 8⁷/₁₆" (21.5 cm). (Philadelphia Museum of Art, gift of American Bell.)

299
MARCO ZANUSO AND RICHARD SAPPER
Grillo telephone, 1965

As the telephone changed from an anonymous instrument to an appliance adapted to individual needs and surroundings, Italtel, the Italian national telephone service, commissioned Marco Zanuso and Richard Sapper to design an alternative to its conventional model. With this provocatively molded, plastic *Grillo* (*Cricket*) telephone the two designers met the project requirements—greatly reduced dimensions and practical simplicity cast in a form that does not insistently advertise its function. Designed to establish a "friendly" relationship between object and user, like a person holding a small, talkative pet, and about half the size of the model then in use, this unit incorporates all necessary functions and fits comfortably into one hand. It was made as small as possible within the dictates of human anatomy—that is, allowing for the necessary span between earphone and mouthpiece. To do this the designers hinged elements together so that when the *Grillo* is not in use the earpiece-and-dial unit folds over the mouthpiece, which becomes the base of the instrument. To scale down the telephone, however, they had to move the calling function to a wall unit, a return to the system used earlier in the century and reintroduced in the *Ericofon* in 1954 (nos. 63, 239). The final hurdle, reducing the size of the dial, was attained with a solution parallel to that of HENRY DREYFUSS ASSOCIATES' *Trimline*, introduced the same year (no. 298).

Made by Italtel, Società Italiana Telecomunicazioni, Milan. ABS plastic housing. Height: 2³/₄" (7 cm); width: 3¹/₈" (8 cm); length (closed): 6⁵/₁₆" (16 cm). (Philadelphia Museum of Art, gift of Italtel.)

300
ROGER TALLON
Chair, 1965

The bizarre and menacing surface of Roger Tallon's chair, suggestive of an instrument of torture or a fakir's bed of nails, is ironic in its relationship to the sitter and brutalist in its use of industrial materials. This imaginative application of polyurethane comes from a designer for whom "rationalism is not the end of design" and "play, fantasy, humor, and eroticism are not forbidden."[23] The 2¹/₂-inch-thick upholstery is made of "egg-box" foam packing material with its papulous inner side turned out and its flat outer side glued to the cast-aluminum frame. Yet what seems so formidable is actually a firm but yielding surface. Tallon's series of aluminum furniture, comprising this chair, a stool, a table, and a bed, as well as a freestanding steel circular staircase, were sold by the Galerie Jacques Lacloche in Paris. The gallery was dedicated to making useful objects designed for series production by contemporary artists available to the public directly and relatively inexpensively.

Made by Jacques Lacloche, Paris. Aluminum and polyure-
  thane foam. 24 x 14¹⁵/₁₆ x 14¹⁵/₁₆" (61 x 38 x 38 cm).
  (Lacloche, Paris.)

301
TADANORI YOKOO
Poster for *Koshimaki Osen*, 1966

Tadanori Yokoo's best-known work, this poster was designed to announce the first performance of an underground theater troupe, the Jōkyō Gekijō, led by the dramatist, producer, and actor Juro Kara. Performed in the open, the play *Koshimaki Osen (Osen in Petticoats)* was deliberately controversial, even scandalous, in its content, style, and rejection of the orthodoxies of contemporary Japanese theater. Yokoo's poster expresses the visual agitation of the performance it promotes by combining garishly colored images and techniques from mass media, popular culture, and even cartoon strips in its densely packed space. The designer's use of such motifs as a peach-and-rose pattern from a penny matchbox cover, a rising sun, an awning from a tenement house, and a string of nude comic-book superwomen flying through the air outraged some Japanese critics who decried the poster's vulgarity and its rejection of the order and logic of prevailing rationalist design theories. Through such posters Yokoo became a popular symbol of protest in the 1960s, a cult hero for a generation of designers who were influenced and liberated by his disregard for convention, his Pop aesthetic, and his use of silkscreen and other printing techniques in collages of photographic elements and illustration.

Screen-print. 41¹/₂ x 29³/₈" (105.4 x 74.4 cm). (Museum of
  Modern Art, New York, gift of the artist.)

235

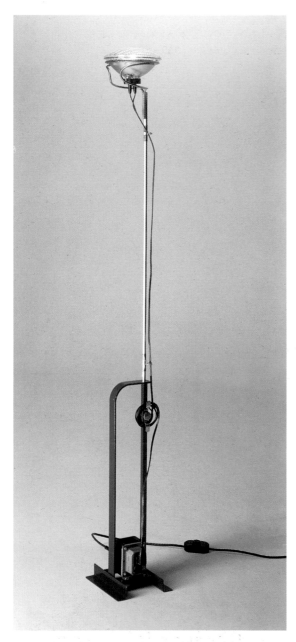

adjustable shaft by fishing-rod coils, the excess looped on a hook from its red base—all stabilized by the heavy transformer required for the bulb's use abroad. In contriving this lamp, the Castiglionis followed methods they used in previous designs, exploiting accessible new lighting technology as they did in their *Tubino* lamp of 1951 (no. 221) and employing an additive construction system as they did in their *Mezzadro* stool design of 1957 (no. 266), which was made of four disparate elements including a domesticated tractor seat.

Made by Flos, Brescia, Italy. Lacquered steel and nickel-plated brass. Height (extended): 78³/₄" (200 cm). (Flos, Brescia, Italy.)

303
GINO VALLE
Cifra 3 table clock, 1966

Using the same technology as the electro-mechanical signboards he devised with the Solari company's planning office for airports and train stations throughout the world, Gino Valle's *Cifra 3* plastic table clock indicates the time with numbers that flip over sequentially, the cylinder to which they are attached being turned by a battery-driven mechanism. The design focuses on legibility, employing large bold white ciphers (designed by Unimark International, the corporate graphic firm founded in 1965 by MASSIMO VIGNELLI and others) to indicate the hours and a lighter face for the minutes. The numbers are silhouetted against a dark ground and are readable at relatively long distances. Valle's series of clocks were models of clarity (his *Cifra 5* was awarded a Compasso d'Oro prize in 1956) and remained in the forefront of the market as the popularity of analog clocks gave way to digital timepieces.

Made by Solari & C., Udine, Italy. Plastic case. Length: 7¹/₁₆" (18 cm); diameter: 3³/₄" (9.5 cm). (Solari & C., Udine, Italy.)

302
ACHILLE CASTIGLIONI AND PIER GIACOMO CASTIGLIONI
Toio floor lamp, 1962

An assemblage of "found" industrial components, Achille and Pier Giacomo Castiglioni's *Toio* floor lamp was one of the most daring design conceptions of the decade. It bespeaks a total denial of accepted principles of formal design, suggesting in very sophisticated terms not that form follows function but that function itself *is* form. Albeit painted and polished, the lamp leaves all its working parts exposed: its bare flood-lamp newly imported into Italy from the United States; its visible electrical connections; and its wire held to the

MARCO ZANUSO AND RICHARD SAPPER
Black 12 television, 1969

The insistent and disturbing presence of the blank television screen, felt especially by the first generation of owners, generated a design problem most often solved by hiding the set in cabinetry. Marco Zanuso took other approaches, however, considering his early sets not as furniture but as equipment that could easily be stored when not in use (such as his compact *Doney 14* for Brionvega of 1962). His *Black 12* model, however, designed in collaboration with Richard Sapper, was conceived as a permanent enriching addition to its environment. Like a piece of contemporary sculpture reduced to the simplest sleekest form, the appliance was transmogrified into a minimalist cube. Sheathed in transparent black plastic, it was in no way intrusive since the screen was revealed only when the set was turned on. A version from 1973, *Black 17*, refined the elegance of this design even further, with controls and appurtenances more fully disguised as part of the black housing and the set's model name less obvious when moved to the top of the set.

Made by Brionvega, Milan. Methacrylite housing. Width: 12⁵/₈" (32.3 cm). (Museum of Modern Art, New York, gift of Brionvega.)

304
MASSIMO VIGNELLI
Compact table service, 1964

When Massimo Vignelli's *Compact* stacking tableware was awarded a Compasso d'Oro in 1964, the jury commended the modular service for its compact solution to stacking, its concentration of functions in simple forms, and the "nobility" of a design that openly communicated its functional characteristics. Vignelli also designed its packaging, which featured the spare graphic presentation for which he is now best known and a full-size outlined drawing of the set as if in a blueprint. The table service was produced for only a short time in Italy because its manufacturer went out of business, but several years later, about 1970, it was revived for production and manufactured with the original molds by Alan Heller, who had just established a housewares firm in New York. As his first product it was marketed in the United States as the *Max 1* dinnerware set, but later was sold as *Hellerware*. Vignelli and his wife, Lella, designed coordinated cups for the service in 1970, mugs in 1972, and a pitcher in 1979.

Made by Articoli Plastici Elettrici, Milan. Melamine. Diameter of dinner plate: 9³/₄" (24.8 cm). (Vignelli Designs, New York.)

306
DE PAS, D'URBINO, LOMAZZI
Blow armchair, 1967

De Pas, D'Urbino, Lomazzi's **Blow** chair was the first completely inflatable piece of furniture to be commercially produced. Totally without a supporting structure, it depended solely on air for its form and cushioning—and its transparent plastic material, sealed with the use of high frequency waves, made this design innovation immediately apparent. While the idea of collapsible furniture may have been appealing—especially in an era of flexibility when structure and formality were becoming suspect—this and the other inflatable plastic chairs that soon followed had major drawbacks: they were uncomfortable, gave the impression of being unstable, were hot to sit on for more than a short time, and liable to slow leaks and blowouts.

Made by Zanotta, Nova Milanese, Italy. PVC plastic. Height: 23⁵/₈" (60 cm). (Museum of Modern Art, New York, gift of the manufacturer.)

307
GAETANO PESCE
Lady armchair, 1969

An "anti-armchair" according to the original sales brochure, Gaetano Pesce's *Lady* armchair from the Up series is made of polyurethane foam without any rigid internal structure; it is able to support a body and to maintain its imprecisely rounded, nontraditional shape, however, because of the high density of the molded foam. What distinguished the six designs in the Up series from other unstructured furniture systems of the same period was the application of plastics technology to the concerns of packaging and transport. After the foam chairs were completely formed and upholstered in tightly stretched jersey, they were totally flattened between vinyl sheets by withdrawing all the air from the foam in a pressurized vacuum chamber and then heat-sealing the sheets; this process made storage and shipping simple and economical, offering a unique solution to one of the most problematic aspects of the furniture industry. After the vinyl package was opened, air entered to fill up each of the polyurethane cells and return the chair to its original, fully upholstered form like an inflatable structure (although the action was not reversible). The continuous unwrapping and inflating of Pesce's Up chairs at the opening of the ninth Milan furniture salon in 1969 was compared by the critic for *Domus* to a contemporary art "happening."[24]

Made by C & B Italia, Como, Italy. Nylon-covered polyurethane foam. Height: 26³/₄" (67.9 cm). (Courtesy Aldo Ballo, Milan.)

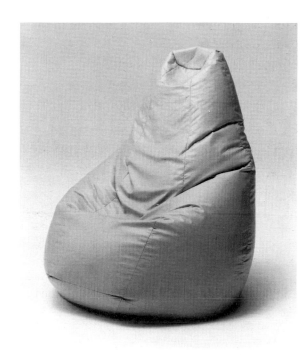

It assumes the form and position of the body resting on it, with its original shape being unrecognizable when it is in use. Thus it is an ambiguous, mimetic, antiformalist object, and because of these characteristics it can be a part of any environment." Small and light, it can also be "loaded into a car and transported anywhere, to a meadow, under a tree, for sleeping, for reading, for making love."[25]

Made by Zanotta, Milan. Leather-covered polystyrene. Width: 31 1/2" (80 cm). (Zanotta, Nova Milanese, Italy.)

308
GATTI, PAOLINI, TEODORO
Sacco seating, 1968–69

If one work can be said to have been created in the spirit of 1968, a year student demonstrators were demanding freedom in every field from education and politics to lifestyle, it would be the *Sacco* (*Sack*) seating unit. A structureless bag filled with polystyrene pellets, this "chair" is a completely nondeterministic alternative to traditional interior furnishings and one designed to be sold at a very low cost. "Universal," as described by the designers in their promotional material, it is "adaptable to any body, in any position, on any surface. . . .

309
JOE COLOMBO
Additional seating system, 1968

The shrinking size of postwar living spaces propelled Joe Colombo's efforts during the 1960s to find flexible furniture systems. Shown in prototype at the *XIV Triennale* exhibition in Milan in 1968 and put into commercial production the following year, his *Additional* system is composed of standardized jersey-covered slabs of polyurethane foam in different heights that can be pegged to rectangular metal bases in infinitely extendable lengths to create a variety of forms. Colombo applied the same principle of composition by segments to his *Tube* chair of 1969, made of plastic cylinders in different diameters that could be hooked together in any sequence. Chairs, chaises, sofas, and ottomans created from both systems were varied and grouped by the user.

Made by Sormani, Como, Italy. Metal with jersey-covered polyurethane-foam upholstery. Height of tallest section: 26 3/8" (67 cm). (Studio Joe Colombo, Milan.)

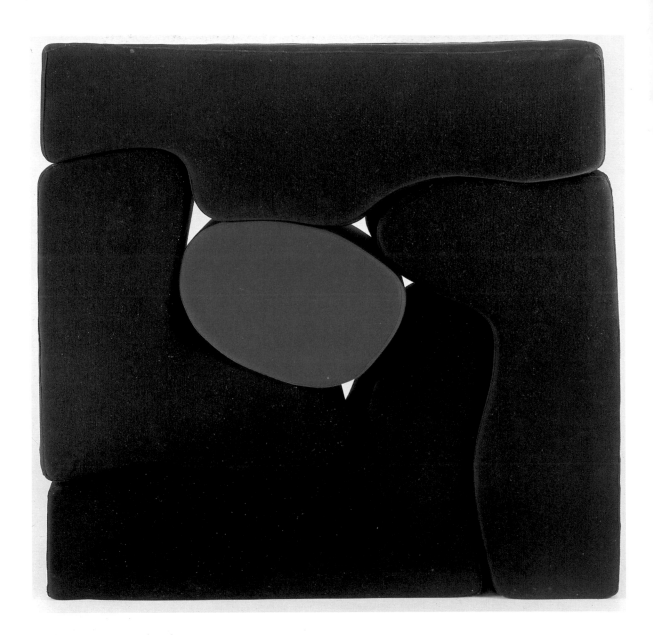

310
ROBERTO SEBASTIAN MATTA
Malitte seating system, 1966

The surrealist painter Roberto Matta's *Malitte* seating system, with its unsupported foam cushions, was one of the earliest conceptions to disregard totally the forms and structure of traditional furniture. The free-form cushions, upholstered in strong saturated colors, are at once sculpture and furniture. Fitted together loosely, they form an upright square for storage and decoration; separated, the units provide five differently shaped seating elements for flexible use in an open unstructured environment. The *Malitte* system was produced by Dino Gavina; the Italian manufacturer, who introduced Matta to furniture design, encouraged new approaches to designing for mass production and advocated universal applications within a variety of interior spaces.

Made by Gavina, Foligno, Italy. Fabric-covered polyurethane foam. Height (stacked): 63" (160 cm). (Philadelphia Museum of Art, gift of Mr. and Mrs. Les J. Cranmer.)

311
LEONARDI-STAGI, ARCHITETTI
Rocking chair, 1967

The ultimate icon in plastic, Leonardi-Stagi's equipoised rocking chair is the formalist triumph of the sophisticated Italian designers who explored the capabilities of this material in the 1960s. Apparently unsupported, the form of this gravity-defying chair implies that its syn-

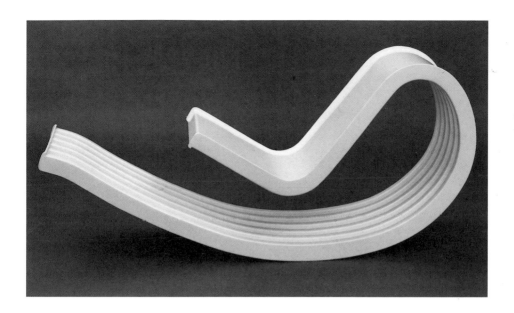

thetic material has extraordinary strength and support-ive ability. Actually, simple molded fiberglass is not strong enough to maintain this daring structure rigidly, with or without the added weight of the user. The boldly expressive shape, conceived on paper and worked out in thick plywood models, could only be reproduced successfully by adding a series of fiberglass ribs; these strengthened the form longitudinally and kept it rigid without the material becoming too thick, the chair too heavy, or the silhouette ungainly.

Made by Arredamenti Arturo G. Bellato & C., Scorze, Italy, for Elco, Venice. Fiberglass. Length: 68⁷/₈" (174.9 cm). (Museum of Modern Art, New York, gift of Stendig, Inc.)

312
JØRN UTZON
Chair and footstool, 1969

With its emphatic, undulating form, Jørn Utzon's exu-berantly sculptural lounge chair molded of plywood and covered with foam cushioning appears to float above its chromed-steel substructure. Accommodating additional pieces that can be linked to create a sofa or a wider seating unit, the design reflects Utzon's con-cept of additive architecture, which he applied most notably in the construction of his flamboyant opera house in Sydney, Australia. Utzon's irregular shapes demonstrated an organic, expressionistic alternative to the geometric angularity of conventional modular sys-tems.

Made by Fritz Hansen, Allerød, Denmark. Plywood and chrome-plated steel with fabric-covered foam upholstery. (Fritz Hansen, Allerød, Denmark.)

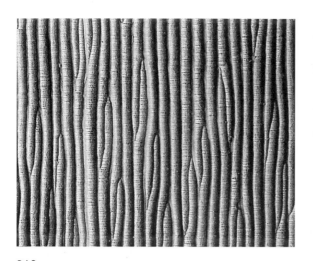

313
SHEILA HICKS
Badagara fabric, 1966–67

An internationally celebrated weaver of complex, sculptural wall hangings, Sheila Hicks has collaborated with craftspeople in developing countries to help them revitalize and modernize their production so that it is more compatible with contemporary design. At the invitation of a large handweaving factory in South India, she designed a range of twenty furnishing fabrics called the Kerala collection, each named after a nearby village and incorporating the unique aspects of local manufacture—their cotton threads, native colors, and traditional factory methods. For *Badagara*, Hicks introduced very thick wefts made up of numerous yarns not unlike those of her own monumental weavings, devising a double-sided fabric with a bold relief effect. One of the benefits of handweaving was that each piece had the handcrafted appearance and individualized production technique that the firm emphasized in its marketing program; *Badagara*, for example, was woven as a broad seamless fabric ten feet wide by several weavers sitting side by side at a large loom. The Kerala collection brought the factory substantial international orders, and it was followed two years later by Hicks's Monsoon collection, which included silk fabrics as well.

Made by Commonwealth Trust, Calicut, India. Cotton. Width: 120" (304.8 cm). (Sheila Hicks.)

314
ISAMU NOGUCHI
Akari hanging lamp, c. 1968

Parallel to but independent of his other ventures into lighting (no. 198), Isamu Noguchi began creating paper lamps based on traditional Japanese folding lanterns during the 1950s. He first saw the traditional lamps being made in the town of Gifu in Japan in 1951 and at that time, at the request of its mayor, provided several new designs to reinvigorate the local industry, for which the town was well known. "I thought lanterns could be luminous sculptures," he explained, "and set about to integrate the use of electricity and methods of support into their structure, to eliminate the traditional wooden rims (Wa), and to utilize Mino or mulberry bark paper which best diffuses the light to the surface—in sum, to ennoble and renew the use of lanterns. These I named Akari, meaning light." During the 1960s the artist's designs took on more independent sculptural shapes, less rigid and no longer symmetrical, like this monumental long spiral lantern. "To me," he remarked, "they were always beyond commercial or industrial design—a medium of art."[26]

Made for Akari Associates, Long Island City, New York. Mulberry-bark paper, bamboo, and wire. Height: 63" (160 cm). (Philadelphia Museum of Art, gift of the designer.)

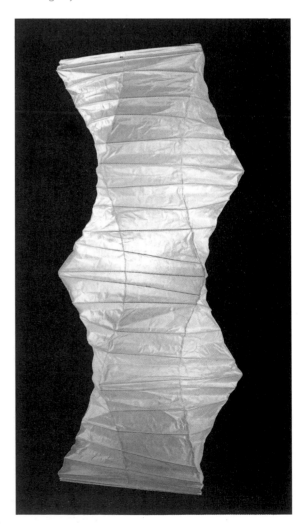

315
TIMO SARPANEVA
Bolero fabric, 1968

Timo Sarpaneva's *Bolero* fabric was produced by a printing technique he devised first for his Ambiente line of decorative papers and then applied to textiles. The Ambiente method employed a rotary perfecting press much like that used for printing newspapers but without the intervention of plates or stencils in what was essentially a type of painting by machine. By positioning each of the fountains of the press individually, Sarpaneva was able to direct and regulate the flow of ink to create soft, constantly varied, and theoretically endless abstract patterns, a process he described as "industrial monotypes." With as many as sixty ink nozzles available, just as many colors could be printed, unlike conventional production methods in which only a few colors could be printed at one time. Because the material was printed on both sides, ink saturation was complete, making the colors more intense, colorfast, and resistant to fading. The economies of Ambiente production were also far reaching: start-up costs were minimal because no plates were required, new designs could be readily implemented, and printing expenses were lowered because no time was lost in stopping and starting presses to change plates and inks. This method could only produce amorphous, abstract designs, however, and thus its application was somewhat limited.

Made by Tampella, Tampere, Finland. Printed cotton. Width: 51" (129.5 cm). (Jack Lenor Larsen, Inc.)

316
LIVIO CASTIGLIONI AND GIANFRANCO FRATTINI
Boalum lamp, 1969

Aptly named *Boalum*, Livio Castiglioni's and Gianfranco Frattini's luminous snakelike fixture can repose on a floor, curl up on a shelf, or hang from a ceiling or wall, theoretically forming an endless lamp since the separate over six-foot-long tubular elements can be joined end to end *ad infinitum*. Made of translucent PVC plastic industrial tubing held in place by metal rings and containing many small bulbs, it has none of the cold glaring qualities usually associated with industrial materials. Rather, *Boalum* is soft, glowing, and romantic and demonstrates that industrial components used in novel ways can go beyond the technological stereotype to produce entirely original imagery.

Made by Artemide, Milan. PVC plastic and metal. Length: 78³/₄" (200 cm). (Philadelphia Museum of Art, gift of Artemide Inc.)

317
ENZO MARI
Pago Pago vase, 1968

The refined and carefully produced plastics of the Milanese manufacturer Danese were heralded for their formal and decorative qualities as much as for their utility (no. 270), challenging on an aesthetic level residual negative attitudes toward a material previously considered of little value. Enzo Mari, when he was first asked by the firm to design a flower vase, questioned whether a mass-produced plastic object could be a commercially viable alternative to the ornamental receptacles usually chosen for this purpose. When he did undertake the commission, Mari approached the design process from a rationalist point of view, exploiting in his *Pago-Pago* vase the strong colors and glowing finish that could be achieved with plastic. His goal was to create vessels for both small and large bouquets and to join the two in one aesthetically satisfying shape; to that end he analyzed various types and sizes of flowers and bouquets and arrived at a double vase that could be used from both sides. Its unusual form— a cone shape with a narrow circular mouth opening on one end and a second wide-mouthed vase wrapped around it that opens on the other—was determined by these functional requirements. With the two shapes sharing interior walls, it could also be manufactured economically in a simple two-part mold.

Made by Danese, Milan. ABS plastic. Height: 11¹³/₁₆"
(30 cm). (Danese, Milan.)

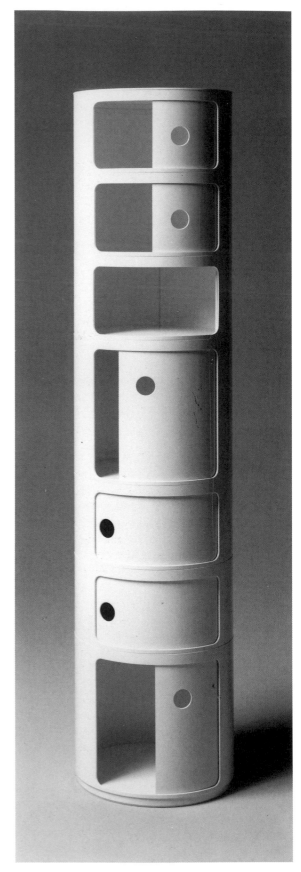

318
ANNA CASTELLI FERRIERI
Round-Up storage system, 1969

Anna Castelli Ferrieri's stylish *Round-Up* storage system refined the concept of free-standing modular units that she explored in a square system in 1967. This was the first furniture to be made of injection-molded ABS, an impact-resistant plastic blend with a shiny but soft surface. Available in the 1950s in the form of sheets or tubes, ABS was adapted to injection molding only in the 1960s; the fully industrialized manufacturing process combined with the material's physical qualities soon made it the most popular plastic for furniture, which could now be produced on a large scale and at a low cost. At the same time the modular system established a completely new, flexible type of household equipment—light, informal, moveable elements that functioned as seats, tables, or storage compartments, and could be put on wheels. The units were used separately or stacked to provide a storage "tower," introducing a new type of snap-together assembly that was accomplished without tools or screws of any kind.

Made by Kartell, Milan. ABS plastic. Diameter: 16 1/2" (42 cm). (Kartell, Milan.)

319
ETTORE SOTTSASS, JR. (WITH PERRY A. KING)
Valentine typewriter, 1969

Having used color and referential shapes to humanize the office equipment he had designed for Olivetti since 1957, Ettore Sottsass, Jr., further personalized it with the *Valentine* typewriter he designed with Perry A. King for use at home. Rejecting the cool efficient image of Olivetti's earlier portable models, he conceived a typewriter that would visually suggest an alternate context and be appreciated less for its function than for its novel design—of orange-red molded plastic accented by two yellow buttons on the ribbon spools ("like the two eyes of a robot"). It was made, he said, "for use any place except in an office, so as not to remind anyone of monotonous working hours, but rather to keep amateur poets company on quiet Sundays in the country or to provide a highly colored object on a table in a studio apartment. An anti-machine machine, built around the commonest mass-produced mechanism, the works inside any typewriter, it may also seem to be an unpretentious toy."[27]

Made by Ing. C. Olivetti & C., Milan. ABS plastic housing. 13 1/4 x 12" (34 x 31 cm). (Ing. C. Olivetti & C., Milan.)

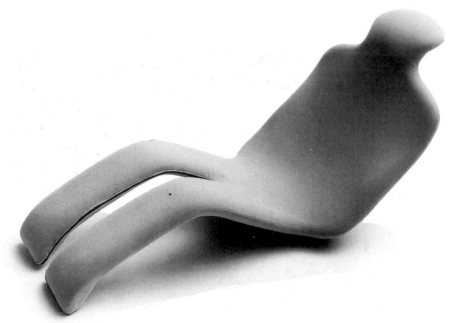

320
OLIVIER MOURGUE
Bouloum chaise longue, 1968

With their anthropomorphic outlines, Olivier Mourgue's witty *Bouloum* lounge chairs populate and humanize interior spaces. Based on the silhouette of one of Mourgue's friends and called by his childhood nickname, these upholstered chairs are engaging and amusing; they are light, easily moveable, and can be stacked and rearranged at will, a factor well suited to the neutral, flexible interiors that Mourgue conceived as the environment for his designs. The jersey-covered foam exterior follows that of Mourgue's earlier Djinn furniture series (no. 296), but in this figurative furniture the earlier interior metal frame construction is replaced with a molded-plastic shell, which can also be used without upholstery out of doors. *Bouloum* forms were the thematic feature of the French pavilion at the *World's Fair* in Osaka in 1970, where they served not only for seating in auditoriums and cafes but also stood vertically like attendants displaying directional and informational signage.

Made by Airborne, Tournus, France. Plastic with nylon-covered polyurethane upholstery. Length: 57" (144.8 cm). (Philadelphia Museum of Art, gift of Arcona Corporation.)

321
ARCHIZOOM ASSOCIATI
Mies armchair, 1969

In giving this chair the name *Mies* at a time when the principles and formal values of modern design were being seriously questioned, the alternative design group Archizoom made it clear that they meant to challenge the past. Using the materials and the geometry preferred by such functionalist designers as LUDWIG MIES VAN DER ROHE, they created a chair that is rational in the uncompromising economy of its structure—a sheet of rubber stretched between two wedge-shaped chrome supports—but is paradoxical in the obfuscation of its function. With a cushion for the head and an accompanying stool for the feet, the chair is provided with traditional comforts, although the slanting rubber surface confounds our expectations of an armchair by appearing uninviting and unyielding. In fact Archizoom provided a fully supportive and flexible seat, which returns to its original shape after the user is gone. The *Mies* chair was introduced at the ninth furniture salon in Milan in 1969, a particularly fertile moment for the showing of innovative designs in Italy.

Made by Poltronova, Pistoia, Italy. Chromed metal and rubber, with upholstered Dacron. $31 \frac{1}{2} \times 29 \frac{1}{8} \times 51 \frac{1}{2}$" (80 x 74 x 131 cm). (Poltronova, Pistoia, Italy.)

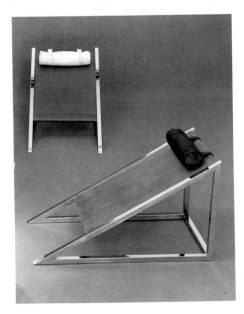

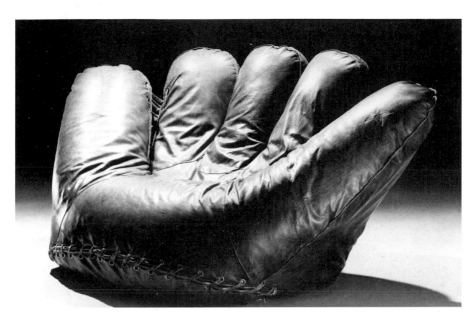

322
DE PAS, D'URBINO, LOMAZZI
Joe chair, 1970

Virtually anyone in Italy in 1970 would have caught the allusion of the *Joe* baseball-glove chair to New York Yankee centerfielder Joe Dimaggio, for as the husband of the movie star Marilyn Monroe, whose fame continued to grow even after her death in 1962, Dimaggio had become an international celebrity. A faithful replica of a baseball mitt down to the label and the player's autograph (here the signatures of its three Italian designers), the leather glove-chair is disarmingly out of context and out of scale; in these aspects it follows the formula of the American Pop art movement, which had first been introduced to Italy at the Venice *Biennale* of 1964, where the work of Claes Oldenburg, Jim Dine, Jasper Johns, and Robert Rauschenberg was shown.

Made by Poltronova Pistoia, Italy. Leather-upholstered polyurethane. Width: 65³/4" (167 cm). (Poltronova, Pistoia, Italy.)

323
BARBARA BROWN
Spiral fabric, 1970

Countering a mid-nineteenth-century dictum, still generally accepted in the 1960s, which declared that fabrics should be conceived as flat patterns, Barbara Brown created oversize illusionistic designs for printed cottons in the style of anonymous technical drawings, many based on mechanical elements. Her supergraphic *Spiral*, a seemingly solid screwlike column delineated solely with parallel lines, rises endlessly as if it were part of a great visionary architectural drawing. Printed in black and white, it won Britain's Council of Industrial Design Award in 1970 along with a second textile, *Automation*, a monochrome gearlike image. Both were produced by Heal Fabrics, whose designs were repeatedly commended by the Design Council during this period for their innovative designs and the virtuosity of their printing.

Made by Heal Fabrics, London. Printed cotton. Width: 48" (122 cm). (Private collection.)

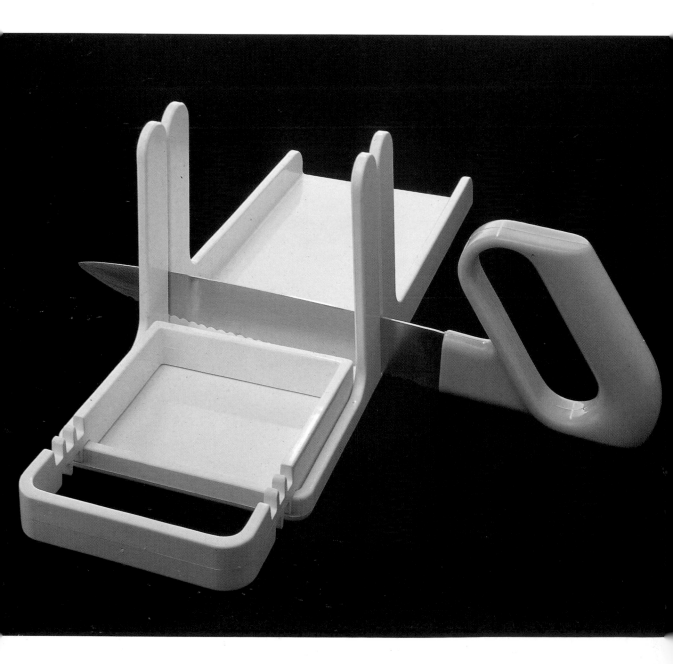

Chapter Eight
Responsible Design 1970–1980

A growing concern for the environment forced designers in the 1970s
to view design as an integral part of wider ecological problems, and to
adopt methodologies that ranged from a deeper consideration of
human needs to a more sophisticated application of technology. The
deterioration of the environment appeared to have reached such a
degree that applying environmental design and planning on a massive
scale seemed to many a matter of survival. While during the 1960s
most industrialized countries had developed some kind of environmental control program, the epicenter of these efforts was located in
the United States. In 1970 the Environmental Protection Agency (EPA)
was created with the power to set and enforce pollution standards,
conduct research, and assist state and local governments in pollution
control; on Earth Day that year, twenty million Americans participated
in antipollution demonstrations. In June 1972, at the Stockholm
Conference on the Human Environment, the United Nations autho-
rized a program to coordinate international environmental activities.
After the conference, Britain's *Architectural Review* editorialized that "as
uniquely qualified individuals in the struggle to improve man's surroundings," architects and designers must seize the opportunities
offered by the ecological movement.[1] The most vociferous designer-
environmental activist was Victor Papanek, an American who took the
design profession to task for fostering planned obsolescence and
impermanence in a world of overproduction and undernourishment in
which the most outward and visible sign of ecological crisis was the
alarming spread of indestructible waste. Attacking the "twin concepts
of 'designed aesthetics' and designed obsolescence" on which the
American "annual model change" is based, in his seminal book *Design
for the Real World* (1972), Papanek complained that "industry, hand-in-
hand with advertising and marketing, teaches us to look for and recognize these superficial changes, to expect them, and ultimately to
demand them. Real changes—basic changes—mean retooling or
rebuilding; in our present system the costs of this are prohibitively
high. . . . Thus the vital working parts of a mechanism (the guts of a
toaster, for instance) will remain unchanged for years while surface finish, exterior embellishments, control mechanisms and skin color and
texture undergo yearly mutations."[2] To Papanek, design and industry
standards had to be shifted from the purely quantitative to a qualitative
approach more in harmony with people and their basic needs.
"Design, if it is to be ecologically responsible and socially responsive,"
he wrote, "must be revolutionary and radical (going back to the roots)

On Earth Day in 1970, twenty
million Americans demonstrated
against the destruction of the
environment.

opposite:
Maria Benktzon and Sven-Eric
Juhlin, Knife and cutting frame,
1974 (no. 333).

249

in the truest sense. It must dedicate itself to nature's 'principle of least effort,' in other words, minimum inventory for maximum diversity . . . or doing the most with the least. That means consuming less, using things longer, recycling materials, and probably not wasting paper printing books such as this."[3] Arguing against the unnecessary duplication of products, Papanek estimated, for example, that "cassette-type tape recorders now come in nearly 40 models. All of these are battery powered (with optional power cords); they all use the same interchangeable tape cassettes, are nearly identical in size and weight, possess identical 'guts'. . . . The casing (or 'skin') of these recorders is the identical black, or sometimes gray, plastic. . . . Nonetheless, they are priced from $22.95 to $149.50."[4] Like other consumer electronics, these were styled for different market echelons—from the low range described by Papanek, which featured chromium, aluminum, and "decorator" colored cases; to the upper-mid-range, which included extra (non-working) control knobs (approaching what the critic Reyner Banham labeled "radio machismo"; no. 348); to the top range, distinguished by a nearly complete absence of chrome parts and a deliberately unostentatious, anonymous, professional appearance (no. 340). Such variety and overabundance seemed particularly unpalatable from the point of view of the underdeveloped and Third World countries where Papanek and other designers volunteered their skills.

Many other designers shared Papanek's concerns although they differed on means to the same end. At the International Design Conference in Aspen in 1970, student activists polemically "forced the conference to vote on a twelve-point resolution covering every current 'problem' from abortion to Vietnam and the abandonment of design for profit."[5] In England, designer and educator Misha Black reported that the Design and Industries Association, celebrating its Diamond Jubilee in 1975, "now concerns itself more with materials and energy resources than with the form and decoration of artefacts; aesthetics have been deposed by social responsibility; its old slogan 'Fitness for Purpose' was replaced, at a recent conference, by 'Fitness for Need.' The majority of students of industrial design choose those projects which are socially desirable, which serve world needs, as they visualize them, rather than encourage the proliferation of consumer products. The Design Council balances its responsibility for consumer products by its involvement in engineering design per se."[6] In the 1960s, in fact, a series of criteria had been introduced by the Council of Industrial Design to ensure that products accepted for exhibition at the Design Centre in London satisfied the consumer's practical needs. Performance headed the list of desiderata and aesthetics came near the bottom: "A. Performance (Does it work well?) B. Safety (Is it safe to use in all likely circumstances?) C. Construction (Is it robust and well made?) D. Ergonomics (Is it well designed for human use: comfortable, convenient, proportioned for human contact?) E. Aesthetics (Does it look good?) F. Cost (Does it cost what people are prepared to pay for it?)"[7] Britain's Design Council gave awards to certain industrial light fittings in 1974 for their "economy, safe and easy mounting and servicing, and minimal maintenance," and to wall coverings that exploited "the

ON PAGE 23 IN THE "SEATING" SECTION OF THIS BOOK, WE HAVE FULLY DESCRIBED ARCHITECT FRANK GEHRY'S "EASY EDGES" MATERIAL. ABOVE IS A DINING TABLE SEATING SIX AND ITS ACCOMPANYING CHAIRS. THESE PIECES ARE ALSO DESIGNED AND MARKETED BY GEHRY'S FIRM IN SANTA MONICA. THE TABLE SELLS FOR ABOUT $100 — [IT IS SO WELL STRUCTURED THAT IT CAN SUPPORT ABOUT 1000 POUNDS], THE CHAIRS ARE LESS THAN $30 EACH.

THIS IS A CASE WHERE THE UNUSUAL SOUND-ABSORBING PROPERTIES, AT THE SOURCE, OF THIS MATERIAL COME TO BE VERY HANDY IN REDUCING THE CLATTER OF DISHES.

WE SHOW IT HERE BOTH AS AN EXCELLENT EXAMPLE OF DESIGN MADE FROM "WASTE", WHICH YOU MIGHT BUY, AS WELL AS A CONCEPT OF LAMINATION FROM WHICH YOU MIGHT DEVELOP YOUR OWN DESIGN IDEAS.

The 1973 book *Nomadic Furniture* offered examples of furniture that could be made at low cost using simple technologies.

practical, fire-resistant, and acoustic properties of wool."[8] Similarly, the magazine *Industrial Design*, in its annual reviews of American products, commended a radio designed for the blind and an educational ecology kit (1970) along with a variety of products that were less extravagant in their use of materials and energy (1976); the publication also argued that furniture design should be more responsive to human anatomy and work habits (1977).[9]

Public concern over the environment reached crisis proportions in 1973 when Arab countries stopped selling oil to the United States and other nations and the dream of an endless supply of low-cost energy came to an abrupt end. The Arab oil embargo proved that the availability of fossil fuels was uncertain and underscored the urgent need to conserve the earth's dwindling natural resources. Conservation and abstinence were proposed as alternatives to resource depletion and the idea of simply producing and consuming less was supported by such strategies as recycling materials, increasing the lifespan of durable goods, and substituting renewable for non-renewable resources. Throughout 1973 and 1974 the cost of fuel—coal, oil, natural gas, and gasoline—continued to rise, and shortages loomed in various parts of the world. This led in 1975 to worldwide recession and inflation. A similar crisis occurred again in 1979 when revolution disrupted oil exports from Iran.

The energy crisis directly affected all of the consumer product industries but most directly the plastics industry. Derived from fossil fuels then in short supply—from oil as well as natural gas and coal—plastics were no longer economically viable as they had been in the 1960s. With the price of oil quadrupling between 1974 and 1979, thermoplastics rose correspondingly in price; other materials such as metals that involved expensive energy-intensive refining processes also became more costly.

Until the energy crisis, new and experimental domestic uses of plastic materials continued to be made widely in Italy just as they had in the 1960s, including the *Serpentone* sofa by CINI BOERI, which developed a natural outward "skin" in the production process when foaming polyurethane came into contact with a hot mold (no. 326). Such innovative designs were celebrated in 1972 at the Museum of Modern Art in New York with the exhibition *Italy: The New Domestic Landscape*, which also featured a series of experimental environments that encouraged, among other things, "exploration into the potentialities of synthetic materials and fibers."[10] Several radical design groups included in the exhibition rejected the whole idea of the designed environment, proposing such conceptual alternatives as an empty room to allow the inhabitant maximum flexibility (SUPERSTUDIO) and a mirrored cube to simulate existence without consumer products (ARCHIZOOM ASSOCIATI). Other designers sought more practical alternatives to complex high energy materials and industrial processes, such as the use of readily available, humble materials and the recycling of industrial wastes. As Papanek graphically demonstrated in the self-help book *Nomadic Furniture* (1973), technology does not necessarily provide superior means of production; what really matters, he explained, is that the means and materials selected should be appropriate to the task. Papanek particularly admired a new furniture material that the American FRANK O. GEHRY developed by laminating layers of corrugated cardboard (no. 327). He described Gehry's work as "an excellent example of design made from 'waste,' which you might buy, as well as a concept of lamination from which you might develop your own design ideas."[11]

Papanek's utopian faith in alternative processes that could reshape the environment and transform society by concentrating on practical fundamentals was realized in vernacular, anonymous "anti-" designs without aesthetic intentions. Subscribing to the convention that technology is neutral, other designers similarly rejected individual expressionism and endorsed the social and economic benefits of using undisguised industrial materials and "found" objects in their designs. As in *Nomadic Furniture*, the underlying premise of this approach was that users could eventually engage in design themselves, assembling industrial objects in high-tech fabrications like the scaffolding in BRUNO MUNARI's *Cockpit* environment (no. 325) or simple boarded furniture, for example in Riccardo Dalisi's experiments with "poor technology" for Global Tools (1973) and in ENZO MARI's *Proposal for Self-Design* (1974).

A late form of functionalism distinguished by novel forms and a special attitude toward materials, this pragmatic "engineering" approach endorsed honesty of expression and economy of means. When it came to the technical equipment revolutionized by advances in miniaturization, however, the ideal of forms displaying the logic of functions became virtually impossible, for those functions were now performed at a scale impractical for human manipulation. Electronics manufacturers everywhere were vying to produce the smallest lightest consumer products. The first pocket-size electronic calculator, by Britain's CLIVE SINCLAIR, included a 7,000-transistor integrated circuit, the most complex then available for commercial application (no. 339); SONY CORPORATION's *Walkman* personal stereo cassette player produced clean unwavering sound even when the user was moving because it included a miniaturized counterbalance mechanism that canceled out vibration and changes in position (no. 342). Designers of consumer electronics were required to provide suitable containers for the engineering wizardry within, and Misha Black among others proposed redefining industrial design as a "specialized activity within the totality of engineering design" and educating designers "in engineering technology as architecture is based on the technology of the building industry."[12] Arthur Drexler, curator of design at the Museum of Modern Art, had already pointed out that, in appliance design, "What is inside the box is what is really interesting. . . . It may even be that the proper subject of good design is the machine itself."[13] To house the high technology of the *Beogram* turntable and other related Bang & Olufsen audio products, the Danish designer JACOB JENSEN created a black box so discreet in appearance and so lacking in articulated detail (even the controls disappear into the overall design) that it seemed as anonymous as any indus-

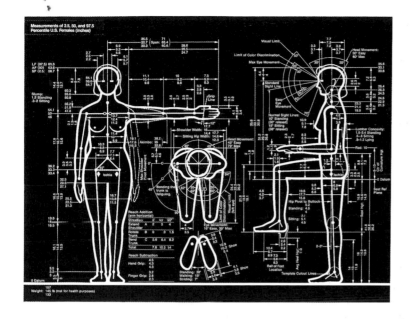

Diagram with percentile measurements of U.S. females, from Henry Dreyfuss Associates' *Humanscale 1/2/3*, 1974.

trial object, revealing as little of its designer as it did of its function. Associated with precision equipment of very high quality, Jensen's anonymous box came to define the aesthetic of the most expensive consumer electronics (no. 340). The retreat into anonymity was taken to the theoretical point of near-nihilism by the Italian group Superstudio, who developed the axonometric grid as a semantically "neutral" (non-commercial–"anti-design") form in their published designs of 1969 and in the furniture they created for Zanotta (no. 324), decorated with an allover three-centimeter silkscreened grid. Superstudio claimed that only through "reduction" could overproduction and other environmental ills be controlled or could the consumer directly experience the "real" world.[14]

Engineering technology as well as common sense of the Papanek variety was also applied to human-systems relationships. The industrial designer was expected to work in collaboration with an ergonomist, or even to function as one himself through the use of such self-help human engineering statistical surveys as those compiled by NIELS DIFFRIENT and other members of HENRY DREYFUSS ASSOCIATES (*Humanscale 1/2/3*, 1974). The increasing importance and complexity of the field of ergonomics was noted by the British designer Bill Moggridge. "If you design, say, a telephone handset, it's best to ask an ergonomist about cheek and finger clearances, or the distance between lips and ears," he said; "when you're considering telephone ringing tones, you've gone into a deeper field where subjective reasoning isn't enough: this means that ergonomic advice is at a premium. By the time you get to designing work stations for data processing, when operator delays are costly and design criteria can only be treated in the context of a total system, ergonomics is absolutely essential."[15] Ergonomics was applied to design situations that benefited from a broader and more responsive view of the human environment, a universal design environment that included infants, the elderly, and the disabled. In Sweden,

Centre Georges Pompidou by Richard Rogers and Renzo Piano, Paris, 1974–76. The museum drew on high-tech imagery by exposing the building's own structural and mechanical systems.

MARIA BENKTZON, SVEN-ERIC JUHLIN, and the cooperative to which they belonged, ERGONOMI DESIGN GRUPPEN, designed kitchen tools and cutlery (nos. 333, 357) for people with limited strength and movement ability, including a weight-adjusted knife and combination cutlery for those with only one functioning hand; their research was funded partly by government organizations (the Swedish Work Environment Fund, the National Board for Occupational Health and Safety) and partly by manufacturers in such fields as mechanical engineering, building equipment, plastics, and medical technology. The Yugoslavian OSKAR KOGOJ designed a curved and channeled baby spoon in response to a baby's motor ability and later developed it into a cutlery series in silver for general use (no. 332). In England in the mid-1970s, Heinz Wolff, director of Brunel University's Institute for Bioengineering, created a consulting practice called Tools for Living to consider other products, such as a bath lift for the elderly, that would benefit a broader population.

In reaction to those designers who used technology to serve human needs and conserve the environment, others claimed a place for the irrational and the subjective as well as for the aesthetic in a science-oriented world. Even a rationalist like Tomás Maldonado argued in his book *Design, Nature, and Revolution* (1972) for recognition of the subjective as a fundamental determinant in the human environment, exemplified by "play, as a free, spontaneous activity: we are speaking of play without a pre-established code, without the 'rules of the game,' without a system of reinforcements or punishments that might suffocate the freedom of the player."[16] From Japan to Italy and Spain designers sometimes created only marginally functional objects that provided scope for the enrichment of life by exploring the realms of personal identity, psychology, and historical continuity, and often by adopting craft techniques. The Japanese designer SHIRO KURAMATA created what he called *Furniture in Irregular Forms*, which distorted the shape of the conventional storage box and freed it from its usual relationship to the user (no. 335); TOSHIYUKI KITA altered the traditional Japanese concept of seating to permit the user greater freedom in his movements (no. 361);

and the Italian ALESSANDRO MENDINI celebrated his freedom from the anti-historicist bias of functionalism by plundering and elaborating on its repertoire of forms and details for the Studio Alchimia Bau.Haus furniture series, largely handmade in limited editions, which also borrowed from a variety of nineteenth-century models (no. 359). At the same time some graphic designers rejected the purely functional aspects of typography, including WOLFGANG WEINGART in Switzerland, who discounted legibility as a primary requirement of graphic communication.

In 1968 Maldonado had predicted the trend toward increased specialization by designers that occurred in the 1970s, and their necessary involvement in such fields as engineering and ergonomics:

> The view that the problems of design can be solved primarily if not exclusively by designing has been shaken. The relationship between the designer and the sciences must be thought out afresh. . . . This can be achieved if the design schools do not train their students merely to make design objects but also to create design knowledge and design organization. In the last analysis design is more than the creation of three-dimensional forms. The activities of the designer will become differentiated. There will be designers who work on the drawing board; there will be designers who research; and there will be designers who organize and plan.[17]

Such specialization, he later argued, was necessary to address the complex reality of the human environment from the multiple viewpoints of ecological science, philosophy, literature, and art, which the responsible designer was required to recognize.[18]

324

SUPERSTUDIO
Misura desk, 1969–71

Superstudio and ARCHIZOOM ASSOCIATI, alternative architecture and design groups founded in Italy in 1966, pursued a radical path designed to neutralize the experience of modern civilization and commodity-based culture in landscapes devoid of superfluous values. Disseminated through graphics and exhibitions, Archizoom's conception of a homogeneous "No-Stop City" and Superstudio's gridded structures monumentally spread over cityscapes and landscapes.[19] prophesied the total urbanization and regularization of the earth. Seemingly in contradiction to Superstudio's sense of futility with commodity-based culture, the Misura (Measure) series of which this desk is a part may as readily be understood as a bid for the elimination of style. A nonspecific design with universal application, it has white plastic surfaces uniformly covered with a three-centimeter (1³/₁₆-inch) silk-screened grid, which appears to be continuous with the larger, neutral environment they postulated. Superstudio recognized that

> to continue to design furniture, objects, and similar household articles was not the solution to the problems of living nor to those of life itself. . . . No cosmetology or *beautification* was sufficient to remedy the ravages of time, the mistakes of man, and the beastliness of architecture. . . . The problem thus was one of becoming ever more detached

from these *design* activities, perhaps adopting the technique of minimum effort in a general reductive process.[20]

Made by Zanotta, Nova Milanese, Italy. Silkscreened plastic and plywood. 49¹/₈ x 49¹/₈" (126 x 126 cm). (Zanotta Collection.)

325

BRUNO MUNARI
Cockpit habitable structure, 1971

As designers faced the challenge of furnishing open interiors and the often undefined loft and industrial spaces that were being rehabilitated for domestic use, they began to think in terms of large self-contained furnishing systems, environments, and complex habitable structures. In 1968 at the *XIV Triennale* in Milan, Bruno Munari presented a proposal for a habitable system—four modular combinable blocks that accommodated all basic daily needs including sanitation, storage, relaxation/sleeping, and food preparation (similar to the *Mini Kitchen* JOE COLOMBO had presented at the previous *Triennale* in 1964; no. 283). Three years later he returned to this concept, which he simplified into the nonspecific, industrially produced *Cockpit* (*Abitacolo*) habitable system. A neutral high-tech structure made of gray epoxy-coated steel that is easily assembled with screws, it comprises four corner uprights, two horizontal platforms, a table top, four bookshelves, two containers, and twenty hooks for attaching other things to

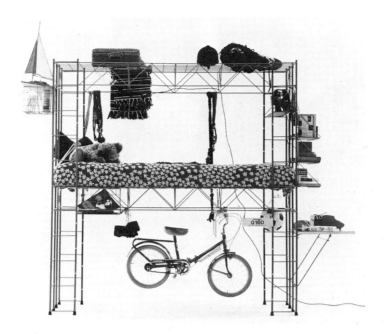

the structure. Except for the uprights, which form the system's support and are used also as ladders for climbing to the top level, the elements are all moveable, meant to give the inhabitants the greatest possible freedom to define their own spaces and lifestyles and satisfy their own needs.

Made by Robots, Milan. Epoxy-coated steel. 90 x 35 1/2 x 85" (200 x 90 x 190 cm). (Courtesy Aldo Balla, Milan.)

326
CINI BOERI
Serpentone seating, 1970–71

The application of technological research within the furniture industry resulted in a new concept of "endless" seating, an example of which is Cini Boeri's standardized *Serpentone* (*Jumbo Snake*) system; the seating was produced by the Arflex firm, which had been founded in 1950 expressly for the purpose of producing upholstered furniture with innovative materials and methods (no. 230). With no internal structure, Boeri's seating system is made up of fifteen-inch-wide injection-molded polyurethane sections, each comprising eight vertical "slices"; glued together, they form a continuous, endlessly extendable unit, which can curve or snake around spaces and create areas suitable for conversation and interaction. Eschewing a covering of conventional upholstery materials for the firm dark foam from which it was made, the *Serpentone* system emphasized the elasticity of polyurethane, which could

be "stretched" in a pleasing curvaceous shape and foamed in a mold to give it springiness.

Made by Arflex, Milan. Polyurethane. Width of section: 15" (38 cm). (Arflex, Milan.)

327
FRANK O. GEHRY
Easy Edges rocking chair, 1971–72

Unlike designers who folded cardboard into boxlike forms as inexpensive and expendable furniture (no. 286), the architect Frank O. Gehry worked with this material in thick laminated layers as if it were a solid, durable substance. Taking his idea from the layered construction of architects' contour models, Gehry used the exposed edges rather than the flat planes as his surface, achieving an effect he particularly liked because it "looked like corduroy, it felt like corduroy, it was seductive."[21] Gehry thoroughly researched the properties of his material, patented his method of construction, and worked out an extremely efficient manufacturing system so that the furniture could be produced quickly and sold at very low prices. The ease of die-cutting the thick corrugated cardboard allowed him to create both regular and eccentric shapes—ribbonlike forms as well as arabesques such as those that define this rocker—and both types were included among the seventeen pieces of Easy Edges furniture he put into production in 1972. Dismayed by the commitment required for him to be an entrepreneur, however, Gehry withdrew the series after three months, although he had received national publicity for his work and sales were beginning to grow.

Made by Jack Brogan. Cardboard. Length: 42" (106.6 cm).
(Museum of Modern Art, New York, gift of the manufacturer.)

328
JACK LENOR LARSEN
Magnum fabric, 1970

A pioneer in the development of new textile materials and technology, Jack Lenor Larsen also showed continuing interest in traditional styles and processes, relying on ancient techniques as varied as wax batik and discharge printing for his African (1962), Andean (1966), and Irish (1969) collections. For his *Magnum* fabric Larsen employed the traditional process of embroidery on the polyester fiber Mylar (polyethylene terephthalate), which has a strong, glassy, flexible surface. Using a schiffli embroidery machine, Larsen covered most of the Mylar ground with numerous stitches forming squares of different colors. "In schiffli embroidery," he wrote, "the decorative yarn does not penetrate the cloth: it is held in place by a binding thread stitched through from the back . . . it is most often sparse, with relatively few stitches and broad open areas of unstitched ground. . . . The thinness is not accidental: costs are based on the number of stitches and the amount of yarn used."[22] Reversing the usual practice, however, Larsen constructed an unusually dense surface of colored yarns and mirrored Mylar, creating in *Magnum* a modern luxury fabric; here the machine process was rendered so slow and costly that it resembled the handcraft of decorative needlework on which it is based.

Cotton, vinyl, nylon, and polyester. Width: 55" (139.5 cm).
(Jack Lenor Larsen, New York.)

329
MARIO BELLINI
Divisumma 18 calculator, 1972

Like MARCELLO NIZZOLI and ETTORE SOTTSASS, JR.,
his predecessors as design consultants for Olivetti,
Mario Bellini approaches design as a complex of con-
sumer-machine relationships that extend beyond technology. The bright yellow, rounded forms of his
Divisumma 18 printing calculator are designed to be
emotionally satisfying and to invite personal response.
In this regard the calculator incorporates one of Bellini's
significant contributions to appliance design—what has
been called a "stretched membrane." Here, a skin of
rubber is drawn taut over the keys to integrate the
mechanical parts into a smooth, sensual, tactile whole.
As a portable machine for personal use, the calculator
was consciously positioned in the market as a product
engendering both visual and physical pleasure, an identity underscored by the images and text of the promotional literature:

> Above all, the *Divisumma 18* is . . . beautiful. A
> unique, functional beauty. Its keys, for example. So
> soft and responsive. . . . Tailored to the human
> hand, and virtually dust-proof. The material itself is
> beautiful, familiar and soft to the touch. In short, the
> whole machine is beautiful, to make it a pleasure to
> have near you.

Made by Ing. C. Olivetti & C., Ivrea, Italy. ABS plastic,
melamine, and rubber. 17/8 x 10 x 43/4" (4.8 x 25.4 x
12.1 cm). (Ing. C. Olivetti & C., S.p.A., Ivrea, Italy.)

330
ARCHIZOOM ASSOCIATI
AEO armchair, 1973

For their somewhat awkward-looking *AEO* armchair,
Archizoom Associati turned from the sophisticated
irony of their *Mies* chair (no. 321) to an innovative
investigation of basic structures and appropriate technologies. The chair featured an additive method of
construction that matched separate functions with separate materials. The chair sits on a wide base of molded plastic, into which is set the structural system—a
painted bent-tubular metal frame to support the seat
(and optional arms) and a flat steel frame for the back.
A loose fabric shell, originally designed of a simple
material resembling shirting or calico, slips over the
back, and a foam cushion upholstered with another
fabric is added for comfort. An assemblage of disparate
elements, the *AEO* chair possessed, as the magazine
Casabella pointed out, "not stylistic unity but structural
unity."[23] Introduced in 1973 by Cassina at the furniture
salon in Milan as an Archizoom design, the chair has
since been credited to one of the group's founders,
Paolo Deganello.

Made by Cassina, Meda, Italy. Plastic, painted metal, and
lacquered steel with fabric-covered foam upholstery. 41 1/2
x 31 1/8 x 22 1/4" (105.4 x 79 x 56.5 cm). (Metropolitan
Museum of Art, New York.)

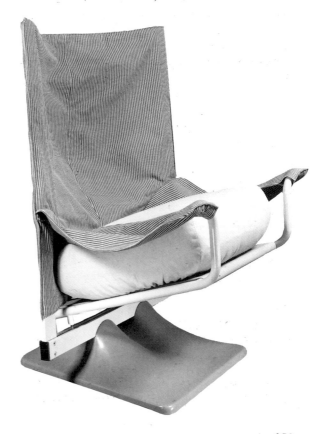

331
LUIGI COLANI
Drop tea service, 1970

Luigi Colani ranks among the most inventive and daring industrial designers of recent years, a visionary whose alternative approach to such fields as transportation has become highly influential. The most advanced of his designs, especially his futuristic automobiles, are nevertheless rarely carried beyond the drawing board or prototype stage. Using what he describes as "hydrodynamic" forms—an aquatic answer to the aerodynamic shapes of the 1930s—Colani also applies his organicism to everyday objects including this tea service commissioned for the Rosenthal Studio Line, which offered it in white, black, and gold. Entitled *Drop*, a name that alludes perhaps to the teardrop, the ideal form of streamlining, the service also recalls RUSSEL WRIGHT's *American Modern* dinnerware of the same period (no. 173). But Colani puts the flowing forms to functional as well as formalist uses. In this flattened teapot, for example, he fully integrates the handle into the unified elongated body, allowing the pot to be grasped very close to its center of gravity and thus making the vessel easy to hold and simple to pour.

Made by Rosenthal, Selb, Germany. Porcelain. Height of teapot: 4 3/16" (10.7 cm). (Rosenthal, Selb, Germany.)

332
OSKAR KOGOJ
Cutlery, 1972

Ergonomic design has for the most part adapted and refined traditional forms, making adjustments for efficiency, ease of use, or bodily comfort based on anatomical and psychological studies. With this organic cutlery design, Oskar Kogoj preferred instead to start anew, drawing on the lessons of more basic precultural attitudes. Challenging Western table habits and manners with a service that is distinctly different in concept, he created cutlery that requires us to relearn the process of eating. After studying the basic shoveling motion of the human hand when designing implements and toys for children, Kogoj determined that curved shapes flow naturally from this motion and better accommodate the introduction of food into the mouth. He first used the concept for a baby spoon that was easy to grip and manipulate and later expanded it into cutlery for adults and children alike. Designed in plastic and published in prototype in 1972, Kogoj's service was not produced commercially until the 1980s.

Made by Rino Greggio Argenterie, Tencarola, Italy. Silver. Length of knife: 6 1/4" (15.9 cm). (Philadelphia Museum of Art, gift of the designer.)

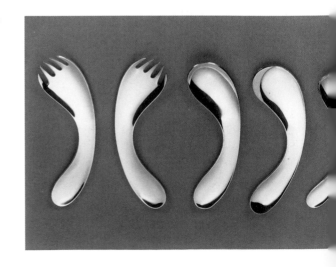

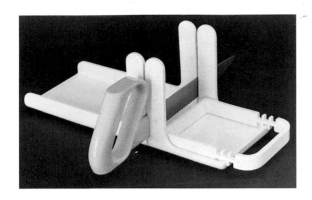

333
MARIA BENKTZON AND SVEN-ERIC JUHLIN
Knife and cutting frame, 1974

Drawing on a research project from 1972 called
"Handles/Grips," which considered the special needs
of those with muscle-strength and mobility impairments, Maria Benktzon and Sven-Eric Juhlin devised a
kitchen knife and cutting frame that fully accommodates these disabilities but in a form that is visually and
physically appealing to the wider public. This
approach—"this 'designing for all' including the
impaired"—which the two specialists pioneered,
involves "nothing more than including the needs of the
impaired people as well as those of the non disabled in
the design of products, machines, and environments."[24]
Their collaborative working method, now adopted by
the ERGONOMI DESIGN GRUPPEN to which they
belong, is based on elaborate research—much of it
funded by governments, institutions, and foundations—
and on extensive product testing in the situations of
daily use for which they are intended. Studies to deter-
mine the type of handle that requires the least strength
established the configuration of the knife, with its sawlike
grip and high blade, while the cutting frame, which
secures food for ease of grasping and slicing, was
designed to extend accessibility even to those with
severe vision impairment and motor disabilities.

Made by Gustavsberg, Gustavsberg, Sweden. Propene plastic
and stainless steel. Length: 13¾" (35 cm). (Gustavsberg,
Gustavsberg, Sweden.)

334
COOK AND SHANOSKY ASSOCIATES
Symbol signs for the United States Department of
Transportation, 1974–76

In 1974 Cook and Shanosky Associates was awarded
the contract to create a program of visual symbols for
the U.S. Department of Transportation. One of the
earliest integrated graphic communications systems
designed in the United States, it was intended to simplify the dissemination of information at domestic and
international travel facilities with symbols that would
be recognizable to all travelers regardless of their language proficiency. Preliminary research was carried out
for the transportation department by a committee
formed by the American Institute of Graphic Arts and
led by Thomas H. Geismar, and its findings served
Roger Cook and Don Shanosky as a guide as they
developed the components of this system. Thirty-four
clearly distinguishable passenger and pedestrian symbol
signs were produced in four categories—public services, concessions, processing activities, and regulations—unified by the consistency of their overall
design. Sixteen additional symbols were added by the
firm between 1979 and 1984. To encourage the adop-
tion of these symbols as a universal system, the transportation department makes them freely available, and
their use has become widespread both in the United
States and abroad. In 1985 Cook and Shanosky was
the recipient of one of the first Presidential Design
Awards for the development of this program.

Printed poster. 29¾ x 21½" (75.5 x 54.6 cm) (Private
collection.)

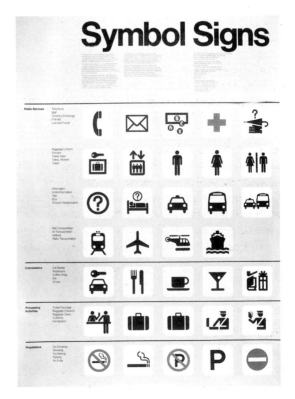

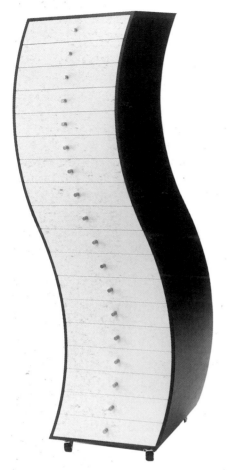

336
RICHARD SAPPER
Tizio table lamp, 1970–71

Richard Sapper's *Tizio* lamp demonstrates the applicability of highly developed engineering skills to consumer goods. The matte black lamp, with red accents where the two robotlike arms pivot, moves effortlessly on snap joints and remains in position anywhere, the arms themselves acting as counterbalances. Conceived with the same general goals and according to the same principles as the flexible, articulated work lights produced in a variety of forms throughout the century, *Tizio* addressed Sapper's desire for a lamp with minimal weight and bulk and a concentrated light source, which was achieved through the use of a small, low-voltage, high-intensity halogen bulb. Because voltage was greatly reduced by the transformer in the base, he could use the metal arms themselves to conduct the power to the bulb. Thus eliminating the need for internal wiring in thick arms, he was able to give his lamp a very thin, elegant structure. Halogen bulbs, first used for consumer lighting by GINO SARFATTI, produce a far whiter and brighter light than incandescent bulbs; because they are small, higher wattages can be used in compact housings with higher output, more efficiency, greater color stability, and a longer bulb life. Sapper's lamp was awarded a Compasso d'Oro prize in 1979.

335
SHIRO KURAMATA
Furniture in Irregular Forms chest of drawers, 1970

Designed just five years after Shiro Kuramata opened his own design office, this double-curved chest of drawers arbitrarily distorts the conventional storage box more for the sake of play than for functional reasons. Kuramata began experimenting with the unusual placement of drawers as early as 1967, attaching them to chairs and tables under the rails where they filled up the empty spaces, and stacking them in tall pyramids. "I've loved drawers ever since I was a child," he reflected. "Mine used to be full of toys and spinning tops and colored cards: they were my hidden treasures. I loved putting my hand into those untidy drawers and rummaging about. Now as an adult I think that maybe I'm still looking for something in the drawers that isn't there."[25] *Furniture in Irregular Forms* was first produced in 1970 by Fujiko, Tokyo, and re-released in 1986 by the Italian manufacturer Cappellini.

Made by Cappellini, Arosio, Italy. Lacquered board. Height: 67" (170 cm). (Cappellini, Arosio, Italy.)

Made by Artemide, Milan. ABS plastic and aluminum. Height (extended): 46 1/2" (118 cm). (Artemide, Milan.)

337
CARLOS RIART
Desnuda chair, 1973

The revival of irrational and individual forms of expression occurred simultaneously in various parts of Europe in the 1970s, including Barcelona, where a progressive group of young designers gave new meanings to the Spanish taste for expressionism. Among them was Carlos Riart who, in his first collection of "special furniture," created whimsical, sometimes anthropomorphic designs—for example, an elephant-footed table, a fan-shaped screen, and this *Desnuda* or *Nude* chair whose dainty brass hooves suggested to the designer "a naked woman, feminine and coquette."[26] (An early design for the seat was dressed in a hoof-length skirt.) According to his description of his *Snark* furniture from the same collection, the sources of Riart's inspiration are many and varied and include historical models: "Japanese art for its subtle system of construction; the so-called functional style for its metrics; neoclassicism for its symmetry; art nouveau for its ambiguity; adhocism for the materials used; tantrism for color; neoplasticism for its spatial projection; magic for its use of the crystal as a repository of psychic

energy."[27] The curved cresting rail, crossed stretchers, and feet suggesting animal hooves are simplified and abstracted from earlier wooden furniture forms; here made of metal, they are combined with an exposed wire back that demonstrates a brutalist, high-tech affection for undisguised industrial materials. Yet the plain metal is not aggressively used: structured in thin elements and painted blue-gray, the chair has a delicacy and awkward grace that is both personal to Riart's style and evocative of the nude that inspired his design.

Made by Termo, Barcelona. Painted and enameled iron and brass with upholstery. Height: 39 3/8" (100 cm). (Philadelphia Museum of Art, gift of the designer.)

338
ALDO VAN DEN NIEUWELAAR
Amsterdamer cupboard system, 1973–79

Aldo van den Nieuwelaar based the form of his *Amsterdamer* (*A'dammer*) storage system on the rounded street barriers of this city. The freestanding cupboards with rolltop polystyrene closures were fitted with dividers that form square compartments and with tops that could be lowered fully or only partially to create open-shelf storage. The cupboards borrow elements of traditional furniture, but they are made of light, inexpensive, modern materials; available in two heights and two widths for use interchangeably in a multifunctional system, they aim for formal anonymity, which van den Nieuwelaar and many other designers felt suitable to mass production. "I try to capture the essence of a utility product with a minimum of material and means," he explained. "Industrial design is a visual realization of that process. I prefer introverted forms, since they have less influence on their surroundings, resulting in more possibilities for those surroundings."[28]

Made by Pastoe, Utrecht. Fiberboard and polystyrene. Height: 87" (221 cm). (UMS-Pastoe, Utrecht.)

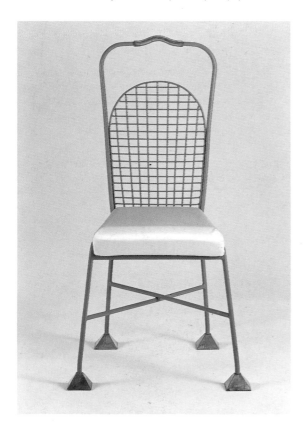

339
CLIVE SINCLAIR
Executive calculator, 1972

One of the first pocket calculators to be manufactured and surely the most elegant, Clive Sinclair's *Executive* calculator, designed with the assistance of his brother Iain, signaled a major step in the miniaturization of electronic equipment. Weighing just two and a half ounces, it was also exceedingly slim, its three-eighths-inch thickness in startling contrast to the bulk of other handheld calculators. Yet with

its 7,000-transistor integrated circuit—according to advertisements the largest that had yet been produced for commercial purposes—the *Executive* also had superior calculating ability. Sinclair was able to pare down its size so radically by reducing the power requirements—while other calculators required larger power sources, the *Executive* could run on tiny hearing-aid batteries. He did this by devising a method to use less power by having the calculator switch itself on and off constantly, working at such a fast pace that the microchip retained its information and the display did not flicker.

Made by Sinclair Radionics, London. Plastic housing. 5 1/2 x 2 1/4 x 3/8" (14 x 5.7 x 1 cm). (Museum of Modern Art, New York, gift of Sinclair Radionics, London.)

340
JACOB JENSEN
Beogram 4000 turntable, 1972

Jacob Jensen's *Beogram 4000* turntable was conceived as a "no-compromise, electronic gramophone featuring absolutely top specifications and obsolescence-proof design" for consumers who "demand utmost fidelity in sound reproduction."[29] With its innovative, electronically guided tangential arm, precision parts, and computerized operating system, the turntable provided very high quality advanced technology to a narrow top market not served by larger American and Japanese audio manufacturers. In designing the housing for this turntable and other related Bang & Olufsen products, Jensen defined the aesthetic of consumer precision equipment. Some critics referred to the uncompromis-

ing asceticism of Jensen's black box as an example of anonymous anti-design born of the engineering industries: for Reyner Banham the solution was so "elegant you can't tell what it is, a completely anonymous plastic box that might well contain paper tissues, did it not appear to have a slide rule glued to one edge."[30]

Made by Bang & Olufsen, Struer, Denmark. Wood, aluminum, and stainless steel housing. Width: 18 7/8" (48 cm). (Bang & Olufsen A/S, Struer, Denmark.)

341
J. C. PENNEY COMPANY
Coffee maker, 1976

J. C. Penney's electric drip coffee maker introduced in its 1976 Christmas catalog was one of a series of the company's products that brought high-quality design and production to the mass market, demonstrating that the discreetly functional look pioneered by such European firms as Braun and Bang & Olufsen (nos. 242, 246, 340) could appeal to a significant segment of the American public. Modest and compact with a rounded white plastic housing embracing the carafe and only an on/off switch and indicator light breaking its smooth surface, the machine is clean in appearance and simple to operate. This reflects the influence on Penney's products of the graphic design program undertaken by Unimark International and implemented by the company between 1970 and 1973. As its annual report explained: "Although we are not a manufacturer, we often redesign hard lines to improve both function and appearance. In certain areas, such as electronics and appliances, we have been able to develop a consistent JCPenney look even though the merchandise comes to us from different manufacturers."[31] Selected by *Industrial Design* magazine for inclusion in

its annual product review of 1978, the coffee maker was one of many award-winning designs to emerge from the J. C. Penney design department under this program.

Made by Munnekata Company, Japan. ABS plastic, painted phenolic plastic, aluminum, and glass. 11 1/4 x 7 1/4 x 10 1/4" (28.5 x 18.4 x 26 cm). (Location unknown.)

342
SONY CORPORATION
Walkman personal cassette player, 1978

Sony's record for technological innovation, for introducing new products such as the transistor radio (no. 258) and the solid-state portable television set (no. 273), depended on a considerable investment in research and development—from 6 to 10 percent of the firm's sales—and on the kind of teamwork proposed by Akio Morita and Masaru Ibuka when they first established the company. The idea for the *Walkman* came about when Morita and Ibuka, unhappy with the weight of their portable stereo tape recorder, refitted an existing model called *Pressman* with a stereo amplifier. According to Morita:

> I outlined the other details I wanted, which included very lightweight headphones that turned out to be one of the most difficult parts of the Walkman project. . . . In a short time the first experimental unit with new, miniature headphones was delivered to

me, and I was delighted with the small size of it and the high-quality sound the headphones produced. In conventional stereo with large loudspeakers, most of the energy used to produce the sound is wasted, because only a fraction of it goes to the listeners' ears. . . . Our tiny unit needed only a small trickle of battery power to the amplifier to drive the tiny lightweight headphones. . . . The idea took hold and from the beginning the Walkman was a runaway success. . . . Soon we could hardly keep pace with the demand and had to design new automated machinery to handle the flood of orders. Of course, we helped stimulate sales by advertising heavily, and in Japan we hired young couples to stroll through the Tokyo Ginza Pedestrian Paradise on Sundays, listening to their Walkmans and showing them off.[32]

Small, light, and exceedingly portable, the *Walkman* produced clean, unwavering sound even when the user was moving because it included a counterbalance mechanism with two flywheels rotating in opposite directions, which canceled out vibration and changes in position.

Anodized-aluminum housing. Height: 5 1/4" (13.3 cm). (Sony Corporation, Tokyo.)

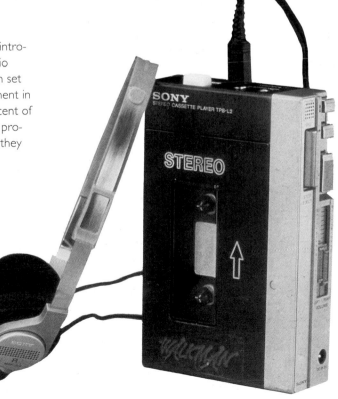

343
GAETANO PESCE
Sit Down armchair, 1975

Gaetano Pesce's Sit Down series of chair, sofa, and ottoman, like many of his other experimental designs (no. 307), proposed a new method for the manufacture of comfortable furniture and a new system of permanent upholstery using the versatility of plastic foam. In this process, cotton-covered quilted polyester placed over a plywood structure was injected with polyurethane foam, which expanded and solidified to form the single integrated unit that gave the chair its final shape. The foam-injection process could not be rigidly controlled to repeat the same shape for each chair; since the manufacturer could only assure a consistency of overall dimensions and look, each buyer was guaranteed a unique object.

Made by Cassina, Meda, Italy. Plywood with cotton-covered polyester and polyurethane foam upholstery. 36 1/4 x 44 7/8 x 35 7/16" (92 x 114 x 90 cm). (Cassina, Meda, Italy.)

344
VICO MAGISTRETTI
Atollo table lamp, 1977

Like many other designers in the mid-1970s, the highly regarded Italian rationalist Vico Magistretti introduced irony as a device to engage the user. In his enameled-aluminum *Atollo* lamp he commented on the use of geometry as an expression of industrial form and function. Direct, with no intrusions to mar the smooth,

engineered surfaces and shapes of the three Euclidean forms—cylinder, cone, and hemisphere—the lamp has all the required ingredients of enduring, timeless, functionalist objects while lacking their underlying stability. The hemisphere precariously balanced on the point of the cone seems to challenge the forces of gravity by masking the structural support that allows it to happen, totally contradicting the security of rationalism as a basis for design. The *Atollo* lamp was awarded a Compasso d'Oro prize in 1979.

Made by O-Luce Italia, Milan. Enameled aluminum. Height: 27 9/16" (70 cm). (Philadelphia Museum of Art, gift of O-Luce.)

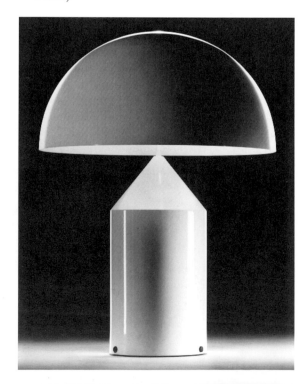

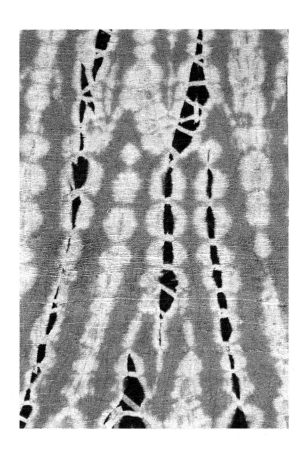

345
MAYA ROMANOFF
Desert Root fabric, 1978

Adapting batik, tie-dying, and other arts that he first saw during his travels to Africa and India in the 1960s, Maya Romanoff brought millenia-old resist dyeing techniques into the contemporary sphere with such fabrics as his *Desert Root* silk, one of the first modern resist-dyed textiles to be generally available. This and other patterns, which were offered in a broad range of scale, colors, and materials, were produced with new techniques that allowed these traditional one-of-a-kind handcraft procedures to be converted into production methods. His technology for resist dying allowed him to maintain a consistency of design over large production runs and to repeat the same pattern whenever required, which had not been possible with this process before.

Dyed silk. Width: 46" (116.8 cm). (Philadelphia Museum of Art, gift of the designer.)

346
VAN NIEUWENBORG/WEGMAN INDUSTRIAL DESIGN
Delight lamp, 1980

Seeking alternatives to the high-tech aesthetic so prevalent in the field of lighting, the Dutch designer-craftsmen Frans van Nieuwenborg and Martijn Wegman ingeniously adapted a piece of heat-resistant, woven fiberglass cloth as a shade for their *Delight* lamp. Like a piece of soft sculpture draped over a bulb, it can hang from a wall or the ceiling or sit crumpled on a table or shelf, where it gives off a soft atmospheric light. The lamp was first produced in small quantities by the two designers in their own studio but it is now made in larger quantities by the German lighting designer and manufacturer INGO MAURER. A small production is still reserved for the studio annually, however, insuring the continued involvement of the designers with their products.

Made by Ingo Maurer, Munich. Fiberglass. Height: 29 1/2" (75 cm). (Ingo Maurer GmbH, Munich.)

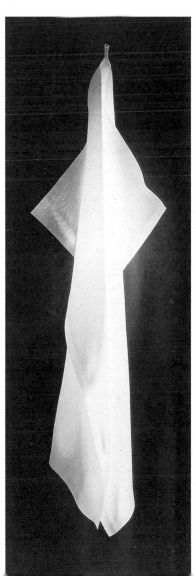

347
MARIO BELLINI
Stereo tape deck, 1974

The crisp wedge shape that Mario Bellini (assisted by his brother Dario) gave to his stereo tape deck for the Japanese firm Yamaha first appeared in his *Logos 50/60* electronic calculator for Olivetti in 1972, a shape well adapted to keyboard and desktop functions. These innovative designs established a coolly efficient formal vocabulary Bellini has repeated in other office equipment and which has been imitated broadly. With its angled form, this tape deck was conceived as a technological desktop fantasy instrument, bringing a well-organized instrumentation panel clearly into view to display the variety of functions available for sound control and suggesting with its black finish the highly specialized equipment of a sound technician. The practice of offering consumers the look of high technology rapidly multiplied in all areas and on all levels of manufacture in Japanese electronic design during the 1970s; in this process it became clear that these appurtenances were not always functionally based but had become the accessories of a new decorative style.

Made by Nippon Gakki Company, Hammatsu, Japan, for Yamaha. ABS plastic housing. 3⁷/₈ x 12¹/₄ x 12¹/₄" (9.8 x 31.2 x 31.2 cm). (Yamaha.)

348
SONY CORPORATION
Jackal television, radio, and cassette player, 1976

The proliferation of knobs, dials, switches, and controls suggestive of an instrument panel imparts Sony's *Jackal* combination television, radio, and cassette player with the "radio machismo" that the critic Reyner Banham identified as pervasive in consumer electronics in the wake of the Vietnam War. Like Panasonic's *Commando* portable television, Sony's *Jackal* concentrated screen and controls "on the narrow front of a case that would drop straight into the instrument racks of a tank or counter-insurgency strike-aircraft."[33] With its black finish and concentric lateral speakers borrowed from recording studio consoles, the components present a gratuitously powerful image designed for immediate appeal to a mass market that placed its confidence in the accoutrements of high technology.

Height: 10⁵/₈" (27 cm). (Sony Corporation, Tokyo.)

logic most notably in his influential experiments at Basel's Kunstgewerbeschule, where he taught, and in his covers for the Swiss graphics journal *Typographische Monatsblätter* (1972–76). In the latter part of the decade he continued to mock the functionalism of the international typographic style with his artistic manipulation of printing techniques, taking the standard moiré or dot patterns used by printers as the means to simulate the effects of collage. For this poster, one of a series he did to celebrate Basel's annual exhibition of its arts grant program, Weingart produced a composition in this complex style, although here its use of overlaid elements heightens the legibility of the message. Using conventional Swiss typographic components, asymmetrically arranged sans-serif type, and a grid structure (clearly acknowledged by the large squared areas), he alternated light and dark grounds and solid reversed type in several sizes to organize the information into a hierarchy, which is emphasized by the "torn paper" forms and the juxtaposition of patterns, colors, shapes, and other "collage" elements.

Printed by Wassermann, Basel. Lithograph. (Museum für Gestaltung, Basel, Plakatsammlung.)

349
FAUSTA CAVAZZA
Parola telephone, 1979

Soft, inviting, and pleasantly tactile, features that make it well suited for being held and used frequently, Fausta Cavazza's *Parola* (*Speech*) telephone confounded expectations by rejecting the smooth, cool, sleek image of virtually all other telephone models then in production. She made her telephone of Santoprene, a soft substance developed by Monsanto that resembles rubber and resists scratches and dirt. A solid black rounded form when not in use, the telephone has luminous pushbuttons and a shoulder rest that opens out from the top (and contains a pencil for messages). Cavazza patented the design in 1979 and in 1982 established her own company to manufacture it.

Santoprene rubber. 2 1/8 x 9 x 2 3/4" (5.5 x 23 x 7 cm). (Cavazza Design, Milan.)

350
WOLFGANG WEINGART
Poster for the city of Basel, 1979

Wolfgang Weingart became known during the 1970s as a typographic maverick, confounding legibility and

Made by Cassina, Meda, Italy. Enameled steel with leather upholstery. 32 1/4 x 20 1/2 x 18 1/2" (82 x 52 x 47 cm). (Atelier International, New York.)

352
KAZUMASA NAGAI
Exhibition poster for Ikeda Museum of Twentieth Century Art, Ito, Japan, 1980

Announcing Kazumasa Nagai's retrospective exhibition at the Ikeda Museum of Twentieth Century Art in Ito, Japan, this poster also serves as a summary of the designer's ongoing exploration of abstract, geometric, linear forms and patterns to create the impression of spatial depth. The surreal landscapes Nagai designs are based on meticulous hand drawings that forecast the use of computers to achieve equally precise technological effects. This highly individual graphic universe of planets and energy forces moving in space represents Nagai's alternative, futuristic view of the environment: "We know that the world's resources are limited, that a depleted natural world is crying out in protest. Somewhere in the infinite universe we must find new sources of energy. I have faith in the resourcefulness of the human race and its efforts to accomplish this objective."[34]

Silkscreen print. 40 3/4 x 28 13/16" (103.5 x 73.3 cm). (Ikeda Museum of Twentieth Century Art, Ito, Japan.)

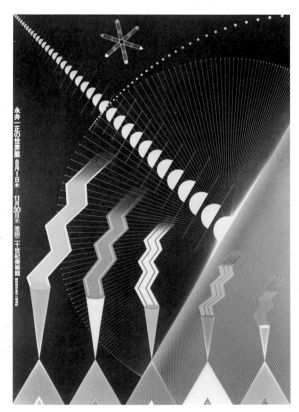

351
MARIO BELLINI
Cab chair, 1976

Like the flexible, synthetic rubber skin stretched over the body of Mario Bellini's electronic calculator (no. 329), leather upholstery tightly sheaths the simple steel frame of his *Cab* chair, a fitted suit that includes even the legs. Conceived like a slipcover, the stitched leather is closed at the legs with four zippers. The chair and its accompanying armchair were developed in collaboration with Cassina's research division, Centro Design e Comunicazione. This was one of several experiments on frames and upholstery that involved Bellini during the 1970s, including the 1972 *Germania* seating prototype for B & B Italia in which both the chair frame and padding were inserted into a single upholstery cover. Designed both for convenience to the user and efficient economical manufacture, the *Cab* chair brought the Italian tradition of innovative upholstery into the 1970s.

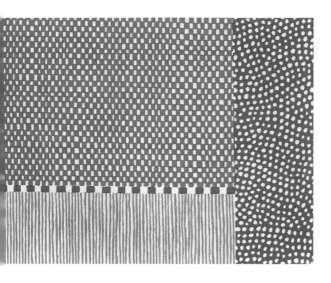

353
KATSUJI WAKISAKA
Ma fabric, 1977

After gaining professional experience in the West at the Finnish textile firm of Marimekko, where he worked between 1968 and 1976, Katsuji Wakisaka returned to his native Japan. There he reasserted his Japanese identity, borrowing for this *Ma (Space)* fabric the small, detailed, geometric stripes, checks, and pin points (*kimon*) of traditional kimono and stencil-resist-dyed patterns but translating them into the clear,

bright colors that he had learned from Marimekko. In addition, Wakisaka also adopted traditional patterns of geometric units or patches. Here as in a *Noh* costume, the patches are placed asymmetrically in a dense, allover combination.

Made by Wacoal Interior Fabrics, Tokyo. Printed cotton. Width: 54" (138 cm). (Philadelphia Museum of Art, gift of Wacoal Interior Fabrics.)

354
RICHARD SAPPER
Espresso coffee maker, 1978

When the columnar espresso pot by Richard Sapper was first sold, it was advertised as "exceptional" and "beautiful . . . an object invented over again, an idea that makes coffee." What was new and convenient, beyond its sleek and stable shape and its dripless spout, was the system Sapper designed for opening the pot: it took "simply a 'click'," the advertisement said, "to open and close." Instead of having to twist open the tight closure of the two parts—the water-boiler bottom and the coffee-container top—Sapper's coffee maker parts are easily separated by a lever device operated by lifting the handle. The stainless steel espresso pot, which is made in sizes of one, three, six, and ten cups, was awarded a Compasso d'Oro prize in 1979.

Made by Alessi, Crusinallo, Italy. Stainless steel and plastic. Height: 8" (20.3 cm). (Alessi, Crusinallo, Italy.)

armchair of about 1934 (no. 150) suffered from "what are believed to be structural and economical as well as esthetic drawbacks." Danko's chair is made from twelve very thin precut layers of wood, "deformed to a desired shape in a single bending operation during which adhesive coatings . . . are activated resulting in a chair that is structurally complete, requiring only finishing operations." The chair was first manufactured by Danko's own company but beginning in 1980 (when Danko's father, a former navy patternmaker, constructed a prototype press to prove that the method would work) it was also produced for a short time by Thonet, the American branch of the Austrian firm responsible for the bentwood revolution in the nineteenth century.

Made by Thonet, York, Pennsylvania. Laminated oak and poplar, with wool-covered foam-rubber upholstery. 31 x 22½ x 24" (78.5 x 55.1 x 61.5 cm). (Musée des Arts Décoratifs, Montreal, gift of the designer.)

355
PETER J. DANKO
Armchair, 1976

Peter Danko updated the use of bent laminated wood as a material for contemporary furniture with this organic, stacking armchair. Produced in a single gluing and bending process by a method he invented in 1976 and patented in 1980,[35] this piece, according to the patent, was the first laminated-wood chair in a single piece designed to be manufactured and marketed widely; previous examples such as GERALD SUMMERS's

356
PETER OPSVIK
Balans Variable chair, 1979

The radical *Balans* concept of seating, which relieves strain on the spine by transferring weight and pressure to the knees and helps to alleviate the discomfort of long hours of sitting, was conceived by Hans Christian Mengshoel for Håg, a Norwegian furniture manufacturer. Demanding a reconsideration of the Western custom of sitting, which Håg's president, T. M. Grimsrud, describes as "static, stiff and at the wrong angles," *Balans* also emphasizes rocking, which "produces dynamic muscle work, that is it creates a muscle-pump effect which influences the blood circulation so that

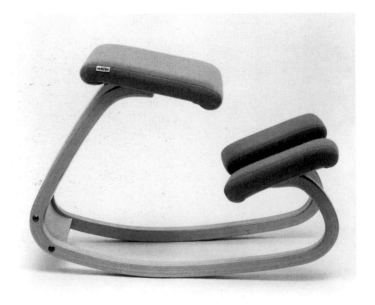

can be used with sawing and rocking motions, are mainly for those with the weak joints and impaired mobility of rheumatoid arthritis. The two other implements are for those with but one functioning hand. The "knork," a fork with a serrated knife edge (available in left- and right-hand models), and the "knoon," a knife-spoon combination, are both designed for cutting food either with short strokes or by twisting; the curved edge of the knoon is easier to use than the tines of the knork and is suited to those with greater impairment.

Made by RFSU Rehab, Stockholm. Stainless steel and poly-carbonate. Length of longer knife: 9 1/4" (23.5 cm). (Philadelphia Museum of Art, gift of RFSU Rehab.)

358
MORISON S. COUSINS & ASSOCIATES
Maxim 4 convection oven, 1980

As part of a trend toward professionalizing the home kitchen, convection ovens were introduced to consumers during the late 1970s. This institutional appliance, which uses a fan to distribute the heat more evenly than conventional ovens, was redesigned, however, to be more appealing to the domestic consumer. In Morison S. Cousins's design for the *Maxim 4* countertop oven, an aura of the professional product is maintained by the use of chrome and black forms and an electronic program control, but in a deliberate effort to make the design "personable" and "fun," a sense of warmth is conveyed by the red detailing and exaggerated feet.[37]

Made by the Maxim Company. Painted steel, chrome, and glass. (Cousins Designs, New York.)

the oxygen supply to the muscles . . . is accelerated."[36] The sitting posture is similar to that projected by ACHILLE CASTIGLIONI in his *Primate* kneeling stool in 1970, but through extensive ergonomic testing Håg developed this concept into a broad scientifically based program for comfortable seating. Peter Opsvik's chair was included in the first *Balans* series of lightweight wood and metal kneeling chairs; several different designers used Mengshoel's concept to create chairs for the series, which was introduced at the Scandinavian Furniture Fair in Copenhagen in 1979.

Made by Håg, Oslo. Wood with fabric covered foam upholstery. 19 x 20 x 28 1/2" (48 x 51 x 72.5 cm). (Håg AS, Oslo.) (Stokke, Skodje, Norway.)

357
ERGONOMI DESIGN GRUPPEN
Eat/Drink cutlery, 1980

In its efforts to design products for the handicapped that are functionally and aesthetically in line with expectations of the broader population, the Ergonomi Design Gruppen follows the goals established earlier by two of its members, MARIA BENKTZON and SVEN-ERIC JUHLIN (no. 333). The forms of their Eat/Drink tableware series, comprising cutlery, dishes, and drinking glasses, are based on clinical studies and extensive testing on people with poor grips, weakness, and muscular disabilities, as well as those with only one hand. The lightweight, safely rounded cutlery is conceived for three types of use: The long knife, fork, and spoon are designed principally for those who need support for their wrist or forearm and thus prefer a "pen" grip to grasp the implements between the fingertips. The shorter, thicker spoon and fork and the folding serrated knife, which is opened by pressing—not pulling—and

359
ALESSANDRO MENDINI
Proust armchair, 1978

In 1976 several Italian designers who had been most involved with radical design activities regrouped and began to create furniture for a new venture, the Studio Alchimia in Milan. Supported by the writings of a group member, Alessandro Mendini, editor of the magazine *Modo*, they took banal everyday reality as their inspiration, rejecting the utopian, modernist design ethos in favor of ornament, symbolism, and craftsmanship. Mendini's *Proust* armchair, unveiled in 1979 in Alchimia's first, ironically titled, Bau.Haus collection, was perhaps the most unexpected of the works shown. While the others used contemporary materials and what seemed like contemporary if eccentric shapes, Mendini reproduced a Victorian armchair in somewhat exaggerated form, hand-painted entirely — carved wooden frame and upholstery alike—with an Impressionistic brushstroke pattern. Mendini explained that he set out to create a chair that Marcel Proust might have sat in. With his own historical research turning up no certain prototypes, however, he chose to allude to the French fin de siècle writer by employing the allover painted pattern on a period-style chair, an obscure reference to the fact that Proust had owned Impressionist paintings. Made like the entire production of Alchimia in relatively few examples, and each painted distinctively, Mendini's *Proust* armchairs exemplify the group's uneasiness with repeated factory production and the commercialization of contemporary design.

Made by Studio Alchimia, Milan. Painted wood with hand-painted upholstery. Height: 42 1/8" (107 cm). (Bangert Collection, Munich.)

360
DAVID ROWLAND
Sof-Tech chair, 1979

Standard flat upholstery springs were the antecedents of this soft stacking chair, whose structural openness

and seemingly hard surface belie its firm but resilient support and its extraordinary comfort. David Rowland's idea for webbed-wire seating dates back to the 1950s when, as a student at the Cranbrook Academy of Art in Bloomfield Hills, Michigan, he experimented with bare zig-zag springs. But it was not until he dipped the wire in PVC plastic, which increased its thickness and gave it a certain elasticity, that he achieved an unupholstered surface that could still be considered truly comfortable. Its application did not become a reality until the 1970s, however, when he was able to combine his "arcuate, continuous, sinuous" wire component system with a lightweight stacking form and arrange to have it produced commercially. Distinguishing in his patent between thin, hard, nonresilient chairs that were truly stackable but uncomfortable, and padded, resilient chairs that were comfortable but too thick to stack tightly, he explained that his chairs had "spring-resilient seats and backs that are truly thin—thinner than the frame" and thus were comfortable and could be stacked compactly.[38]

Made by Thonet, York, Pennsylvania. Chrome-plated steel and PVC-covered metal. Height: 29³/4" (75.5 cm). (Philadelphia Museum of Art, gift of Thonet.)

361
TOSHIYUKI KITA
Wink chair, 1980

Like a number of other young, progressive Japanese designers, Toshiyuki Kita left his country to work in Italy, where the small craft-based furniture industry routinely accepted innovative products discouraged in Japan and elsewhere because of high engineering costs. The extraordinarily cheerful *Wink* chair demonstrated Kita's ability to combine Japanese and Western elements in an ingeniously modern way. An adjustable chair with but a few components, *Wink* can be flexed and bent, offering the user several options: by tilting the base forward the chair becomes a chaise, and the headrest, which is divided in two parts, allows it to take both a reclining and a forward "winking" position. For convenience, the upholstery fabric is also zip fastened and can be removed for cleaning. Kita sees the flexibility offered by the differently positioned supports as a Westernized form of the Japanese practice of sitting on the floor.

Made by Cassina, Meda, Italy. Steel with polyester-covered polyurethane foam upholstery. Length (extended): 78" (200 cm). (Cassina, Meda, Italy.)

Chapter Nine
Postmodernism and Pluralism
Since 1980

The label almost uniformly applied to design since 1980 has been "postmodern," despite the lack of real cohesion or of a single direction in the period's aesthetics or philosophy. The polymorphous direction and appearance of design in the 1980s and 90s owe something to the origins of postmodernism itself, where risk-taking and posturing, the invention of new forms and the recasting of old ones, produced a grab-bag of alternative styles.

In the context of architecture and design the phrase "postmodern" dates at least from 1949; it was used by Nikolaus Pevsner in 1966 to attack those whom he called "neo-expressionist" and by other writers in the mid-1970s.[1] But the British architect-historian Charles Jencks gave it currency in the first edition of his book *The Language of Post-Modern Architecture* (1977). Jencks described postmodernism as a hybrid style concerned with issues of historical (sometimes specifically architectural) memory, local context, metaphor, and ambiguity. Endorsing "radical eclecticism" to allow a wider understanding of the variety of human culture, Jencks described postmodernism as pluralistic, "variegated rather than homogeneous, witty rather than sombre, messy rather than clean, picturesque but not necessarily without a classical, geometric order."[2]

The return to symbolism and allusion that Jencks documented in the late 1970s was further legitimized in two exhibitions realized at Venice's *Biennale* in 1980, which gave postmodernism its most characteristic expression and put Italy at the center of the movement: *La Presenza del Passato* (*The Presence of the Past*), an international architecture show organized by the architect Paolo Portoghesi, and *L'Oggetto Banale* (*The Banal Object*), an exhibition of experimental furniture and objects by the Italian group Studio Alchimia, under the leadership of ALESSANDRO MENDINI, editor of the magazine *Modo*. Whereas both exhibitions demonstrated a free spirit of reaction against what were deemed the constrictions and purist values of traditional modernism, the architectural designs were largely based on classical forms and vocabulary, while Mendini's tongue-in-check presentation featured altered objects from everyday life, such as an espresso pot painted in several colors and appliances sporting colored arrows to accentuate their shapes. Inspired by various sources, from 1950s laminate patterns to pre–World War I cubist designs, these objects and Alchimia's first collection, introduced in 1979 under the title "Bau.Haus," aimed a

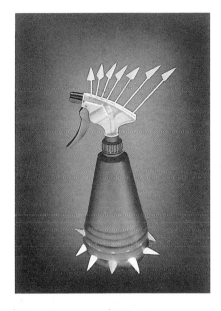

In the *Oggetto Banale* (*Banal Object*) exhibition at the Venice *Biennale* of 1980, colored vectors were used to accentuate the profiles and the banality of familiar objects.

opposite:
Ettore Sottsass, Jr., *Casablanca* sideboard, 1981 (no. 362)

riposte at the institution against which the prefix *post* in postmodernism was most specifically directed (no. 359). Their color as well as screen-printed and painted decorations, applied by hand, announced a return to surface decoration and elaboration. The handcraftsmanship involved in their manufacture was meant to appeal directly to the senses, and the historical borrowings to the intellect of the consumer, who was expected to recognize and respond to the comforting symbols of tradition and the past. The Alchimia manifesto, published retrospectively in 1985, celebrated " 'sentimental thought'. . . . Alchimia believes that memory and tradition are important. . . . Alchimia believes in despecialization: 'confused' methods of creation and production can live side by side; crafts, industry, informatics, new and obsolete techniques and materials. Alchimia believes in the concept of 'variation'."[3]

In late 1980 ETTORE SOTTSASS, JR., who had designed a number of objects for Alchimia's Bau.Haus collection, organized his own radical design group, Memphis, which was funded principally by Artemide, the Milanese lighting and furniture manufacturer. Compared to the self-limiting, more experimental approach of Studio Alchimia, Memphis from the outset was intended as a commercial venture aimed at international distribution. In its first highly publicized collection of 1981, called "Memphis, The New International Style," the group presented

Alessandro Mendini added painted extensions to Marcel Breuer's armchair of 1925 (no. 104).

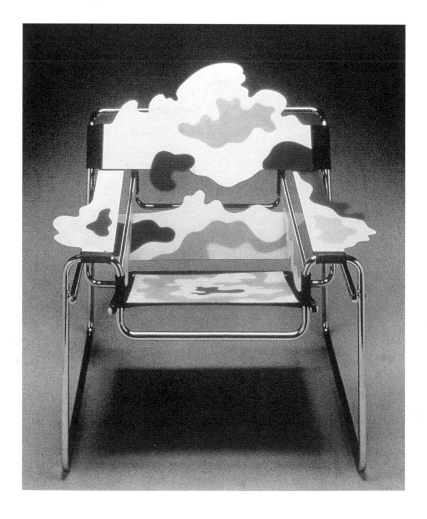

furniture, lighting fixtures, and ceramics by Sottsass, Michele De Lucchi, and Andrea Branzi that reflected the earlier work of these artists for Alchimia. Other designers who had not been associated with Alchimia also collaborated with Memphis, including such international figures as the Japanese Arata Isozaki, SHIRO KURAMATA, and Masanori Umeda; the Spaniard JAVIER MARISCAL; the Americans MICHAEL GRAVES and Peter Shire; the Austrians HANS HOLLEIN (no. 363) and Matteo Thun; and the Briton George James Sowden. From Sottsass's monumental *Casablanca* sideboard decorated with patterned plastic laminate (no. 362) and Umeda's wooden boxing-ring bed with a traditional tatami floor to Thun's pyramidal *Nefertiti* tea service, Memphis proclaimed the aesthetic and metaphysical values of color, symbol, ornamented surfaces, heterogeneous materials, and irregular shapes. In an interview that year, Sottsass delineated his differences with Alchimia: "There are no quotations from the past in these works," he insisted. "We are not going back to history . . . or attempting a folkloric/ecological approach."[4] Like postmodernism in general and Studio Alchimia in particular, however, Memphis did not present itself as a homogeneous movement or fashion, "nor is it a clearly defined programme," said the group's spokeswoman, Barbara Radice. "It operates in a gelatinous, rarefied area whose very nature precludes set models and definitions." Regarding the characteristics of the new "international style," she explained, "Next to the traditionally functional argument Memphis introduces color and decoration, and opens up infinite scope for enrichment and semantic dynamics. The decoration, in almost all these designs, is not a conceptual ploy. . . . It is not even (save a few exceptions) a cultivated quotation, as in the canonical examples of postmodernism in architecture, which dip into the heritage of classical cultures and tradition. The decoration starts and evolves as a game, a crust, ornament and possibly, as a reference to the themes and motifs of contemporary industrial and urban iconography."[5]

The Italian forms of postmodern design were influential out of all proportion to the size or commercial success of either Studio Alchimia or Memphis. As a style Italian postmodernism proved effortless to imitate and anyone, from High Point, North Carolina, to London and Milan, could and did practice with license its eclectic, decorative, and self-consciously novel formulas. "Art" furniture makers in the United States and elsewhere also produced designs after the Italian fashion that needed no tooling and could be made economically in very limited quantities. In part because of the popularization of this style, postmodernism faced a critical controversy similar to that inspired by the French "cubist" style at the Paris *Exposition Internationale des Arts Décoratifs* in 1925. Critics attacked the supposed lack of integrity and moral purpose of its practitioners, claiming that function and cost were irresponsibly ignored in favor of fashionable and expensive aesthetic gimmicks. References to the past or to tradition, they charged, were made at the level of the lowest common public denominator and were hence superficial and limited; references to popular culture and the industrial world, on the other hand, glorified a realm that was hardly

Team Disney Building by Arata Isozaki, Lake Buena Vista, Florida, 1991. Isozaki used whimsical and familiar forms, such as the Mickey Mouse ears, in his building at Disneyworld.

worth preserving or emulating. In reply to Portoghesi's exhibition of postmodern architecture at Venice's *Biennale* as well as to his series of advocative publications on the subject,[6] Manfredo Tafuri argued that postmodernism was merely a "'gay errancy,' . . . annulling history in reducing it to a field of visual incursions . . . informed by television." By taking the most superficial characteristics of modernism to extremes, he said, "There is good reason to label such a mixture of components as hypermodern. . . . And this is the point: the important themes carelessly assembled by the hypermodern synthesis . . . have been turned into an organ grinder's song. All of this may explain the success of the formula among those on the margins of the profession, seeking a forum and confronting a public eager for eccentric novelties."[7]

From as early as 1986, the death of postmodernism was broadly and variously reported,[8] despite the persistence of many of the stylistic features that appeared to define it. Advanced by the idea that design could be practiced on a high plane of fantasy, untrammeled by practical limitations, postmodernism did not disappear but reinvented itself in new imaginative forms that celebrated the inspiration of the designer and the value of communication over the object itself.

The value that postmodernism gave to symbol, temporality, and other "human" elements transformed and invigorated 1970s high tech during the 1980s. This idiom and its designers considered structure and the materials and processes of high technology to be absolute values in the functionalist sense; however, like other postmodernists, they came increasingly to explore the possibilities of integrating aesthetics, subjective expression, and communication into their design process, reinterpreting their technological vocabulary for expressive purposes. Creating domestic objects and appliances that depended on technology but approached sculpture, certain designers began to exploit the aesthetic effects of dynamic tension, movement, and the insubstantiality of structural materials. Using expanded steel mesh for interior and furniture design, Shiro Kuramata constructed ghostly immaterial forms like his *How High the Moon* chair (no. 392), which confounded conventional expectations of form and function. In his architecture and furniture—most notably a series of steel chairs for Alias—the Swiss designer MARIO BOTTA reduced his compositions to tense, mannered geometric silhouettes, producing designs that resembled deconstructed graphic symbols (no. 391). In an interview in 1982 Botta described his design process: "When I approach a design, I always look for the objective elements . . . those that have been transmitted to me. But I also know that perhaps the most important factor is the emotional one . . . it's the more sensitive." As a structuralist, however, Botta rejected the styles of postmodernism that exploited the surface: "It is important to find a solution to problems deep down," he said, "and not merely the skin of a problem. The Post-Modernists who try to find in the facade, in nostalgia, a solution to problems are merely looking at the skin. . . . The critical issue is never the facade, but always the structure."[9]

The concern for structural minimalism or the "deconstructed" object also appeared in several innovative high technology lighting systems. The Munich-based designer INGO MAURER freed the electric light from its source: stringing pendant lamps like holiday ornaments on thin, almost invisible low-voltage wires, Maurer created a magical atmosphere (no. 375). "I see this kind of lighting as having a spiritual feeling," he said when the system was introduced in 1984. "It's a way of choosing one's own light and a move towards individualism."[10] The American ALBERTO FRASER developed a lamp of a thin extruded ribbon of colored plastic containing electric wiring, an open display of structure and technology that he derived from computers, having seen colored computer ribbons and what he described as "magical black boxes" inside the machines" (no. 368). The Dutch designer RENÉ KEMNA reduced his lamp's thin fiberglass arm—which is also the electrical conductor—to a sweeping calligraphic sign (no. 387) not unlike Botta's graphic statements. Other designers humanized technological forms by deconstructing them in another sense, that is, by softening their contours. The application of ergonomics to consumer electronic equipment resulted in sculptural, organic forms that mimicked the shape and impressions of the human hand and fingers—such as DONALD BOOTY, JR.'s hand-held undulating calculator made in left- and right-handed models (no. 395).

To make its products more user-friendly, high-tech electronics also participated to some degree in the metaphorical and referential aspects of postmodernism. SONY CORPORATION's *Palmtop* computer and AT&T's personal communicator (no. 400), for example, employed a traditional stylus as the means of data input on a touch-sensitive screen, while TECHNOLOGY DESIGN drew on typological antecedents—paper, pencil, and books—as the formal inspiration for components of its personal computer (no. 396).

At its most innovative, this effort by high-tech designers to preserve the appearance of continuity with the past restored a kind of honesty to the sleekness and glossiness that technology could produce. Valued particularly in tradition-based Japan, this "retro-tech" approach was developed by the textile designer JUNICHI ARAI, who engineered high-tech layered fabrics into dimensional reliefs by computer, and finished them by chemical burn-out and melt-off processes and in vacuum heat-set machines that left wrinkled, curled, buckled, and shrunken surfaces with the appearance and texture of handcraft (no. 397). With Mitsubishi Petrochemical, Tatsugi Mizobe developed a speaker system from a plastic square printed with a resonating strip that is hand-rolled by the consumer into a funnel like a traditional Japanese paper product or sushi. In the United States, APRIL GREIMAN developed a new style of graphic design that looked back to handmade collage in its hybrid combinations of photographic, video, typographic, and computer-generated images (no. 373).

At the same time, traditional craft industries surviving into the 1980s and 1990s sought to make themselves more economically viable with high-tech processes and marketing techniques while preserving the craft values of authenticity, continuity, intimacy, and dignity in their products. The village of Wajima, Japan's traditional center of lacquer production, invited TOSHIYUKI KITA and other well-known designers to create a series of "modern" handcrafted lacquer tablewares (no. 388) in simpler, less labor-intensive styles that could be mass-marketed. The Italian designer GAETANO PESCE became concerned with developing less costly low technologies for what he termed "the third industrial revolution,"[11] creating the *Feltri* chair (no. 389) out of ordinary felt soaked with polyester resin, a process that he intended for semi-craft production in nonindustrialized countries. The Czech designer Bořek Šípek adapted traditional basketry techniques and materials from the Philippines to commercial furniture production in Italy, preserving the craft's aesthetic if not its means of production. Likewise the American architect FRANK O. GEHRY adopted basketry techniques to commercial production for his line of woven-wood furniture for Knoll (no. 398).

As they combined hand processes and industrial materials, "post-industrial" designers sought truthfulness and direct expression in a different way. Defying prettiness of form or manufacture by employing brutal new forms and low technologies, they intended to shake up the design world sometimes for simple shock value. RON ARAD in London (no. 393) and Elisabeth Garouste and Mattia Bonetti in Paris were among those who created furniture and objects in limited editions and as one-of-a-kind pieces, using metal (iron, steel, brass, and copper) and simple tools (hammer, tongs, and blowtorch). Their designs were deliberately raw and often crudely joined with welding and solder seams plainly visible. Invigorating and innovative at their best, these calculatedly abrasive objects demanded a reaction from the consumer. A graphic counterpart to these postindustrial furniture designs was the work of the French group GRAPUS, which exploited sometimes sloppy and unfinished freehand drawing and popular images with startling frankness (no. 378).

What linked these heterogeneous styles of postmodernism together, from Alchimia to the postindustrial, was their inventive fantasy, expressiveness, and almost universal acceptance of artifice. Plastic laminates in bright colors disguised fiberboard, fabrics that looked handmade were designed and made with fast modern machines, and metal furniture was carefully conceived to take on the aura of the salvage yard while high-tech functions were encased in humanized referential forms. These were designs that shouted rather than whispered, that could be abrasive and ironic, and that seemed to reflect all the complexity of a period that communicated in sound-bites and the virtual realities of computerized images.

362
ETTORE SOTTSASS, JR.
Casablanca sideboard, 1981

The centerpiece of the Memphis group's first collection in 1981, Ettore Sottsass, Jr.'s *Casablanca* sideboard is a totally original, fully developed, confident creation. The tall, bright, irregular wooden form containing a cupboard and three drawers features oblique, radiating arms that have been arbitrarily added. Its conception may have been influenced by Giacomo Balla's futurist designs for painted furniture (1918–22), but its only clear antecedents were the designs of the Studio

Alchimia, to which Sottsass himself had contributed. The sideboard is veneered with three differently colored printed plastic laminates in the *Spugnato* or *Sponge* pattern, which Sottsass designed in 1979 for Abet Laminati, a firm that later became one of Memphis's industrial collaborators. Memphis claimed that it was open to any stylistic option provided it involved aesthetic risks: the group favored discordant and unlikely combinations of acid with pastel colors, modest, vernacular materials in unsystematic shapes, and an abundance of ornament, usually in the form of fabrics with complex, small-scale patterns (no. 364) and laminates like this.

Made by Memphis, Milan. Wood and plastic laminate. 90$\frac{1}{2}$ x 59$\frac{1}{8}$ x 15$\frac{3}{4}$" (230 x 150 x 40 cm). (Philadelphia Museum of Art, gift of COLLAB and Abet Laminati.)

363
HANS HOLLEIN
Schwarzenberg side table, 1981

Hans Hollein was one of eight non-Italians (including MICHAEL GRAVES, SHIRO KURAMATA, and the Los Angeles architect Peter Shire) invited to contribute to the first Memphis collection, which was envisioned as its 1982 catalog stated as "a kind of anthology of the most contemporary researches in furniture and interior design." Ironically contrasting industrialized and "noble" decorative techniques, Hollein's stepped *Schwarzenberg* side table made for the collection creates a visual counterpoint between its pink veneered brierwood top, gilded legs, and black aniline-dyed base. Unlike the other Memphis designers, who exploited a playful popular asymmetry and bright discordant colors, Hollein reflected seriously on the communicative power of historical forms, suggesting with this table the virtues of

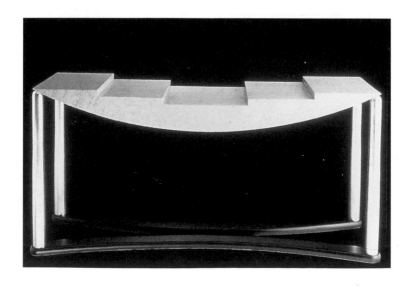

permanence and solemnity for the "elite,"[12] which Hollein conceives as the audience for his buildings, interiors, and surely for this Memphis design.

Made by Memphis, Milan. Gilded and dyed wood veneered with bricrwood. 32 1/4 x 63 x 18 1/2" (82 x 160 x 47 cm). (Memphis, Milan.)

364
NATHALIE DU PASQUIER
Gabon fabric, 1982

The fabrics of Nathalie du Pasquier, the first textile designer associated with Memphis, signified a new type of decorative thinking, which drew on a mixed and diverse set of ornamental precedents—from the arts of Africa and India, where she had traveled, to cubism, graffiti, and comic book illustrations. But du Pasquier recombined them in an original, often naive, way that seemed to ignore all conventions of Western design. "Some designers," explained Memphis's art director and spokesperson Barbara Radice, "are introducing colour and decoration without referring to contemporary iconographies, but freely and more or less insistently resuming themes and motifs that belong to the tradition of history of architecture and of the applied arts. They recompose these themes and motifs . . . in the form of eclectic collages; and they redevelop them so that they are barely recognizable . . . until absolutely new objects have been imagined."[13] Du Pasquier's fabrics, introduced as coverings for George Sowden's *Oberoi* armchair and *Chelsea* bed in Memphis's initial collection in 1981, were made available independently in its second collection the next year. Named after African countries, the seven designs shown in 1982, which included her frenetic *Gabon* fabric printed in six colors on cotton, were dense, angular, and irregular patterns with strongly discordant palettes. They were produced by Rainbow, the firm founded in 1972 by

Fabio Bellotti, which also provided fabrics for such fashion designers as Issey Miyake, Giorgio Armani, and Gianni Versace.

Made by Rainbow, Milan, for Memphis. Printed cotton. Width: 55 1/8" (140 cm). (Philadelphia Museum of Art, gift of Furniture of the Twentieth Century.)

365
MARCO ZANINI
Alpha Centauri vase, 1982

Marco Zanini's rich, deeply colored *Alpha Centauri* vase was one of several designs he created for the Murano glass industry that were included in the second Memphis collection, expanding the group's initial focus on furniture, lamps, and clocks to embrace fabrics, silver, porcelain, and glass. Zanini, who had no training as a glass craftsman, approached this project from the point of view of an industrial designer: instead of conceiving his glasswares as integral creations blown and formed at the furnace in a single operation, he followed an additive method as if he were assembling a simple appliance or piece of furniture. Toso, the Muranese glasshouse that made this vase, is one of the firms that supported Memphis by manufacturing its products; founded in the 1930s to breathe new life into Venetian glassblowing, it produces both traditional wares and innovative designs such as this.

Made by Toso Vetri d'Arte, Murano, Italy, for Memphis. Blown colored glass. Height: 15 5/8" (39.7 cm). (Philadelphia Museum of Art, gift of COLLAB.)

366
GIORGETTO GIUGIARO
Logica electronic sewing machine, 1981

Styled with acute angles and hard edges more attuned to the spirit of the Volkswagen *Rabbit* (which he designed) than to conventional sewing machines, Giorgetto Giugiaro's *Logica* introduced electronic functions and a pictorial display to this appliance, expanding the flexibility and speed of domestic sewing. The machine's memory includes instructions for basic stitches and functions, for intricate decorative embroidery, and for monogramming, any of which can be produced singly or in succession by programming the keyboard and then guiding the material under the needle. The machine's functions are separated into two distinct areas, programming at right, and sewing, using an arm that extends forward close to the operator, at left. Most of the hand controls have been eliminated—indeed only a few mechanical parts remain—and the hand wheel, traditionally at the extreme right, has been moved adjacent to the needle so that all manual activity involved in the sewing process is efficiently located in one place.

Made by Necchi, Pavia, Italy. Plastic and aluminum housing. 10 x 16 1/2 x 9 5/8" (25.5 x 42 x 24.5 cm). (Necchi, Pavia, Italy.)

367
I.D. TWO
Compass personal computer, 1982

Industrial design and engineering rather than computer technology were the keys to producing Grid's *Compass,* the world's first truly portable computer: technological miniaturization had already been accomplished by 1982 but the physical elements of the product had to be greatly compacted and tightly organized. The *Compass* computer was conceived by Grid Systems for a business executive to use at home or while traveling. The I.D. Two design firm was then asked to make the powerful computer thin enough to fit into a briefcase and light enough so there would be no resistance to carrying it, with a flat panel display, large memory, and modems for voice and data transmission by telephone lines. The housing material became a major consideration: plastic, which was light, was not sufficiently rugged and would not easily dissipate the heat, while aluminum exceeded the weight limit established for the project. By its innovative use of magnesium, which was light, strong, and had adequate heat transfer characteristics, the firm created a product that weighed under ten pounds. The lighter metal had the added advantage of being well suited to precision casting, accommodating a second innovative design feature, involving the pivoting hinge assembly through which the electric cables are guided and which regulates the opening and closing of the display. The *Compass* computer,[14] with its black housing and amber electroluminescent display, won the Industrial Designers Society of America's Industrial Design Excellence Award in 1982.

Made by Grid Systems Corporation, Mountain View, California. Magnesium housing. 2 x 15 x 11 1/2" (5 x 38 x 29 cm). (Grid Systems Corporation, Mountain View, California.)

368
ALBERTO FRASER
Nastro table lamp, 1983–84

Supple extruded plastic allows the body of Alberto Fraser's *Nastro* (*Ribbon*) halogen lamp to be moved easily into any position, making it as flexible as the counterbalanced and articulated adjustable lamps that function by mechanical means. The unusual, colorful plastic form that supports the bulb was an unintended by-product of Fraser's work as a consultant designer for the computer industry. "I was fascinated by the imagery of these machines in their naked state," he recalled, "that is, without their outer coverings or housings. They were full of magical black boxes and ribbons of a colored, co-extruded wire, harnessings which electrically connected the various electro-mechanical components." Taking the computer ribbons as his model and wanting "to make a light which has all electrical and mechanical components enclosed and manufactured in one production process,"[15] Fraser developed an extruded plastic ribbon containing electrical wiring that could be made to rotate, would remain in any position, and became both its structure and decoration.

Made by Stilnovo, Lainate, Italy. Plastic. Length of reflector: 8¹/4" (21 cm); length of base: 5¹/2" (14 cm). (Stilnovo, Lainate, Italy.)

369
VERNER PANTON
Mira-Columba fabric, 1983

Verner Panton's *Mira-Columba* pattern was one of eight woven, printed, or burn etched fabrics introduced by the Swiss firm Mira-X in 1983 as part of his Orbit collection, all elements of which were based on a rigorous double-square design and all bearing astronomical names. Overlying the clearly delineated regular grid structure of *Mira-Columba* is a complex arrangement of color variations, which may be read as large horizontal, vertical, or diagonal areas syncopated with the colors of the small squares within. The lively pattern of *Mira-Columba*, printed in flat colors, glossy enamels, and gold and silver, recalls the electronic digitalized displays and computer graphics that had become familiar by the early 1980s.

Made by Mira-X, Suhr, Switzerland. Printed cotton cretonne. Width: 52" (129.5 cm). (Philadelphia Museum of Art, gift of the manufacturer.)

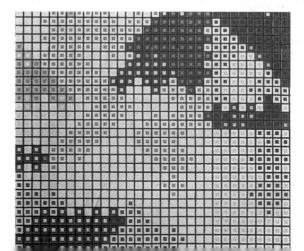

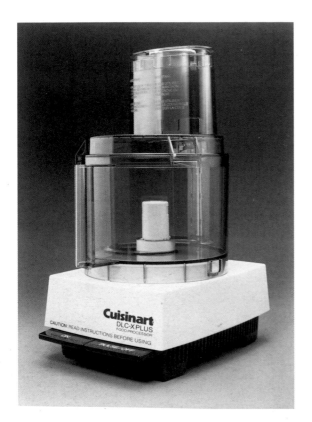

United States as a consumer appliance in 1973. Invented ten years earlier in France for professional use, it was modified for the American consumer market by the Cuisinarts company's president Carl Sontheimer. But the machine was never fully reconsidered until Marc Harrison was called in to create a deluxe model with large food capacity that was safer and easier to use. In approaching this design problem, Harrison chose to examine the needs of the disabled, including those with arthritis and visual impairments, realizing that if he could address his product to the requirements of this group it would be suited to and benefit the entire consumer population. Harrison studied the operations and parts of the machine closely for function and safety. With the aid of anthropometric data he designed the handle of the work bowl to fit better into the palm of the hand, made the controls into long flat bars so that they could be operated with simple motions, and used large prominent graphics for the controls and warning label.

Made by Cuisinarts, Greenwich, Connecticut. Polycarbonate plastic and nylon housing. Height: 17 1/4" (43.8 cm). (Cuisinarts Corporation, Stamford, Connecticut.)

370
MARC HARRISON
Cuisinart DLC-X food processor, 1981

The *Cuisinart* food processor has had a phenomenal sales success virtually since it was introduced in the

371
EUREKA COMPANY
Mighty Mite vacuum cleaner, 1982

A strong, compact unit that greatly reduced the size and weight of a standard vacuum cleaner, Eureka's *Mighty Mite* introduced a new friendly format for appli-

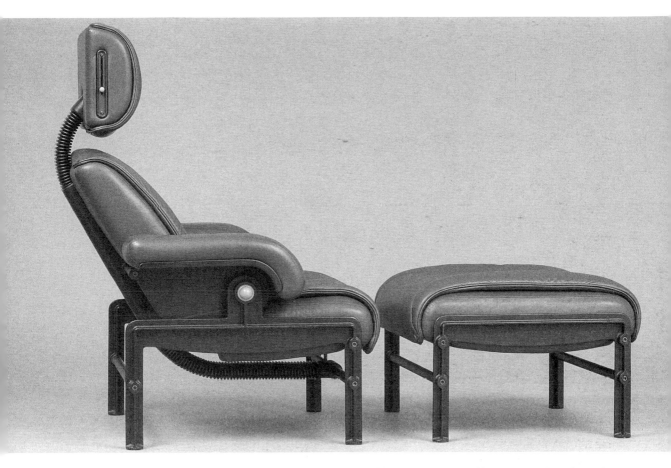

ances with its stylish, up-to-date appearance, large, readable graphics, and a visual vocabulary borrowed from sports and portable aerospace equipment. Its vivid, glossy red or yellow plastic housing posed on large, easy-turning wheels gives the vacuum a unique witty presentation contrived by the company's designers Samuel E. Hohulin and Kenneth R. Parker. It is small enough to be moved about easily and to sit on a step, and light enough to be hand held or carried on a shoulder strap for the entire cleaning process. While using this small appliance may have seemed like child's play, the consumer must have needed reassurance about its power and utility, for a national advertising campaign proclaimed: "This is no toy. The new Eureka Mighty Mite is a mighty serious vacuum cleaner."

ABS plastic housing. 11 x 11 1/2 x 6 3/4" (28 x 29.2 x 17.2 cm). (The Eureka Company, Detroit.)

372
NIELS DIFFRIENT
Jefferson armchair and ottoman, 1984

For half a century, ergonomic design in America was led by the firm of HENRY DREYFUSS, where Niels Diffrient worked and collaborated on the *Humanscale* series. These volumes provide extensive data about the human body and have become standard tools for designers concerned with human factors engineering. Diffrient's own design has focused primarily on seating in transportation and the workplace, where people must sit in one position for a long time; the two office chairs he designed for SunarHauserman and Knoll have been especially praised for their comfort and suitability for office tasks. With his *Jefferson* chair, Diffrient brought ergonomic studies and seating technology closer to the home. While the chair was produced for business executives and comes with accessory stands for computers and lights, it was also designed for the home office and for relaxation. It is soft but supportive, mimicking the postures of the human body as it reclines. Diffrient called the chair *Jefferson* because he derived the concept of a multifunction lounge-work center from the famous chair and ottoman with candle lights and writing table designed by Thomas Jefferson for Monticello, his home in Virginia.

Made by SunarHauserman, Cleveland, Ohio. Aluminum and steel with leather-covered polyurethane upholstery. Height: 40 1/2" (102.9 cm). (Niels Diffrient.)

289

373
APRIL GREIMAN
Poster for Pacific Design Center, 1983

The leading exponent of the new style of graphic design that emerged in California in the late 1970s, April Greiman works with what she calls "hybrid imagery." She combines geometric shapes, sophisticated color combinations, and type into highly energetic, original compositions with a deep, uncanny space of her own construction. Greiman creates distinct and contradictory perspectives by angling the shapes and images (sometimes photographs), establishing figures and planes that tilt, overlap, and carry type that conforms to the illusion, further defining the intricate layering of spatial information that has become her trademark. Greiman's original approach is a decisive break with the long-standing convention mandating the flatness of the picture plane as a support for graphics. Her fascination with depth is playfully exaggerated here by the seemingly out-of-register typography and imagery that produces an extreme three-dimensional effect when viewed through the special glasses distributed with the poster, a throwback to the 3-D craze of the 1950s. Greiman's work has succeeded because the space she composes is convincing; likewise the clarity of her message, linked to the discipline of her typographic studies in the early 1970s with Armin Hofmann and WOLFGANG WEINGART in Switzerland, is not compromised.

Offset lithograph. 36.x 24" (91.3 x 61.2 cm). (April Greiman.)

374
ACHILLE CASTIGLIONI
Gibigiana table lamp, 1980

Gibigiana, the Italian term for a flash of light reflected from a mirror, precisely describes the principle of Achille Castiglioni's lamp: contained within its conelike form is a small halogen bulb directed upward at a circular mirror, which reflects the light and concentrates it onto a particular spot. The angle of reflection, and thus the direction of the path of light, is controlled by a thumbscrew on the circular housing holding the mirror, while the intensity of the light is adjusted by moving a lever along the flat side of the lamp. Insistently eccentric in its formal design, *Gibigiana* was engineered as thoroughly as if it were an instrument designed for a scientific purpose.

Manufactured by Flos, Brescia, Italy. Enameled steel and aluminum. Height: 16½" (41.9 cm). (Flos, Brescia, Italy.)

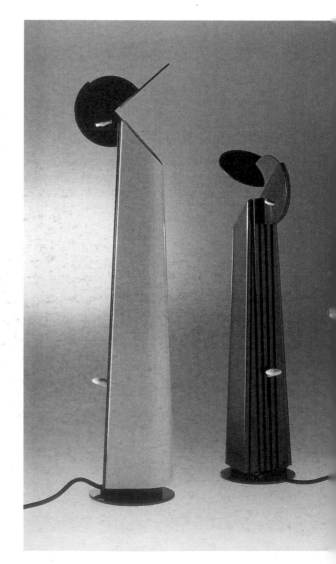

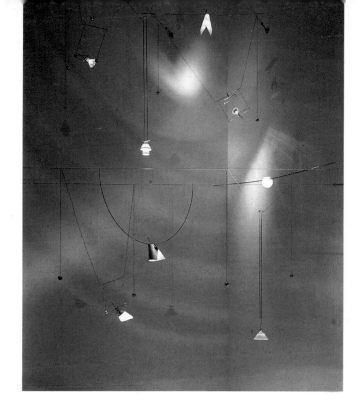

375
INGO MAURER
YaYaHo lighting system, 1981–84

One of the most innovative lighting designers of recent years, Ingo Maurer combined expressionism and high technology in his *YaYaHo* system of conductive low-voltage cables and pendant lamps. With a variety of clip-on miniature glass and metal light sources that can be arranged at will by the user, the strung cables have the magical appearance of Christmas lights or a light mobile. In development for almost three years, *YaYaHo* was first exhibited at the Euroluce lighting fair in Milan in 1984 where it challenged the traditional concept of lamps as objects that are simply plugged into interiors. Instead, a work of art as well as technology, the *YaYaHo* itself defines interior space and creates a broadly evocative visual mood.

Made by Design M Ingo Maurer, Munich. Glass, ceramic, metal, and plastic. Length of cables: 118¹/₈" (6 m); height of fixtures: 19¹/₂" (50 cm). (Ingo Maurer.)

376
FUJIWO ISHIMOTO
Maisema fabric, 1982

Since 1974 the Japanese designer Fujiwo Ishimoto has been working for Marimekko, introducing patterns of visible, uneven brushstrokes and subtle, sometimes dissonant colors into the firm's textile design. This squared *Maisema* (*Landscape*) design is translated directly from the artist's crayon sketches and visibly communicates the freshness and spontaneity of the act of drawing, which many artists in the 1980s considered the most important part of the design process. Ishimoto conceived of this design as a four seasons series, abstractly representing seasonal changes in climate, vegetation, and lighting by changes in color-way and density of line. His reverence for the landscape bridged the difference between Finnish and Japanese cultures, both of which highly value the relationship of man with nature.

Made by Marimekko, Helsinki. Printed cotton. Width: 54" (137.2 cm). (Philadelphia Museum of Art, gift of Marimekko, Helsinki.)

377
VICO MAGISTRETTI
Sindbad armchair, 1981

Sindbad is "a chair without upholstery,"[16] according to Vico Magistretti, who came by his idea for the design after buying a group of horse blankets in an equestrian shop in London and using them to throw over sofas and chairs as loose covers. Instead of conventional fixed upholstery, the chair has an ingenious blanketlike cover that is removable and can be changed at will, thrown over a flexible steel-framed foam padding and attached to the seat by means of hooks, with an adhesive strip and two clips near the back as anchors. Like MARIO BELLINI's *Cab* chair of 1976, which he reduced to a steel frame and zippered-leather cover (no. 351), Magistretti's *Sindbad* design boils the chair down to its typological essentials—structural frame and cover—and offers its soft colorful surface as a friendly concession to functional necessity.

Made by Cassina, Meda, Italy. Lacquered beechwood with steel-framed wool and grosgrain-covered upholstery over foam padding of polyester and polyurethane. 41³/8 x 43⁵/16 x 33¹/2" (105 x 110 x 85 cm). (Cassina, Meda, Italy.)

378
GRAPUS
Poster for the Musée de l'Affiche, Paris, 1982

Grapus, an alternative French design collective founded in 1970, invented a visual language that distinguished the work it did for leftist political organizations and small cultural groups from the slickness of commercial advertising. By the 1980s their approach had become one of the most influential new forces in French graphic design. By focusing on process, the group sought to engage the viewer with its deconstructed graphic images. Among the tricks Grapus devised to arouse curiosity and draw the viewer closer to its work were handwritten messages (which expanded on, or sometimes even interfered with, the primary text), quixotic areas of seemingly unfinished freehand drawing, and a sloppy or imprecise execution. Here, in a poster for an exhibition of its work at Paris's Musée de l'Affiche (Poster Museum), Grapus used these techniques and an agglomeration of metaphorical elements to summarize the group's history and radical design approach: its sense of humor, its social commitment (the hammer and sickle), its national allegiance (the blue, white, and red target), its graphic simplicity (primary colors and basic symbols such as sun, moon, and arrow), and its affection for recognizable imagery (Mickey Mouse, the Hitlerian mustache and hair, and the television antennae).

Lithograph. 23³/8 x 31¹/4" (60 x 80 cm). (Musée de la Publicité, Paris.)

379
SINYA OKAYAMA
Kazenoko stool, 1984

This stool was first in a series of furniture designs by
Sinya Okayama that take their shape from kanji—the
Japanese written system of pictographs—to which he
gives highly finished three-dimensional form. Like other
postmodern designers, Okayama is interested in creating a dialogue between the object and the user
through the use of familiar symbols, here directed
specifically at the Japanese audience who can "read"
the object as a graphic code and understand its literal
meaning, "child of the wind" (*kazenoko*). The stool was
first exhibited at the *Phoenix* exhibition in Toronto in
1984 and attracted international attention, including
that of ALESSANDRO MENDINI, with whom Okayama
subsequently collaborated. He shares with Mendini a
fundamental interest in design as the act of conception,
creating symbols that have the power to communicate,
as Mendini described in the opening passage of his
manifesto for Alchimia, the radical design group he
founded: "The act itself of 'drawing' is what counts
today. To draw, meaning the act of making signs, is not
to design', nor to 'project': it is instead a free and continuous expression of thought, made visual."[17]

*Made by Interior Object, Tokyo. Painted steel with plastic
upholstery. 11 13/16 x 18 x 16 1/2" (30 x 46 x 42 cm).
(Philadelphia Museum of Art, gift of COLLAB.)*

380
JAVIER MARISCAL AND PEPE CORTÉS
Araña floor lamp, 1985

Javier Mariscal began his career as a cartoonist, and
most of his product designs, like this lamp in the form
of a spider (*araña*), translate his humorous graphic lines
into three dimensions. Employing the cartoonist's stock
tools of lightning bolt and zigzag, used here for the spider's red steel legs, Mariscal communicates the awkward industriousness of his domesticated insect. This is
one of a series of lamps Mariscal designed with his collaborator, Pepe Cortés, for the B.D. furniture manufacturer in Barcelona, using steel in varying finishes and
thin, quirky, cartoonlike forms. His expressive, often figurative forms relate to the imagery of such Spanish
artists as the surrealist painter Salvador Dalí and the
filmmaker Luis Buñuel as well as ANTONÍ GAUDÍ,
although the sketchy, linear, graphic style Mariscal
employs is his entirely personal contribution to the
recent renaissance in Spanish design.

*Made by BD Ediciones de Diseño, Barcelona. Epoxy-coated
steel. 10 1/2 x 23 1/2 x 8" (27 x 60 x 20 cm). (Estudio
Mariscal, Barcelona.)*

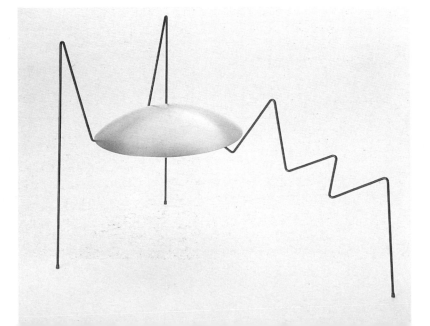

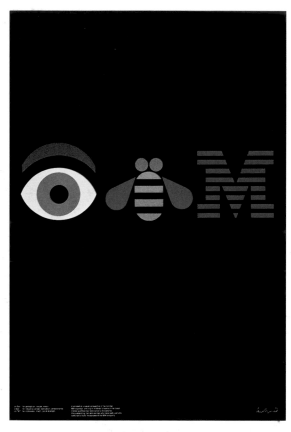

381
PAUL RAND
Poster for International Business Machines, 1982

As consultant designer for International Business
Machines, Paul Rand has conceived a remarkably intelligent and successful corporate identity program, establishing the company's solid image through the high
quality of its displays, promotional materials, product
identity, packaging, and advertisements over several
decades and across the continents. The IBM logo that
he designed for the corporation in 1956 (and later
revised) was based on the letterforms of a geometric,
slab-serif typeface called City Medium, designed by
Georg Trump in 1930. It became so universally recognizable that when he deconstructed it into a rebus in 1982
there was little doubt that this poster (eye-bee-M)
would not be immediately understood. By choosing to
work with humor—one of Rand's favorite graphic
devices—he added an aura of user-friendliness to a conservative company that dealt in high technology.

*Lithograph. 37³/₈ x 26¹/₄" (95.9 x 67.3 cm). (Museum of
Modern Art, New York, gift of the designer.)*

382
MARIO BELLINI
ET Personal 55 **electronic typewriter, 1985–86**

Those industrial designers in the 1980s who created
housings for sophisticated electronics were largely free
to invent forms independent of the miniaturized technologies within. Unlike their predecessors, who were
required to accommodate sizable internal mechanical
functions, designers like Mario Bellini were faced primarily with engaging the consumer on a visual and
practical level. His *ET Personal 55* portable electronic
typewriter, Olivetti's lightweight contender in the highly competitive market of personal computers and

word processors, introduced a dashing new look to the firm's products. Taking the wedge shape he had used for earlier equipment (no. 347), Bellini (working with Alessandro Chiarato) restricted his typewriter to structural essentials to ensure its lightness. He reduced the machine to a thin stepped profile boldly articulated with sculptured corrugated bands and introduced selective coloration (gray keyboard and base, light blue top, and yellow knobs for the paper roller) to make the product user-friendly.

Made by Ing. C. Olivetti & C., Ivrea, Italy. ABS plastic housing. 4⁷/₈ x 16¹/₈ x 13" (12.5 x 41 x 33 cm). (C. Olivetti & C., Ivrea, Italy.)

383
FROGDESIGN
Apple IIc personal computer and Imagewriter II printer, 1982–85

The compact, clear presentation and ease of operation of the *Apple IIc* made it the first truly user-friendly computer. Its scaled-down components, including keyboard and disk drive, are integrated into one portable unit, whose handle folds to support it at an efficient angle for typing; the separate monitor fits over it on a special stand. The integrated form was the idea of Apple's president Steven P. Jobs, who at a meeting in 1982 simply "took an Apple II logic board, slapped a keyboard on top, then put a disk drive over the remaining space and said, 'This should be our next computer! Isn't that a great idea?'"[18] Carried out by frogdesign along with the Apple design staff, the computer was given an expressive sculptural form, sophisticated surface and graphic treatments, and the off-white color imitated almost immediately by rival computer manufacturers. The active, articulated forms of the *Imagewriter II* printer show the consistent design attitude that has been applied to Apple's entire line. The *Apple IIc* was voted "Best of Category" in *Industrial Design* magazine's annual design review of 1985, and the *Imagewriter* was included the next year.

Made by Apple Computer, Cupertino, California. ABS plastic housing. Width of computer: 11³/₈" (29 cm); width of printer: 17⁵/₈" (44.8 cm). (Apple Computer, Cupertino, California.)

384

PHILIPPE STARCK

Président M table, 1981–84

Philippe Starck was one of five young interior architects chosen in 1981 to refurbish the private apartments of the French presidential residence, the Elysée Palace in Paris, a commission responsible for his early celebrity and for refocusing international attention on modern French furniture design. Starck insisted on a broader distribution for his work, making many of the presidential pieces available to the public at the same time through a mail-order catalog and other distributors. His *Président M* table, designed for the bedroom of Danielle Mitterand, the president's wife, has a glass top that seems to hover perversely over the pyramidal structure, supported not on its apex but on the points of the four die-cast fins attached to tubular sections, which fit into the black metal legs. The construction of these expressive elements gives an indication of Starck's involvement with furniture mechanics—with the hinges and joints that make many of his designs flexible, foldable, and disassemblable—and with the economics of manufacture, sale, and delivery. Both clear and contradictory in conveying the way it functions, the table partakes of an intellectualism that Starck identifies as a national characteristic: "Not being a Minimalist like the Scandinavians, nor serious like the Germans, nor austere like the Spanish, nor creative like the Italians, the French can only claim the qualities of thoughtfulness and balance. . . . I aim for my work to have this French quality."[19]

Made by Baleri Italia, Bergamo, Italy. Varnished steel and glass. 29 1/2 x 53 1/2 x 53 1/2" (75 x 136 x 136 cm). (Baleri Italia, Bergamo, Italy.)

385

ROBERT VENTURI

Sheraton chair, 1979–84

The series of nine plywood chairs that Robert Venturi designed for Knoll stands as a manifesto of postmodern historicism, recapitulating the progress of historic styles and rejecting the modernist bias against tradition. Like Red Grooms's caricature constructions or silhouettes lined up on a chart of furniture styles, the chairs express in broad outline and selective detail the salient features of each era—Queen Anne, Chippendale, Gothic Revival, Hepplewhite, Sheraton, Empire, Biedermeier, Art Nouveau, and Art Deco—but only as flat false fronts or facades, Venturi's witty way of presenting the past in contemporary terms. Viewed from the side, the structure of the chairs is exposed and they appear virtually alike as thin factory-made molded-plywood forms. This, the *Sheraton* chair, has a multicolor silkscreen pattern of neoclassical ornament with column, swag, molding, and vase. It and the entire series further confound historical accuracy when furnished with alternative solid finishes or allover laminates in Venturi's own floral *Grandmother* pattern. The values of historical style and ornament had first been introduced to the postwar generation with Venturi's *Complexity and Contradiction in Architecture* (1966). This book became one of the basic treatises of postmodernism, leading such architects as Robert Stern and MICHAEL GRAVES to adopt the forms and often the materials of the historical past, and to introduce color and ornament into their work.

Made by Knoll International, New York. Painted plywood. Height: 33 1/4" (88.4 cm). (Philadelphia Museum of Art, gift of COLLAB.)

386
MICHAEL GRAVES
Tea kettle, 1984–85

The bird-whistle tea kettle designed by the architect Michael Graves is one of the few successful mass market products associated with postmodernism, with annual sales of 100,000 posted by its Italian metalware manufacturer, Alessi. The concept could hardly be simpler: the prosaic red molded-plastic bird whimsically suggests a source for the teapot's whistle—calling up precedents in ceramic bird whistles and in ornaments on American nineteenth-century Federal tea and coffee services—and at the same time brings the object figurative relief, fantasy, and humor. The kettle itself employs a classical motif, the well-metered line of raised dots encircling the conical stainless steel vessel at its base; color was added with the insulated blue plastic grip, red spherical accents, and black ball on top. An alternative whistling teapot from Alessi, designed by RICHARD SAPPER the previous year, emulates an old-fashioned train whistle in its brass pipe form and its tone.

Made by Alessi, Crusinallo, Italy. Stainless steel and polyamide. Height: 87/8" (22.5 cm). (Alessi, Crusinallo, Italy.)

387
RENÉ KEMNA
Sigla table lamp, 1986

Insistent in its bold calligraphic gesture or sign (*sigla*), René Kemna's lamp represents a form of technological expressionism. Made of a thin fiberglass material developed for this purpose, the sweeping arm, which adjusts both horizontally and vertically, is itself the electrical conductor, while the nylon friction joint, also a new invention, allows the arm to be locked securely into any position. Produced in table, clip-on, and floor models, the Sigla series greatly refines the concept of the adjustable work lamp, providing a considerably more sensitive system than articulated arms in order to position and rotate the halogen bulb properly for close illumination.

Made by Sirrah, Imola, Italy. Painted metal, anodized aluminum, fiberglass, and nylon. Height (extended): 331/2" (85 cm). (Sirrah, Imola, Italy.)

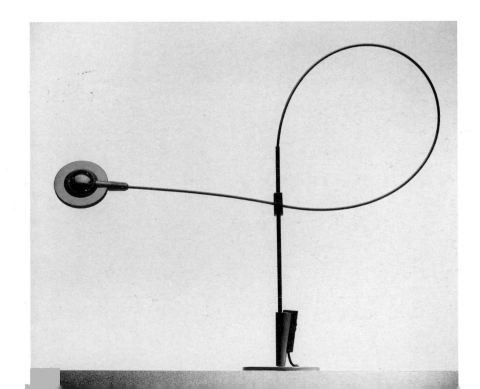

crafts, but to use such materials to pave the way for a new era in articles for daily use," he declared.[20] One of a series of lacquerwares he designed for the Japanese table, including a tray with lid for sushi, nesting boxes for food, and chopsticks, this bowl is handmade in the slow, costly, traditional way. But these tablewares are given sleeker, broader silhouettes and proportions than the forms on which they are based. Rejecting the instability and technological bias of modern culture, Kita discovered in the Japanese village and its artistic handcraft the virtues of authenticity, continuity, intimacy, and order.

Made by Koshudo Company, Wajima, Japan. Lacquered wood. Height of covered bowl: 3³/₄" (8 cm); diameter: 5³/₄" (13 cm). (Toshiyuki Kita.)

388
TOSHIYUKI KITA
Urushi table service, 1986

By reinterpreting traditional materials and techniques in his Urushi (Lacquer) series, Toshiyuki Kita was engaged in establishing a modern cultural identity and market for the local industry of Wajima, Japan's most important center of lacquer production, just as he had with his Kyo paper lamps designed between 1971 and 1983. "I want not only to simply preserve traditional

389
GAETANO PESCE
Feltri chair, 1987

Continuing to experiment with innovative fabricating techniques and materials, especially plastics, an interest that has characterized his career as a furniture designer (nos. 307, 343), Gaetano Pesce devised a method for using ordinary felt as a structural substance by soaking it with polyester resin. Sheets of thick felt precut into the form of his *Feltri* (Felt) chairs are impregnated with liquid resin in different quantities, more on the bottom

to make it rigid for support, less on the top to keep it supple so that the back of the chair can be turned like a collar. The tub-shaped forms are hardened in a mold, sprayed with color, laced with twine for decoration, and upholstered with a quilted pad. Pesce's manufacturing concept, with its relatively low start-up costs and semi-craft-based production methods, is a simple manufacturing process to follow, even in nonindustrialized countries, and underscores his view of the future role of technology: "Many people say the future will be more complex. I don't believe that. Instead, we will have shorter production runs—not millions of copies but 3000 or 4000. Technologies must therefore be inexpensive. . . . Feltri represents this idea very well. To make 10 copies of it is the same price as to make a million copies."[21]

Made by Cassina, Meda, Italy. Wool felt, polyester resin, and hemp, with fabric-covered down upholstery. 55 1/8 x 29 1/8 x 25 3/16" (140 x 74 x 64 cm). (Cassina, Meda, Italy.)

390

KING-MIRANDA ASSOCIATI
Expanded Line Network lighting system, 1983

King-Miranda's total illumination system, the *Expanded Line Network*, was the first significant advance in envi-

ronmental track lighting since LIGHTOLIER introduced it in 1963 (no. 284). The suspended fixtures draw power from a track of 1.25-meter modules, a concept inspired by Dodgem or bumper cars at amusement parks, "with that pole which took energy from the net ceiling. . . . Expanded Line uses this principle in a new way to distribute light and energy in space."[22] Its principal advance was the ability to combine standard and low-voltage light sources, both fluorescents and halogens, in the same system, and to house them not only at the track but suspended on poles from it. King-Miranda developed a range of light fittings of varied materials and colors as well as several special bulbs for this flexible system, including miniature dichroic (heat and color dissipating) spots, low-voltage halogen fixtures that give a spot effect below and a flood above, ceramic incandescent fixtures with direct and indirect lighting, and coupled fluorescent-tube fittings with louver shields or plastic diffusers to provide background lighting.

Made by Arteluce, Brescia, Italy. Aluminum, steel, ceramic, plastic and glass. Length of longer track: 71" (180.3 cm). (Flos, Brescia, Italy.)

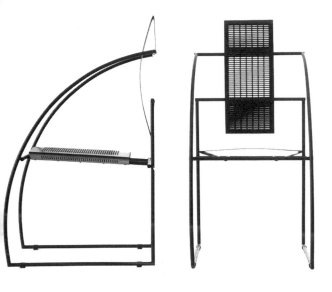

391
MARIO BOTTA
Quinta armchair, 1985

When Mario Botta, the Swiss structural-rationalist architect, was asked by Alias to design furniture, he applied the universal principles of functionalism—geometry, formal order, and structural clarity—to highly expressive ends. Radically reduced to a tense, thin metal outline, his *Quinta* (*Fifth*) chair has the clear structural rigor and the same type of continuous frame as tubular-steel chairs designed in the 1920s—although the Botta piece, reflecting the significant voids in his own buildings, is perversely interrupted so that the arms do not rest on the back member. Using industrial materials such as perforated sheet metal for the seat, Botta bares them in a cooly elegant, mechanistic display. Assessing his *Prima* (*First*) chair, designed for Alias in 1982, but equally descriptive of this one, Botta observed: "This is a very vain chair. It wants to show everything of itself. It was built to show all points of attachment; nothing is hidden. Therefore, the seat is perforated, to reveal a glimpse of the understructure. Its two colors distinguish support from that which is supported."[23]

Made by Alias, Milan. Painted iron and copper. 36 1/4 x 17 3/4 x 20 1/2" (92 x 45 x 52 cm). (Alias, Milan.)

392
SHIRO KURAMATA
How High the Moon armchair, 1986

Shiro Kuramata's innovative transformations of common industrial materials—including steel mesh, terraz-

zo, corrugated aluminum, and steel cables—pushed material technologies to new limits as design possibilities. Asked whether the materials themselves, as opposed to his own ideas, determined his design process, Kuramata replied, "The design image comes first. Once I get my idea, I find materials literally by the roadside and can utilize information gleaned from daily life."[24] The designer first began experimenting with steel mesh in 1984 when he completely fitted out the interior of the Esprit boutique in Hong Kong with mesh grid—walls and ceiling, hanging and shelving units; three years later, for the Issey Miyake boutique in Tokyo's Seibu department store, Kuramata created another mesh interior with tall, shaped mesh columns growing from the floor up to airy ceiling canopies. Part of the same series of experiments, which also included his *North Latitude* table in 1985, *How High the Moon* shares their effect of immateriality. Its metal mesh surface is reduced to a series of crossing points and finished with a custom paint that includes nickel or copper. The transparent, shimmering, apparently weightless volume of the chair is otherworldly, suggesting, perhaps, its name. Dematerialization and the ironies of function and form were constant themes of Kuramata's during the 1980s.

Made by IDÉE (Kurosaki Trading Company), Tokyo. Painted steel. 27 3/8 x 37 1/2 x 32 1/2" (69.5 x 95.5 x 82.5 cm). (Kuramata Design Office, Tokyo.)

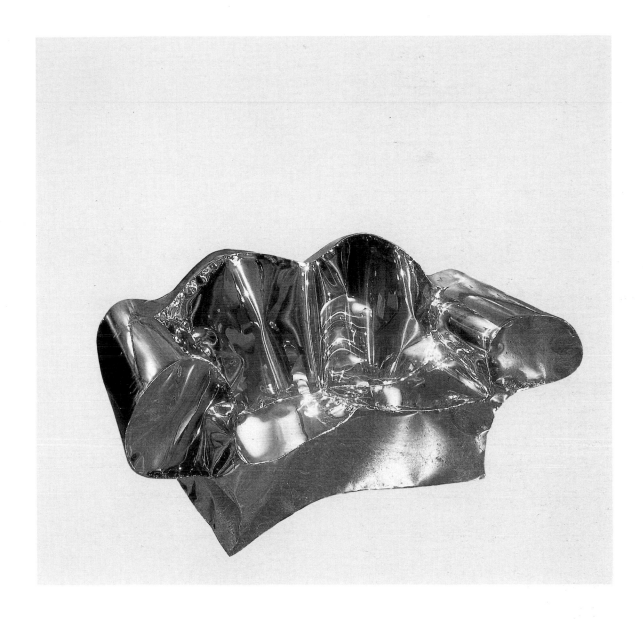

393
RON ARAD
Big Easy Volume 2 sofa, 1988

Ron Arad's Big Easy Volumes series of chairs are hollow, welded-steel forms, some partly filled with sand, which can be shifted to alter their center of gravity—and their equilibrium. Mimicking the rounded silhouettes of traditional overstuffed upholstered furniture, this sofa offers an unexpectedly comfortable seat given its hard surface. Although all the components of the series are cut from the same coarsely flamboyant patterns, the chairs and sofas acquire individuality as the metal pieces are put together in the process of welding. Indeed Arad compares his use of the blowtorch to the idiosyncracies of freehand drawing. "The whole collection came from a series of freehand sketches," he explained. "I wanted to do furniture that would be true to the original drawing and yet be refined. I used the drawing line as the welding line."[25] The shapes and seams are irregular, and the surface finish is also reflective; since the polished sides are uneven, the reflections mirrored in them are distorted. Like other postmodern designers, Arad confounds handcraft processes and industrial materials for expressive purposes, and the result is that his designs lose their technological quality and take on the aspects of one-of-a-kind pieces. Arad's aesthetic vocabulary, which can be both raw and brutal, challenges conventional assumptions about such crafted objects. "I like creating expectations," Arad says, "and then breaking them."[26]

Made by One Off, London. Stainless steel and steel. Height:
34 1/4" (87 cm). (One Off, London.)

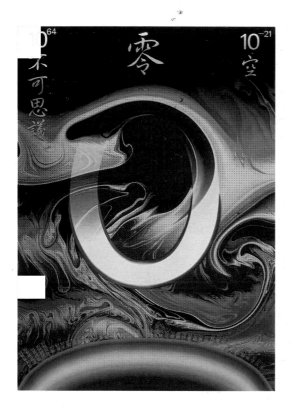

394
MITSUO KATSUI
Poster for Morisawa, 1985

Created with a multiplicity of functions and with a mind to the individuality of the user, Donald Booty, Jr.'s *Double Plus* calculator has a contoured edge that makes it comfortable to grasp in either a right- or left-handed model. With its one straight and one sinuously curved edge, the calculator shares two formal aspects of late 1980s product design—hard-line technology in a box and ergonomic, expressive forms. By particularizing the models for left- or right-handed users and including a display that tilts upward to adjust legibility, the design recognizes individual needs rather than satisfying a homogeneous consumer profile. The keys, color-coded and with different dimensions and shapes, respond to the psychology of human perception: their relative size, arrangement, intensity, and legibility are correlated with hierarchies of function, frequency of need, and user familiarity. A special key—a second add (or "plus") key from which the calculator takes its name—allows the hand holding the instrument to participate in and increase the speed of calculation.

Made by Zelco Industries, Mount Vernon, New York. Plastic housing. Length: 5¹¹/₁₆" (14.8 cm). (Zelco Industries, Mount Vernon, New York.)

Japan's leading designer in computer graphics, Mitsuo Katsui exercised the broad range of his medium in this poster for Morisawa, a manufacturer of phototypesetting equipment. The ground of the poster is a visible bitmap composed of pixels, the smallest possible dot the computer can display and the fundamental building block of computer graphics. Normally invisible to the eye, the dot pattern is enlarged by Katsui to create a busy ornamental surface onto which is positioned an oversize zero. This bold number advertises the fact that point size in computerized typesetting has lost its fixed meaning since any size type is obtainable by digitized enlargement or reduction. Using an image of reflections on a soap bubble scanned into the computer, he manipulated it to create the flames that leap around and through the zero. With the digital red-green-blue component color system, Katsui subtly controlled the levels of color in these images and demonstrated his ability to mix them in any combination. They vibrate against the dark ground and make the shapes jump out at the spectator, eloquently testifying to the aesthetic and expressive power technology can wield if imaginatively applied by an artist.

Printed by Dai Nippon, Tokyo. Offset lithograph. 40¹/₂ x 28⁵/₈" (103 x 72.8 cm). (Katsui Design, Tokyo.)

396

TECHNOLOGY DESIGN
Emily, Julie, and Max personal computer, 1989

Espousing the need to return meaning and ideals as well as psychological and emotional values to design, Technology Design has envisioned products that go beyond the functional object encased in a box to those that communicate visually the processes and historical associations underlying modern technology. The design of their *Emily, Julie, and Max* personal computer is a metaphor for the tools that the word processor has all but replaced: pencils, notebooks, paper, and books. The screen's design has its origin in a sheet of three-ring notebook paper; the keyboard in a spiral-bound notebook; and the central processor with disk drive, where information is stored, in a row of books—traditional elements of communication that this generation at least still finds meaningful. Matching the functions of the three components with their typological antecedents and adding a large yellow pencil-like support, the designers hope to humanize technology and thereby enrich the relationship between man and machine.

Made by Manufacturing Alternatives, Redmond, Washington. ABS plastic, urethane, polyurethane, and sheet metal. Height of central processor: 10" (25.4 cm). (Technology Design, Bellevue, Washington.)

397
JUNICHI ARAI
Big Wave fabric, 1988

One of the most technologically inventive textile designer-engineers today, Junichi Arai has become known for developing new techniques of making and weaving metallic yarns, for which he has received thirty-six patents. At the same time, he continues to explore earlier techniques and to combine them with high-technology processes. In *Big Wave*, Arai applied traditional tie-dye (*shibori*) resists to a high-tech base fabric of sheer flat polyester, vacuum-sealed with aluminum. Using the ancient tie-dye technique, Arai preserved pattern areas of the fabric from dye; in other areas the aluminum coating was selectively stripped from the cloth with an alkali solution, leaving the nearly transparent, filmy polyester yarns exposed. To the surface patterns and iridescent variations created by these processes, Arai added the textural effect of heat-set, permanently pleated wrinkles. "Paradoxically," one critic has written, "with each stage of the process, the fabrics lose their impersonal machine-made quality and gain a singular hand-crafted flavor from their very advanced technology. Herein lies the heart of Arai's retro-tech approach to textile creation,"[27] a postmodern paradigm.

Dyed titanium and polyester. Width: 50" (127 cm). (Philadelphia Museum of Art, gift of Nuno Corp.)

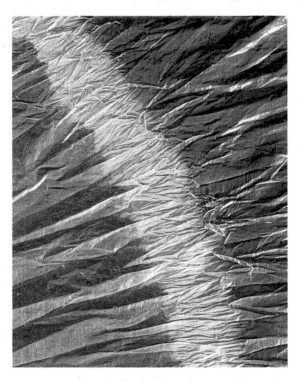

398
FRANK O. GEHRY
Cross Check armchair, 1989–91

Developed over a two-and-a-half-year period in a workshop adjacent to his architectural office established by the manufacturer Knoll (not unlike its arrangement with HARRY BERTOIA four decades earlier), Frank O. Gehry's bentwood furniture is structurally expressive and highly decorative. His plans for woven-wood furniture date back to 1984, when the German furniture manufacturer Vitra asked him to create a chair that would be comparable to GIO PONTI's light, best-selling *Superleggera* design of 1957 (no. 265) but then rejected his proposal, which was based on the structure of the bushel basket. In 1989 Gehry returned to this concept for his Knoll commission, working closely with the firm's technicians, who created as many as 120 full-scale bentwood prototypes to test successive schemes as Gehry conceived them. Using a laminate of seven layers of maple, each $1/32$ inches thick, he completed five chairs and two tables for production (each, like the *Cross Check* armchair, distinguished by a hockey term for its name). According to Gehry, "the material forms a single and continuous idea. What makes all this work and gives it extraordinary strength is the interwoven, basketlike character of the design. Now structure and material have freed bentwood furniture from its former heaviness and rigidity. It really is possible to make bentwood furniture pliable, springy and light."[28]

Made by Hasty Plywood, Maxton, North Carolina, and Marshall Group, Bern, North Carolina, for Knoll. Maple. $33 1/8 \times 26 \times 25 1/2$" (84.2 x 66 x 64.8 cm). (Knoll Group, New York.)

399
WATER STUDIO
Television, 1991

Replacing bulky cathode-ray tubes with tiny color liquid-crystal screens, the Sharp Corporation was able to develop the industry's long-sought flat television, a compact and portable system that produces high-quality, high-resolution pictures. Using this technology, Sharp worked with Naoki Sakai of the Japanese design firm Water Studio to produce a new type of television, one conceived as an art object. The screen is like an electronic picture that can be hung on the wall, and it is offered with a choice of frames ranging from this sleekly modern model in stainless steel to a gilt rococo version designed for more traditional connoisseurs. Kiyoshi Sakashita, director and general manager of Sharp's Corporate Design Center, has led the firm to a more design-conscious position somewhere between

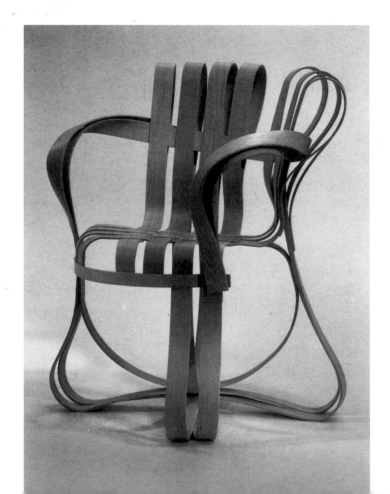

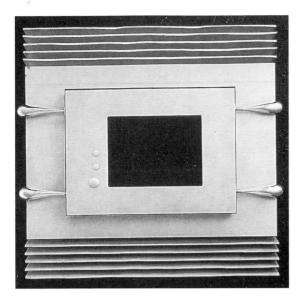

"art" and industry, and considers the role of the designer as that of an innovator: "Picasso, Matisse and other geniuses of modern art, with their keen perception and foresight . . . became the triggering force that brought about trends in the century we live in. Will designers, as the artists of the industrialized age, be trendsetters with the foresight necessary for the upcoming age of information?"[29]

Made by the Sharp Corporation, Osaka. Stainless steel. Screen: 8⁵/₈" (22 cm). (Sharp Corporation, Osaka.)

400
FROGDESIGN AND AMERICAN TELEPHONE AND TELEGRAPH
Personal communicator, 1992

A multifunctional household secretary, AT&T's personal communicator, introduced in 1993, combines voice, data, and handwriting transmission—the principal elements of modern electronic communication—in one consumer product. While serving as a standard telephone it also sends messages by fax or electronic mail and can keep an appointment calendar as well as telephone numbers and addresses. The portable instrument with its touch sensitive screen incorporates sophisticated miniaturized computer and communications technologies including handwriting-recognition software, advances that were almost inconceivable for home application even a decade earlier. But its friendly charcoal-gray plastic form created by frogdesign (with the handset by AT&T) attempts to humanize these technologies with its visual references to the activities it performs—earlike appendages seem to be listening and a "pen" and "pad" are included for making notes and sending messages. Elements of this technology were explored in such earlier systems as the stylus-based data-input *Palmtop* computer, developed in 1980 by SONY CORPORATION to recognize Japanese characters, and in the prototypes for a direct-writing glass-topped facsimile machine created by I.D. TWO. Producing such equipment in the 1990s has come to mean extensive collaboration between a number of specialized hardware and software firms, in this instance, with AT&T contributing its *Hobbit* microprocessor communications chip, GO corporation providing its manual input system as well as its fax and record-keeping software, and Matsushita participating with its manufacturing and assembly capabilities, all coordinated by the EO corporation.

Made by EO, Mountain Valley, California, for AT&T. Plastic housing. 9¹/₂ x 10¹/₂ x 1³/₄" (24.1 x 26.2 x 4.5 cm). (AT&T Archives, Warren, New Jersey.)

BIOGRAPHIES OF DESIGNERS

Note: The bibliographical citations that follow the biographies are meant to present a variety of sources on the life and career of each designer as well as to document the objects illustrated in this book. Ephemeral materials such as catalogs, product descriptions, biographies, and statements supplied by manufacturers and designers have not been cited.

AINO MARSIO AALTO
Finnish, 1894–1949

Aino Marsio received her architect's degree in 1920 from what is now the Helsinki University of Technology and afterwards worked in the office of Oiva Kallio. In 1923 she joined the office of ALVAR AALTO, whom she married in 1924. Like the results of the relationship between CHARLES EAMES and Ray Eames, the respective areas of collaboration in the subsequent work of the Aalto office are often difficult to distinguish. Nevertheless Aino Aalto specialized in interior design and pursued projects independent of her husband—including a prize-winning design for household pressed glassware that was first produced by Karhula-Iittala in 1934 (no. 148) and has recently been reissued. Aino Aalto was a partner in the firm of Artek, founded to produce and distribute the office's product designs, and served as its managing director from 1941 until her death in 1949.

References: Paul David Pearson, *Alvar Aalto and the International Style* (New York, 1978), passim; Museum of Finnish Architecture, Helsinki, *Profiles: Pioneering Women Architects in Finland* (1983), pp. 56–59.

ALVAR AALTO
Finnish, 1898–1976

One of the giants of twentieth-century architecture and design, Alvar Aalto is ranked by historians alongside LE CORBUSIER, WALTER GROPIUS, and LUDWIG MIES VAN DER ROHE, although his work shared few of the formal usages and structural methods for which his peers were known. Boldly independent, Aalto was a self-described humanist who emphasized organic forms (no. 177), the use of wood as a medium, and the relationship of architecture to nature. He was trained as an architect at what is now the Helsinki University of Technology and after his graduation in 1922 set up his practice first in the small town of Jyväskylä followed by Turku (1927–33) and Helsinki (1933–76). In 1924, Aalto married Aino Marsio (AINO MARSIO AALTO), an architect practicing in his office with whom he collaborated on furniture and interior design commissions. By the end of the 1920s Aalto had already begun the avant-garde buildings that catapulted him into international prominence in the 1930s—the Turun-Sanomat newspaper office in Turku (1928–30), the

tuberculosis sanatorium at Paimio (1929–33), and the city library at Viipuri (1927–35). At the same time, for the Huonekaluja Rakennustyötendas furniture company, he began to design experimental furniture in laminated woods, which first appeared at the firm's exhibition display in Turku in 1929 in the form of a chair with a seat and back formed from a single curved piece of bent plywood. Considering interior furnishings as "architectural accessories," part of the "biology of building," Aalto went on to develop plywood furniture for the Paimio sanatorium (no. 141), pieces he considered more humane than the metal furniture then regarded as hygienic for institutional use. When shown for the first time at exhibitions in London (1933) and Zurich (1934), and at the *V Triennale* in Milan in 1933, his furniture met with such immediate popular and critical success that English and Swiss firms made arrangements to import it on a regular basis; in 1935, Aalto himself, his wife, the art critic Nils Gustav Hahl, and the financier Harry Gullichsen and his wife, Maire Gullichsen, founded a company called Artek to produce and distribute Aalto's designs. The firm continues to this day, and more than half of Aalto's original models are still in production (no. 140).

While the 1930s are sometimes described as Aalto's "heroic" period, the architect had a long and distinguished career, designing libraries, churches, concert halls, university buildings, and community centers in and outside Finland. He also taught architecture at the Massachusetts Institute of Technology in Cambridge between 1946 and 1948. During the 1950s, Artek put into production a number of the lighting fixtures he had designed for his buildings, which show the same meticulous concern for detail as those of his other product designs.

References: Museum of Modern Art, New York, *Alvar Aalto: Architecture and Furniture* (1938); Siegfried Giedion, *Space, Time, and Architecture*, 2d ed. (Cambridge, Mass., 1949), pp. 453–92; Paul David Pearson, *Alvar Aalto and the International Style* (New York, 1978); *Alvar Aalto, 1898–1976* (Helsinki, 1978); Malcolm Quantrill, *Alvar Aalto: A Critical Study* (New York, 1983); Juhani Pallasmaa, ed., *Alvar Aalto Furniture* (Cambridge, Mass., 1985).

EERO AARNIO
Finnish, born 1932

A designer of furniture and interiors, Eero Aarnio created notable designs in entirely original shapes for production in plastic and steel by the Finnish firm Asko, Scandinavia's largest producer of furniture. Aarnio attended the School for Industrial Arts (Taideteollinen oppilaitos) in Helsinki from 1954 to 1957 and opened his own studio in 1962, designing furniture for manufacture in a variety of materials. His work found an international audience with two designs in fiberglass, his *Ball* chair of 1965 (no. 289) and

Gyro of 1968, for Asko. In his later work he returned to the use of traditional materials with such designs as his wooden *Viking* dining table and chairs for Polardesign (1982).

References: Whitechapel Art Gallery, London, *Modern Chairs, 1918–1970* (July 22–August 30, 1970), no. 89; "A Designer's Home Is His Showcase, Too," *New York Times*, December 16, 1970, p. M 50; Colin Naylor, ed., *Contemporary Designers*, 2d ed. (Chicago, 1990), pp. 2–3.

ADVISORY COMMITTEE ON UTILITY FURNITURE
Established London, 1942–1953

The Advisory Committee on Utility Furniture, comprising furniture designers and manufacturers, planners, and a member of a housing estate council, was established on July 8, 1942, by the British Board of Trade, charged under the wartime civilian rationing and manufacturing regulations "to produce specifications for furniture of good, sound construction in simple but agreeable designs for sale at reasonable prices, and ensuring the maximum economy of raw materials and labour." Within five months the committee had created designs in prototype for a range of domestic furniture (no. 187) to be produced uniformly by all manufacturers in Britain; its first catalog was published in January 1943 and by the end of February, 25,000 pieces of furniture had already been sold. In mid-1943 a design panel, headed by the designer and manufacturer Gordon Russell, was established by the committee to oversee the creation of additional furniture designs and to prepare for the postwar period. Textiles were also brought into the Utility program, most created by ENID MARX, a member of the design panel beginning in 1944 (no. 188). Because of persistent shortages and exceedingly high demand, Utility continued well into the period of recovery, but as materials became more readily available, regulations changed and restrictions on the manufacturing of furniture became less stringent (no. 189). The Utility scheme was abolished by an act of Parliament in 1953.

References: Geffrye Museum, London, *CC41: Utility Furniture and Fashion, 1941–1951* (September 24–December 29, 1974); "Utility CC41," *Design* 309 (September 1974): 62–71.

AGA HEAT LIMITED
Established London, 1934

Formed to manufacture and distribute the AGA stove in Britain on license from its originator in Sweden, AGA Heat Limited introduced the *New Standard* model about 1934 (no. 153). This firm was the successor to Bell's Heat Appliances, established in 1931, which had previously been the store's distributor and manufacturer. AGA solid-fuel stoves gained steady popularity and the mostly handmade units were produced in relatively large numbers, with an estimated fifty thousand in use in Great Britain by 1948.

References: Herbert Read, *Art and Industry: The Principles of Industrial Design* (New York, 1935), p. 105; Joni Miller, "Hail to the AGA: You Never Have To Turn It Off," *Connoisseur* 219 (March 1989): 150–51.

ANNI ALBERS
German, later American, 1899–1994

Through the example of her work (no. 97), her teaching, and her writings, Anni Albers has been one of the most influential weavers of this century. She attended the Kunstgewerbeschule in Hamburg (1919–20) and was admitted to the Bauhaus in Weimar in 1922 where she married the painter Josef Albers in 1925. A student in the Bauhaus weaving workshop, Albers was trained chiefly by her fellow student GUNTA STÖLZL, who became head of the workshop in 1926. Albers's achievement at the Bauhaus lay in her investigation of new fibers and finishes for both practical and aesthetic purposes. In 1930 she received her Bauhaus degree for a sound-absorbing and light-reflecting cotton, chenille, and cellophane drapery fabric she developed for use in a school auditorium at Bernau. After February 1930, Albers held a part-time teaching position in the weaving workshop and in 1931, after Stölzl's resignation, became its temporary head. When the Bauhaus was closed in 1933, she and her husband left Germany for the United States, where she introduced the style of regular geometric patterns that she practiced at the Bauhaus and developed the "pictorial" weaving she taught at Black Mountain College in North Carolina from 1933 to 1949. From 1950 she lived in Connecticut, where she continued to weave independently and design for industry, including a leno weave drapery fabric for Knoll (1958). From 1963 she largely gave up weaving for printmaking, and in 1970, sold her looms. Albers wrote two important books on her craft, *On Designing* (1959) and *On Weaving* (1965).

References: *Anni Albers: Pictorial Weavings* (Cambridge, Mass., 1965); Hans M. Wingler, *The Bauhaus: Weimar, Dessau, Berlin, Chicago* (Cambridge, Mass., 1969), pp. 461–62, 503, 519, 544, 574; Renwick Gallery of the National Museum of American Art, Washington, D.C., *The Woven and Graphic Art of Anni Albers* (June 1985–January 1986).

AMERICAN TELEPHONE AND TELEGRAPH, *see* BELL TELEPHONE COMPANY

KAREL APPEL
Dutch, lives in France, born 1921

Karel Appel was one of the founders of the Cobra group in 1948, formed primarily by avant-garde artists from Copenhagen, Brussels, and Amsterdam. An expressionistic painter whose strong colors and harsh brushstrokes are influenced by the works of Vincent van Gogh, Appel has also created sculpture, constructions with found objects, ceramics, wood reliefs, and murals. As a young but already well known painter—he represented the Netherlands at the Venice *Biennale* in 1954—Appel was one of a number of artists hired by Dutch textile firms to provide fresh textile patterns during the 1950s; his abstract designs were printed by 't Paapje for the exhibition of the work of Dutch designers at the Bijenkorf department store in 1953 (no. 236).

References: Alfred Frankenstein, ed., *Karel Appel* (New York, 1980); Gert Staal and Hester Wolters, eds., *Holland in Vorm: Dutch Design, 1945–1987* (The Hague, 1987), pp. 146, 148, 166.

RON ARAD
Israeli, lives in England, born 1951

Challenging the conventions of the machine aesthetic, Ron Arad makes powerfully expressive furniture of metal, glass, and even concrete in tortured shapes with jagged edges and raw surfaces. He relies on simple technologies like welding to create objects that are at once primitive and futuristic; indeed Arad has been hailed as a leader of "postindustrial" design. After attending the Jerusalem Academy of Art (1971–73), Arad moved to London in 1973 where he studied architecture under Peter Cook and Bernard Tschumi at the Architectural Association (1974–79). He then practiced architecture from 1979 until 1981, when he met the furniture entrepreneur Dennis Groves and the two founded the company One Off to design and manufacture low-budget, custom, experimental furniture. Using industrial elements in novel applications, Arad rapidly gained a reputation for invention in the manner of Marcel Duchamp and Jean Tinguely. While appropriation and reuse were constant themes in his early designs, since about 1988 his furniture has become increasingly sculptural—and costly—including the Big Easy Volumes series (no. 393). In 1989 he founded Ron Arad Associates to support architectural projects, including the interior design of the new opera house foyer in Tel Aviv. At the same time the One Off workshop continues to produce and market Arad's furniture designs in limited editions, "constantly speeding through ideas, sometimes merely noting them by a crude artifact, sometimes processing them to a greater degree."[1]

References: Deyan Sudjic, *Ron Arad: Restless Furniture* (London, 1989); Alexander von Vegesack, ed., *Sticks & Stones, One Offs & Short Runs: Ron Arad, 1980–1990* (Weil am Rhein, Germany, 1990).

JUNICHI ARAI
Japanese, born 1932

The most technologically innovative textile designer of the 1980s, Junichi Arai was born to a family of weavers in the traditional textile center of Kiryu. He started his career in his father's kimono factory and audited textile courses at Kiryu's Gunma University. From the mid-1950s to the mid-1960s, Arai began the experiments with metallic

yams and chemically altered fibers for which he became known, eventually receiving thirty-six patents for his inventions. In the 1970s he first applied computers to the design and production of fabrics. Using highly complex computer-generated punch cards to drive the Jacquard looms, Arai broadened the horizons of the textile industry, weaving quadruple-cloths with different designs on each surface and other fabrics of unparalleled complexity. Since the 1980s, Arai has also experimented with a number of high-tech finishing techniques, using the heat-transfer-print machine, for example, to produce extraordinary patterns and textures such as those created by overlapping layers of permanently pleated wrinkles (no. 397). "Arai's conscious rejection of the conventional," the textile designer Reiko Sudo writes, "leads him to deny total and dispassionate perfection. His subversions of heat-set and chemical-finished processes allow for spontaneity and ever-changing expressions. He sometimes, for example, ties fabrics for tie-dying, then purposely omits all dying, putting the tied fabrics directly into the tumble-dryer for finishing. This culminates in unpredictably shrunken and buckled textures. He is truly the enfant terrible of Japanese textiles."[2] Arai has supplied fabrics for the fashion designers Issey Miyake and Rei Kawakubo. In 1983 he was awarded the Mainichi Fashion Grand Prix Special Prize and in 1987 named an honorary Royal Designer for Industry.

References: Maria Tulokas, *Textiles for the Eighties* (Providence, RI, 1985), p. 61; Chloë Colchester, *The New Textiles: Trends and Traditions* (New York, 1991), pp. 20–21, 39–40, 170, figs. 61–63, 117, 119; Yurakucho Asahi Gallery, Tokyo, *Hand and Technology: Textile by Junichi Arai '92* (March 7–25, 1992).

ARCHIZOOM ASSOCIATI
Established Florence, 1966–1974

Archizoom was one of the first Italian avant-garde groups to challenge conventional attitudes about the built environment in their architecture, design, and urban-planning projects, and in theoretical writings published in *In*, *Domus*, *Design Quarterly*, and other international magazines. The studio was founded in 1966 by four graduates of the architectural faculty of the University of Florence—Andrea Branzi, Gilberto Corretti, Paolo Deganello, and Massimo Morozzi (with two industrial designers, Dario and Lucia Bartolini, joining in 1968). Their earliest projects were exhibitions: with SUPERSTUDIO they organized *Superarchitettura (Superarchitecture)* in Pistoia (1966) and Modena (1967), which presented colorful architectural projects and large graphics in the Pop style; in 1968 they created a meditative space, the "Center of Eclectic Conspiracy," for Milan's *XIV Triennale*. The next year Archizoom began their most provocative project, the "No-Stop City," a physical and sociological investigation of urbanization that postulated the endless extension of the city as industrial spatial organization. Their design work included pop objects, such as the foam *Superonda*

(*Superwave*) sectional couch of 1966, *Safari* environmental seating of 1967, and their super-rationalist *Mies* chair (no. 321) of 1969, all for Poltronova, as well as the *AEO* seating of 1973 for Cassina (no. 330). In 1972 Archizoom contributed a conceptual piece to *Italy: The New Domestic Landscape* at the Museum of Modern Art in New York, proposing liberation from cultural dictates as the goal of vanguard architecture, and in 1973 they joined with other countercultural architecture groups in a collective called Global Tools.

References: Emilio Ambasz, ed., *Italy: The New Domestic Landscape* (New York, 1972), pp. 101, 103, 108, 232–39; "AEO," *Casabella* 382 (October 1973): 54–55; Andrea Branzi, *The Hot House: Italian New Wave Design* (Cambridge, Mass., 1984), p. 151 et passim.

CHARLES ROBERT ASHBEE
English, 1863–1942

Inspired by the romantic socialism of William Morris and John Ruskin, Charles Robert Ashbee was one of the leaders of the Arts and Crafts Movement in England through the school and cooperative workshop for craftsmen he founded in London in 1888, the Guild and School of Handicraft. His writings also helped establish him as one of the movement's most respected figures, as did the example of his work as a designer, chiefly of metalwares (no. 28). Ashbee spread the influence of English Arts and Crafts through his contacts, travels, and exhibitions abroad: he visited the United States in 1896, 1900, and 1908–9, meeting Frank Lloyd Wright and Charles Sumner Greene (see Greene & Greene); in 1897 the Guild was commissioned to make furniture after the designs of M. H. Baillie Scott for the grand duke of Hesse at Darmstadt; and Ashbee exhibited furniture and objects in 1898 at the Glaspalast in Munich and in 1900 at the eighth Secession exhibition in Vienna. Trained as an architect in the office of G. F. Bodley, Ashbee established the Guild and School of Handicraft to improve the quality of English applied arts, producing furniture and metalwork on commission that were shown in most of the Arts and Crafts Exhibition Society displays (Ashbee was an active committee member). The Guild also inspired other workshops in Great Britain such as the Birmingham Guild of Handicraft (established in 1890). From its warehouse on Commercial Street in London, the workshop moved to larger premises at Essex House in 1891, where Ashbee added the Essex House Press in 1898. At the same time Ashbee practiced architecture, opening his first office in London in 1890 and designing middle-class private houses, notably in Cheyne Walk, Chelsea (London); one called The Ancient Magpie and Stump was designed for his mother (1893–94), furnished by the Guild, and published in both the *Studio* (1895) and the German magazine *Dekorative Kunst* (1898). Although the school attached to the Guild was forced to close in 1895 for financial reasons, the Guild itself flourished throughout the 1890s. In 1902, when the lease expired on Essex House, the Guild,

which then employed some seventy craftsmen, moved to Chipping Campden in Gloucestershire, but in 1907, faced with economic depression and competition from industry (as Ashbee described in his 1909 book, *Craftsmanship and Competitive Industry*), it was forced to close. Although the organization was restructured as a trust in 1908, it never regained the commercial success or reputation it had earlier enjoyed. While Ashbee continued to defend the principle of the craftsman's guild and cooperative workshop, his book *Should We Stop Teaching Art?* (1911) indicated that he had reconsidered the role of handcrafts in light of modern economic and technical changes.

References: Gillian Naylor, *The Arts and Crafts Movement* (London, 1971), pp. 166–77; Alan Crawford, *C. R. Ashbee: Architect, Designer, and Romantic Socialist* (New Haven, Conn., 1985).

ATELIER MARTINE
Established Paris, 1911–c. 1928

A design school and workshop for young women created by Paul Poiret, the Atelier Martine was inspired by the design workshops that Poiret had seen in Berlin and Vienna, but which he criticized for their "monotonous repetition" of geometrical figures and "criminal" restrictive teaching methods. At Poiret's workshop, students were encouraged to respond freely to nature, to translate what they saw directly into designs for printed fabrics, carpets, wallpaper (no. 55), lamps, and porcelain—work Poiret claimed in his autobiography had "influenced all fashion and the whole of modern decorative art."[3] Founded in 1911 with a few teenage girls as students, the Atelier Martine was represented the following year at the Salon d'Automne with a series of "decorative projects intended for industrial reproduction." With murals and objects that reflected a primitivism and exoticism unlike any other contemporary decorative activity, Martine furnished Poiret's fashion salon and designed interiors on commission, often under the direction of the painter Guy-Pierre Fauconnet. The workshop's products, including somewhat more conservative furniture designs, were sold by Martine shops from Paris to Biarritz, at a franchise in London, and in department store boutiques throughout Europe and in America. In 1925 Martine, along with Raoul Dufy, furnished the barges in the Seine Poiret created for the *Exposition Internationale des Arts Décoratifs*, and in 1927, decorated cabins on the *Ile de France*. In 1926, when Poiret's own fashion business was failing, he sold his interest in the Martine shops.

References: *King of Fashion: The Autobiography of Paul Poiret* (Philadelphia, 1931), pp. 161–64; Musée de la Mode et du Costume, Palais Galliera, Paris, *Paul Poiret et Nicole Groult: Maîtres de la mode art déco* (July 5–October 12, 1986), pp. 224–26; Yvonne Deslandres, with Dorothée Lalanne, *Poiret: Paul Poiret, 1879–1944* (New York, 1987), pp. 17–18, 259–307.

BARTOLUCCI & WALDHEIM
Established Chicago, 1944–c. 1951

Established in 1944 by two students at the Institute of Design in Chicago, the partnership of Edgar Bartolucci and John J. Waldheim designed interiors, exhibits, and furniture, most notably, the tilting *Barwa* lounge chair (no. 199), which was patented under the name of Waldheim. In 1947 the firm founded Barwa Associates to manufacture this and other tubular metal furniture, but the partnership was short-lived— Waldheim returned to his hometown of Milwaukee to teach art in 1951 and Bartolucci moved to New York, where he was co-publisher of *Furniture Forum* and worked as designer and producer of exhibits and displays.

References: Buffalo Fine Arts Academy, Albright Art Gallery, *Good Design Is Your Business* (1947), p. 48; "Inventiveness—A Design Essential," *Interiors* 107 (October 1947): 126–31; "New Versions of the Barwa," *Interiors* 110 (November 1950): 161; David A. Hanks, *Innovative Furniture in America: From 1800 to the Present* (New York, 1981), pp. 103 5.

SAUL BASS
American, born 1920

A pioneer in the creation of titling graphics for feature films, among them *The Man with the Golden Arm* (1955; no. 250) and *Exodus* (1960), Saul Bass is known for his simple, powerful pictographic images and logos, which identify and convey the essence of his subjects. Bass studied at the Art Students' League, New York (1936–39), and under Gyorgy Kepes at Brooklyn College (1944–45). In 1946 he moved to Los Angeles and founded his own graphic design firm, Saul Bass and Associates (since 1978, Saul Bass/Herb Yager and Associates), which has designed and developed corporate identification programs for such clients as Alcoa, AMERICAN TELEPHONE AND TELEGRAPH, Celanese, Exxon, Minolta, Quaker Oats, United Airlines, the United Way, and Warner Communications; the firm has also created packaging for Hunt Food and Industries and Dixie Paper Products, among others. His graphics and titles for the motion picture industry were perhaps most influential: *The Man with the Golden Arm* is credited as being the first film with a comprehensive design program, ranging from print advertisement (posters, newspapers, and magazines) to the media graphics (animated titles coordinated with music). Bass himself has made and directed short films, including *Why Man Creates* (1969), which received the Academy Award for a documentary short.

References: Herb Yager, "Saul Bass," *Graphis* 33 (February–March 1978): 392–407; Colin Naylor, ed., *Contemporary Designers*, 2d ed. (Chicago, 1990), pp. 36–37; Philip B. Meggs, *A History of Graphic Design*, 2d ed. (New York, 1992), pp. 355–57.

HERBERT BAYER
Austrian, active Germany, later American, 1900–1985

A pioneer of modern graphic design and the most eminent graphic designer associated with the Bauhaus, Herbert Bayer was made a master at the school in 1925, charged with creating a new Bauhaus workshop for printing and advertising (renamed the workshop for typography and advertising design in 1927). From 1925 to 1928, Bayer designed and produced all of the Bauhaus's typographical material and executed commissions for private industry as well. Bayer's most significant typographical innovations were his insistence on a single lowercase alphabet and sans-serif typefaces; adopted in the interest of functional legibility and universality, these elements soon became identified as the Bauhaus graphic style (no. 119). Bayer had entered the Bauhaus as a student in 1921 after apprenticing in a craft workshop in Linz, Austria (1919–20), and an architectural office in Vienna (1920–21). At the Bauhaus, Bayer belonged to the wall-painting workshop directed by Wassily Kandinsky and produced designs for the 1923 Bauhaus exhibition and publication, including postcards, the cover of the catalog (no. 90), and a number of drawings published in it. In 1925 after passing his journeyman's examination and being appointed master, Bayer accompanied the move of the Bauhaus from Weimar to Dessau, where he designed signage for the new Bauhaus building complex.

Bayer left the Bauhaus after the resignation of WALTER GROPIUS in 1928 and worked for a decade in Berlin as art director of the German *Vogue*, design director of the international advertising agency Dorland Studio, and freelance designer for the type foundry H. Berthold. In 1938 he immigrated to the United States, where he became consultant art director to the N. W. Ayers, J. Walter Thompson, and Dorland International advertising agencies in New York. After 1946, when he moved to Aspen, Colorado, he served as art director to the Container Corporation of America (from 1956 to 1965 as chairman of its design department) and the Atlantic Richfield Corporation. Bayer had numerous independent commissions, architectural as well as graphic, and designed two major retrospective Bauhaus exhibitions: *Bauhaus, 1919–1928* (Museum of Modern Art, New York, 1938) and *50 Years Bauhaus* (organized by the Württembergischer Kunstverein Stuttgart, 1968–71). He served as adviser to the Aspen Institute of Humanistic Studies and was cofounder of the International Design Conference at Aspen.

Reference: Arthur A. Cohen, *Herbert Bayer: The Complete Work* (Cambridge, Mass., 1984).

LESTER BEALL
American, 1903–1969

Lester Beall applied his intelligence and knowledge of the history of art to graphic design, and his work had a particularly invigorating effect in the areas of corporate identity and advertising. With a degree in art history from the University of Chicago (1926) but virtually self-taught as an artist, Beall at first had only moderate success as a freelance graphic designer working in Chicago for such clients as the *Chicago Tribune* and R. R. Donnelley. With his move to New York in 1934, however, his work began to be recognized for its fresh approach—particularly his application of the tenets of modern European advertising design and especially the use of photography and its adventuresome combination with type. Beall received numerous awards for his advertisements for the Columbia Broadcasting System and Marshall Field, and was featured in articles in the German magazine of advertising art *Novum Gebrauchsgraphik* and the trade journal *PM*. In addition, in November 1937 an exhibition devoted to his work was held at the Museum of Modern Art in New York, which included several of his posters for the Rural Electrification Administration (no. 164). Beall's extensive corporate involvement began in the 1940s; especially notable was the design, layout, and typography he did for Upjohn Pharmaceuticals' *Scope* magazine (1941–55), for which he drew on a wide range of historical imagery and typography. His corporate identity program for the International Paper Company (1958–60) was one of the first fully worked out systems, coordinated through his development of a company design manual and applied to all aspects of the company's communications—printed matter, advertisements, and the identification of vehicles and even of trees.

References: E. Holscher, "Lester Beall," *Novum Gebrauchsgraphik* 16 (April 1939): 17–24; *Current Biography* (1949), s.v. "Beall, Lester (Thomas)"; R. Roger Remington and Barbara J. Hodik, *Nine Pioneers in American Graphic Design* (Cambridge, Mass., 1989), pp. 86–103; Philip B. Meggs, *A History of Graphic Design*, 2d ed. (New York, 1992), pp. 313–14, 385, 387, 389–90.

PETER BEHRENS
German, 1868–1940

Architect, industrial designer, and teacher, Peter Behrens has been recognized as the first person to practice industrial design in the modern sense. From 1907 to 1914 he served as artistic adviser to the Allgemeine Elektricitäts-Gesellschaft (AEG) in Berlin, a vast industrial concern that manufactured generators, cables, transformers, motors, light bulbs, arc lamps, and electrical appliances for a large portion of the world market. In his consultant capacity, Behrens designed factory and office buildings, housing, appliances (no. 46), and graphics (no. 45). Even at the time, his association with the firm was hailed as having great significance for the relationship between art and industry, and he became a role model for the Deutscher Werkbund, of which he was a founding member in 1907. His monumental steel, glass, and concrete turbine factory for the AEG (1908) influenced the course of architecture in the twentieth century both because it was an early expression of frank industrial architecture and for the fact

that two of this century's greatest architects and designers were employed in Behrens's office during the time it was built, WALTER GROPIUS and LUDWIG MIES VAN DER ROHE (as was LE CORBUSIER shortly thereafter). Behrens's achievements were recognized during his lifetime by exhibitions of his work at the world's fair in Ghent in 1913 and in Berlin in 1928, with monographs on his work published in the same years.

Behrens had studied painting in Hamburg, Karlsruhe, and Düsseldorf before moving to Munich in 1889. There, inspired by the new reform Jugendstil movement, he turned to graphics and the applied arts, creating a series of large color woodcuts, bookbindings, illustrations, and, in 1898, his first furniture and objects (no. 11), which were displayed in a dining-room ensemble at the Munich Glaspalast the following year. In 1899 Behrens was invited by Grand Duke Ernst Ludwig of Hesse to join the artists' colony in Darmstadt, where he stayed until 1903, designing his own house and furnishings in the manner of HENRY VAN DE VELDE. Behrens left Darmstadt to become director of the Kunstgewerbeschule in Düsseldorf, the first of several important teaching posts he would hold, including the directorships of the Meisterschule für Architektur at the Akademie der Bildenden Künste in Vienna (1922–36) and the Meisteratelier für Baukunst at the Akademie der Künste, Berlin (1936–40). Behrens led and then followed the major movements in architecture and design in the first decades of this century, from Jugendstil to functionalism and expressionism, and he was a founding member of many of the organizations that promoted them. Behrens was described as among the "most German" of artists,[4] and throughout his career he received a number of official government commissions, including the design of exhibition rooms for the *Esposizione Internazionale*, Turin (1902); the German imperial exhibition catalog at the *Louisiana Purchase Exhibition*, Saint Louis (1904); the German embassy in Saint Petersburg (1911–12); and exhibition rooms for the international exhibition at Brussels (1910).

References: Fritz Hoeber, *Peter Behrens* (Munich, 1913); Paul Joseph Cremers, *Peter Behrens: Sein Werk von 1900 bis zur Gegenwart* (Essen, 1928); Alan Windsor, *Peter Behrens: Architect and Designer* (New York, 1981); Tilmann Buddensieg, *Industriekultur: Peter Behrens and the AEG, 1907–1914* (Cambridge, Mass., 1984); Gisela Moeller, "Peter Behrens," in Kathryn B. Hiesinger, ed., *Art Nouveau in Munich* (Philadelphia, 1988), pp. 31–36.

VANESSA BELL
English, 1879–1961

Sister of Virginia Woolf and a central figure in the Bloomsbury group, Vanessa (Stephen) Bell studied painting in London at the Royal Academy schools under John Singer Sargent (1901–4). Through the close association she and her husband, the critic Clive Bell, had with DUNCAN GRANT and ROGER FRY, and her experiences traveling abroad, she developed a colorful, decorative style influenced by French avant-garde painting, and four of her works were shown in Fry's *Second Post-Impressionist Exhibition* in London in 1912. Competitions and commissions for murals led to other endeavors, such as decorating boxes and painting pottery, and to the creation of the Omega Workshops, of which she became a director on its founding in 1913. An active participant in its exhibitions, activities, and commissions, Bell designed two of the six textiles for the workshops' opening; she also painted screens, furniture, boxes, pottery, and designed rugs and clothing. After the demise of the Omega Workshops, Bell and Grant continued to collaborate on commissions for interior decoration, often creating furnishings specifically for these interiors. In the 1930s she provided designs for screen-printed textiles for the designer-manufacturer Allan Walton (no. 162) and pottery decorations for Foley China, shown in an exhibition, *Modern Art for the Table*, at Harrods in London in 1934. From 1919 she exhibited her paintings annually with the London Group, and over the next decade she also designed covers and provided illustrations for many of the books printed and published by Leonard and Virginia Woolf's Hogarth Press.

References: Richard Shone, *Bloomsbury Portraits: Vanessa Bell, Duncan Grant, and Their Circle* (New York, 1976), passim; Arts Council of Great Britain, Hayward Gallery, London, *Thirties: British Art and Design before the War* (October 25, 1979–January 13, 1980), p. 285, nos. 2.14, 2.68, 2.100; Judith Collins, *The Omega Workshops* (London, 1983), passim; Crafts Council Gallery, London, *The Omega Workshops, 1913–19: Decorative Arts of Bloomsbury* (January 18–March 18, 1984), passim.

BELL TELEPHONE COMPANY
Established New York, 1876

The Bell Telephone Company, founded by Alexander Graham Bell, began to expand immediately after Bell received his telephone patent in 1876 and slowly gained control of all aspects of the telephone industry. In 1881 when he bought out Gray and Barton, the manufacturing company of his rival telephone developer Elisha Gray, Bell gained a supplier of telephone equipment (Western Electric; no. 63), and over the next two decades he built up both the equipment and the transmission industry virtually as a monopoly. Forming the American Telephone and Telegraph Company in 1900, Bell established the structure of the communications corporation, which would remain intact until the United States Supreme Court's ruling on divestiture took effect in 1984. The company has been known for the high quality of the work done at Bell Telephone Laboratories, a research arm established as a separate company in 1925. Bell Labs has been responsible for the design of Bell's equipment, sometimes with outside consultants such as HENRY DREYFUSS (no. 294), and the development of new technology, including early advances in television transmission, the invention of the transistor in 1947, and more recently,

refinement of microprocessors such as those used in the firm's personal communicator (no. 400).

References: Don Wallance, *Shaping America's Products* (New York, 1956), pp. 31–40; John Brooks, *Telephone: The First Hundred Years* (New York, 1976); H. M. Boettinger, *The Telephone Book: Bell, Watson, Vail and American Life, 1876–1976* (Croton-on-Hudson, N.Y., 1977); Anthony Ramirez, "Rethinking the Plain Old Telephone," *New York Times*, January 3, 1993, 3, pp. 1, 6.

MARIO BELLINI
Italian, born 1935

The third principal consultant designer working for Olivetti, Mario Bellini is as versatile as his predecessors, MARCELLO NIZZOLI and ETTORE SOTTSASS, JR. He too has produced a range of electronic equipment (for Brionvega and Yamaha), lighting (for Flos and Artemide), furniture (for Cassina, C & B Italia, and Marcatré), and ceramics (for Rosenthal), products that are known for the quality of their formal inventiveness (no. 382). Bellini graduated from the Milan Politecnico's architecture faculty in 1959 and was hired by Olivetti in 1963, having already won the first of several Compasso d'Oro awards the year before. In his designs for Olivetti he used organic shapes with stretched rubber and plastic membranes to unify the surfaces of his computers, display terminals, and calculators (no. 379) and to provide a friendly, tactile surface for their users. Later, in the early 1970s, he introduced a geometric wedge shape as the basic form of this equipment (no. 347). Bellini has been particularly innovative in developing new forms of upholstered furniture, from a modular armchair without supporting structure that was made of leather cushions held together by belts (1965) to the Cab series (1976) whose zipped leather covers shrouded simple welded-metal frames (no. 351). In 1981 Bellini founded the magazine *Album*, and in 1986 he became editor-in-chief of *Domus*.

References: Alfonso Grassi and Anty Pansera, *Atlante del design italiano, 1940–1980* (Milan, 1980), p. 277 et passim; Cara McCarty, *Mario Bellini: Designer* (New York, 1987); Sibylle Kicherer, *Olivetti: A Study of the Corporate Management of Design* (New York, 1990), pp. 51–58 et passim.

MARIA BENKTZON, *see* ERGONOMI DESIGN GRUPPEN

EMILE BERLINER
American, born Germany, 1851–1929

A significant contributor to the field of telephonics and sound transmittal, Emile Berliner was a self-taught inventor who first traveled to America in 1870. Having seen a demonstration of Alexander Graham Bell's telephone at Philadelphia's Centennial Exposition in 1876, Berliner began to work on the means of improving its sound transmission, developing the principle of microphonics (patented in 1891). After a return trip to Germany to establish a telephone manufacturing company, Berliner was back in America by 1883, making improvements to the cylinder phonograph that Thomas A. Edison had invented in 1877. He devised the flat-disc recording system (patented in 1887), refining a number of processes that had been used for Edison's phonograph. Publicly demonstrated at Philadelphia's Franklin Institute in 1888, the gramophone was first manufactured commercially in a rudimentary form by Berliner's United States Gramophone Company about 1891; this took place after he had perfected a method for duplicating the original recordings, first using celluloid, then rubber, and finally a shellac composition. Improvements were also made to the machine when Eldridge Johnson of Camden, New Jersey, devised a clockwork motor for the instrument, which was much quieter than the previous mechanism and solved the earlier problem of maintaining a constant speed. With new financing, the Berliner Gramophone Company was established about 1896, and sales of the first satisfactory disc record player (no. 4) began to mount after a campaign was initiated to record performances of the world's greatest musicians and licenses were sold for the manufacture of gramophones throughout the world. While the company was a success, Berliner's own finances faltered and the firm was taken over about 1900 by Johnson, who renamed it the Victor Talking Machine Company.

References: Emile Berliner, "The Development of the Talking Machine," 1913, in *Three Essays* (n.p., n.d.); Orrin E. Dunlap, Jr., *Radio's 100 Men of Science* (New York, 1944), pp. 99–102; *Neue Deutsche Biographie* (1955), s.v. "Berliner, Emile"; Lawrence A. Schlick, *A Portfolio of Early Phonographs*, 2d ed. (n.p., 1969); Daniel Marty, *The Illustrated History of Phonographs* (New York, 1981), pp. 39–53 et passim.

BERNADOTTE & BJØRN
Established Copenhagen, 1949–1964

Founded in 1949 by the Swedish designer Sigvard Bernadotte and the Danish architect and planner Acton Bjørn, Bernadotte & Bjørn was Denmark's first industrial design firm to concentrate on work for production in diversified areas and soon became an international company with affiliates in Stockholm and New York (with the firm of DONALD DESKEY). Bernadotte himself had been a designer of handmade objects, including silver for GEORG JENSEN, but the firm specialized in design of mass-produced consumer goods and products for industry. It provided Scandinavian companies with designs that moved them beyond craft-oriented manufacturing systems and a dependence on natural resources and toward the use of new materials and technologies that allowed them to compete in the growing international postwar markets. Among the goods they designed were kitchen equipment (for Elektro-Helios), appliances, telephones (for L M ERICSSON), office equipment (for Facit), plastics (for Rosti;

no. 216), cutlery, and sanitary fixtures. They also conceived corporate interiors as well as those of the steamship *Gripsholm* for the Swedish American Line.

References: "Designs from Abroad," *Industrial Design* 3 (February 1956): 76–79; Jens Bernsen, *Design: The Problem Comes First* (Copenhagen, 1982), pp. 68–71.

LUCIAN BERNHARD
German, later American, 1883–1972

Designer of posters, trademarks, some thirty-six typefaces, textiles, packaging, and interiors, Lucian Bernhard first studied at the Akademie der Kunst in Munich. He then moved to Berlin in 1901 where, influenced by the reductive imagery of the English Beggarstaffs group, he developed his own distinctive approach to posters, introducing a modern pictorial style to Germany. Most characteristically, he placed a flatly drawn product image on a solid ground accompanied by large bold type, as in his prizewinning entry for a Priester matches competition of 1905 and his poster for Bosch spark plugs of 1914 (no. 70). His work gained renown through its reproduction in *Das Plakat* (The Poster), a magazine for collectors he helped found in 1909 and that was printed in his only text typeface, Bernhard Antiqua (for Bauer, Frankfurt). Bernhard was one of a stable of graphic artists who regularly supplied designs for the Berlin printer Hollerbaum & Schmidt, which built its reputation as a leader of progressive advertising art by publishing their work. About 1923 Bernhard moved to New York where he opened a second studio (the first he kept open). He continued to design advertising graphics (notably billboards for Amoco gasoline for almost two decades), logos, and typefaces (for American Typefounders), and did stage and interior design. In 1928 he joined the German designer Bruno Paul as well as PAUL POIRET and the American artist Rockwell Kent in establishing Contempora, a design firm conceived to supply complete domestic interiors, from furniture to pictures, in up-to-date styles.

References: Robert Foster, "The Matchless Art of Lucian Bernhard," *American Artist* 34 (December 1970): 54–59, 65; Helga Hollmann et al., eds., *Das frühe Plakat in Europa un den USA*, vol. 3, *Deutschland* (Berlin, 1980), pp. 14–26, pls. 119–272.

HARRY BERTOIA
American, born Italy, 1915–1978

A designer of furniture, jewelry, silver, and graphics, Harry Bertoia was primarily a sculptor, whose metal constructions were made both as monumental architectural commissions and on a more domestic scale. Bertoia attended the art school of the Detroit Society of Arts and Crafts in 1936 and then in 1937 began to study at the Cranbrook Academy of Art in Bloomfield Hills, Michigan. There, at the request of its director, ELIEL SAARINEN, he reestablished the metal shop in 1939, teaching both jewelry and metalwork. Bertoia left in 1943 to work in California with former Cranbrook student CHARLES EAMES, first doing wartime work on plywood airplane and medical equipment and then helping Eames develop the bent-plywood chair (no. 194) that would be exhibited in New York in 1946. Disappointed at what he felt was a lack of recognition for his contribution to the chair's design, Bertoia later left Eames and at the invitation of Knoll Associates moved to a studio near its factory in Pennsylvania, where he worked as a sculptor and created his line of wire-mesh furniture in 1951–52 (no. 222). The commissions for architectural sculpture that he began to receive in 1953 allowed him to devote himself entirely to sculpture, and although he remained a consultant to Knoll he did not create any more furniture for the firm.

References: June Kompass Nelso, *Harry Bertoia, Sculptor* (Detroit, 1970); Eric Larrabee and Massimo Vignelli, *Knoll Design* (New York, 1981), pp. 66–71.

MAX BILL
Swiss, born 1908

Architect, sculptor, painter, designer, and theorist, Max Bill was trained first as a silversmith at the Kunstgewerbeschule in Zurich (1924–27) and at the Bauhaus in Dessau, where he studied painting and architecture, and worked in the stage and metal workshops (1927–29). In 1929 he returned to Zurich where he established a studio initially for architecture, painting, and sculpture. He won a grand prize at Milan's *VI Triennale* in 1936 for his design of the Swiss exhibition, winning a similar prize at the *IX Triennale* of 1951. Bill's formative years in Germany made a lasting impact on the products he has designed (no. 211): following WALTER GROPIUS (and the Deutscher Werkbund) he consistently argued that the search for universally valid forms, satisfying proportions, good materials, and workmanship within the constraints of function and production would result in "good" designs like those of the Bauhaus and the simple, functional wares he saw illustrated in magazines like *Die Form* during the 1920s. After World War II, Bill organized a traveling exhibition called *Die Gute Form* (*Good Design*) for the Schweizer Werkbund (1949) and published a record of it under the title *Form* in 1952. "Against the meretricious falsity of so much which passes for 'industrial' design," he wrote in the introduction, "we set the simple, straightforward ideal of good forms, honest designing, for everything mankind requires to shape or reshape, from plastic tea-cups to the planning of better towns for the next generation to live in."[5] Between 1950 and 1956 Bill was cofounder, director, architect, and head of the departments of architecture and product design at the Hochschule für Gestaltung (Institute of Design) in Ulm, Germany, which he conceived as a "lineal continuation of the Dessau Bauhaus"[6] and where he assembled an international faculty that included Tomás Maldonado, Otl Aicher, HANS GUGELOT, and Abraham Moles. At the same time Bill created designs for industry, including clocks for Junghans (no. 257), lamps for BAG, and furni-

ture for Horgen-Glarus and Wohnbedarf. His major work, however, has been as a painter, sculptor, and architect; notable among his designs was the Bilden und Gestalten (Educating and Creating) pavilion at the *Swiss National Exhibition* in Lausanne in 1964. He has also been professor of environmental design at the Staatliche Hochschule für Bildende Künste, Hamburg (1967–74), and served as a member of the Swiss parliament (1967–74).

References: Tomás Maldonado, *Max Bill* (Buenos Aires, 1955); Margit Staber, *Max Bill* (Saint Gall, Switzerland, 1971); Eduard Hüttinger, *Max Bill* (New York, 1978).

THORVALD BINDESBØLL
Danish, 1846–1908

Trained as an architect at the Copenhagen academy, Thorvald Bindesbøll was also a designer of bookbindings, illustrations, and graphics (including labels for Carlsberg beer), as well as silver, furniture, textiles, and ceramics. A member of the Arts-and-Crafts-inspired Dekorationsforening (Decorative Society), founded in 1887, Bindesbøll was employed during the 1890s at the Københavns Lervarefabrik, a pottery for which he created ceramics with floral slip-painted and sgraffito patterns. These designs were planned out in quick, flat, wash drawings, many of which have survived. By the later 1890s he had achieved his own powerful, more graphically abstract style (no. 25), which he also applied to his textile designs. Bindesbøll created silver beakers, bowls, and flatware for A. Michelsen and Holger Kyster in patterns that were usually more discrete and dependent on oriental motifs than those he did in other mediums.

References: Karl Madsen, *Thorvald Bindesbøll* (Copenhagen, 1943); Meret Bodelsen, "Thorvald Bindesbøll: A Forerunner of Abstract Art," *Connoisseur* 149 (February 1962): 92–96; Marianne Ertberg Pedersen, "Thorvald Bindesbøll, 1846–1908," *Du* 36 (March 1976): 56–63; Reto Niggl, *Thorvald Bindesbøll: Keramik und Silber* (Starnberg, Germany, 1989).

CINI BOERI
Italian, born 1924

As a designer for Arflex from the mid-1960s, Cini Boeri has conceived of furniture in terms of systems—endlessly extendable elements, modular furnishing families, or environments. Her polyurethane *Bobo* seating of 1967 was one of the earliest pieces of furniture made of foam blocks without internal structure, while her *Serpentone* seating of 1970–71 (no. 326), comprising widths of polyurethane slices glued together, could be extended without end. Most successful commercially was Strips, a large family of armchairs, sofas, and beds with informal, quilted covering, designed in 1972 (with Laura Griziotti), which was awarded a Compasso d'Oro prize in 1979. An architect with a degree from the Milan Politecnico (1951), Boeri was associated with the studio of MARCO ZANUSO from 1952 until 1963, when she became a freelance designer. She has also designed lighting (for Arteluce), hardware (for Fusital), and more recently (with Tomu Katayanagi) a bent-glass armchair, *Ghost* (for Fiam).

References: Alfonso Grassi and Anty Pansera, *Atlante del design italiano, 1940–1980* (Milan, 1980), pp. 162, 165, 176, 187, 278; *Arflex '51 '81* (Milan, 1981), pp. 38–39, 48–57, 64–65; *The International Design Yearbook*, vol. I (1985–86), p. 178; vol. 4 (1988), p. 33.

THEODOR BOGLER
German, 1897–1968

In 1919 Theodor Bogler became one of the first students at the Bauhaus, working from 1920 in the pottery workshop at Dornburg an der Saale and eventually, in 1923, taking charge of the model production as a co-journeyman with Otto Lindig. One of the Bauhaus's earliest advocates of design for industry, Bogler was first to put theory into practice, creating prototypes at Dornburg that were made by ceramics factories around Berlin. Bogler's ceramics, illustrated in the first Bauhaus publication, *Staatliches Bauhaus, Weimar, 1919–1923* (1923), and later in the *Neue Arbeiten der Bauhaus Werkstätten* (1925), included containers for kitchen supplies made at the Steingutfabrik, Velten-Vordamm, teapots made of interchangeable elements (no. 96), a coffee machine made by the Staatliche Porzellanmanufaktur, Berlin, and storage containers made by the Älteste Volkstedter Porzellanmanufaktur. In 1924 Bogler left the Bauhaus to work as artistic director at Velten-Vordamm. There he remained until 1927 when he entered the Benedictine order at Maria Laach, although he continued to supply designs to ceramic factories in Karlsruhe and Höhr-Grenzhausen.

References: Annagrete Janda, "Bauhauskeramik," *Kunstmuseen der Deutschen Demokratischen Republik, Mitteilungen und Berichte* 2 (1959): 101; Art Gallery of Ontario, Toronto, *50 Years Bauhaus* (December 6, 1969–February 1, 1970), p. 342.

KAY BOJESEN
Danish, 1886–1958

Silversmith and woodworker, Kay Bojesen was known popularly throughout his country for the droll wooden toy soldiers and articulated animals he designed and sold, and internationally as a pioneer and promoter of modern Danish design. He began his career as a silversmith, training in the workshop of GEORG JENSEN and then abroad at the Royal Craft School for Precious Metals in Württemberg and in Paris. Bojesen opened his own studio in Copenhagen in 1913, designing silver in the Danish art nouveau tradition, but in the later 1920s and '30s he altered his work to follow a deliberate modernist style of smooth undecorated forms. His work was also produced in stainless steel (by Motala Verkstad, Sweden, and Universal Steel), and his silver *Grand Prix* cutlery, designed

in 1938 and honored at the *IX Triennale* in Milan in 1951 (no. 167) was adapted to this material virtually unaltered. Bojesen also created wooden tablewares, particularly salad bowls, which he manufactured along with those of other Danish designers in his own workshops. In his efforts to promote modern design, Bojesen founded Den Permanente, one of the first design centers in Europe, which opened in Copenhagen in 1931 to exhibit examples of Danish craftsmanship and industrial design.

References: Edgar Kaufmann, Jr., "Kay Bojesen: Tableware to Toys," *Interiors* 112 (February 1953): 64–67; Mary Lyon, "A Master Plays Wide Field: Bojesen of Denmark Designs Toys, Silverware, Woodenware, Glass," *Craft Horizons* 13 (July 1953): 26–31; Esbjørn Hiort, *Modern Danish Silver* (New York, 1954), pp. 8–9, pls. 1–6; Arne Karlsen, *Made in Denmark* (New York, 1960), pp. 44–49, 122.

DONALD BOOTY, JR.
American, born 1956

President of Booty Design Associates (founded in 1988), Donald Booty, Jr., studied industrial design at the Illinois Institute of Technology's Institute of Design in Chicago. The firm has worked in the areas of consumer electronics, housewares, storage, lighting, and industrial equipment, following the traditional approach of designing on commission but also developing product and system concepts that it markets to manufacturers, as well as manufacturing on its own, under the name PHORM, products it has developed. Two of Donald Booty, Jr.'s ergonomically conceived designs for small electronic products are of particular note, his *Double Plus* calculator (no. 395) and *Thumper* alarm clock, both for Zelco.

Reference: "Design Portfolio," *Business Week*, June 15, 1990, p. 191.

MARIO BOTTA
Swiss, born 1943

The organic, rationalist buildings of Mario Botta—geometric and strongly volumetric, with a sense of materials, light, and locale that relates them to their surroundings—reveal the influence of three architectural mentors: his thesis adviser at the University of Venice, Carlo Scarpa, LE CORBUSIER, and the American Louis Kahn. The last two he met, and assisted, in Venice, and he also worked for a short time in Corbusier's studio in Paris. Apprenticed to the architectural firm of Carloni & Camenisch in Lugano when he was fifteen, Botta attended the Liceo Artistico in Milan from 1961 to 1964. He studied architecture at the University of Venice from 1964 to 1969 and then returned to Lugano, where he established his own firm and constructed the monumental houses in the Ticino that soon brought him international recognition. In 1982 Botta began to design furniture for Alias, and his *Prima* (*First*) chair—expressive but rigorously geometric, made of thin tubular steel and sheet metal—established the vocabulary that would continue for the series of chairs (no. 391), tables, and lamps (for Artemide) that followed.

References: Paul Goldberger, "Design Notebook," *New York Times*, March 17, 1983, p. C12; Pierluigi Nicolin, *Mario Botta: Buildings and Projects, 1961–1982* (New York, 1984); Stuart Wrede, *Mario Botta* (New York, 1986); Francesco Dal Co, *Mario Botta: Architecture, 1960–1985* (New York, 1987).

WILL H. BRADLEY
American, 1868–1962

Designer, typographer, art director, and publisher, Will Bradley was one of the leading proponents of the art nouveau graphic style in America, seen in the illustrations, posters, and covers he provided for *The Chap-Book, Harper's Bazaar, The Echo,* and other magazines. Self-taught as an artist, Bradley learned the printer's trade as an apprentice in his early teens, picked up engraving at Rand McNally, and then became a typographic designer and illustrator for the Chicago printer Knight & Leonard. In 1894, influenced by the latest illustrations appearing in magazines from abroad, especially those of Aubrey Beardsley, Bradley adopted the sinuous art nouveau line and areas of flat color, most notably for the art and literary magazine *The Chap-Book* (no. 6) and *The Inland Printer,* introducing a style that had broad and immediate success. Bradley then moved to Springfield, Massachusetts, where in 1895 he established the Wayside Press specifically to print and publish his own art and literary magazine, *Bradley: His Book.* At the same time he became interested in period typography, particularly the typefaces used in books printed in colonial New England, which he studied at the Boston Public Library. A member of the Arts and Crafts Society of Boston, Bradley participated in its exhibitions, showing his printing in Caslon and other early typefaces, which he revived and also used for his job printing for such firms as Strathmore paper and Towle silversmiths.

Forced by poor health to relinquish his successful printing business, Bradley returned to graphic design in 1898, providing covers for *Collier's,* creating a series of Arts and Crafts designs for interiors and furnishings for *Ladies' Home Journal,* and undertaking the total effort of publishing a trade journal for American Type Founders called *The American Chap-Book* (1904–5). Bradley became art director of *Collier's* in 1907, later also working for *Good Housekeeping, Cosmopolitan,* and other Hearst magazines.

References: Metropolitan Museum of Art, New York, *Bradley: American Artist & Craftsman* (June 16–July 31, 1972); Clarence P. Hornung, ed., *Will Bradley: His Graphic Art* (New York, 1974); David W. Kiehl, *American Art Posters of the 1890s* (New York, 1987), nos. 13–35.

MARIANNE BRANDT
German, 1893–1983

Marianne Brandt is best remembered today for the lamps and metalwork she designed as a student in the Bauhaus metal workshop from about 1924 in Weimar (no. 91) through about 1928 in Dessau. Her designs were among those actually produced by industry, notably the *Kandem* bedside-table lamp made by Körting & Matthiesen in Leipzig (no. 118). Brandt studied painting and sculpture at the Kunstakademie in Weimar before entering the Bauhaus, and served as assistant master of the metal workshop in 1928 before leaving to work in WALTER GROPIUS's office in Berlin (1928–29). Between 1929 and 1932 she designed metalwares for the Ruppelberg factory in Gotha, and after World War II taught at the Hochschule für Freie und Angewandte Künste in Dresden (1949–51) as well as the Institut für Angewandte Kunst in Berlin (1951–54).

References: Hans M. Wingler, *The Bauhaus: Weimar, Dessau, Berlin, Chicago* (Cambridge, Mass., 1969), pp. 98, 293, 314, 318, 320, 456–58; Art Gallery of Ontario, Toronto, *50 Years Bauhaus* (December 6, 1969–February 1, 1970), pp. 44, 105–8, 342–43; Marianne Brandt, statement, in Eckhard Neumann, ed., *Bauhaus and Bauhaus People* (New York, 1970), pp. 97–101.

CARL-ARNE BREGER
Swedish, born 1923

Carl-Arne Breger studied industrial design at the Konstfackskolan (School of Arts, Crafts and Design) in Stockholm from 1943 to 1948, later designing interiors for the Swedish film industry and working independently before joining the design staff of Gustavsberg in 1953. There he designed sanitary fittings as well as plastic housewares, including both products for the table (no. 268) and utility wares such as a square bucket that was named the best-designed plastic product of the decade in 1960 by the Swedish Plastic Association. From 1957 to 1959 Breger was chief designer for the Stockholm office of BERNADOTTE & BJØRN, and since then has had his own design consultancy with offices in Malmö, Stockholm, and Rome. Breger has been responsible for thousands of products including a well-known telephone for L M ERICSSON and a handsaw for Sandvik that was awarded a Bundespreis Gute Form in 1975.

References: Nationalmuseum, Stockholm, *Gustavsberg 150 år* (1975), nos. 306, 309–10, 317; Carl-Arne Breger, "The Story behind a Design," *Tele* 2 (1979): 212–15.

MARCEL BREUER
Hungarian, active Germany and England, later American, 1902–1981

Among the first students to benefit from the entire educational program of the Bauhaus, Marcel Breuer was one of its most influential graduates and the one whose work is most broadly associated with its philosophy. Born in Hungary, Breuer enrolled at the Academie der Bildenden Künste in Vienna in 1920 but left shortly, the same year entering the school of the Bauhaus in Weimar, where he studied furniture design (no. 89). He soon became the protégé of the director, WALTER GROPIUS, and, after graduating in 1924 and traveling to Paris, was asked back to become master of the carpentry workshop at the Bauhaus's new quarters constructed by Gropius in Dessau. Between 1925 and 1928, the years he taught at the school, Breuer independently created a series of revolutionary tubular-steel furniture designs (nos. 104, 124), simple, light, rational, resilient, and sleekly modern in appearance and manufacture. His later lightweight furniture made of aluminum bars won both the industry and the designer first prizes at the Paris international competition for the best aluminum chair in 1934.

Breuer moved to England in 1935, where he practiced architecture and designed plywood furniture for Isokon (no. 158), and in 1937 he came to America to join the faculty of the Harvard University School of Design under Gropius. More and more he concentrated on architecture, while continuing to design furnishings for his own interiors and to experiment with plywood. His design for an economical, resilient plywood chair (in conjunction with the U.S. Forest Products Laboratory) was included in the 1950 exhibition, *Prize Designs for Modern Furniture*, at the Museum of Modern Art in New York.

References: Edgar Kaufmann, Jr., *Prize Designs for Modern Furniture* (New York, 1950), pp. 56–57; Eric Larrabee and Massimo Vignelli, *Knoll Design* (New York, 1981), pp. 168–73; Christopher Wilk, *Marcel Breuer: Furniture and Interiors* (New York, 1981); Derek E. Ostergard, ed., *Bent Wood and Metal Furniture, 1850–1946* (New York, 1987), passim.

BARBARA BROWN
English, born 1932

A freelance textile designer, Barbara Brown studied at the Canterbury College of Art and then at the Royal College of Art in London (1953–56). She sold her first design to Heal Fabrics while she was still a student and for years she continued to supply them regularly with her work, winning two Council of Industrial Design awards for *Complex* in 1968 and for *Spiral* (no. 323) and *Automation* in 1970. Her printed fabrics of the early 1960s used configurations familiar from op art—flat geometric forms in small repeating units—while later in the decade she introduced a sense of depth and solidity in both her geometric and illusionistic designs. More recently she has created pieced knitted fabrics for shawls and clothing.

References: Whitworth Art Gallery, Manchester, England, *Brown/Craven/Dodd: 3 Textile Designers* (1965), pp. 6–10; "Furnishing Fabrics: Heal's Chevron, Complex and Extension," *Design* 233 (May 1968): 42–43; "Furnishing Textiles," *Design* 258 (June 1970): 49.

GREGORY BROWN
English, 1887–1941

Graphic artist and textile designer, Gregory Brown worked virtually throughout his career, from 1916 to 1940, creating advertising and poster designs for Frank Pick, commercial manager of the London Underground, who, like Brown, was a founding member of the British Design and Industries Association. Brown studied at the North London School of Art and then apprenticed to an art metalworker (1903), but soon gave that up for work as an illustrator. In the 1920s and 30s he worked as a freelance designer for the textile manufacturer William Foxton. His fabrics for Foxton won a gold medal at the 1925 Paris exhibition (no. 87), and they were also included in the 1930–31 *International Exhibition of Decorative Metalwork and Cotton Textiles* organized by the American Federation of the Arts.

References: Obituary, *Times* (London), March 7, 1941, p. 7; Arts Council of Great Britain, Hayward Gallery, London, *Thirties: British Art and Design before the War* (October 25, 1979–January 13, 1980), p. 286, nos. 4.15, 4.16, 17.6; Donald King et al., *British Textile Design in the Victoria and Albert Museum*, vol. 3: *Victorian to Modern (1850–1940)* (Tokyo, 1980), pp. xviii, xxxv, xxxviii; Oliver Green, *Art for the London Underground: London Transport Posters, 1908 to the Present* (New York, 1990), pp. 37, 45, 138–39.

CARLO BUGATTI
Italian, 1856–1940

The best known internationally among Italian designers around the turn of the century, Carlo Bugatti created exotic furniture that was a completely original contribution to the art nouveau style. Bugatti studied at the Accademia di Brera in Milan and then at the Ecole des Beaux-Arts in Paris, but instead of becoming an architect as most of his colleagues did he began to design furniture and interiors. In 1888, the year he established his own cabinetmaking workshop and decorating business in Milan, he was awarded a diploma of honor for his furniture at the *Italian Exhibition* at Earl's Court in London. His works of the next decade, which were highlighted in an 1895 article on "quaint" continental furniture in the British journal *Furniture and Decoration*, were characterized by eclectic combinations of asymmetrically placed Moorish motifs; parchment surfaces painted with Japanese-inspired natural decoration; the use of copper and brass; and decorative tassels. Bugatti won a silver medal in 1900 in Paris and a diploma of honor in 1902 in Turin, where he created four complete rooms and showed numerous individual pieces, which were widely illustrated in international publications and noted for their bizarre motifs and materials, perfection of workmanship, and stylistic unity (no. 24). Shortly after achieving this success, Bugatti sold his business to the firm of De Vecchi (which continued to use his furniture designs for a short time) and moved to Paris. There he opened a cabinetry workshop, supplying luxury items to such clients as the Bon Marché department store, but put his energy into silverwork, which was shown first in 1907 at the Galerie Hébrard and then regularly at the Salon des Artistes Décorateurs.

References: Simon Jervis, "Carlo Bugatti," *Arte Illustrata* 3 (October–December 1970): 80–87; Philippe Dejean, *Carlo-Rembrandt-Ettore-Jean Bugatti* (New York, 1982); Museum für Kunst und Gewerbe, Hamburg, *Die Bugattis: Automobile, Möbel, Bronzen, Plakate* (June 8–August 28, 1983).

EDOUARD-WILFRID BUQUET
French, active 1920s–1930s

The designer Edouard-Wilfrid Buquet is known only from the French patent he received for the design of his celebrated adjustable lamp (no. 117), dated July 11, 1927 (no. 628,883).

Reference: Alastair Duncan, *Art Nouveau and Art Deco Lighting* (London, 1978), p. 147, fig. 89.

LUIGI CACCIA DOMINIONI
Italian, born 1913

A designer associated closely with the studio of LIVIO and PIER GIACOMO CASTIGLIONI when it was founded in 1938, Luigi Caccia Dominioni collaborated with them on the design of radios for Phonola (no. 180) and the organization of the radio exhibition at the *VII Triennale* in Milan in 1940, where they were shown. He continued to collaborate intermittently with the studio into the 1950s, winning a Compasso d'Oro with them in 1960 for a school chair designed for Palini in 1959. His independent work included furniture designs (for Azucena) and metalware (for Miracoli), and he was also one of the organizers of the exhibition of household objects at the *VIII Triennale* in 1947.

References: "Lezione sulla natura e profezia sulla forma degli apparecchi radio," *Domus* 151 (July 1940): 84–87; Antonio Grassi and Anty Pansera, *Atlante del design italiano, 1940–1980* (Milan, 1980), pp. 17, 23, 43, 106, 114, 156.

CAPPELLIN-VENINI & C., see PAOLO VENINI

JEAN CARLU
French, 1900–1989

Jean Carlu is best known for the body of graphic work he created from the 1920s through the 1940s, applying the stylized geometries of cubism to a series of spare strong poster images with equally concise texts. Carlu studied architecture at the Ecole des Beaux-Arts in Paris until he lost his right arm in a trolley accident at the age of eighteen. He taught himself to draw with his left hand and achieved a significant reputation as a graphic designer within a decade, creating poster and publicity materials for clients as varied as toothpaste manufacturers (Glycodont, 1918; Gellé Frères, 1927), the aquarium in Monaco (1926), and the newspaper *Paris-Soir* (1928). A member of the avant-garde Union des Artistes Modernes, Carlu

was also a political activist, founding in 1932 the Office de Propagande Graphique pour la Paix for which his controversial poster *Désarmement (Disarmament)*—an early use of photomontage in France—was created the same year. Peace propagandist Carlu later became a dedicated anti-Fascist, serving as artistic adviser to the French Information Service, which sent him in 1940 to the United States to organize an exhibition on France at war. With the collapse of France, Carlu remained in America, serving his country as a propagandist through such organizations as the Free French Movement in America, the American-French War Relief, the Committee to Defend America by Aiding the Allies, and the United States Division of Information, Office for Emergency Management (no. 186). In 1952 Carlu returned to Paris, where his later work included designs for Air France (1957–59) and the publisher Larousse (1952–72).

References: W. H. Allner, "Jean Carlu," *Graphis* 3 (January–March 1947): 24–29; Stanley Mason, "Jean Carlu," *Graphis* 35 (November–December 1979): 272–76; Musée de l'Affiche, Paris, *Rétrospective Jean Carlu* (November 26, 1980–March 29, 1981).

GEORGE CARWARDINE
English, 1887–1948

In 1932 George Carwardine, an automotive engineer and one of the directors of Carwardine Associates in Bath, England, patented his design for the articulated *Anglepoise* lamp (no. 143), which was put into production by Herbert Terry in Redditch, England. Little else is known of his design activities.

References: Jeremy Myerson and Sylvia Katz, *Lamps and Lighting* (New York, 1990), pp. 16, 49, 73; Richard Newbury, "Design Classic: A Desktop Icon," *Design* 508 (April 1991): 79.

A. M. CASSANDRE
French, born Ukraine, 1901–1968

Celebrated for his strong, emblematic posters, which blanketed the kiosks and billboards of Paris for two decades, A. M. Cassandre also designed typefaces, which likewise encapsulated the decorative style of their period. Cassandre (born Adolphe-Jean-Marie Mouron) studied painting in Paris, for a short time at the Ecole des Beaux-Arts and then at the Académie Julian, supporting himself as a graphic artist. In 1923, working for the printer-publisher Hachard, he designed *Au Bucheron*, the first poster in what would become his characteristic style; it brought him almost instant celebrity and numerous commissions for other advertisements. With a sequence of exclusive contracts with Hachard, Danel, Nicholas, Draeger, and other publishers in France, as well as those in several other countries, Cassandre produced notable travel and product posters. Prominent among them were the many he did for the French national railways (no. 114) and his well-known witty designs for the aperitif Dubonnet. His typefaces—Bifur (1929), Acier (1930), and Peignot (1937)—were designed for Deberney et Peignot, and in 1968 he also designed a calligraphic photo face that bears his name. Among his other works were magazine covers (for *Harper's Bazaar* and *Fortune*, done when he was in America during the winters of 1936–37 and 1937–38), stage designs (for the Comédie Française, Théâtre National de l'Opéra, and other theaters in Paris, mostly in the postwar period), and logos (for Yves Saint Laurent, 1963). Major retrospective exhibitions of Cassandre's work were held at the Museum of Modern Art in New York in 1936 and at the Musée des Arts Décoratifs in Paris in 1950.

References: Robert K. Brown and Susan Reinhold, *The Poster Art of A. M. Cassandre* (New York, 1979); Henri Mouron, *Cassandre* (Paris, 1985).

ANNA CASTELLI FERRIERI
Italian, born 1920

A designer specializing in plastics, notably furniture and modular storage systems for the firm of Kartell but tablewares as well, Anna Castelli Ferrieri is also an architect and urban planner. She received her architecture degree from the Milan Politecnico (1942), where she studied under Franco Albini, later working in his studio, and in 1954 became an associate in the firm of Ignazio Gardella. In 1947 and 1950 Castelli Ferrieri was awarded gold medals at the *Triennale* exhibitions in Milan, first for a tubular steel armchair and later modular kitchen furniture. Her modular storage units of 1967 and the elaborated *Round-Up* system of 1969 (no. 318) allowed Kartell to introduce a new mobile storage form with snap-together construction. Under her artistic direction—she has been the firm's art director since 1976—the company itself was awarded the Compasso d'Oro prize in 1979 for its "policy based on coherence of product design and constant research and development."[7] From 1969 to 1971 Castelli Ferrieri was president of the Associazione per il Disegno Industriale (ADI).

References: Palazzo delle Stelline, Milan, *Design & design* (May 29–July 31, 1979), pp. 130–31, 157; Augusto Morello and Anna Castelli Ferrieri, *Plastic and Design* (Milan, 1988), passim.

ACHILLE CASTIGLIONI
Italian, born 1918

One of Italy's most inventive postwar industrial designers, Achille Castiglioni has created an astonishing variety of domestic products in a dazzling array of forms, repeatedly accommodating new technology as he closely defines the function and context of each of his products, especially in the area of lighting. In 1944, the year he received his degree in architecture from the Milan Politecnico, he joined the studio of his two older brothers, LIVIO (who

worked with the two until 1952) and PIER GIACOMO (who would be his close collaborator until his death in 1968). Early on, the brothers, who focused primarily on exhibition and product design, experimented with the use of industrial elements and specialized light sources, finding solutions to specific design problems through a simplification of the forms they used. Castiglioni's work received broad recognition: he won seven Compasso d'Oro awards between 1955 and 1979 and medals at successive *Triennale* exhibitions in Milan. His work includes lighting, for Flos (nos. 221, 276, 281, 302, 374); furniture, for Gavina, BBB Bonacina, and Zanotta (no. 266); electrical equipment, for Rem and Brionvega; glass, for Danese; and metal tablewares, for Alessi.

As a champion of Italian industrial design—whose success is "due to the fact that design . . . is not a discipline but an attitude growing out of one's humanistic, technological, economic, and political beliefs"[8]—he became a founding member of the Associazione per il Disegno Industriale (1956) and an organizer of the Compasso d'Oro award, whose jury in 1989 gave him a special mention "for having raised design to the highest levels of culture with his irreplaceable experience."[9] He places great emphasis on designers as teachers, and he himself has been on the faculty of the Politecnico of Turin (from 1969) and the Politecnico of Milan (from 1981).

References: Paolo Fossati, *Il design in Italia, 1945–1972* (Turin, 1972), pp. 122–27, 224–33, pls. 310–54; Daniele Baroni, *L'oggetto lampada* (Milan, 1981), pp. 128–36, figs. 292–321; Paolo Ferrari, *Achille Castiglioni* (Milan, 1984).

LIVIO CASTIGLIONI
Italian, 1911–1979

Working mostly independently of his two younger brothers, ACHILLE and PIER GIACOMO, Livio Castiglioni specialized in the design of electrical equipment, radios, and televisions, although like his brothers he was also a lighting consultant and designer—noted especially for his *Boalum* lamp (with GIANFRANCO FRATTINI; no. 316). Having received a degree in architecture from the Milan Politecnico in 1936, Livio established a design studio with Pier Giacomo in 1938 and became design consultant to Phonola radio in 1939, a relationship that lasted until 1960. With their associate LUIGI CACCIA DOMINIONI, the brothers organized an exhibition of radios at the *VII Triennale* in Milan in 1940, which offered new design possibilities for these instruments independent of furniture cabinetry; the three also showed their own molded-plastic Phonola radio (no. 180), receiving a gold medal and a grand prize for their efforts as designers and exhibition organizers. Livio remained with the studio (which had been joined by Achille after the war) until 1952, when he left to work as a freelance designer and consultant variously for Brionvega, Osram, Artemide, Philips, and Radio Television Italia (RAI), among others. He was a founding member (1956) and president (1959–60) of the Associazione per il Disegno Industriale.

References: "Lezione sulla natura e profezia sulla forma degli apparecchi radio," *Domus* 151 (July 1940): 84–87; Antonio Grassi and Anty Pansera, *Atlante del design italiano, 1940–1980* (Milan, 1980), pp. 17, 42, 178; Vittorio Gregotti, "Traviamenti interpretativi," in Paolo Ferrari, *Achille Castiglioni* (Milan, 1984), pp. 9–14; Colin Naylor, ed., *Contemporary Designers*, 2d ed. (Chicago, 1990), p. 99.

PIER GIACOMO CASTIGLIONI
Italian, 1913–1968

Less well known than his younger brother ACHILLE, with whom he collaborated almost exclusively for over twenty years, Pier Giacomo Castiglioni was nonetheless equally responsible for the design of some of the best-known Italian products of the 1950s and '60s, including the *Arco* (no. 276), *Taccia* (no. 281), and *Toio* (no. 302) lamps, and the *Mezzadro* stool (no. 266). A graduate in architecture from the Milan Politecnico (1937), he and his elder brother LIVIO opened a design studio in 1938, working at times with LUIGI CACCIA DOMINIONI, notably on the design of a molded-plastic radio for Phonola in 1939 (no. 180) and the organization of the exhibition of radios at the *VII Triennale* in Milan in 1940, where their Phonola model was first shown. After the war the two brothers were joined by Achille, and the three collaborated until the early 1950s when Livio left to work on his own. Achille and Pier Giacomo continued together, working mainly in the area of lighting (no. 221) but also producing designs for interiors, furniture, sanitary fixtures, electrical equipment, and tableware; they won numerous prizes at successive *Triennale* exhibitions as well as Compasso d'Oro awards. A founding member of the Associazione per il Disegno Industriale (1956), Pier Giacomo was a member of the faculty of architecture of the Milan Politecnico from 1946 until his death in 1968.

References: Vittorio Gregotti, "Ricordo di Pier Giacomo Castiglioni," *Ottagono* 12 (January 1969): 20–23; Agnoldomenico Pica, "Piergiacomo Castiglioni," *Domus* 470 (January 1969): 1–2; Paolo Fossati, *Il disegno in Italia, 1945–1972* (Turin, 1972), pp. 122–27, 224–33, pls. 310–54; Paolo Ferrari, *Achille Castiglioni* (Milan, 1984), passim; Colin Naylor, ed., *Contemporary Designers* (Chicago, 1990), pp. 100–101.

FAUSTA CAVAZZA
Italian, active from 1970s

Fausta Cavazza, designer of the *Parola* telephone (no. 349), lives in Milan and St.-Paul-de-Vence, France. To manufacture this product, which she patented in 1979, she formed her own company in 1982.

References: *Industrial Design* 33 (July–August 1986): 26; *The International Design Yearbook*, vol. 3 (1987), pp. 196, 225.

PIERRE CHAREAU
French, 1883–1950

Architect, decorator, and designer, Pierre Chareau was considered a leader of French avant-garde designers in the mid-1920s. His extraordinary Maison de Verre (House of Glass) in Paris (1928–33), a townhouse reconstructed with the Dutch architect Bernard Bijvoet, brought together modern ideas about lighting, modular spatial organization, built-in furnishings, and the use of industrial materials. From 1900 to 1908 Chareau studied at the Ecole des Beaux-Arts in Paris and then apprenticed in the decorating department of the French branch of Waring & Gillow, working there until the beginning of World War I. He exhibited interior designs and furnishings influenced by the Wiener Werkstätte at the Salon d'Automne (from 1919), and from 1923 showed works of a markedly different modern note with the Société des Artistes Décorateurs, for whom he designed the library-study of their pavilion, "A French Embassy," at the 1925 Paris exhibition (no. 107). Chareau's nontraditional forms (no. 85), often made of metal, which like JEAN PROUVÉ he began to use as early as 1923, were angular, unornamented, and architectural in conception. Chareau did not successfully design for large-scale industrial manufacture; instead his pieces were generally crafted for specific clients in small quantities. His work was included in the first exhibition of the Union des Artistes Modernes in 1930.

Reference: Marc Vellay and Kenneth Frampton, *Pierre Chareau: Architect and Craftsman, 1883–1950* (New York, 1985).

ILIA CHASHNIK
Russian, 1902–1929

A student and then assistant of KAZIMIR MALEVICH, founder of suprematism, Ilia Chashnik followed his teacher from Moscow to Vitebsk, where he became a member of the short-lived UNOVIS artists' collective, and then to Petrograd. There he became a researcher at the Institute of Artistic Culture, founded by Malevich for scholarly study of contemporary art, and worked with his teacher at the State Porcelain Factory, creating suprematist decorations (no. 95) for its products. Chashnik assisted Malevich on the development of his concepts of a suprematist architecture (*arkhitektons*) and made his own parallel suprematist spatial constructions. Chashnik also created posters and advertising, work that was shown at the 1925 Paris exposition.

References: Leonard Hutton Galleries, New York, *Ilya Grigorevich Chashnik, Lyucite/1902–Leningrad/1929: Watercolors, Drawings, Reliefs* (November 2, 1979–March 15, 1980); Deborah Sampson Shinn, *Revolution, Life and Labor: Soviet Porcelains (1918–1985)* (New York, 1992), p. 33.

WELLS COATES
British, born Japan, 1895–1958

The architect most firmly associated with the modern movement in England in the 1930s, Wells Coates was an engineer by training and saw his buildings and interiors as well as the furniture and appliances he designed as works of technology. Raised in Japan, the son of a missionary, he attended the University of British Columbia in Vancouver, and after serving as a pilot in World War I, settled in London, where he worked intermittently as a journalist and a draftsman. Coates was in Paris as a journalist during the 1925 exhibition, where he was undoubtedly influenced by LE CORBUSIER's Pavillon de l'Esprit Nouveau. His first major architectural commission, the Lawn Road flats in Hampstead, London (1932–34), built by Isokon, was clearly involved in playing out Corbusier's ideas on housing as a "machine for living."

Coates was one of the principals of Isokon (an acronym for Isometric Unit Construction), a firm established with Jack Pritchard in 1931 to build modular housing and unit furnishings designed by Coates; the firm expanded into the Isokon Furniture Company in 1935 to manufacture and distribute furniture by other designers as well (no. 158). Coates's major work in industrial design was for E. K. Cole. Having won the firm's radio competition in 1932 with a unique circular design, he created a series of circular plastic radios between 1934 and 1946 (no. 145), the portable *Princess-Handbag* model in 1947 (no. 196), and plastic electric heaters (1937).

References: J. M. Richards, "Wells Coates 1893–1958," *Architectural Review* 124 (December 1958): 357–60; University of East Anglia, Norwich, England, *Isokon Exhibition* (January–February, 1975), passim; Sherban Cantacuzino, *Wells Coates* (London, 1978); Arts Council of Great Britain, Hayward Gallery, London, *Thirties: British Art and Design before the War* (October 25, 1979–January 13, 1980), pp. 267–68, 287, nos. 4.57, 10.3, 10.4, 11.9–14, 11.44, 11.63, 11.76, 14.12, 21.8; Adrian Forty, *Objects of Desire* (New York, 1986), pp. 204–5.

LUIGI COLANI
German, born 1928

Combining ergonomics with strangely curved, organic forms, Luigi Colani has created a diverse range of products that share the same distinctly individual character—from personal accessories (sunglasses) and household equipment (glasswares and faucets) to visionary forms of transportation (sharklike heavy transport planes, space shuttles, hydrofoils, high-speed trains, a record-setting propeller plane, and experimental racing cars, motorcycles, and bicycles). Although most have progressed no further than models and prototypes, his ideas for transport nonetheless have inspired the thinking of many other designers and manufacturers. Colani's passion for aerodynamic styling dates to his study at the Sorbonne in Paris and his later work as an airplane engineer, and it has affected everything he has designed, including the *Drop* porcelain service for Rosenthal (no. 331) and his cameras for Canon.

References: "Things Seen," *Design* 271 (July 1971): 92; Kestner-Museum, Hanover, *Rosenthal: Hundert Jahre Porzellan* (April 29–June 13, 1982), pp. 171–72; *The Colani Line* (Tokyo, 1983); Tommaso Trini, "Il design post-diluviano di Luigi Colani," *Domus* 636 (February 1983): 48–50; G.K.K., "A Case Apart: Luigi Colani," *Ottagono* 83 (December 1986): 40–43.

JOE COLOMBO
Italian, 1930–1971

Perhaps the most original and technologically inventive of the artists who defined Italian design during the 1960s, Joe Colombo concurrently studied painting at the Accademia di Belle Arti di Brera and architecture at Milan's Politecnico. He joined the painting group Movimento Nucleare (Nuclear Movement), founded in 1951 by Enrico Baj and Sergio Dangelo, and exhibited his paintings with the group from 1952 to 1954. In 1958 Colombo gave up painting, first to run his father's company, which manufactured electrical equipment, and, from 1962 when he opened his first studio in Milan, to practice interior and product design; the latter he had precociously attempted in 1954, creating a "Television Shrine" open-air rest area with benches for the X Triennale in Milan. Colombo's prolific career as a designer, which spanned less than a decade, was marked by an innovative use of materials (no. 294), particularly the then-new plastics such as fiberglass, ABS, methacrylate (no. 282), polyethylene, and PVC. He employed them in elegant, formal solutions often distinguished by flexibility of function—from his *Universal* plastic chair (1965), with unscrewable legs made in different heights for use as a low child's chair or as a high barstool, to the *Ciclope* lamp (1970), which slides vertically along two parallel cables for variable positioning. Driven by concern for man's "total" domestic environment and by the need for economy of cost and careful space planning, Colombo designed "systems" furnishings made of elements that could be combined in different ways to produce different objects. His *Additional* seating system (1968; no. 309), for example, links together six cushions of different sizes to create couches or armchairs. Colombo also designed multifunctional units like the *Mini Kitchen* (1963; no. 283), which provides all necessary functions for food preparation in a single unit. These ideas he integrated into the experimental habitats he created for the Bayer plastics company's "Visiona 69" installation in Cologne and into the *Roto-Living* unit for Sormani, both in 1969. His *Total Furnishing Unit* designed for the Museum of Modern Art's *Italy: The New Domestic Landscape* exhibition in New York in 1972 also reflected these concerns.

Reference: Ignazia Favata, *Joe Colombo and Italian Design of the Sixties* (Cambridge, Mass., 1988).

COOK AND SHANOSKY ASSOCIATES
Established New York, 1967

A design partnership specializing in graphic design and corporate communications, Cook and Shanosky

Associates received its first important national and international notice for the series of symbols they designed for the United States Department of Transportation between 1974 and 1976 (no. 334). Roger Cook and Don Shanosky first met at a design firm, Graphic Directions, in New York, where both worked for several years until they began their partnership in 1967. Their own firm provides full-service graphic design capabilities, including annual reports, corporate collateral material, logo and identity development, print advertising, and architectural signage systems, and has counted among its corporate and institutional clients Black & Decker, BASF, Volvo, Ithaca College, and the Educational Testing Service. In 1992 Cook and Shanosky designed the identity program for the New Jersey State Aquarium in Camden.

Reference: E. K. Carpenter, "Travelers' Aid, Courtesy DOT and AIGA," *Print* 29 (March 1975): 25–31.

HANS CORAY
Swiss, born 1906

Artist and industrial designer, Hans Coray designed one of this century's most successful all-weather chairs (no. 168), the aluminum *Landi* chair, created for the *Schweizerische Landesausstellung*, the Swiss national exhibition of 1939. Self-taught, Coray began designing chair models about 1930; a course in metalwork in Zurich in 1911 led to exhibition designs for several Swiss chemical firms during World War II. After the war Coray created sculptures largely in metal that were shown in exhibitions in Zurich (from 1950 to 1985), Bern (1951), and Cologne (1981). Coray was most active as an industrial designer in the 1950s, creating and producing furniture in tubular steel, wood, and aluminum, which was sold through Wohnbedarf.

Reference: Museum für Gestaltung, Kunstgewerbemuseum, Zurich, *Hans Coray: Künstler und Entwerfer* (August 20–October 5, 1986).

CORNING GLASS WORKS
Established Corning, New York, 1868

One of the world's largest manufacturers of glass products, both under its own name and that of its many subsidiaries, the Corning Glass Works was established as the Corning Flint Glass Company in 1868, the successor to glassworks in Massachusetts and New York in which its founder, Amory Houghton, Sr., had financial interests. The firm, which manufactured blanks for decorative cut glass, was not successful and went bankrupt in 1872. After its reorganization as the Corning Glass Works the same year, however, great effort was directed to research and to finding broader commercial applications of glass. The company became the first manufacturer of light bulbs for Thomas A. Edison (1878) and later developed a heat-resistant glass with numerous industrial uses that was

introduced as Pyrex ("fire-glass") cookware in 1915 (no. 64). Corning's landmark research laboratories were established in 1908 under Eugene C. Sullivan, and its developments have included virtually all aspects of glass manufacture and production.

One of Corning's subsidiaries, Steuben Glass, was founded in 1903 by Frederick Carder for the manufacture of art glass and acquired by Corning in 1918. It was reorganized in 1933 by Arthur A. Houghton, Jr., with the advice of WALTER DORWIN TEAGUE and the collaboration of the designer Sidney Waugh. Following the lead of Scandinavian glasshouses such as Orrefors and using a heavy glass body, Steuben became America's most prominent producer of luxury engraved glass.

References: "The Battery Jar That Built a Business," *Corning Glass Works Gaffer* (July 1946): 3–6, 18; Don Wallance, *Shaping America's Products* (New York, 1956), pp. 57–64; Estelle Sinclaire Farrar and Jane Shadel Spillman, *The Complete Cut & Engraved Glass of Corning* (New York, 1979); Mary Jean Madigan, *Steuben Glass: An American Tradition in Crystal* (New York, 1982).

PEPE CORTÉS
Spanish, born 1946

Pepe Cortés has collaborated frequently with his Spanish compatriots JAVIER MARISCAL and Oscar Tusquets. Like them, he has been an influential protagonist in the design renaissance that has taken place in Barcelona since the early 1980s, participating in such exhibitions as *Design in Catalogna*, which opened in Milan in 1987. Trained at the Eina School in Barcelona, Cortés has practiced as both an interior and product designer, creating furniture and lighting for BD Ediciones de Diseño, including *Roberto* furniture (1983) and the *Araña* floor lamp (1985; no. 380).

References: Michael Collins and Andreas Papadakis, *Post-Modern Design* (New York, 1989), p. 245; Emma Dent Coad, *Javier Mariscal: Designing the New Spain* (New York, 1991), pp. 80–81.

MORISON S. COUSINS & ASSOCIATES
Established New York, 1963

Morison S. Cousins & Associates has been the recipient of innumerable awards for products and packaging designed for American corporate clients. Specializing in the consumer market, they have created appliances (for Gillette and Honeywell), housewares (for Heller), hardware, lighting, and communications equipment, and their packaging as well. With such notable products as the familiar *Promax* hair dryer for Gillette in 1975, the *Maxim 4* convection oven in 1980 (no. 358), and the *Space Tel* telephone for Atari in 1985, all of which were given Excellence of Design awards by *Industrial Design* magazine, their work draws on European design approaches interpreted for the American mass market.

References: *Industrial Design* 28 (July–August 1981): 16; Nada Westerman and Joan Wessel, *American Design Classics* (New York, 1985), pp. 114–15; *Industrial Design* 32 (July–August 1985): 76.

PETER J. DANKO
American, born 1949

Peter J. Danko studied fine arts at the University of Maryland, graduating in 1971, and since 1976 has had his own studio where he works as a cabinetmaker and a designer of furniture, both one-off and production pieces manufactured by his own concern. Choosing bentwood as his medium, Danko has engaged in much technical research, patenting the production process for his one-piece plywood chair (no. 355) in 1980. His subsequent designs include the plywood *Bodyform*, *Fan*, and *Waveform* chairs and coordinated tables.

References: Christopher Wilk, *Thonet: 150 Years of Furniture* (New York, 1980), pp. 132–33; J. K., "A One-Piece Chair: They Said It Couldn't Be Done," *Fine Woodworking* 20 (January–February 1980): 46–47; David A. Hanks, *Innovative Furniture in America: From 1800 to the Present* (New York, 1981), pp. 72–73; Susan Goodman, "Chairs with Souls for the Computer Age," *New York Times*, March 31, 1988, p. C10; Dick Burrows, "Peter Danko: Props in the Play of Life," *American Craft* 53 (April–May 1993): 54–57.

IVAN DA SILVA BRUHNS
French, 1881–1980

One of the best-known carpet designers during the 1920s and '30s, Ivan da Silva Bruhns was a medical student turned painter turned designer who exhibited with the Société des Artistes Décorateurs in 1911 and 1912 and almost without exception between 1920 and 1939. After World War I he studied carpet making, established his own workshops for the production of his carpets, and opened a shop in Paris in 1925 to sell them. Designs for his tightly woven, geometrically patterned carpets, usually in close tonal harmonies, were derived from both oriental examples and the art of Africa, and were inspired also by cubist painting (no. 133). Da Silva Bruhns was awarded a diploma of honor at the *Exposition Internationale des Arts Décoratifs* in 1925, and provided carpets for the most important interior designers and the decoration of French ocean liners, including one for the reading room of the *Ile de France* in the "Congolese" style (1926) and others for the *Normandie* (1935).

References: M. Valotaire, "Carpets by M. Da Silva Bruhns," *Studio* 91 (1926): 87–89; G. Rémon, "Les Dernières Créations de Da Silva Bruhns," *Mobilier & Décoration* 91 (1929): 97–104; Pierre Cabanne, *Encyclopédie art déco* (Paris, 1986), p. 183.

LUCIENNE DAY
English, born 1917

Named Royal Designer for Industry in 1963, Lucienne Day is best known for her colorful abstract fabrics for furnishing and apparel. Trained at the Croydon School of Art (1934–37) and the Royal College of Art (1937–40) in London, she first worked as an art teacher and then became a freelance textile designer, joining with her husband Robin Day in a design studio in 1948. About 1950 she became associated with Heal Fabrics, which printed the *Calyx* pattern she created for the *Festival of Britain* (no. 227) and for whom she provided numerous other designs over several decades. Day collaborated with her husband on interior design for BOAC aircraft and the two served as consultants to the John Lewis Partnerships department stores; she also designed linens (for Thos. Somerset of Belfast), carpets (for Tomkinsons and Wilton), wallpaper, and porcelain (for Rosenthal). More recently she has concentrated on unique abstract wall hangings, which she calls "silk mosaics." At the Milan *Triennale*, Day was awarded a gold medal and grand prize in 1951 and 1954 respectively, and she has been the recipient of three Council of Industrial Design awards.

References: "Lucienne Day," *Design Quarterly* 36 (1956): 9–10; "Furnishing Fabrics: Heal's Chevron, Complex and Extension," *Design* 233 (May 1968): 42–43; Fiona MacCarthy, *British Design since 1880: A Visual History* (London, 1982), figs. 17, 165; Jennifer Harris, *Lucienne Day: A Career in Design* (Manchester, 1993).

SONIA DELAUNAY
French, born Russia, 1885–1979

A painter and close collaborator of her husband Robert, Sonia Delaunay brought the results of their orphist experiments with geometrical shapes and abstract color contrasts to the fields of textiles, clothing, and theatrical design. After studying at the Karlsruhe academy in Germany (1903–4), she moved to Paris in 1905, attending the Académie de la Palette there. She produced the first of her "simultaneous" clothing in 1913, and later in the decade created the first of her costumes for the theater. In 1923 she provided a series of fabric designs for a textile manufacturer in Lyons and the next year decided to produce fabrics herself (no. 101) for sale at her Paris shop, the Atelier Simultané, and for distribution to shops abroad. Delaunay shared a boutique with the couturier Jacques Heim at the Paris exhibition in 1925, when the reviewer for *L'Art Vivant* praised her work: "Printed fabrics, embroidered fabrics, they both obey the same principles: the balance of volumes and color. Here is the realm of abstraction, of a constant but supple geometry, alive, excited by the gaiety of its inspiration, the capricious play of the brush, the triumphant joy of its color."[10] The same year she gained more popular notice by accepting the commission to paint a Citroën B 12 automobile with multicolored "simultaneous" decorations. In 1930 Delaunay closed her shop to devote herself principally to painting.

References: Michel Hoog, "Les Tissus de Sonia Delaunay," *Bulletin des Musées et Monuments Lyonnais* (1968): 85–93; Albright-Knox Art Gallery, Buffalo, *Sonia Delaunay: A Retrospective* (1980); Musée de l'Impression sur Etoffes, Mulhouse, France, *Sonia Delaunay: Etoffes imprimées des années folles* (1980); Jacques Damase, *Sonia Delaunay: Fashion and Fabrics* (London, 1991).

DE PAS, D'URBINO, LOMAZZI
Established Milan, 1966

The firm of Jonathan De Pas, Donato D'Urbino, and Paolo Lomazzi has worked almost from its inception for Italian industry; nevertheless in their writings and communal approach the three architects, who founded the firm in their twenties, continuously projected an unconventional outlook focused on environmental, symbolic, and communicative values. Turning to furniture design when commissions for buildings were not forthcoming, in 1967 the firm created the first fully inflatable chair to be commercially produced (no. 306), an innovation that led to further experimentation with inflatable structures for use in their exhibition designs—at the *XIV Triennale* in Milan (1968) and for the Italian pavilion at *Expo '70* in Osaka. While they have most consistently focused on flexible and interchangeable designs—for example, modular foam seating and component storage systems for BBB Bonacina in the early 1970s—their detour into pop imagery in 1970 with the *Joe* baseball-mitt chair for Poltronova (no. 322) brought them their best-known creation. A number of their works were included in *Italy: The New Domestic Landscape*, at the Museum of Modern Art in New York in 1972, and the firm was awarded the Compasso d'Oro in 1979 for their *Sciangai* folding coat rack, unfolding *Flap* chair, and *Jointed* drawer system. During the 1980s they began to design furniture that seems deliberately luxurious, principally for Zanotta, and joined with Cast Design to create a series of beds and accompanying furnishings in a postmodern idiom.

References: Emilio Ambasz, ed., *Italy: The New Domestic Landscape* (New York, 1972), pp. 34, 44, 57, 95, 114; Gerd Hatje, *New Furniture 11* (New York, 1973), nos. 103, 168–69, 354–55, 390–93, 424–25; Alfonso Grassi and Anty Pansera, *Atlante del design italiano, 1940–1980* (Milan, 1980), p. 299 et passim; *The International Design Yearbook*, vol. 1 (1985–86), pp. 29, 50; vol. 2 (1986), pp. 75, 115, 220; vol. 3 (1987), pp. 48, 80–81.

DONALD DESKEY
American, 1894–1989

The creator of America's quintessential art moderne interior, Radio City Music Hall in New York (1932), Donald Deskey was also responsible for some of the country's most familiar advertising imagery, including the packaging for Crest toothpaste, first designed in the mid-1950s and still in use. Erratically schooled, with some engineering and some architectural study, Deskey attended various painting academies in Paris in 1921–22 and became a painter and art teacher there. He returned to the U.S., but after a second trip to Paris in 1925, where he visited the *Exposition Internationale des Arts Décoratifs*, he began to create window displays for New York's Franklin Simon and Saks & Company department stores using industrial materials and geometrical designs influenced by his exposure to cubism and other modern movements in France. The next year PAUL T. FRANKL commissioned a series of painted screens from him for sale at his gallery, and at the same time Deskey began to design metal furniture and lighting (no. 132) for Deskey-Vollmer, a company he established with Phillip Vollmer that was in business from 1927 to 1931. His work expanded to include interiors, wallpapers, and fabrics, and he became a founding member of and exhibitor with the American Designers' Gallery (1928 and 1929) and the American Union of Decorative Artists and Craftsmen (1930 and 1931). His reputation was fully established in 1932 as the winner of the competition for Radio City Music Hall's interiors, and many more commissions for residential interiors and furniture followed (notably, for W. & J. Sloane and Widdicomb). During World War II he formed Donald Deskey Associates, which by the 1950s had become one of America's largest design firms, working in architectural, exhibition, and industrial design as well as packaging and advertising. Deskey's archives are in the Cooper-Hewitt Museum in New York.

References: Michael Komanecky, "The Screens and Screen Designs of Donald Deskey," *Antiques* 131 (May 1987): 1064–77; David A. Hanks and Jennifer Toher, *Donald Deskey: Decorative Designs and Interiors* (New York, 1987).

NIELS DIFFRIENT
American, born 1928

A leader in the field of human factors engineering, Niels Diffrient was associated for a quarter of a century with HENRY DREYFUSS ASSOCIATES, where he worked on the design of industrial and transportation equipment, architectural interiors, and corporate identity programs, and contributed to the anthropometric data compiled in the *Humanscale* volumes (1974, 1981). Diffrient studied architecture and design at the Cranbrook Academy of Art in Bloomfield Hills, Michigan, and then worked as an assistant to EERO SAARINEN and, for a time, with MARCO ZANUSO. His independent designs have included office seating systems in newly derived forms that emphasize support of the body, for Knoll (1979) and Sunar (1982), and the *Jefferson* armchair and ottoman of 1984 (no. 372).

References: Eric Larrabee and Massimo Vignelli, *Knoll Design* (New York, 1981), pp. 50, 56–57, 244, 271–81; *Designer's Choice '82* (New York, 1982), pp. 22–27; Wolf von Eckardt, "A Chair with All the Angles," *Time*, August

20, 1984, p. 97; *Industrial Design* 32 (July–August 1985): 116.

MARION DORN
American, active also England, 1899–1964

After graduating from Stanford University in 1916, Marion Dorn, one of the leading textile and carpet designers in England during the 1930s, became a freelance designer working with resist-dyed fabrics first in America and then England, where she moved about 1924. Dorn and her husband, the American graphic designer EDWARD MCKNIGHT KAUFFER, then began to design carpets, which were handmade by Wilton and first shown in London in 1929. Successive commissions for private and then commercial interiors (frequently for hotels and ocean liners, including the *Queen Mary*) brought her much publicity, and in 1934 she opened her own shop in London where her carpets were sold. At the same time she supplied designs for woven and printed textiles to many leading manufacturers, including Warners, Old Bleach Linen (no. 171), Edinburgh Weavers, and Donald Brothers. Dorn returned to America in 1940, where she continued to design fabrics, some of which were produced by Greeff.

References: "New Rug Designs by E. McKnight Kauffer and Marion V. Dorn: A Conversation with a 'Studio' Representative," *Creative Art* 14 (January 1929) [*Studio* 97]: 35–39; Dorothy Todd, "Marion Dorn: Architect of Floors," *Architectural Review* 72 (September 1932): 107–14; Arts Council of Great Britain, Hayward Gallery, London, *Thirties: British Art and Design before the War* (October 25, 1979–January 13, 1980), p. 288, nos. 4.36–41, 4.45–48; *A Choice of Design, 1850–1980: Fabrics by Warner & Sons Limited* (London, 1981), nos. 175, 176, 178, 179, 185, 190, 198, 204, 218, 224.

HENRY DREYFUSS
American, 1904–1972

Of the group of industrial designers who developed the profession in the 1930s, Henry Dreyfuss was the most concerned with the relationship between man and his environment. His approach, based on technical research and the establishment of "universal" standards, made him a pioneer in the field of human factors engineering, or ergonomics, which he described in his autobiography *Designing for People* (1955) and promoted through the publication of his *Measure of Man* (1960). The latter, which included life-size charts detailing the measurements of the average man and woman, advised designers to accommodate their products to human bodies. An apprentice in the theater under NORMAN BEL GEDDES, Dreyfuss was also a stage designer before he established his own industrial design office in 1929. Like RAYMOND LOEWY, he became celebrated for his streamlined designs for transportation, including the *Twentieth Century Limited* and other trains for the New York Central Railroad. He garnered a wealth of prestigious clients through the seri-

ousness of his proposals and pursuits, and counted among his consultancies BELL TELEPHONE COMPANY (no. 298), John Deere, Hoover (no. 165), and American Airlines. In 1969 Dreyfuss retired from his firm, which continues today under his name.

References: K. O. Tooker and F. L. Pierce, "The Hoover One Fifty," *Modern Plastics* 14 (November 1936): 32–33, 62–63; Don Wallance, *Shaping America's Products* (New York, 1956), pp. 30–40; C. L. Krumreich and L. W. Mosing, "The Evolution of a Telephone," *Bell Laboratories Record* (January 1966): 9–14; "Henry Dreyfuss 1904–1972," *Industrial Design* 20 (March 1973): 37–43; Jeffrey L. Meikle, *Twentieth Century Limited: Industrial Design in America, 1925–1939* (Philadelphia, 1979), passim.

HENRY DREYFUSS ASSOCIATES, see HENRY DREYFUSS

RAOUL DUFY
French, 1877–1953

While Raoul Dufy is known chiefly as a painter, his work in the decorative arts, especially textile design, demonstrates the breadth of his inventive abilities. After studying at the Ecole des Beaux-Arts in Paris, Dufy exhibited along with the Fauve artists Henri Matisse, André Derain, and Maurice de Vlaminck from 1903 to 1909, and then unsuccessfully turned to a cubist style. The influence of the traditional peasant-inspired designs that he saw in Munich in 1909 and that made a sensation at the Salon d'Automne in Paris the following year led him to turn to a simple, folklike style in a series of large-scale woodcut illustrations he did for Guillaume Apollinaire's *Bestiare*. In 1911, when PAUL POIRET established a small textile workshop for him, Dufy continued to work in this style, creating free, colorful patterns not unlike those of Poiret's own ATELIER MARTINE and using unusual materials for printing them—linen, silk, satin, velvet, and even brocades—which Poiret adopted for his fashions. In a friendship and patronage lasting over a decade Poiret also gave Dufy commissions for decorative paintings, elaborate costume spectacles, and finally, in 1925, a series of fourteen painted wall hangings for his barge *Orgues*, moored in the Seine for the *Exposition Internationale des Arts Décoratifs*. In 1912 Dufy signed a contract to work for the Lyons textile firm of Bianchini-Férier, providing them with an extraordinary corpus of imaginative textile designs until 1928 (no. 76). Publicity for Dufy's fabrics came with their publication in 1920 in the prestigious fashion magazine *Gazette de Bon Ton* and in art journals; he exhibited them as well at the Salon des Artistes Décorateurs (1921–23). Dufy also created tapestries (for Beauvais) and ceramics (for Artigas, 1923–30), and from 1930 to 1933 had an association with the American textile manufacturer Onondaga.

References: Musée de l'Impression sur Etoffes, Mulhouse, France, *Raoul Dufy: Créateur d'étoffes* (n.d.); Arts Council of Great Britain, Hayward Gallery, London, *Raoul Dufy* (November 9, 1983–February 5, 1984).

JEAN DUNAND
French, born Switzerland, 1877–1942

This century's most important specialist in lacquer, Jean Dunand led the French revival of this traditional technique during the 1920s, decorating an astonishing variety of furniture, screens, panels, and small objects with motifs ranging from geometric and planar abstractions to animals, portraits, and figurative images inspired by exotic sources. He also created tour de force interiors, including a smoking room in black lacquer for the "French Embassy" pavilion at the *Exposition Internationale des Arts Décoratifs* in Paris in 1925 and a smoking room for the *Normandie* in 1935 (panels now in the Metropolitan Museum of Art, New York).

Trained as a sculptor at the Ecole des Arts Industriels in Geneva, Dunand began his career as a coppersmith in Paris, showing his first metalwork in 1905 and exhibiting finely inlaid and patinated vessels, some with sculptural embellishments, at the salons before World War I. In 1912 he began to learn the technique of lacquer from Sugawara, a Japanese craftsman in Paris who had previously instructed EILEEN GRAY, using it at first to enhance the coloration of the metalwork designs he continued to produce throughout his career (no. 108). After the war he also began to apply lacquer to wooden forms such as furniture, screens, and panels, exhibiting these lacquerworks first at the Salon des Artistes Décorateurs in Paris in 1921. As commissions came in he greatly expanded his shop, employing scores of workers to follow the arduous procedure of this oriental technique and establishing a reputation and a loyal following that would continue undiminished until the end of the 1930s.

References: Howard S. Cresswell, "Oriental Lacquer on Modern Furniture," *Good Furniture Magazine* 31 (June 1928): 291–95; Galerie du Luxembourg, Paris, *Jean Dunand—Jean Goulden* (May–July, 1973); K. M. McClinton, "Jean Dunand: Art Deco Craftsman," *Apollo* 116 (September 1982): 177–80; Anthony DeLorenzo, *Jean Dunand* (New York, 1985).

NATHALIE DU PASQUIER
French, lives in Italy, born 1957

One of the first textile designers to define the postmodern idiom, Nathalie du Pasquier drew on a wealth of diverse sources for her harsh, naive, close patterns, which in the early 1980s became synonymous with the Memphis group. Du Pasquier traveled extensively in Africa, Australia, and India between 1975 and 1978 and then studied drawing and design for a short time in her native Bordeaux before settling in Milan, where in 1980 she began to design textiles for Rainbow. Her work appeared in 1981 in the first Memphis collection as fabric coverings on the furniture of her frequent collaborator, the British designer George Sowden; a line of her fabrics, printed by Rainbow, was presented in the Memphis 1982 collection (no. 364). Du Pasquier has also designed furniture with decorative plastic laminates, and ceramics for Memphis, fabrics for Fiorucci and Esprit, and clocks for Lorenz (with Sowden).

References: Barbara Radice, *Memphis: Research, Experiences, Results, Failures and Successes of New Design* (New York, 1984), p. 88 et passim; *The International Design Yearbook*, vol. 1 (1985–86), pp. 54, 57, 148–49; vol. 2 (1986), pp. 86–87, 151, 174–75, vol. 3 (1987), pp. 82, 156–57, 177–78; Michael Collins and Andreas Papadakis, *Post-Modern Design* (New York, 1989), pp. 39–40.

CHARLES EAMES
American, 1907–1978

An inventor and designer of consummate originality, Charles Eames was one of the most influential figures in American twentieth-century design. His far-ranging achievements in architecture, film making, interior and exhibition design, and product design, particularly with furniture and toys, created a new modern stylistic idiom at midcentury based on Eames's firsthand knowledge of materials technology and production techniques. Technically brilliant, his work was characterized by pure colors, whimsical expression, lightness, and mobility.

Eames studied architecture at Washington University in Saint Louis (1925–27) and worked for the architectural firm of Trueblood and Graf as a draftsman. In 1930 he opened his own architectural office in Saint Louis with Charles M. Gray (Gray and Eames), designing sets for the Saint Louis Municipal Opera outdoor theater, stained-glass windows and mosaics for the Pilgrim Congregational Church, and small residences (1933). In 1935 Eames opened a new architectural firm with Robert T. Walsh (Eames and Walsh); the firm designed churches and residences including the Meyer house (1936–37), which involved consultation with ELIEL SAARINEN. In 1938 Saarinen offered Eames a fellowship to study architecture and design at the Cranbrook Academy of Art in Bloomfield Hills, Michigan, where he remained until 1941, becoming an instructor of design (1939) and head of the department of industrial design (1940). In 1940 Eames and EERO SAARINEN collaborated on designs for the Museum of Modern Art's "Organic Design in Home Furnishings" competition, winning first prize for furniture that involved molding plywood shells in compound curves.

Eames married Ray Kaiser in 1941, with whom he formed a lifelong professional partnership, and moved to southern California where he continued his experiments with molded plywood under contract to the United States Navy and as director of the Molded Plywood Division of the Evans Products Company (1943–47). His interest in mass-producing molded plywood shapes that could be used in low-cost, high-quality furniture resulted in plywood shell chairs shown in the exhibition *New Furniture Designed by Charles Eames* at the Museum of Modern Art in New York in 1946 (no. 194). Two years later he also experimented with stamped metal for the Museum of Modern Art's "International Competition for Low-Cost Furniture Design"; a variant of his prototype competition chair was produced not in metal but in molded fiberglass, an early use of the material (1950; no. 210). Eames's reputation as an architect rests on two houses designed initially with Eero Saarinen as "Case Study Houses" for *Arts and Architecture* magazine in 1945; they were built for Eames (1949) and John Entenza, the magazine's editor and publisher (1950), in Pacific Palisades, California, and were influential for their use of standardized prefabricated parts.

During the 1950s, Eames produced other notable furniture designs including a wire mesh chair (1951–53), a plywood shell lounge chair and ottoman (1956; no. 256), and aluminum furniture (1958). At the same time, he began the series of exhibition and "communication" projects for which his office became known: the "Information Machine" film, produced for IBM and shown in its pavilion at the 1958 Brussels world's fair (1957); the "India Report," on the impact of Western design and technology on Indian culture, commissioned by the Indian government (1958) and resulting in the foundation of the National Institute of Design in Ahmedabad (1961); the exhibition *Mathematica*, designed for the California Museum of Science and Industry in Los Angeles (1961); the IBM pavilion, created for the *New York World's Fair* (1964–65); and *The World of Franklin and Jefferson*, an international traveling exhibition produced for the American Revolution Bicentennial Administration (1975–77), the last major project Eames undertook before his death.

References: "Eames Celebration," *Architectural Design* (special issue) 36 (September 1966); Arthur Drexler, *Charles Eames: Furniture from the Design Collection* (New York, 1973); Frederick S. Wight Art Gallery, University of California, Los Angeles, *Connections: The Work of Charles and Ray Eames* (December 7, 1976–February 6, 1977); John Neuhart, Marilyn Neuhart, and Ray Eames, *Eames Design: The Work of the Office of Charles and Ray Eames* (New York, 1989).

JAN EISENLOEFFEL
Dutch, active also Germany, 1876–1957

The industrial character of Jan Eisenloeffel's metalwork held a strong appeal in pre–World War I Germany, where certain advanced designers and manufacturers, some connected with the Deutscher Werkbund, sought to develop designs for machinery and mass production. Eisenloeffel had been trained in Amsterdam in the silver studio of W. Hoeker, and spent a year in Russia learning enameling techniques. In 1896 he became head of metal-

wares at the Amstelhoek workshops, which Hoeker had set up two years earlier, and from 1900 he designed metalwares for such Dutch firms as 't Binnenhuis, De Woning, and C. J. Begeer, along with ceramics for De Distel. In 1903 he became a member of Kunst aan het Volk (Art to the People), an organization dedicated to improving the quality of everyday mass-produced utensils. Between 1908 and 1911 Eisenloeffel worked in Munich at the Vereinigte Werkstätten für Kunst im Handwerk, where some ninety-three of his model drawings are still preserved. His well-known tea service for the workshops, with its severe, straight shapes (no. 48), was developed out of his earlier Dutch designs. Among his other works were lamps with enamel for the city hall in Amsterdam (c. 1911), a crystal service for Kristalunie in Maastricht (c. 1928), and cutlery for Gerofabriek (1929).

References: Willem Vogelsang, "Metallarbeiten von Jan Eisenloeffel," *Dekorative Kunst* 11 (1903): 383–89; Nederlands Goud-, Zilver- en Klokkenmuseum, Utrecht, *Klokken, zilver, sieraden uit de Nederlandse art nouveau en art deco* (July–September 1976), n.p.; Irmela Franzke, ed., *Jugendstil* (Karlsruhe, 1978), pp. 242, 285; Stedelijk Museum, Amsterdam, *Industry & Design in the Netherlands, 1850–1950* (December 21, 1985–February 9, 1986), passim.

EKCO PRODUCTS COMPANY
Established Chicago, 1888

Founded in 1888 as a manufacturer of pots and pans, Ekco Products began to expand significantly in the 1920s by acquiring other housewares firms and by the 1950s had become the largest kitchenware manufacturer in America. Ekco's lead in the industry was signaled in 1935, when it introduced a simple but significant feature in its kitchen spoons—a hole in the handle from which they could be hung—which was soon widely imitated. The firm's dominance was fully attained with the markedly successful *Flint 1900* kitchen tools of 1946 (no. 202). In 1956 Ekco revised its corporate structure to include a product planning group charged with planning, developing, and merchandising the company's products; design remained, as it always had been, a team endeavor rather than an individual effort.

References: Eliot Noyes, "Good Design in Everyday Objects: Eleven Cases in Point," *Consumer Reports*, January 1949, p. 27; Don Wallance, *Shaping America's Products* (New York, 1956), pp. 129–31; "The Change at Ekco: Merchandising Bows to a Unique Planning Group," *Industrial Design* 3 (October 1956): 103–5; Jay Doblin, *One Hundred Great Product Designs* (New York, 1970), pp. 64–65.

ERGONOMI DESIGN GRUPPEN
Established Bromma, Sweden, 1979

Dedicated to the design of safe, reliable, and efficient products for the disabled and for use in hospitals, transportation systems, and the general workplace, the Ergonomi Design Gruppen amalgamated two earlier firms, Designgruppen and Ergonomi Design, into a collective in 1979. Using research funded by the Swedish government, foundations, and industry, the firm thoroughly examines user-systems problems, by building full-scale models to evaluate designs in experimental situations and through field testing. MARIA BENKTZON and SVEN-ERIC JUHLIN, members of the group who had studied at the Konstfackskolan (School of Arts, Crafts and Design) in Stockholm, pioneered design for the handicapped with a study in 1972 of muscular strength and mobility as it related to holding and gripping; from this they developed their cutting frame and knife designed in 1974 (no. 333). Previous to their collaboration, Benktzon had studied clothing for the disabled and Juhlin had worked for nine years as a designer for Gustavsberg, where his many products included institutional services in plastic and pistol-grip tongs for the disabled (with Per-Olof Bjurling). They have since worked on the Ergonomi Design Gruppen's Eat and Drink series of dishes, drinking vessels, and cutlery (no. 357).

References: Nationalmuseum, Stockholm, *Gustavsberg 150 år* (1975), nos. 302, 313 16, 318–20, 322–24, 332–34, 336, 338–39; Lennart Lindkvist, "Maria Benktzon and Sven-Eric Juhlin," in Nationalmuseum, Stockholm, *Contemporary Swedish Design* (1983), pp. 52–55.

L M ERICSSON
Established Stockholm, 1876

Founded as a telegraph repair shop in 1876 by Lars Magnus Ericsson, the L M Ericsson company began to manufacture telephones two years later, basing its early models on Alexander Graham Bell's prototype but soon creating independent designs. The firm developed a large export business, supplying telephones to much of Europe and opening factories as far away as Mexico. Ericsson has grown into one of the world's largest producers of communications equipment, and among its many innovative products were the standard European cradle desk telephone of 1909, one of the first plastic telephones, designed by the sculptor JEAN HEIBERG in 1930 (no. 134), and the one piece *Ericofon*, introduced in 1956 (no. 239).

Reference: *Ericsson Review* (special issue) 33 (1956): 95–124.

EUREKA COMPANY
Established Detroit, 1909

Founded in 1909 by real estate entrepreneur Fred Wardell, the Eureka Company entered the new home vacuum cleaner market with relatively light and versatile machines sold with an array of attachments. Eureka gained prestige by winning medals at hygiene product and home expositions in Brussels, Amsterdam, and London in the early 1920s, but advertising and aggressive door-to-door selling is what gave the company one-third of the American market by 1927. More recently, design recognition has come with the introduction of the *Mighty Mite* models (no. 371) in 1982. Since 1974 Eureka and its parent company, National Union Electric Corporation, have been part of the Swedish appliance firm Electrolux, a European pioneer in the manufacture of vacuum cleaners.

References: Wolf von Eckardt, "Fashionable Is Not Enough," *Time*, January 3, 1983, pp. 76–77; *Industrial Design* 30 (September–October 1983): 24, 85; Nada Westerman and Joan Wessel, *American Design Classics* (New York, 1985), pp. 118–19.

PAUL FOLLOT
French, 1877–1941

Faced with successive controversies among French designers over the threat of competition from Germany and standardization in the decorative arts, Paul Follot consistently spoke out for the French tradition of individualism, fine hand craftsmanship, and decoration. A designer of costly objects for wealthy clients, he nonetheless considered his ornamental aesthetic universally applicable and hoped that eventually "through technical processes and new materials" French genius would bring "objects of luxury and art into the homes of those with modest incomes."[11]

Follot was a student of the illustrator and poster designer Eugène Grasset, whom he later succeeded as instructor of the advanced decorative arts course at the Ecole Normale d'Enseignement du Dessin in Paris. He then taught himself the techniques of sculpture that would serve to distinguish his work from that of his competitors. From 1901 he created metalwork, jewelry, and fabrics for La Maison Moderne, Julius Meier-Graefe's shop in Paris, and a portfolio of his designs for what he called "modern" jewelry and silverwork was published in 1905. His earliest interior design—an art nouveau ensemble—was created for the first exhibition of the Société des Artistes-Décorateurs in 1904. Within a short time he turned to a style of restrained classicism based on eighteenth- and nineteenth-century models in interiors praised for their logic and sobriety. Large-scale flowers, leaves, and garlands were his principal decorative motifs, and his furniture was made of light woods either decorated with marquetry or carved in high relief with lacquer or gilding (no. 74). He also designed textiles (for Cornille et Cie), carpets (for Savonnerie), bronzes, silver, and ceramics (for Wedgwood and Limoges). In 1923 Follot became director of Pomone, the new design studio at the Paris Bon Marché department store, and conceived its presentation at the 1925 *Exposition Internationale des Arts Décoratifs*. At the exhibition he also furnished the antechamber for "A French Embassy," the pavilion of the Société des Artistes Décorateurs. Follot was instrumental in bringing the modern French decorative style to England through an exhibition organized in 1928 at the decorating firm of Waring & Gillow in London, in collaboration with Serge Chermayeff, director of what the firm called its Modern Art Studio between 1928 and 1931. Follot managed the Paris branch of Waring & Gillow during the same period.

References: C. Genuys, "L'Exposition de la Société des Artistes Décorateurs," Art et Décoration 15 (January–June 1904): 78–92; Paul Follot, Documents de bijouterie et orfèvrerie modernes (Paris, 1905); Guillaume Janneau, "Notre Enquête sur le mobilier moderne: Paul Follot," Art et Décoration 40 (November 1921): 141–48; Léon Riotor, Paul Follot (Paris, 1923); Jessica Rutherford, "Paul Follot: Traditional Art Deco in France," Connoisseur 204 (June 1980): 86–91.

KAJ FRANCK
Finnish, 1911–1989

Kaj Franck had an extraordinary influence on tableware through the popular ceramics (no. 234) and decorative glass (no. 261) he created for two major Finnish manufacturers. The ceramics he produced as head of the design department for utility wares at Arabia from 1945 to 1960, and the glassware he designed as artistic director at Nuutajärvi beginning in 1950 (when it joined the Wärtsilä group). Focusing primarily on simple shapes and inexpensive, multifunctional forms that were fully adapted to mass production, Franck saw design in terms of social not individualistic goals, and he argued in an article in 1967 for the anonymity of factory products and clearly distinguished between them and the unique works of the craftsman. "It is wrong to make the designer the salesman of the [manufactured] article," he wrote. "This offends against the object, the consumer, and the designer. It deprives the article of its value as an article. It inhibits objective judgment by the consumer and restricts his freedom of choice."[12]

Franck studied interior design at the Taideteollinen Keskuskoulu (Central School of Industrial Arts) in Helsinki from 1929 to 1932, and then worked as an independent interior and product designer creating lighting fixtures (for Taito), furniture (for Tema), glass (for Riihimaen Lasi), and textiles before going to work for Arabia in 1945. He worked for the Wärtsilä firms until 1978. Franck was awarded a gold medal in 1951, a diploma of honor in 1954, and a grand prize in 1957 at the Triennale in Milan; a Compasso d'Oro in 1957; and the Lunning Prize in 1955.

References: Erik Zahle, ed., A Treasury of Scandinavian Design (New York, 1961), pp. 34–35, 273, nos. 207–9, 232–35, 325–28, 343–46; Finnish Society of Crafts and Design, Helsinki, Finland: Nature, Design, Architecture (1980–81), pp. 60–66; Jennifer Hawkins Opie, Scandinavia: Ceramics & Glass in the Twentieth Century (London, 1989), pp. 56, 62–65, 68, 72–76, 155.

PAUL T. FRANKL
American, born Austria, 1887–1958

Paul T. Frankl was among the first progressive designers in America to reject European precedents and create new furniture forms inspired directly by the American scene. "Decorative arts and furniture design," he wrote, "are already under the powerful modern architectural influence. This can only resolve into one thing: a decorative art that is in keeping with the country and the people who live in it. It will resolve into an American decorative art, original and at the same time satisfying."[13] Educated as an architect in Berlin, Vienna, Paris, and Munich, Frankl came to the United States in 1914, designing several interiors for Helena Rubinstein and, in 1915–16, stage sets for the Theatre Guild in New York. He worked primarily as a decorator, but as early as 1925 he began to design geometric cabinetwork with flat surfaces, sharp angles, and stepped silhouettes, which he called "skyscraper" furniture (no. 130). These he sold in his midtown New York gallery and exhibited at the first Art in Trade exhibition at Macy's department store in 1927. Frankl was an influential spokesperson for modern design, which he explained and promoted through two books, New Dimensions: The Decorative Arts of Today (1928) and Form and Re-Form (1930), copiously illustrated with examples of his own work.

References: "American Modernist Furniture Inspired by Sky-scraper Architecture," Good Furniture Magazine 29 (September 1927): 119–21; Karen Davies, At Home in Manhattan: Modern Decorative Arts, 1925 to the Depression (New Haven, 1983), nos. 16, 29, 46.

ALBERTO FRASER
American, lives in Italy, born Scotland 1945

Alberto Fraser studied architecture and industrial design at the Rhode Island School of Design in Providence and has since worked as a consultant designer for American and foreign clients (he has lived in Milan since 1984). His designs include sunglasses (for Bausch and Lomb), computer housing components (for Wang), pens (for Mont Blanc), lighting (for Stilnovo; no. 368), and kitchen appliances (for Ariston).

References: The International Design Yearbook, vol. 1 (1985–86), pp. 98–99; vol. 3 (1987), p. 121.

GIANFRANCO FRATTINI
Italian, born 1926

An architecture graduate from the Milan Politecnico (1953), Gianfranco Frattini worked in the office of GIO PONTI between 1952 and 1954, opened his own architectural firm, and turned to furniture design to produce pieces for his own interiors. He has worked in the area of interior design, creating apartments, boutiques, and restaurants in Rome, Milan, and Genoa. But he has simultaneously been involved in product design as a consultant designer for numerous Italian firms, including Cassina, G. B. Bernini, C &

B Italia, and Artemide, for whom he created the *Boalum* lamp (with LIVIO CASTIGLIONI) in 1969 (no. 316). Frattini was awarded a gold medal at the Milan's *XI Triennale* in 1957, a grand prize at the *XII Triennale* in 1960, and a silver medal (for cutlery for Ricci) at the *XV Triennale* in 1973.

References: Alfonso Grassi and Anty Pansera, *Atlante del design italiano, 1940–1980* (Milan, 1980), pp. 31, 38, 74, 178, 224, 282; *The International Design Yearbook*, vol. 2 (1986), pp. 30, 32; vol. 3 (1987), p. 83; vol. 4 (1988), pp. 61, 124; vol. 5 (1990), p. 104; Colin Naylor, ed., *Contemporary Designers*, 2d ed. (Chicago, 1990), pp. 184–85.

FROGDESIGN
Established Altensteig, Germany, 1969

An international design firm with offices in Altensteig, Germany, Campbell, California (since 1982), and Tokyo (since 1986), frogdesign was founded by Hartmut Esslinger in 1969 (the *frog* in the firm's name is an acronym for the Federal Republic of Germany). Frogdesign made a global impact in the 1980s by virtue of the visual expressiveness and ergonomic success of its products, traits that attracted a large and prestigious client list—Apple Computer, AMERICAN TELEPHONE AND TELEGRAPH (no. 400), RCA, Eastman Kodak, Polaroid, Motorola, and General Electric in the United States; AEG, ERCO, Koenig & Neurath, PHILIPS, and Louis Vuitton in Europe; and Matsushita, NEC, Olympus, Seiko, and SONY CORPORATION in Japan. Esslinger had been trained as an electrical engineer at the University of Stuttgart and studied industrial design at the Fachhochschule Schwabisch Gmund, winning the German Bundespreis Gute Form in 1969 for a portable radio. His first client was Wega, a West German electronics company (owned by Sony since 1975) for whom he designed color televisions, stereos, and accessories (1971) that brought the firm a reputation for sleek, innovative electronics design; the line also brought Esslinger further commissions, among them the Sony *Trinitron* television. In 1982, Steven P. Jobs of Apple Computer hired Esslinger to design the firm's new product line, which catapulted frogdesign to international prominence: the off-white *Apple IIc* personal computer (no. 383) was featured on the cover of *Time* magazine as "design of the year" in 1984, with the companion *Scribe* and *Imagewriter* printers later cited for their good design by *Industrial Design* magazine. From snub-snouted *frollerskates* for Indusco to an aggressive black computer monitor for Jobs's NeXT, Inc., frogdesigns are calculated as user experiences. "The purpose of design," explained Esslinger, "is to make our artificial environment more human. My goal is and always was to design mainstream products as art."[14]

References: Steven Holt, "Leapfrogging to Fame," *Metropolis* 6 (September 1986): 39–40, 48–50; Stuart I. Frolick, "The World According to Esslinger," *Graphis* 43 (March–April 1987): 39–49; Rosenwald-Wolf Gallery, University of the Arts, Philadelphia, *frogart*

(November 4–December 3, 1988); Joan O. Hamilton, "Rebel with a Cause: Hartmut Esslinger Remodels Industrial Design," *Business Week*, December 3, 1990, pp. 130–35.

ROGER FRY
English, 1866–1934

Roger Fry studied natural sciences at Cambridge where he was a friend of CHARLES ROBERT ASHBEE, but then turned to painting, which he pursued in England and at the Académie Julian in Paris. However, it was his activities as editor (*Burlington Magazine*), art historian, museum curator (Metropolitan Museum of Art, New York), connoisseur, and critic—particularly his formalist theories of aesthetics—for which he became better known. Discovering Cézanne (about 1906) and the French avant-garde painters, he introduced their work to British audiences in an exhibition of postimpressionism (a term he coined) in 1910. He showed them again in 1912 along with British progressive painters, some of whom—including VANESSA BELL, DUNCAN GRANT, and Wyndham Lewis—participated in his artistic design studio, the Omega Workshops, which opened at 33 Fitzroy Square in London in 1913. Fry had no overriding social program; his goals were purely artistic and economic, aimed at promoting the new spirit of postimpressionism in the applied arts and providing financial support for his younger Bloomsbury friends. Omega products, many of which Fry designed himself, were anonymous—signed only with the Omega mark—and the artists were free to use each other's designs. Omega products included painted furniture, screens (no. 56), boxes, marquetry work, rugs, textiles (no. 57), embroideries, clothing, and pottery. By the outbreak of World War I the Omega Workshops had attracted a number of commissions for interior decorations and some good reviews, but Fry then had to sustain the workshop almost single-handedly. Despite the success of the pottery table service he made between 1916 and 1918, he had to liquidate the salesrooms in 1919, and dissolved the association in 1920.

References: Frances Spalding, *Roger Fry: Art and Life* (London, 1980); Judith Collins, *The Omega Workshops* (London, 1983); Crafts Council Gallery, London, *The Omega Workshops, 1913–19: Decorative Arts of Bloomsbury* (January 18–March 18, 1984).

KENJI FUJIMORI
Japanese, 1919–1993

Introducing modern industrial materials to Japanese postwar furniture (no. 279), Kenji Fujimori reinterpreted the traditional Japanese custom of sitting on the floor by creating in plywood the first chair designed for floor-level use. Fujimori graduated from Waseda University (1941) and worked in the general planning division of Toshiba Machinery Company before opening his own design office in 1948. In 1954–55 he was sent by the Japanese government to study product design in Helsinki, initiating a life-long involvement in international—particularly Finnish—design institutions and programs. From 1963 until his retirement in 1985, Fujimori was professor at the Kanazawa College of Arts. Alongside practicing and teaching industrial design, he studied and promoted traditional handcrafts both in Japan and internationally: in 1972 he was named Japanese delegate to the World Crafts Council, subsequently serving as vice-president and honorary director of that organization (1980, 1984). Between 1974 and 1984 he served as adviser to the Japanese government for the promotion of traditional crafts. His many honors include medals from the Finnish government (1962, 1967) and the World Crafts Council (1978).

Reference: *Structure of Dexterity: Industrial Design Works in Japan* (Tokyo, 1983), p. 130.

FULPER POTTERY COMPANY
Established Flemington, New Jersey, c. 1805–1930

William Hill Fulper began to experiment at his family's pottery around the turn of the century with decorative glazes and shapes, and by 1909 had added the Vase Kraft line of stoneware art pottery to the utilitarian wares that had been made by the Fulper Pottery Company and its predecessor for almost a century. Like Artus van Briggle and a number of other art potters at the time, Fulper was inspired by oriental—particularly Chinese—ceramics; he adapted many of his shapes directly from Chinese examples and set out to reinvent a number of the glazes he admired on them. The allover effects of these Chinese-inspired glazes, fired in one operation with the green clay body, gave Fulper wares their distinction, and when occasionally figurative ornamentation was added, drawn from historical and exotic sources, it was modeled, not painted. While Fulper vases, bowls, and lamps (no. 54) were mostly commercially molded, they were offered in a wide variety of colors and glazes—listed in the catalogs and advertisements as Mirror, Flambe, Lustre, Matte, Wistaria, and Crystal—which gave them the seeming individuality of an art pottery. Fulper won a bronze medal in 1904 at the *Louisiana Purchase Exhibition* in Saint Louis for his wares, and a medal of honor at the 1915 *Panama-Pacific International Exposition* in San Francisco. Fulper pottery continued to be made through the 1920s, but a fire in 1929 destroyed the factory and the firm was sold in 1930, with most of the Vase Kraft line replaced by utilitarian wares.

Reference: Robert W. Blasberg, *Fulper Art Pottery: An Aesthetic Appreciation, 1909–1929* (New York, 1979).

SABURŌ FUNAKOSHI
Japanese, born 1931

Since 1957 Saburō Funakoshi has made his career at the Hoya glassworks, where he became head of Hoya's Musashi factory design department in 1982, designing sleek, refined,

table glasswares for mass production as well as decorative pieces for manufacture by hand in limited series. His functional glass (no. 278) raised industrial tablewares to a new level of quality in Japan and won many distinctions there, including the Osaka Design House prize of 1970; exhibitions of his work have been held at the Matsuya Department Store (1969, 1982), Tokyo Museum of Modern Art (1980), and Hokkaido Museum of Modern Art (1982). Funakoshi was trained in the crafts department of Tokyo University of the Arts (1954) and worked from 1954 to 1957 at the Shizouka Prefectural Industrial Testing Institute.

References: Corning Museum of Glass, Corning, N.Y., *New Glass: A Worldwide Survey* (April 26–October 1, 1979), p. 255, no. 63; National Museum of Modern Art, Tokyo, *Modern Japanese Glass* (Tokyo, 1982), no. 142; Crafts Gallery, National Museum of Modern Art, Tokyo, *Contemporary Vessels: How To Pour* (February 10–March 22, 1982), nos. 189–90; Japan Design Committee, Tokyo, *Design 19* (September 3–8, 1982), n.p.; Matsuya Ginza, Tokyo, *Design Collection* (1989), pp. 10–11; Kogei Zaidan, ed., *Japanese Industrial Design: 100 Famous Products of the Showa Era* (Tokyo, 1989), p. 92.

EMILE GALLÉ
French, 1846–1904

The most technically innovative artist-glassmaker of the nineteenth century, Emile Gallé created a personal art nouveau style in Nancy that combined a Romantic floral naturalism with the poetic feeling of the contemporary symbolists. Gallé considered himself a symbolist and inscribed the verses of such symbolist poets as Charles Baudelaire, Robert de Montesquiou, and Maurice Maeterlinck on many of his works. Like Baudelaire, Gallé was also particularly drawn to the poetry of Victor Hugo, whose love of nature in all its moods, mystical experience of infinity, and vision of the universe he shared. Throughout his artistic career Gallé was a member of the Société Centrale d'Horticulture de Nancy and the Société Nationale d'Horticulture de France, writing botanical notes in the bulletins of these organizations and participating in their exhibitions.

Son of a ceramics and glass dealer in Nancy, Gallé collaborated in the design and decoration of faience and glass supplied to his father from the pottery at Saint-Clément and from the glasshouse at Meisenthal, whose proprietor, Mathieu Burgun, is thought to have trained Gallé in his craft. In 1871 he represented his father in the French section of the international exhibition in London and in 1877 took over direction of the family firm. Like his father, Gallé showed ceramics and glass, executed after his own designs, at national and international exhibitions for some thirty years, achieving his first important critical success at the *VIIIᵉ Exposition de l'Union Centrale des Arts Décoratifs* in 1884 where he won two gold medals—one for ceramics, one for glass—and was described as the "revelation, the event" of the exhibition.[15] In the same year Gallé purchased land for the addition to his ateliers of a cabinetmaking workshop, which was completed in 1886—inspired, he said, by searching for wood bases for his glasswares. At the 1889 Paris *Exposition Universelle*, Gallé made a tour-de-force presentation in three mediums, winning a grand prize for glass, a gold medal for ceramics, and a silver medal for his furniture, which included both luxury pieces and an inexpensive commercial line. In his glasses, Gallé employed a variety of decorative techniques that he combined in highly novel ways: flashing and clouding colors; exploiting air bubbles, crazing, and other "imperfections" in the glass; acid etching, wheel engraving, and enamel painting; and (invented in 1898) a process he called glass or crystal "marquetry" (no. 40). Inspired by nature, Gallé continued to create masterworks that were sought in his lifetime by museums and collectors (no. 39). At the Paris *Exposition Universelle* of 1900, the critic Roger Marx described Gallé as an "innovator" who had liberated French art from the "despotic supremacy of dead styles" through his "modern" applications of stylized plant forms.[16]

References: Emile Gallé, *Ecrits pour l'art, floriculture—art décoratif—notices d'exposition (1884–1889)* [1908], reprint (Marseilles, 1980); Janine Bloch-Dermant, *L'Art du verre en France, 1860–1914* (Lausanne, 1974), pp. 52–132; Philippe Garner, *Emile Gallé* (London, 1976); Musée du Luxembourg, Paris, *Gallé* (November 1985–February 1986).

AKSELI GALLEN-KALLELA
Finnish, 1865–1931

Akseli Gallen-Kallela, Finland's leading romantic painter at the turn of the century, was also a furniture and textile designer, glass painter, and graphic artist. He studied at the Taideyhdistyksen Piirustuskoulu (School of Fine Arts Society) in Helsinki from 1881 to 1884, and from 1884 to 1890 in Paris at the Academie Julian, where he became friends with the Swede Louis Sparre. Together, Gallen-Kallela and Sparre visited remote regions of Finland, which inspired their use of traditional Finnish sources for pictorial themes and the decorative arts. In 1894 Gallen-Kallela built his wilderness studio—Kalela, a landmark of Finnish national architecture—and furnished it himself in the Arts and Crafts tradition. He painted frescoes with the theme of Finland's national epic for his country's pavilion at the 1900 Paris *Exposition Universelle*; he also won a gold medal there for the plain furnishings, based on indigenous styles and created in natural materials and colors, that he designed for the exhibit of the Iris factory in Porvoo (no. 22), which Sparre had founded in 1897 for the production of simple, well-designed objects for everyday use. Gallen-Kallela was awarded a diploma of honor for book design at the 1925 Paris exhibition.

References: Onni Okkonen, *Akselli Gallen-Kallelan Taidetta* (Porvoo, Finland, 1948); Ulf Hård af Segerstad, *Modern Finnish Design* (New York, 1969), pp. 7–8, 15–21, pl. 2; John Boulton Smith, *The Golden Age of Finnish Art: Art Nouveau and the National Spirit* (Helsinki, 1976), especially pp. 32–42.

GATTI, PAOLINI, TEODORO
Established Turin, 1965

The firm of Piero Gatti, Cesare Paolini, and Franco Teodoro has undertaken work in architecture, city planning, industrial design, product development, and graphics. International notice came early with their design of the soft *Sacco* seating in 1968–69 (no. 308), manufactured by Zanotta, which was widely successful, although more often in the copy than the original. Respectful of the behavior of the consumer, the firm attempts to create objects that will fit into any environment and disturb it as little as possible, objects that in their own literature are described as "spontaneous as well as lucid, free of monumentality as well as anxiety."

References: Whitechapel Art Gallery, London, *Modern Chairs, 1918–1970* (July 22–August 30, 1970), no. 94; Victor Papanek, *Design for the Real World* (New York, 1974), pp. 103–4.

ANTONÍ GAUDÍ
Spanish, 1852–1926

Celebrated for the highly personal and regional form of art nouveau that he developed in Barcelona, most conspicuously in the Parque Güell (1900–1914), Casa Milá apartment house (1906–10), and Church of the Sagrada Familia (begun in 1883), Antoní Gaudí has also been embraced by recent postmodern architects for his rich and surprising distortions of form and space, historical reminiscences, and colorful decorative detailing. Gaudí also designed furniture, some expressly for his buildings and some independent of them, that was as fantastic and sculptural as his architecture.

Gaudí was trained as an architect at the University of Barcelona in the Facultad de Ciencias (1869–72) and in the new Escuela Provincial de Arquitectura (1873–74, 1876–77). His first independent commission was a house for Manuel Vicens (1878–80), which he designed in a neo-medieval, Mudéjar style that drew on local precedents and the fact that his patron was a wealthy tile merchant; at the same time he designed church furniture for the chapel at Comillas (Santander) in a neo-Gothic style suited to the building for which it was conceived. In 1883 he was made director of works for the new Gothic church in Barcelona, the Sagrada Familia, a project that would occupy him throughout his career and mark the transition from a more conventional historicizing approach to one increasingly unconventional and imaginative. In 1885 he was commissioned to design the residence in Barcelona of Eusebio Güell (1885–90), an important industrialist and art patron who would employ Gaudí over and over again—in the outbuildings of his estate in the Barcelona suburbs (1887), the park he intended as the site of a garden city, and the family church and crypt at Santa Coloma de Corvelló (1898–1916). Among Gaudí's numerous private commissions was the Casa Calvet (1898–1900), in which he demonstrated his independence from historicism and for which he designed an important body of furniture for the family's offices and private apartments (no. 18); in 1901 the house received the first annual architectural prize offered by the city of Barcelona. For Gaudí, the deciding "character" of architecture and design was ornamentation, which should, as he wrote in 1878, "remind us of poetic ideas that constitute motives—historical, legendary, active, emblematic, mythological—motives that relate to man, his life, actions, and passion."[17]

References: Henry-Russell Hitchcock, *Antoní Gaudí* (New York, 1957); James Johnson Sweeney and Josep Lluis Sert, *Antoní Gaudí* (London, 1960); José F. Ráfols, *Antoní Gaudí* (Barcelona, 1960); Cesar Martinell y Brunet, *Gaudí: Su vida, su teoria, su obra* (Barcelona, 1967).

NORMAN BEL GEDDES
American, 1893–1958

A prolific and visionary designer, Norman Bel Geddes created hundreds of theatrical productions, principally between 1916 and 1927, and then, after turning to industrial design, numerous streamlined and futuristic products—many too experimental to be put into production. His work culminated in the *Futurama* exhibit at the *New York World's Fair* in 1939, which projected the world of 1960 in scale model and was the most popular attraction at the fair.

Geddes studied art briefly at the Cleveland Institute of Art and the school of the Art Institute of Chicago, and worked as an advertising illustrator and portrait painter before deciding on a career in the theater. He wrote plays, devised new lighting techniques, invented sound devices, and created stage designs that were internationally recognized in exhibitions at museums in Chicago, New York, London, Amsterdam, and Vienna. His move to industrial design and architecture in 1927 was influenced by his early contact with FRANK LLOYD WRIGHT, with whom he had worked in 1916 (on the Aline Barnsdall theater project), and his friendship with Erich Mendelsohn, the German expressionist architect whom he met in New York during the 1920s. His designs include a proposal of 1928 for a five-year sequence of streamlined style implementations for the Graham-Paige automobile company, the modular *Oriole* stove (no. 151), prefabricated service stations for Socony-Vacuum oil (1934), interiors for the Pan American Airways *China Clipper* (1934), and housewares, among them a line of decorative metalwork for Revere. His book *Horizons* (1932) was the first to chronicle the field of industrial design, and in it he presented a justification of the teardrop as the ideal streamlined form, which he gave to the aerodynamic trains, ships, airplanes, and automobiles he designed. Geddes's papers are housed at the University of Texas in Austin.

References: Kenneth Reid, "Masters of Design 2— Norman Bel Geddes," *Pencil Points* 18 (January 1937):

2–32; "Norman Bel Geddes, 1893–1958," *Industrial Design* 5 (June 1958): 48–51; University of Texas, Austin, *Norman Bel Geddes: An Exhibition of Theatrical and Industrial Designs* (June 10–July 22, 1979).

FRANK O. GEHRY
American, born Canada, 1929

An architect inspired by contemporary art, Frank O. Gehry creates angular "deconstructed" forms in his buildings using commonplace materials such as chain-link fencing, corrugated metal, raw wood—paradigmatically in his own house in Santa Monica, California (1977–78). He has also collaborated with sculptors (including Claes Oldenburg and Richard Serra) on competitions and projects, and designed stage sets, lighting, and exhibitions (the latter for the Los Angeles County Museum of Art, 1965–83). A graduate of the University of Southern California School of Architecture (1954) and a student at the Harvard University Graduate School of Design (1956–57), Gehry worked for Victor Gruen Associates in Los Angeles and André Remondet in Paris before opening his own office in Los Angeles in 1962. National recognition first came not for buildings but for his innovative Easy Edges line of corrugated-cardboard furniture introduced in 1972 (no. 327); its unexpected success involved him with the requirements of manufacture, distribution, and marketing, and called into question his own aspirations as an architect—with the result that he withdrew the furniture within several months. Gehry's experimentation with furniture is ongoing, and in 1982 in New York he exhibited a baroque exaggerated parody of his earlier work called the Rough Edges series (created in collaboration with the architect Richard Saul Wurman). Featuring the fish motif that had already appeared in a number of his architectural and sculptural conceptions, a series of Fish lamps, again exhibition pieces, was begun in 1984 on commission from Formica, which was seeking inventive uses for its Colorcore material. In 1989–91 he returned to the design of production furniture with his series of bentwood chairs and tables for Knoll (no. 398). Gehry was awarded the Pritzker Architecture Prize in 1989.

References: "Paper Currency," *Industrial Design* 19 (May 1972): 53; Walker Art Center, Minneapolis, *The Architecture of Frank Gehry* (1986), especially Joseph Giovannini, "Edges, Easy and Experimental," pp. 62–81; Montreal Museum of Decorative Arts, *Frank Gehry: New Bentwood Furniture Designs* (1992).

GIORGETTO GIUGIARO
Italian, born 1938

Perhaps the most influential designer of automobiles today, Giorgetto Giugiaro has more than one hundred models to his name, sleek sports cars for Alfa Romeo and Maserati as well as angular designs for Volkswagen (*Rabbit*) and Fiat (*Uno*). He has also turned his attention to a wide range of consumer products, among them appliances for SONY CORPORATION, cameras for Nikon, watches for Seiko, sewing machines for Necchi (no. 366), lighting for Luci, and even a patented grooved, double-barreled pasta shape, *Marille*, for Voiello. Giugiaro studied painting at the Accademia di Belle Arti in Turin and concurrently took courses in technical drawing. His drafting skill brought him an offer from the Fiat styling center, where he remained from 1955 to 1959 before becoming a designer for Bertone (1959–65), and head designer for Ghia (1965–68). In 1968 Giugiaro founded his own design firm, Ital Design, offering design, models, testing, and fabrication for automobile manufacturers internationally. In 1971 he organized Giugiaro Design, which is devoted to industrial design. Giugiaro received Compasso d'Oro awards in 1980 and 1984.

References: Wolf von Eckardt, "Creation, Italian-Style," *Time*, February 22, 1982, pp. 62–63; Paul Kunkel, "Driven," *Industrial Design* 34 (November-December 1987): 28–35; National Museum of Modern Art, Kyoto, *Giugiaro Design* (April 25–May 28, 1989); Colin Naylor, ed., *Contemporary Designers* (Chicago, 1990), pp. 214–15.

JOSEF GOČÁR
Czechoslovakian, 1880–1945

Architect, city planner, teacher, and, with Pavel Janák, principal designer of buildings and furniture in the cubist style, Josef Gočár studied until 1905 in Prague with Jan Kotěra, the founder of modern architecture in Czechoslovakia, and then worked as his assistant between 1906 and 1908. Gočár was one of the Prague artists and architects who in 1911 established the Skupina Výtvarných Umělců (Group of Avant-Garde Artists), an organization that created works in all mediums reflecting the influence of cubism, which was first exhibited in Prague in 1912. Drawings for architecture and furnishings show Gočár's involvement with cubism from 1911; his spa at Bohdaneč of 1911–12 and his furniture of 1913 for the actor Otto Boleška (no. 52) were his most expressive works in this style. By the mid-1920s Gočár had altered his approach under the influence of De Stijl design and German functionalism, a development exemplified by his Czech pavilion at the Paris exhibition of 1925 and subsequent buildings in his homeland.

References: Zdeněk Wirth, *Josef Gočár* (Geneva, 1930); Mathildenhohe, Darmstadt, Germany, *Tschechische Kunst der 20er + 30er Jahre: Avantgarde und Tradition* (November 20, 1988–January 29, 1989), pp. 90–95; Alexander von Vegesack, ed., *Czech Cubism: Architecture Furniture Decorative Arts, 1910–1925* (New York, 1992), passim.

JEAN GOULDEN
French, 1878–1947

Jean Goulden is best known for his application of the geometrical forms of cubism and constructivism to the design of enamel wares in the 1920s. With the security of an income from his family's Alsatian farms, Goulden abandoned medicine after World War I to become a painter and designer. He spent several months at the monasteries of Mount Athos, where he learned to admire Byzantine enamels, and on his return to Paris convinced JEAN DUNAND to teach him the techniques of enameling; eventually he became Dunand's friend, patron, and his collaborator as well. The majority of Goulden's works are metal objects with enamel decoration in simple, flat, angular designs—small boxes, vases, plaques, cigarette cases, table lamps (no. 129), and clocks—but he also designed furniture, which was made in Dunand's workshops. Goulden joined with Dunand, the animal painter Paul Jouve, and the Swiss book designer and printer François-Louis Schmied in regular exhibitions in Paris at the Galerie Georges Petit from 1921 to 1932 and at the Galerie Jean Charpentier in 1933 and 1934; these artists were frequent collaborators and they continually influenced each other's work. In 1928 Goulden moved his studio to Rheims, where he worked independently until his death in 1947.

References: Galerie de Luxembourg, Paris, *Jean Dunand—Jean Goulden* (May–August 1973), pp. 109–21; Lynne Thornton, "Jean Dunand and His Friends," *Apollo* 98 (October 1973): 294–99; Bernard Goulden, *Jean Goulden* (Paris, 1989).

DUNCAN GRANT
English, 1885–1978

A highly regarded English painter with a career that spanned some seventy years, Duncan Grant studied in London at the Westminster School of Art (1902–5) and in Paris with Jacques-Emile Blanche (1906–7). In 1905 he met VANESSA BELL, soon joining the English progressive painters and becoming part of the Bloomsbury group. Probably introduced to ROGER FRY by Bell, Grant showed six paintings at Fry's *Second Post-Impressionist Exhibition* in London in 1912. He collaborated with Fry and Bell on mural decorations and with Bell on designing small domestic articles. Grant was one of the directors of the Omega Workshops when it opened in 1913, and his works were included among its products: painted screens (no. 56) and furniture; marquetry, embroidery, and rugs (which Fry praised as the "high-water mark of applied design in England"[18]); and painted pottery. In the 1920s and 30s Grant and Bell collaborated on numerous commissions for interior decorative schemes furnished with objects of their own design; their conception for a "Music Room" was shown at the Lefevre Galleries in London in 1932. Grant was one of a number of artists commissioned to design screen-printed textiles for Allan Walton, and one of his six, *Apollo and Daphne* (1932–33), was awarded a medal of merit at the 1937 Paris *Exposition Internationale*. Grant created painted decorations for Foley and Wilkinson's pottery (shown at Harrods in 1934) and he continued to decorate pottery himself into the 1950s.

References: Tate Gallery, London, *Duncan Grant: A Retrospective Exhibition* (May 12–June 20, 1959); Richard Shone, *Bloomsbury Portraits: Vanessa Bell, Duncan Grant, and Their Circle* (New York, 1976), passim; Judith Collins, *The Omega Workshops* (London, 1983), passim; Crafts Council, London, *The Omega Workshops, 1913–19: Decorative Arts of Bloomsbury* (January 18–March 18, 1984), passim.

GRAPUS
Established Paris, 1970–1992

Emerging from the student demonstrations in Paris during 1968, when the three designers who would form Grapus worked together daily to produce political posters, this Marxist design collective survived for over two decades working for political and cultural organizations. Established in 1970 by Pierre Bernard, Gérard Paris-Clavel, and François Miehe, each of whom had studied in Poland with the poster designer Henryk Tomasczewski, the group expanded its membership and changed over the years, with their original philosophy of collective decisions on all projects yielding to a team method of working. Their client base grew, too, during the 1980s from a host of small left-wing political groups, social causes, and small theaters to include establishment cultural organizations (the Musée du Louvre, for which they designed an identity system and handbook) and the city of Paris (identity for the Parc de la Villette, 1984). Grapus devised its own graphic conventions, rejecting the slick methods of commercial advertising for unexpected imagery, odd juxtapositions, and for attention-getting effects that looked as if they had been done by hand—childlike drawing, scribbles over their poster designs, and messages combining type and handwriting that could be understood on several levels (no. 378). Grapus was disbanded in 1992.

References: Musée de l'Affiche et de la Publicité, Paris, *Grapus* (October 27, 1982–February 7, 1983); F.H.K. Henrion, *Top Graphic Design* (Zurich, 1973), pp. 70–77; Agence pour la Promotion de la Création Industrielle and Centre Georges Pompidou, Paris, *Design français, 1960–1990: Trois décennies* (June 22–September 26, 1988), pp. 148–51; Steven Heller, "Grapus," *Graphis* 44 (September–October, 1988): 48–57; Alain Weill, "Grapus," *Creation* 8 (1991): 76–97; Ronald Labuz, *Contemporary Graphic Design* (New York, 1991), pp. 9–11.

MICHAEL GRAVES
American, born 1934

In 1977 Michael Graves turned from a crisp, white, late-modern formalism based on technology and the machine metaphor to what he called "figurative" architecture, implementing a decorative, colorful building vocabulary with historic, cultural, and thematic associations. In tandem with ROBERT VENTURI, Charles Jencks, and HANS HOLLEIN, he has become one of the leading figures of the postmodern movement. Until the completion in

1982 of his first major postmodern architectural commission, the Portland Building in Portland, Oregon, Graves had been best known as a teacher of architecture at Princeton University (from 1962) and, through his elegantly colored drawings, as an architectural fantasist. Graves, who received a degree from the Graduate School of Design at Harvard University in 1959, had drawn furniture designs in his sketchbooks during the 1970s and created custom pieces for residential commissions. But the first independent furnishings he produced were his art deco *Plaza* dressing table and *Stanhope* bed for Memphis, included respectively in its first collection in 1981 and its second in 1982, and his neoclassical tables and chairs designed along with his showrooms for Sunar (1979–81). Graves was one of the architects included by Alessi in its much publicized series of silver coffee and tea services, and it was for Alessi that he created specifically for the American market the popular bird-whistling teapot in 1984–85 (no. 386), followed by a family of tablewares in the same materials. He has also designed ceramics (for Swid Powell), carpets (for V'Soske), lighting, and jewelry (for Cleto Munari).

References: Karen Vogel Wheeler, Peter Arnell, and Ted Bickford, eds., *Michael Graves: Buildings and Projects 1966–1981* (New York, 1982); Michael Collins and Andreas Papadakis, *Post-Modern Design* (New York, 1989), pp. 126–29; Laura Polinoro, *L'officina Alessi* (Crusinallo, Italy, 1989), pp. 141–44; Karen Vogel Nichols, Patrick J. Burke, and Caroline Hancock, eds., *Michael Graves: Buildings and Projects 1982–1989* (New York, 1990).

EILEEN GRAY
Irish, active France, 1878–1976

Allied with the most advanced French designers of the 1920s, Eileen Gray was nonetheless totally independent in her remarkably inventive work. Born in Ireland, Gray enrolled in the Slade School of Fine Arts in London in 1901 and between 1902 and 1905 studied in Paris, where she attended classes at the Ecole Colarossi and then the Académie Julian. During a short interval in London in 1906, she worked in a lacquer repair shop and when she returned to Paris arranged to have a young Japanese lacquer worker, Sugawara, teach her his traditional craft (as he later would JEAN DUNAND). Mastering this difficult medium over a period of years, she became entrepreneur as well as designer, and with Sugawara in her employ produced elegant lacquer screens, panels, and tables; these began to receive publicity—for example, in the British edition of *Vogue* in August 1917—and were acquired by such notable collectors as the couturier Jacques Doucet. Many of her designs were sold in the shop Jean Désert, which she operated in Paris between 1922 and 1930. However, it was the unified interiors she designed on commission after World War I and the objects she created for them (no. 84) that established her position in the history of design.

Gray's most important work was the house she

built in the south of France (1926–29) for her friend Jean Badovici, architectural critic and publisher of *L'Architecture Vivante*. This was her first essay into architecture and was, like so many of her endeavors, virtually self-taught. She furnished the house with her own work: carpets (which she had been designing and selling for over a decade); built-in units calculated to serve multiple specific functions; and furniture, notably the lacquered *Transat* (no. 109) and padded *Bibendum* chairs as well as the adjustable metal and glass table known by the name of the house, *E.1027*. With her own house at Castellar following, she continued to work on architectural and design projects during the 1930s and just after World War II. Gray's work was included by LE CORBUSIER in his Pavillon des Temps Nouveaux at the *Exposition Internationale* in Paris in 1937.

References: Eileen Gray and Jean Badovici, "E1027: Maison en bord de mer," *L'Architecture Vivante* (winter 1929) (special issue); Joseph Rykwert, "Un ommagio a Eileen Gray—Pioniera del design," *Domus* 468 (December 1966) [irregular pagination]; J. Stewart Johnson, *Eileen Gray, Designer* (London, 1979); Peter Adam, *Eileen Gray, Architect/Designer* (New York, 1987).

GREENE & GREENE
Established Pasadena, California, 1894–1916

In 1894 the brothers Charles Sumner Greene and Henry Mather Greene, who had recently arrived in California after completing their architectural training at the Massachusetts Institute of Technology, opened an office in Pasadena and developed in the next decade, principally between 1907 and 1909, the most refined expression of Arts and Crafts building in America. Turning from the Queen Anne and Colonial Revival styles of their early works and the chalet and California patio styles that followed, they devised a new structural type based heavily on Chinese and Japanese sources—a picturesque "bungalow" with a large pitched roof, overhanging eaves, and visibly articulated structural members, built of rare woods and rustic materials with fine workmanship. Greene & Greene gave equal care to the interior fittings, conceiving carved woodwork, built-in and freestanding furniture (no. 47), stained glass, carpets, and other furnishings as part of a unified interior design; this they supplemented with other suitable Arts and Crafts lamps, vases, and decorative objects. Their trim, simple, stained and oiled furniture was fabricated by John and Peter Hall with native woods, ebony, and subtle inlays.

References: Robert Judson Clark, ed., *The Arts and Crafts Movement in America, 1876–1916* (Princeton, N.J., 1972), pp. 83–87; Karen Current, *Greene & Greene: Architects in the Residential Style* (Fort Worth, 1974); Alan Marks, "Greene and Greene: A Study in Functional Design," *Fine Woodworking* 12 (September 1978): 40–45.

GREGOTTI, MENEGHETTI, STOPPINO, ARCHITETTI
Established Novara, Italy, 1954–1967

Through a series of expressive, historicizing structures built in the city of Novara, the architectural firm founded by Vittorio Gregotti, Lodovico Meneghetti, and Giotto Stoppino was associated with the Italian neo-Liberty movement of the 1950s; the connection was strengthened by the group's furniture design of the later 1950s (no. 274) shown at the controversial exhibition *Nuovi Disegni per il Mobile Italiano (New Designs for Italian Furniture)* in Milan in 1960. Earlier, at the *X Triennale* in Milan in 1954, they had exhibited bookshelf systems and technologically innovative plywood tables and chairs, designs that were rationalist in conception. Their other work included furnishings and interiors for retail stores, housing, planning, and exhibition design, notably the introductory section on the theme of leisure for the *XIII Triennale* in 1964 (with Peppe Brivio, Umberto Eco, and MASSIMO VIGNELLI). They also created furniture for La Rinascente and lighting for Arteluce.

References: "Furniture 'mobile singolo'," *Interiors* 114 (November 1954): 92–93; Gillo Dorfles, "Una mostra di mobili a Milan," *Domus* 367 (June 1960): 33–34; Vittorio Gregotti, *Il disegno del prodotto industriale: Italia 1860–1980* (Milan, 1982), p. 289; Manfredo Tafuri, *Vittorio Gregotti: Buildings and Projects* (New York, 1982), passim; Sergio Crolli, ed., *Vittorio Gregotti* (Bologna, 1986), passim.

APRIL GREIMAN
American, born 1948

April Greiman drew on the layering concepts of the experimental "new wave" Swiss graphics, created in the 1970s by such designers as WOLFGANG WEINGART, and combined them with a funky California outlook and color sensibility to create a dense, spatially complex style (no. 373) that proved to be one of the most influential design movements of the 1980s. Greiman studied at the Kansas City Art Institute (1966–70) and then with Weingart and Armin Hofmann at the Kunstgewerbeschule in Basel (1970–71). After working as a freelance designer in New York (1971–75), she moved to Los Angeles in 1976, where she built a reputation as one of the foremost young designers on the West Coast through the startling graphic illusionism of her identity programs for restaurants (China Club, 1980–81), retail shops, and other clients, along with such ambitious work as the publications of the California Institute of Arts (1982–84). She was invited to contribute a poster design for the 1984 Los Angeles Olympics (in collaboration with Jayme Odgers, with whom she frequently worked), and in 1986 created a special issue of *Design Quarterly*. With the arrival of the Macintosh computer in 1984, Greiman began to use electronic technology instead of hand craftsmanship to create her intricate collages, and she has since experimented widely with the possibilities of computers, fax machines, and electronic graphics systems. She has created sculpture internationally by fax (for the *Pacific Wave-California Graphic Design* exhibition at the Museo Fortuny in Venice, 1987), generated designs by computer and video for textiles (for the Polyester Institute of Japan, 1985), and used video to develop imagery that she then transferred to print for posters.

References: Marc Treib, "California Graphic Design," *Studio International* 195 (June 1982): 60–61; Annetta Hanna, "April Greiman," *Industrial Design* 34 (March–April 1987): 54–59; April Greiman, *Hybrid Imagery: The Fusion of Technology and Graphic Design* (New York, 1990); Ronald Labuz, *Contemporary Graphic Design* (New York, 1991), pp. 34–37.

WALTER GROPIUS
German, later American, 1883–1969

One of the leading protagonists in the development of modem design, Walter Gropius first defined the vocabulary of modem architecture in the Fagus factory at Alfeld, Germany (1911–12), creating an engineering aesthetic with great expanses of glass and a curtain wall construction that has been widely influential in this century. Gropius also founded the century's most important design school, the Staatliches Bauhaus Weimar, which he directed between 1918 and 1928 and where he assembled an international faculty that included Paul Klee, Wassily Kandinsky, GERHARD MARCKS, Johannes Itten, and later Josef Albers, HERBERT BAYER, MARCEL BREUER, and LÁSZLÓ MOHOLY-NAGY.

Born in Berlin, the son of an architect, Gropius studied architecture at the Technische Hochschule in Munich (1903) and the Technische Hochschule in Berlin (1905–7) before working as an assistant in the office of PETER BEHRENS at the beginning of Behrens's program of factory buildings for the AEG (1908–10). Gropius opened his own office in Berlin in 1910 in association with Adolf Meyer, joining the Berliner-Architekten-Verein (Berlin Architects Union) and the Deutscher Werkbund the following year. He served as editor of the Werkbund's yearbook in 1912, 1913, and 1914, and designed a factory and office building for the Werkbund exhibition in Cologne in 1914, which further developed the glass and metal idiom of the Fagus factory. At the same time he designed furniture and interiors in a stripped-down style for a variety of clients, including Fagus (no. 58) and the Vereinigte Werkstätten für Kunst im Handwerk (United Workshops for Art in Handicraft) in Munich; for the latter he designed a showroom at the world exhibition in Ghent in 1913, which won a gold medal. As early as 1916 HENRY VAN DE VELDE had suggested Gropius as his successor at the Grossherzogliche Sächsische Kunstgewerbeschule (Grand-Ducal Saxon School of Arts and Crafts) in Weimar, which was combined with the Grossherzogliche Sächsische Hochschule für Bildende Kunst (Grand-Ducal Saxon School for the Fine Arts) under Gropius's direction in 1918 and restructured as the Bauhaus in 1919. Gropius's changing attitudes toward art and industry were reflected in the Bauhaus curriculum, which at Weimar initially stressed individual handcraft and workshop training. Opposed by local critics and an increasingly hostile and reactionary press, the Bauhaus was forced to leave Weimar and move to Dessau in 1925, where Gropius declared the school a "laboratory for industry," with textiles, lamps, metalwares, ceramics, and furniture designed at the Bauhaus actually put into commercial production. He also designed the building for the school at Dessau along with houses for the director and masters (1925–26).

In 1928 Gropius resigned from the Bauhaus to practice architecture and design independently, including developing automobile bodies for the Adler Automobilwerke, Frankfurt (1930–33). Under criticism by the Nazis, he emigrated to England in 1934 where he practiced architecture in partnership with Maxwell Fry, published *The New Architecture and the Bauhaus* (1935), and designed furniture for Isokon. In 1937 he came to the United States, where he became professor of architecture in the Graduate School of Design at Harvard University, then served as chairman of the department (1938–52) and at the same time established a private architectural practice with Breuer (1938–41). In 1946 Gropius established a firm called The Architects Collaborative (TAC), which in 1948–50 built Harvard's Graduate Center. Later he undertook such other large commissions as the comprehensive plan for the New University of Baghdad (from 1957) and the American Embassy in Athens (1956–61).

References: Herbert Bayer, Walter Gropius, and Ise Gropius, eds., *Bauhaus, 1919–1928* (New York, 1938), passim; Hans M. Wingler, *The Bauhaus: Weimar, Dessau, Berlin, Chicago* (Cambridge, Mass., 1969), passim; Winfried Nerdinger, *Walter Gropius* (Berlin, 1985).

GRUEBY FAIENCE COMPANY
Established Boston, c. 1895–1909

At a time when the ROOKWOOD POTTERY and other American art potteries were promoting painted ornament, William H. Grueby focused on the decorative effects of glazes, developing in particular a rich, dense, matte green glaze that brought him international recognition. Having learned the craft and business of pottery manufacture at the Low Art Tile Works in Chelsea, near Boston, where he apprenticed at the age of fifteen, by 1892 Grueby was a partner in Atwood & Grueby, a firm that supplied tile and glazed bricks, often in historical styles, for architectural decoration. The following year at the *World's Columbian Exposition* in Chicago, Grueby became acquainted with the robust wares of the French art potters Ernest Chaplet and Auguste Delaherche, and it was to these (along with oriental ceramics) that he turned for models after he founded his own pottery and tileworks about 1895. Reorganized and incorporated in 1897, with one of its principals, George Prentiss Kendrick, serving as chief designer (until about 1901), the Grueby pottery specialized in handmade wares decorated with applied naturalistic ornament, which gave a certain individuality to each piece (no. 20). Published in American art journals beginning in 1898, Grueby's wares were shown at the *Exposition Universelle* of 1900 in Paris, where the firm was awarded two gold medals and one silver. Grueby also won medals at the *Pan-American Exposition* in Buffalo and the international exhibition of ceramics in Saint Petersburg in 1901; at Turin in 1902; and at the *Louisiana Purchase Exposition* in Saint Louis in 1904. Despite its critical success, the company could not sustain itself financially; the pottery was bankrupt by 1909, although Grueby himself incorporated a new firm, Grueby Faience and Tile Company, in Boston that same year.

References: Arthur Russell, "Grueby Pottery," *House Beautiful* 5 (December 1898): 3–9; Martin Eidelberg, "The Ceramic Art of William H. Grueby," *Connoisseur* 184 (September 1973): 47–54; Everson Museum, Syracuse, N.Y., *Grueby* (March 21–May 31, 1981).

GRUPO AUSTRAL
Established Buenos Aires, c. 1938–40

Grupo Austral was the name used by the designers Jorge Ferrari-Hardoy, Antonio Bonet, and Juan Kurchan when they filed an Argentinian copyright application for the B.K.F. chair (no. 175). The designers had worked together in Paris with LE CORBUSIER, but little else is known about the activities of the group.

Reference: Peter Blake and Jane Thompson, "More Than You May Want to Know about a Very Significant Chair," *Architecture Plus* 1 (May 1973): 73–80.

HANS GUGELOT
Dutch, born Indonesia, active Switzerland and Germany, 1920–1965

Architect, industrial designer, and teacher, Hans Gugelot was considered one of the world's leading systems designers, creating families of products and modular systems that ranged from furniture to musical instruments. Gugelot's concerns for standardized systems, mathematical order, and clarity of design also made him a leading exponent of neo-Bauhaus functionalism in the immediate postwar era. From his *M125* cabinet system (no. 244) and a series of radios, record players, and televisions for Braun (with DIETER RAMS; no. 242) to the Frankfurt U-Bahn transit system, Gugelot designed advanced technical equipment that lent itself to multiple combinations.

Born of Dutch parents in Indonesia, Gugelot moved with his family to Switzerland, where he was educated at the engineering school in Lausanne and in the department of architecture at the Technischen Hochschule in Zurich (1945–46). Between 1948 and 1950 he worked with several architects, including MAX BILL, and designed furniture for Horgen/Glarus, among other firms.

In 1950 he opened his own office in Zurich and began work on the *M125* system, sponsored by Wohnbedarf, which was put into commercial production by Bofinger in 1956. In 1954 Bill invited Gugelot to teach at the still-unfinished Hochschule für Gestaltung in Ulm, West Germany, where Gugelot remained as teacher and, later, director of the department of product development until his death. In 1955 with his Ulm colleague Otl Aicher, Gugelot began a highly successful association with the Braun firm, designing radios and record players first shown that year at a radio exhibition in Düsseldorf and afterwards at the *XI Triennale* in Milan in 1957, where the firm won a grand prize for its entire production. In 1959 Gugelot, with a team of collaborators, began work on the Frankfurt U-Bahn transportation system; at the same time he designed sewing machines for Pfaff and Gritzner-Kayser and a music system for Johannes Link. His other clients included Agfa, Lumoprint, Kodak, Girard, and Weishaupt.

Reference: Hans Wichmann, ed., *System-Designer Bahnbrecher. Hans Gugelot, 1920–1965* (Munich, 1984).

HECTOR GUIMARD
French, 1867–1942

Hector Guimard gave art nouveau its most complete and characteristic expression in the entrances to the Paris Métro stations (1900–1901), which he designed in picturesque semi-abstract forms derived from nature and realized in painted cast iron. The *style Guimard*, as he himself called it, first emerged in the Castel Béranger apartment building (1894–98) for which Guimard was not only the architect but also the interior and furniture designer (nos. 7, 8), creating a total unity based on curvilinear forms. Guimard, who had studied in Paris at the Ecole des Arts Décoratifs (1882–85) and trained as an architect at the Ecole des Beaux-Arts (1885–89), acknowledged that his new principles of decoration had been inspired by the example of Victor Horta, whose work he had seen in Belgium in 1895. In 1898 Guimard published an album of sixty-five plates fully illustrating the Castel Béranger and the following year held an exhibition devoted to the building in the salon of the French newspaper *Le Figaro*, which included drawings, photographs, and furniture that he described as "compositions in a new style." The Castel Béranger also won a facade competition in 1899, which brought Guimard further commissions: vases for the Manufacture Nationale de Sèvres (no. 30), the first two of which were shown in 1900 at the Paris *Exposition Universelle*; a series of private townhouses and villas; the Coilliot residence and ceramics shop in Lille (1898–1900); and the Jassedé apartment building in Paris (1903–5), among others. In his buildings Guimard made extensive use of cast iron, and in 1907 published a catalog of ornamental ironwork designs.

Guimard was a founding member of the Salon d'Automne in 1903, showing furniture, designs, and objects in the Salon exhibitions until World War I, just as he did in the salons of the Société des Artistes

Décorateurs during the same period. While he continued to practice architecture, designing his own house on the avenue Mozart (1909–12) in Paris and the villa "La Guimardière" at Vaucresson (1930), the art nouveau *style Guimard* fell out of fashion and Guimard's practice declined. In 1938 he left Paris for New York, where he died in 1942.

References: F. Lanier Graham, *Hector Guimard* (New York, 1970); Sherban Cantacuzino, "Hector Guimard," in J. M. Richards and Nikolaus Pevsner, eds., *The Anti-Rationalists* (Toronto, 1973), pp. 9–31; Ralph Culpepper, *Hector Guimard—Bibliographie* (Paris, 1975); Yvonne Brunhammer, *Art Nouveau: Belgium, France* (Houston, 1976), pp. 405–63 et passim; David Dunster, ed., *Hector Guimard* (London, 1978); Musée d'Orsay, Paris, *Guimard* (April 13–July 26, 1992).

EDWARD HALD
Swedish, 1883–1980

Hired to improve the aesthetic production of the Orrefors glassworks in 1917, Edward Hald was an established painter when he joined Simon Gate in the factory's design studio. Hald had studied in Dresden (first architecture, then painting), Copenhagen (with JOHAN ROHDE), Stockholm, and Paris (with Henri Matisse), and had exhibited paintings, most notably with the gallery Der Sturm in Berlin in 1915. At Orrefors he created both decorative pieces (no. 78) and utilitarian wares, specializing in engraved designs on thin clear glass, as in his early *Strawberry* service (1918) and his *Fireworks* bowl (1921). Concurrent with his work at Orrefors, Hald provided designs for the Rörstrand porcelain factory, including his *Turbine* table service shown at the influential *Hemutställningen* (*Home Exhibition*) in Stockholm in 1917. From his first years at Orrefors, Hald had also experimented with colored glass, as had Gate and the company's glassblowers, and he later designed cut glass for the firm as well. His work was among that exhibited successfully by Orrefors at the *Exposition Internationale des Arts Décoratifs* in Paris in 1925, where he won a grand prize, and in Stockholm in 1930, where he unveiled his large glass globe engraved with images of the constellations (Nationalmuseum, Stockholm). In Stockholm he also exhibited engraved green glass with a thicker body than that hitherto produced at Orrefors, as well as a collection of decorated porcelain wares for Karlskrona. Hald became managing director of Orrefors in 1933, giving up further work in ceramics; he held this position until he retired in 1944, but returned to Orrefors as a consultant in 1947 when the firm changed hands, and continued this association until his death in 1980.

References: Nationalmuseum, Stockholm, *Edward Hald: Målare Konstindustripionjär* (September 14–November 6, 1983); Helmut Ricke and Ulrich Gronert, eds., *Glas in Schweden, 1915–1960* (Munich, 1987), passim; Helena Dahlbäck Lutteman, "Orrefors Engraved Glass," *FMR* 35 (November-December, 1988): 49–68.

MARC HARRISON
American, born 1936

Principal designer for Cuisinarts since 1978, Marc Harrison brought a concern for ergonomics and safety to the firm's line of food processors (no. 370). A graduate of the Pratt Institute in New York (1958), he received a master's degree from the Cranbrook Academy of Art, Bloomfield Hills, Michigan, in 1959. Harrison has patented designs for equipment for the handicapped as well as the blood-collecting system used by the American National Red Cross, and has also designed silver, medical products, industrial equipment, and electronics. He has taught industrial design at the Rhode Island School of Design in Providence since 1959, and has concurrently maintained a design and engineering practice in Portsmouth, Rhode Island.

References: Edward K. Carpenter, *Industrial Design: 25th Annual Design Review* (New York, 1979), pp. 50–51; *Industrial Design* 28 (July–August 1981): 20; Nada Westerman and Joan Wessel, *American Design Classics* (New York, 1985), pp. 178–79.

AMBROSE HEAL
English, 1872–1959

Designer and retailer, Ambrose Heal transformed his family bedding firm into one of the most progressive furniture businesses in England, one committed to producing and selling solid, undecorated furniture of high quality to a mass market. As a young man Heal showed an interest in furniture-making and between 1890 and 1891 he apprenticed to the firm of Plucknett in Warwick, where he learned the craft, and in 1892 at Graham and Biddle in London, where he learned the trade. He joined Heal & Son in 1893. The first furniture following his designs was produced in 1897, the Newlyn and St. Ives lines of bedroom furniture made in oak with wrought steel handles and hinges. Admitted to the partnership by his father in 1898, Heal was given a small area of the shop in which to show his work, which was also exhibited by the Arts and Crafts Exhibition Society in London and at the Paris *Exposition Universelle* of 1900. After the turn of the century Heal's designs enjoyed both public recognition and commercial success. His work, including a Cottage furniture line (c. 1919; no. 77), had a traditional English vernacular character although it was not specifically historicizing; like certain examples of German "machine" furniture of about the same date, it was considered advanced for its geometric simplicity, squared corners, flush surfaces, and absence of surface decoration. In 1915 Heal became a founding member of the Design and Industries Association (DIA), dedicated to improving British design and to promoting contacts between designers and manufacturers after the example of the Deutscher Werkbund. Heal continued to design furniture until 1939, when the outbreak of war restricted all but Utility production. He wrote on a variety of topics and received numerous honors and awards: in 1933 he was knighted, in 1939 he was elected to the Faculty of Royal Designers for Industry, and in 1954 he received the Albert Gold Medal for services to industrial design from the Royal Society of Arts.

References: *Heal's Catalogues, 1853–1934* (London, 1972); *A Booklet to Commemorate the Life and Work of Sir Ambrose Heal, 1872–1959* (London, 1984); Nikolaus Pevsner, "Patient Progress Three: The DIA," in *Art, Architecture, and Design: Victorian and After* (Princeton, N.J., 1982), passim.

JEAN HEIBERG
Norwegian, active also France, 1884–1976

Jean Heiberg studied painting in Munich and then with Henri Matisse in Paris (1908–10), where he remained until 1929, gaining considerable renown as a painter. His design for the housing of the desk telephone introduced by L M ERICSSON in 1931 (no. 134), made after his return to Norway, established an object-type that remained the principal telephone form until the 1950s.

References: *Raben & Sjögrens Lexikon över Modern Skandinavisk Konst* (Stockholm, 1958), pp. 87–89; Michael Collins, "1931: Six Products That Have Stood the Test of Time," *Design* 392 (August 1981): 24; Boilerhouse Project, Victoria and Albert Museum, London, *Art & Industry* (January 18–March 2, 1982), pp. 42–45; Hans Wichmann, *Industrial Design, Unikate, Serienerzeugnisse: Die Neue Sammlung, ein neuer Museumstyp des 20. Jahrhunderts* (Munich, 1985), pp. 287, 499; Design Museum, London, *Telephone Study Notes* (n.d.), n.p.

PIET HEIN
Danish, born 1905

A mathematician, scientist, and poet, who in the 1960s gained an extensive following abroad with the publication of international editions of his "grooks" (short aphoristic poems written under the name Kumbel), Piet Hein is above all a problem solver. For him, the creative process is "the solving of implicit problems," ones "that cannot be formulated before they have been solved. The shaping of the question is part of the answer."[19] With his roots in theoretical problem-solving, Hein came to design through city planning when in 1959, he collaborated on devising the configuration of the Sergels Torg, a great urban space being constructed at the meeting of two arteries in central Stockholm. The "superellipse," the shape he created mathematically for the Sergels Torg, mediated between rectangle and ellipse and offered a solution to the square's traffic flow problem while giving it the maximum possible dimension. The benefits of this new harmonious form did not go unremarked; later it was adapted for use in furniture (with BRUNO MATHSSON, no. 291); silver (for Jensen);

lighting; wooden bowls (for the firm of KAY BOJESEN); textiles; and china and glassware.

References: Carl E. Christiansson, "Bruno Mathsson: Furniture Structures Ideas," *Design Quarterly* 65 (1966): 5–9; Renwick Gallery, National Collection of Fine Arts, Washington, D.C., *Georg Jensen—Silversmithy: 77 Artists 75 Years* (February 29–July 6, 1980), nos. 48–49; "The Solution Comes First," *Mobilia* 323 (1984): 10–12.

POUL HENNINGSEN
Danish, 1894–1967

Trained as an architect at the Danmarks Tekniske Højskole (Technical University of Denmark) in Copenhagen, Poul Henningsen practiced architecture from 1920, creating theaters, restaurants, and houses, as well as lighting designs, which made his international reputation. After winning all six prizes in a Danish competition for lighting in 1924, his lamps produced from those prototypes were shown at the *Exposition Internationale des Arts Décoratifs* in Paris in 1925, where he won a gold medal. The next year he was awarded the contract for lighting the Forum, a large exhibition hall being constructed in Copenhagen; the elegant fixtures shown there and manufactured by Louis Poulsen were mass-produced and brought to the market as the PH series the same year (no. 116). The other PH lamps that followed, designed in hanging, wall, and table versions, were based on similar principles of directing rather than diffusing light. Several of Henning-sen's lamps were created for his own interior spaces, which were given specific tonalities by the use of different colored metals for the shades (no. 263).

References: "When Darkness Falls," *Mobilia* (special issue) 295 (December 1980); David Revere McFadden, ed., *Scandinavian Modern Design, 1880–1980* (New York, 1982), nos. 100, 202–4.

RENÉ HERBST
French, 1891–1982

René Herbst was allied with those French designers in the 1920s who defended undecorated forms and the use of industrial materials and methods in their work. Trained in architectural offices in Frankfurt and London, Herbst first exhibited his furniture at the Salon d'Automne in Paris in 1921. He was awarded a diploma of honor for his furniture at the Paris *Exposition Internationale des Arts Décoratifs* of 1925, and designed a number of the special shops on the pont Alexandre III, including his own. These stores he provided with "modern" architectonic furniture and geometric decor, introducing a new artistry to shop-window and display techniques, for which he won a grand prize. He later created interiors and windows for other fashionable shops in Paris, including that of JEAN PUIFORCAT.

Herbst used metal in his furniture designs as early as 1925, but it was his display in Paris at the Salon des

Artistes Décorateurs in 1928 that placed him among the avant-garde in his use of the material; adjacent to the stand of CHARLOTTE PERRIAND, and almost as an adjunct to it, he showed an interior furnished with nickel-plated bent-tubular-steel furniture. From this came his later metal frame furniture designs (no. 126), which Herbst manufactured himself in limited numbers. In 1929, revolting against the opposition to such new materials within the conservative Société des Artistes Décorateurs, Herbst became one of the founders of the Union des Artistes Modemes, and he and FRANCIS JOURDAIN were in charge of its first Salon in 1930. Herbst was made president of the group in 1946, and he served as president of the UAM's Formes Utiles exhibitions of industrial design beginning in 1950.

References: André Boll, "René Herbst," Art et Décoration 62 (June 1933): 161–70; Derek E. Ostergard, ed., Bent Wood and Metal Furniture, 1850–1946 (New York, 1987), pp. 141–42, 287–88; Musée des Arts Décoratifs, Paris, Les Années UAM, 1929–1958 (September 27, 1988–January 29, 1989), pp. 194–95.

SHEILA HICKS
American, lives in France, born 1934

One of the most influential hand weavers of the postwar period, Sheila Hicks has also contributed to the design of production textiles, mainly as a consultant and designer helping traditional weavers accommodate their work to industry. A student of painting under Josef Albers and Rico Lebrun at Yale University, where she was awarded a bachelor's degree in 1957 and master of fine arts in 1959, Hicks began to weave on a small scale in 1955, but it was not until the early 1960s that the craft started to dominate her work. She has spent much of her time traveling abroad studying prehistoric and traditional weaving. Living and working in Mexico, India, Chile, and Morocco, she has collaborated with local weavers, designed textiles for production (no. 313), joined in a weaving cooperative, and provided unique rug designs for weaving by local artisans. Since 1964 Hicks has lived in Paris where her studio, the Atelier des Grands Augustins, has supplied large hangings on commission for important architectural installations, notably working with the American architect Warren Platner on interiors for the Ford Foundation building in New York (1966–68) and the Rochester Institute of Technology (1967). In addition she has created hangings for the Banque de Rothschild in Paris (1970), King Saud University in Saudi Arabia (1982–85), and Fuji City Cultural Center in Japan (1992–93).

References: Betty Werther, "Radical Rugs from Rabat," Design 270 (June 1971): 48–53; Mildred Constantine and Jack Lenor Larsen, Beyond Craft: The Art Fabric (New York, 1973), pp. 172–93; Monique Lévi-Strauss, Sheila Hicks (New York, 1974); Uměleckoprůmyslové Muzeum, Prague, Sheila Hicks (October 22–November 22, 1992).

JOSEF HOFFMANN
Austrian, born Moravia, 1870–1956

An architect and designer in all branches of the applied arts whose work was based on cubic forms and geometric constructions, Josef Hoffmann developed a personal style of great elegance that was highly influential before World War I and again in the 1970s and 1980s through exhibitions and reproductions of his work. He studied architecture in Vienna first as a pupil of Karl Freiherr von Hausenauer and then of OTTO WAGNER, in whose office he worked from 1896 to 1899. In 1899 Hoffmann was appointed professor of architecture at the Vienna Kunstgewerbeschule, a post he held until 1941. He became a pioneer of design reform in Vienna: a member of the Vienna Secession (1897) and a founding member of such groups as the Wiener Werkstätte (1903), the Kunstschau (1905), the Deutscher Werkbund (1907), and the Österreichischer Werkbund (1912), the last based on the Deutscher Werkbund. Inspired by British models and the English Arts and Crafts Movement, Hoffmann's work around the turn of the century included residential buildings with half-timbering in Hohenberg (1900), exhibition rooms for the Vienna Secession, and products for the Wiener Werkstätte (nos. 31, 36). The Werkstätte had been founded by Hoffmann with KOLOMAN MOSER and Fritz Wärndorfer after the example of CHARLES ROBERT ASHBEE's Guild of Handicraft. Hoffmann's use of elementary geometrical forms and their multiple repetition and framing owed much to CHARLES RENNIE MACKINTOSH. However it was in the architecture and interior design of the Purkersdorf Sanatorium (1903–6) and the Palais Stoclet, Brussels (1905–11), his greatest and most famous buildings, that Hoffmann found his own voice. In the sanatorium, Hoffmann pioneered a style of clear, unified, and simple cubic forms enriched with decorative borders of blue and white tile, stenciled friezes, and leaded glazed windows. His tendency toward decorative enrichments increased in the opulent Stoclet house with the collaboration of Carl Otto Czeschka and Gustav Klimt, the latter providing a celebrated stone-and-glass mosaic for the dining room. Both buildings were furnished by the Wiener Werkstätte, Purkersdorf with the collaboration of Moser. Hoffmann also provided designs for leading Viennese furniture, glass, and textile firms, among them Jacob & Josef Kohn, who produced Hoffman's bentwood chairs (nos. 43, 44); Johann Backhausen & Sohne, who produced his carpets for the Palais Stoclet; and J. & L. Lobmeyr. Hoffmann's most important later projects included the Austrian state pavilions for exhibitions in Cologne (1914), Paris (1925), and Stockholm (1930).

References: Werner J. Schweiger, Wiener Werkstaette: Design in Vienna, 1903–1932 (New York, 1984), passim; Eduard F. Sekler, Josef Hoffmann: The Architectural Work (Princeton, N.J., 1985); Historisches Museum der Stadt Wien, Vienna, Traum und Wirklichkeit: Wien, 1870–1930 (March 28–October 6, 1985), passim; Museum of Modern Art, New York, Vienna 1900: Art Architecture & Design

(July 3–October 21, 1986), passim; Peter Noever, ed., *Josef Hoffmann Designs* (Munich, 1992).

HANS HOLLEIN
Austrian, born 1934

Winner in 1985 of the most prestigious contemporary architecture award, the Pritzker Architecture Prize, Hans Hollein was cited by the jury as a "master of his profession" who "in the design of museums, schools, shops, and public housing . . . mingles bold shapes and colors with an exquisite refinement of detail and never fears to bring together the richest of ancient marbles and the latest in plastics."[20] Since 1964 Hollein has had his own practice in Vienna, where he has designed luxurious interior settings in marble, fine woods, and metal with elements quoting other styles for emotive purposes. His design is also replete with allusion: the *Zauberflute* dressing table (for Möbel Industrie Design) is an art deco confection surrounded by ostrich feathers, and his *Marilyn* and *Mitzi* sofas of 1981 (for Poltronova) are similarly evocative.

Hollein received a degree in architecture from the Akademie der Bildenden Künste in Vienna (1956), and then studied in the United States at the Illinois Institute of Technology in Chicago and the University of California at Berkeley. His *Transformations* of 1963, photomontages showing cityscapes altered by the addition of common objects used as monuments, drew on pop imagery like that of Claes Oldenburg and anticipated the radical architectural statements of ARCHIZOOM ASSOCIATI and SUPERSTUDIO in Italy toward the end of the decade. Hollein was one of the foreign architects and designers invited to participate in the first Memphis collection in 1981, where his *Schwarzenberg* table was first presented (no. 363).

References: Charles A. Jencks, *The Language of Post-Modern Architecture*, 3d ed. rev. (New York, 1981), pp. 32, 33, 133, 142–45; Centre de Création Industrielle, Centre Georges Pompidou, Paris, *Hans Hollein: Métaphores et métamorphoses* (March 18–June 8, 1987); Gianni Pettena, *Hans Hollein: opere 1960–1988* (Milan, 1988); Michael Collins and Andreas Papadakis, *Post-Modern Design* (New York, 1989), pp. 225–30.

VILMOS HUSZAR
Dutch, born Hungary, 1884–1960

Painter and designer of both graphics and interiors, Vilmos Huszar was a founding member of De Stijl and best known for his contributions to the group's monthly magazine. These included the cover design used from the magazine's inception in 1917 until 1921 (no. 73) and a series of articles, "Aestheticische Beschouwingen" (Aesthetic Considerations), published between 1917 and 1919. A Hungarian who immigrated to the Netherlands in 1905, Huszar was already known as a cubist painter in 1916 when he joined the artists' society De Anderen (The Others), founded by Theo van Doesburg. In 1917 his designs for stained-glass windows were published by van Doesburg in an essay on new painting, and the following year Huszar designed the color scheme for a boys' bedroom in the house of Cornelis Bruynzeel, Jr., Huszar's neighbor in Voorburg, near The Hague. Using flat unbroken rectangles of primary color as well as black, white, and gray on walls, ceiling, and rug, Huszar also painted the furniture that the architect P.J.C. Klaarhammer designed for the room, creating one of the earliest applications of De Stijl color theory to interior design. In 1920 and 1921, Huszar collaborated with the architect Piet Zwart on furniture designs, and in 1923 with GERRIT RIETVELD on an exhibition in Berlin. In 1923 he left De Stijl to paint and practice interior design independently.

Reference: Mildred Friedman, ed., *De Stijl: 1917–1931, Visions of Utopia* (New York, 1982), passim.

I.D. TWO
Established Palo Alto, California, 1979

Founded in 1979 by Bill Moggridge as an offshoot of his London-based industrial design firm Design Developments, I.D. Two was situated until 1984 in Palo Alto, the heart of California's Silicon Valley (now it is in San Francisco). The firm first specialized in design for technology, working on hardware for companies such as Conversion Technologies, Decision Data, and Grid Systems, for which it created the *Compass* portable computer (no. 367). I.D. Two's other work has included communication, office, and laboratory equipment, and in recent years the firm has also become involved in software and interactive design. Moggridge, a graduate of London's Central School of Design in 1965, started his own firm in 1969, designing scientific equipment and consumer products; in 1977 he added Industrial Design Models, a facility for appearance modelmaking and prototyping, and both are now subsumed under Design Developments.

References: Central School of Art and Design, London, *Central to Design, Central to Industry* (1983), pp. 95–96; "The Compass Computer: The Design Challenges behind the Innovation," *Innovation* (winter 1983): 4–8; "ID Two," *Design* 440 (August 1985): 65; Chee Pearlman, "Silicon Valley Stories," *International Design* 37 (January–February 1990): 38–39; Mike Jones, "The One-Stop ID Shop," *Design* 512 (August 1991): 18–21.

PAUL IRIBE
French, active also United States, 1883–1935

A prolific and talented self-taught graphic designer, Paul Iribe created advertisements, political cartoons, fashion illustrations (for PAUL POIRET), posters, packaging, satirical drawings, and caricatures. His first caricature was published when he was only seventeen (in *Le Rire*, 1901), with others following in many of the leading French weeklies. In 1906 he himself became the publisher of a new satirical journal, *Le Témoin*, founded to rival such popular weeklies as the German *Simplicissimus*. But by 1910 Iribe had turned to the applied arts, designing jewelry for Robert Linzeler (exhibited in Turin in 1911), floral fabrics for André Groult (later, also for Bianchini-Férier), stage settings, and furniture; the last he designed mainly on commission and sold along with fabrics, glass, and objets d'art at his decorating shop in the Faubourg Saint-Honoré. With the aid of PIERRE LEGRAIN, who had collaborated with him on *Le Témoin*, Iribe decorated the apartment of Jacques Doucet in 1912, gathering an ensemble of contemporary decorative arts for the couturier's home. Many of the pieces Iribe created for Doucet, and for other notable Parisians as well, were sophisticated reinterpretations of the past (no. 61), works made of exotic woods and precious materials including shagreen (sharkskin), which Iribe revived for the design of furniture carried out for him by CLÉMENT ROUSSEAU. By 1919 Iribe had moved to America, where for almost a decade he applied his creative resources to the Hollywood film industry. As art director for Paramount, he gave form to the grandiose conceptions of the silent films, working with Cecil B. De Mille on twelve productions, notoriously clothing Gloria Swanson in a dress of pearls (for *Male and Female*, 1919), and executing the magniloquent sets for *The Ten Commandments* (1923). The last years of Iribe's life were spent in France, where he designed posters for Ford automobiles, steamships, Wagons-Lits trains, and the wine merchant Nicolas. He also created diamond jewelry for Chanel (1932), and returned to publishing and political satire.

References: Raymond Bachollet, Daniel Bordet, and Anne-Claude Lelieur, *Paul Iribe* (Paris, 1982); Bibliothèque Fomey, Paris, *Paul Iribe: Précurseur de l'art déco* (October 6–December 31, 1983).

FUJIWO ISHIMOTO
Japanese, born 1941

A textile designer whose career has been made in Finland at Marimekko, Fujiwo Ishimoto introduced Japanese-style brushstroke patterns into the firm's formal vocabulary. Ishimoto studied graphic design at the Tokyo National University of Art and subsequently worked as a commercial artist in the advertising department of the Ichida textile company (1964–70). In 1970 he left Japan for Finland, joining Marimekko's sister company, Décembre, as a textile designer, where he collaborated on the design of a popular series of canvas carry bags. Joining Marimekko in 1974, Ishimoto began independently to design dress and furnishing fabrics—his *Sumo* and *Jama* (1977) and *Taiga* (1978) fabrics revealing the calligraphic nature of the designs for which he became known at Marimekko (no. 376). Ishimoto was awarded the American Roscoe prize in 1983 and given awards at the *Finland Designs* exhibitions of 1983 and 1989.

References: Pekka Suhonen and Juhani Pallasmaa, eds., *Phenomenon Marimekko* (Helsinki, 1986);

pp. 130–31; Matsuya Ginza, Tokyo, *Design Collection* (1989), pp. 14–15.

MAIJA ISOLA
Finnish, born 1927

A painter, Maija Isola was a principal designer for the textile firm Printex since its inception in 1949, contributing greatly to the international success that it and its sister company Marimekko achieved in the 1950s and 1960s. A student of painting at the Taideteollisuuskeskuskoulu (Central School of Industrial Arts) in Helsinki (1946–49), Isola turned her abstractions into printed-cotton textile designs, at first small geometrics and flat patterns inspired by nature and then the large-scale bold prints in flat colors (no. 248) that came to signify Printex and Marimekko. Other designs were inspired by Byzantine and Finnish motifs and decorations, anticipating a return to traditional and folk-inspired designs in the 1970s. With FUJIWO ISHIMOTO, Isola remains one of the few staff designers in this large international firm. She was awarded the International ID prize in 1965 and 1968.

References: Charles S. Talley, *Contemporary Textile Art: Scandinavia* (Stockholm, 1982), pp. 129–31; Pekka Suhonen and Juhani Pallasmaa, eds., *Phenomenon Marimekko* (Helsinki, 1986), pp. 118–19.

ARNE JACOBSEN
Danish, 1902–1971

Denmark's leading International Style architect, Arne Jacobsen graduated in 1927 from the Kongelige Danske Kunstakademi (Royal Danish Academy of Fine Arts) in Copenhagen, but even as a student he had won a silver medal for a chair exhibited at the 1925 Paris *Exposition Internationale des Arts Décoratifs*. Inspired both by the pavilion of LE CORBUSIER in Paris and the work of the rationalist architects he saw on a visit to Berlin (1927–28), Jacobsen introduced modernist designs to Denmark, winning first prize for a circular "House of the Future" (with Flemming Lassen) in the building exhibition sponsored by the Akademisk Arkitektforening (Academic Association of Architects) in Copenhagen in 1929. The following year for one of his very first commissions, the Rothenborg house in Ordrup, he designed a low, functionalist building with large expanses of glass, and created compatible interior furnishings, which he would continue to do frequently throughout his career. His best known—and most fully integrated work—was the glass-sheathed Scandinavian Airlines System Air Terminal and Royal Hotel in Copenhagen (1956–60), for which he designed all of the furnishings—textiles, furniture (no. 252), lighting, tableware (no. 253), and other utilitarian objects. Jacobsen also designed directly for factory production: his range of designs for the furniture manufacturer Fritz Hansen, including his most successful piece, the three-legged *Ant* chair of 1951 (no. 228), won a grand prize at the *XI Triennale* in Milan in 1957. Among his other designs for industry were lighting (for Louis Poulsen), metalware (for Stelton; no. 293), textiles (for Grautex, Millech, and C. Olesen), and sanitary fittings (for I. P. Lunds).

References: Arne Karlsen, *Made in Denmark* (New York, 1960), pp. 94–103, 147; Tobias Faber, *Arne Jacobsen* (New York, 1964); Rebecka Tarschys and Henry End, "Arne Jacobsen: From Stainless Flatware to the Royal Hotel in Copenhagen," *Interiors* 122 (October 1962): 112–22; Danish Society of Industrial Design, *ID Prizes, 1965–1969* (Copenhagen, 1970), pp. 38–39, 130–31; Musée des Arts Décoratifs, Paris, *Arne Jacobsen: Architecte et designer danois, 1902–1971* (November 16, 1987–January 31, 1988).

PIERRE JEANNERET
Swiss, active France, 1896–1967

Pierre Jeanneret worked as an architect, planner, and furniture designer with his cousin Charles Edouard Jeanneret (LE CORBUSIER). In the 1920s the two chiefly designed individual dwellings in the suburbs of Paris for upper-middle-class clients, homes that included the Villa Stein-de-Monzie at Garches (1926–28) and the Villa Savoye at Poissy (1928–30); they also shared first prize in the much disputed competition for the League of Nations building in Geneva (1926–27). The firm's well-known tubular-steel-framed furniture, designed in collaboration with CHARLOTTE PERRIAND, who joined the office in 1927, was first shown at the Salon d'Automne of 1929 under the title "interior equipment of a dwelling" (nos. 125, 131), where it was praised for its audacious scorn of traditionalism and its logic. Like Perriand, Jeanneret joined the breakaway organization of architects and designers known as the Union des Artistes Modernes (UAM), and exhibited architectural designs, photographs, and models of projects conceived in collaboration with Le Corbusier at its salons: projects included the Villa Savoye, the Palace of Soviets in Moscow (1931–32); an urban scheme for Algiers (from 1932); and the *Radiant City* (1930–35). In 1940 Jeanneret joined the French Resistance, making a temporary break in the partnership, and during the 1940s he also worked briefly in association with JEAN PROUVÉ, Perriand, and Georges Blanchon. After the war, Jeanneret continued his collaboration with Prouvé on prefabricated housing and with Blanchon on an urban design for Puteaux, France. In 1951 Jeanneret joined Le Corbusier in the planning and design of the new state capital of the Punjab, Chandigarh, and spent the next fourteen years largely in India realizing Le Corbusier's grand scheme, which included the city plan, four government buildings, several monuments, two museums, two colleges, low-income housing, and a clubhouse. While in India, Jeanneret also designed experimental low-cost furniture made of native materials such as cord and bamboo.

References: Willi Boesiger, ed., *Le Corbusier et Pierre Jeanneret: Oeuvre complète*, 8 vols. (Zurich, 1930–69); Ecole Nationale Supérieure des Beaux-Arts, Paris,

Architectures en Inde (November 27, 1985–January 19, 1986), pp. 105–10; Catherine Cortiau, "Pierre Jeanneret," in *Le Corbusier: Une encyclopédie* (Paris, 1987), pp. 213–15; Musée des Arts Décoratifs, Paris, *Les Années UAM, 1929–1958* (September 27, 1988–January 29, 1989), pp. 198–99 et passim.

GEORG JENSEN
Danish, 1866–1935

The founder of the celebrated Danish silver firm that bears his name, Georg Jensen began as a goldsmith's apprentice and then became a student of sculpture at the Kongelige Danske Kunstakademi (Royal Danish Academy of Fine Arts) in Copenhagen. Afterward he worked as a modeler for the Bing & Grøndhal porcelain factory, and later, with his friend the painter Joachim Petersen, opened a small pottery, whose works were exhibited with honorable mention at the *Exposition Universelle* in Paris in 1900. After the turn of the century Jensen returned to metalwork, making jewelry with interlaced and naturalistic decoration, which in 1904 was exhibited at, and then bought by, the Kunstindustrimuseum in Copenhagen. That same year he opened his own shop and in about 1904–5 created the first of his hollowware pieces, the *Blossom* teapot (no. 35). Jensen became so well known for the high quality of his craftsmanship—with the first of his shops abroad opening in Berlin in 1909, followed by Paris in 1919, London in 1921, and New York in 1924—that he was required to enlarge the scale of his workshop and add machine techniques to his production. His silver was shown at major international exhibitions, winning a gold medal in Brussels in 1910, first prize in San Francisco in 1915, and grand prize in Paris in 1925. Jensen had several important early collaborators, including his brother-in-law Harald Nielsen, and most notably JOHAN ROHDE, who from about 1907 created a series of hollowware and cutlery designs that brought both classical and simplified, unornamented forms to the silversmith's line (nos. 67, 82). Jensen retired in 1926, leaving the firm to be run by his family.

References: Emile Sedeyn, "L'Orfèvre Georg Jensen," *Art et Décoration* 36 (July 1914): 15–20; Ivan Munk Olsen, *Sølvsmeden Georg Jensen* (Copenhagen, 1937); Renwick Gallery, National Collection of Fine Arts, Washington, D.C., *Georg Jensen—Silversmithy: 77 Artists 75 Years* (February 29–July 6, 1980), pp. 9–16, nos. 62–80.

JACOB JENSEN
Danish, born 1926

The sleek, refined audio products Jacob Jensen created for Bang & Olufsen from 1964 so successfully defined the look of high technology and performance that they still remain the standard for the industry (no. 340). While he is best known for his Bang & Olufsen work (he has designed most of their audio equipment), Jensen has also provided designs for other Danish products, including the pushbutton *E76* telephone for Alcatel-Kirk (1972), a wristwatch for Max René (1983), an ergonomic office chair for Labofa (1979), and an ultrasound scanner for Bruel & Kjaer (1982). A graduate of the Kunsthåndvaerkerskolen (School of Arts, Crafts and Design) in Copenhagen, where he studied industrial design (1952), Jensen worked as chief designer for BERNADOTTE & BJØRN from 1952 to 1959. From 1959 to 1961 he concurrently taught at the University of Illinois in Chicago and practiced there with Richard Latham and several others in an international design firm. On his return to Copenhagen in 1961 Jensen opened his own office, later joined by his son, Timothy Jacob Jensen. Jensen has won numerous international design awards, from Denmark's ID prize and Germany's Die Gute Industrieform prize to the American I.D.S.A. prize (1978).

References: Svend Erik Moller, "A Non-Specializing Specialist," *Danish Journal* 76 (1973): 30–32; Jens Bernsen, *Design: The Problem Comes First* (Copenhagen, 1982), pp. 90–95; Michael Evamy, "North Star," *Design* 516 (December 1991): 26–28.

FRANCIS JOURDAIN
French, 1876–1958

Francis Jourdain was an early proponent of rationalist design in France, introducing the concept of standardized furniture made by industry. Son of Frantz Jourdain, architect of the iron-and-glass Samaritaine department store in Paris (1905), Jourdain studied painting with a number of artists in his father's circle, principally Eugène Carrière, and exhibited in the salons between 1897 and 1913. In 1902 he showed furniture for the first time at the Salon d'Automne and continued to create decorative objects, winning a grand prize at the *Esposizione Internazionale* in Turin in 1911. The following year in Esbly, not far from Paris, he founded the Ateliers Modernes, a workshop for the manufacture of simple furnishings devoid of historical precedent and artistic or symbolic associations. This reflected a new, rational approach to decoration, as exemplified by the interiors of his own apartment, which he presented at the Salon d'Automne in 1913 (no. 59). Jourdain designed furniture that could be used interchangeably (a concept he continued to refine as late as 1937, exhibiting a small modularly furnished room at the *Exposition Internationale* in Paris). In 1916, following his social concerns and supported by the populist newspaper *L'Humanité*, he manufactured furniture in series that was designed for workers, but inexpensive as it was it still proved too costly for broad distribution. After World War I the Ateliers Modernes expanded into wider factory production, and a shop, Chez Francis Jourdain, was opened in Paris to sell its products and to furnish complete interiors; Jourdain also designed printed fabrics, carpets, and lighting that were sold there. For the *Exposition Internationale des Arts Décoratifs* in Paris in 1925, he designed a gymnasium for the "French Embassy" exhibit and a smoking-car for the Chemins de Fer de Paris-

Orléans. Along with a group of progressive designers, Jourdain was a founder of the Union des Artistes Modernes in 1929, organizing its first salon (with RENÉ HERBST) in 1930; he continued to show his rationalist furnishings with the group throughout the 1930s.

References: Léon Moussinac, *Francis Jourdain* (Geneva, 1955); Claire Doré, "Un Ensemblier a l'avant-garde des années 20: Francis Jourdain," *Connaissance des Arts* 322 (December 1978): 121–26; Pierre Kjellberg, *Art déco: Les maîtres du mobilier, le décor des paquebots* (Paris, 1986), pp. 97–100; Musée des Arts Décoratifs, Paris, *Les Années UAM, 1929–1958* (September 27, 1988–January 29, 1989), pp. 200–202; Suzanne Tise, "Francis Jourdain," in Arlette Barré-Despond, *Jourdain* (New York, 1991), pp. 213–343.

KARL J. JUCKER
German, active 1922–25

Karl J. Jucker is known only as a student in the Bauhaus metal workshop from 1922 to about 1925 and by the works he made there, including a samovar, electric samovar, piano lamp, and glass table lamp; the latter was designed with WILHELM WAGENFELD in 1923–24 (no. 94) and remains his best-known work. From the evidence of his lighting devices, which were published in *Neue Arbeiten der Bauhauswerkstätten* (1925) and those that survive, primarily in the Bauhaus-Archiv in Berlin, Jucker seems to have been particularly interested in developing new mechanisms. His piano lamp of 1923, for example, was constructed with a swivel stand and arm, and his experimental extension wall-lamp was described by LÁSZLÓ MOHOLY-NAGY as having "devices for pushing and pulling, heavy strips and rods of iron and brass, looking more like a dinosaur than a functional object."[21]

References: *Neue Arbeiten der Bauhauswerkstätten* (Munich, 1925), pp. 65–66, 68; Herbert Bayer, Walter Gropius, and Ise Gropius, eds., *Bauhaus, 1919–1928* (New York, 1938), pp. 54, 57, 136; Hans M. Wingler, *The Bauhaus: Weimar, Dessau, Berlin, Chicago* (Cambridge, Mass., 1969), pp. 98, 314, 317.

FINN JUHL
Danish, born 1912

One of the best-known designers of the "Danish modern" style that became popular internationally after World War II, Finn Juhl studied architecture at the Kongelige Danske Kunstakademi (Royal Danish Academy of Fine Arts) in Copenhagen under KAARE KLINT. In the late 1930s he turned to furniture design, beginning a long-standing collaboration with the cabinetmaker Niels Vodder, who produced his series of organic chairs (no. 220), sofas, and tables in the 1940s and 50s. Juhl's sculptural designs, superbly crafted of handsome native and imported woods, won fourteen successive prizes from the Copenhagen Cabinetmakers Guild during this period as well as six Milan *Triennale* gold medals. His furniture was also adapted for large-scale manufacture in America by Baker in 1951 (and shown in the *Good Design* exhibitions in Chicago and New York in the early 1950s). Juhl's other work includes interior and exhibition designs, wooden bowls (for the firm of KAY BOJESEN), appliances (for General Electric), carpets (for Unika-Vaev), porcelain (for Bing & Grøndahl), glassware (for Jensen), and lighting.

References: Edgar Kaufmann, "Finn Juhl of Copenhagen," *Interiors* 108 (November 1948): 96–99; O.G., "Finn Juhl," *Interiors* 110 (September 1950): 82–91; "Finn Juhl," *Interiors* (November 1951): 84–93; Esbjørn Hiort, *Danish Furniture* (New York, 1956), pp. 8–9, 52–65; Enzo Frateili, "Finn Juhl: Architect and Designer," *Zodiac* 5 (1960): 106–15; Esbjørn Hiort, *Finn Juhl: Furniture, Architecture, Applied Art* (Copenhagen, 1990).

SVEN-ERIC JUHLIN—*see* ERGONOMI DESIGN GRUPPEN

DORA JUNG
Finnish, 1906–1980

A weaver and creator of patterns for textile production, Dora Jung devoted herself exclusively to the damask technique throughout her career. From 1929 to 1932 she studied at the Taideteollisuuskeskuskoulu (Central School of Industrial Arts) in Helsinki, and then opened her own weaving studio, where she and her assistants made utilitarian articles, ecclesiastical textiles, and ornamental hangings in discrete patterns and restricted colors. Her ideas for handwoven damasks exceeded the possibilities of the standard looms so she devised new tools and techniques to achieve her decorative goals, which in her later years included bright, large-scale, often pictorial, designs. From 1936 to 1941 and again between 1956 and 1972, Jung worked for the Finnish textile manufacturer Tampella, conceiving linens for production (no. 241). She also received commissions to decorate public buildings in Finland and worked with ALVAR AALTO on a number of these projects. Jung won a gold medal at the Paris *Exposition Internationale* in 1937 and was awarded three grand prizes at the *Triennale* exhibitions in Milan, in 1951, 1954, and 1957. In 1979 she was given the British title of Honorary Royal Designer for Industry. Jung's archives are in the Taideteollisuusmuseo in Helsinki.

References: Erik Zahle, ed., *A Treasury of Scandinavian Design* (New York, 1961), p. 279, nos. 123–25, 127, 181–82, 344, 408; Eeva Siltavuori, "I Never Tire of Watching a Gull's Glide," *Form Function Finland* 2 (1981): 58–63; "Charles S. Talley, *Contemporary Textile Art: Scandinavia* (Stockholm, 1982), pp. 107–13; Taideteollisuusmuseo, Helsinki, *Dora Jung* (1983).

WILHELM KÅGE
Swedish, 1889–1960

Like his contemporaries Simon Gate and EDWARD HALD at Orrefors, Wilhelm Kåge was hired by the Gustavsberg ceramic factory to breathe new life into their products, encouraged by the campaign of the Svenska Slöjdföreningen (Swedish Society of Industrial Design) to improve domestic objects by employing artists in industry. A student of painting in Göteborg, Stockholm, and Copenhagen (where he studied with JOHAN ROHDE) and of graphics in Munich, Kåge was the most influential of Swedish ceramic designers, creating art pottery, including his distinctive, robust Farsta stoneware, which showed the influence of Mexican and Chinese ceramics, and the Surrea series of fragmented pieces inspired by cubism and surrealism. He also developed many well-thought-out table services for mass production (nos. 66, 139), most traditional in their inspiration but with simplified forms and decoration. Among the features he introduced to Swedish ceramics were stacking services, oven-to-table ware (the *Pyro* service, first shown at the 1930 Stockholm exhibition), and the concept of "open stock." Kåge was awarded a grand prize at the *Exposition Internationale des Arts Décoratifs* in Paris in 1925.

References: Nils Palmgren, *Wilhelm Kåge: Konstnar och Hantverkare* (Stockholm, 1953); Nationalmuseum, Stockholm, *Wilhelm Kåge, Gustavsberg* (April 17–May 14, 1953); Björn Hedstrand, *Servisgods från Gustavsberg av Wilhelm Kåge, 1917–1945* (Motala, Sweden, 1975); Boilerhouse Project, Victoria and Albert Museum, London, *Art & Industry* (January 18–March 2, 1982), pp. 14–20; Jennifer Hawkins Opie, *Scandinavia: Ceramics & Glass in the Twentieth Century* (London, 1989), passim.

YUSAKU KAMEKURA
Japanese, born 1915

Yusaku Kamekura pioneered the field of modern graphic design in Japan, raising offset and silkscreen processes in the public mind to the level of fine art and setting the high standards for printed production for which Japanese graphics have since become known. As the critic Masaru Katsumi has noted, "there has been almost no important development in postwar design in which he [Kamekura] has not played an active role . . . creat[ing] Japanese design as we know it today."[22] Kamekura was a founding member of Tokyo's Japan Advertising Artists Club in 1951 and of the Japan Graphic Designers Association in 1978. In 1960 he cofounded the Nippon Design Center, which afterwards became Japan's largest graphic design firm.

Kamekura studied at the Shin Kenchiku Kogei Gakuin (New Architecture and Industrial Arts School; 1935–37), Tokyo, which had been established by Renshichiro Kawakita in 1931 as a Japanese Bauhaus. There Kamekura learned the pure geometric forms and design systems of European avant-garde graphics on which he would base his later work. From 1938 to 1949 he worked as art director for several Japanese magazines, including *Nippon* (1938) and *Commerce Japan* (1949), and from 1940 to 1960 he served as head of the art department of the publishing firm Nippon Kobo. Under its influential founder, Yonosuke Natori, in 1954 Kamekura began his long association with Nippon Kogaku (later Nikon), designing posters (no. 269), packaging, and other commercial graphics in an abstract, geometric style that captured the clarity and precision of the camera mechanism and brought the designer national recognition. Kamekura has also held a similar long-term relationship with Yamagiwa, a light-fixture manufacturing company where since 1970 he has served as director of the LD Yamagiwa laboratory.

In 1962 Kamekura left the Nippon Design Center to practice independently in Tokyo. He came to international attention with his design work for the 1964 Olympics in Tokyo, including the Olympic Symbol (1961) and posters (1962, 1963) that were the first in Olympic history to use photographs. Other of Kamekura's government commissions include the G (Good Design) Mark for the Ministry of International Trade and Industry (1959); the interior display of the Japanese pavilion at the *New York World's Fair* (1964); posters for the Sapporo Winter Olympics (1969, 1970); and the symbol marks for *Expo '75* in Okinawa (1972) and *Expo '89* in Nagoya (1988).

References: *The Graphic Design of Yusaku Kamekura* (New York, 1973); Masataka Ogawa, Ikko Tanaka, and Kazumasa Nagai, eds., *The Works of Yusaku Kamekura* (Tokyo, 1983).

MITSUO KATSUI
Japanese, born 1931

Known for his creative digital designs (no. 394), Mitsuo Katsui used computer and photographic technology to challenge traditional Japanese graphic concepts as early as 1971, when he was awarded a medal by the Japanese typography institution for his computer-designed posters. Katsui graduated from the Tokyo University of Education (1955), where he studied design and photography. He joined the Ajinomoto Company in 1956 and received national recognition when he was awarded the eighth Japan Advertising Artists Club's gold medal in 1958. In 1961 he established his own design office in Tokyo and at the same time began lecturing and teaching at Tokyo (now Tsukuba) University and Musashino Art University. Katsui was made art director of the Japanese government pavilion, Orgorama, at *Expo '70* in Osaka, the Okinawa *International Ocean Exposition* in 1975, and the Kodansha pavilion, Brain House, at *Expo '85* in Tsukuba. His many awards range from the Mainichi industrial design prize (1965) to the grand prize at the graphics biennial in Brno, Czechoslovakia (1990).

References: Art Directors Club of Tokyo, *Art Direction Today* (Tokyo, 1984), pp. 166–67; *Best 100 Japanese Posters, 1945–1989* (Tokyo, 1990), pp. 94–95, 160–61, 198–99, 228–29, 246; National Museum of Modern Art, Tokyo, *Graphic Design Today* (September 26–November 11, 1990), pp. 50–53, 112; Richard S. Thornton, *The Graphic Spirit of Japan* (New York, 1991), pp. 109, 224–25; Hiroshi Kashiwagi, "Mitsuo Katsui," *Creation* 9 (1991): 112, 143–65, 167–68.

EDWARD McKNIGHT KAUFFER
American, active England, 1890–1954

For a period of twenty-five years Edward McKnight Kauffer was the leading poster designer for London's transportation network, creating over a hundred placards encouraging ridership and advertising destinations that could be reached by tube, tram, and omnibus. An American, Kauffer traveled to Europe in 1913 after studying painting at the Art Institute of Chicago, but in 1914 the outbreak of World War I forced him to leave Paris, where he had enrolled at the Académie Moderne, for London . The following year saw the beginning of his career as a graphic designer when he received the first of his numerous commissions from Frank Pick, head of publicity for the Underground. At the same time Kauffer continued painting, joining the London and the Cumberland Market groups of painters, and having his drawings offered for sale by ROGER FRY at the Omega Workshops. Throughout his career Kauffer's work responded to a succession of modern styles (he had first been introduced to European modernism at the Armory Show when it traveled to Chicago in 1913). His paintings and his poster designs, which were featured in solo exhibitions in the 1920s and 30s, reflected the influence of postimpressionism, cubism (no. 71), futurism, vorticism, and surrealism, and during the later 1920s he introduced photomontage and a purist aesthetic to his repertoire. Among Kauffer's other clients, for whom he produced book illustrations and jackets in addition to posters, were the publishers Chatto & Windus, Nonesuch Press, and the Hogarth Press, as well as Shell oil, Bass brewers, and Heal and Son. Kauffer also designed carpets for Wilton beginning in 1929, along with his wife MARION DORN. At the onset of World War II, Kauffer returned to the United States, where he designed book jackets (for Random House, Modern Library, Pantheon, and others). Beginning in 1948 he again created series of posters on the theme of transportation, this time for American Airlines and Pan American Airways.

References: "New Rug Designs by E. McKnight Kauffer and Marion V. Dorn: A Conversation with a 'Studio' Representative," *Creative Art* 14 (January 1929) [*Studio* 97]: 35–39; Museum of Modern Art, New York, *Posters by E. McKnight Kauffer* (1937); Mark Haworth-Booth, *E. McKnight Kauffer: A Designer and His Public* (London, 1979); Arts Council of Great Britain, Hayward Gallery, London, *Thirties: British Art and Design before the War* (October 25, 1979–January 13, 1980), pp. 293—94, nos. 4.42, 4.43, 10.20, 11.78, 13.4, 16.3, 16.12, 17.2, 20.12–14; Oliver Green, *Art for the London Underground: London*

Transport Posters, 1908 to the Present (New York, 1990), pp. 36, 48, 60, 68, 69, 141.

RENÉ KEMNA
Dutch, born 1956

René Kemna, a graduate of the industrial design program at the polytechnic school in Delft (1981), specializes in lighting design and works in both the Netherlands and Italy. He has designed extensively for the Italian lighting firm Sirrah, in Imola, for whom he created the Sigla series of lamps in 1986 (no. 387).

References: *The International Design Yearbook*, vol. 2 (1986), p. 114; *Industrial Design* 34 (July–August, 1987): 71.

WALTER MARIA KERSTING
German, 1892–1970

Architect, designer, engineer, and graphic artist, Walter Maria Kersting attended the Technische Hochschule in Hanover (1912–14), where he began to work as a graphic designer and served as art director for a printing plant. Between 1922 and 1932, in Weimar and then Cologne, he also worked as an architect, and during the same period designed furniture, lighting, and the first version of a plastic radio that later was produced in great numbers throughout Germany to serve the informational purposes of the Nazi regime (no. 144). Between 1933 and 1944 Kersting taught graphics and book design at the Staatliche Kunstakademie in Düsseldorf, and then opened up a studio for industrial design. Among the products he created in the postwar period were audio equipment (for Telefunken), sewing machines (for Adler), and telephones (for Telefonbau und Normalzeit).

References: Heinz G. Pfaender et al., *Walter Maria Kersting: Architekt, Formgestalter, Ingenieur, Grafiker* (Darmstadt, 1974); Haus der Kunst, Munich, *Die dreissiger Jahre: Schauplatz Deutschland* (February 11–April 11, 1977), pp. 186–87; Hans Wichmann, *Industrial Design, Unikate, Serienerzeugnisse: Die Neue Sammlung, ein neuer Museumstyp des 20. Jahrhunderts* (Munich, 1985), p. 502, nos. 266, 289; Heinz Fuchs and François Burkhardt, *Product—Design—History: German Design from 1870 down to the Present Era* (Stuttgart, 1986), pp. 251, 288.

FREDERICK KIESLER
American, born Romania, 1890–1965

Trained in Vienna, Frederick Kiesler was profoundly international in outlook; he was a member of the De Stijl group and later associated with the surrealists and was continually involved with European avant-garde movements. Architect, sculptor, and designer of stage sets, interiors, and furniture, he is best known for his biomorphic designs, the most influential being the *Endless House* (first designed in 1923). This project featured freely flowing spaces rather than rectangular rooms, a new conception of spatial planning that he continually redesigned and exhibited in the form of drawings and models but never built.

Kiesler attended the Technische Hochschule in Vienna (1908–9) and then the Akademie der Bildenden Künste (from 1910), where he studied painting and printmaking. After World War I he created stage and theater designs in Vienna and Berlin, and his utopian De Stijl environment, *City in Space*, was built for the Paris exposition of 1925. Kiesler moved to the United States in 1926 where his activities were extremely diverse. In 1929 he constructed the Film Guild Cinema in New York, the first theater in America designed specifically for film projection. He created window displays for Saks Fifth Avenue (1928–30), one of several designers including DONALD DESKEY and NORMAN BEL GEDDES to bring advances in European design to America through this medium. As he explained in his book on the subject, "the department store acted as the interpreter for the populace of a new spirit in art."[23] He began to design furniture in 1929, showing an office with a suspended desk as well as tubular-steel furniture at the 1930 exhibition of the American Union of Decorative Artists and Craftsmen (AUDAC), of which he was a founder and director. During the 1930s he patented several designs for multifunctional furniture and created a series of biomorphic cast-aluminum tables (no. 176), experimenting with such new materials and techniques as director between 1937 and 1942 of the Laboratory for Design Correlation in the School of Architecture at Columbia University. His inventiveness in the area of display techniques was reasserted in 1942 in the interior designs and organic modular furnishings he created for Peggy Guggenheim's Art of This Century Gallery in New York. From 1934 to 1957 Kiesler was director of scenic design at the Juilliard School of Music in New York.

References: "New Display Techniques for 'Art of This Century' Designed by Frederick J. Kiesler," *Architectural Forum* 78 (February 1943): 49–53; Frederick Kiesler, "Pseudo-Functionalism in Modern Architecture," *Partisan Review* 16 (July 1949): 731–42; Cynthia Goodman, "Frederick Kiesler: Designs for Peggy Guggenheim's Art of This Century Gallery," *Arts Magazine* 51 (June 1977): pp. 90–95; Dieter Bogner, ed., *Friedrich Kiesler: Architekt Maler Bildhauer, 1890–1965* (Vienna, 1988); Lisa Phillips, *Frederick Kiesler* (New York, 1989).

PERRY A. KING, *see* KING-MIRANDA ASSOCIATI

KING-MIRANDA ASSOCIATI
Established Milan, 1975

Designers closely associated with high-technology lighting, the King-Miranda partnership was established in 1975 by Perry A. King, an Englishman who had moved to Milan in 1965 to work with ETTORE SOTTSASS, JR., as a consultant to Olivetti (no. 319), and Santiago Miranda, a Spaniard who had arrived in 1971. Before their partnership became formalized, the two had collaborated on typeface designs for Olivetti's dot matrix printers, including one that has become the European standard for optical character recognition; at the same time they worked together on a long-term research project they called "Unlimited Horizons," which explored the relationship of products and their environments. King and Miranda have since designed computers and keyboard consoles for Olivetti, and continued to work on the firm's graphics. They have also designed a series of light fixtures for Arteluce/Flos that are technologically innovative and inventive in their form and use of materials. For these, including their best-selling *Jill* floor lamp of 1977, they adapted pressed glass and halogen bulbs for domestic use, while their *Expanded Line Network* of 1983 (no. 390), a flexible track lighting system, accommodates various voltages and kinds of illumination. Other designs include furniture for Marcatré and Disform; interiors, also for Marcatré; and power tools for Black and Decker. Their cumulative experience in lighting technology led to their being chosen to design the lighting for the international exposition in Seville in 1992.

References: James Woudhuysen, "Priests at Technology's Altar," *Design* 410 (February 1983): 40–42; John Thackara, "Lighting: Inspired by Dodgem Cars," *Design* 421 (January 1984): 38–40; Annetta Hanna, "The Vision of King-Miranda," *Industrial Design* 33 (May–June 1986): 34–39; Hugh Aldersey-Williams, *King and Miranda: The Poetry of the Machine* (New York, 1991).

TOSHIYUKI KITA
Japanese, born 1942

The most international of Japanese furniture and product designers of the 1980s, Toshiyuki Kita has nonetheless continued to assert his cultural identity, inventing asymmetrical animistic forms for Western products while contributing to the revival of traditional Japanese crafts. With regard to the latter, he has designed lamps for IDK (1983) and Kosyudo (1986) with shades made of Japanese paper, as well as a series of lacquer tablewares made at Wajima by traditional means (1986; no. 388). Like many other designers of his generation, Kita left Japan to work in Italy, where he readily found manufacturers for his designs, among them Bernini and Bilumen. He first gained international success with his *Wink* chair for Cassina (1980), a legless lounge with adjustable back, head, and footrest that has been compared to a gigantic insect (no. 361). Kita was trained in the industrial design department of Naniwa College (1964) and established his first office in Osaka in 1967.

Reference: *Toshiyuki Kita: Movement as Concept* (Tokyo, 1990).

POUL KJAERHOLM
Danish, 1929–1980

Architect as well as designer, Poul Kjaerholm apprenticed as a joiner, attended the Kunsthåndvaerkerskolen (School of Arts, Crafts and Design) in Copenhagen (1949–52), and, while beginning his career as a designer and teacher, continued his studies at the furniture school of the Kongelige Danske Kunstakademi (Royal Danish Academy of Fine Arts; 1953–59). Virtually all his furniture was created for mass production, principally for E. Kold Christensen in Copenhagen beginning in 1955 (no. 251). The simplicity of intent and structural honesty of his work connect him with the International Style, although it presents a fresh interpretation of that tradition. The extensive series of chairs, sofas, and tables he designed over a twenty-five-year period favored steel structure, but with natural upholstery—leather, cane, canvas; as early as 1953, however, he had experimented with more innovative materials, including colored cast aluminum, steel wire, and poured concrete (for outdoor use). Kjaerholm was awarded the Lunning Prize in 1958, and a grand prize and gold medal at, respectively, Milan's *XI Triennale* in 1957 and *XII Triennale* in 1960.

References: Per Mollerup, "Poul Kjaerholm's Furniture," *Mobilia* 304–5 (1982): 1–24; "Poul Kjaerholm," in Nationalmuseum, Stockholm, *The Lunning Prize* (1986), pp. 94–97.

KAARE KLINT
Danish, 1885–1954

The father of modern Danish furniture design, Kaare Klint promoted practical cabinetry with straight lines, simple construction, and waxed natural finishes, introducing at the same time the concept of human factors research and data collection as the basis of his work (no. 137). He looked to stylistic sources as diverse as eighteenth-century English furniture, Shaker designs, and oriental cabinetry; he also introduced his own versions of vernacular types, including his deck and *Safari* chairs and his camp stool, all of 1933, lightweight designs that folded or could be easily disassembled for storage.

Son of the architect P. V. Jensen Klint, he was active as a painter before turning to the study of architecture with his father and the Danish architect Carl Petersen; he collaborated with the latter on furnishings for the Fåborg Museum (1914). Other early work was also done as commissions for furnishing museums, including Copenhagen's Thorvaldsen Museum (1922–25) and Danske Kunstindustrimuseum (1924–54). Klint's influence was strongly felt through his courses as a lecturer in furniture at the Kongelige Danske Kunstakademi (Royal Danish Academy of Fine Arts) in Copenhagen beginning in 1924, where with his students he carried on his ergonomic research. He also designed and manufactured paper lamps in a family cottage industry (no. 191).

References: Sigvard Bernadotte, ed., *Moderne dansk Boligkunst*, vol. 1 (Odense, Denmark, 1946), pp. 147–55, 204; Arne Karlsen, *Made in Denmark* (New York, 1960), pp. 126–29; Erik Zahle, ed., *Scandinavian Domestic Design* (London, 1963), pp. 10–11, 92, 112, 114, 116, 124, 280; Svend Hansen, "Le Klint," *Mobilia* 206 (1972): n.p.

ARCHIBALD KNOX
English, 1864–1933

Born and educated on the Isle of Man, Archibald Knox introduced "Celtic" ornament into the vocabulary of English design at the turn of the century, ornament that he promoted through his writings and through the metal-wares he designed for Liberty and Company in London. Knox's stylized interlacing patterns provided an alternative to the art nouveau and Jugendstil decorations that Liberty's continental competitors were selling at the time with great success. The two important ranges of Celtic-inspired designs with which Knox was chiefly involved were Liberty's Cymric silverwares (no. 30) and Tudric pewter (1901), examples of which were shown in the Arts and Crafts Society exhibitions in London in 1899 and 1903. Knox lived periodically in London, first between 1897 and 1900, when he taught at the Redhill School of Art and later served as head of the design department at the art school at Kingston-upon-Thames, and then between 1904 and 1912, when he taught again at Kingston and concurrently at Wimbledon Art School. In 1912–13 Knox traveled to the United States, where he taught briefly in Philadelphia, but returned to live on the Isle of Man.

Reference: A. J. Tilbrook, *The Designs of Archibald Knox for Liberty & Co.* (London, 1976).

OSKAR KOGOJ
Yugoslavian, born 1942

Oskar Kogoj, a designer of graphics and ergonomic products, studied industrial design at the University of Venice, graduating in 1966. One of his early works, a plastic wagon-toy that he called *Red Object*, won an international competition in 1969 for the design of children's products; the competition was cosponsored by *Abitare* magazine and by the Baby Mark Studio in Milan, for whom he provided subsequent designs. Kogoj has worked as an independent designer since 1971, specializing in designs for children—wooden and plastic toys, furniture, and tableware, all conceived to widen physical awareness and develop motor and sensory skills. These projects have also had applications to a broader range of design problems. His curved and channeled utensils for babies, for instance, led to a rethinking of contemporary eating habits that resulted in a revolutionary design for adult cutlery, which has been made in plastic and silver (no. 332). Kogoj has concentrated on the use of plastics in sculptural forms, and his *Gondola* easy chairs, with a seating shell derived from the impression of the human body at rest, shows his continuing interest in relating design to comfortable use.

References: Moderna Galerija, Ljubljana, *Oblikovalec Oskar Kogoj* (1972); "Design in Action," *Industrial Design* 19 (October 1972): 60–61; Scot Haller, "Child Care," *Industrial Design* 24 (May 1977): 49–51.

JURRIAAN JURRIAAN KOK
Dutch, 1861–1919

Jurriaan Jurriaan Kok was general director of the Rozenburg porcelain factory in The Hague from 1895 to 1913, introducing in 1899 the "egg shell" porcelain for which the factory became best known and for which it received critical acclaim and commercial success. Kok was trained as an architect at the polytechnical school in Delft, and afterwards worked in The Hague in the office of the architect D. P. van Ameijden van Duym, who had occasionally done work for the Rozenburg factory. Through him, Kok was appointed artistic adviser to Rozenburg in either 1893 or 1894 and named its acting director in 1894. In 1900 the firm was granted the title "royal" and its name was changed from the N.V. Haagsche Plateel-bakkerij Rozenburg to Koninklijke Porselein-en Aardewerkfabriek Rozenburg. Kok himself designed most of the highly unconventional attenuated and angular forms that identified the firm with international art nouveau (no. 12). After his retirement from Rozenburg in 1913, he served as commissioner of public works in The Hague until his death.

Reference: Haags Gemeentemuseum, The Hague, *Rozenburg 1883–1917: Geschiedenis van een Haagse fabriek* (1983), p. 27 et passim.

HENNING KOPPEL
Danish, 1918–1981

The first artist to join the design staff of Georg Jensen after World War II, Henning Koppel studied sculpture at the Kongelige Danske Kunstakademi (Royal Danish Academy of Fine Arts) in Copenhagen (1936–37) and at the Académie Ranson in Paris (1938–39). In Sweden during the war, he worked for Orrefors and designed bracelets on commission for the Svenskt Tenn store in Stockholm, which he continued to do for Jensen on his return to Denmark in 1945. The silver hollowware he designed from 1948 (no. 217) and his flatware, notably the *Caravel* service of 1957, brought a new, expressive style to the Jensen line. His later work for the firm included stainless steel utensils, wristwatches (1978), and a group of coordinated measuring devices in lacquered metal marketed as a weather station (1980). Koppel also worked as a ceramics designer for Bing & Grøndahl (from 1961), creating the sculptural white *Form 24* service (1962) as well as dishes and vases with freely painted decoration. He also designed glass for Orrefors (from 1971), graphics (including Danish postage stamps), and furniture. Koppel won the Lunning Prize in 1953, gold medals at the *Triennale* exhibition in Milan in 1951, 1954, and 1957, and the International

Design Award from the American Institute of Interior Designers in 1963.

References: Esbjørn Hiort, *Modern Danish Silver* (New York, 1954), pp. 12, 96–101; Arne Karlsen, *Made in Denmark* (New York, 1960), pp. 38–43, 141, 150, 152; Renwick Gallery, National Collection of Fine Arts, Washington, D.C., *Georg Jensen—Silversmithy: 77 Artists 75 Years* (February 29–July 6, 1980), pp. 18–19, nos. 88–97; Kunstindustrimuseet, Copenhagen, *Henning Koppel: A Commemorative Exhibition* (May 27–August 22, 1982); Nationalmuseum, Stockholm, *The Lunning Prize* (1986), pp. 54–57.

SHIRO KURAMATA
Japanese, 1934–1991

One of the most daringly original interior and furniture designers of the 1980s, Shiro Kuramata used industrial materials—steel mesh, corrugated aluminum, steel cables, and glass—to create unexpected effects, often those of transparency and dematerialization. Kuramata was given traditional training in the woodcraft department of the Tokyo Municipal Polytechnic High School and worked in the furniture factory of Teikokukizai in 1953. After studying interior design at the Kuwasawa Design Institute (1956), he worked first for San-Ai (from 1957) and then in the interior design department of Matsuya department store (1964) before opening his own design office in Tokyo in 1965. Kuramata's earliest manufactured furniture designs, Furniture with Drawers (1967), fitted drawers unexpectedly in and around otherwise conventional forms and stacked them in tall pyramids on wheels (1968). By 1970 he was designing furniture in boldly irregular forms (no. 335) and from the mid-1970s he was using materials in contexts that subverted their meanings. His work included a glass table with bullet-shaped rubber legs (1976); illuminated acrylic shelves that appeared to float (1978); the *Homage to Hoffmann* chair (1985), made of steel rods embracing the ghost-space of a burnt-out wooden core; the *North Latitude* table (1985), apparently precariously supported on cone-shaped steel-mesh legs; and the *How High the Moon* chair, constructed entirely of airy steel mesh (1986; no. 392). From his Club Judd nightclub in Tokyo (1969), with walls of overlapping stainless steel pipes, to the series of boutiques he created for the fashion designer Issey Miyake in Tokyo, Paris, and New York (most notably Issey Miyake Men, with steel mesh columns, in the Seibu department store, Tokyo; 1987), Kuramata's interior spaces were as experimental and novel as his furniture.

References: Shiro Kuramata, Itsuko Hasegawa, and Minoru Ueda, "A Talk on Materials," *Axis* 23 (spring 1987): 6–8; Chee Pearlman, "Shiro Kuramata," *Industrial Design* 35 (September–October 1988): 31–33; *Shiro Kuramata 1967–1987* (Tokyo, 1988).

RENÉ LALIQUE
French, 1860–1945

A celebrated designer of extravagant art nouveau jewelry at the turn of the century, René Lalique had a second career as a designer of production glass. Lalique trained as a jeweler by apprenticing to the Parisian silversmith Louis Aucoc, studying at the Ecole des Arts Décoratifs (1876–78), and then, between 1878 and 1880, at Sydenham College in London. After his return to France he supplied models for jewelry to leading Parisian firms while studying sculpture, and in 1885 took over the business of the jeweler Jules Destape, which he had managed the previous year. Lalique established his own exquisite style, introducing new combinations of materials, adding silver and even base metals to the customary gold, and using ivory, a variety of stones, and enameling, in addition to diamonds. He exhibited his work at the salons from 1894, with Siegfried Bing at L'Art Nouveau, at the *Exposition Universelle* of 1900 in Paris, and in 1905 at Agnew's in London, the last major showing of his jewelry. Having experimented with glass, primarily for sculptural pieces, in a workshop he established in 1902, Lalique was commissioned around 1908 to supply perfume bottles to François Coty, with such success that he had to purchase a factory to produce bottles for Coty and other perfumers as well. After World War I, Lalique opened a second factory, in Wingen-sur-Moder, France, where he manufactured a range of decorative objects of a fine-quality "demi-crystal" primarily by industrial molding techniques. He produced vases (no. 111), bowls, tablewares, lamps, statuettes, and jewelry, using both abstract and figurative styles, with some 1,500 different designs being listed in his 1932 catalog. At the *Exposition Internationale des Arts Décoratifs* in Paris in 1925, where he served as president of the jury for the glass section, Lalique provided a dining room for the Sèvres pavilion and a monumental glass fountain, and also had his own pavilion. His firm supplied glass panels and chandeliers for the *Normandie* ocean liner (1932). Lalique was given a retrospective exhibition at the Musée des Arts Décoratifs in Paris in 1933.

References: Christopher Vane Percy, *The Glass of Lalique: A Collector's Guide* (New York, 1977); Victor Arwas, *Glass: Art Nouveau to Art Deco* (New York, 1977), pp. 121–32; Museum Bellerive, Zurich, *René Lalique: Schmuck und Glas aus Paris vom Art Nouveau zum Art Déco* (May 25–August 13, 1978); Félix Marcilhac, *René Lalique 1860–1945, maître-verrier: Analyse de l'oeuvre et catalogue raisonné* (Paris, 1989); Musée des Arts Décoratifs, Paris, *René Lalique: Jewelry, Glass* (October 22, 1991–March 8, 1992).

JACK LENOR LARSEN
American, born 1927

Since establishing the firm that bears his name in 1952, Jack Lenor Larsen has been a teacher and writer as well as the world's most influential commercial textile designer, known for the technical ingenuity of his designs and his ability to adapt traditional handwoven styles and processes to mass production. His innovations include printed velvet upholstery fabrics (1959), stretch upholstery (1961), and the development of warp-knit casements (most notably his *Interplay*, a Saran monofilament of 1960; no. 275). Trained at the University of Washington in Seattle, where he first studied weaving under Ed Rossbach (1945–49) and at the Cranbrook Academy of Art, Bloomfield Hills, Michigan, under Marianne Strengell (1950–51), Larsen moved to New York in 1951. In 1952 he received his first major architectural commission in the form of draperies for New York's Lever House, which was followed by fabric wall panels for Louis Kahn's First Unitarian Church of Rochester, New York (1966); theater curtains for the Filene Center for the Performing Arts, Wolf Trap Farm Park, Vienna, Virginia (1971), and the Phoenix (Arizona) Civic Plaza concert hall (1970; no. 328); and silk hangings for the Sears Bank & Trust Company, Sears Tower, Chicago (1974). In 1958 he established the Larsen Design Studio to develop new materials and processes and to expand the firm's operation as fabric consultants and designers. That year he designed upholstery fabrics for Pan American Airlines, as he did again in 1969 and 1972–78, and for Braniff Airlines (1969). By the late 1960s his firm had branches in Zurich, Stuttgart, and Paris. To diversify its product line Larsen established Larsen Carpet and Larsen Leather in 1973 followed by Larsen Furniture in 1976. He has also designed linens for J. P. Stevens (1965), porcelain tablewares for Dansk International (1980), upholstery collections for Cassina and Vescom (1982), and seating for I. M. Pei's Myerson Symphony Center, Dallas (1989). Larsen's many distinctions range from a gold medal at the *XIII Triennale* in Milan in 1964 to nomination as honorary Royal Designer for Industry in 1983.

References: Larry Salmon, "Jack Lenor Larsen in Boston," *Craft Horizons* 23 (April 1971): 14–23; Mildred Constantine, "Jack Lenor Larsen: The First 25 Years," *American Fabrics and Fashions* (special issue) 113 (summer 1978); Musée des Arts Décoratifs, Paris, *Jack Lenor Larsen: Thirty Years of Creative Textiles* (September 24–December 28, 1981); Robert Judson Clark et al., *Design in America: The Cranbrook Vision, 1925–1950* (New York, 1983), pp. 205–11, 270–71.

LE CORBUSIER (CHARLES EDOUARD JEANNERET)
Swiss, later French, 1887–1965

Le Corbusier was one of the most influential architects of the twentieth century, a man whose achievements in architecture and urban planning, furniture design, painting, and sculpture, as well as his writings, continue to inspire and provoke decades after his death. A key figure in the development of the International Style in the 1920s, Le Corbusier championed the forms of modern industrialization—materials technology, standardization, and rationalization—and sought universal ordered solutions in their application. Charles Edouard Jeanneret was not trained as

an architect, but in 1908 he worked in Paris for the French architect Auguste Perret, from whom he learned the value of the reinforced concrete frame; in 1910 he worked in Berlin for PETER BEHRENS, who was then designing products for mass production and buildings for the AEG and who was closely connected to the Deutscher Werkbund. Jeanneret wrote about his German experiences in *Etude du mouvement d'art décoratif en Allemagne* (*Study of the Decorative Arts in Germany*, 1912) and admired the numerous attempts he saw to improve the quality of the German national product through educational programs and the application of design to industry. In 1917 he moved to Paris, and with Amédée Ozenfant published the manifesto *Après le cubisme*; he also painted Purist still-life pictures of mass-produced objects in simplified, generalized forms. He took the name of Le Corbusier in 1920 and, with Ozenfant, founded the magazine *L'Esprit Nouveau*. In the essays he published there, Le Corbusier laid down the critical theories that were developed in his four seminal books, *Vers une architecture* (*Towards a New Architecture*, 1923) *Urbanisme* (1924), *L'Art décoratif d'aujourdhui* (*The Decorative Art of Today*, 1925), and *L'Almanach d'architecture moderne* (*Almanac of Modern Architecture*, 1925). Le Corbusier set up an architectural office in partnership with his cousin PIERRE JEANNERET in 1922, chiefly designing private houses, which, like the Villa Savoye at Poissy (1928–30), fulfilled the ideas and images set out in his books. Defining and arranging these buildings like the geometrical shapes in his paintings and drawing inspiration from engineering functionalism, he developed the idea of the mass-produced "machine for living" that would be formally analogous to ocean liners, automobiles, and other machines of the period and demonstrated it in his Pavillon de l'Esprit Nouveau at the 1925 international exhibition in Paris. This standardized dwelling unit was furnished with ready-made mass-produced furniture (Thonet bentwood chairs) and prototype standardized fittings. In collaboration with CHARLOTTE PERRIAND, who joined the office in 1927, the partnership created a small group of tubular-steel-framed furniture (nos. 125, 131) that constituted his most important manufactured solution to the problem of furnishing his new technocratic interior. The furniture was first exhibited at the Salon d'Automne of 1929 under the title "interior equipment of a dwelling" and was used by Le Corbusier and Jeanneret to furnish the villa for the Church family at Ville d'Avray the same year. While the furniture was in theory inspired by ideas of mass production and mass market, it was highly uneconomical and ultimately produced in only very limited quantities.

From the early 1930s, Le Corbusier grew increasingly involved with great public projects and international town planning studies, from the Palace of Soviets competition design, Moscow (1931–32), and urban planning for Algiers (from 1932) to the Unité d'Habitation public housing in Marseilles (1945–52) and the plan and design of Chandigarh, the new state capital of the Punjab (1951–64). In his later work Le Corbusier broke with the purist-machinist vision with which he is most commonly associated and developed a richly expressive formal vocabulary that incorporated vernacular and regional elements.

References: Willi Boesiger, ed., *Le Corbusier et Pierre Jeanneret: Oeuvre complète*, 8 vols. (Zurich, 1930–69); Renato De Fusco, *Le Corbusier, Designer: Furniture, 1929* (Woodbury, N.Y., 1977); Darlene Brady, *Le Corbusier: An Annotated Bibliography* (New York, 1985); Hayward Gallery, London, *Le Corbusier: Architect of the Century* (March 5–June 7, 1987); *Le Corbusier: Une encyclopédie* (Paris, 1987).

PIERRE LEGRAIN
French, 1889–1929

Perhaps best known for his African-inspired furniture created in the 1920s (no. 86), Pierre Legrain was also a pre-eminent designer of bookbindings and of furnishings in a progressive mode. A student at the Ecole des Arts Appliqués Germain Pilon in Paris, Legrain contributed satirical drawings to the publications of PAUL IRIBE and collaborated as well with him on interior decoration, including the furnishing of the apartment of the couturier Jacques Doucet in 1912–13. From 1917 to 1919 Legrain worked again for Doucet, designing contemporary bookbindings for over three hundred manuscripts and first editions in his collection (the projects carried out by several binders, including René Kieffer). He would continue this work for other bibliophiles and exhibited the designs regularly in the salons. During the 1920s Legrain concentrated on furnishings for Doucet and others, designing in the African style or in solid, lacquered forms. (After World War I and Iribe's departure for America, Doucet depended on Legrain to oversee the decoration of his new apartment in 1919 and the studio he constructed between 1926 and 1929.) Legrain also worked in metal and glass, leather, vellum, and sharkskin. He joined with PIERRE CHAREAU, JEAN PUIFORCAT, Dominique, and the jeweler Raymond Templier in the Group des Cinq, which cooperated on interior designs and furnishings.

References: Lynne Thornton, "Negro Art and the Furniture of Pierre-Emile Legrain," *Connoisseur* 181 (November 1972): 166–69; Philippe Garner, "Pierre Legrain—Decorateur," *Connoisseur* 189 (June 1975): 130–37.

LEONARDI–STAGI, ARCHITETTI
Established Modena, Italy, 1962

The studio of Cesari Leonardi and Franca Stagi, architecture graduates from the University of Florence (1970) and the Politecnico of Milan (1962) respectively, has engaged in both architectural projects and product design. Their architectural practice has included urban planning and the creation of parks, schools, swimming pools, and sports facilities in the region of Modena, as well as the restoration of historical structures. Their major design activity has been in the field of furniture, for Bernini and Fiarm and most notably their rocking chair for Elco (no. 311). They have also designed lamps (for Lumenform) and plastics (for Elco).

References: "In laboratorio: Dal disegno al pezzo finito," *Casa Arredamento Giardino* 19 (November 1969): 57–59; Whitechapel Art Gallery, London, *Modern Chairs, 1918–1970* (July 22–August 30, 1970), no. 119.

EMILE LETTRÉ
German, 1876–1954

Emile Lettré's career spanned the transition in German design from manufacture by hand to high-quality mass production. Apprenticed as a goldsmith in Hanau, Lettré left in 1896 to study in Vienna, and after extensive traveling, worked in Paris between 1898 and 1900. Financed by the French jewelry firm Schurmann, Lettré opened his own shop in Berlin in 1900. His most important early commission was table silver made for presentation by the cities of Prussia to the Prussian crown prince and princess, Friedrich Wilhelm and Cäcilie, as a wedding gift in 1905. Over the years from his shop in Berlin, Lettré supplied silver and jewelry to German aristocrats and officials. Ironically, it is less for his typical handmade luxury wares than for a simple, straight-edged table service designed for production by the Bruckmann firm in Heilbronn (no. 138) that Lettré is best remembered today. His shop, with its archives, models, and designs, was destroyed during World War II.

Reference: Museen der Stadt Köln, Kunstgewerbemuseum, Cologne, *Emile Lettré—Andreas Moritz: Zwei deutsche Silberschmiede im 20. Jahrhundert* (December 10, 1976–February 13, 1977).

DOROTHY LIEBES
American, 1899–1972

Just over a decade after Dorothy Liebes had opened her studio in 1930, *House and Garden* described her as "America's acknowledged leader in the field of hand-loomed fabrics."[24] Liebes had studied applied design at the University of California (1919–23), learning to weave during a summer at Hull House in Chicago. She worked in Paris with Paul Rodier in 1929 and the following year set up a studio in San Francisco, where she soon became known for custom fabrics woven in unusual techniques and materials (no. 223), textiles often designed for architects and decorators (including FRANK LLOYD WRIGHT and HENRY DREYFUSS). Liebes became involved with industrial production in 1940 when she was hired by Goodall Fabrics in Sanford, Maine, as a designer and stylist, working with the factory to adapt handwoven prototypes to the capabilities of the power loom. Liebes went on to work with numerous other factories, designing wallpaper (for United Wallpaper); furnishing fabrics using metallics and synthetics (the former for Dobeckmun, creators of Lurex, the latter for Du Pont); rugs (for Bigelow); and fabrics for apparel (for Jantzen and Jasco) and for automobiles (for the 1957 Plymouth *Fury*). She opened a second studio in New York in 1948 where she began to concentrate on production work, and in 1958 ended her hand weaving completely. Liebes then began to work for Du Pont, beginning a whole new area of experimentation, and her reputation as a colorist and handweaver was supplanted by her reputation as a pioneer in the use of synthetics.

References: Elizabeth McCausland, "Dorothy Liebes: Designer for Mass Production," *Magazine of Art* 40 (April 1947): 130–35; "Dorothy Wright Liebes, First Lady of the Loom," *Interiors* 106 (July 1947): 87–91, 134, 136; *Current Biography* (1948), s.v. "Liebes, Dorothy (Wright)"; Museum of Contemporary Crafts, New York, *Dorothy Liebes: Retrospective Exhibition* (March 20–May 10, 1970).

LIGHTOLIER
Established New York, 1904

Founded as a gaslight sales and supply shop in 1904 but soon selling electric light fixtures as well, the New York Gas Appliance Company started to manufacture lighting in 1919, the year after its name was changed to Lightolier. After World War II Lightolier expanded its market, supplementing residential designs with commercial and institutional lighting. The company's large design staff developed products in a clean style geared to architects, and Lightolier gained a reputation as a supplier of modern fixtures and new technology, including the first track lighting system, developed in 1963 (no. 284). Lightolier is now a major developer and manufacturer of lighting products for diverse applications, with numerous factories and thousands of employees.

References: "Lightolier Design Staff," *Industrial Design* 116 (June 1957): 108–13; *Industrial Design* 123 (December 1963): 52; *Lightolier: The First 75 Years* (New York, 1979).

VICKE LINDSTRAND
Swedish, 1904–1983

Vicke Lindstrand, a sculptor by training, was hired by Sweden's Orrefors glassworks in 1928, the result of its policy of relying on designers with backgrounds in the fine arts. Lindstrand introduced a thick, smooth, clear body to Orrefors glass, for which he provided robust designs for engraved decoration, most notably his *Pearl Diver* (1935; no. 169) and *Shark Killer* (1937) vases. He also worked in colored glass and on a monumental scale, creating glass sculpture and windows, and a fountain for the Swedish pavilion at the *New York World's Fair* in 1939. Lindstrand left Orrefors in 1940 to work for the Uppsala-Ekeby ceramics firm, and then in 1950 became director of design for the Kosta glassworks,

contributing designs for engraved glass in abstract and figurative patterns.

References: Philip Gustafson, "The Glassmakers of Småland Woods," *Arts & Decoration* 50 (June 1939): 16–17, 47; Helmut Ricke and Ulrich Gronert, eds., *Glas in Schweden, 1915–1960* (Munich, 1987), passim.

EL LISSITZKY
Russian, 1890–1941

A pioneer of modern typography, graphic design, and abstract painting, El Lissitzky was also an innovative exhibition designer and architect. From 1909 to 1914 he studied architecture in Darmstadt, Germany, but at the outbreak of World War I he returned to Moscow, graduating as an engineer-architect in 1918 from the Riga Polytechnic Institute (then in Moscow) and also exhibiting paintings on Jewish themes and providing cover designs and illustrations for Yiddish publications. In 1919 as a teacher of graphic arts, printing, and architecture in Vitebsk, he met KAZIMIR MALEVICH, whose suprematist constructions most likely inspired his abstract graphics (no. 82) and architectonic designs, which he called *prouns*. Between 1921 and 1925 Lissitzky traveled in Germany and Switzerland, where he introduced contemporary Soviet art and theory to the West through painting, graphics (including advertisements for Pelikan ink [no. 98] and a children's book, *Of Two Squares*), and exhibition spaces based on his *proun* theory, which he constructed in Berlin (1923), Dresden (1926), and Hanover (1927–28). In Moscow after 1925, Lissitzky was active in architecture and urban planning, notably a proposal to redesign and color-coordinate street signs in the Soviet capital, as well as exhibition design and graphics, in which he made inventive use of photomontage. For his furnishing designs he projected and analyzed a variety of standardized furniture—built-in, multipurpose, modular, mobile, and even disposable. In his Soviet trade exhibitions of the late 1920s he used constructivist techniques (photomontage, light, lettering, and movement) to create bold innovative presentations, just as he did with propaganda posters and magazine illustrations in the 1930s.

References: Christina Lodder, *Russian Constructivism* (New Haven, Conn., 1983), pp. 248–49 et passim; Harvard University Art Museums, Busch-Reisinger Museum, Cambridge, Mass., *El Lissitzky, 1890–1941* (September 26–November 29, 1987); Frank Lubbers, *El Lissitzky, 1890–1941* (New York, 1991).

RAYMOND LOEWY
American, born France, 1893–1986

Raymond Loewy was the best known and the most flamboyant of those who in the 1930s created the profession of industrial designer in the United States and through his work and prolific writing he also did the most to promote the new field. An engineering graduate, Loewy came from

France to America in 1919, where he supported himself in the world of fashion by creating illustrations and advertisements for various department stores and for *Vogue, Harper's Bazaar, Vanity Fair,* and other magazines. His breakthrough came in 1929 when he was able to mock up, within a week, a redesign for the Gestetner company's mimeograph machine, a successful sheathing of its mechanism in a clean, sculptural form. "Industrial design was being born," he wrote in his book *Never Leave Well Enough Alone,* "and I worked on it frantically."[25] Later he called his process of streamlining, or enveloping the inner workings of products with sleek designs, the "self-expression of the machine."[26] Loewy sometimes sunk large amounts of his own money into his projects, as he did to get the Hupmobile contract in 1931 by constructing a full-scale working model of his design, which won prizes in automobile competitions across the world. His streamlined equipment for the Pennsylvania Railroad, steamship lines, and airline companies, along with those of HENRY DREYFUSS and Otto Kuhler, changed the face of American transportation in the 1930s. In 1944, with four other partners, he founded the firm of Raymond Loewy Associates (renamed Loewy/Snaith in 1961), and in 1952 he established the independent Compagnie de l'Esthétique Industrielle (CEI) in Paris, an important stimulus to industrial design in France. While he was sometimes criticized for excessive styling, the *Coldspot Super Six* refrigerator he designed for Sears (no. 152), his redesign of the Lucky Strike cigarette package (no. 184), his Greyhound buses, and his Studebaker and Avanti automobiles became classics of the profession, and his creations have pervaded almost every aspect of American life (no. 197). Loewy's most satisfying achievement, according to his own reckoning, was the work he did for NASA on the interior design of the Saturn-Apollo Skylab project, a project that gave him responsibilities for the physical and psychological well-being of the astronauts (1968–73).

References: C.F.O. Clarke, "Raymond Loewy Associates: Modern American Industrial Designing," *Graphis* 2 (January–February, 1946): 94–97; David Pleydell-Bouverie and Alec Davis, "Popular Art Organised: The Manner and Methods of Raymond Loewy Associates," *Architectural Review* 110 (November 1951): 319–26; Don Wallance, *Shaping America's Products* (New York, 1956), pp. 47–50; Renwick Gallery, National Collection of Fine Arts, Washington, D.C., *The Designs of Raymond Loewy* (August 1–November 16, 1975); Angela Schonberger, ed., *Raymond Loewy: Pioneer of American Industrial Design* (Munich, 1990).

RAYMOND LOEWY ASSOCIATES, see RAYMOND LOEWY

CHARLES RENNIE MACKINTOSH
Scottish, 1868–1928

Architect and designer of interiors, furniture, and graphics, Charles Rennie Mackintosh led an independent modern movement in Glasgow at the turn of the century that soon became widely influential in Europe. The abstract style of rectilinear forms and geometrical motifs for which he is known was markedly different from the organic naturalism of continental art nouveau, although Mackintosh did occasionally use the stylized floral motifs and curves of that style, particularly in his early graphic designs (no. 9).

From 1884 to 1889 Mackintosh was apprenticed to an architect in Glasgow, John Hutchison. He joined the firm of Honeyman and Keppie in 1890, later winning the important competition for the new Glasgow School of Art building for his firm (1897). Mackintosh also studied at the Glasgow School of Art, where he met Herbert J. MacNair and the sisters Frances and Margaret Macdonald (the latter of whom he married in 1900). "The Four" formed a collaborative group of similar style, which was given its first public showing at the Arts and Crafts Exhibition Society in London in 1896. The same year, he received an independent commission to convert, decorate, and furnish the interiors of Miss Catherine Cranston's Argyle Street Tea Rooms. The high back dining chair with oval back rail that Mackintosh designed for the Tea Rooms was entirely original in its exaggerated proportions (no. 10) and was reused by the architect in several variations. Known to readers of the German magazine *Dekorative Kunst* from an article about The Four in 1898, Mackintosh became even better known in Europe when he and his three collaborators exhibited at the Eighth Secession exhibition in Vienna in 1900. His use of white in the interior of the display there, combined with the use of the square as a decorative motifs, profoundly influenced JOSEF HOFFMANN and other Viennese designers. (In 1901 an issue of the Secession magazine *Ver Sacrum* was entirely devoted to the work of the group.) In 1900 Mackintosh also began work on another of Miss Cranston's tea rooms, at Ingram Street, which included a white dining room. This was followed by a series of domestic commissions for chiefly Scottish clients—Windyhill at Kilmacolm (1900); Kingsborough Gardens, Glasgow (1901–2; no. 27); Hill House at Helensburgh (1903–4); and his last major residence, Hous' Hill at Nitshill (1904). Mackintosh also designed the most elegant of Miss Cranston's tea rooms, the Willow Tea Rooms (1903–4), and the library of the Glasgow School of Art (1907–11). In 1913 Mackintosh left the firm of Honeyman and Keppie in which he had become a partner in 1904, but did not succeed as an independent architect. From 1916 to 1919 he converted a house in Northampton for W. J. Bassett-Lowke (no. 65) but, unable to find further commissions for furniture, interiors, and buildings, he retired to the south of France in 1923.

References: Thomas Howarth, *Charles Rennie Mackintosh and the Modern Movement,* 2d ed. (London, 1977); Roger Billcliffe, *Charles Rennie Mackintosh: The Complete Furniture, Furniture Drawings and Interior Designs* (Guildford, England, 1979).

VICO MAGISTRETTI
Italian, born 1920

An architect by training, Vico Magistretti received his diploma from the Milan Politecnico in 1945 and studied under Ernesto Rogers at the Champ Universitaire Italien in Lausanne. He worked first in Switzerland with Alfred Roth and then in his father's design office in Milan. While his earliest independent commissions involved designing commercial interiors, he soon established a reputation as an architect as well as a product designer. Strongly rationalist in his approach, Magistretti has emphasized structure in every area of his practice. In the realm of products, for instance, early in his career he created a freestanding bookcase supported on iron poles and held in place by tension between floor and ceiling, a piece he showed at the exhibition of low-cost furnishings organized by the Riunione Italiana Mostre Arredamento (Italian Association for Exhibitions of Furnishings) in Milan in 1946. More recently he designed his *Sinbad* armchairs and sofas of 1981 for Cassina (no. 377) with skeletal structures separated from their minimal, blanketlike covers thrown over as upholstery. Like GIO PONTI, he has also sought inspiration in vernacular forms, as shown by his lacquered wooden chair with woven seat of 1964. Magistretti was one of the first Italian designers to use plastic for furniture (for Artemide), valuing it over wood for its greater possibilities for mechanized production. He has also designed lighting (for O-Luce), which displays the same rationalized approach as his furniture (no. 344).

References: D. A., "Given Four Walls and a Ceiling, Magistretti Props Up the Present amid the Past," *Interiors* 110 (December 1950): 86–92; *The International Design Yearbook*, vol. 1 (1985–86), pp. 15, 38, 93–94; vol. 2 (1986), pp. 36–37, 216; vol. 4 (1988), pp. 109, 218; vol. 5 (1990), p. 72; Vanni Pasca, *Vico Magistretti: Designer* (New York, 1991).

ERIK MAGNUSSEN
Danish, active also in the United States, 1884–1961

Eric Magnussen brought Danish craftsmanship to the American silverware industry. Like his compatriot GEORG JENSEN, Magnussen studied sculpture before becoming a silversmith and shortly after the turn of the century began to fashion jewelry with naturalistic motifs in an art nouveau style. He worked as a chaser in 1902 for the silversmith Viggo Hansen in Copenhagen and with Otto Rohloff in Berlin at the Kunstgewerbeschule from 1907 to 1909 before opening his own workshop in 1909. His silver was shown internationally, in exhibitions in Berlin (1910 and 1911), Paris (1922), and Rio de Janeiro (1922), among others. From 1925 to 1929, Magnussen was a designer for the Gorham Manufacturing Company in Providence, Rhode Island, creating silver hollowware services in both modernist (no. 128) and Danish styles that were unlike any of the company's traditional products. After leaving Gorham in 1929 he designed and executed

silver for the German firm of August Dingeldein and Son, which had a showroom in New York, and then worked in Chicago and, from 1932 to 1938, in Los Angeles. Magnussen returned to Denmark in 1939.

References: Charles H. Carpenter, Jr., *Gorham Silver, 1831–1981* (New York, 1982), pp. 256–64; Karen Davies, *At Home in Manhattan: Modern Decorative Arts, 1925 to the Depression* (New Haven, Conn., 1983), nos. 14–15.

LOUIS MAJORELLE
French, 1859–1926

Louis Majorelle was the leading designer of art nouveau furniture in France, with a large high-quality commercial production that continued until 1916 when his workshops in Nancy were destroyed during World War I. Trained as a painter at the Ecole des Beaux-Arts in Paris (1877–79), Majorelle was the son of a cabinetmaker and ceramist in Nancy, whose business he and his brother Jules inherited in 1879. The firm continued to produce furniture in historicizing styles until the mid-1890s, when Majorelle took up the "new" naturalist style of curving, decorative forms practiced by his compatriot EMILE GALLÉ and other craftsmen in Nancy. Inspired by the work of Gallé, who first exhibited furniture at the *Exposition Universelle* in Paris in 1889, Majorelle developed a similar decorative style of naturalistic pictorial marquetries, applying shaped pieces of wood in mosaic patterns of vegetation, flowers, insects, and animals, according to individual themes. At the Paris *Exposition Universelle* of 1900, he exhibited an impressive bedroom suite with orchid flowers and leaves created in amaranth, purpleheart, metal, and mother-of-pearl inlays, carved in relief and cast as gilt-bronze mounts (no. 14). Majorelle exhibited his work regularly in Paris at the salons of the Société des Artistes Français, the Société Nationale des Beaux-Arts, the Société des Artistes Décorateurs, and the Société du Salon d'Automne. After purchasing Siegfried Bing's celebrated Paris shop L'Art Nouveau in 1904, Majorelle began to establish a retail network and by 1910 had outlets in Nancy, Paris, Lille, and Lyons. After World War I, Majorelle rebuilt his ateliers in Nancy, but could not regain the market or reputation his firm had earlier enjoyed.

References: Yvonne Brunhammer et al., *Art Nouveau: Belgium France* (Houston, 1976), pp. 270–72, 484 et passim; Alastair Duncan, *Louis Majorelle: Master of Art Nouveau Design* (New York, 1991).

KAZIMIR MALEVICH
Russian, 1878–1935

Kazimir Malevich was one of the first nonfigurative artists of the twentieth century, deriving from analytical cubism and futurism a totally abstract, geometric language of forms that exploited strong colors and dynamic elements. Malevich studied at the art institute in Kiev (1895–96) and at the School for Painting, Sculpture, and Architecture in Moscow (1904–5). From 1907 he exhibited with various groups, including the Moscow Association of Artists (1907–9), whose participants included Natalya Goncharova and Wassily Kandinsky, and the Knave of Diamonds (1910–17). He joined the Union of Youth with Vladimir Tatlin in 1913, and designed stage sets and costumes for a cubo-futurist opera, "Victory over the Sun," which was performed for the St. Petersburg Union of Youth in December 1913. In 1915 at the futurist exhibition *0.10* in Petrograd, Malevich exhibited thirty-nine completely nonrepresentational paintings, which consisted of geometric forms in pure colors against a white background. These he described as the "supremacy of pure emotion," and called the style *suprematism*, "the new painterly realism." After the Revolution, Malevich taught at the Free State Art Studios in Petrograd and Moscow and from 1919 to 1922 at the art school in Vitebsk. In 1920 at Vitebsk he founded the UNOVIS group, a collective that included EL LISSITZKY, ILIA CHASHNIK, and Nikolai Suetin among its members. From 1922, when Malevich returned to Petrograd, until the late 1920s, he abandoned painting for urban and product design as well as architecture. In 1923 in collaboration with the Petrograd State Porcelain Factory, he and other UNOVIS members designed geometric forms and decorations for porcelains based on suprematist principles (no. 95). Malevich also taught at the Petrograd Academy of Arts and became a member of the State Institute of Artistic Culture, which he directed from 1923, and worked in a studio provided him in the Russian State Museum in Leningrad.

References: Stedelijk Museum, Amsterdam, *Kazimir Malevich, 1878–1935* (March 5, 1989–May 29, 1989); Christina Lodder, *Russian Constructivism* (New Haven, Conn., 1983), p. 251 et passim.

ROBERT MALLET-STEVENS
French, 1886–1945

A leader of the modernist school of French designers and architects during the 1920s, Robert Mallet-Stevens was a founder and the first president of the secessionist Union des Artistes Modernes, established in 1929. As an architect he was particularly interested in the relationship of interior furnishings to architectural spaces; his design was spare, geometric, and free of extraneous objects, employing modern materials like tubular steel, sheet metal, and concrete that were softened, however, by the use of paint, lacquer, leather, and fine woods.

Mallet-Stevens studied at the Ecole Speciale d'Architecture in Paris (where he himself later taught) and was acquainted early with the work of JOSEF HOFFMANN and his Palais Stocklet, which was being built for Mallet-Stevens's uncle in Brussels. Later he absorbed other influences from abroad—the architecture of Japan, of FRANK LLOYD WRIGHT (for whose work he wrote a foreword in the Dutch magazine *Wendingen* in 1925), and of the De Stijl group. Mallet-Stevens exhibited at the Salon

d'Automne before and after World War I; he was also involved in the 1925 Paris exposition, where he was responsible for the hall of the "French Embassy" exhibit, and the 1937 Paris *Exposition Internationale*, for which he designed five pavilions. Among his clients were supporters of avant-garde art, among them the vicomte Charles de Noailles (for whom he built a villa in the south of France; no. 103), the couturiers PAUL POIRET and Jacques Doucet, and Marcel Herbier, for whose futuristic film, *L'Inhumaine*, he provided the exterior settings.

References: Léon Deshairs, "Une Villa moderne à Hyères," *Art et Décoration* (July 1928): 1–24; *Rob Mallet-Stevens, Architecte* (Brussels, 1980); Pierre Kjellberg, *Art déco: Les maîtres du mobilier, le décor des paquebots* (Paris, 1986), pp. 120–22.

MAN RAY
American, active also in France, 1890–1976

One of this century's most important avant-garde artists, Man Ray was equally at ease as a painter, photographer, sculptor, and filmmaker, in New York, Paris, or Hollywood. He embraced a succession of modern styles but he must be counted primarily among the dada and surrealist artists.

Man Ray studied art in New York and then worked in publishing as a calligrapher and layout artist. Visits to Alfred Stieglitz's Gallery 291 and the New York Armory Show in 1913 put him firmly in the camp of European modernism, and his friendship with the painters Francis Picabia and Marcel Duchamp pushed him further into the enigmatic art of dada. In 1915 he taught himself photography; his later experiments with images he called "rayographs," made directly on the film without the aid of a lens (like the work of EL LISSITZKY, LÁSZLÓ MOHOLY-NAGY, and Christian Schad), were truly original contributions to the genre. He claimed to have invented this technique accidentally while printing fashion plates he took for PAUL POIRET in Paris, where he went in 1921. Photography helped Man Ray support himself during the 1920s and 30s, and his photographs of friends and fashionable society were illustrated first in *Charm* and then in *Harper's Bazaar*, *Vanity Fair*, and other fashion magazines. In the late 1930s, Man Ray was commissioned to design a poster for the London Passenger Transport Board (no. 174), most likely through his friendship with EDWARD MCKNIGHT KAUFFER.

References: Merry Foresta et al., *Perpetual Motif: The Art of Man Ray* (New York, 1988); Oliver Green, *Art for the London Underground: London Transport Posters, 1908 to the Present* (London, 1990), pp. 77, 142–43.

GERHARD MARCKS
German, 1889–1981

Director of the Bauhaus pottery workshop from 1919 to 1925, Gerhard Marcks was responsible for design at the

Dornburg an der Saale facility from the time it opened in 1920 until the Bauhaus moved to Dessau. Marcks had studied sculpture in Berlin with Richard Scheibe (1907), often using terracotta as his medium. He was one of several artists, including Scheibe and Georg Kolbe, who provided sculpture, paintings, and reliefs for the model factory and office building designed by WALTER GROPIUS for the Deutscher Werkbund exhibition in Cologne in 1914. Following military service in World War I, Marcks taught at the Kunstgewerbeschule in Berlin under Bruno Paul. After his years with Gropius at the Bauhaus, Marcks taught at the Kunstgewerbeschule at Burg Giebichenstein, becoming director of the school in 1930, but was dismissed in 1933 by the Nazis. Primarily a sculptor and graphic artist, Marcks also provided designs for the Staatliche Porzellanmanufaktur Berlin between 1929 and 1938, and in 1925 designed an exceptional glass coffee maker for the Jenaer Glaswerk Schott & Gen. in Jena, in the simple, spare, geometric style he practiced and taught (no. 93).

References: Wallraf-Richartz-Museum, Cologne, *Gerhard Marcks: Skulpturen und Zeichnungen* (April–May 1964); Hans M. Wingler, *The Bauhaus: Weimar, Dessau, Berlin, Chicago* (Cambridge, Mass., 1969), p. 249 et passim; Art Gallery of Ontario, Toronto, *50 Years Bauhaus* (December 6, 1969–February 1, 1970), p. 352; Margarete Jarchow, "Die Staatliche Porzellanmanufaktur Berlin (KPM), 1918–1938: Institution und Produktion," diss., Hamburg, 1984, p. 139.

ENZO MARI
Italian, born 1932

Enzo Mari is an artist and designer of impeccable refinement as well as a theoretician (his contribution to the environment section of the Italian design exhibition held at the Museum of Modern Art in New York in 1972 involved a philosophical "counterdesign" statement on art as communication). A graduate of the Accademia di Belle Arti di Brera in Milan (1956), Mari has worked as a painter and sculptor, and became a member of the Nuova Tendenza group of artists during the 1960s. Toys, games, and books for children have been a strong area of interest for him and in 1957 he created his first work for Danese, a wooden puzzle in the shape of sixteen interlocking animals; he continued with Danese as one of only a few designers asked to work for the firm. His objects in plastic, begun in 1964–65—small, technologically inventive containers for desk and table (no. 317)—helped define the aesthetic and the formal direction of the firm's production. Mari has also designed furniture (for Driade and Gavina), lamps (for Artemide), ceramics (for Gabbianelli), as well as books, posters, and other graphics.

References: Emilio Ambasz, ed., *Italy: The New Domestic Landscape* (New York, 1972), pp. 54, 76–77, 83, 89–91, 262–65; Ida Faré, "L'artigianato non esiste" [interview], *Modo* 56 (January–February 1983): 22–25; Arturo Carlo Quintavalle, *Enzo Mari* (Parma, 1983).

MAURICE MARINOT
French, 1882–1960

France's most original art-glass maker of the twentieth century, Maurice Marinot developed a modern abstract idiom within the tradition of his craft, inventing, like EMILE GALLÉ before him, novel decorative techniques that ranged from the use of freely ascending internal bubbles (no. 100) to unusually deep acid-etching and surface coatings of metallic oxide. Trained as a painter at the Ecole des Beaux-Arts in Paris (from 1901), Marinot continued to paint throughout his career. He took up glassmaking in 1911 in Troyes through the offices of his friends, the brothers Viard, who operated a glasshouse at Bar-sur-Seine. Marinot began by decorating glass with colored enamels, which he showed in the celebrated *Maison Cubiste* at the Salon d'Automne of 1912. From about 1919 to 1927, he learned to blow his own glass and decorate it in a variety of other techniques, but then abandoned cold forms of decoration, working the hot glass in a malleable state at the furnace like sculpture, with only a few simple tools. Between 1912 and 1935, Marinot exhibited his glass at the salons of the Société des Artistes-Décorateurs. In 1925 he was named a member of the Conseil des Manufactures Nationales et des Arts Appliqués à l'Industrie, and in 1932 he received the cross of the chevalier of the Legion of Honor.

References: R. J. Charleston, "The Glass of Maurice Marinot," *Victoria and Albert Museum Bulletin* 1 (July 1965): 1–8; Musée de l'Orangerie, Paris, *Maurice Marinot: Peintre et verrier* (February 27–May 21, 1990).

JAVIER MARISCAL
Spanish, born 1950

A leader in Spanish design since the 1980s, Javier Mariscal created the whimsical canine symbol and the signage program for the 1992 Olympics in Barcelona, where he had opened his first design studio in 1976. Mariscal studied graphic design at the Escuela de Grafismo Elisava in Barcelona (1971–73). As a member of the group El Rrollo Enmascarado (Masked Tedium), he gained a reputation for his underground comics that brought him commissions for printed textiles (for Marieta, 1978–83) and the interior decoration of bars in Barcelona (Merbeyé, with Fernando Amat, 1978) and Valencia (Duplex, with Fernando Salas, 1981). For the last, Mariscal designed a barstool produced by B D Ediciones de Diseño with wobbly, inebriated, asymmetrical legs in colored metal—a three-dimensional translation of his irreverent cartoons and an approach that has since characterized his product designs from ceramics (for Porcelanas del Bidasoa) to lighting fixtures (no. 380). Mariscal was invited by ETTORE SOTTSASS, JR., to participate in the Memphis exhibition of 1981, for which he created his metal and glass *Hilton* trolley in collaboration with the industrial designer PEPE CORTÉS, bringing him an international audience in addition to his already considerable following in Spain. In 1988

Mariscal moved and enlarged his studio to accommodate work on the Olympic graphic identity program and for the major Olympic sponsors, IBM, Xerox, Coca-Cola, and Kodak. He also took on a series of interior projects created in collaboration with the architect Alfredo Arribas, including a children's room in Barcelona's science museum (1989) and the nightclub Las Torres de Avila (1990).

References: Michael Collins and Andreas Papadakis, *Post-Modern Design* (New York, 1989), p. 245; Colin Naylor, ed., *Contemporary Designers,* 2d ed. (Chicago, 1990), pp. 368, 370; Guy Julier, *New Spanish Design* (New York, 1991), p. 181 et passim; Emma Dent Coad, *Javier Mariscal: Designing the New Spain* (New York, 1991).

ENID MARX
English, born 1902

Enid Marx came to fabric design through her interest in wood engraving and is as well recognized for her graphic work as for her textiles. A student at the Central School of Arts and Crafts in London in 1921 and the Royal College of Art from 1922 to 1925, she apprenticed to the textile printers Phyllis Barron and Dorothy Larcher in Hampstead in 1925, and within a few years had her own studio and shop where she made and sold hand block-printed textiles. During the later 1930s she also supplied designs for lively printed linens, organdies, and velvets to Dunbar Hay and for plush upholstery fabrics commissioned by the London Passenger Transport Board for passenger seating. During World War II, Marx became the primary supplier of designs for civilian furnishing fabrics under the design panel of the ADVISORY COMMITTEE ON UTILITY FURNITURE (no. 188), of which she was a member from 1944 to 1947. After the war she concentrated on graphic work (book jackets for Penguin, stamp designs for the accession of Elizabeth II and for Christmas 1976), and wrote and illustrated children's books as well. But she also supplied fabric designs for Morton Sundour and for the Royal Pavilion of the Festival of Britain in 1951. As a collector of popular arts and through her books, especially *English Popular Art*, written with Margaret Lambert (1951), she did much to heighten the awareness of Britain's folk traditions. Marx was named a Royal Designer for Industry in 1945.

References: Geffrye Museum, London, *CC 41: Utility Furniture and Fashion, 1941–1951* (September 24–December 29, 1974), pp. 30–31; Jacqueline Herald, "A Portrait of Enid Marx," *Crafts* 40 (September 1979): 17–21; Camden Arts Centre, London, *Enid Marx* (October 3–November 25, 1979); Cynthia Weaver, "Enid Marx: Designing Fabrics for the London Passenger Transport Board in the 1930s," *Journal of Design History* 2 (1989): 35–46.

BRUNO MATHSSON
Swedish, 1907–1988

Sweden's best known furniture designer for over half a century, Bruno Mathsson applied functionalist principles to organic design, responding as did ALVAR AALTO to regional demands of purpose, place, culture, and materials. Mathsson apprenticed as a cabinetmaker in his family's workshop, but went beyond their traditional methods to new modes of design derived from physiological research on the comfort of sitting. His research led to the use of bent and laminated wood and woven webbing, which he felt gave the proper support that was dictated by the shape of his chairs (no. 159). Mathsson's chairs were first shown at the Gothenburg Museum in 1936, where his innovative designs met with critical acclaim but no offers of manufacture. Instead he decided to produce the furniture himself in his family shop, establishing a system of quality production and economical distribution by direct sales to customers. Mathsson's other work included beds, tables, and shelving systems of bentwood, and in the 1960s he created furniture of other materials including tubular metal, for other manufacturers as well as his own firm (no. 291).

References: *Design Quarterly* (special issue) 65 (1966); Derek E. Ostergard, ed., *Bent Wood and Metal Furniture* (New York, 1987), pp. 323–24.

ROBERTO SEBASTIAN MATTA
French, born Chile, 1911

Roberto Matta received a degree in architecture from the University of Chile in 1931 and worked in France from 1934 to 1935 in the office of LE CORBUSIER. Deciding to follow his earlier ambition to be a painter, he met and became closely associated with the surrealists, although his later work took an independent course into mechanistic and fantastic imagery. In the 1960s he was one of a number of artists and architects invited by the founder of the Gavina firm to create innovative designs for furniture, at which time he produced his puzzlelike *Malitte* foam-cushion seating system, which was named after his wife (no. 310). In 1970 he returned to design with his *MAgriTTA* lounge chair (for Simon International through Domus Locus), which paid tribute to his friend the painter René Magritte both in its portmanteau name and in its Pop imagery. Borrowing two of the artist's well-known recurring motifs, Matta created a black fiberglass bowler-hat chair with an inset green foam-rubber apple seat.

References: *Progressive Architecture* 56 (February 1975): 84; Eric Larrabee and Massimo Vignelli, *Knoll Design* (New York, 1981), pp. 172, 176, 178–79.

HERBERT MATTER
Swiss, later American, 1907–1984

Herbert Matter was a pioneer in the use of photography for advertising, producing heightened imagery through the technique of photomontage and combining it with color and his own version of the spare Swiss typography. Most notable were the series of travel posters he created for the Swiss national tourist office in 1932–36 (no. 166) as well as the posters and advertisements he conceived as design consultant for Knoll (along with its logo) over a period of two decades, from 1946 to 1966.

Matter studied painting at the Ecole des Beaux-Arts in Geneva (1925–27) and at the Académie Moderne in Paris (1928–29). Afterwards he worked for the design firm Deberny et Peignot (1929–32), where he collaborated on posters with A. M. CASSANDRE and on architecture and exhibition display with LE CORBUSIER. He returned to Switzerland in 1932 when he began his work for the Swiss tourist office. Matter immigrated to America in 1936, working first as a freelance photographer for *Vogue, Harper's Bazaar,* and other magazines, and between 1946 and 1957 as staff photographer for Condé Nast Publications. He also designed exhibitions, for the *New York World's Fair* in 1939 and for the Museum of Modern Art in New York, for whom he also did typography and book design. Matter was a professor of photography at Yale University from 1952 to 1982.

References: A & A Gallery, School of Art, Yale University, New Haven, Conn., *Herbert Matter: A Retrospective* (January 16–February 3, 1978); Eric Larrabee and Massimo Vignelli, *Knoll Design* (New York, 1981), pp. 108–17; Martin Eidelberg, ed., *Design 1935–1965: What Modern Was* (Montreal, 1991), pp. 44, 226, 386–87.

INGO MAURER
German, born 1932

Ingo Maurer has been one of the most innovative lighting designers in recent years, particularly with his remarkable *YaYaHo* system of low-voltage cables and small suspended halogen light sources, developed over a three-year period between 1981 and 1984 and produced from 1985 (no. 375). Trained as a typographer in Germany and Switzerland (1954–58), Maurer worked as a freelance designer in New York and San Francisco (1960–63) before establishing his "Design M" office in Munich in 1966. The first lamps produced by the firm borrowed ideas from Pop culture, the oversize *Bulb Clear* (1966) encasing an ordinary incandescent bulb within another bulb of giant proportions. Maurer is typically interested in engaging and amusing users while involving them in the design process, as revealed by the touch-sensitive *Grasl Vulgaris* lamp of 1973, the *Ilò Ilù* lamp of 1986, and the *YaYaHo*'s component elements, which can be purchased separately and installed at will. As they did in the *YaYaHo*, Maurer and "Design M" have adopted new technologies, including a miniaturized electronic transformer for the operation of *Ilò Ilù*. Maurer has also applied his inventive fantasy to lighting installations, including one in the Munich airport (1991–92).

References: Ingo Maurer, "L'Abat-Jour cauchemar de Thomas Edison," in Centre de Création Industrielle and Agence pour la Promotion de la Création Industrielle, Paris, *Lumières, je pense à vous* (June 3–August 5, 1985), pp. 54–55; Valeria Cosmelli, "Ingo Maurer: Punto, linea, forza e luce," *Domus* 685 (July–August 1987): 53–57; Helmut Bauer, ed., *Ingo Maurer: Making Light* (Munich, 1992).

PAUL McCOBB
American, 1917–1969

Paul McCobb created a mass market in the United States for clean, modern furnishings through his durable, economical component-furniture groups, which were sold in department stores throughout the country during the 1950s and shown as well at the "Good Design" exhibitions in New York and Chicago. As was done with RUSSEL WRIGHT's *Modern Living* ensembles, McCobb's name was widely advertised in conjunction with the sample rooms for these stores, which presented modular groups, wall systems (called "living walls"), and room dividers and were furnished and fully accessorized with his own designs—ceramics, metalware, fabrics, and low, light-wood furniture with trim foam cushions. McCobb's work was admired equally by professionals, for he achieved unified furniture systems that were meant to endure and were designed specifically for mass production and mass marketing. A student of painting who had worked as a department-store display and interior designer and a plastics engineer before forming his own industrial design company in 1945, he later joined with a partner, B. G. Mesberg, to launch his Planner Group (no. 213) in 1949, which became the best selling contemporary furniture in America during the next decade. Several other component groups followed—Directional, Predictor, Linear, and Perimeter—based on similar concepts but manufactured with costlier materials for an upscale market.

References: O.G., "McCobb's Predictor," *Interiors* 111 (October 1951), pp. 126–29; George Nelson, ed., *Storage* (New York, 1954), pp. 32, 48, 60, 62, 67, 76, 92; *Current Biography* (1958), s.v. "McCobb, Paul (Winthrop)"; Jay Doblin, *One Hundred Great Product Designs* (New York, 1970), pp. 78–79.

ALESSANDRO MENDINI
Italian, born 1931

Alessandro Mendini has been one of the most influential figures in Italian design for the last two decades through his work as editor of important design magazines, his involvement in radical design, and his participation in the semantic rebellions of the Alchimia and Memphis groups. A graduate of the architecture faculty of the Milan Politecnico, Mendini worked with the firm of MARCELLO NIZZOLI on design and architectural projects until 1970, when he became editor of *Casabella* (until 1976); there he used his position to help establish and promote the radical design group Global Tools. Mendini moved to the magazine *Modo* (of which he was a founder), winning a Compasso d'Oro award in 1979 for its design, and then to *Domus* (1980–85). Working with Alchimia from its founding in 1976, he became a partner in the group and its principal theoretician (writing its manifesto after the fact in 1985). Drawing on the banal as the common element of contemporary society, he relied on precedents established in the previous century for the design and decoration of his *Proust* armchair (no. 359) and played with the icons of twentieth-century furniture for ironic "redesigns." These he exhibited as part of Alchimia's Bau.Haus collection in 1979. The following year he was one of the organizers of the *Oggetto Banale* (*Banal Object*) exhibition at the Venice *Biennale*. Mendini's *Cipriani* bar was included in the first Memphis collection in 1981, and his more recent work includes lighting for Segno, metalware for Alessi, and furniture for Matteo Grassi.

References: Gilles de Bure, "Alchymia, ou le crime de l'ornement," *Architecture d'Aujourd'hui* 210 (September 1980): 28–31; Andrea Branzi, *The Hot House: Italian New Wave Design* (Cambridge, Mass., 1984), passim; Guia Sambonet, *Alchimia, 1977–1987* (Turin, 1986), passim; *The International Design Yearbook*, vol. 1 (1985–86), pp. 62–64, 165; vol. 2 (1986), p. 74; vol. 4 (1988), p. 114; Groninger Museum, Groningen, *Alessandro Mendini: Sketchbook* (October 1–November 27, 1988).

ROBERTO MENGHI
Italian, born 1920

A graduate in architecture from Milan's Politecnico in 1944, Roberto Menghi is an architect and a teacher (at Venice, 1953–57, and at Milan, 1964–71) who has also contributed to the field of design. His earliest design, the *Libra Lux* lamp of 1948 (no. 205), was followed in the 1950s by a number of works exploring the possibilities and technology of plastics for the home. He exhibited a series of plastic housewares in the *Mostra Internazionale per l'Estetica delle Materie Plastiche* (*International Exhibition of the Aesthetics of Plastic Materials*) in Milan in 1956 and won a Compasso d'Oro award for his polyethylene pail (by Moneta) in 1956. He has also designed exhibitions, furniture (for Arflex), radios (for Siemens), and kitchen equipment (for Merloni).

References: Alfonso Grassi and Anty Pansera, *Atlante del design italiano, 1940–1980* (Milan, 1980), pp. 37, 134, 139, 170, 232–33, 252–53, 285; Andrea Branzi and Michele De Lucchi, eds., *Il design italiano degli anni '50* (Milan, 1981), passim.

LUDWIG MIES VAN DER ROHE
German, later American, 1886–1969

Although popularly associated with the Bauhaus, Ludwig Mies van der Rohe did not actually join the school until a decade after it was founded, when he succeeded WALTER GROPIUS as director in 1930. By then he had established a totally independent style most fully expressed in two major buildings—an apartment house for the 1927 Weissenhof experimental housing development in Stuttgart, sponsored by the Deutscher Werkbund (which as its vice-president he directed); and the German national pavilion at the Barcelona world's fair in 1929. Both of these structures included revolutionary metal furniture designed specifically for them (nos. 120, 123).

Trained first as a stonemason in his father's shop, Mies apprenticed to the furniture designer Bruno Paul and, from 1908 to 1911, worked for the firm of PETER BEHRENS, where he was exposed to product design as well as architecture. While Mies generated a wealth of furniture designs (now at the Mies van der Rohe Archives at the Museum of Modern Art in New York), only fifteen models, all essentially conceived between 1927 and 1931, were put into production, first by the metal shop of Joseph Müller in Berlin. By 1931 most of the pieces appeared in the catalog of the Bamberg Metallwerkstätten, and later that year Mies contracted with Thonet-Mundus in Zurich for their manufacture. He achieved broad distribution with this international firm, although disputes over patents for tubular-steel furniture and royalties dogged him throughout the 1930s. Mies remained in Germany after the Nazi regime forced him to close the Bauhaus in 1933, but he had little work and in 1937 he immigrated to the United States. It was here that he triumphed with his International Style architecture—most notably the plan and buildings of the Illinois Institute of Technology in Chicago (from 1940), where he taught; his Lake Shore Drive apartment houses (1957); and the Seagram Building in New York (1958), which was endlessly imitated. After the war Mies's furniture was introduced in America by Knoll, beginning in 1948 with the *Barcelona* chair, based on new drawings prepared by Mies's office under his supervision.

References: Ludwig Glaeser, *Ludwig Mies van der Rohe: Furniture . . .* (New York, 1977); Franz Schulze, *Mies van der Rohe: A Critical Biography* (Chicago, 1985).

LÁSZLÓ MOHOLY-NAGY
Hungarian, active Austria, Germany, the Netherlands, England, United States, 1895–1946

In his eulogy at László Moholy-Nagy's funeral, WALTER GROPIUS, who in 1924 had made Moholy the youngest master at the Bauhaus and head of both its metal workshop and its foundation course, praised his contribution to Bauhaus teaching methods and ideas: "The Bauhaus and what it has achieved cannot be thought of without bringing back into one's mind the fiery spirit of Moholy, the great stimulator. In painting, sculpture, and architecture, in theatre and industrial design, in photography and film, in advertising and typography, he constantly strove to interpret space in its relation to time, that is, motion in space.

We see that at all times he was successful as a thinker and inventor, as a writer and teacher. That seems almost to be too vast a field for one man to fill, but this abundant versatility was uniquely his."[27]

When Moholy was wounded during World War I, his law studies at the University of Budapest were interrupted and he began to produce drawings. In 1917 he organized an artists' group, MA, and cofounded a literary review. He then lived in Vienna and Berlin in 1919 and 1920 where he continued to draw, paint, and experiment with photograms (images produced directly on light-sensitive paper without a camera). During these years he was influenced by KAZIMIR MALEVICH, EL LISSITZKY, and other constructivist designers, as well as by Kurt Schwitters and the Berlin Dada group. In 1922 Moholy's work was first exhibited in Berlin, where Gropius saw it and invited the twenty-seven-year-old artist to join the faculty of the Bauhaus. Moholy taught at the Bauhaus in Weimar and Dessau from 1923 until 1928, working in photography and typography (no. 90), collaborating with other faculty members on murals as well as ballet and stage design, and working with Gropius on the design of the *bauhaus* magazine along with a series of fourteen books (*Bauhausbucher*, two volumes of which were written by Moholy). After leaving the Bauhaus, he worked as a stage and exhibition designer in Berlin until 1933 and produced photograms, films, paintings, and sculpture. He moved to Amsterdam the next year where he experimented with color film and photography, and there he was given a retrospective exhibition at the Stedelijk Museum. In 1935 he immigrated to London, where he designed graphics for International Textiles, Imperial Airways, and London Transport as well as interiors and displays for Simpson's department store. Two years later he moved again, this time to Chicago where he became director of the New Bauhaus, which closed the following year for lack of funds. In 1939 Moholy himself established the School of Design in Chicago (renamed the Institute of Design in 1944), where its distinguished faculty included György Kepes and HERBERT BAYER and its preliminary course continued Bauhaus teaching methods in the United States.

References: Richard Kostelanetz, ed., *Moholy-Nagy* (New York, 1970); Krisztina Passuth, *Moholy-Nagy* (New York, 1985).

CARLO MOLLINO
Italian, 1905–1973

Carlo Mollino took a highly individualistic position in the forums of architecture and design in the 1940s and 50s, opposing the Italian rationalism of the past two decades with expressive, organic, and eccentric forms. An architect, designer, and urban planner, Mollino received his degree from the Regia Scuola Superiore d'Architettura of the Accademia Albertina in Turin (1931), and then worked in the office of his father, a civil engineer, before establishing his own design studio. His furniture especially—

rolltop desks with hybrid forms, dining chairs sculpted into organic shapes, bent and pierced plywood tables with glass tops (no. 208)—expressed his conviction that the "fantastic" should also be considered as inspiration for the field of design.

References: "Turinese Baroque," *Interiors* 107 (July 1948): 93–95; "Forme di mobili," *Domus* 238 (1949): 10–12; Roberto Aloi, *Esempi di arredamento*, vols. 1–4 (Milan, 1950), passim; L.L.P., "Nuovi mobili di Mollino," *Domus* 270 (1952): 50–53; *Carlo Mollino, 1905–1973* (Milan, 1989).

MONTAGNI, BERIZZI, BUTTÈ, ARCHITETTI
Established Milan, 1950s

The Italian architects Dario Montagni, Sergio Berizzi, and Cesare Buttè worked for the Phonola company in the mid-1950s, designing their new shop in Milan in 1956 with freestanding, swivel supports to display the company's wares. This interior repeated the effect of the television they designed for the firm the same year, with a swivel picture tube separated from its chassis (no. 249). Montagni continued to work for Phonola, designing the company's display at the Fiera di Milano in 1960 (with Ernesto Griffini).

References: Gio Ponti, "Un nuovo televisore," *Domus* 323 (October 1956): 45; "Nuovo negozio per apparecchi radio e televisivi," *Domus* 323 (October 1956): 46–47.

KOLOMAN MOSER
Austrian, 1868–1918

Koloman Moser, one of the leaders of the modern movement in turn-of-the-century Viennese design, was closely connected to the three institutions that promoted it: he was a founding member of the Secession in 1897; a pupil, then teacher (from 1899), at the Kunstgewerbeschule; and a cofounder in 1903 of the Wiener Werkstätte. Unlike JOSEF HOFFMANN and JOSEPH MARIA OLBRICH, who were similarly involved in the reform movement, Moser was trained not as an architect but first as a painter (at the Akademie der Bildenden Künste, 1888–92) and then as a graphic designer (at the Kunstgewerbeschule, 1893–95); he practiced various forms of handcraft as well. In the postcards, vignettes, furniture, and other designs that he contributed to the Secession exhibitions (between 1898 and 1905) and the Secession magazine (*Ver Sacrum*) as well as in his work for the Wiener Werkstätte from 1903 to 1908, Moser displayed a remarkable talent for ornament, for close repeating organic designs, and for the rectilinear, geometric style that he practiced with Hoffmann (no. 36). He also designed textiles for Backhausen, glass for Bakalowits, and furniture for Portois & Fix. In 1904–5 he designed stained-glass windows for OTTO WAGNER's Steinhof Church, and later, for the Austrian government, he created several sets of postage stamps (1906–14) and the Imperial Jubilee postcard (1908).

After 1908 Moser continued to teach at the Kunstgewerbeschule until his death and was active chiefly as a painter.

References: Oswald Oberhuber and Julius Hummel, *Koloman Moser, 1868–1918* (Vienna, 1979); Galerie Metropol, Vienna, *Kolo Moser: Maler und Designer* (1982); Daniele Baroni and Antonio D'Avria, *Kolo Moser: Grafico e designer* (Milan, 1984); Werner Fenz, *Koloman Moser: Graphik, Kunstgewerbe, Malerei* (Salzburg, 1984); Werner J. Schweiger, *Wiener Werkstaette: Design in Vienna, 1903–1932* (New York, 1984), passim.

OLIVIER MOURGUE
French, born 1939

Designer and dreamer, Olivier Mourgue has brought wit and fantasy to product, environmental, and interior design. After studying interior architecture at the Ecole Boulle in Paris (1954–58), Mourgue attended the Ecole Nationale Supérieure des Arts Décoratifs (1958–60), where as a student he created the prototype for the first of his chairs to be produced by the furniture manufacturer Airborne (nos. 296, 320). He then apprenticed as an interior designer at the Nordiska Kompaniet department store in Stockholm (1960). In 1964 he went to work for Airborne but began to feel uneasy about designing objects "that claim to be perfect." Instead he began to explore experimental alternatives (the sitting-rug of 1966), a mobile studio (1970), and environmental habitats for open living spaces (notably one shown at "Visiona 3" of 1971). Fantasy has informed Mourgue's more recent production, with creations of colorful "toy seats" (painted wood and canvas constructions using animal, plant, and human forms) and a captivating, portable, silent "theatre of design." "Gaiety in objects, enjoyment in their construction, in making them work—this to me seems very important," he has explained, "unlike repetitive objects or systems in which I don't have much interest. . . . In their life and humor they touch people endlessly, not just a tiny group but the man in the street and the child."[28]

References: B.A., "An Interview with Olivier Mourgue," *Industrial Design* 15 (October 1968): 44–45; "Visiona 3," *Industrial Design* 19 (May 1972): 42–45; Musée des Arts Décoratifs, Nantes, France, *Olivier Mourgue* (March 12–April 19, 1976); *Olivier Mourgue's Little Theatre of Design* (London, n.d.); Sainsbury Centre for Visual Arts, University of East Anglia, Norwich, England, *Olivier Mourgue: Imaginary Gardens and Little Theatres* (June 2–August 30, 1992).

GERD ALFRED MÜLLER
German, born 1932

As a designer of kitchen appliances for Braun, Gerd Alfred Müller developed his family of products with simple, ordered, rational forms and white finishes following the company aesthetic as defined by its chief designer DIETER RAMS. Müller completed an apprenticeship as a furniture maker in 1952 and then studied interior design at the Werkkunstschule in Wiesbaden. Part of the Braun design team from 1955 to 1960, where he was responsible for a line of electric shavers in addition to the *Kitchen Machine*, a food processor with multiple attachments (no. 246), Müller established his own studio in Eschborn, Germany, designing graphics, appliances, and communications equipment.

References: François Burkhardt and Inez Franksen, *Design: Dieter Rams &* (Berlin, 1981), pp. 154–55, 163; *75 Jahre Deutscher Werkbund* (Frankfort, 1983), n.p.

JOSEF MÜLLER-BROCKMANN
Swiss, born 1914

Josef Müller-Brockmann was one of the leaders of the Swiss typographic movement during the 1950s. Through his writings and his work he advanced an approach to graphic design that was intended to be universal and thoroughly calculated, based on "objective and functional criteria"[29] and free from the vagaries of personality, individual expression, and manipulative communications techniques. His use of large photographs turned into graphic symbols and his understanding of design as visual problem-solving had profound international influence. But so too did the discreet sans-serif typography he employed in layouts based on sophisticated grid structures, a technique most clearly presented in the series of concert posters he created for the Tonhalle in Zurich (from 1951; no. 245). Müller-Brockmann studied in Zurich at the Kunstgewerbeschule (where he later taught) and at the University of Zurich before opening his own studio in 1936, where his work also included stage and exhibition design. He was a founder and editor of the journal *Neue Grafik* in 1959, which documented and defined the new Swiss graphics.

References: Josef Müller-Brockmann, *The Graphic Designer and His Design Problems* (New York, 1983); Colin Naylor, ed., *Contemporary Designers*, 2d ed. (Chicago, 1990), pp. 412, 414–15.

PETER MÜLLER-MUNK
American, born Germany, 1904–1967

One of America's first industrial designers, Peter Müller-Munk had the dual careers of industrial designer and silversmith, and during the 1930s he readily moved back and forth between both fields. Trained under the silversmith Waldemar Raemisch at the Kunstgewerbeschule in Berlin, Müller-Munk came to New York in 1926, where he worked for a short time as a silver designer for TIFFANY AND COMPANY. His silver was shown in 1929 at the Newark Museum's exhibition *Modern American Design in Metal*; in 1937 in the exhibition of contemporary American silver at the Metropolitan Museum of Art in

New York; and in 1939 at the *Golden Gate International Exposition* in San Francisco. At the same time he designed decorative production metalwork for the Revere Copper and Brass Company (no. 155). Müller-Munk's industrial design encompassed a wide range of endeavors: plastics, appliances (including the well-known Waring blender), interiors, exhibitions, and transportation. In 1935 he taught in the first industrial design program in America, organized the previous year at the Carnegie Institute of Technology in Pittsburgh, where he remained until 1945. He left to establish his own industrial design firm, Peter Müller-Munk Associates, which is still in operation.

References: Dorothy Grafly, "Peter Müller-Munk, Industrial Designer," *Design* 47 (May 1946): 8–9; "Designers in America: Part 3," *Industrial Design* 19 (October 1972): 32–33; Karen Davies, *At Home in Manhattan: Modern Decorative Arts, 1925 to the Depression* (New Haven, Conn., 1983), nos. 9, 18, 68.

BRUNO MUNARI
Italian, born 1907

Artist and creator of games, toys, and picture books for children, Bruno Munari is also a designer of graphics, plastics, furniture, and environments who in his work and writings tries to bridge the gap between art and industrial design. "The artist has to regain the modesty he had when art was just a trade," he wrote in 1970, "and instead of despising the very public he is trying to interest he must discover its needs and make contact with it again. This is the reason why the traditional artist is being transformed into the designer, and . . . I myself have undergone this transformation in the course of my working career."[30] Self taught as an artist and a designer, Munari was connected with the later futurist artists, showing paintings with the group from 1927 and exhibiting a number of "useless machines" in 1933. He also joined in the program of futurist ceramics with his series of droll animals about 1929, and his better-known cup with shutters of 1933–34. Munari designed the first product made by Danese, the *Cube* ashtray of 1957 (no. 270), and continued to work primarily for the firm. He showed an environmental system in 1968 at the *XIV Triennale* in Milan and in 1971 designed a habitable structure (no. 325), which won additional Compasso d'Oro prizes for him in 1979. It was manufactured by Robots, the firm that also manufactured his *Divanetta* sofa of 1988 with a similar metal-frame structure.

References: Paolo Fossati, *Il design in Italia, 1945–1972* (Turin, 1972), pp. 84–90, pls. 78–94; Enrico Crispolti, ed., *La ceramica futurista da Balla a Tullio D'Albisola* (Florence, 1982), pp. 29–30, 49, 112–17, 190–91; Musée des Arts Décoratifs, Bordeaux, et al., *Objets Danese: Profil d'une production* (1988–89), passim; Mirella Loik, "Intervista: Bruno Munari," *Disegno* 17–18 (March–April 1989): 32–39.

PETER MURDOCH
English, born 1940

Best known internationally for his graphic communications systems—particularly that for the 1968 Mexican Olympics (with Lance Wyman)—Peter Murdoch has designed product packaging, corporate identity programs, and graphics as well as architecture, interiors, and furniture. While a student at the Royal College of Art in London in 1963 he devised a paper chair, the first to be produced commercially (in 1964–65 in New York; no. 286). Since 1969 he has had his own design office in London and has been a consultant designer to government agencies and businesses. Murdoch is the recipient of two Council of Industrial Design awards, one for Those Things, the second line of fiberboard furniture he developed, and the other for door hardware.

References: "Children's Table, Chair and Stool: Perspective Design's Those Things," *Design* 233 (May 1968): 33; Whitechapel Art Gallery, London, *Modern Chairs, 1918–1970* (July 22–August 30, 1970), no. 69.

KAZUMASA NAGAI
Japanese, born 1929

One of Japan's leading graphic designers and art directors since the 1960s, Kazumasa Nagai joined the Nippon Design Center when it was established in 1960 and served as president (1975–86) and director (since 1986) of what then became the largest and most influential design production company in Japan. Nagai studied sculpture at the Tokyo National University of Fine Arts and Music (1951) but left to work as a graphic designer for the Daiwa Spinning Company in Osaka (1951–60). When he returned to Tokyo, Nagai had already developed his personal style of cool, abstract, geometric forms and linear patterns. This style appeared in his early poster for the Nippon Kogaku Company (later Nikon) and in a poster series created for the *Life* science library of Time-Life Books (1966), where it was perfectly suited to the high-quality optical products and scientific subjects the posters advertised. During the late 1960s Nagai began to combine photographs largely of the sea, sky, and horizon with geometrical compositions, as in his posters for *GQ* magazine, setting his forms in a vast space. In addition to his commercial work with posters, trademarks, and advertisements, Nagai continued independently to create prints and drawings that have been widely exhibited in Japan and elsewhere, images that display the technical and production quality for which he is so justly famous. Nagai's research into geometric forms in space continued throughout the 1970s and early 1980s (no. 352). By the late 1980s, however, realistic elements had entered his formal vocabulary, first, notably, in the fantastic animal posters he created for the annual exhibition of the Japan Graphic Designers Association in 1988 (each animal composed of traditional small-scale decorative textile patterns), and later in his one-man exhibition, *The World of Kazumasa Nagai*, held at the Museum of Modern Art, Toyama, in 1990. Among the most premiated of Japanese designers, Nagai has won awards ranging from the gold medal in the first international poster biennial in Warsaw, the Mainichi industrial design prize, and the Asahi advertising prize (1966), to the grand prize in the first Moscow international poster triennial (1992).

References: Tadanori Yokoo, "Kazumasa Nagai, His Works and Personality," *Design* 95 (April 1967): 18–33; Art Directors Club of Tokyo, *Art Direction Today* (Tokyo, 1984), pp. 162–65, 238–41; *The Works of Kazumasa Nagai* (Tokyo, 1985); *Best 100 Japanese Posters, 1945–1989* (Tokyo, 1990), pp. 84–85, 134–35, 138–39, 166–67, 210–11, 220–21, 250; Museum of Modern Art, Toyama, *The World of Kazumasa Nagai* (September 1–October 7, 1990); National Museum of Modern Art, Tokyo, *Graphic Design Today* (September 26–November 11, 1990), pp. 66–69, 114.

GEORGE NAKASHIMA
American, 1905–1990

Trained as an architect, George Nakashima chose to pursue the career of wood craftsman, and for almost five decades designed and produced furniture of original design in limited quantity that represented the high quality of a craft workshop system. Nakashima studied architecture at the University of Washington in Seattle and received a master's degree from the Massachusetts Institute of Technology in 1930. In the mid-1930s he traveled abroad, to Europe and the East, working in Japan and then India for the office of the architect Antonin Raymond, who had assisted FRANK LLOYD WRIGHT on the construction of the Imperial Hotel in Tokyo. He returned to Seattle in 1940 where he opened his first furniture workshop, but following his internment at the beginning of World War II, along with other Japanese-Americans, he moved to New Hope, Pennsylvania. There, in 1946, he began to design and manufacture furniture himself, at the same time designing a mass-production line for Hans Knoll (this he did again in 1957, for Widdicomb-Mueller, but it did not prove successful). Using carefully chosen woods, mainly native walnut and cherry, Nakashima created simple, sometimes Japanese-inspired designs, for chairs, tables (no. 207), and storage pieces, first in organic shapes but later more rationalized ones. (His cantilevered *Conoid* chair of about 1960 is a good example.) His later, extremely expressive work was based on an increasingly individualistic approach, taking inspiration for his forms from the particular character of pieces of exotic woods rather than using predetermined designs drawn on paper. In 1986 Nakashima completed his monumental *Altar for Peace*, commissioned for the Cathedral of Saint John the Divine in New York. His autobiography, *The Soul of a Tree: A Woodworker's Reflections*, was published in 1981.

Reference: Derek E. Ostergard, *George Nakashima: Full Circle* (New York, 1989).

UMBERTO NASON
Italian, 1898–1967

Umberto Nason was a founder and director of the Murano, Italy, glasshouse Nason & Moretti, which was established in 1923 for the manufacture of utilitarian glass, creating tablewares that were designed particularly for production by factory methods. The firm was awarded a gold medal at Milan's *IX Triennale* in 1951 and a silver medal in 1954; Nason also won an individual Compasso d'Oro award in 1955 for his bicolored cocktail set (no. 240).

References: *Industrial Design* 3 (April 1956): 65; Palazzo delle Stelline, Milan, *Design & design* (May 29–July 31, 1979), p. 42.

GEORGE NELSON
American, 1908–1986

George Nelson became one of the most influential figures in postwar American design through his research, writing, and design. His published analyses of design problems made a tremendous impact on the profession, as did his books on modern living spaces (1952), on chairs (1953), and on storage (1954). Through his long-standing association with the furniture manufacturer Herman Miller, he showed that good contemporary design could be profitable, and his own designs, ranging from early modular storage systems (no. 195) to his *Action Office* (1961), were met with wide acclaim. A graduate of Yale University School of Fine Arts (1931), Nelson first worked as associate editor (1935–43) and co-managing editor (1943–44) of *Architectural Forum*. Following the publication in 1945 of his built-in storage wall, a concept he originated, he was hired by Herman Miller to succeed GILBERT ROHDE as director of design, a consultancy he held for twenty years and during which he brought in other top designers, among them CHARLES EAMES. Nelson was always production-oriented, offering the factory ideas for standardized elements and economical production systems along with his designs (nos. 247, 292).

In 1947 Nelson established his own office in New York, providing designs for clocks (for Howard Miller—an extensive series of decorative table and wall clocks designed over a period of two decades; no. 200), housewares (notably, his melamine *Florence Ware* table service), furniture, and office equipment. He also worked extensively as an exhibition designer, creating the umbrella-shaped fiberglass structures for the United States national exhibition in Moscow in 1959, several pavilions at the *New York World's Fair* in 1964, and the installation of the exhibition *Design since 1945* at the Philadelphia Museum of Art in 1983.

References: "Storage Wall," *Life*, January 22, 1945, pp. 64–71; "Mass Produced—Custom Tailored," *Interiors* 105 (June 1946): 90–93; O.G., "Merchandise Cues," *Interiors* 109 (November 1949): 128, 130–31; *Industrial Design* 3 (December 1956): 100; "Nelson's Way," *Interiors* 123 (November 1963): 115–17; Jay Doblin, *One Hundred Great Product Designs* (New York, 1970), nos. 58, 59, 98; Ralph Caplan, *The Design of Herman Miller* (New York, 1976), passim.

ALDO VAN DEN NIEUWELAAR
Dutch, born 1944

Aldo van den Nieuwelaar studied at the Academie voor Beeldende Kunsten St Joost in Breda and then worked for the architectural firms of Spier & Lammersen and Premsela Vonk in Amsterdam, where he has had his own design firm since 1969. He has designed exhibitions and created lighting for Artimeta, carpets for the German firm Teunen & Teunen, and furniture for Pastoe; notable among the latter are his *Amsterdamer* cupboard system (no. 338) and his minimalist modular seating of 1986.

References: *Industrial Design* 27 (May–June 1980): 20; Visual Arts Office for Abroad, Amsterdam, *Design from the Netherlands* (1981), pp. 38–41; Metz & Co., Amsterdam, *Aldo van den Nieuwelaar* (1984); Gert Staal and Hester Wolters, eds., *Holland in Vorm: Dutch Design, 1945–1987* (The Hague, 1987), pp. 149, 151, 155, 163, 170, 231.

MARCELLO NIZZOLI
Italian, 1887–1969

Designer of Olivetti's products and some of its publicity materials during the 1940s and 50s, Marcello Nizzoli was responsible for creating a progressive, integrated corporate image considered the best of its time. Having studied architecture, painting, and decoration at the Accademia di Belli Arte in Parma, Nizzoli became a painter, first exhibiting with the Nuove Tendenze group in Milan in 1914; he also created decorative and graphic designs, including posters (for Campari), tapestries, and fabrics. During the 1920s and 30s he was associated with the Italian rationalist architects, among them GIUSEPPE TERRAGNI and Edoardo Persico, collaborating with the latter on interior and exhibition design. It was as a graphic artist that Adriano Olivetti hired him about 1938 (he had done freelance design for the company with Persico as early as 1931), but by 1940 he had created the model for his first product, the *Summa 40* adding machine. His *Lexikon 80* typewriter of 1948 and *Lettera 22* portable of 1950 (no. 214) introduced fluid sculptural lines that rejected the accepted formulas of technological equipment, an approach he followed until 1959 when his geometric about-face, the faceted *Diaspron 82* typewriter, appeared. Nizzoli's designs for Olivetti also included office buildings and the workers' housing that reflected the firm's continuing social consciousness. Nizzoli also worked for other companies, designing sewing machines for Necchi (no. 238), cigarette lighters for Ronson (1959), furniture for Arflex (1960), and a stove and gas pumps for Agip (1960).

References: "Olivetti: Design in Industry," *Museum of Modern Art Bulletin* (special issue) 20 (fall 1952); Germano Celant, *Marcello Nizzoli* (Milan, 1968); Frederick S. Wight Art Gallery, University of California, Los Angeles, *Design Process: Olivetti, 1908–1978* (March 27–May 6, 1979), p. 262 et passim; Irene de Guttry, Maria Paola Maino, and Mario Quesada, *Le arti minori d'autore in Italia dal 1900 al 1930* (Rome, 1985), pp. 248–51; Sibylle Kicherer, *Olivetti: A Study of the Corporate Management of Design* (New York, 1990), pp. 25–30 et passim.

ISAMU NOGUCHI
American, 1904–1988

With the hope that "originality might survive mass production," Isamu Noguchi periodically turned from his abstract sculptures and contemplative garden designs to the creation of "things for everybody's enjoyment."[31] Among his earliest work in this area was a home intercom in biomorphic form called *Radio Nurse*, commissioned by the Zenith Radio Company (1937), but it was his experiments with environmental light sculptures, which he called "Lunars," that led to an involvement with lighting design (no. 198) sustained throughout his career. He also designed furniture, both unique pieces on commission and production work—coffee tables (no. 193), upholstered seating, dining tables and chairs, as well as occasional tables—for Herman Miller, Knoll, and Alcoa. Because his work was both distinctive and successful, imitations and unauthorized copies repeatedly dogged him. To elude his imitators he developed his Akari lighting designs to more and more intensely particular, formalistic shapes (no. 314). Noguchi was also concerned with the continuation of traditional craft industries and conceived of designs that would use such talent in Japan, not just his Akari lighting but furniture as well, which he intended to be of international interest.

References: "Art into Living: Sculptor-Designed Table," *Art News* 46 (May 1947): 36; D. Pleydell Bouverie, "Demountable Table by Noguchi," *Architectural Review* 107 (February 1950): 135; "Japanese Akari Lamps," *Craft Horizons* 14 (September 1954): 16–18; Sam Hunter, *Isamu Noguchi* (New York, 1978); "Shapes of Light: Noguchi's New Akari Sculptures," *Interiors* 128 (January 1969): 12; Stewart Johnson, "Noguchi: Light," *Architectural Review* 162 (December 1977): 369–71.

ELIOT NOYES
American, 1910–1977

Eliot Noyes was responsible for overseeing America's first integrated corporate design system—for IBM—and through this and his other work became one of America's most influential postwar designers. After graduating from the Harvard University Graduate School of Design in 1938, Noyes went to work in the Cambridge office of MARCEL BREUER and WALTER GROPIUS. Recommended soon after by Gropius for the new position of curator of industrial design at the Museum of Modern Art in New York, in 1940 he organized the "Organic Design in Home Furnishings" competition, and exhibition, which introduced the talents of EERO SAARINEN and CHARLES EAMES. After the war Noyes joined the firm of NORMAN BEL GEDDES as design director, and there he worked on his first typewriter design for IBM, which he continued after he opened his own office in 1947. As product designer for IBM, he created the standard *Executive* (1959) and *Selectric* (1961; no. 280) typewriters, along with computers and other equipment; as design consultant for the company he established its new corporate image, recommending the hiring of well-known designers for other aspects of the firm's design work. Noyes's other clients included Westinghouse, Xerox, and Mobil, for which he created a new image in 1969, including the familiar round gasoline pump with its clear graphic presentation. He also won significant awards for his innovative architecture, including his own house in New Canaan, Connecticut (1955). Between 1947 and 1954 Noyes brought common sense to design criticism in the series of columns he wrote for *Consumer Reports*.

References: Walter McQuade, "An Industrial Designer with a Conspicuous Conscience," *Fortune* (August 1963): 135–38, 183–88, 190; Scott Kelly, "Eliot Noyes and Associates," *Design* 210 (June 1966): 38–43; "Eliot F. Noyes (1910–1977)," *Industrial Design* 24 (September–October 1977): 42–43; Boilerhouse Project, Victoria and Albert Museum, London, *Art & Industry* (January 18–March 2, 1982), pp. 72–79.

HERMANN OBRIST
Swiss, active Germany, 1862–1927

One of the principal spokesmen for design reform in Munich at the turn of the century, Hermann Obrist was a designer of furniture and decorative arts and a sculptor as well as an influential teacher. An exhibition of his embroideries (no. 2), held in 1896 in Munich and afterwards in Berlin and London, was acclaimed as the "birth" of a new applied art and focused international attention on Munich as the birthplace and center of the Jugendstil movement. Decrying historicism and "style-notions" of any kind, Obrist lectured widely, calling for an expressive art of "intensified emotions." In his embroideries, drawings, and studies for fountains and monuments, Obrist created expressive designs of great originality that bordered on abstraction.

Born in Switzerland, the son of a physician, Obrist briefly studied medicine at the University of Heidelberg, but in 1887, determined to devote himself to applied art, he traveled to Scotland and England. Over the next five years Obrist alternately worked independently and took formal instruction (at the Kunstgewerbeschule in Karlsruhe and at the Académie Julian in Paris, where he studied sculpture). In 1892 with the assistance of a family friend, Berthe Ruchet, Obrist set up a studio to make embroideries in Florence and at the same time, experimented with marble sculpture there. With the move of his studio to Munich in 1894 and the enormously successful exhibition of his embroideries, Obrist became a central figure in the new Jugendstil movement. In 1897 he served on the committee that selected decorative arts for the annual art exhibition in the Glaspalast and directly afterwards became a founding member of the Vereinigte Werkstätten für Kunst im Handwerk, established to produce and market the new designs. In 1898–99 Obrist commissioned RICHARD RIEMERSCHMID and Bernhard Pankok to design furniture (which was produced by the Vereinigte Werkstätten) for his new house in Munich's Schwabing district. Together with Wilhelm von Debschitz, a painter and interior designer, in 1902 Obrist founded the Lehr- und Versuch-Ateliers für Angewandte und Freie Kunst, a school for applied arts, which has since been seen as a major antecedent of the Bauhaus. Because of a hearing loss, Obrist left the school in 1904.

References: Museum Villa Stuck, Munich, *Hermann Obrist: Wegbereiter der Moderne* (1968); Silvie Lampe-von Bennigsen, *Hermann Obrist: Erinnerungen* (Munich, 1970); Peg Weiss, *Kandinsky in Munich* (Princeton, N.J., 1979), pp. 28–34; Kathryn B. Hiesinger, ed., *Art Nouveau in Munich* (Philadelphia, 1988), pp. 79–87.

SINYA OKAYAMA
Japanese, born 1941

Sinya Okayama worked in the design department of the Mitsukoshi Department Store Corporation before 1970, when he opened his own office in Osaka. After a decade of interior design practice, both commercial and residential, he turned to product design, inaugurating in 1981 a range of postmodern furniture and lighting fixtures under his own name. While his earliest designs shared the formal vocabulary of the "new international style," launched by the Italians ALESSANDRO MENDINI and ETTORE SOTTSASS, JR., by 1984 Sinya had found his own voice, infusing his work with a personal and distinctly Japanese identity. In that year his *Kazenoko* stool (no. 379) and *Crocodile* bench were exhibited in the Phoenix exhibition held in Toronto, where they attracted international attention. The *Kazenoko* was the first piece in what would become a series of furniture designs that translated pictographic Japanese brushstrokes into three-dimensional forms, allowing the user to "read" the object. In 1985 Sinya served as artistic director of an exhibition of Mendini's Infinite furniture in Kyoto and afterward was invited by Mendini to collaborate with him in the design of *Six Small Pieces of Furniture* (1986) and *7 + 7 Jewels* (1987).

Reference: Yurakucho Asahi Gallery, Tokyo, *Interior Objects by Sinya Okayama* (April 28–May 17, 1989).

JOSEPH MARIA OLBRICH
Austrian, born Silesia, 1867–1908

Trained in architecture at the Akademie der Bildenden Künste in Vienna (1893), Joseph Maria Olbrich was one of the leaders of progressive Viennese architecture, along with OTTO WAGNER, before the turn of the century, and was a founding member of the radical artists' exhibition society, the Secession, in 1897. Two years later Olbrich was one of six designers, including PETER BEHRENS, invited to Darmstadt by Grand Duke Ernst Ludwig of Hesse to form an artists' colony and to prepare an exhibition, *Ein Dokument deutscher Kunst (A Document of German Art)*, for 1901. Architect of the colony, Olbrich laid out the whole site and designed almost all the buildings, including the Ernst Ludwig House, the colony's central studio and exhibition building. In addition, for the exhibition Olbrich designed furniture, lighting, and objects for many of the buildings (no. 23). He brought to Darmstadt the unified Viennese rectilinear style of geometric forms and decoration that he had developed as an assistant to Wagner and in the exhibition building he designed for the Secession (1897–98). Olbrich was also a brilliant interior designer and represented the Darmstadt colony at Paris's *Exposition Universelle* of 1900 with a furnished interior, which won a gold medal; he also showed interiors at Turin in 1902 and again at the *Louisiana Purchase Exhibition* in Saint Louis in 1904, where he won a grand prize and gold medal. A four-volume book of his work, published by Wasmuth in 1904, was influential in disseminating Olbrich's style in Germany. Olbrich's late work, including furniture and interiors in the Altes Schloss Giessen executed for Grand Duke Ernst Ludwig (1906), indicated a turn toward the monumental classicism that German architects, including Behrens, adopted before World War I.

References: Hessisches Landesmuseum, Darmstadt, *Joseph Maria Olbrich, 1867–1908: Das Werk des Architekten* (1967); Hessisches Landesmuseum, Darmstadt, *Ein Dokument deutscher Kunst: Darmstadt, 1901–1976* (1976), passim; Ian Latham, *Joseph Maria Olbrich* (New York, 1980); *Joseph Maria Olbrich, 1867–1908* (Darmstadt, 1983).

CAMILLO OLIVETTI
Italian, 1868–1943

An 1891 graduate in electrical engineering from the Turin Politecnico, Camillo Olivetti traveled to the United States in 1893, where he attended the *World's Columbian Exposition* and the International Congress on Electricity in Chicago, afterwards becoming a teaching assistant at Stanford University. Back in Italy in 1894, he opened a factory for the manufacture of electrical measuring devices, and later, in 1908, founded Italy's first typewriter compa-

ny, which he organized industrially around the methods of the large typewriter factories he had visited on a return trip to America that year. With his model *M1* typewriter (no. 49), introduced at the *Esposizione Universale* in Turin in 1911, Olivetti built up a successful business, establishing the corporate approach to design and publicity that would give his firm its unique, lasting identity. A socialist and an outspoken reformer, Olivetti enjoyed continued good relations with his employees, and the policies he established for their benefit were among the most progressive in the world. Olivetti retired as president of the firm in 1938 and was succeeded by his son Adriano.

References: Frederick S. Wight Art Gallery, University of California, Los Angeles, *Design Process: Olivetti, 1908–1978* (March 27–May 6, 1979), pp. 10–15, 262–63; Sibylle Kicherer, *Olivetti: A Study of the Corporate Management of Design* (New York, 1990), pp. 1–6.

PETER OPSVIK
Norwegian, born 1939

Peter Opsvik is one of three designers (along with Svein Gusrud and Oddvin Rykken) who have worked with Hans Christian Mengshoel to give form to his Balans concept—ergonomic seating that offers an alternative sitting position in which the body's weight rests on the knees. Introduced in 1979 at the Scandinavian furniture fair in Copenhagen, Balans chairs by these designers have been manufatured by Håg (no. 356) and by Stokke Fabrikker. Opsvik designed some seven different Balans chairs between 1979 and 1984. After studying at the Kunsthåndverksskole (School of Art and Design) in Bergen (1959–63) and the Statens Håndverks -og Kunstindustriskole (National School of Art and Design) in Oslo (1963–64), Opsvik worked first as a designer of radios for Tandberg (1965–70). His interest in ergonomics developed after studies in England in the 1970s and at the Volkwangschule für Kunstgewerbe in Essen, Germany.

References: David Revere McFadden, ed., *Scandinavian Modern Design, 1880–1980* (New York, 1982), p. 269, no. 343; Nanna Segelcke, *Made in Norway* (Oslo, 1990), pp. 48–49.

ERNEST PAILLARD & CIE
Established Sainte-Croix, Switzerland, 1814

Founded in the early nineteenth century as a manufacturer of music boxes and clockworks, the firm of Ernest Paillard began the production of phonographs around the end of the nineteenth century, later adding radios, photographic equipment, and office machinery to its products. Typewriter manufacture was developed in 1920 when a new factory was built at Yverdon, and from 1923 the company introduced a succession of personal and commercial models that steadily increased its market. Paillard's first portable model was issued in 1933, but the considerably scaled-down *Hermes Baby* (no. 146) brought impressive international sales and recognition to the firm. By the beginning of World War II it had gained an important share of the world export market.

References: Jay Doblin, *One Hundred Great Product Designs* (New York, 1970), pp. 45–46; Wilfred A. Beeching, *Century of the Typewriter* (New York, 1974), pp. 113–18; Museum für Gestaltung, Kunstgewerbemuseum, Zurich, *Unbekannt—Vertraut: "Anonymes" Design im Schweizer, Gebrauchsgerät seit 1920* (January 21–March 8, 1987), pp. 25–33.

VERNER PANTON
Danish, lives in Switzerland, born 1926

A Danish designer and architect who lives in Switzerland, Vernon Panton has worked in many areas and with many manufacturers, providing numerous designs for furnishing fabrics (Unika-Vaev), carpets, lighting (Louis Poulsen), and furniture (Fritz Hansen; Thonet). A student at the Kongelige Danske Kunstakademi (Royal Danish Academy of Fine Arts) in Copenhagen, Panton worked with ARNE JACOBSEN between 1950 and 1952 and opened his own office in 1955. He has repeatedly experimented with the concept of the single-piece cantilevered chair, and his bright, flowing plastic design introduced by Herman Miller in 1967 (no. 288) was the first to be commercially produced; he later made versions in plywood, including playful painted models jigsawed in abstract and natural shapes (1982). The experimental "Visiona" interiors he created for the plastics firm of Bayer in 1968 and 1970 introduced his concept of the integrated interior environment with flowing furniture forms and electric colors. Panton has since developed his own complex color system for interior design, which he applies to furniture, walls, and furnishing fabrics, choosing parallel or sequential hues from his spectrum of eighty-four colors for an interior palette. This color system (with the later addition of a structural grid system) has been the basis for an extensive line of fabrics Panton created for Mira-X (no. 369).

References: "Una sedia di Verner Panton per Herman Miller," *Domus* 459 (February 1968): 24–25; Centre de Création Industrielle, Paris, *Qu'est-ce que le design?* (October 24–December 31, 1969), n.p.; Sylvia Katz, *Plastics: Designs and Materials* (London, 1978), pp. 87, 138, 142–43, 156, 169; Jan Blaich, "Verner Panton: Color by Number," *Industrial Design* 31 (May–June 1984): 52–55; *Verner Panton* (Copenhagen, 1986).

PIERRE PAULIN
French, born 1927

One of France's most successful postwar industrial designers, Pierre Paulin is best known for his furniture, but he has also designed automotive interiors (for Citroën), appliances (for L M ERICSSON and Calor), packaging (for Christian Dior), signage (for the Musée d'Orsay, Paris), and textiles. A graduate of the Ecole Nationale Supérieure

des Arts Décoratifs in Paris, Paulin began to design furniture in the late 1950s for the Dutch manufacturers A. Polak and Artifort, his early molded-plywood chairs being followed by a series of innovative soft furnishings—tubular-metal structures covered with foam and upholstered in stretch fabrics (no. 296). In 1969 Paulin was commissioned by the Mobilier Nationale to create interiors and furniture for the private apartments of the Elysée Palace, the French presidential residence, and his office worked on other prestigious commissions such as visitor seating for the Musée du Louvre in 1968 and furniture for the French pavilion at the Osaka world's fair in 1970. In the 1980s Paulin worked again with the studios of the Mobilier Nationale to create a line of handcrafted limited-production furniture; for this he employed contemporary forms as well as those evoking eighteenth-century and oriental precedents, and used lacquer, fine woods, and leather in the tradition of French *ébénisterie*. Paulin established the design firm ADSA + Partners in 1975, which ROGER TALLON and the clothing designer Michel Schreiber joined in 1984.

References: Musée des Arts Décoratifs, Paris, *Les Assises du siège contemporain* (May 30–July 29, 1968), pp. 94–96; Monelle Hayot, "Les Nouvelles Créations de Pierre Paulin," *L'Oeil* 334 (May 1983): 46–51; Gert Staal and Hester Wolters, eds., *Holland in Vorm: Dutch Design, 1945–1987* (The Hague, 1987), pp. 149–51, 161–62; Agence pour la Promotion de la Création Industrielle and Centre Georges Pompidou, Paris, *Design français, 1960–1990: Trois décennies* (June 22–September 26, 1988), pp. 244–45.

DAGOBERT PECHE
Austrian, 1887–1923

An ornamental designer of particular brilliance, Peche entered the Wiener Werkstätte in 1915, where he created a vast array of products ranging from silver (no. 67), jewelry, and embroideries to wallpapers, costumes, textiles, bookbindings, ceramics, and glasswares. His playful designs, favoring gaily colored and delicately drawn plants and animals and based on historical models, were responsible for a new stylistic phase in the Wiener Werkstätte, one that shifted the emphasis away from the geometric manner pioneered there by JOSEF HOFFMANN and KOLOMAN MOSER. Peche had studied architecture in Vienna at the Technische Hochschule from 1906 to 1908 and at the Akademie der Bildenden Künste until 1911. By 1913, as a freelance designer in Vienna, Peche was producing textile designs for Johann Backhausen & Söhne and Philipp Haas & Söhne, wallpapers for Max Schmidt, and ceramics for the porcelain manufactory of Josef Bock. That same year Peche made his public debut with wallpapers and a lady's salon at an exhibition in the Österreichisches Museum für Kunst und Industrie and with interiors at the Secession exhibition. The following year, in 1914, he created another interior—a lady's boudoir for the Austrian pavilion at the Deutscher Werkbund exhibition in Cologne. As a member of the Wiener Werkstätte, Peche continued to participate in exhibitions, displaying the many aspects of his talent at the Vienna *Kunstschau* (1920) and the *Deutsche Gewerbeschau* in Munich (1922). He managed the Zurich branch of the Wiener Werkstätte from 1917 to 1919.

References: Österreichisches Museum für Kunst und Industrie, Vienna, *Ausstellung von Arbeiten des modernen österreichischen Kunsthandwerks: Dagobert Peche Gedächtnis Ausstellung* (September–November 1923); Max Eisler, *Dagobert Peche* (Vienna, 1925); Werner J. Schweiger, *Wiener Werkstaette: Design in Vienna, 1903–1932* (New York, 1984), passim; Eduard F. Sekler, *Josef Hoffmann: The Architectural Work* (Princeton, N.J., 1985), pp. 164–67 et passim.

J. C. PENNEY COMPANY
Established Kemmerer, Wyoming, 1902

Founded as a small retail store in a Wyoming mining town by James Cash Penney and two partners, the J. C. Penney Company expanded rapidly as a chain by grooming managers to buy one-third of the shares in the new stores they would manage (as Penney himself had done). By 1930 there were over 1,100 Penney stores in the country and by 1951 at least one in every state. In 1970 the company initiated the development of an overall design program, created by Unimark International under the direction of senior vice president Jay Doblin, who continued to act as consultant to the firm after leaving Unimark in 1971. The J. C. Penney Design System, according to the 1973 employee manual, was "much more than rubber-stamping a logotype on every Penney package, truck, and ad. The Design System expresses the Penney image and personality. Its influence must permeate all our design activities [and] . . . we can already see the effect of the Design System on certain merchandise lines."[32] The effect on its merchandise was most strongly apparent during the 1970s and early 1980s in the design of small appliances that carried the store's name (no. 341), manufactured for Penney to its original designs, or, as was often the case, its redesigns.

References: S.M., "J. C. Penney," *Graphis* 173 (1974–75): 232–37; Barry Dean, *Industrial Design: 24th Annual Design Review* (New York, 1978), pp. 63, 65.

CHARLOTTE PERRIAND
French, born 1903

A collaborator in the office of LE CORBUSIER and PIERRE JEANNERET between 1927 and 1937, Charlotte Perriand is widely regarded as the catalyst that prompted the firm to design the metal furniture for which it became widely known (nos. 125, 131). An exhibitor at the Société des Artistes Décorateurs from 1926, Perriand first displayed metal furniture in chromed steel and anodized aluminum at the 1927 Salon d'Automne in her rooftop bar interior,

provoking a critical uproar and attracting the attention of Le Corbusier, who took on the recent graduate of the Ecole de l'Union Centrale des Arts Décoratifs.

Perriand had studied under Henri Rapin at the Ecole (1925), and at the same time took courses offered by Maurice Dufrène, artistic director of La Maîtrise at the Galeries Lafayette. The first works designed by Perriand after entering Le Corbusier's office were shown in a dining-room interior at the 1928 Salon of the Société des Artistes Décorateurs, a room that included a telescoping table and four revolving tubular-steel chairs (produced after 1929 by Thonet). At the Salon d'Automne of 1929 the Corbusier-Perriand-Jeanneret partnership made its definitive statement about the furnishing and arrangement of the modern interior with its "interior equipment of a dwelling," which featured storage units, chairs, a chaise longue, and tables made almost entirely of glass and metal. Perriand had initially planned to present the prototypes for these furnishings at the Salon of the Société des Artistes Décorateurs, along with work by other avant-garde designers, but when the jury refused to grant this group sufficient exhibition space, they resigned from the Société, forming the Union des Artistes Modernes (UAM). Perriand participated in the UAM exhibition of 1930 with Le Corbusier and Jeanneret and in 1931 under her own name. Through her work in their office, she continued to experiment with industrial materials, using aluminum in a mountain shelter she presented with Jeanneret and others at the Paris international exhibition of 1937 and studying its use in prefabricated housing and in other projects in an office with JEAN PROUVÉ, Jeanneret, and Georges Blanchon in 1940.

That same year she was invited to Japan by the Japanese Ministry of Commerce and Industry as an industrial design adviser. Blocked by the war, Perriand spent the years 1940–42 in Japan, where she organized an exhibition in Tokyo and Osaka, and from 1943 to 1946 in Indochina. On her return to France after the war, Perriand continued her work with Jeanneret and Blanchon and worked independently as well, designing and furnishing a hotel at Mérebel-les-Allues (1946–49); designing a prototype kitchen for Le Corbusier's Unité d'Habitation at Marseilles (1950); creating furniture for Steph Simon in Paris (1955–74); furnishing the interior of the Air France office in London (1957); and developing a hotel facility at Arcs, in Savoy (1967–82).

References: Charlotte Perriand, "Wood or Metal?" *Studio* 97 (April 1929): 278–79; Musée des Arts Décoratifs, Paris, *Charlotte Perriand: Un Art de vivre* (February 5–April 1, 1985); Musée des Arts Décoratifs, Paris, *Les Années UAM, 1929–1958* (September 27, 1988– January 29, 1989), pp. 232–33 et passim; Yvonne Brunhammer and Suzanne Tise, *French Decorative Art: The Société des Artistes Décorateurs, 1900–1942* (Paris, 1990), pp. 122, 132–33, 137, 143, 150.

JEAN PERZEL
French, born Bohemia, 1892–1986

One of the leading lighting designers and manufacturers of the 1920s and 30s, Jean Perzel used the experience he gained studying glass painting in Munich and Paris and working in his family's glassmaking establishment to develop special types of glass that would provide evenly diffused light and increased illumination. His production was limited to relatively few styles, mainly geometric shapes with metal fixtures, which he produced in quantity as ceiling lights, table lamps, chandeliers, and wall lights (no. 112). He also worked on commission for other design firms and designed lighting for such interiors as the League of Nations building in Geneva and the ocean liner *Normandie*, gaining an international reputation and clients worldwide. Perzel began to work in lighting in 1923, and he exhibited at the principal Paris salons between 1924 and 1958. He received first prize in the decorative lighting competition organized by the Société pour le Perfectionnement de l'Eclairage at the Salon des Artistes Décorateurs in 1928 and four first prizes in the decorative lighting competition in Paris in 1936.

References: B.D., "Appareils d'éclairage de Jean Perzel," *Mobilier et Décoration* 9 (May 1929): 107–10; *Dictionnaire des artistes décorateurs*, s.v. "Jean Perzel"; Alastair Duncan, *Art Nouveau and Art Deco Lighting* (London, 1978), pp. 180–81, 203, figs. 118–19; Yvonne Brunhammer, *The Art Deco Style* (New York, 1984), pp. 172–75.

GAETANO PESCE
Italian, born 1939

Architect, artist, and designer, Gaetano Pesce has taken an extraordinarily inventive approach to the use of new materials and techniques in the design, manufacture, and distribution of furniture (nos. 307, 343, 389). Pesce studied architecture and industrial design in Venice and in 1961 worked at the Hochschule für Gestaltung in Ulm, Germany. His activity as a designer, which began in 1962, included semantic investigations (having contributed overscale familiar objects and referential furnishings to the Pop design movement) as well as technological ones, both of which continue to inform his work. Simultaneously visionary and pragmatic, Pesce has considered technology on both an immediate and a global scale, suggesting in recent years that attitudes toward mass production and design are changing and that designers must respond to these concerns: "In the future, customers will expect original objects. What I call the third industrial revolution will give people the opportunity to have a unique piece. The technology we have today gives us the possibility to produce in this way."[33]

References: Emilio Ambasz, ed., *Italy: The New Domestic Landscape* (New York, 1972), pp. 35, 97–98, 212–22; Musée des Arts Décoratifs, Paris, *Gaetano Pesce: "The Future Is Perhaps Past"* (January 8–March 9, 1975); "Talking with Four Men Who Are Shaping Italian Design," *Industrial Design* 28 (September–October 1981): 30–35; Marco Romanelli, "Gaetano Pesce: Le poltrone I Feltri per Cassina," *Domus* 686 (September 1987): 98–101; B. F., "Gaetano Pesce vers un nouvel art du siège: Les Feltri," *Architecture d'Aujourd'hui* 254 (December 1987): 83; Suzanne Slesin, "Modern Notions of Design: The Furniture of Gaetano Pesce," *New York Times*, November 10, 1988, pp. C1, C10.

TRUDE PETRI
German, 1906–1968

Known for the standardized porcelain tablewares she designed for the state porcelain factory in Berlin during the 1930s, Trude Petri studied first at the Hochschule für Bildende Künste in Hamburg and, from 1927, in the ceramics department of the Vereinigte Staatsschule für Angewandte und Bildende Kunst (United School for Applied and Fine Arts) in Berlin. In 1929 she was appointed designer for the state porcelain factory and during the next decade created the simple but elegantly shaped, white "modern" services for which she remains best known today, including the *Rheinisches* (1929–30), *Neu-Berlin* (1931–32), *Urbino* (1931; no. 136), and *Arkadisches* (1938, with Siegmund Schütz) services. In 1953 she immigrated to the United States, where she became an independent industrial designer.

References: Margarete Jarchow, "Die Staatliche Porzellanmanufaktur Berlin (KPM), 1918–1938: Institution und Produktion," Ph.D. diss., Universität Hamburg, 1984, pp. 142–44; Hans Wichmann, *Industrial Design, Unikate, Serienerzeugnisse: Die Neue Sammlung, ein neuer Museumstyp des 20. Jahrhunderts* (Munich, 1985), pp. 120, 511.

PHILCO CORPORATION
Established Philadelphia, 1892

Founded in 1892 as a manufacturer of electrical equipment, Philco began to produce radios in the 1920s and by 1930 was one of the leaders of the industry, selling its products made by assembly-line procedures at low prices on the appeal of its period cabinetry. In 1930 NORMAN BEL GEDDES began to design Philco radios, and his *Lazy Boy* table model of 1931 was its best-seller for the next two years. In the later 1930s the company diversified into the production of air conditioners, stoves, and refrigerators, and in 1948 produced its first television with conventional cabinetry designs. Philco's Predicta models of 1958–59 (no. 267) were the first American televisions to break through the box format and take a totally independent technological and design approach. In 1961 Philco was bought out by Ford.

References: "REdesign," *Industrial Design* 5 (June 1958): 52–53; Hubert Luckett, "Two-Piece TV Has Portable Picture Tube," *Popular Science* 173 (August 1958): 177–80.

GIOVANNI PINTORI
Italian, born 1912

As designer (1936–50) and then director of publicity (1950–67) for Olivetti, Giovanni Pintori introduced a boldly modern graphic imagery that came to symbolize the high quality and innovation of the company's products. Pintori was hired by Adriano Olivetti after completing his study at the Istituto Superiore per le Industrie Artistiche in Monza. He developed major advertising campaigns for a succession of Olivetti products with graphics influenced first by the unexpected juxtapositions of surrealism and then by abstract painting. Symbolic and conceptual, his work focused on abstracted machine elements to represent products and employed oblique typological parallels—an abacus to advertise an adding machine (1947) and hieroglyphics to publicize a typewriter (1953). He also reduced visual images to great masses of numbers (no. 215) and letterforms to represent the rapid functions of calculation and typography performed by Olivetti's products. Pintori's work for Olivetti included print advertisements, manuals, billboards, exhibition design, and a new lowercase sans-serif Olivetti logo (1947). He opened his own design studio in Milan in 1968.

References: "Olivetti: Design in Industry," *Museum of Modern Art Bulletin* (special issue) 20 (fall 1952); Giovanni Pintori, "Olivetti: A Designer's View," *Print* 15 (March 1961): 35–43; Frederick S. Wight Art Gallery, University of California, Los Angeles, *Design Process: Olivetti, 1908–1978* (March 27–May 6, 1979), pp. 265–66 et passim; Colin Naylor, ed., *Contemporary Designers*, 2d ed. (Chicago, 1990), p. 452.

PAUL POIRET
French, 1879–1944

One of the great fashion designers of the century, Paul Poiret also had a strong impact on the design of interiors, graphics, and textiles before World War I. He developed his talents in the salon of the noted couturier Jacques Doucet, where he not only designed clothing but also provided theatrical costumes for celebrated actresses, including Mistinguett and Sarah Bernhardt. For a short time he worked for the House of Worth and at the beginning of the century opened his own salon, achieving celebrity in 1906 when he began to design reform clothing without corsets. Poiret is credited with the liberation of the female figure by returning to the loose lines of the Empire styles.

Poiret's business flourished during the first two decades of the century, and he introduced new modes of presenting his collections, hiring PAUL IRIBE in 1908 to draw his fashion plates and EDWARD STEICHEN in 1911 to bring the fine art of photography to fashion illustration. He broadened his interests to include a millinery line; a textile-printing workshop, which he established for RAOUL DUFY; the Rosine perfume house, the first to be connected with a fashion designer; and the ATELIER MARTINE, a school and workshop founded in 1911, which introduced the taste for bold, bright exotic furnishings (no. 55). After the interruptions of World War I, Poiret was never successful in reestablishing his position, and although he made a final grand gesture at the *Exposition Internationale des Arts Décoratifs* in 1925, presenting three barges on the Seine furnished by Martine and with decorations by Dufy, he had to sell his businesses. He tried to recoup his career with a variety of commercial involvements, contributing a startling bedroom suite to the Contempora collection shown in New York in 1929 (no. 115), but he died impoverished in 1944.

References: Art Center, New York, *Contempora Exposition of Art and Industry* (1929), n.p.; Musée de la Mode et du Costume, Palais Galliera, Paris, *Paul Poiret et Nicole Groult: Maîtres de la mode art déco* (July 5–October 12, 1986); Yvonne Deslandres, with Dorothée Lalanne, *Poiret: Paul Poiret, 1879–1944* (New York, 1987).

FLAVIO POLI
Italian, 1900–1984

Flavio Poli became head designer for Seguso Vetri d'Arte in 1934, and after the war was recognized with prizes at international exhibitions for bringing simple, vigorous forms to Murano glass production (no. 271). His designs were generally produced in thick glass of a brilliant clarity, which featured strongly contrasting colors and no additional decoration. Among his earlier works were glass sculpture, especially a large opalescent crystal relief of the zodiac, as well as latticework (*vetro traliccio*) chandeliers and ornamental glass in futuristic shapes (*vetro astrale*), both of which styles he introduced. Poli was awarded a Compasso d'Oro prize in 1954.

References: Hans Heilmaier, "Kunstgläser aus der Manufaktur Ernesto Seguso nach Entwürfen von Flavio Poli," *Die Kunst und das schöne Heim* 54 (May 1956): 300–303; Corning Museum of Glass, Corning, New York, *Glas 1959* (1959), nos. 182–87; Gio Ponti, "Alta fedeltà: Vetro di Flavio Poli," *Domus* 410 (1964): 50–52; Palazzo delle Stelline, Milan, *Design & design* (May 29–July 31, 1979), p. 30; Rosa Barovier Mentasti et al., *Mille anni di arte del vetro a Venezia* (Venice, 1982), pp. 273–77.

GIO PONTI
Italian, 1891–1979

For more than half a century Gio Ponti championed modern design in Italy through his own work as an architect and designer of products, graphics, and interiors, and through the architecture and design magazines he directed: *Domus*, which he founded in 1928 and, with the exception of six years, edited until his death, and *Stile*, which he established in 1941 and edited until 1947. In addition, from 1936 to 1961 he was professor in the faculty of architecture at the Milan Politecnico and wrote nine books and some three hundred articles, the earliest in 1923.

Ponti graduated from the Politecnico in Milan with a degree in architecture (1921) and opened his first office in Milan with the architects Mino Fiocchi and Emilio Lancia. He first came to public attention through his work for the ceramic firm of Richard-Ginori (1923–30), where as artistic director he was engaged to modernize the firm's production. Ponti not only designed a broad range of important pieces (no. 110) but introduced Richard-Ginori to the concept of standardized product series, published the firm's first catalog of "modern" ceramics, and designed advertisements for Richard-Ginori products in Domus when it appeared in 1928. Ponti's ceramics were shown at the first Biennale exhibition of the decorative arts in Monza in 1923 and afterwards in the subsequent Triennale exhibitions in Monza and Milan, which Ponti helped to organize.

Like other rationalist Italian designers of the 1920s and 30s, Ponti sought to achieve a synthesis between the traditional, nationalistic values of Italian classicism and the structural logic of the machine age—a middle ground between historicism and the vocabulary of industrial form bequeathed by the futurists. During this period, he drew on the legacy of the Vienna Secession and the Wiener Werkstätte, practicing a stripped form of neoclassicism that paralleled the work of JOSEF HOFFMANN and others. After World War II Ponti's designs grew increasingly expressionistic although they remained simple in form and rationally conceived. His legendary espresso coffee machine for La Pavoni (1948) was compared at the time to "certain wind instruments," and his sanitary fixtures for Ideal Standard (1953; no. 237) to ancient sculpture. Ponti's prodigious design work included furniture (no. 265), ceramics, appliances, lighting, metalwares, glass, and textiles for numerous firms in Italy and abroad.

References: D. Guarnati, ed., "Espressione di Gio Ponti," Aria d'Italia (special issue) 8 (1954); Nathan H. Shapira, "The Expression of Gio Ponti," Design Quarterly (special issue) 69–70 (1967); Rossana Bossaglia, Omaggio a Gio Ponti (Milan, 1980); Paolo Portoghesi and Anty Pansera, Gio Ponti alla Manifattura di Doccia (Milan, 1982); Gio Ponti, Ceramiche 1923–1930 (Florence, 1983); Arata Isozaki, ed., Gio Ponti: From the Human Scale to the Postmodernism (Tokyo, 1986); Ugo La Pietra, ed., Gio Ponti: L'arte si innamora dell'industria (Milan, 1988); Lisa Licitra Ponti, Gio Ponti: The Complete Work, 1923–1978 (Cambridge, Mass., 1990).

JEAN PROUVÉ
French, 1901–1984

Engineer and designer, Jean Prouvé worked primarily in metal, conceiving of architecture and design pragmatically as products to be fabricated of industrial materials with industrial techniques at reasonable prices. The son of Victor Prouvé, a versatile artist-decorator of the Ecole de Nancy, Prouvé learned the trade of ironworker in Paris, between 1916 and 1919 with Emile Robert and from 1919 to 1921 with Adalbert Szabo. In 1923 he opened a workshop in Nancy, where he executed decorative metalwork for architects and designers, in 1925 meeting ROBERT MALLET-STEVENS, who gave him his first major decorative commission, and LE CORBUSIER. Between 1923 and 1953 Prouvé designed and manufactured furniture in a totally original form using bent and welded sheet steel, at first producing residential seating in limited quantities (no. 102) and then adding office and school furniture, which he manufactured in large numbers. His ideas for the use of prefabricated architectural elements and the construction of metal buildings during the 1930s brought him numerous commissions before and after World War II, and he remained unique within the French construction trades for his combined activity as architect, manufacturer, and builder. Prouvé was a founding member of the Union des Artistes Modernes in 1929.

References: Reyner Banham, "On Trial: Jean Prouvé, the Thin, Bent Detail," Architectural Review 131 (April 1962): 249–52; Benedikt Huber and Jean-Claude Steinegger, eds., Jean Prouvé, Prefabrication: Structures and Elements (New York, 1971); Museum Boymans-van Beuningen, Rotterdam, Jean Prouvé, Constructeur (1981); "Jean Prouvé: Sedie tra il 1924 e il 1930," Domus 697 (September 1988): 86–89; Jean Prouvé: Möbel, Furniture, Meubles (Cologne, 1991).

JEAN PUIFORCAT
French, 1897–1945

The most celebrated French silversmith of this century, Jean Puiforcat followed his family's craft, learning his trade as an apprentice in his father's studio. He attended the Central School of Arts and Crafts in London and studied the art of sculpture, apparently with Louis-Aimé Lejeune. Working at first in an angular, geometric mode, he exhibited in Paris in 1925, where he had his own display and also contributed to the "Hôtel du Collectionneur" of EMILE-JACQUES RUHLMANN. Puiforcat was a member of Les Cinq—a group that included Dominique (André Domain and Maurice Genèvrière), PIERRE LEGRAIN, PIERRE CHAREAU, and the jeweler Raymond Templier—who exhibited together in 1926 and 1927 and were associated with the founding of the Union des Artistes Modernes in 1929.

Puiforcat's silverware is noted for its combinations with rare wood, ivory, rock crystal, lapis lazuli, jade, carnelian, amber, and other unusual materials; he exploited these contrasts in his flatware, tea and coffee services, tureens (no. 157), and trays, which generally are otherwise devoid of decoration. As he matured his approach became increasingly intellectual, his designs mathematical and almost mystical, as he searched for perfect forms based on his understanding of Platonic ideals and the ratios of the golden section. More and more he turned to a fluidity of line, for, as he explained, "I continue to think that the circle, which explains the entire world, is the ideal figure, and the curve, which approaches it, is more noble than the straight line."[34] At the 1937 Paris *Exposition Internationale*, Puiforcat showed his work in a separate pavilion, where he exhibited not only domestic silver but also a large number of ecclesiastical pieces, which he first began to produce in 1934.

References: *Jean Puiforcat, orfèvre sculpteur* (Paris, 1951); Françoise de Bonneville, *Jean Puiforcat* (Paris, 1986).

ERNEST RACE
English, 1913–1964

One of the most successful early post–World War II furniture designers in Great Britain, Ernest Race had to overcome the substantial obstacles imposed by the wartime Utility system to begin his career. Designed with alternative materials, his furniture received Board of Trade approval, and it came to the attention of progressives who saw his use of these materials as modern and innovative. His first and ultimately most successful design was the lightweight *BA* chair (no. 189) in cast surplus aluminum produced by the company he formed with J. W. Noel Jordan, an engineer, under the name Ernest Race Limited. Other early designs included component storage units awarded an honorable mention in the "International Competition for Low-Cost Furniture Design" at New York's Museum of Modern Art in 1948 and a range of upholstered seating with welded steel-rod structure. This use of bent and welded metal was applied in 1951 to his two *Festival of Britain* designs, the *Antelope* (no. 226) and *Springbok* chairs. Much of Race's later work was in the area of contract furniture, including the *Neptune* deck chair (1953) and *Cormorant* chair (1959) for the Orient Line, and the *Sheppey* line of modular, easily assembled upholstered furniture (1961). Race left the firm in 1962 to become a freelance designer.

References: "Trends in Factory Made Furniture by Ernest Race," *Architectural Review* 103 (May 1948): 218–20; L. Bruce Archer, "Theory into Practice: Design and Stress Analysis," *Design* 101 (May 1957): 18–21; Hazel Conway, *Ernest Race* (London, 1982).

DIETER RAMS
German, born 1932

Trained as an architect and interior designer at the Werkkunstschule in Wiesbaden (1947, 1951–53), Dieter Rams made his career at the consumer appliance firm of Braun, which he joined in 1955. Rams became head of Braun's product design division in 1961, director of product design in 1968, and a general manager of the firm in 1988. Although Braun's corporate image had been defined before Rams's arrival by a collaboration between the designers HANS GUGELOT and Otl Aicher of the Hochschule für Gestaltung in Ulm and the firm's management—Artur Braun, Erwin Braun, and Fritz Eichler—it was Rams who developed many of the austerely beautiful and functional appliances for which Braun's design program

became so well known (nos. 242, 259). One of Germany's best-known industrial designers, Rams has been a leading practitioner and spokesperson for the aesthetic of neofunctionalism, writing in 1978, "the aesthetic requirement of an industrial product is that it should be simple, carefully made, honest, balanced and unobtrusive. . . . I regard it as one of the most important and most responsible tasks of a designer today to help clear the chaos we are living in."[35] In addition to his work for Braun, Rams has designed furniture for Otto Zapf and Modus.

References: François Burkhardt and Inez Franksen, eds., *Design: Dieter Rams &* (Berlin, 1981); Industrie Forum Design, Hannover, Germany, *Dieter Rams, Designer: Die liese Ordnung der Dinge* (Göttingen, Germany, 1990).

PAUL RAND
American, born 1914

The preeminent American corporate designer, Paul Rand has created intelligent, practical, and witty identity programs for such companies as IBM (no. 381), Westinghouse, and UPS that have become models of the genre. Rand was one of the first to apply European modernism to American graphic design and advertising, drawing on the aesthetic of LÁSZLÓ MOHOLY-NAGY (whose 1932 book *The New Vision* greatly influenced him), LE CORBUSIER, cubism, De Stijl, and Paul Klee in his manipulation of abstract forms and his reliance on humor as a communication tool. Rand studied in New York at the Pratt Institute (1930–32) and Parsons School of Design (1932). From 1936 to 1941 he was art director and designer for Esquire-Coronet and *Apparel Arts* magazine, and between 1938 and 1945 he created bimonthly covers for *Direction* magazine (no. 182). Between 1941 and 1954, when he worked as creative director of the William H. Weintraub advertising agency, his work achieved a level of quality that set new standards for this burgeoning field. Introduced to IBM by its design consultant ELIOT NOYES in 1956, Rand restructured the company's image and established the basis for a consistent but flexible program of corporate design. He designed its logo, advertising, and packaging, and developed the IBM annual report into a vital marketing tool, which would be much imitated throughout the industry. Rand has been professor of graphic design at Yale University since 1956.

References: Paul Rand, *Thoughts on Design* (New York, 1946); Steven Heller, interview, in Mildred Friedman et al., *Graphic Design in America: A Visual Language History* (New York, 1989), pp. 193–95; Paul Rand, *Paul Rand: A Designer's Art* (New Haven, Conn., 1985).

ARMAND-ALBERT RATEAU
French, 1882–1938

Remaining independent of the confraternity of Parisian designers (he never, for example, exhibited at the salons), Armand Rateau created an original style—exotic, sumptuous, mysterious—that found favor with a succession of important clients. After studying drawing and wood sculpture at the Ecole Boulle in Paris, he began to provide designs independently for a number of decorators, including Georges Hoentschel; then from 1905 to 1914 he managed the workshops of the prestigious decorating firm Maison Alavoine. After the war, in 1919, he opened his own decorating business and within a year received a major commission from the couturiere Jeanne Lanvin. Between 1920 and 1922 he provided her house with furnishings inspired by the orient and the antique, including a celebrated marble bathroom and numerous pieces of his signature bronzework—lamps, furniture (no. 83), accessories, all sculpted and chased with animal and floral decoration. (Several complete rooms are now in the Musée des Arts Décoratifs in Paris.) The bronzework was made at the Ateliers Neuilly-Levallois, which he acquired in 1922 and where he employed over one hundred workers. Simultaneously Lanvin made him director of her newly established decorating salon, Lanvin-Décoration. Bronze furnishings similar to those designed for Lanvin's house appeared in the presentations of the firms of Jenny and Callot Soeurs in the Pavillon de l'Elégance at the 1925 *Exposition Internationale des Arts Décoratifs* in Paris, where he won two grand prizes, for ensembles of furniture and metal. Other clients for whom he worked between 1920 and 1938 included the duchess of Alba (a Persian bathroom for her Palacio Liria in Madrid, 1925–26), Baron Eugène de Rothschild, and the American collectors Mr. and Mrs. George Blumenthal.

References: Eveline Schlumberger, "Au 16 Rue Barbet-de-Jouy avec Jeanne Lanvin," *Connaissance des Arts* 138 (August 1963): 63–71; Pierre Kjellberg, *Art déco: Les maîtres du mobilier, le décor des paquebots* (Paris, 1986), pp. 148–51; Alastair Duncan, *A. A. Rateau* (New York, 1990).

RUTH REEVES
American, 1892–1966

Painter as well as textile designer, Ruth Reeves attended the Pratt Institute in Brooklyn, the San Francisco School of Design, and the Art Students' League in New York, and between 1920 and 1927 lived in Paris where she was a student at the Académie Moderne under Fernand Léger. The modern style of her paintings was adopted for many of the decorative patterns she designed for block printing after her return to New York. Reeves was one of the founders of the American Designers' Gallery in New York, and in its first exhibition in 1928 she showed an ensemble of block-printed fabrics, metal lamps, and a daybed made of silver-lacquered steel tubing. A series of twelve printed textiles designed for W. & J. Sloane for the *International Exhibition of Decorative Metalwork and Cotton Textiles* was shown by Sloane's in New York in 1930 (no. 135), and eight subsequently toured the country in the exhibition. In 1932 she designed a tapestry and the carpet for the grand foyer of the Radio City Music Hall in New York. Reeves also traveled widely on foundation grants to study other cultures' weaving and decorative techniques, which she often adapted for her own work; in 1934 she went to Guatemala, in 1941 to Ecuador, Peru, and Bolivia, and in 1956 to India, where she worked for the All-India Handicrafts Board.

References: "Exhibit of American Designers' Gallery: An Ambitious Program in Art Moderne," *Good Furniture Magazine* 32 (January 1929): 43; W. & J. Sloane, New York, *Exhibition of Contemporary Textiles* (December 1930); Harry V. Anderson, "Ruth Reeves," *Design* 37 (March 1936): 24–26, 39; Obituary, *New York Times*, December 24, 1966, p. 19; Karen Davies, *At Home in Manhattan: Modern Decorative Arts, 1925 to the Depression* (New Haven, Conn., 1983), nos. 34, 47, 60, 70.

FREDERICK HURTEN RHEAD
American, born England, 1880–1942

Born to a family of potters and ceramic painters in the English pottery center of Staffordshire, Frederick Hurten Rhead trained and apprenticed there and in 1899 took his first position as art director of the Wardle Pottery. He left for America in 1902 to manage Vance/Avon Faience in Tiltonville, Ohio, and over the next decades made his way as manager and designer for some eight other American art potteries, basing his wares mainly on British commercial models and favoring incised and slip-trailed techniques. He was art director of the Roseville Pottery in Zanesville, Ohio (1904–8); organized a therapeutic pottery program at the Arequipa Sanatorium in Marin County, California (1911–13); had his own studio in Santa Barbara (1914–17); and, back in Zanesville, became designer and director of research at the American Encaustic Tiling Company (1917–27). Rhead also taught at the People's University in University City, St. Louis (1909–11), with his friend the potter Adelaide Alsop Robineau, and contributed numerous articles to her journal, *Keramic Studio*, between 1904 and 1912. When in 1927 he became art director of the Homer Laughlin China Company in East Liverpool, Ohio, Rhead abandoned the arts and crafts aspects of his designs and embarked on a series of low-priced dinnerware services that were totally industrial in manufacture and often modern in appearance. The colorful, popular *Fiesta* ware (no. 170), introduced in 1936 and produced for the next three decades, was followed by several variations, most notably, *Harlequin* dinnerware (c. 1938), and Kitchen Kraft mixing, serving, and storage items (1939).

Reference: Sharon Dale, *Frederick Hurten Rhead: An English Potter in America* (Erie, Pa., 1986).

CARLOS RIART
Spanish, born 1944

A leader of Barcelona's postmodern design movement, Carlos Riart has created highly original furniture for

Tecmo in Barcelona (no. 337), Société Ecart International in Paris, and Knoll International in New York as well as interiors and exhibitions. Riart studied industrial design and cabinetry and taught industrial design at the Escuela de Deseño Eina (1976–78). His *1° Colección de muebles especiales* in 1976 first brought him critical notice, with furniture, he said, "of ambiguous use conceived as space dividers," which had the attributes of "meaning, personality, criticism, and historicism."[36]

References: "A Barcelona Workshop," *Domus* 546 (May 1975): 28; *1° Colección de muebles especiales de Carlos Riart* (Barcelona, n.d.), pp. 48–49; "Knoll Presents: Three Diverse Furniture Groups," *Interior Design* 53 (December 1982): 134–35.

RICHARD RIEMERSCHMID
German, 1868–1957

An architect and designer for industry, Richard Riemerschmid introduced a practical style of smooth, simple, and undecorated forms that bridged the distance between Jugendstil and industry products and set standards for progressive German design in the first decade of the twentieth century. His designs were described by contemporary critics as *sachlich*, or functional, a word that would endure in twentieth-century design theory through the products of the Deutscher Werkbund (of which Riemerschmid was a founding member [1907] and chairman [1921–26]) and of the Bauhaus. Trained initially as a painter at the Munich academy between 1888 and 1890, Riemerschmid was a cofounder in 1897–98 of Munich's Vereinigte Werkstätten für Kunst im Handwerk which was to produce and market industrial designs. His first products for the Vereinigte Werkstätten were metalwares (no. 16), the earliest of which appeared in the spring of 1898 and among which was a candlestick that was criticized at the time for its "unnatural" decorative restraint.[37] Riemerschmid came to full artistic maturity with the design in 1899 for the Dresden *Deutsche Kunst-Ausstellung* of a music room considered remarkable for the unity of its interior decoration and for the highly original chairs that furnished it (no. 15). Other interiors that brought Riemerschmid international recognition followed, including his Room of an Art Lover for the *Exposition Universelle* in Paris in 1900; a theater in Munich, the Schauspielhaus of 1900–1901, which today remains Germany's finest Jugendstil building; and exhibition rooms for the Dresdner Werkstätten in 1903 and 1906. For the latter, Riemerschmid created a revolutionary program of machine-made furniture (*Maschinenmöbel*; no. 38). With its ready-made suites aimed at a middle market, the series pioneered modern production furniture. Until World War I Riemerschmid's practice was highly varied: he designed metal wares (no. 51) and lighting for the Dresden workshops, porcelains for the Meissen factory (1903–4), glasswares for the firm of Benedikt von Poschinger (1900–1914), ceramics for Reinhold Merkelbach (1900–1908), and linoleum (no. 50), and was involved in the planning of Germany's first garden city at Hellerau near Dresden (1907–13). After the war Riemerschmid was active principally as an architect and teacher, serving as director of the Munich Kunstgewerbeschule (1912–24) and head of the Cologne Werkschule (1926–31).

References: Hermann Muthesius, "Die Kunst Richard Riemerschmid," *Kunst* 10 (1904): 249–83; Paul Johannes Ree, "Richard Riemerschmid," *Kunst* 14 (1906): 265–303; Winfried Nerdinger, ed., *Richard Riemerschmid: Vom Jugendstil zum Werkbund: Werke und Dokumente* (Munich, 1982); Kathryn B. Hiesinger, ed., *Art Nouveau in Munich* (Philadelphia, 1988), pp. 107–47.

GERRIT RIETVELD
Dutch, 1888–1964

Gerrit Rietveld designed the two best-known and most widely influential monuments associated with the De Stijl group, which he joined in 1919—the *Red/Blue* chair of 1918 (no. 81) and a house on the outskirts of Utrecht and its furnishings for Truus Schröder-Schräder, of 1924–25 (no. 88). The chair and building share the same formal aesthetic in which planar and linear elements are clearly differentiated by the use of color and the way they overlap, creating a highly original effect of objectivity and openness since considered fundamental to modern design. In describing his chair in 1919, Rietveld wrote that he had attempted to make every part simple and its most elementary form in accordance with function and material so that the whole would stand freely and clearly in space, an elementarist philosophy that the De Stijl theoretician Theo van Doesburg later expanded.

Rietveld was the son of a Utrecht cabinetmaker and apprenticed with his father as well as with the architect P. J. Klaarhammer. He opened his own studio in 1911, making furniture first to the designs of Klaarhammer and others, even versions of the work of FRANK LLOYD WRIGHT, before executing his own designs. While the De Stijl group began to disband in the mid-1920s, Rietveld continued to produce avant-garde designs and experiment with modern industrial materials and construction techniques; he built a garage and chauffeur's quarters in Utrecht of prefabricated concrete planks and steel I-beams (1927–28) and designed chairs with plywood shells and tubular-metal frames. In 1928 he became a founding member of C.I.A.M. (International Congress of Modern Architecture), and from 1930 was associated with Amsterdam's Metz & Company department store, for which he created low-cost furniture, including the boldly cantilevered *Zig-Zag* chair (1934; no. 160) and wooden *Crate* furniture (1935), the latter marketed in kits with instructions for assembly at home. After World War II Rietveld taught variously in Rotterdam, The Hague, Arnhem, and Amsterdam, and practiced as an architect, designing the Netherlands' Pavilion at the *Biennale*, Venice (1954), the Institut voor Kunstnijverheidsonderwijs, Amsterdam (1956–68), the Akademie voor Beeldende

Kunsten, Arnhem (1957–63), and De Zoohehof exhibition hall (1959–60) in Amersfoort.

References: T. M. Brown, *The Work of G. Rietveld, Architect* (Utrecht, 1958); Stedelijk Museum, Amsterdam, *G. Rietveld, Architect* (November 26, 1971–January 9, 1972); Daniele Baroni, *The Furniture of Gerrit Thomas Rietveld* (Woodbury, N.Y., 1978); Mildred Friedman, ed., *De Stijl, 1917–1931: Visions of Utopia* (New York, 1982), pp. 124–45 et passim; Marijke Küper and Ida van Zijl, *Gerrit Th. Rietveld, 1888–1964: The Complete Works* (Utrecht, 1992).

JENS RISOM
American, born Denmark, 1916

One of the first designers to bring Scandinavian values and traditions to American furniture manufacture, Jens Risom studied design and interior planning at the Nordiska Kompaniet in Stockholm (1935) along with furniture and interior design at the Kunsthåndvaerkerskolen (School of Arts, Crafts and Design) in Copenhagen (1937). He immigrated to the United States in 1939 where he worked for the Dan Cooper studio, designing textiles, furniture, and interiors. He also collaborated on interior design projects with Hans Knoll, another recent immigrant, and developed the first line produced by Knoll's new furniture company; fifteen of his designs were included when it was introduced in 1942 (no. 185). In 1946 Risom established his own firm, which designed, manufactured, and distributed furniture to contract as well as residential clients in the United States and abroad. Since 1973, when his firm was acquired by Dictaphone, Risom has headed a consulting and design firm, Design Control, in New Canaan, Connecticut.

References: "Modern Doesn't Pay, or Does It?," *Interiors* 105 (March 1946): 70–71; Buffalo Fine Arts Academy, Albright Art Gallery, Buffalo, *Good Design Is Your Business* (1947), p. 46; "In the Showrooms," *Interiors* 110 (March 1951): 104–5; George Nelson, ed., *Chairs* (New York, 1953), pp. 92, 94, 159; Eric Larrabee and Massimo Vignelli, *Knoll Design* (New York, 1981), pp. 40–43; Martin Eidelberg, ed., *Design 1935–1965: What Modern Was* (Montreal, 1991), p. 51.

HANS ROERICHT
German, born 1932

From 1955 to 1959 Hans Roericht studied at the Hochschule für Gestaltung at Ulm, Germany; his diploma project, a compact, modular institutional table service (*Kompaktgeschirr*), was adopted by Rosenthal, introduced in 1961 (no. 260), and has since been widely imitated. Remaining at Ulm as a member of the school's design development program, he worked on corporate identity and product design systems, and in 1964 became a teaching assistant with additional responsibilities for curriculum development. In 1967 he founded his own firm in Ulm, and his work has included visual communications, trans-port, and production systems for Lufthansa, WMF, AEG, and Rosenthal. Since 1973 he has taught industrial design at the Hochschule der Künste in Berlin, specializing in office products and environments. Roericht designed the NCR *Decision Mate V* personal computer, which won a Bundespreis Gute Form in 1983.

References: "Designs from Abroad: 'New Bauhaus' Dinnerware," *Industrial Design* 8 (July 1961): 70–75; Hans Wichmann, *Industrial Design, Unikate, Serienerzeugnisse; Die Neue Sammlung, ein neuer Museumstyp des 20. Jahrhunderts* (Munich, 1985), pp. 445, 451.

GILBERT ROHDE
American, 1894–1944

With experience in photography, advertising, and journalism, Gilbert Rohde turned to furniture design in 1927, disseminating the French style of decorative arts in the United States by basing his early custom furniture and interiors on the progressive styles he saw on a trip to France that year. Rohde opened his own studio in New York in 1929, and through the contacts he made with a number of important furniture manufacturers, among them Heywood-Wakefield, Troy Sunshade, John Widdicomb, Thonet, and Herman Miller (no. 161), was one of the first to bring modern design to American mass-produced furniture. Using both wood and metal in simple rectilinear forms, he pioneered component systems for home and office use, including an early version of the sectional sofa. His closest ties were with Herman Miller, for whom he designed storage units, modular desks, and upholstered furniture as well as showrooms, and it was he who established the design direction that the company would follow in the postwar period. Rohde also created a large series of electric clocks for the Herman Miller Clock Company. In addition he designed interiors for exhibitions, including A Music Room Corner for the 1934 exhibition of industrial design at the Metropolitan Museum of Art in New York and the "Design for Living" house at the 1933 *Century of Progress* exhibition in Chicago. He also created interiors for department stores, where at R. H. Macy's in New York and John Wanamaker's in Philadelphia his work became known to a popular audience.

References: Ralph Caplan, *The Design of Herman Miller* (New York, 1976), pp. 24–29; Washburn Gallery, New York, *Gilbert Rohde* (September–October 1981); Derek Ostergard and David A. Hanks, "Gilbert Rohde and the Evolution of Modern Design, 1927–1941," *Arts Magazine* 56 (October 1981): 98–107; Derek E. Ostergard, ed., *Bent Wood and Metal Furniture, 1850–1946* (New York, 1987), pp. 290, 298–99, 302, 314–15.

JOHAN ROHDE
Danish, 1856–1935

Mentor and associate of GEORG JENSEN, Johan Rohde

studied painting and graphics at the Kongelige Danske Kunstakademi (Royal Danish Academy of Fine Arts) in Copenhagen and was the founder of the Kunstnernes Studieskole (Artists' Studio School) in 1882, which he directed between 1908 and 1912. In 1905, as part of the highly refined furnishings he was designing for his own house, he commissioned Jensen to produce silver flatware and hollowware from the models he had created. This led to further collaboration when Rohde began to supply designs for the Jensen firm in 1907; he continued to work with the silversmith until his death in 1935. Rohde was responsible for Jensen's most popular cutlery, the *Acorn* pattern (no. 68), designed in 1915, and numerous other pieces, many of which reveal traditional elements of Scandinavian historicism, and neoclassicism in particular. Later, especially in the 1930s, Rohde adopted a sleek undecorated style, which had been suggested in his work as early as 1920 (no. 79). He also redesigned the Jensen shop in Copenhagen in 1918 at a time when the firm was beginning to establish its international reputation.

References: Sigurd Schultz, *Johan Rohde Sølv* (Copenhagen, 1951); Renwick Gallery, National Collection of Fine Arts, Washington, D.C., *Georg Jensen—Silversmithy: 77 Artists 75 Years* (February 29–July 6, 1980), nos. 123–30.

ALFRED ROLLER
Austrian, 1864–1935

Alfred Roller was a graphic designer, painter, and teacher who spent his entire artistic career in Vienna in the circle of those artists who created a Viennese "modern" style at the turn of the century. A member of the radical Vienna Secession, Roller is best known for the five posters he designed to advertise Secession exhibitions between 1899 and 1903 (no. 33), as well as for his contributions to *Ver Sacrum*, the Secession journal. At the fourteenth Secession exhibition in 1902, Roller designed a mural decoration for the central exhibition space. The following year he designed the stage sets for a production of Wagner's *Tristan and Isolde* directed by Gustav Mahler at Vienna's Hof-Operntheater. In 1907, after the opening of the Fledermaus cabaret, which the Wiener Werkstätte furnished, Roller, a collaborating decorator, supplied designs for sets and costumes along with Karl Otto Czeschka, JOSEF HOFFMANN, Gustav Klimt, Oskar Kokoschka, KOLOMAN MOSER, and EDUARD JOSEF WIMMER. Professor at the Kunstgewerbeschule since 1893, Roller was made the school's director in 1909.

Reference: Werner J. Schweiger, *Wiener Werkstaette: Design in Vienna, 1903–1932* (New York, 1984), pp. 45, 94, 145, 188, 265.

MAYA ROMANOFF
American, born 1941

A specialist in the resist dyeing of diverse materials—silk, leather, suede, canvas, velvet—Maya Romanoff came to textile design through anthropology and classical archaeology, which he studied at the University of California in Berkeley, and through his travels in the third world, where he saw these ancient techniques being used. He experimented with resist methods and adapted them for modern production, creating both one-off designs and textiles in series (no. 345). Romanoff has used his dyed fabrics as floor and wall coverings as well as upholstery and drapery fabrics, and he has also executed environments (including the "Garden Room" commissioned by *House and Garden* in 1971) and site-specific sculptural installations (the Arsenal in New York's Central Park in 1980).

References: The Arsenal, New York, *Maya Romanoff: Fabric Impressionist* (1979); "Maya Romanoff: A Textile Artist," *Interior Design* 52 (September 1981): 194–95; Janet Koplos, "Maya Romanoff's Odyssey," *FiberArts* 15 (January–February 1989): 33–36.

ROOKWOOD POTTERY
Established Cincinnati, 1880–1967

Choosing Rookwood's name from her father's estate (but also because "it reminded one of Wedgwood"), Maria Longworth Nichols transformed an association of amateur ceramists into a thriving business and one of America's most celebrated art potteries. Rookwood was founded in 1880 with the support of Nichols's father, and production built up quickly, with vases being sold in the leading stores of major American cities within a few years. The pottery sent a display to the *Exposition Universelle* in Paris in 1889 where it was awarded a gold medal, followed in 1893 by the highest award given at the *World's Columbian Exposition* in Chicago. In 1890 the company was given to William Watts Taylor, the manager who had been hired in 1883 and had brought it financial success. By the turn of the century Rookwood's output had become enormous (seven thousand Rookwood shapes have been cataloged) and some thirty-five decorators were working at the pottery, most important among them being Albert Valentien, Artus van Briggle, and Katara Shirayamadani (no. 21). Rookwood won prizes at the international expositions in Paris in 1900 (grand prize), Turin in 1902 (diploma of honor), and Saint Louis in 1904 (two grand prizes).

References: *Rookwood: An American Art* (Cincinnati, 1904); Herbert Peck, *The Book of Rookwood Pottery* (New York, 1968); Catherine Hoover Voorsanger, "Dictionary of Architects, Artisans, Artists, and Manufacturers," in Doreen Bolger Burke et al., *In Pursuit of Beauty: Americans and the Aesthetic Movement* (New York, 1986), pp. 464–65.

CLÉMENT ROUSSEAU
French, 1872–1950

Clément Rousseau is known as a designer of luxury furniture, although he first worked as a sculptor and did not begin to create furniture until he was forty. About 1910 he began to assist PAUL IRIBE in the preparation of sha-green (sharkskin), a technique Iribe reintroduced in this century for the decoration of furniture and the one that would bring renown to Rousseau's refined designs. He combined natural and colored skins with other rare materials—ebony, rosewood, marquetries of exotic woods, ivory, and copper—in forms very much rooted in the eighteenth and nineteenth centuries but adapted to the modern style (no. 105). During the 1920s Rousseau exhibited with the Société des Artistes Françaises and contributed to the furnishing of the studio of Jacques Doucet at Neuilly about 1925, when he also exhibited at the Galerie Charpentier in Paris. Later in the decade he was associated with the decorator Clément Mère.

References: Pierre Kjellberg, *Art déco: Les maîtres du mobilier, le décor des paquebots* (Paris, 1986), pp. 152–53; Gaston Derys, "Le Galuchat," *La Demeure Française* 4 (1927), quoted in Raymond Bachollet, Daniel Bordet, and Anne-Claude Lelieur, *Paul Iribe* (Paris, 1982), p. 230, n. 59; Frederick R. Brandt, *Late Nineteenth and Early Twentieth Century Decorative Arts: The Sydney and Frances Lewis Collection in the Virginia Museum of Fine Arts* (Richmond, 1985), pp. 180–81.

DAVID ROWLAND
American, born 1924

Since the beginning of his involvement in industrial design, David Rowland has been interested in creating comfortable seating for the great diversity of the adult human form, especially as it relates to accommodating large numbers of people. When he was still in high school he took summer courses with LÁSZLÓ MOHOLY-NAGY, which led to his enrollment, after he completed a college degree in physics, at the Cranbrook Academy of Art, Bloomfield Hills, Michigan (1950–51). Afterward he worked for NORMAN BEL GEDDES in New York, mostly doing architectural renderings, before opening his own office in 1954. Rowland designed interiors and pursued experiments with seating, exploring designs for metal chairs that did not require conventional upholstery and could easily be ganged and stacked; he succeeded admirably with his much premiated *40 in 4* chair of 1963 (no. 277). Early essays with wire seating at Cranbrook, including a chair with seat and back of woven wire and yarn (in collaboration with fellow student JACK LENOR LARSEN), developed into a related work exhibited at the *XI Triennale* in Milan in 1957 and ultimately into the *Sof-Tech* chair of 1979 (no. 360), which used a system of plastic-coated zig-zag spring components. His other works include a patented weatherproof (*Drain-Dri*) cushion and the *Modulus* molded-wood seating system manufactured by Martela in Finland.

References: "The Padded Spring Chair That Isn't," *Interiors* 113 (November 1953): 101; *Industrial Design* 12 (November 1965): 7–9; Olga Gueft, "Thonet Sof-Tech Stacker," *Interiors* 139 (August 1979): 66–67, 84; "David Rowland Designs the Sof-Tech Chair for Thonet," *Interior Design* 50 (August 1979): 167; Robert Judson Clark et al., *Design in America: The Cranbrook Vision, 1925–1950* (New York, 1983), pp. 108, 129–30; Nada Westerman and Joan Wessel, *American Design Classics* (New York, 1985), pp. 140–41.

EMILE-JACQUES RUHLMANN
French, 1879–1933

The foremost French furnituremaker of the twentieth century, Emile-Jacques Ruhlmann is often compared to Riesener, Boulle, and other great craftsmen of the eighteenth century. Like them, he used precious and exotic materials for his veneers and inlays, and only the highest craftsmanship was given to his pieces. While acknowledging traditional means and forms, he created lavish furniture in simplified modern forms (no. 69) that helped shift the French taste for expensive antiques to a fashion for equally expensive contemporary furnishings. Son of a prosperous interior contractor, Ruhlmann took over the business after his father's death in 1907. He first exhibited his own designs for furniture, lamps, and printed linens at the Paris Salon d'Automne in 1913, and by the 1919 Salon he was able to show a significant collection of his work (no. 75). The war years had been fertile for him, and although little was actually constructed, the inspiration for many of his later pieces can be found in sketches of this period (now in the Bibliothèque Nationale and Musée des Arts Décoratifs in Paris). In 1919 he joined with Pierre Laurent, a decorating contractor, to form the firm of Ruhlmann & Laurent, which engaged in both decorating and cabinetmaking; after 1921, however, furniture was labeled solely under the name of Ruhlmann. A designer rather than a craftsman himself, Ruhlmann employed a staff of architects and draftsmen to translate his sketches into plans and elevations, and meticulous full-scale drawings for the craftsmen who, until 1923 when he opened his own workshops, were outside contractors.

It was at the 1925 Paris *Exposition Internationale des Arts Décoratifs* that Ruhlmann achieved international celebrity. There, as an *ensemblier*, or decorator, he created the "Hôtel du Collectionneur" ("House of a Collector"), a separate pavilion furnished with his own works and those of some forty collaborators, which is now considered one of the landmarks of the art deco style. This brought him increased orders from a fashionable clientele and public commissions as well, for Paris's Chambre de Commerce and salons for the *Ile-de-France*, among others. The late 1920s saw the introduction of an even more simplified style and the addition of metal, glass, and laminated wood to the materials he used. With the onset of the Depression, Ruhlmann's business decreased, and before his death in 1933 he had decided that the firm should be dissolved.

References: Exposition des Arts Décoratifs de 1925, *L'Hôtel du Collectionneur: Groupe Ruhlmann* (Paris, 1926); Pavillon de Marsan, Paris, *Retrospective Ruhlmann*

(October–December 1934); Guillaume Janneau, "Chroniques: D'André-Charles Boulle à Ruhlmann," *La Revue de l'Art* 46 (December 1934): 185–91; Florence Camard, *Ruhlmann: Master of Art Deco* (New York, 1984).

R. D. RUSSELL
English, 1903–1981

Working first for his brother's firm, Gordon Russell, Ltd. (founded in 1929), which was commissioned in 1930 to produce cabinets for Murphy radios, and then on the design staff of Murphy itself, R. D. Russell developed the distinctive wooden cabinets (no. 181) that set this company apart from other radio manufacturers in England during the 1930s. Russell attended the school of the Architectural Association in London between 1924 and 1927 and then headed his brother's furniture design staff, continuing as an independent designer and consultant for Gordon Russell and others after joining Murphy. Between 1948 and 1964 he was professor of furniture design at the Royal College of Art, afterwards working as an independent designer and architect until his death in 1981. Russell was appointed Royal Designer for Industry in 1944.

References: John Gloag, *Industrial Art Explained,* 2nd ed. (London, 1946), pl. 5; Nikolaus Pevsner, "Patient Progress Two: Gordon Russell" [1962], in *Studies in Art, Architecture and Design,* vol. 2: *Victorian and After* (London, 1968), pp. 210–25; David Joel, *Furniture Design Set Free,* rev. ed. (London, 1969), p. 94; Obituary, *Times* (London), October 20, 1981, p. 16.

EERO SAARINEN
American, born Finland, 1910–1961

During the era most dominated by the International Style in America, the alternative approach, humanism, and genius of the architect Eero Saarinen were also widely recognized. He was awarded commissions for major monumental structures, which he executed in a daring, freely organic style; like Pierluigi Nervi, he exploited the properties of concrete for large open shell structures such as the undulating Trans World Airlines terminal at New York's John F. Kennedy Airport (1962) and the soaring parabolic Gateway Arch in the Jefferson National Expansion Monument in Saint Louis (completed 1964). Son of ELIEL SAARINEN, architect and president of the Cranbrook Academy of Art in Bloomfield Hills, Michigan, Saarinen attended Yale University, graduating with a degree in architecture and pursuing this career from 1936 until his death. Concurrently he worked as a furniture designer, collaborating in 1940 with CHARLES EAMES on developing a body-molded plywood-shell chair, which was awarded both first prizes in the "Organic Design in Home Furnishings" competition at the Museum of Modern Art in New York. Similarly organic and sculptural in conception, his succeeding works included the upholstered *Womb* chair of 1948 (no. 201) and his series of pedestal

chairs and tables of 1957 (no. 243) in which he aimed to eliminate "the ugly clutter of . . . legs going in different directions."[38]

References: Allan Temko, *Eero Saarinen* (New York, 1962); Robert A. Kuhner, *Eero Saarinen: His Life and Work* (Monticello, Ill., 1975); Robert Judson Clark et al., *Design in America: The Cranbrook Vision, 1925–1950* (New York, 1983), passim.

ELIEL SAARINEN
American, born Finland, 1873–1951

Finland's leading protagonist of nationalist romanticism at the turn of the century, Eliel Saarinen was a partner in the architectural firm of Gesellius, Lindgren, and Saarinen (established 1896), which won international recognition for the design of the Finnish pavilion at the Paris *Exposition Universelle* in 1900. The office was also highly regarded for domestic houses and furniture in a rustic, vernacular style, including Hvitträsk, their own studio and residences near Kirkkonummi (from 1902), and for the Helsinki central railway station (1904–14). The partnership dissolved in 1907 and Saarinen practiced independently, designing city plans for Helsinki (1916–18) and the Kästyöläispankki store in Helsinki (1920), among other projects. In 1922 Saarinen won second prize in the Chicago Tribune Tower competition and the following year moved with his family to the United States.

There he was appointed visiting professor in architectural design at the University of Michigan in 1923 and the next year was commissioned by George G. Booth, proprietor of the *Detroit News,* to develop plans for his Cranbrook Educational Community, including the Cranbrook Academy of Art, at Bloomfield Hills, Michigan. Saarinen essentially spent the rest of his career at Cranbrook, where he served as chief architect and architectural adviser. He also served as president of Cranbrook Academy (1932–46), which he developed into one of the most influential art schools in America, counting among its faculty and students Carl Milles, Maija Grotell, Marianne Strengell, CHARLES EAMES, HARRY BERTOIA, EERO SAARINEN, JACK LENOR LARSEN, DAVID ROWLAND, and Florence Knoll. Saarinen also worked on a smaller scale, designing furniture, carpets (with his wife, LOJA SAARINEN; no. 121), and metalwares (no. 154), mostly to furnish the structures of Cranbrook. In addition to teaching in the Academy's department of architecture, Saarinen maintained an independent architectural and design practice in which he was joined by his son Eero in 1936. Among the firm's commissions awarded in recognition of the Cranbrook buildings were master campus plans for Drake University in Des Moines, Iowa (1946–c. 1955), and Brandeis University in Waltham, Massachusetts (1948–c. 1951). After his resignation as Cranbrook's president, Saarinen continued as director of its department of architecture and urban design until his death.

References: J. S. Siren, ed., *Eliel Saarinen, Muistonäyttely* (Helsinki, 1955); Robert Judson Clark et al., *Design in America: The Cranbrook Vision, 1925–1950* (New York, 1983), passim.

LOJA SAARINEN
American, born Finland, 1879–1968

Trained as a sculptor and photographer at the Konstforeningen school and Taideteollinen keskuskoulu (Central School of Industrial Arts), Helsinki (1898–99), Louise (Loja) Gesellius Saarinen also studied at the Taideyhdistyksen Piirustuskoulu (School of the Fine Arts Society; 1899–1902) and in Paris at the Académie Colarossi (1902–3). She then worked in the Helsinki office of her brother, the architect Herman Gesellius, partner to ELIEL SAARINEN, whom she married in 1904. After continuing to work in Finland for nineteen years, in 1923 she and her family came to the United States, settling in 1925 in Bloomfield Hills, Michigan, at the Cranbrook Academy of Art, where her husband was chief architect. A few years later, in 1928, she turned to textile design and production, establishing the Studio Loja Saarinen to produce textiles for the new Cranbrook buildings, including handwoven fabrics, rugs, and window hangings, which she also did for others by special commission. The studio produced furnishing fabrics for the Saarinen residence and a rug (no. 121) designed in collaboration with her husband in the simplified vernacular style for which she became known. In 1930 she also became director of the department of weaving and textile design at Cranbrook, a post she held until her retirement in 1942. Among the most important commissions realized by the studio were textiles and carpets for a girls' preparatory school, the Kingswood School (1929–31). In her own work, that of the Scandinavian weavers whom she employed at her studio, and in the weaving department at Cranbrook, Saarinen introduced traditional Scandinavian craft styles, materials, and techniques into the vocabulary of pre–World War II American textile design.

Reference: Robert Judson Clark et al., *Design in America: The Cranbrook Vision, 1925–1950* (New York, 1983), pp. 173–211, 274–275 et passim.

LINO SABATTINI
Italian, born 1925

One of Italy's most prolific and original silver designers, Lino Sabattini has maintained a successful independent studio for over a quarter of a century, where his work is both produced and sold. With no schooling in design but with years of apprenticeship as an artisan in a metalwares shop, Sabattini opened his first workshop in Milan in 1955. There he was brought to the attention of GIO PONTI, editor of *Domus*, who published his work in 1956 and arranged for it to be shown in Paris. From 1956 to 1963 Sabattini was director of design for the Parisian silver firm of Christofle (no. 254), and on his return to Italy he established a studio in Bregnano, near Como, where he continues to work today. Sabattini's *Eskimo* ice bucket was awarded a Compasso d'Oro prize in 1979.

References: "Ottone e argento," *Domus* 321 (August 1956): 41; Enrico Marelli, *Intimations and Craftsmanship* (Mariano Comense, Italy, 1979); Filippo Alison, "Lino Sabattini," *Domus* 711 (December 1989): 64–71; Filippo Alison and Renato De Fusco, *L'Artidesign: Il caso Sabattini* (Naples, 1991).

ROBERTO SAMBONET
Italian, born 1924

Roberto Sambonet is a painter and an industrial designer with a degree in architecture from the Politecnico in Milan (1945). Before he joined his family metalware firm in Vercelli in 1954 he worked in Finland with ALVAR AALTO. Once at the firm Sambonet introduced new contemporary forms to the company's products, treating his stainless steel table and cookware—among them, his fish cooker and server of 1954 (no. 231) and his concentric, nesting *Center Line* cookware of 1964 (no. 290)—as part of an ongoing design system (which includes their packaging). Sambonet received a Compasso d'Oro award for his production in 1970. He has also designed glasswares for Baccarat (1977) and Seguso (1979) as well as ceramics for Bing & Grøndahl (1974) and Richard-Ginori (1979).

References: Pier Carlo Santini, *Roberto Sambonet* (Milan, 1970); Regione Lombardia, Comune de Milano, *Roberto Sambonet: Design, grafica, pittura, '74–79* (Milan, 1980).

RICHARD SAPPER
Italian, born Germany, 1932

Richard Sapper has been responsible for a number of the most recognizable Italian designs of the past decades, both those he designed with MARCO ZANUSO (no. 305) and those created independently. He has been the recipient of many Compasso d'Oro awards: in 1960 for his *Static* table clock (for Lorenz) and in 1979 for his *Tizio* lamp and espresso pot (nos. 336, 354); and with Zanuso, in 1962 for their *Doney 14* television (for Brionvega), in 1964 for their child's chair (no. 287), in 1967 for their *Grillo* telephone (no. 299), and in 1979 for their *Ariante* fan (for Vortice). Trained in economics and engineering at the University of Munich, Sapper worked for Daimler-Benz (1956–58) before moving to Italy, where he was first associated with GIO PONTI and La Rinascente and then, until 1977, with Zanuso. From 1970 to 1976 Sapper also worked on the development of experimental vehicles and automobile equipment for Fiat and Pirelli, and he collaborated with Gae Aulenti in 1972 on a proposal for new urban transportation systems that was presented at Milan's *XVI Triennale* in 1979. Sapper was hired by IBM as consultant for product design in 1980.

References: "La caffettiera," *Abitare* 173 (April 1979): 3; Alfonso Grassi and Anty Pansera, *Atlante del design italiano, 1940–1980* (Milan, 1980), p. 289 et passim; Jane Lott, "Fifties Fantasist Turned Design Houdini," *Design* 381 (September 1980): 37; *Richard Sapper: 40 progetti di design, 1958–1988* (Milan, 1988).

GINO SARFATTI
Italian, 1912–1985

Gino Sarfatti dominated the field of lighting in Italy in the 1950s, both through his own designs and those of the designers (among them the architects Franco Albini, GIANFRANCO FRATTINI, and MARCO ZANUSO) he commissioned to create lamps for his firm, Arteluce. A student of aero-naval engineering at the University of Genoa until he was forced by Fascist laws to leave, Sarfatti opened a glass showroom in Milan in 1939 and began by chance to create original lamps with Murano glass. Interrupted by World War II, he reopened the shop afterwards, producing functionalist lacquered-metal lamps with movable arms and then more adventurous, innovative designs, two of which were the recipients of the first two Compasso d'Oro awards for lighting, in 1954 (no. 232) and 1955. Sarfatti introduced a variety of new materials and forms, pioneering the use of plastics, neon tubes, and halogen bulbs for domestic lighting. He later concentrated on large interior commissions, creating lighting for office buildings, hotels, and the Italian ocean liners *Andrea Doria*, *Michelangelo*, and *Raffaello*.

References: "Lamps in a Milan Shop," *Interiors* 108 (November 1948): 114–15; Andrea Branzi and Michele De Lucchi, eds., *Il design italiano degli anni '50* (Milan, 1981), pp. 221, 223, 225–27, 229, 232; Jean François Grunfeld, "Gino Sarfatti, l'artisan" [interview], in Centre de Création Industrielle and Agence pour la Promotion de la Création Industrielle, Paris, *Lumières, je pense à vous* (June 3–August 5, 1985), pp. 56–62.

TIMO SARPANEVA
Finnish, born 1926

A masterly glass artist whose creativity has been equally applied to the production of decorative and utilitarian wares, Timo Sarpaneva has also designed ceramics, metalware (no. 272), textiles, graphics, and interiors. A graduate in graphics from the Taideteollinen keskuskoulu (Central School of Industrial Arts) in Helsinki (1948), Sarpaneva first worked in the area of textiles, producing figurative works designed by him and embroidered by his mother that were awarded a silver medal at Milan's *IX Triennale* in 1951; his Karelia series of simple weaves in close colors won a similar prize in 1957. Sarpaneva began to work in glass in 1950, creating at the littala factory a series of smooth rounded sculptures he called Devil's Churns. He has continued to produce sculptural works of great variety, introducing a truly distinctive series blown in wooden molds in 1963. His i-line of fine glass in misty colors, which brought a new elegance and refinement to littala's utilitarian wares, was launched in 1956, with Sarpaneva designing all of its coordinated packaging as well as the red trademark that appears on each piece of the continuing line (no. 262). Sarpaneva opened his own firm in 1962, producing among other designs his Ambiente lines; these were decorative papers (for Rosenlew) and textiles (for Tampella) that were freely "painted" with a mechanical printing process he developed (no. 315) and which received the International Design Award of the American Institute of Interior Designers in 1969. The *Suomi* porcelain service he designed for Rosenthal over a period of two years was introduced in 1974.

Reference: Kaj Kalin, *Sarpaneva* (Helsinki, 1986).

EGON SCHIELE
Austrian, 1890–1918

One of the most distinguished painters and draftsmen of Vienna's turn-of-the-century cultural renaissance, Egon Schiele, with Oskar Kokoschka, defined expressionism in Austria. Together they turned the course of progressive Viennese painting from the style of decorative linearity initiated by the Secession a decade earlier. Admitted to the Akademie der Bildenden Künste (Academy of Fine Arts) in Vienna at sixteen, Schiele first showed his work publicly in a group exhibition of local artists at Klosterneuburg in 1908, and again the following year at the Vienna international *Kunstschau*, where works of Gustav Klimt and Kokoschka influenced the young artist. In 1909 Schiele withdrew from the academy and with some of his classmates formed an independent exhibition organization, the Neukunstgruppe (New Art Group). During this period, Schiele also designed postcards for the Wiener Werkstätte (although only three were accepted for publication). Schiele continued to exhibit his work before and during World War I: in the Secession exhibitions in Munich (1912) and Vienna (1913) and in a *War Exhibition* in Vienna (1917), which Schiele, then attached to the Imperial and Royal Military Supply Depot, organized on behalf of the Army Museum. The artist's most productive years came in 1917 and 1918, culminating in the Vienna Secession exhibition of 1918, which Schiele organized and which served as a retrospective of his work (no. 72). The exhibition was a resounding critical and commercial success, the most important of Schiele's career, bringing him widespread recognition before his untimely death from the influenza epidemic that same year.

Reference: Jane Kallir, *Egon Schiele: The Complete Works* (New York, 1990).

PETER SCHLUMBOHM
American, born Germany, 1896–1962

Like a latter-day Benjamin Franklin, Peter Schlumbohm could not help putting things right. An inventor who amassed some three hundred patents, rather than a designer ("inventors are original, non-compromising pioneers," he asserted; "designers are parasitic politicians"),[39] he was concerned with how things work and how to make them work more efficiently. At the same time he had a talent for making things *look right*, convinced that an appropriate design would result from the process of invention itself. Schlumbohm first turned to invention to support himself when he lost his family's study allowance after receiving a doctorate in chemistry from the University of Berlin at the age of thirty; his first patents were granted in the area of refrigeration. Throughout his career he preferred to maintain control over his inventions and to nurture them through his own manufacturing and distribution company. In the 1940s, after he had come to the United States in 1939, he began to make a name for himself through a combination of entrepreneurship, proselytizing, and adaptive design, particularly with his now best-known product, the glass *Chemex* coffeemaker (no. 183). Its success let him add additional items, some successful, others not, for what he called the "Chemist's Kitchen"—most, like the coffeepot, based on laboratory glassware (no. 203). He also created products for such diversified purposes as environmental control, transportation (propane-powered automobile), and health improvement (*Phlebette* apparatus for improving blood circulation). His products were accompanied by explanatory literature about their beneficial values and by promotional literature advertising other "startling products, too highbrow for mass distribution." Although he often thought up secondary uses for his products, most of them were directed to very specific, narrow needs—for example, his *Soupette* (c. 1960), a kind of electric double boiler designed for warming canned condensed soup. Schlumbohm's products regularly appeared in the yearly design reviews of *Industrial Design* magazine, and his company's design program was shown along with that of Braun in an exhibition at the Museum of Modern Art in New York in 1964.

References: Ralph Caplan, "Chemex and Creation," *Industrial Design* 9 (December 1962): 121–22; Victor Papanek, *Design for the Real World* (New York, 1974), pp. 105–6.

GERTRAUD VON SCHNELLENBÜHEL
German, 1878–1959

Gertraud von Schnellenbühel studied painting in Munich with Angelo Jank and became one of the first students to take up applied arts at the Lehr- und Versuch-Ateliers für Angewandte und Freie Kunst (Teaching and Experimental Ateliers for Applied and Fine Art), the school founded in Munich in 1902 by HERMANN OBRIST and Wilhelm von Debschitz. Specializing in metalwork, Schnellenbühel designed a silver tea service with bare surfaces and angular handles as well as jewelry composed of small chains and multiple ornaments that was shown with other Debschitz school products at the 1906 Bayerische

Jubilaums-Landes-Ausstellung in Nuremberg. The decorativeness and clear sense of formal, geometric structure that appeared in these early works were combined in Schnellenbühel's later exhibition pieces. A critic for *Die Kunst* noted in 1914: Schnellenbühel "displayed a number of beautifully shaped unique objects in metal and wood, creations showing a delicate feeling for the possibilities of the material and exemplary in the way they combine construction with decorative ornament."[40] Her master work, a twenty-four-light candelabrum (no. 60), was exhibited with these objects at the Deutscher Werkbund exhibition of 1914 in Cologne.

References: G.J.W., "Zu den Arbeiten aus der Ausstellung 'Raumkunst,'" *Kunst* 30 (1914): 328–31; Kathryn B. Hiesinger, ed., *Art Nouveau in Munich* (Philadelphia, 1988), pp. 156–57; Graham Dry, ed., *Münchner Schmuck, 1900–1940* (Munich, 1990), pp. 39–41.

PAUL SCHRECKENGOST
American, 1908–1983

Paul Schreckengost studied at the Cleveland School of Art, and in the early 1930s began to work for the Gem Clay Forming Company in Sebring, Ohio, manufacturers of china tableware. He later became its chief designer, working there until his retirement in 1979. Over the years the company expanded its products from tablewares to earthenware lamps and decorative objects, among which his streamlined glazed earthenware pitcher (no. 172) is particularly outstanding.

Reference: Richard Guy Wilson, Dianne H. Pilgrim, and Dickran Tashjian, *The Machine Age in America, 1918–1941* (New York, 1986), p. 310.

BEN SHAHN
American, born Lithuania, 1898–1969

A painter and graphic artist, Ben Shahn is also known for his espousal of social and political causes. Shahn immigrated to the United States with his family from czarist Lithuania in 1906 and worked as a lithographer's apprentice while attending high school at night (1913–17). He attended New York University, the City College of New York, the National Academy of Design, and the Art Students' League, supporting himself with commissions for lettering, illustrations, posters, and commercial advertisements. During the 1920s Shahn traveled in Europe and North Africa, living in Paris in 1925 and again in 1927–29. He returned to New York in 1929 and shared a studio with the photographer Walker Evans. From 1930 he began to show his work at the Downtown Gallery and elsewhere, attracting considerable attention in 1932 with a series of paintings about the Sacco and Vanzetti trial. The labor movement, race relations, and atomic warfare were other of Shahn's themes, developed in posters such as *We Demand the National Textile Act* (1935), *This is Nazi Brutality* (1942), and during the 1960s, *Stop H Bomb Tests*.

During the 1930s and 40s, Shahn received numerous government commissions: from New York City, to design murals for the Riker's Island Penitentiary (1934–35); from the Farm Security Administration, to paint a mural for the community center at Roosevelt, New Jersey; from the Treasury Department, for murals at the Bronx Central Annex Post Office (1938–39); and from the Office of War Information, for posters (1942–44). After World War II, Shahn's clients were largely corporate; he produced illustrations for *Harper's* (1947–48), CBS (1947–59), and *Time* (1955–68), but also created posters for many cultural organizations (no. 264). Shahn's work was widely exhibited, and he received numerous honors and awards, including membership in the National Institute of Arts and Letters (1956), the American Institute of Graphic Arts Gold Medal (1958), and membership in the American Academy of Arts and Sciences (1959).

Reference: Kenneth W. Prescott, *The Complete Graphic Works of Ben Shahn* (New York, 1973).

CLIVE SINCLAIR
English, born 1940

A prodigious inventor whose formal schooling ended before university, Clive Sinclair was at the forefront of consumer electronics in the 1970s and early 1980s, personally developing the technology required to reduce the scale of his products and to offer them at low cost. Establishing Sinclair Radionics in 1962 after working as a technical journalist, Sinclair first sold mail-order radio and amplifier kits. In 1972 he introduced what is said to have been the first true pocket calculator, the *Executive* (no. 339), followed by the luxury *Sovereign* model and his *Microvision* pocket television, both designed by John H. Pemberton and all of which received Design Council awards. Financial problems led Sinclair to leave the firm in 1979, but the same year he established a new business, Sinclair Research, and introduced a series of small and very low priced personal computers—*ZX 80* (1980), *ZX 81* (1981), and *Spectrum* (1984)—which rivaled IBM and Apple products by selling millions of units within the following decade. Sinclair simultaneously developed a small, flat-screen television and an electric vehicle (unveiling the one-person *C5* in 1985), and continues to work in areas of computer technology.

References: "Clive Sinclair's New Leaf," *Design* 389 (May 1981): 26–27; Myron Magnet, "Clive Sinclair's Little Computer That Could," *Fortune* 105 (March 8, 1982): 78–84; Barnaby Feder, "Inventing the Future," *New York Times Magazine*, May 19, 1985, pp. 101, 110–11, 114, 116, 132–33.

SONY CORPORATION
Established Tokyo, 1945

Known for high-quality technological innovation in audio and video equipment, Sony was founded by Masaru Ibuka as Tokyo Tsushin Kenkyusho (Tokyo Telecommunications Research Laboratories) in 1945 and incorporated with Akio Morita as Tokyo Tsushin Kyogo (Tokyo Telecommunications Engineering Corporation) the following year. The company changed its name to Sony in 1958 after the name of its successful "pocket" transistor radio (no. 258). Ibuka, an electronics engineer, and Morita, a physicist and heir to a sake brewing concern, developed imported technology after the war to produce magnetic tape and transistors: in 1950 the firm marketed Japan's first magnetic tape recorder (initially making its own paper tapes) and in 1954, under license from Western Electric, produced Japan's first transistor. The following year Sony manufactured Japan's first transistor radio, the *TR-55*, which was also the firm's first export.

Building its reputation on the consistent quality of its products, its emphasis on miniaturization, and its aggressive consumer education and marketing techniques (no. 348), the company created a series of innovative products over the next decades: the first all-transistor television set (1959; no. 273); the first home video recorder (1964); a color television system using a single electron gun and a cylindrical picture tube for improved color and resolution (*Trinitron*, 1968); a portable cassette player (*Walkman*, 1978; no. 347) and its descendants, including a flat-screen portable micro television (*Watchman*, 1982); a component television system (*Profeel*, 1980); a portable compact disc player (*Discman*, 1990); and a notebook-size, portable computer with a touch-sensitive screen instead of a keyboard (*Palmtop*, 1990). While Sony's first products were designed largely by the firm's engineers, by 1961 the firm had seventeen designers, a number that increased significantly between 1968 and 1977. In 1978 Morita created a central design department for product planning and design under the direction of Yasuo Kuroki and increased the design staff to over a hundred.

Sony has electronics production, sales plants, and subsidiaries across the globe, particularly in the United States. The firm entered the American entertainment industry by purchasing CBS Records in 1987 and Columbia Pictures Entertainment in 1989 to provide software programming for its audio and video products.

References: Wolfgang Schmittel, *Design Concept Realisation* (Zurich, 1975), pp. 169–96; Boilerhouse Project, Victoria and Albert Museum, London, *Sony Design* (London, 1982); Akio Morita with Edwin M. Reingold and Mitsuko Shimomura, *Made in Japan: Akio Morita and Sony* (New York, 1986).

ETTORE SOTTSASS, JR.
Italian, born Austria, 1917

Ettore Sottsass, Jr., is one of Italy's most versatile and expressive contemporary designers, a leader of postmodernism during the 1980s. He has consistently brought his own intuitive approach to his work, whether it is one of the office machines he designed for Olivetti (from 1957 to 1969) or a ceramic vase inspired by his experiences in India, which he created at the same time; a Pop cabinet for Poltronova (1966); an unconventional sideboard with radiating shelves covered with laminated plastic for Memphis (1981; no. 362); or a watch for Cleto Munari (1988). The personal expressiveness of his creations means that even his most rationalized technological designs frequently display referential shapes and strong colors intended to communicate the poetic and spiritual values that Sottsass contends are fundamental to his work.

Sottsass graduated from the Turin Politecnico in 1939 with a degree in architecture and in 1947 opened a design studio in Milan, participating in postwar reconstruction projects as well as exhibition and product design. After working in New York in the office of GEORGE NELSON (1956), he returned to Milan and was hired as a consultant for Olivetti (1957), designing the Elea computer series (1959), typewriters (no. 319), adding machines, and total office systems, products that won him the Compasso d'Oro award in 1959 and 1970. A founding member of the reductive Global Tools group in 1975, he became associated with the Studio Alchimia in 1978, exhibiting lamps, bowls, and furniture with the first Bau.Haus collection in 1979 but disassociating himself the following year. With Sottsass as its inspiration, the Memphis group was founded in 1981, exhibiting its collections of "new design" annually with an impact that, through imitation and publicity, went far beyond the products they actually produced and sold. In 1980 Sottsass and four young architects, MARCO ZANINI, Matteo Thun, Aldo Cibic, and Marco Marabelli, formed an industrial design partnership, Sottsass Associati, which has created interiors, exhibitions, and high-technology products. In recent years Sottsass has designed numerous consumer products, including furniture (for Zanotta), ceramics (for Swid Powell), and metalware (for Alessi).

References: Paolo Fossati, Il Design in Italia, 1945–1972 (Turin, 1972), pp. 114–21, 220–23, pls. 250–74, 296–309; Frederick S. Wight Art Gallery, University of California, Los Angeles, Design Process: Olivetti, 1908–1978 (March 27–May 6, 1979), p. 267 et passim; Barbara Radice, ed., Memphis: The New International Style (Milan, 1981), passim; Penny Sparke, Ettore Sottsass, Jnr. (London, 1982); Barbara Radice, Memphis: Research, Experiences, Results, Failures and Successes of New Design (New York, 1984), passim; Sottsass Associati (New York, 1988).

PHILIPPE STARCK
French, born 1949

France's most stylish and celebrated contemporary designer, Philippe Starck first became known for his interiors, nightclubs (the Starck Club in Dallas), cafés (Costes in Paris), and hotels (the Royalton and the Paramount in New York), furnished with his own boldly unconventional designs. Starck studied interior architecture at the Ecole Camondo in Paris, and then served as artistic director at Pierre Cardin, designing sixty-five pieces of furniture for the company in a short time. In 1981 he was one of five young designers chosen to furnish the private apartments of the president of France at the Elysée Palace (no. 384), a commission that brought him international celebrity, and in 1985 he won a government competition for street furniture for the Parc de la Villette in Paris. Starck has continued to challenge the public with offbeat, unexpected, and slightly disconcerting designs, especially his spare three-legged furniture forms. In 1980 he established his own company, Starck Products, to produce and distribute the furniture he designed over the previous years, but his more recent works, often labeled with the odd-sounding names of characters from the science-fiction novels of Philip K. Dick, have been distributed by such firms as Driade, Baleri, Kartell, Vitra, and the French mass-market mail-order house Les 3 Suisse. Starck has also designed lighting (for Flos), glass (for Daum) and a pasta shape, Mandala (for Panzani), as well as shop and sailboat interiors. He was the first recipient of France's national prize for design.

References: Andrea Truppin, "Five Uneasy Pieces," Interiors 144 (August 1984): 140–45, 178, 182; Daralice D. Boles, "Starck Contrasts," Progressive Architecture 66 (September 1985): 141–46; Agence pour la Promotion de la Création Industrielle and Centre Georges Pompidou, Paris, Design français, 1960–1990: Trois décennies (June 22–September 26, 1988), pp. 268–69; Andrea Truppin, "Starck Struck," Interiors 148 (February 1989): 121–29, 156; Christine Colin, Starck (Tübingen, Germany, 1989); Laura Polinoro, L'officina Alessi (Crusinallo, Italy, 1989), pp. 229–36.

EDWARD STEICHEN
American, born Luxembourg, 1879–1973

A photographer and a great promoter of the art of photography, Edward Steichen was born in Luxembourg but came to the United States with his family when he was two. He trained as a commercial lithographer between 1894 and 1898, at the same time studying painting and beginning to take photographs. Within a few years after his debut at the second Philadelphia Photographic Salon in 1899, Steichen had gained an enormous reputation through his participation in international exhibitions, the sequence of important prizes he was awarded, and exuberant critical praise. Creator of such renowned artistic photographic icons as Rodin's Balzac in the moonlight and the dancer Isadora Duncan on the Acropolis, Steichen was also a commercial photographer. He brought fine photography to fashion illustration with the publication of his shots of PAUL POIRET's creations in Art et Décoration in 1911. Later, commanding unprecedented prices for his photographic work, he was hired as chief photographer for Condé Nast, publishers of Vanity Fair and Vogue, and as advertising photographer for the J. Walter Thompson agency (both beginning in 1923). Steichen made no distinction between his "art" photography and his commercial activity, which included a series of photographs of common objects to be used as fabric designs commissioned by the Stehli Silk Corporation about 1927 (no. 127) "If my technic, imagination and vision is any good," Carl Sandburg quotes him as saying, "I ought to be able to put the best values of my non-commercial and experimental photographs into a pair of shoes, a tube of tooth paste, a jar of face cream, a mattress, or any object that I want to light up and make humanly interesting in an advertising photograph. . . . I welcome the chance to work in commercial art."[41] Steichen gave up his own photographic work in 1947 when he became director of the photography department at the Museum of Modern Art in New York, where he organized numerous important exhibitions, including *The Family of Man* in 1955.

References: Carl Sandburg, *Steichen: The Photographer* (New York, 1929); Grace M. Mayer, "Biographical Outline," in Carl Sandburg et al., *Steichen the Photographer* (New York, 1961), pp. 69–75.

VARVARA STEPANOVA
Russian, born Lithuania, 1894–1958

One of the founders and theorists of constructivism, Varvara Stepanova applied its principles to stage, textile, costume, and graphic design. After studying for a short time at the art school in Kazan, she moved to Moscow where she continued her art studies and joined the ranks of the literati, creating a type of visual poetry, illustrating books, and painting. Her costumes for the play *The Death of Tarelkin* (1922), exhibited in Paris in 1925, were the earliest expression of her own theories of clothing based on function, which she later worked out to include distinctive designs for trades and professions, and were most boldly realized in the creation of sports uniforms. Her work at the First State Textile Printing Factory in Moscow in 1923–24 (no. 92) brought her directly into the area of textile manufacture, and she both created fabric designs for the factory and advised on the improvement of its production techniques. Stepanova taught at the textile faculty of the Vkhutemas (Higher State Artistic and Technical Workshops) in 1924–25, and was a staff member of the journals *LEF* (1923–25) and *Novyi LEF* (1927–28). With her husband, Alexander Rodchenko, she collaborated on poster and book design and jointly developed the techniques of photomontage used in their journals, books, and commemorative albums.

References: John E. Bowlt, "From Pictures to Textile Prints," *Print Collector's Newsletter* 7 (March–April 1976): 16–20; Christina Lodder, *Russian Constructivism* (New Haven, Conn., 1983), pp. 261–63 et passim; Alexander Lavrentiev, *Varvara Stepanova: The Complete Work* (Cambridge, Mass., 1988).

GUSTAV STICKLEY
American, 1857–1942

Gustav Stickley was the prime spokesman for Arts and Crafts principles in America. Unlike the Englishman William Morris, however, he accepted the necessity of combining machine manufacture with hand production. A manufacturer of eclectic furniture and then historicizing reproductions in the 1880s and 90s, Stickley returned from a trip to Europe in 1898 determined to make original furniture from his own designs. He first employed ornament based on the art nouveau style and then, taking a reductive, structuralist approach based on English Arts and Crafts examples, introduced his Craftsman, or Mission, furniture and established the United Crafts workshops (later Craftsman Workshops) in Eastwood, New York, near Syracuse. In the foreword to the first issue of *The Craftsman*, the monthly magazine he founded in 1901, Stickley announced its purpose: "The United Crafts endeavor to promote and to extend the principles established by Morris, in both the artistic and the socialistic sense. In the interests of art, they seek to substitute the luxury of taste for the luxury of costliness; to teach that beauty does not imply elaboration or ornament; to employ only those forms and materials which make for simplicity, individuality and dignity of effect." Stickley's undecorated oak furniture (no. 29) quickly became popular and almost as soon was imitated and commercialized by other factories, including those of his brothers, L. & J. G. Stickley (Fayetteville, New York), Stickley Bros. (Grand Rapids), and Charles Stickley (Binghamton, New York). With offices in New York after 1905, Stickley led the field of Mission furniture for over a decade, with national sales representatives and an enormous production. In 1913 at the height of his success he opened a twelve-story building in New York that housed salesrooms for Craftsman furniture and interior furnishings (no. 53) and the offices of *The Craftsman*. By 1915, however, with Stickley's overexpansion and a rising taste in America for colonial revival styles (which he unsuccessfully tried to market) Stickley was forced into bankruptcy and his entire assets were later sold.

References: Samuel Howe, "A Visit to the Workshops of The United Crafts at Eastwood, New York," *Craftsman* 3 (October 1902): 59–64; Samuel Howe, "A Visit to the House of Mr. Stickley," *Craftsman* 3 (December 1902): 161–69, pls. iv–v; *What Is Wrought in the Craftsman Workshops* (Syracuse, 1904); John Crosby Freeman, *The Forgotten Rebel: Gustav Stickley and His Craftsman Mission Furniture* (Watkins Glen, N.Y., 1966); David M. Cathers, *Furniture of the American Arts and Crafts Movement: Stickley and Roycroft Mission Oak* (New York, 1981), passim.

GUNTA STÖLZL
German, later Swiss, 1897–1983

As a student (1919–23), journeyman (1923–25), instructor (1925–26), and master (1926–31), Gunta Stölzl gave direction to the Bauhaus weaving workshop through her work (no. 122) and her teaching, exerting considerable influence on the development of both hand-loom and industrial weaving there. Stölzl studied at the Kunstgewerbeschule (1914–16) in Munich and at the Bauhaus, initially under Johannes Itten and Paul Klee. In 1922, the year in which she passed her journeyman's examination, and again in 1924, she and a fellow worker, Benita Otte, were sent to attend special courses in dye-work and production techniques in Krefeld at the Preussische Höhere Fachschule für Textil-Industrie (Prussian Higher Technical School for Textiles). Put in charge of the entire Bauhaus weaving workshop in 1927 after the departure of Georg Muche, Stölzl took her students to Berlin to see collections of historical material as well as to the Leipzig trade fair and the factories that manufactured Bauhaus textiles. She resigned from the Bauhaus in 1931 for political reasons and established a design studio that year in Zurich under the name S-P-H-Stoffe with her Bauhaus colleagues Gertrud Preiswerk and Heinrich-Otto Hürlimann. Among the firm's commissions were curtains for a Zurich cinema (1934) and a series of commercial furnishing fabrics for Wohnbedarf. From 1937 Stölzl ran the studio alone and was active in the Schweizer Werkbund, exhibiting dress and furnishing fabrics at the Schweizerische *Landesausstellung* (*Swiss National Exhibition*) in 1939. She maintained her studio until 1967 and continued to weave privately afterwards.

Reference: Magdalena Droste, ed., *Gunta Stölzl: Weberei am Bauhaus und aus eigener Werkstatt* (Berlin, 1987).

MARIANNE STRAUB
British, born Switzerland, 1909

One of the central figures in the field of British textile design for industry, Marianne Straub chose the career of industrial designer rather than craft weaver or printer while still a student at the Kunstgewerbeschule in Zurich under Heinrich-Otto Hürlimann, a former Bauhaus student. Pursuing this goal, she gained admittance to the Bradford Technical College in England (1932), where she learned the rigors of power loom production. After a year in the handweaving studio of Ethel Mairet, she took the position of consultant designer to the Welsh woolen mills, which were in great need of both technical upgrading and a new design image (1934–37). In 1937, Straub became head designer at Helios, the firm established in 1936 as a subsidiary of Barlow & Jones to develop a range of contemporary cotton fabrics, and was made managing director in 1947, moving to Warner's in 1950 when Helios was taken over by them. It was as a representative of Warner's that she, along with the firm's production director Alec Hunter, participated in the Festival Pattern project in 1951 (no. 225), soon after her arrival. Straub remained at Warner's for twenty years, principally designing contract furnishing fabrics, and from 1964 she also designed for Tamesa Fabrics, which were manufactured at Warner's factories.

Straub was named Royal Designer for Industry in 1972.

Reference: Mary Schoeser, *Marianne Straub* (London, 1984).

S. STRUSEVICH
Russian, active 1920s

Virtually nothing is known about this fabric designer who worked for the Sosnevsk Amalgamated Mills in Ivanovo, Russia (no. 113).

References: I. Yasinskaya, *Revolutionary Textile Design: Russia in the 1920s and 1930s* (New York, 1983), pp. 32–33; Museum of Modern Art, Oxford, *Art into Production: Soviet Textiles, Fashion and Ceramics, 1917–1935* (December 9, 1984–February 3, 1985), p. 54.

SÜE ET MARE
Established Paris, 1919–1928

Architect and painter respectively, Louis Süe and André Mare formed the Compagnie des Arts Français in 1919, a decorating firm that succeeded Süe's Atelier Français, which had been founded in 1911 but had closed at the onset of World War I. At the Salon d'Automne in 1912, Mare himself had collaborated on the much-publicized *Maison Cubiste (Cubist House)*, a structure with a prismatic facade and a furnished interior hung with cubist paintings and entitled "A Bourgeois Salon." Süe et Mare was rivaled only by EMILE-JACQUES RUHLMANN in its impact on interior design after the war, and in its 1925 presentation at the Paris *Exposition Internationale des Arts Décoratifs*. There, in its domed pavilion titled "Musée d'Art Contemporain," the firm showed interiors in a lavish, personal adaptation of the Louis XIV and Louis XV styles. Its furniture was created of rare woods with sculpted, gilded, and inlaid decoration in traditional albeit exaggerated motifs (no. 106), and it provided tapestries and luxurious accessories by many associates, among them MAURICE MARINOT and the sculptor Aristide Maillol.

References: L'Ancienne Douane, Strasbourg, *André Mare et la Compagnie des Arts Français (Süe et Mare)* (April 1–June 13, 1971); Pierre Kjellberg, *Art déco: Les maîtres du mobilier, le décor des paquebots* (Paris, 1986), pp. 177–81.

GERALD SUMMERS
English, 1899–1967

Gerald Summers founded a London firm called Makers of Simple Furniture in 1929 and there he produced a range of unusual plywood furniture of his own design. He seems to have used this material exclusively throughout the 1930s, and when supplies of plywood imported from Eastern Europe began to dwindle at the onset of World War II, Summers gave up furniture production entirely. His earliest bent-plywood products were brought to market in England about the same time as ALVAR AALTO'S plywood chairs were introduced in London at Fortnum & Mason in 1933, and his work, too, was marketed abroad—advertised in American magazines and sold in such stores as Marshall Field in Chicago. Summers's best-known products are an armchair from about 1934 constructed of a single piece of plywood (no. 150) and a three-tiered serving trolley, designed about 1935 and formed of a piece of plywood bent in an S shape, which also appeared along with furniture by MARCEL BREUER and WALTER GROPIUS among the products distributed by the Isokon company.

Reference: Derek E. Ostergard, ed., *Bent Wood and Metal Furniture, 1850–1946* (New York, 1987), pp. 156, 163, 317–20, 327, 330.

SUPERSTUDIO
Established Florence, 1966

Composed of a group of young designers in Florence (Gian Piero Frassinelli, Alessandro Magris, Roberto Magris, Adolfo Natalini, and Cristiano Toraldo di Francia), Superstudio was formed in 1966 to engage in theoretical work involving architecture, interior and industrial design, and planning. The group joined with ARCHIZOOM ASSOCIATI to organize an exhibition entitled *Superarchitettura* (*Superarchitecture*), held in Pistoia in 1966 and Modena in 1967, and they designed objects derived from Pop culture such as their *Bazaar* couch (for Giovanetti) and *Passiflora* (*Passionflower*) lamp (for Poltronova), both of 1968. By 1969 Superstudio had turned to conceptual projects, conceiving a series of gridded never-ending spatial structures projected over landscapes that suggested the eventual urbanization of the entire planet; this in turn spawned their *Misura* furniture produced by Zanotta (no. 324), their series of depictions of *Twelve Imaginary Cities* of 1971, and an abstract "microevent" for the exhibition *Italy: The New Domestic Landscape* at the Museum of Modern Art in New York in 1972. Superstudio was one of the initiators of the design laboratory and cooperative Global Tools in 1975, and later joined the University of Florence.

References: "Dai cataloghi del Superstudio: Istogrammi," *Domus* 497 (April 1971): 46; Emilio Ambasz, ed., *Italy: The New Domestic Landscape* (New York, 1972), pp. 100, 240–51; "Superstudio: Dal catalogo degli istogrammi la serie 'Misura,'" *Domus* 517 (December 1972): 36–38; Gianni Pettena, ed., *Superstudio, 1966–1982: Storie, figure, architettura* (Florence, 1982); Andrea Branzi, *The Hot House: Italian New Wave Design* (Cambridge, Mass., 1984), p. 155 et passim; Albrecht Bangert, *Italian Furniture Design* (Munich, 1988), pp. 50, 53, 54, 56, 132, 160, 164.

ROGER TALLON
French, born 1929

Roger Tallon was one of the first industrial designers to practice in France, opening a design office in Paris in 1953 after having studied electrical engineering (1947–50). His initial clients were international and multinational corporations—Du Pont, Caterpillar, General Motors. From 1963 to 1973 Tallon worked with Jacques Vienot as director of research of the Technès design agency in Paris. In 1973 he founded Design Programmes, and since 1984 has been associated with PIERRE PAULIN and Michel Schreiber in the design firm ADSA + Partners. His most important work has been in the field of transportation, having prepared studies for the Mexico City subway in 1969 and recently designed the *TGV-Atlantique* high-speed train for the French national railways as well as the train for the Euro-Tunnel. Tallon has also designed a wide range of products, appliances (for Téléavia and Japy), seating (for the Mobilier National), glass (for Daum), furniture (for Lacloche; no. 300), and watches (for Lip).

References: Centre de Création Industrielle, Paris, *Qu'est-ce que le design?* (October 24–December 31, 1969), n.p.; Centre de Création Industrielle, Centre Georges Pompidou, Paris, *Mobilier National: 20 ans de création* (May 29–September 24, 1984), pp. 46–48; Agence pour la Promotion de la Création Industrielle and Centre Georges Pompidou, Paris, *Design français, 1960–1990: Trois décennies* (June 22–September 26, 1988), pp. 270–71; Colin Naylor, ed., *Contemporary Designers*, 2d ed. (Chicago, 1990), pp. 554–55.

WALTER DORWIN TEAGUE
American, 1883–1960

More than any other American industrial designer of the 1930s, Walter Dorwin Teague was concerned with the formalism of proportion, line, and symmetry. In his lectures and in his book *Design This Day: The Technique of Order in the Machine Age* (New York, 1940), he spoke about the need to create a new formal order out of the Machine Age: "Out of our machines themselves and the things our machines can do best we are producing a new and thrilling style so right and so easy and so natural that there is no reason why we should not make over the world in its image."[42]

Teague attended classes at the Art Students' League in New York, and after working for an advertising agency, opened his own studio in 1912. A classicist by training, he became interested in modern design after a trip to Paris in 1926, the year he left graphics for industrial design. His first client was Eastman Kodak, for whom he designed a series of popular cameras, the best known being the streamlined *Bantam Special* of 1936. Teague served as consultant to CORNING GLASS WORKS in 1932, advising the company on the future direction of their Steuben Division and designing engraved vases and glassware along with a complete crystal table setting of dishes, cutlery, and glasses in undecorated geometrical forms. The line of blue-mirrored radios he created for the Sparton radio company between 1933 and 1936 (no. 156) similarly reflected his concerns with streamlined formalism. Teague also worked on architectural projects and

389

designed machinery and transportation, counting among his other clients Texaco (for whom he conceived standardized service stations and exhibition buildings), Ford, and the New Haven Railroad.

References: Kenneth Reid, "Walter Dorwin Teague, Master of Design," *Pencil Points* 18 (September 1937): 540–70; Jeffrey L. Meikle, *Twentieth Century Limited: Industrial Design in America, 1925–1939* (Philadelphia, 1979), passim.

TECHNOLOGY DESIGN
Established Bellevue, Washington, 1982

Technology Design was in the forefront of those firms that worked to return content to technological products, most graphically illustrated by their prototype *Elaine* computer printer with a stand in the shape of an unfolding scroll of computer paper. Founded by Loyd Moore in 1982, the firm offers a range of design solutions, from the high-tech black box to visually referential products such as the *Emily, Julie, and Max* personal computer (no. 396), solutions that generally elicit positive responses but find few manufacturers who will risk producing the most innovative of their proposals. Technology Design works in four areas: medical equipment, instrumentation for industrial applications, consumer products (*Accelerator* ski speedometer-odometer for Insight), and technological office machinery.

References: Hugh Aldersey-Williams, *New American Design: Products and Graphics for a Post-Industrial Age* (New York, 1988), pp. 126–31; Nicholas Backlund, "Northwest by Design," *International Design* 37 (January–February 1990): 55–57.

GIUSEPPE TERRAGNI
Italian, 1904–1943

Giuseppe Terragni introduced modern architectural forms and technology in Italy during the 1930s, drawing on the ideas of LE CORBUSIER's *Vers une architecture* (1923) and WALTER GROPIUS's *Internationale Architektur* (1925). A graduate in architecture of the Politecnico in Milan (1926), Terragni was one of the architects who formed the Gruppo 7 in 1926, publishing a series of articles in *Rassegna Italiana* that proclaimed a new era in Italian architecture. Self-described "rationalists," Terragni and the others advocated the use of modern industrial materials and pure geometric forms as both timeless and expressive of the machine age. From the start they declared they did not want to break with the nationalist classical tradition, however, but rather to transform it. Terragni's first building, the Novocomum apartment block in Como (1927–29), exploited reinforced concrete and introduced glass-walled cylinders at the corners. In 1932, he was given his most important commission, the Fascist party headquarters and its furnishings (Casa del Fascio) for Como (no. 149). There he combined a perfectly square

plan with a central glazed atrium, concrete construction, and extensive fenestration to create one of the most advanced Italian buildings of its time, a transparent structure that symbolized for Terragni the "Mussolinian concept that Fascism is a house of glass into which all may look."[43] During the later 1930s Terragni designed several apartment buildings in Milan and, in Como, the Sant'Elia Nursery School (1936–37) and Giuliani-Frigerio apartments (1939–40). He joined the Italian armed forces when his country entered World War II, and died just after the fall of the Fascist government in 1943.

References: Enrico Mantero, ed., *Giuseppe Terragni e la città del razionalismo italiano* (Bari, Italy, 1969); Diane Yvonne Ghirardo, "Italian Architecture and Fascist Politics: An Evaluation of the Rationalist's Role in Regime Building," *Journal of the Society of Architectural Historians* 39 (May 1980): 109–27; Richard A. Etlin, "Italian Rationalism," *Progressive Architecture* 64 (July 1983): 86–94; Giorgio Ciucci, "Italian Architecture during the Fascist Period," *Harvard Architecture Review* 6 (1987): 77–87.

ANGELO TESTA
American, 1921–1983

The work of Angelo Testa had considerable influence during the 1940s, being reproduced widely in design periodicals and included in survey exhibitions of modern design. A graduate of the Institute of Design in Chicago (1945)—the former New Bauhaus—Testa promoted the use of printed fabrics in contemporary interiors. His early patterns (no. 190), both figurative abstractions and linear designs (some created while he was still a student), were screen-printed by hand in the workshop he founded in 1943 and sold—some with matching wallpapers— in the shop he opened in Chicago. Testa's 1943 *Campagna* was part of Knoll's original fabric production, and in 1947 he designed one of the first mass-produced American contemporary textile collections. Following Bauhaus precepts he also experimented with weaving, and in the late 1940s and 1950s created patterns for both woven and printed textiles for Greeff, Cohn-Hall-Marx, Monsanto, and a number of additional manufacturers. His other designs included plastic laminates, fiberglass panels, vinyls, ceramic tiles, and graphics, and he was also a painter and sculptor.

References: "Angelo Testa," *Everyday Art Quarterly* 25 (1953): 16–17; College of Architecture, Art and Urban Planning Gallery, University of Illinois, Chicago, *Angelo Testa: 40 Years as a Designer/Painter/Weaver* (April 13–May 6, 1983); Mary Schoeser, *Fabrics and Wallpapers* (London, 1986), pp. 85–86.

LOUIS COMFORT TIFFANY
American, 1848–1933

A master of the many mediums through which he expressed his personal vision of international art nouveau,

Louis Comfort Tiffany worked as a designer of decorative objects in glass, stained glass, jewelry, metalware, and ceramics. Son of Charles Louis Tiffany, founder of TIFFANY AND COMPANY, he turned his back on the family business in 1866 and decided to become a painter, studying first with the American artist George Inness and then in Paris with Léon Belly. Between 1867, when he first exhibited at the National Academy of Design in New York, and 1880, when he was made an academician, Tiffany pursued the career of an artist, painting oil and watercolor landscapes, many based on his travels in Europe and North Africa.

In 1880 he went into business as one of the founders of Associated Artists, a group that created interiors, mostly in exotic styles, for prominent clients. After it was dissolved in 1883 he opened his own firm, Louis C. Tiffany & Company. He himself devoted most of his effort to glass design, establishing a factory to execute large stained-glass commissions primarily for architects and in 1892 developing a lustrous blown glass made in sinuous art nouveau forms (no. 5), which was sold under his trademark "Favrile." His products expanded during the 1890s to include leaded-glass lamps, which, as made by his Tiffany Studios after 1900 (no. 41), became a large part of the firm's work. Tiffany showed a range of decorative objects and stained glass to great acclaim at the Exposition Universelle in Paris in 1900 (no. 19), and his production was represented in Europe by Siegfried Bing's Paris shop, L'Art Nouveau.

References: "Louis C. Tiffany's Coloured Glass Work," in S. Bing, Artistic America, Tiffany Glass, and Art Nouveau (Cambridge, Mass., 1970), pp. 193–212; Egon Neustadt, The Lamps of Tiffany (New York, 1970); Robert Koch, Louis C. Tiffany's Glass-Bronzes-Lamps (New York, 1971); Michael Komanecky and Virginia Fabbri Butera, The Folding Image: Screens by Western Artists of the Nineteenth and Twentieth Centuries (New Haven, Conn., 1984), pp. 163–64; Catherine Hoover Voorsanger, "Dictionary of Architects, Artisans, Artists, and Manufacturers," in Doreen Bolger Burke et al., In Pursuit of Beauty: Americans and the Aesthetic Movement (New York, 1986), pp. 474–75; Martin Eidelberg, Masterworks of Louis Comfort Tiffany (New York, 1989).

TIFFANY AND COMPANY
Established New York, 1837

The shop founded in New York in 1837 by Charles Louis Tiffany (father of LOUIS COMFORT TIFFANY) and John B. Young first sold stationery and fancy goods, much of it imported, and soon grew into a fashionable store with branches in Paris (1850) and London (1868). Tiffany and Young (which became Tiffany and Company in 1853 when Young was bought out) began to sell silver about 1847, contracting in 1851 with the New York silversmith John Chandler Moore to manufacture hollowware exclusively for the store; Moore was succeeded almost immediately by his son Edward Chandler Moore, who was

responsible for the majority of Tiffany's most innovative silver until the end of the century. Tiffany exhibited its wares at the Paris exhibition of 1867, where it won a silver medal, the first American firm to be so premiated abroad, and in 1878 it won a grand prize in Paris for its spectacular display of silverwares, which by that time had come to include grand presentation pieces and ornate silver services with decoration in revival, oriental, and aesthetic movement styles. Native American designs were first shown at the Paris exhibition of 1889, a thematic interest that continued to expand throughout the 1890s (no. 32). About the turn of the century, when the displays of Tiffany and Company and Tiffany Studios adjoined each other at the Paris Exposition Universelle, the firms of father and son drew closer together, and Louis Comfort Tiffany became vice president and artistic director of Tiffany and Company after his father's death in 1902. Over the past century Tiffany's reputation has continued to grow, and it now stands as a world-renowned symbol of luxury for jewelry, silver, and household wares.

References: Charles H. Carpenter, Jr., with Mary Grace Carpenter, Tiffany Silver (New York, 1978); Catherine Hoover Voorsanger, "Dictionary of Architects, Artisans, Artists, and Manufacturers," in Doreen Bolger Burke et al., In Pursuit of Beauty: Americans and the Aesthetic Movement (New York, 1986), pp. 472–74; John Loring, Tiffany's 150 Years (New York, 1987).

TIFFANY STUDIOS, see LOUIS COMFORT TIFFANY

TOKYO TELECOMMUNICATIONS ENGINEERING CORPORATION, see SONY CORPORATION

TADEUSZ TREPKOWSKI
Polish, 1914–1954

The work of Tadeusz Trepkowski inspired the flourishing poster movement that emerged in Poland after World War II, and his method of communicating with direct imagery and spare messages underlies the work of his successors. A student at the State School of Decorative Art and Painting in Warsaw, Trepkowski first worked as a commercial artist, finding his métier in the art of the poster during the 1930s. The stirring posters he designed immediately after the war expressed the concerns of a nation catapulted into a socialist state. Working with the state art and graphics publisher Wydawnictwo Artystyczno-Graficzne (WAG), Trepkowski created posters on broad social themes including peace (no. 229), nationalism, and socialism as well as posters advertising concerts, cultural events, films, and the theater.

References: Jan Lenica, "Tadeusz Trepkowski," Graphis 12 (January 1956): 78–79, 85; Jan Lenica, Plakat: Tadeusza Trepkowskiego (Warsaw, 1958).

EARL S. TUPPER
American, later Costa Rican, 1907–1983

Devising a process for the manufacture of polyethylene that prevented it from cracking and made it exceedingly durable, Earl S. Tupper began to produce objects with his new material (called "Poly-T") through the company he founded in 1942, and by 1947 was making millions of inexpensive plastic items annually as giveaway premiums for large corporations. With the introduction of his own Tupperware line of houseware products after the war, he provided simple, flexible table and storage containers (no. 204) that would become known worldwide after he began to distribute them through Tupperware home sales parties in 1951. In 1958 the Tupper corporation was sold to the Rexall Drug Company.

References: "Tupperware," *Time*, September 8, 1947, pp. 90, 92; Elizabeth Gordon, "Fine Art for 39¢," *House Beautiful* 89 (October 1947): 130–31; Obituary, *New York Times*, October 7, 1983, p. B8.

JØRN UTZON
Danish, born 1918

Jørn Utzon's sculpturally conceived opera house in Sydney, Australia, was perhaps the most expressive architectural statement of the early post–World War II era; the winner of an international competition in 1956, it was built with prefabricated concrete elements according to Utzon's principle of additive construction. Utzon, a graduate of the Kongelige Danske Kunstakademi (Royal Danish Academy of Fine Arts) in Copenhagen, drew inspiration broadly: from the work of the architects ALVAR AALTO, Gunnar Asplund (with whom he studied in Stockholm), LE CORBUSIER, and both FRANK LLOYD WRIGHT and LUDWIG MIES VAN DER ROHE (whom he visited in the United States in 1949). He was also influenced by the sculptor Henri Laurens and by great architectural monuments of other cultures and ages, which he visited extensively and wrote about in his book *The Eternal Present: The Beginnings of Architecture* (1964). Like his buildings, much of his furniture has been based on additive principles, notably his organic foam serpentine Utsep Møbler flexible furniture components (1968), his plywood and steel lounge chairs (no. 312), and his metal-framed Floating Dock line (1967).

References: Siegfried Giedion, "Jørn Utzon and the Third Generation," in *Space, Time and Architecture*, 5th ed., rev. and enl. (Cambridge, Mass., 1967), pp. 668–95; Karl Mang, *History of Modern Furniture* (New York, 1979), pp. 138, 158–59.

GINO VALLE
Italian, born 1923

Gino Valle received his diploma in architecture from the University of Venice in 1948 and studied city planning as a Fulbright Scholar at the Harvard Graduate School of Design in 1951–52. Since 1955 he has had his own architectural studio in Udine, where with several collaborators he has designed public buildings, factories, and housing, principally for the region of northern Italy. He has also worked on the design of electro-mechanical clocks (no. 303) and transportation signboards; he was awarded Compasso d'Oro prizes in 1956 for the *Cifra 5* clock, one of the early versions in his series for Solari; in 1962 for his direct-reading indicator boards for train stations and airports, also for Solari; and in 1963 for a stove for Rex Zanussi, for whom he also worked as an architect.

References: "Un nuovo orologio da tavolo," *Domus* 437 (April 1966): 54–55; Padiglione d'Arte Contemporanea, Milan, *Gino Valle: Architetto, 1950–1978* (1979).

HENRY VAN DE VELDE
Belgian, 1863–1957

A pioneer of international art nouveau and a propagandist for modernism, Henry van de Velde studied painting at the academy in Antwerp (1881–84) and with Carolus Duran in Paris (1884–85). About 1893, influenced by the writings of William Morris and John Ruskin, van de Velde gave up painting for graphic and decorative arts and architecture. Subsequently he followed Morris's example by building and furnishing his own house, Bloemenwerf, at Uccle (1894–95) in a style that combined the rustic simplicity of the English Arts and Crafts Movement with abstract and elegant curvilinear forms (no. 1). The Parisian art dealers Siegfried Bing and Julius Meier-Graefe visited van de Velde at Uccle, and Bing afterwards commissioned van de Velde to design interiors—a smoking room, dining room, and study—for his shop in Paris, L'Art Nouveau, which opened in December 1895. Van de Velde again showed furnished interiors and objects at the Dresden exhibition (1897) and the Secession exhibition in Munich (1899; no. 17), which brought him German clients and a reputation as the leading exponent of "abstract line" in ornamental design.[44] Among van de Velde's German clients were the furniture firm of Löffler (1899) and the Königliche Sächsische Porzellanmanufaktur, Meissen, for whom he designed a porcelain service in the "modern" style in 1902–4. Van de Velde opened an office in Berlin (1900) and designed the Folkwang Museum in Hagen (1900–1902). In 1904 he was named director of the new school of applied arts at Weimar, where he remained until 1914; his successor, WALTER GROPIUS, later restructured the school as the Bauhaus.

Van de Velde was a founding member of the Deutscher Werkbund in 1907 and designed a theater in 1914 for the Werkbund exhibition in Cologne, a building that combined curvilinear art nouveau forms with an expressionist sculptural use of reinforced concrete. His aims for the Werkbund were articulated during a famous debate held at the 1914 exhibition between van de Velde and Hermann Muthesius over the aims of the organization, van de Velde arguing successfully at the time for individual creativity against Muthesius's call for standardization. Van de Velde was exiled during World War I and settled first in Switzerland (1917) and then in the Netherlands (1921), where he designed the Kröller-Muller Museum (1923, 1937–54). Repatriated in 1925, he established the Institut Supérieur des Arts Décoratifs in Brussels (1926) and was a professor of architecture at the University of Ghent (1926–36). In 1947 van de Velde retired to Switzerland, where he wrote his memoirs (1956); with the exhibition *Um 1900: Art Nouveau und Jugendstil* at the Kunstgewerbemuseum in Zurich in 1952, he witnessed the reappraisal of the style he had helped to create.

References: Henry van de Velde, *Geschichte meines Lebens* (Munich, 1962); A. M. Hammacher, *Le Monde de Henry van de Velde* (Antwerp, 1967); Ministère de l'Education Nationale, Galerie l'Ecuyer, Brussels, *Henry van de Velde, 1863–1957* (1970); Yvonne Brunhammer et al., *Art Nouveau: Belgium France* (Houston, 1976), pp. 368–77 et passim.

VAN NIEUWENBORG/WEGMAN INDUSTRIAL DESIGN
Established Leiden, the Netherlands, 1973

The industrial design partnership of Frans van Nieuwenborg and Martijn Wegman works independently, creating designs for lighting, furniture, and primarily jewelry, which they generally produce themselves in limited quantities but also have manufactured commercially (no. 346). Artists who were trained respectively at the Academy of Industrial Design in Eindhoven and the Gerrit Rietveld Academy in Amsterdam, they attempt to meld the concerns of craftsmanship with those of industrial production.

References: Gert Staal and Hester Wolters, eds., *Holland in Vorm: Dutch Design, 1945–1987* (The Hague, 1987), pp. 201, 208, 211, 217, 220, 239, 246; *The International Design Yearbook*, vol. 1 (New York, 1985–86), p. 95.

PAOLO VENINI
Italian, 1895–1959

Paolo Venini, a young lawyer from a family of glassblowers, and Giacomo Cappellin, a Venetian businessman, bought out the Muranese glass furnace of Andrea Rioda in 1921, forming the partnership of Cappellin-Venini & C., with the Muranese designer Vittorio Zecchin as artistic director and Giovanni Seguso as studio master. Much of the initial production was simple, clear glassware based on sixteenth-century Venetian forms, but the firm also made an effort to align itself with the major currents of progressive styles (no. 99). Cappellin-Venini glass was exhibited at the Monza *Biennale* in 1923 and again, after Venini established his own company, in Paris in 1925, where the glassworks received a grand prize and five of its collaborators won gold medals. On his own, Venini began to collaborate with architects and designers, including GIO PONTI

(from 1927) and Carlo Scarpa (from 1932), and their glasswares with spare shapes and subtle decorations won prizes successively in the *Biennale* and *Triennale* exhibitions. At the same time Venini revived traditional Venetian glassblowing techniques, which he used to add color and texture to his production. By the end of World War II, the factory had become the leading manufacturer of colored glassware in Venice, developing a series of vases (no. 209), figurines, and bottles created by Venini and the firm's designers, among them Fulvio Bianconi, who was hired in 1948. After Venini's death in 1959 the firm was continued by his wife, Ginette, and his son-in-law, Ludovico de Santillana, who have maintained the high standards set by Venini and likewise collaborated with well-known designers, among them TAPIO WIRKKALA.

References: Robert Linzeler, "Les Verreries de Cappellin Venini," *La Renaissance de l'Art Français et des Industries de Luxe* 5 (December 1922): 666–68; N. G. Fiumi, "Messrs. Venini's Muranese Glass," *Studio* 92 (1926): 166–67; Venini International and Smithsonian Institution Traveling Exhibition Service, Washington, D.C., *Venini Glass* (1981), passim.

ROBERT VENTURI
American, born 1925

In his 1966 study, *Complexity and Contradiction in Architecture*, Robert Venturi set out the text that would become the theoretical touchstone of postmodernism, arguing for elements of design that are "hybrid rather than 'pure,' compromising rather than 'clean,' distorted rather than 'straightforward,' ambiguous rather than 'articulated,' perverse as well as impersonal, boring as well as 'interesting,' conventional rather than 'designed,' accommodating rather than excluding, redundant rather than simple, vestigial as well as innovating, inconsistent and equivocal rather than direct and clear."[45] In his architectural works illustrated in the book and in his subsequent buildings, Venturi conveyed this attitude, and structures as diverse as the Guild House in Philadelphia of 1963 and the 1990 addition to the National Gallery in London partake of this allusive, symbolic, and at the same time ordinary design. Venturi, a graduate of Princeton University with a master's of fine arts degree, has brought his respect for the past to the field of design through a series of historicizing chairs he designed for Knoll (no. 385) and his Queen Anne silver tea service and *Campidoglio* platter for Alessi. His partiality for the banal is reflected in the floral *Grandmother* pattern used as a laminate on the Knoll chairs, which also appears, along with his *Notebook* pattern, on ceramics for Swid Powell and textiles for the Fabric Workshop in Philadelphia.

References: Stanislaus von Moss, *Venturi, Rauch & Scott Brown: Buildings and Projects* (New York, 1987); Michael Collins and Andreas Papadakis, *Post-Modern Design* (New York, 1989), pp. 103–10.

MASSIMO VIGNELLI
Italian, lives in United States, born 1931

Massimo Vignelli has brought a sophisticated European refinement to American design through the graphics, packaging, and products he has produced with his wife Lella since they came to the United States in 1965. Vignelli studied at the Accademia di Belle Arti di Brera in Milan and then at the school of architecture at the University of Venice. He began in the 1950s to design products, including glasswares for Venini, which won a Compasso d'Oro award in 1956, and a plastic tableware service with coordinated packaging similarly honored in 1964 (no. 304). Vignelli was cofounder of the design and marketing corporation Unimark International in 1965, and in 1971 the Vignellis established Vignelli Associates in New York. Their consistent, high-quality design approach has resulted in notable corporate identity programs (Bloomingdale's department store, American Airlines), book and magazine design (Industrial Design), packaging, transportation signage (New York City subway), interiors (showrooms for Knoll and Artemide in New York), and products such as plastics (for Heller), metalwares (for San Lorenzo), and furniture (for Knoll).

References: Design: Vignelli (New York, 1981); Stephen Kliment, "The Vignellis—Profile of a Design Team," Industrial Design (special issue: Designers' Choice, 1981), pp. 6–12; Barbaralee Diamonstein, Interior Design: The New Freedom (New York, 1982), pp. 176–91; Stan Pinkwas, "King and Queen of Cups," Metropolis (January–February 1983), pp. 12–17; The International Design Yearbook, vol. 2 (New York, 1986), pp. 29, 55, 139.

C.F.A. VOYSEY
English, 1857–1941

An architect primarily of country houses, C.F.A. Voysey was also a designer of ornamental patterns, furniture, and silver, whose work was known and much praised abroad as well as in England. Apprenticed to the architect John Pollard Seddon from 1873 to 1878, he opened his own office in 1881 or 1882. With architectural commissions slow in coming, he began to create patterns for wallpaper about 1883, receiving technical advice from his friend A. H. Mackmurdo, founder of the Century Guild, and selling his designs to Jeffrey and Company. Over the next decades Voysey sold numerous patterns to various manu-facturers for wallpapers, woven and printed textiles, and carpets. He worked on contract as well for Essex & Company (from 1893) and Alexander Morton (from 1895), taking plants (no. 3), birds, and, in his later years, narrative themes as the inspiration for his designs. Popular almost immediately in England, Voysey's decorative work soon became known abroad through exhibitions (as early as 1889 at the Paris Exposition Universelle) and reproduc-tions in art journals. When a group of Jeffrey wallpapers was shown at the Salon de l'Association pour l'Art in Antwerp in 1893, HENRY VAN DE VELDE praised Voysey's

work, seeing in his patterns a "new orientation"[46] quite unlike the other British papers on exhibit, and there is lit-tle doubt that he had a significant, early impact on the decorative direction of art nouveau. Voysey himself, how-ever, later repudiated this style: "I think the condition which has made l'Art Nouveau possible is a distinctly healthy development, but at the same time the manifesta-tion of it is distinctly unhealthy and revolting."[47] Voysey was among the first to receive the designation Royal Designer for Industry (in 1936).

References: "An Interview with Mr. Charles F. Annesley Voysey, Architect and Designer," Studio 1 (September 1893); 231–37; Nikolaus Pevsner, "C.F.A. Voysey" [1940], in Studies in Art, Architecture and Design, vol. 2: Victorian and After (Princeton, N.J., 1982), pp. 141–51; Peter Floud, "The Wallpaper Designs of C.F.A. Voysey," Penrose Annual, vol. 52 (1958), pp. 10–14; John Brandon-Jones et al., C.F.A. Voysey: Architect and Designer, 1857–1941 (London, 1978); Stuart Durant, The Decorative Designs of C.F.A. Voysey (New York, 1991).

WILHELM WAGENFELD
German, 1900–1990

Throughout his long career, Wilhelm Wagenfeld has pro-moted rational design for industry, applying the principles of functional efficiency and clear, geometrical form that he learned in the Bauhaus metal workshop as a student and journeyman (1923–25) and designing broad ranges of glass and metalwares distinguished by their consistent quality. Wagenfeld apprenticed in the silverwares firm of Koch & Bergfeld while attending classes at the Kunstgewerbeschule in Bremen (1916–17); receiving a stipend, he attended the Staatliche Zeichenakademie in Hanau (1919–22) where he designed woodcuts in an expressionist style. In 1923 Wagenfeld entered the Bauhaus at Weimar. Under the direction of LÁSZLÓ MOHOLY-NAGY in the metal workshop, he produced one of his most famous designs in collaboration with KARL J. JUCKER, a metal and glass table lamp in simplified form (no. 94). When the Bauhaus moved to Dessau in 1925, Wagenfeld remained in Weimar as assistant in the metal workshop of the Weimar Staatliche Bauhochschule (he became a teacher and director of the workshop in 1929). From 1927 he began to design independently for industry, for the metalwares firms of Walter & Wagner in Schliez and S. A. Loevy in Berlin, and he opened his own studio in 1930. He designed glasswares from 1931 for Jenaer Glaswerk Schott & Gen., creating tablewares in ovenproof glass, some of which are still in production today (no. 147), as well as a porcelain service in 1934 for Fürstenberg in Weser that was produced until 1958. He was professor at the Staatliche Kunsthochschule Grunewaldstrasse in Berlin (1931–35), but gave up teach-ing to become artistic director of the Vereinigte Lausitzer Glaswerke in Weisswasser, where he designed economi-cal pressed glass (no. 178), bottles, hollowwares, and stemwares that were recognized for their high quality as well as economy. In 1938 Wagenfeld designed the *Daphne* porcelain service for Rosenthal, which was produced for export until 1956.

After refusing to join the Nazi party, in 1944 Wagenfeld was sent as a political undesirable to the war front, and became a Russian prisoner of war. After the war, from 1947–49, he was professor of industrial design at the Hochschule für Bildende Künste in Berlin, and in 1949–50 a lecturer for industrial design at the Landesgewerbeamt in Stuttgart. During these years he continued designing the unadorned clear-lined products he made before the war, creating his first designs for the Württembergische Metallwarenfabrik (WMF) in Geislingen. With WMF as his major client, in 1954 he founded a consulting studio for the research and development of industrial design, and there he created numerous metal hollowwares, flatwares, glass, and silver until 1970. Among his other clients were Peill & Putzler in Düren and Lindner in Bamberg, for whom he created lighting fixtures from 1955 to 1970. Wagenfeld closed his workshop in 1978.

References: Kunstgewerbemuseum, Zurich, *Industrieware von Wilhelm Wagenfeld* (October 7–November 13, 1960); Kunstgewerbemuseum, Cologne, *Wilhelm Wagenfeld: 50 Jahre Mitarbeit in Fabriken* (October–December 1973); Württembergisches Landesmuseum, Stuttgart, *Wilhelm Wagenfeld: Schöne Form, gute Ware* (April 4–June 8, 1980); Beate Manske and Gudrun Scholz, eds., *Täglich in der Hand: Industrieformen von Wilhelm Wagenfeld aus sechs Jahrzehnten* (Worpswede, Germany, 1987).

OTTO WAGNER
Austrian, 1841–1918

From the 1880s Otto Wagner led Vienna's progressive movement in architecture, promoting through his work and writings, notably *Moderne Architektur* (1895), the rational use of modern materials and techniques and a rectilinear style of flat, simple surfaces with geometric ornament. Wagner's work influenced not only his assistants and pupils, including JOSEPH MARIA OLBRICH and JOSEF HOFFMANN, but the generation of German designers that established the Deutscher Werkbund. Trained as an architect at the Vienna Polytechnic (1860), Berlin Bauakademie (1861), and Vienna Akademie der Bildenden Künste (1862), Wagner spent the early years of his career designing apartment and office buildings in the Vienna Ringstrasse in a monumental classical style derived from Karl Friedrich Schinkel, the Bauakademie's most famous teacher. Wagner also took part in many competitions for public works throughout Europe and in Vienna, including a development plan for the city, and from 1893 he designed the track and stations of the Stadtbahn, Vienna's urban transport system. In 1894 he was named professor of architecture at the Akademie, where he was in turn influenced by his pupils, whom he joined in the Secession in 1899. He was also inspired by the art nouveau decorative styles then sweeping Europe, as demonstrated in the facade of his Majolika Haus

(1899), decorated with colored floral majolica tiles. Although classicism seemed Wagner's natural style, after the turn of the century he grew increasingly independent of it, particularly in his most famous building, the Österreichische Postsparkasse (Imperial Austrian Postal Savings Bank; 1904–6, 1910–12). This influential building relied on the use of aluminum for the large exposed bolts that secured the white marble cladding of the facade, the crowning statues at roof level, and the canopy of the main doorway. With its frank exhibition of an industrial material for decorative purposes and the extreme simplicity of its wall treatment, the building was considered boldly modern by contemporaries and a landmark of its period by later historians. Wagner designed furniture for the Postal Savings Bank that was as radically simple in form as the building, some of which was similarly decorated with aluminum fittings (no. 37).

References: Heinz Geretsegger and Max Peintner, *Otto Wagner, 1841–1918: The Expanding City and the Beginnings of Modern Architecture* (New York, 1979); Paul Asenbaum et al., *Otto Wagner: Möbel und Innenräume* (Salzburg, 1984); Gustav Peichl, ed., *Die Kunst des Otto Wagner* (Vienna, 1984); Hessisches Landesmuseum, Darmstadt, Germany *Otto Wagner: Das Werk des Architeckten* (1985).

KATSUJI WAKISAKA
Japanese, born 1944

Trained in textile design at the Kyoto School of Arts and Crafts (1960–63), Katsuji Wakisaka worked as a designer of apparel fabrics first for Itoh in Osaka (1963–65) and subsequently for the Samejima Textile Design Studio in Kyoto (1965–68). In 1968 he went to Finland where he spent the next seven years designing furnishing and dress fabrics for Marimekko. His first designs, including *Yume* (1969), were figurative and Western in style and aimed at the children's market, as was his popular pattern of cars and trucks, *Bo Boo* (1975). Gradually, however, Wakisaka returned to small-scale, abstract Japanese patterns, even creating a kimono and kimono sashes for the Finnish firm. From 1976 Wakisaka worked concurrently for Jack Lenor Larsen, New York, and the Wacoal Interior Fabric Company, Tokyo, relying increasingly on Japanese traditional textile patterns for inspiration (no. 353). In 1980 Wakisaka's designs for Wacoal were selected by the Japan Design Committee for exhibition in the Matsuya Ginza gallery, Tokyo.

Reference: Pekka Suhonen and Juhani Pallasmaa, eds., *Phenomenon Marimekko* (Helsinki, 1986), pp. 132–33.

DON WALLANCE
American, 1909–1990

Designer of furniture and metalware, Don Wallance was also a commentator on industrial design, surveying the relationship between craft and industry in his book

Shaping America's Products (1956). In this volume he presented case studies of thirty products, studies originally undertaken in 1950 on commission from the Walker Art Center in Minneapolis and the American Craftsman's Educational Council. Trained at the Design Laboratory in New York (1935–39), Wallance was awarded a prize in 1938 by the Museum of Modern Art in New York for a chair design for its new building. During World War II he researched furniture mass production for the United States armed forces, work that carried over to his study of plywood storage units (with the Midwest Research Institute, Kansas City, Missouri, and Yale University School of Forestry), which won a prize in the Museum of Modern Art's low-cost furniture competition in 1948. Wallance designed cutlery for Lauffer from 1954, his organic stainless-steel *Design 1* service (no. 224) being the first in a succession of flatware designs, which by 1979 with *Design 10*, had expanded to include plastic utensils. The furniture that Wallance designed was mostly for contract use, the best known being seating for Philharmonic Hall in New York's Lincoln Center (1964).

References: Edgar Kaufmann, Jr., *Prize Designs for Modern Furniture* (New York, 1950), p. 48; Ada Louise Huxtable, "Stainless Comes to Dinner," *Industrial Design* 1 (August 1954): 29– 37; Colin Naylor, ed., *Contemporary Designers*, 2d ed. (Chicago, 1990), pp. 596–98; Obituary, *New York Times*, May 28, 1990, p. 42.

WATER STUDIO
Established Tokyo, 1973

Founder and principal of the design firm Water Studio, Naoki Sakai studied at Kyoto University of Fine Art (1966). In 1973 he established Water Studio, which initially specialized in textile and fashion design but has since become known for its highly original product and automotive designs, ranging from the Nissan *Pao* automobile and Suzuki's *SW-1* motorcycle to the Olympus *O–Product* camera, Seiko *Asterisk* wristwatch, and Sharp's liquid crystal television (no. 399).

Reference: *The International Design Yearbook*, vol. 6 (New York, 1991), p. 213.

GILBERT A. WATROUS
American, born 1919

An exhibition and industrial designer as well as a sculptor, Gilbert A. Watrous graduated from the Institute of Design at the Illinois Institute of Technology in Chicago. His work includes museum exhibitions, landscape architecture (San Diego's children's zoo), and product design—a floor lamp that won a special award in the 1950 lighting competition at the Museum of Modern Art in New York (no. 212). Between 1957 and about 1962 he worked on product design as a partner in the firm VID (Visual and Industrial Design).

References: A.D., "Lamp Competition: A New Flexibility in Machines for Lighting," *Interiors* 110 (April 1951): 136–39; H. M. Dunnett, "Lamp Design Competition," *Architectural Review* 111 (January 1952): 57.

KEM WEBER
American, born Germany, 1889–1963

One of the leading exponents of advanced European art and design principles on the West Coast during the 1920s and 30s, Kem Weber first adapted the "cubist" trends he saw in Paris at the 1925 *Exposition Internationale des Arts Décoratifs* and then introduced the use of tubular steel, plywood, and other modern materials in a streamlined style. Weber apprenticed as a cabinetmaker in his native Germany, becoming a journeyman in Potsdam in 1907 and then studying at the school of the Kunstgewerbemuseum in Berlin with Bruno Paul, whom he assisted on the design and construction of the German section at the Brussels world's fair in 1910. On the recommendation of Paul, in whose studio he had worked since his graduation in 1912, Weber was sent in 1914 as a designer for Germany's exhibit at the *Panama-Pacific International Exposition* in San Francisco, where he was stranded by the outbreak of World War I and where he then settled. From 1922 to 1927, Weber acted as art director for Barker Brothers, a large decorating and furniture store in Los Angeles, where he introduced his version of the "modern" style in the Modes and Manners shop he designed. His national reputation was established when he exhibited in New York at Macy's second *International Exposition of Art in Industry* in 1928, along with a group of international exhibitors including Paul, JOSEF HOFFMANN, PETER MÜLLER-MUNK, and the American furniture designer Eugene Schoen. Weber continued as an independent consultant designer for Barker after 1927, but over the next decade created numerous designs for manufacturers across the country, among them the Bentlock furniture line produced by Higgins in San Francisco; furniture for Baker, Berkey and Gay, Mueller, and Widdicomb, all of Grand Rapids, Michigan; silver for Friedman in New York; and clocks for Lawson of Los Angeles. Toward the end of the 1930s Weber's work was centered mostly on interiors and architecture, and in 1939–40 he designed the Walt Disney Studios in Burbank, from site plan to its furnishings; among the latter he included a version of his best-known work, the *Airline* chair of 1934 (no. 142).

References: "Airline Chair of Wood by Kem Weber," *Architectural Record* 77 (May 1935): 31; "Disney Studios, Burbank, Calif.," *Architectural Forum* 81 (September 1944): 123–28, 142; David Gebhard and Harriette Von Breton, *Kem Weber: The Moderne in Southern California, 1920 through 1941* (Santa Barbara, Calif., 1969); David Gebhard, "Kem Weber: Moderne Design in California, 1920–1940," *Journal of Decorative and Propaganda Arts* 2 (summer-fall 1986): 20–31.

HANS J. WEGNER
Danish, born 1914

With his furniture of natural wood, simple, pure forms, expressive lines, high-quality manufacture, and regard for tradition, Hans J. Wegner became synonymous with Danish modern design during the 1950s. Apprenticed at the age of fourteen to a cabinetmaker, Wegner worked in the trade between 1932 and 1935, and from 1936 to 1938 studied furniture design at the Kunsthåndvaerker-skolen (School of Arts, Crafts and Design) in Copenhagen. Between 1938 and 1943 he worked for ARNE JACOBSEN and Erik Møller in Aarhus, where he then opened his first studio, moving to Copenhagen in 1946. He was associated from 1940 with the cabinetmaker Johannes Hansen, who from 1941 produced the designs Wegner submitted annually to the Copenhagen Cabinetmakers Guild competitions, showing his *Peacock* chair (no. 219) there in 1947. But it was the armchair he designed in 1949 (no. 218) and showed at the guild exhibition that year that brought him broad recognition and the beginning of a large production to satisfy the international market; eventually six separate factories—Hansen's and those of Salesco, a distribution organization—were devoted solely to manufacturing his work. Wegner was awarded numerous design prizes, including the Lunning Prize in 1951.

References: Arne Karlsen, *Made in Denmark* (New York, 1960), pp. 56–63, 136–37, 142–43, 150–51; Johan Møller-Nielsen, *Wegner: En dansk møbelkunstner* (Copenhagen, 1965); Henrik Sten Møller, *Tema med variationer: Hans J. Wegner's møbler* (Tonder, Denmark, 1979); Irving Sloane, "Hans Wegner: A Modern Master of Furniture Design," *Fine Woodworking* 20 (January–February 1980): 36–42.

WOLFGANG WEINGART
German, lives in Switzerland, born 1941

An independent graphic designer and a very influential teacher at the Kunstgewerbeschule in Basel (from 1968), Wolfgang Weingart revised and expanded the Swiss typographic style, challenging the tenets of a movement that by the late 1960s had become in many ways formulaic. With a background in typography, specifically hand composition, but otherwise self-taught, Weingart questioned what had become conventional in the Swiss style: "Type must not always be set flush left/ragged right, nor in only two type sizes, nor in necessarily right-angle arrangements, nor printed either black or red. Typography must not be dry, tightly ordered or rigid. Type may be set center axis, ragged left/ragged right, perhaps sometimes in a chaos. But even then, typography should have a hidden structure and visual order."[48] In the late 1970s Weingart's approach became more pictorial (no. 350), creating a kind of photo-mechanical collage by using a layering process to join type, illustration, and later computer-generated graphic images. In the process he creates new complex compositions and what he postulated might perhaps be "the language of a new world of typography."[49]

References: Peter von Kornatzki, "Wolfgang Weingart: A Typographic Rebel," *Graphis* 39 (September–October 1983): 80–87; F.H.K. Henrion, *Top Graphic Design* (Zurich, 1983), pp. 150–57; Wolfgang Weingart, "My Typography Instruction at the Basle School of Design/Switzerland, 1968 to 1985," *Design Quarterly* 130 (1985).

W. ARCHIBALD WELDEN
American, active 1920s–1950s

W. Archibald Welden became associated with the Revere Copper Company as an independent designer in the mid-1930s, after having had his own metal fabricating business, Kantack, in the later 1920s. Kantack manufactured metalwork for architecture, lighting, and giftwares and had produced models of the metal accessories designed by NORMAN BEL GEDDES for Revere in 1934; Welden himself had designed giftware for the company. At Revere, Welden worked with the company's engineers on the design of the copper-bottom stainless steel *Revere Ware* cooking utensils (no. 179) and also created an institutional variant in 1954.

References: Don Wallance, *Shaping America's Products* (New York, 1956), pp. 41–45; Jay Doblin, *One Hundred Great Product Designs* (New York, 1970), no. 40.

WES WILSON
American, born 1937

One of the originators and leading designers of the California psychedelic poster craze during the 1960s, Wes Wilson was a graduate of San Francisco State University whose experience included working for a small printing firm. In early 1966 he designed the first poster commissioned by the rock promoter Bill Graham, and he was responsible for most of Graham's posters the next year, primarily for concerts at San Francisco's Fillmore Auditorium. Wilson's most characteristic posters embraced a dense art nouveau–inspired style (no. 297) suggesting an origin in the visual excitement and hallucinations of the LSD experience. Wilson's work was included along with that of Rick Griffin, Victor Moscoso, Stanley Mouse, and Alton Kelley in the first important exhibition of psychedelic graphics at the Moore Gallery in San Francisco in July 1967.

References: Peter Selz, "The Hippie Poster," *Graphis* 135 (1968): 70–74, 91; Paul D. Grushkin, *The Art of Rock: Posters from Presley to Punk* (New York, 1987), passim.

EDUARD JOSEF WIMMER
Austrian, 1882–1961

Known for his successful direction of the Wiener Werkstätte's fashion department after its establishment in 1910, Eduard Josef Wimmer independently designed products for a number of other Viennese firms, including furniture for Wilhelm Niedermoser (no. 62), glass for J. and L. Lobmeyer, and graphics for the printing company Graphische Industrie. A student of JOSEF HOFFMANN, Wimmer attended the Kunstgewerbeschule in Vienna where he later taught almost continuously between 1912 and 1953. Wimmer began his association with the Wiener Werkstätte in 1907 by helping in the decoration of the Fledermaus Cabaret. He became one of Hoffmann's closest collaborators, specializing in decorative painting and other wall treatments in such projects as the *Kunstschau* exhibition buildings (1908), exhibition rooms for the Wiener Werkstätte in the Österreichische Museum für Kunst und Industrie (1910–11), a new show-room for the Wiener Werkstätte's fashion department on the Kärntnerstrasse (1916), and rooms for the Öster-reichische Werkbund exhibition (1929–30). Wimmer also designed an exhibition room for the Wiener Werkstätte at the Deutscher Werkbund exhibition in Cologne (1914). Between 1923 and 1925 he lived in the United States, where he taught briefly at the Art Institute of Chicago and created stage sets for Joseph Urban in New York. A gifted ornamental designer, Wimmer often super-imposed one pattern over another—in the apartment for the actress Mimi Marlow, arcades of flowers and leaves were painted over a network of lozenges. This interest in dense pattern and color persisted in the costumes, tex-tiles, bookbindings, and metalwork as well as the interiors that Wimmer designed for the Wiener Werkstätte.

References: Werner J. Schweiger, *Wiener Werkstaette: Design in Vienna, 1903–1932* (New York, 1984), passim; Eduard F. Sekler, *Josef Hoffmann: The Architectural Work* (Princeton, N.J., 1985), passim.

TAPIO WIRKKALA
Finnish, 1915–1985

Craftsman and designer of glass, ceramics, metal, wooden objects, lighting, furniture, appliances, graphics, and exhibi-tions, Tapio Wirkkala was Finland's most versatile and influential designer in the second half of the twentieth century, evoking a national identity in his work by drawing on the materials and processes of Finnish handcraft and naturalistic forms. Educated at the Taideteollinen kesku skoulu (Central School of Industrial Arts), Helsinki (1933–36), where he was later artistic director (1951–54), Wirkkala became glass designer for Iittala in 1947 after sharing first prize with KAJ FRANCK in a com-petition organized by the glassworks. He achieved interna-tional recognition in the late 1940s and 1950s with his *Kantarelli* (*Chanterelle*) glasses (no. 206) and laminated wooden dishes (no. 233), as well as for his role as design-er and commissioner of the Finnish sections at the *IX* and *X Triennale* exhibitions in Milan in 1951 and 1954. He was awarded three grand prizes at each exhibition—for exhi-bition design, glass, and wood carving in 1951, and glass, sculpture, and exhibition design in 1954. The exhibitions brought Wirkkala various commissions—from RAYMOND LOEWY, with whom Wirkkala was associated in New York in 1955–56; from the Rosenthal porcelain factory (initially through Loewy) for designs throughout Wirkkala's career, including the firm's centennial (*Century*) service of 1979; from Venini, with whom Wirkkala had a similar longstanding relationship for glass design; from the lighting firm Airam, for whom Wirkkala designed opalescent glass bulbs to be used without shades; and from Hackman, for whom Wirkkala designed versions of the traditional Finnish *puukko* knife (from 1963). Wirkkala married the noted Finnish ceramicist Rut Bryk in 1945 and collaborat-ed with her on several projects; she provided the *Cumulus* decorations for his Rosenthal *Century* service.

References: Smithsonian Institution, Washington, D.C., *Rut Bryk–Tapio Wirkkala* (1956–59); Finnish Society of Crafts and Design, Helsinki, *Tapio Wirkkala* (1981); "Interview with Tapio Wirkkala," *Domus* 619 (July–August 1981): 6–7; Pekka Suhonen, "Counterpoints in Tapio Wirkkala's Output," *Form Function Finland* 2 (1981): 38–43.

FRANK LLOYD WRIGHT
American, 1867–1959

When Frank Lloyd Wright, undisputably America's great-est twentieth-century architect, wrote in 1908 of making "a building, together with its equipment, appurtenances and environment, an entity which shall constitute a com-plete work of art,"[50] he was expressing a design principle learned from abroad, where French and German design-ers especially were creating entire interiors and exhibiting them at national and international expositions. Admired early on for his simple and geometric designs, particularly by critics writing in American journals such as *The House Beautiful* that promoted Arts and Crafts principles, Wright nonetheless broke with the movement on the issue of hand craftsmanship, believing that "the art of the future will be the expression of the individual artist through the thousand powers of the machine, the machine, doing all those things that the individual workman cannot do."[51] Wright's designs in fact share the machine aesthetic; they are simple and based on geometric forms then thought most suitable for machine manufacture, although few were made entirely by machine. In creating his interiors Wright provided built-in furnishings wherever possible and where necessary designed freestanding, coordinated pieces, which were manufactured for him by a succession of small firms.

Raised to be an architect, Wright studied engineer-ing for a short time at the University of Wisconsin and then worked for a draftsman, but ran off to Chicago to work first for J. L. Silsbee and then for Louis Sullivan in the firm of Adler and Sullivan, becoming the firm's specialist in house design. From his earliest independent work Wright conceived of his buildings as complete entities, as organic architecture that demanded equal attention and quality for all parts. It was for Wright's Prairie houses, the sequence of residences that he began to build mainly in Chicago and Oak Park, Illinois, around the turn of the century, that most of his best-known furnishings were created (nos. 13, 26, 42)—chairs and tables, lamps, stained glass, and metalwork. He continued to furnish his own interiors throughout his career, including the Imperial Hotel in Tokyo of 1916–22 (no. 80); Fallingwater in Bear Run, Pennsylvania, the most eloquent American domestic creation of this century; the S. C. Johnson Administration Building in Racine, Wisconsin, of 1936–39 (no. 163); and his homes, Taliesen East, in Wisconsin, and Taliesen West, in Arizona. His one major venture into commercial production, the Taliesin Ensemble series introduced in the pages of *House Beautiful* in 1955, provided furniture, carpeting, wall coverings, fabrics, and accessories—everything necessary for the public to construct their own Wrightian interiors. Wright's great final achievement was the Solomon R. Guggenheim Museum in New York (1956–59).

References: "Frank Lloyd Wright Designs Home Furnishings You Can Buy," *House Beautiful* 98 (November 1955): pp. 282–90, 336–40; Irma Strauss, "Husser House Dining Room Set," *Frank Lloyd Wright Newsletter* 2 (1979): 5–9; David Hanks, *The Decorative Designs of Frank Lloyd Wright* (New York, 1979).

RUSSEL WRIGHT
American, 1904–1976

With the conviction that "good design is for everyone," Russel Wright created his products for all Americans and championed modern design for the new informal lifestyle of the 1930s. Like several other first-generation industrial designers, he came to the profession with experience in the theater, gained at Princeton (which he entered in 1921) and in New York, as an apprentice to NORMAN BEL GEDDES (then a stage designer). In the early 1930s, encouraged by his wife, Mary (who was to be his business partner), he began to design and produce spun-aluminum accessories for the home; these introduced oven-to-table ware as well as new forms such as cheese boards, bun warmers, "sandwich humidors," "tid-bit trays," wares that fostered the philosophy of informal living and entertaining he outlined in *A Guide to Easier Living*, which he wrote with his wife in 1951. His ideas about flexibility were explored in his 1934 upholstered furniture (for Heywood-Wakefield), a collection conceived as coordinated elements rather than matched suites and one that introduced the sectional sofa; it was shown in 1934 at Bloomingdale's in New York in a series of room settings fully accessorized with products he designed. The blonde *Modern Living* (later *American Modern*) maple furniture line produced for R. H. Macy's (through Conant Ball) the following year was promoted widely, and for the first time his name—which was to become "famous" and advertised that way—was associated with his design.

But it was in the area of tableware that Wright achieved true renown. His distinctive, organic *American Modern* ceramic dinnerware (no. 173), designed in 1937 but not produced until 1939, sold in enormous quantities.

It was followed by his more restrained but also very popular *Casual China* of 1946 (for Iroquois China)—cleverly marketed with a "replaced free if it chips or breaks" guarantee. Accessories to *American Modern* were also marketed: flatware produced by John Hull Cutlery (1951); glassware by Morgantown Glass Guild (1951); and table linens by Leacock (1946–48). *Meladur*, the melamine dinnerware designed for American Cyanamid in 1945 and marketed first in 1949 (by General American Transportation), was one of the earliest attempts to bring plastic to the dining table; later his melamine *Residential* service of 1953 (no. 235) had a resounding success. Wright continued to design into the 1960s—household accessories, furniture (folding metal chairs for Samsonite), small appliances, fabrics, interiors, as well as advertising and packaging, but his consultancy as a planner for the National Park Service (beginning in 1967) marked the effective end of his design career. He did, however, continue to work on Dragon Rock, the experimental house in Garrison, New York, that he built with a sensitivity toward nature and materials deriving from his experiences in Japan; here he also applied the principles of informal living he had championed throughout his career.

References: *Current Biography* (1950), s.v. "Wright, Russel"; Dianne Cochrane, "Designer for All Seasons," *Industrial Design* 23 (March–April 1976): 46–51; William J. Hennessey, *Russel Wright: American Designer* (Cambridge, Mass., 1983); Ann Kerr, *Russel Wright Dinnerware: Design for the American Table* (Paducah, Ky., 1985).

SORI YANAGI
Japanese, born 1915

Since winning first prize in the inaugural Japanese Competition for Industrial Design in 1952 (with the design of a record player for Columbia, Japan), Sori Yanagi has pioneered the design field in Japan. After studying architecture and painting at the Tokyo Academy of Fine Art (1936–40), he worked in the architectural office of Junzo Sakakura and then as assistant to CHARLOTTE PERRIAND when she was caught in Japan by the outbreak of the war. Yanagi opened his own office in Tokyo in 1952, and the following year was a founding member of the Japan Industrial Designers Association (JIDA) and the Japan Design Committee. He also taught at the Tokyo Women's College of Art (1953–54) and at Kanazawa University of Art and Crafts (from 1954).

In the works he has created as an independent designer, Yanagi combines Japanese forms with Western methods and technology. In his *Butterfly* stool (no. 255), for example, he suggests a Japanese furniture type (which it is not) while following a sophisticated method of plywood molding to achieve its organic shapes. Although prizing the technical and practical side of industrial design, he resists its marketing determinations, commercialism, and the heavy emphasis placed on efficiency and economy; indeed his works always retain an underlying sense of fine craftsmanship and artistic design. Yanagi's wide range of products— notably an extensive line of ceramics, plastic stacking stools, wooden furniture, metal tableware, appliances, and tractors—all share understated organic forms that bespeak their Japanese origins. He also designed the torches for the Olympics in Tokyo (1964) and Sapporo (1972). Yanagi's keen interest in the traditions of his native land brought him the position of director of the Japan Folk Crafts Museum in Tokyo in 1977, which his father, Soetsu Yanagi, founded.

References: "Produzione recente di Sori Yanagi," *Stile Industria* 28 (August 1960): 42–45; Katzumie Masaru, "Yanagi Sori's Milan Exhibit—Symbol of Good Design in Japan," *Gurafuikku Dezain* 80 (winter 1980): 2–7; Sori Yanagi, *Dezain: Yanagi Sori no Sakuhin to Kangae (Design: Sori Yanagi's Works and Philosophy)* (Tokyo, 1983); Colin Naylor, ed., *Contemporary Designers*, 2d ed. (Chicago, 1990), pp. 618–20.

TADANORI YOKOO
Japanese, born 1936

Painter, printmaker, and graphic designer, Tadanori Yokoo led the movement toward a Pop aesthetic in Japan during the 1960s, winning the admiration and following of young graphic designers and the criticism of Japanese traditionalists who decried the vulgarity of the images he created (no. 301). Yokoo became a Pop celebrity, acting in film and on the stage and starring in Takashi Ichiyanagi's performance work *Tadanori Yokoo Sings—An Opera*. Yokoo produced posters, commercial illustrations, and book designs for clients ranging from theater and dance companies (Tenjo Sajiki, Jokyo Gekijo, Ankoku Buto-Ha) to department stores (Seibu, Matsuya, Tokyu, Sogo) and industrial corporations (Toshiba Machine Company, Yamagiwa Electric, Takeda Chemical Industry, Suntory).

Yokoo's design sources, which during the 1960s included matchbox covers, beer and sake bottle labels, playing cards, and *ukiyoe* woodblock prints, became increasingly religious and metaphysical in the 1970s, with references to Hindu, Buddhist, and Zen images. A sometime collaborator of the fashion designer Issey Miyake, Yokoo has provided designs for Miyake's printed fabrics; in 1970, he was commissioned to design the Textile Pavilion for *Expo '70* in Osaka.

Born in Nishiwaki, Yokoo worked as an artist at Seibundo Printing Company, Kakogawa City (1954–56), for the newspaper *Kobe Shimbun*, Kobe (1956–59), and the National Advertisement Laboratory, Osaka (1959–60), before moving to Tokyo and the Nippon Design Center (1960–64). He established two graphic design studios during the later 1960s, Studio Illfill, with Akira Uno and Chunao Harada (1964–65), and the End Studio, with Masamichi Oikawa (1968–71). Since 1971, he has practiced independently, and since 1981, has devoted himself to painting, employing an expressive, painterly style focused on the human figure.

References: Y. Tono, "Tadanori Yokoo," in S. Takashina, Y. Tono, Y. Nakahara, eds., *Art in Japan Today* (Tokyo, 1974), pp. 178–80; Koichi Tanikawa, *100 Posters of Tadanori Yokoo* (Tokyo, 1978); Tadanori Yokoo, *All About Tadanori Yokoo and His Graphic Works* (Tokyo, 1989); *Best 100 Japanese Posters, 1945–1989* (Tokyo, 1990), pp. 80–83, 96–97, 104–5, 126–29, 258; Colin Naylor, ed., *Contemporary Designers*, 2d ed. (Chicago, 1990), pp. 623–25; Mark Holborn, *Beyond Japan: A Photo Theater* (London, 1991), pp. 76–77, 118, 168, 172.

MARCO ZANINI
Italian, born 1954

Marco Zanini was one of the young architects who joined the firm of Sottsass Associati when it was first organized in 1980 by ETTORE SOTTSASS, JR.. The two designers met in 1975 at a workshop of the radical Global Tools group when Zanini was a student at the University of Florence, from which he graduated in 1978. Zanini has simultaneously designed graphics, products, and interiors for Sottsass Associati and created furniture and decorative objects for other firms as well. A member of the Memphis group, he was represented in the first collection in 1981 with a sofa and in the second collection of 1982 primarily with a series of glass vessels (no. 365). Zanini has also worked with Sottsass as an associate in the production firm Enorme, which makes high-technology appliances for the consumer market.

References: Barbara Radice, ed., *Memphis: The New International Style* (Milan, 1981), pp. 65–66; *Memphis: Research, Experiences, Results, Failures and Successes of New Design* (New York, 1984), passim; *Sottsass Associati* (New York, 1988), passim; Nally Bellati, *New Italian Design* (New York, 1990), pp. 150–55.

MARCO ZANUSO
Italian, born 1916

Italy's leading rationalist designer of the post–World War II period, Marco Zanuso has based his design activities on materials and technology research. Exploring new materials, manufacturing methods, forms of construction, and the implementation of technological developments, Zanuso's work in these areas at times has pushed considerably beyond the limits of the commissions that inspired them. Zanuso received a diploma in architecture from the Milan Politecnico in 1939 and established his own design office in 1945. He approached his work with a technical intensity that allowed him to solve problems such as the applicability of rubber for upholstery (no. 230) and the use of shell construction (no. 285) and polyethylene for furniture (no. 287), the latter in collaboration with RICHARD SAPPER who worked with him from 1958 to 1977. Zanuso and Sapper collaborated on a large number of electronic products (no. 305), using miniaturization technology to rethink totally the typology for their *Doney 14* television for Brionvega and *Grillo* telephone (no. 299).

References: Gillo Dorfles, *Marco Zanuso, Designer* (Rome, 1971); Paolo Fossati, *Il design in Italia, 1945–1972* (Turin, 1972), pp. 107–13, 207–19, pls. 177–235; "Imbottito," *Domus* 686 (September 1987): 79–80; Augusto Morello and Anna Castelli Ferrieri, *Plastic and Design* (Milan, 1988), pp. 134–37.

EVA ZEISEL
American, active Germany and Soviet Union, born Hungary, 1906

While Eva Zeisel's career as a ceramic designer mirrored currents in international modern design, particularly the geometric forms she had created in Germany around 1930, her work consistently retained a particular organic character with a striking sense of material and place. Like Scandinavian designs, some of her work was specifically folklike, as in the humorous animal forms she adopted, but more often it was abstract and fluidly sculptural. Zeisel studied painting at the Képzomuveszeti Academia in Budapest in 1923 and apprenticed herself to the pottery firm of Jakob Karapancsik before opening her own pottery in 1925. Between 1928 and 1930 she worked in Germany as ceramic designer at the Schramberger Majolika Fabrik, and in 1930–31 in Berlin for the Christian Carstens Kommerz.Gesellschaft. The next year Zeisel left Germany for the Soviet Union, where she worked first at the Lomonosov factory in Leningrad and from 1934 at the Dulevo factory near Moscow. Like other foreign experts, Zeisel left Russia when she was removed from her government position in 1937, and in 1938 she arrived in New York, where she was to settle permanently.

In the United States Zeisel first designed ceramic wares for the Bay Ridge Specialty Company, Trenton, New Jersey (c. 1939); Sears, Roebuck and Company (1942); and the Castleton China Company of New Castle, Pennsylvania—the latter bringing Zeisel national attention through its connection with the Museum of Modern Art in New York (no. 192). Other commissions for ceramic dinnerwares and accessories came from the Riverside Ceramic Company, Riverside, California (1946–47), and Hall China of East Liverpool, Ohio (c. 1952). While her ceramic designs remain the work for which she is best known, Zeisel also designed glasswares (Bryce Brothers, c. 1952; Federal, c. 1954) and a patented metal chair shown at the *XIII Triennale* in Milan in 1964. Between 1938 and 1953 she also taught at the Pratt Institute, New York, before largely retiring from practice in the mid-1960s.

References: Musée des Arts Décoratifs, Montreal, *Eva Zeisel: Designer for Industry* (1984); Suzannah Lessard, "Profiles," *New Yorker*, April 13, 1987, pp. 36–59.

GENERAL BIBLIOGRAPHY

Ades, Dawn. *The Twentieth-Century Poster: Design of the Avant-Garde.* New York, 1984.

Agence pour la Promotion de la Création Industrielle and Centre Georges Pompidou, Paris. *Design français, 1960–1990: Trois décennies.* June 22–September 26, 1988.

Aldersey-Williams, Hugh. *New American Design: Products and Graphics for a Post-Industrial Age.* New York, 1988.

Ambasz, Emilio, ed. *Italy: The New Domestic Landscape.* New York, 1972.

Art Gallery of Ontario, Toronto. *50 Years Bauhaus.* December 6, 1969–February 1, 1970.

Arts Council of Great Britain, Hayward Gallery, London. *Thirties: British Art and Design before the War.* October 25, 1979–January 13, 1980.

Banham, Reyner. *Theory and Design in the First Machine Age.* New York, 1960.

———, ed. *The Aspen Papers: Twenty Years of Design Theory from the International Design Conference in Aspen.* New York, 1974.

———. *Design by Choice.* New York, 1981.

Bauhaus-Archiv Museum für Gestaltung, Berlin. *Sammlungs–Katalog.* Berlin, 1981.

Bayer, Herbert, Walter Gropius, and Ise Gropius, eds. *Bauhaus, 1919–1928.* New York, 1938.

Bayley, Stephen. *In Good Shape: Style in Industrial Products, 1900 to 1960.* London, 1979.

Beard, Geoffrey. *International Modern Glass.* London, 1976.

Beer, Eileene Harrison. *Scandinavian Design: Objects of a Life Style.* New York, 1975.

Benton, Tim, ed. *History of Architecture and Design, 1890–1939.* Units 1-20. Milton Keynes, England, 1975.

Bill, Max. *Form—A Balance Sheet of Mid-Twentieth Century Trends in Design.* Basel, 1952.

Bouillon, Jean Paul. *Art Nouveau, 1870–1914.* New York, 1985.

———. *Art Deco, 1903–1940.* New York, 1989.

Brandt, Frederick R. *Late Nineteenth and Early Twentieth Century Decorative Arts: The Sydney and Frances Lewis Collection in the Virginia Museum of Fine Arts.* Richmond, 1985.

Branzi, Andrea. *The Hot House: Italian New Wave Design.* Cambridge, Mass., 1984.

———, and Michele De Lucchi, eds. *Il design italiano degli anni '50.* Milan, 1981.

Brunhammer, Yvonne. *1925.* Paris, 1976.

———, et al. *Art Nouveau: Belgium France.* Houston, 1976.

———, and Suzanne Tise. *French Decorative Art, 1900–1942: The Société des Artistes Décorateurs.* Paris, 1990.

Buddensieg, Tilmann, ed. *Berlin 1900–1933: Architecture and Design.* New York, 1987.

Bush, Donald J. *The Streamlined Decade.* New York, 1975.

Campbell, Joan. *The German Werkbund: The Politics of Reform in the Applied Arts.* Princeton, 1978.

Centre de Création Industrielle, Paris. *Qu'est-ce que le design?* October 24–December 31, 1969.

Centre de Création Industrielle and Agence pour la Promotion de la Création Industrielle, Paris. *Lumières, je pense à vous.* June 3–August 5, 1985.

Clark, Robert Judson. *The Arts and Crafts Movement in America, 1876–1916.* Princeton, 1972.

———, et al. *Design in America: The Cranbrook Vision, 1925–1950.* New York, 1983.

Collins, Michael, and Andreas Papadakis. *Post-Modern Design.* New York, 1989.

Davies, Karen. *At Home in Manhattan: Modern Decorative Arts, 1925 to the Depression.* New Haven, Conn., 1983.

de Noblet, Jocelyn, ed. *Industrial Design: Reflection of a Century.* Paris, 1993.

de Noblet, Jocelyn, with Catherine Bressy. *Design: Introduction à l'histoire de l'évolution des formes industrielles de 1820 à aujourd'hui.* Paris, 1974.

DiNoto, Andrea. *Art Plastic: Designed for Living.* New York, 1984.

Doblin, Jay. *One Hundred Great Product Designs.* New York, 1970.

Eidelberg, Martin, ed. *Design 1935–1965: What Modern Was.* Montreal, 1991.

Elzea, Rowland, and Betty Elzea. *The Pre-Raphaelite Era, 1848–1914.* Wilmington, Del., 1976.

Encyclopédie des arts décoratifs et industriels modernes au XXe siècle. 12 vols. Paris, 1927–1931; rpt., New York, 1977.

Fanelli, Giovanni, and Rosalia Fanelli. *Il tessuto moderno: Disegno modo archittetura, 1890–1940.* Florence, 1976.

Farr, Michael. *Design in British Industry: A Mid-Century Survey.* Cambridge, 1955.

Finnish Society of Crafts and Design, Helsinki. *Finland: Nature, Design, Architecture.* 1981.

Fossati, Paolo. *Il design in Italia, 1945–1972.* Turin, 1972.

Friedman, Mildred, ed. *De Stijl: 1917–1931, Visions of Utopia.* New York, 1982.

———, et al. *Graphic Design in America: A Visual Language History.* New York, 1989.

Fuchs, Heinz, and François Burkhardt. *Product—Design—History: German Design from 1820 down to the Present Era.* Stuttgart, 1986.

Giedion, Siegfried. *Mechanization Takes Command: A Contribution to Anonymous History.* New York, 1948.

———. *Space, Time, and Architecture.* 2d ed. Cambridge, Mass., 1949.

Gloag, John. *Industrial Art Explained*. London, 1934.

Grassi, Alfonso, and Anty Pansera. *Atlante del design italiano, 1940–1980*. Milan, 1980.

Gregotti, Vittorio. *Il disegno del prodotto industriale: Italia 1860–1980*. Milan, 1982.

Gunther, Sonja. *Das Deutsche Heim: Luxusinterieurs und Arbeitermöbel von der Gründerzeit bis zum 'Dritten Reich.'* Berlin, 1984.

Hald, Arthur. *Swedish Design*. Stockholm, 1958.

Hanks, David A. *Innovative Furniture in America: From 1800 to the Present*. New York, 1981.

Hård af Segerstad, Ulf. *Scandinavian Design*. Stockholm, 1961.

Henry Ford Museum and Greenfield Village, Dearborn, Michigan. *Streamlining America*. September 1986–December 1987.

Heskett, John. *Industrial Design*. New York, 1980.

———. *German Design, 1870–1918*. New York, 1986.

Hiesinger, Kathryn B., and Felice Fischer. *Japanese Design: A Survey Since 1950*. Philadelphia, 1994.

Hiesinger, Kathryn B., and George H. Marcus, eds. *Design since 1945*. Philadelphia, 1983.

———, ed. *Art Nouveau in Munich: Masters of Jugendstil*. Philadelphia, 1988.

Hillier, Bevis. *The Decorative Arts of the Forties and Fifties*. New York, 1975.

Hughes, Graham. *Modern Silver throughout the World, 1880–1967*. New York, 1967.

Jackson, Lesley. *The New Look: Design in the Fifties*. London, 1991.

Jencks, Charles A. *The Language of Post-Modern Architecture*. 3d ed. rev. New York, 1981.

Jensen, Robert, and Patricia Conway. *Ornamentalism: The New Decorativeness in Architecture and Design*. New York, 1983.

Kaplan, Wendy. *"The Art that Is Life": The Arts and Crafts Movement in America, 1875–1920*. Boston, 1987.

Karlsen, Arne. *Made in Denmark*. New York, 1960.

Katz, Sylvia. *Plastics: Designs and Materials*. London, 1978.

———. *Plastics: Common Objects, Classic Designs*. New York, 1984.

Kjellberg, Pierre. *Art déco: Les Maîtres du mobilier, le décor des paquebots*. Paris, 1986.

Kron, Joan, and Suzanne Slesin. *High-Tech*. New York, 1978.

Labuz, Ronald. *Contemporary Graphic Design*. New York, 1991.

La Jolla Museum of Contemporary Art, La Jolla, California. *Italian Re Evolution: Design in Italian Society in the Eighties*. September 10–October 31, 1982.

Le Corbusier. *Towards a New Architecture*. London, 1970.

Lindkvist, Lennart, ed. *Design in Sweden*. Stockholm, 1972.

Lodder, Christina. *Russian Constructivism*. New Haven, Conn., 1983.

MacCarthy, Fiona. *A History of British Design, 1830–1970*. London, 1979.

———. *British Design since 1880: A Visual History*. London, 1982.

McFadden, David Revere, ed. *Scandinavian Modern Design, 1880–1980*. New York, 1982.

Madsen, Stephan T. *Sources of Art Nouveau*. Oslo, 1956.

Mang, Karl. *History of Modern Furniture*. New York, 1979.

Marcus, George H. *Functionalist Design: An Ongoing History*. Munich, Germany, 1995.

Massobrio, G. *Album degli anni cinquanta*. Rome, 1977.

Meggs, Philip B. *A History of Graphic Design*. 2d ed. New York, 1992.

Meikle, Jeffrey L. *Twentieth Century Limited: Industrial Design in America, 1925–1939*. Philadelphia, 1979.

Mentasti, Rosa Barovier. *Venetian Glass, 1890–1990*. Venice, 1992.

Miller, R. Craig. *Modern Design in The Metropolitan Museum of Art 1890–1990*. New York, 1990.

Mumford, Lewis. *The City in History*. 1966.

———. *Technics and Civilization*. 1967.

Musée des Arts Décoratifs, Paris. *Cinquantenaire de l'Exposition de 1925*. October 15, 1976–February 2, 1977.

———, Paris. *Les Anneés UAM, 1929–1958*. September 27, 1988–January 29, 1989.

———, Paris. *Techniques discrètes: Le Design mobilier en Italie, 1980 1990*. April 24– September 1, 1991.

Museo Poldi Pezzoli, Milan. *Milano 70/70: Un secolo d'arte*. From May 30, 1972.

Museum of Modern Art, New York. *The Design Collection: Selected Objects*. New York, 1970.

Nationalmuseum, Stockholm. *The Lunning Prize*. 1986.

Naylor, Colin, ed. *Contemporary Designers*. 2d ed. Chicago, 1990.

Naylor, Gillian. *The Bauhaus*. London, 1969.

———. *The Arts and Crafts Movement*. London, 1971.

Opie, Jennifer Hawkins. *Scandinavia: Ceramics & Glass in the Twentieth Century*. London, 1989.

Ostergard, Derek E., ed. *Bent Wood and Metal Furniture, 1850–1946*. New York, 1987.

Palazzo delle Stelline, Milan. *Design & design*. May 29–July 31, 1979.

Papanek, Victor. *Design for the Real World*. New York, 1974.

Pevsner, Nikolaus. *An Inquiry into Industrial Art in England*. Cambridge, England, 1937.

———. *Studies in Art, Architecture and Design*. London, 1966.

———. *Pioneers of Modern Design*. London, 1972.

Pica, Agnoldomenico. *Storia della Triennale di Milano: 1918–1957*. Milan, 1957.

Polak, Ada. *Modern Glass*. London, 1962.

Préaud, Tamara, and Serge Gauthier. *Ceramics of the Twentieth Century*. New York, 1982.

Pulos, Arthur J. *American Design Ethic: A History of Industrial Design to 1940*. Cambridge, Mass., 1983.

———. *The American Design Adventure 1940–1975*. Cambridge, Mass., 1988.

Radice, Barbara, ed. *Memphis: The New International Style*. Milan, 1981.

Read, Herbert. *Art and Industry: The Principles of Industrial Design*. New York, 1935.

Richards, J. M., and Nikolaus Pevsner, eds. *The Anti-Rationalists*. Toronto, 1973.

Rudoe, Judy. *Decorative Arts, 1850–1950: A Catalogue of the British Museum Collection*. London, 1991.

Schaefer, Herwin. *The Roots of Modern Design*. London, 1970.

Schmittel, Wolfgang. *Design Concept Realisation*. Zurich, 1975.

Schmutzler, Robert. *Art Nouveau*. London, 1964.

Schoeser, Mary. *Fabrics and Wallpapers*. London, 1986.

Schweiger, Werner J. *Wiener Werkstaette: Design in Vienna, 1903–1932*. New York, 1984.

Sparke, Penny. *An Introduction to Design and Culture in the Twentieth Century*. New York, 1986.

Staal, Gert, and Hester Wolters, eds. *Holland in Vorm: Dutch Design, 1945–1987*. The Hague, 1987.

Stedelijk Museum, Amsterdam. *Industry & Design in the Netherlands, 1850–1950*. December 21, 1985–February 9, 1986.

Thackara, John, ed. *Design after Modernism: Beyond the Object*. London, 1988.

Thornton, Richard S. *The Graphic Spirit of Japan*. New York, 1991.

Troy, Nancy J. *Modernism and the Decorative Arts in France: Art Nouveau to Le Corbusier*. New Haven, 1991.

Venturi, Robert. *Complexity and Contradiction in Architecture*. New York, 1966.

Victoria and Albert Museum, London. *Two Centuries of Danish Design*. April 18–June 3, 1968.

———. *British Art and Design, 1900–1960*. 1983.

Wallance, Don. *Shaping America's Products*. New York, 1956.

Weisberg, Gabriel P. *Art Nouveau Bing*. Washington, D.C. 1986.

Westerman, Nada, and Joan Wessel. *American Design Classics*. New York, 1985.

Whitechapel Art Gallery, London. *Modern Chairs: 1918–1970*. July 22–August 30, 1970.

Whitney Museum of American Art, New York. *High Styles: Twentieth Century American Design*. September 19, 1985–February 16, 1986.

Wichmann, Hans. *Aufbruch zum neuen Wohnen: Deutsche Werkstätten und WK-Verband: Ihr Beitrag zur Kultur unseres Jahrhunderts*. Basel, 1978.

———. *Industrial Design, Unikate, Serienerzeugnisse: Die Neue Sammlung, ein neuer Museumstyp des 20. Jahrhunderts*. Munich, 1985.

Wilson, Richard Guy, Dianne H. Pilgrim, and Dickran Tashjian. *The Machine Age in America, 1918–1941*. New York, 1986.

Wingler, Haus M. *The Bauhaus: Weimar, Dessau, Berlin, Chicago*. Cambridge, Mass., 1969.

Zahle, Erik, ed. *A Treasury of Scandinavian Design*. New York, 1961.

Zilliacus, Benedict. *Decorative Arts in Finland*. Helsinki, 1963.

NOTES

FOREWORD

1. Le Corbusier *Towards a New Architecture* (London, 1927), p. 240.
2. Walter Gropius, *The New Architecture and the Bauhaus* (London, 1935), pp. 26–27.

CHAPTER 1

1. Philippe Burty, in Union Centrale des Beaux Arts Appliqué à l'Industrie, *Exposition de 1865 au Palais de l'Industrie* (Paris, 1866), p. 400.
2. François Ducuing, *L'Exposition Universelle de 1867 illustrée* (Paris, 1868), vol. 2, p. 227.
3. Richard Redgrave, "Supplementary Report on Design," in *Exhibition of the Works of Industry of All Nations, 1851* (London, 1852), p. 708.
4. William Morris, "The Beauty of Life," in G.D.H. Cole, ed., *William Morris* (London, 1948), p. 564.
5. Hermann Muthesius, "Kunst und Machine," *Dekorative Kunst* 10 (1902): 142.
6. Hermann Muthesius, "Englische und Kontinentale Nutzkunst," *Kunst und Handwerk* 49 (1898–99): 321.
7. Richard Graul, "Deutschland," in Richard Graul, ed., *Die Krisis im Kunstgewerbe* (Leipzig, 1901), p. 40.
8. Gustav Stickley, *Chips from the Craftsman Workshops* (New York, 1906), quoted in David M. Cathers, *Furniture of the American Arts and Crafts Movement* (New York, 1981), p. 55.
9. Charles Robert Ashbee, *Should We Stop Teaching Art?* (London, 1911), p. 2.
10. Henry van de Velde, "Ein Kapitel ueber Entwurf und Bau moderner Moebel," *Pan* 3 (1897): 260–64, translated in Tim and Charlotte Benton, eds., *Architecture and Design, 1890–1939* (New York, 1975), p. 18.
11. Frank Lloyd Wright, "The Art and Craft of the Machine," 1901; reprinted in Wright, *Modern Architecture* (Princeton, 1931), pp. 10–11, 16.
12. Van de Velde, op. cit., p. 18.
13. Julius Meier-Graefe, "Floral-Linear," *Dekorative Kunst* 4 (1899): 169.
14. Muthesius, "Kunst und Machine," op. cit.
15. Ernst Zimmermann, "Künstlerische Maschinenmöbel," *Deutsche Kunst und Dekoration* 17 (1905–6): 253, 257.
16. Hermann Muthesius, "Die Bedeutung des Kunstgewerbes," lecture at Handelshochschule, Berlin, 1907, translated as "The Meaning of the Arts and Crafts," in Tim and Charlotte Benton, eds., op. cit., pp. 48–51.
17. Hermann Muthesius, "Wo Stehen Wir?," *Jahrbuch des Deutschen Werkbundes* (Jena, Germany, 1912), p. 23.
18. Georg Fuchs, "Hermann Obrist," *Pan* 1 (1896): 318, 324.
19. Mary Logan, "Hermann Obrist's Embroidered Decorations," *Studio* 9 (November 1896): 105.
20. "An Interview with Mr. Charles F. Annesley Voysey, Architect and Designer," *Studio* 1 (September 1893): 233–34.
21. "Die Kunstgläser von Louis C. Tiffany," *Kunst und Kunsthandwerk* 1 (1898): 105–11; reprinted as "Louis C. Tiffany's Coloured Glass Work," in S. Bing, *Artistic America, Tiffany Glass, and Art Nouveau* (Cambridge, Mass., 1970), p. 211.
22. Victor Champier, "Le Castel Béranger et M. Hector Guimard," *Revue des Arts Décoratifs* 19 (1899): 6.
23. Roger de Félice, "L'Art appliqué au Salon d'Automne," *L'Art Décoratif* 63 (December 1903): 234.
24. Hector Guimard, "An Architect's Opinion of 'L'Art Nouveau'," *Architectural Record* 12 (1902): 126, 131.
25. Gleeson White, "Some Glasgow Designers and Their Work," *Studio* 11 (1897): 98–99.
26. Julius Meier-Graefe, "Peter Behrens," *Dekorative Kunst* 5 (1900): 3.
27. "Le Meuble français à l'exposition," *L'Art Décoratif* 22 (July 1900): 145.
28. Ibid., p. 147.
29. "Neues aus den Vereinigten Werkstätte für Kunst im Handwerk, Munchen," *Dekorative Kunst* 3 (1899): 145, 153.
30. *Kunst und Handwerk* 51 (1900–1901): 356.
31. Henry van de Velde, "Prinzipielle Erklarungen" in *Kunstgewerblichen Laienpredigten* (Leipzig, 1902), p. 188.
32. Octave Maus, "Le Salon de la Libre Esthétique à Bruxelles," *Revue des Arts Décoratifs* 20 (1900): 173.
33. Quoted in Robert Koch, *Louis C. Tiffany's Glass— Bronze—Lamps* (New York, 1971), p. 34.
34. Program for L'Art Nouveau, in Gabriel P. Weisberg, *Art Nouveau Bing: Paris Style 1900* (New York, 1986), p. 90, fig. 88.
35. *Rookwood: An American Art* (Cincinnati, 1904), n.p.
36. Ibid.
37. Vittorio Pica, *L'arte decorativa all'Esposizione di Torino: La sezione italiana*, part 4 (Bergamo, 1903); excerpted in Francesca R. Fratini, *Torino 1902: Polemiche in Italia sull'arte nuova* (Turin, 1970), p. 270.
38. Julius Meier-Graefe, "Dänemark auf der Weltausstellung," *Dekorative Kunst* 3 (1899–1900): 427.
39. Frank Lloyd Wright, "In the Cause of Architecture," *Architectural Record* 23 (March 1908): 161.
40. Samuel Howe, "A Visit to the House of Mr. Stickley," *Craftsman* 3 (December 1902): 166.
41. Victoria and Albert Museum, London, *Liberty's, 1875–1975* (July–October 1975), p. 5.
42. October 17, 1906, quoted in Waltraud Neuwirth, *Josef Hoffmann* (Vienna, 1982), p. 29.
43. October 11, 1906, quoted in ibid., p. 31.
44. Zimmermann, op. cit.
45. Emile Gallé, "Le Mobilier contemporain orné d'après la nature," *Revue des Arts Décoratifs* 20 (November 1900): 333–42; (December 1900): 305–78.
46. Emile Gallé, *Ecrits pour l'art: Floriculture, art décoratif,*

notices d'exposition 1884–1889 (1908), reprint (Marseille, 1980), pp. 352, 350.

47. Frank Lloyd Wright, *An Autobiography* (New York, 1932), p. 143.

48. Wright, "In the Cause of Architecture," op. cit., pp. 157, 162.

49. Ludwig Hevesi, "Neubauten von Josef Hoffmann," in *Altkunst-Neukunst, Wien 1894–1908* (Vienna, 1909), p. 215.

50. Peter Behrens, *Berliner Tageblatt*, August 29, 1907, translated in Tilmann Buddensieg, *Industriekultur: Peter Behrens and the AEG, 1907–1914* (Cambridge, Mass., 1984), pp. 207–8.

51. Quoted in Robert W. Winter, "American Sheaves from 'C.R.A.' and Janet Ashbee," *Journal of the Society of Architectural Historians* 30 (December 1971): 321.

52. Willem Vogelsang, "Metallarbeiten von Jan Eisenloeffel," *Dekorative Kunst* 11 (1903): 389.

53. Camillo Olivetti, 1912, quoted in Frederick S. Wight Art Gallery, University of California, Los Angeles, *Design Process: Olivetti, 1908–1978* (March 27–May 6, 1979), p. xvii.

CHAPTER 2

1. "Modern German Applied Arts," *Art and Progress* 3 (May 1912): 586.

2. Nikolaus Pevsner, "Patient Progress Three: The DIA," in *Art, Architecture, and Design: Victorian and After* (Princeton, 1982), p. 228.

3. L. Deubner, "German Architecture and Decoration," *"The Studio" Year Book of Decorative Art* (1912): 123.

4. Louis Vauxcelles, "L'Art décoratif au Salon d'Automne," *Art et Industrie* (November 1910), n.p., translated in Yvonne Brunhammer and Suzanne Tise, *French Decorative Art, 1900–1942* (Paris, 1990), p. 23.

5. Deubner, op. cit.

6. Francis Jourdain, *Sans remords ni rancune* (Paris, 1953), p. 272, translated in Suzanne Tise, "Francis Jourdain," in Arlette Barré-Despond, *Jourdain* (New York, 1991), p. 251.

7. André Vera, "Le Nouveau Style," *L'Art Décoratif* 14 (January 1912): 31–32.

8. F. T. Marinetti, "The Founding and Manifesto of Futurism 1909," in Umbro Apollonio, ed., *Futurist Manifestos* (London, 1973), pp. 21–22.

9. Henry van de Velde, "Counter-Propositions," translated in Charlotte Benton, ed., *History of Architecture and Design, 1890–1939: Documents* (Milton Keynes, England, 1975), p. 6.

10. Walter Gropius, *Programm des Staatlichen Bauhauses in Weimar* (Weimar, 1919), translated in Hans M. Wingler, *The Bauhaus: Weimar, Dessau, Berlin, Chicago* (Cambridge, Mass., 1969), pp. 31–32.

11. Walter Gropius, *Idee und Aufbau des Staatlichen Bauhauses Weimar* (Munich, 1923), translated in Herbert Bayer, Walter Gropius, and Ise Gropius, eds., *Bauhaus, 1919–1928* (New York, 1938), p. 27.

12. A.P., "Hellerauer Zinn," *Kunst* 28 (1913): 229.

13. In David M. Cathers, ed., *Stickley Craftsman Furniture Catalogues* (New York, 1979), p. 122.

14. Patent number 1,045,965.

15. Mary W. Mount, "The Artistic Unity of Lamp Shades and Bases," *Arts and Decoration* 2 (December 1911): 82–83.

16. Advertisement in *Vogue*, 1913, reproduced in Robert W. Blasberg, *Fulper Art Pottery: An Aesthetic Appreciation, 1909–1929* (New York, 1979), p. 65.

17. *King of Fashion: The Autobiography of Paul Poiret* (Philadelphia, 1931), pp. 161–62.

18. Roger Fry, quoted in Judith Collins, *The Omega Workshops* (London, 1983), p. 30.

19. Roger Fry, quoted in ibid., p. 44.

20. Quoted in Léon Moussinac, *Francis Jourdain* (Geneva, 1955), p. 18.

21. Herthe von Wersin, Daybook, Stadtarchiv, Munich.

22. G.J.W., "Zu den Arbeiten aus der Ausstellung 'Raumkunst'," *Kunst* 30 (1914): 329.

23. G. Rémon, "Exposition Internationale des Arts Décoratifs: Le Meuble," *L'Art Vivant* 1 (September 15, 1925): 20.

24. Edward McKnight Kauffer, in Museum of Modern Art, New York, *Posters by E. McKnight Kauffer* (1937), n.p.

25. Theo van Doesburg, "De nieuwe beweging in de schilderkunst," 1917, translated in Joop Joosten, "Painting and Sculpture in the Context of De Stijl," in Mildred Friedman, ed., *De Stijl: 1917–1931, Visions of Utopia* (New York, 1982), p. 55.

26. Translated in Kees Broos, "From De Stijl to a New Typography," in ibid., p. 149.

27. Ibid.

28. Emile Henriot, "Le XIe Salon des Artistes Décorateurs," *Art et Décoration* 37 (April 1920): 115.

29. Jean-Louis Vaudoyer, "Le Salon d'Automne II—L'Art décoratif," *Art et Décoration* 36 (December 1919): 188.

30. Frank Lloyd Wright, *An Autobiography* (New York, 1932), p. 218.

31. Theo van Doesburg, "Aanteekeningen bij een leun-stoel van Rietveld," *De Stijl* 2 (September 1919): 439.

CHAPTER 3

1. See L. H., "L'Art décoratif allemand moderne," *L'Architecture* 38 (August 1925): 225.

2. "Modernism in Industrial Art," *American Magazine of Art* 15 (October 1924): 540.

3. International Exposition of Modern Decorative and Industrial Art, Paris, *Report of Commission* (Washington, D.C., 1925), p. 16.

4. Waldemar George, "L'Exposition des Arts Décoratifs et Industriels de 1925. Les Tendances générales," *L'Amour de l'Art* 6 (1925): 288–89.

5. American Association of Museums, New York, *A Selected Collection of Objects from the International Exposition of Modern Decorative and Industrial Art at Paris 1925* (1926), p. 32.

6. Advertisement, *New York Times*, May 1, 1927.

7. Le Corbusier, *The Decorative Art of Today* (Cambridge, Mass., 1987), pp. 186, 87.

8. Gabriel Mourey, "L'Esprit de l'Exposition," *L'Amour de l'Art* 6 (1925): 297.

9. Le Corbusier, op. cit., p. 73.

10. Varst, "Rabochii klub," 1926, translated in Christina Lodder, *Russian Constructivism* (New Haven, 1983), p. 156.

11. Central State Archive of Literature and Art, Moscow, fond 681, op. 3, ed. Khr. 26, list 320, translated in ibid., p. 135.

12. Le Corbusier, *Almanach d'architecture moderne* (Paris, 1925), p. 145.

13. Ibid.

14. Walter Gropius, "Grundsätze der Bauhaus Produktion," in *Neue Arbeiten der Bauhauswerkstätten* (Munich, 1925), pp. 7–8.

15. László Moholy-Nagy, "Metal Workshop: From Wine Jugs to Lighting Fixtures," in Herbert Bayer, Walter Gropius, and Ise Gropius, eds., *Bauhaus, 1919–1928* (New York, 1938), p. 136.

16. Walter Gropius, op. cit., p. 5, translated in Art Gallery of Ontario, Toronto, *50 Years Bauhaus* (December 6, 1969– February 1, 1970), p. 20.

17. Marcel Breuer, "Metallmöbel," in Werner Gräff, *Innenräume* (Stuttgart, 1928), pp. 133–34, translated in Tim and Charlotte Benton, eds., op. cit., p. 226.

18. John Gloag, "Wood or Metal," *Studio* 97 (1929): 50.

19. Musée des Arts Décoratifs, Paris, *Les Années UAM, 1929–1958* (September 27, 1988–January 29, 1989), p. 21.

20. Le Corbusier, *The Decorative Art of Today*, op. cit., p. 114.

21. László Moholy-Nagy, "Die neue Typographie," in László Moholy-Nagy and Walter Gropius, eds. *Staatliches Bauhaus in Weimar, 1919–1923* (Munich and Weimar, 1923), translated in Richard Kostelanetz, ed., *Moholy-Nagy* (New York, 1970), p. 75.

22. F. H. Ehmke, translated in Arthur A. Cohen, *Herbert Bayer: The Complete Work* (Cambridge, Mass., 1984), p. 408, n. 12.

23. Hildegard Schwab-Felisch, "Formen und Form," *Form* 8 (August 1928): 244.

24. Moholy-Nagy, "Metal Workshop: From Wine Jugs to Lighting Fixtures," op. cit., p. 136.

25. V. V. Filatov, "Soviet Porcelain," translated in Museum of Modern Art, Oxford, *Art into Production: Soviet Textiles, Fashion and Ceramics, 1917–1935* (December 9, 1984–February 3, 1985), p. 14.

26. Anni Albers, "The Weaving Workshop," in Herbert Bayer, Walter Gropius, and Ise Gropius, eds., *Bauhaus, 1919–1928* (New York, 1938), pp. 143–44.

27. Anni Albers, *On Weaving* (Middletown, Conn., 1965), p. 47.

28. *Encyclopédie des arts décoratifs et industriels modernes au XXème siècle*, repr. (New York, 1977), vol. 3, p. 88

29. Ibid., vol. 5, p. 83.

30. Maurice Marinot, "Réponse à une enquête de cette revue à propos de l'Exposition de 1925," *Courrier de la Vie Artistique* 14 (July 15, 1924).

31. Ibid.

32. Robert Delaunay, "The 'Simultaneous' Fabrics of Sonia Delaunay (Second Version)," in Arthur A. Cohen, ed., *The New Art of Color: The Writings of Robert and Sonia Delaunay* (New York, 1978), pp. 138–39.

33. Quoted in Benedikt Huber and Jean-Claude Steinegger, *Jean Prouvé, Prefabrication: Structures and Elements* (New York, 1971), p. 142.

34. Robert Mallet-Stevens, *Bulletin de la Vie Moderne* (1924): 532–34, translated as "Architecture and Geometry," in Tim and Charlotte Benton, eds., op. cit., p. 131.

35. G. Rémon, "Exposition Internationale des Arts Décoratifs: Le Meuble," *L'Art Vivant* 1 (September 15, 1925): 20.

36. Marie Dormoy, "Les Intérieurs à l'Exposition Internationale des Arts Décoratifs, *L'Amour de l'Art* (August 1925): 316; quoted in Marc Vellay and Kenneth Frampton, *Pierre Chareau: Architect and Craftsman, 1883–1950* (New York, 1985), p. 139.

37. Eileen Gray and Jean Badovici, "E1027: Maison en bord de mer," *L'Architecture Vivante* (winter 1929) (special issue): 23.

38. *Gio Ponti, Ceramiche 1923–1930* (Florence, 1983), p. 10.

39. Jean Perzel, *Lux* (August 1928): 8, translated in Alastair Duncan, *Art Nouveau and Art Deco Lighting* (London, 1978), p. 180.

40. B. D., "Appareils d'éclairage de Jean Perzel," *Mobilier & Décoration* 9 (May 1929): 108.

41. A. A. Fyodorov-Davidov, "Introduction to the First Art Exhibition of Soviet Domestic Textiles," Moscow, 1928, quoted in Museum of Modern Art, Oxford, *Art into Production: Soviet Textiles, Fashion and Ceramics, 1917–1935* (December 9, 1984–February 3, 1985), p. 93.

42. Art Center, New York, *Contempora Exposition of Art and Industry* (1929), n.p.

43. Walter Rendell Storey, "Making Modern Rooms 'All of a Piece'," *New York Times Magazine*, July 7, 1929, p. 17.

44. No. 628, 883, patented in France, July 11, 1927.

45. Walter Gropius, op. cit., p. 7.

46. Ibid., p. 6.

47. Ibid., p. 8.

48. Gunta Stölzl, "Die Entwicklung der Bauhausweberei," *Bauhaus Zeitschrift für Bau und Gestaltung* 2 (1931), translated in Hans M. Wingler, *The Bauhaus: Weimar, Dessau, Berlin, Chicago* (Cambridge, Mass., 1969), p. 465.

49. Quoted by Ludwig Glaeser, *Ludwig Mies van der Rohe: Furniture. . .* (New York, 1977), p. 9.

50. Marcel Breuer, op. cit.

51. Fabien Sollar, "Le Salon d'Automne," *Les Echos d'Art* 53 (December 1929): 25.

52. René Drouin, "Le Salon de l'U.A.M.," *Architecture d'Aujourd'hui* 5 (June 1933): 95–96.
53. Carl Sandburg, *Steichen: The Photographer* (New York, 1929), pp. 55–56.
54. William H. Baldwin, "Modern Art and the Machine Age," *Independent* 119 (July 9, 1927): 39.
55. "A New York Diary," *New Republic* 53 (January 4, 1928): 192.
56. "American Modernist Furniture Inspired by Sky-Scraper Architecture," *Good Furniture* 29 (September 1927): 119.
57. *New Dimensions: The Decorative Art of Today* (New York, 1928), pp. 56, 37.
58. Le Corbusier, *The Decorative Art of Today*, op. cit., pp. 76, n. 2, 72–73, 114.
59. Helen Sprackling, "Modern Art and the Artist," *House Beautiful* 65 (February 1929): 154.
60. "Exhibit of American Designers' Gallery: An Ambitious Program in Art Moderne," *Good Furniture* 32 (January 1929): 45.
61. G. Rémon, "Les Dernières Créations de Da Silva Bruhns," *Mobilier & Décoration* 91 (1929): 98–100.

CHAPTER 4

1. Nikolaus Pevsner, *An Enquiry into Industrial Art in England* (New York, 1937), p. 207.
2. Lewis Mumford, "Art in the Machine Age," *Saturday Review of Literature*, September 8, 1928, p. 102.
3. Henry Ford Museum's Greenfield Village, Dearborn, Michigan, *Streamlining America* (September 1986–December 1987), p. 7.
4. See Adrian Forty, "The Electric Home: A Case Study of the Domestic Revolution of the Inter-War Years," in *British Design* (Milton Keynes, England, 1975), pp. 49–62.
5. "Lezione sulla natura e profezia sulla forma degli apparecchi radio," *Domus* 151 (July 1940): 84–87.
6. Harold van Doren, *Industrial Design: A Practical Guide* (New York, 1940), p. 137.
7. Sheldon and Martha Chandler Cheney, *Art and the Machine: An Account of Industrial Design in Twentieth-Century America* (New York, 1936), pp. 57–58.
8. Walter Dorwin Teague, *Design This Day: The Technique of Order in the Machine Age* (New York, 1940), pp. 39–40.
9. Ibid., p. 215.
10. Jeffrey L. Miekle, *Twentieth Century Limited: Industrial Design in America, 1925–1939* (Philadelphia, 1979), pp. 104–6.
11. Walter Gropius, *The New Architecture and the Bauhaus* (London, 1935), p. 38.
12. Philip Johnson, *Machine Art* (New York, 1934), n.p.
13. P. Morton Shand, "Stockholm 1930," *Architectural Review* 68 (August 1930): 72.
14. Alvar Aalto, in *Åbo Underrättelser*, 1930, translated in *Alvar Aalto, 1898–1976* (Helsinki, 1978), p. 101.
15. Alvar Aalto, "Rationalism och människan" (Rationalism and Man), lecture, Swedish Society of Industrial Design, May 9, 1935, translated in Juhani Pallasmaa, ed., *Alvar Aalto Furniture* (Cambridge, Mass., 1985), pp. 115–16.
16. Jacques de Brunhoff, "L'Union des Artistes Modernes à l'Exposition de 1937," *Le Décor d'Aujourd'hui* 24 (August–September 1937): 49.
17. Paul Bromberg, "Terug naar het Ornament," *Binnenhuis en Buitenwereld* 18 (1936): 120, translated in Stedelijk Museum, Amsterdam, *Industry and Design in the Netherlands, 1850–1950* (December 21, 1985–February 9, 1986), p. 71.
18. Lewis Mumford, *Technics and Civilization* (New York, 1934), p. 356.
19. Eliot F. Noyes, *Organic Design in Home Furnishings* (New York, 1941), n.p.
20. *Deutsche Kunst und Dekoration* 7 (1900–1901): 119.
21. John McAndrew, Foreword, *Alvar Aalto: Architecture and Furniture* (New York, 1938), p. 4.
22. Alvar Aalto, "The Humanizing of Architecture," *Technology Review* (1940), quoted in Pallasmaa, op. cit., p. 118.
23. Wilhelm Wagenfeld, "Industrielle Formgebung," *Form* 4 (1958): 41.
24. Wilhelm Wagenfeld, "Jenaer Glas," *Schaulade* (1932): 199, quoted in Beate Manske and Gudrun Scholz, eds., *Täglich in der Hand: Industrieform von Wilhelm Wagenfeld aus sechs Jahrzehnten* (Bremen, 1987), p. 239.
25. Norman Bel Geddes, *Horizons* (New York, 1932), p. 251.
26. No. 103,123, patented February 2, 1937.
27. Peter Müller-Munk, "Machine—Hand," *Creative Art* 5 (October 1929): 710–11.
28. Walter Dorwin Teague, *Industrial Art and Its Future*, lecture, School of Architecture and Allied Arts, New York University, November 18, 1936, pp. 5–6.
29. Metz archive, Amsterdam, translated in Stedelijk Museum, op. cit., p. 274.
30. Quoted in Derek Ostergard and David A. Hanks, "Gilbert Rohde and the Evolution of Modern Design, 1927–1941," *Arts Magazine* 56 (October 1981): 99.
31. The desk's patent, number 114,203, was submitted in December 1937 and received in April 1939. The three-legged armchair received patent number 108,473 in February 1938.
32. *Report of Rural Electrification Administration, 1938* (Washington, D.C., 1939), pp. 3, 11.
33. "Museum of Modern Art Shows Canvases by Americans—Posters Exhibited," *New York Times*, November 21, 1937, 2, p. 10.
34. Quoted in K. O. Tooker and F. L. Pierce, "The Hoover One Fifty," *Modern Plastics* 14 (December 1936): 33.
35. Frederick Hurten Rhead, "More about Color," *Crockery and Glass Journal* 120 (May 1937): 13, 38.
36. Quoted in Oliver Green, *Art for the London Underground: London Transport Posters, 1908 to the*

Present (London, 1990), p. 12.

37. Frederick Kiesler, "Pseudo-Functionalism in Modern Architecture," *Partisan Review* 16 (July 1949): 738.

38. No. 2,272,609, patented February 10, 1942.

CHAPTER 5

1. Geffrye Museum, London, *CC41: Utility Furniture and Fashion, 1941–1951* (September 24–December 29, 1974), pp. 7–8.

2. Ibid., p. 12.

3. Gordon Russell, *Designer's Trade* (London, 1968), p. 200.

4. Ibid., p. 199.

5. Albert Speer, *Inside the Third Reich* (New York, 1970), p. 57.

6. Ibid., p. 214.

7. Ibid., p. 222.

8. Jerome B. Cohen, *Japan's Economy in War and Reconstruction* (Minneapolis, 1949), p. 362.

9. Ibid., p. 412.

10. See John Neuhart, Marilyn Neuhart, and Ray Eames, *Eames Design: The Work of the Office of Charles and Ray Eames* (New York, 1989), pp. 139–41 et passim.

11. H. McG. Dunnett, "Furniture since the War," *Architectural Review* 109 (March 1951): 152.

12. Edgar Kaufmann, Jr., *Prize Designs for Modern Furniture from the International Competition for Low-Cost Furniture Design* (New York, 1950), p. 6.

13. Ibid., p. 44.

14. André Hermant, Preface, in Union des Artistes Modernes, Paris, *UAM—Exposition Formes Utiles, 1949–1950*, quoted in Musée des Arts Décoratifs, Paris, *Les Années UAM, 1929–1958* (September 27, 1988–January 29, 1989), p. 100.

15. Paul Rand, *A Designer's Art* (New Haven, 1985), p. 72.

16. The original patent, no. 2,241,368, was granted May 6, 1941, while a later design patent covering the coffee maker form itself dates from May 23, 1944, no. 137,943.

17. Raymond Loewy, *Never Leave Well Enough Alone* (New York, 1951), pp. 148–49.

18. Risom's patent, no. 141,839, was filed in 1943 and awarded July 10, 1945.

19. Hugh Dalton, Introduction, in Board of Trade, London, *Utility Furniture* (1943), p. 1.

20. Angelo Testa, "Design vs. Monkey Business," *Interiors* 107 (February 1948): 84.

21. "Photographs of Industrial Design Exhibitions, 1946," *Museum of Modern Art Bulletin* 14 (fall 1946): 6.

22. Ibid.

23. Eva Zeisel, "Registering a New Trend," *Everyday Art Quarterly* (fall 1946): 5–7.

24. Isamu Noguchi, *A Sculptor's World* (London, 1967), p. 26.

25. George Nelson, *Storage* (New York, 1954), p. 56.

26. Noguchi, op. cit., p. 27.

27. Buffalo Fine Arts Academy, Albright Art Gallery, *Good Design Is Your Business* (1947), p. 48.

28. No. 2,482,306, patented September 20, 1949, assigned to Bartolucci & Waldheim.

29. "New Furniture: Top American Designers Make It Simple, Slim, and Comfortable," *Life*, November 15, 1948, p. 115.

30. Eero Saarinen, "Furniture Design 1947 to 1958," in Aline B. Saarinen, ed., *Eero Saarinen on His Work* (New Haven, 1962), p. 66.

31. No. 2,566,035, patented August 28, 1951.

32. Elizabeth Gordon, "Fine Art for 39¢," *House Beautiful* 89 (October 1947): 131.

33. No. 2,487,400, patented November 8, 1949.

34. Tapio Wirkkala, in National Collection of Fine Arts, Smithsonian Institution, Washington, D.C., *An Exhibition of Finnish Arts and Crafts* (June 5–26, 1952), pp. 6–7.

35. George Nakashima, *The Soul of Tree: A Woodworker's Reflections* (Tokyo, 1981), pp. 72–73.

36. Meyric R. Rogers, *Italy at Work: Her Renaissance in Design Today* (Rome, 1950), p. 26.

37. Kaufmann, op. cit., pp. 19–20.

38. Patented January 29, 1952, no. 165,806.

39. Hans J. Wegner, "Furniture," in Kathryn B. Hiesinger and George H. Marcus, eds., *Design since 1945* (Philadelphia, 1983), p. 118.

CHAPTER 6

1. John and Avril Blake, *The Practical Idealists* (London, 1969), p. 43.

2. Hugh Dalton, speech, December 19, 1944, quoted in Jonathan M. Woodham, "Design Promotion 1946 and After," in Penny Sparke, ed., *Did Britain Make It?* (London, 1986), p. 23.

3. Hugh Dalton, speech, January 12, 1945, in Council of Industrial Design, London, *Annual Report* (1945–46), quoted in ibid.

4. The prizes were renamed the Council of Industrial Design awards in 1967.

5. The organization's original name, changed in 1951, was the Stichting Industriële Vormgeving (Industrial Design Foundation).

6. In 1963 the committee was given its present name, the Japan Design Committee. See Katzumie Masaru, *The Japan Design Committee* (Tokyo, 1977), n.p.

7. Norman Bel Geddes, *Horizons* (New York, 1932), pp. 242–58.

8. Edgar Kaufmann, Jr., *What is Modern Design?* (New York, 1950), p. 9.

9. Museum of Modern Art, New York, *Good Design: An Exhibition of Home Furnishings Selected by the Museum of Modern Art, New York, for the Merchandise Mart, Chicago* (1953), inside cover.

10. Palazzo delle Stelline, Milan, *Design & design* (May 29–July 31, 1979), pp. 22, 30.

11. Max Bill, "The Bauhaus Idea: From Weimar to Ulm," in *The Architect's Year Book*, vol. 5 (London, 1953): p. 32.

12. Ibid.

13. George Nelson, ed., *Chairs* (New York, 1953), p. 30.

14. Quoted in Marja Kaipainen, "Generations in Design," *Form Function Finland* 2 (March 1982): 12.

15. Translated in Vittorio Gregotti, "Italian Design, 1945–1971," in Emilio Ambasz, ed., *Italy: The New Domestic Landscape* (New York, 1972), p. 323.

16. Charles Eames, quoted in "News," *Industrial Design* 20 (April 1973): 11; Eero Saarinen, "Furniture Design 1947 to 1958," in Aline B. Saarinen, ed., *Eero Saarinen on His Work* (New Haven, 1962), p. 66.

17. Helen Megaw, "The Investigation of Crystal Structure," *Architectural Review* 109 (April 1951): 236.

18. Marco Zanuso, "Design and Society," in Kathryn B. Hiesinger and George H. Marcus, eds., op. cit., pp. 18–19.

19. See Reyner Banham, "Neoliberty," *Architectural Review* 125 (April 1959): 231.

20. Harry Bertoia, quoted in Eric Larrabee and Massimo Vignelli, *Knoll Design* (New York, 1981), p. 71.

21. "Dorothy Wright Liebes, First Lady of the Loom," *Interiors* 106 (July 1947): 89.

22. Zanuso, op. cit., p. 18.

23. Jean-François Grunfeld, "Gino Sarfatti, l'artisan" (interview), in Centre de Création Industrielle and Agence pour la Promotion de la Création Industrielle, Paris, *Lumières, je pense à vous* (June 3–August 5, 1985), p. 59.

24. "The Most Beautiful Object of 1951," *House Beautiful* (January 1952): 67.

25. Edgar Kaufmann, Jr., "The Wonderworks of Tapio Wirkkala," *Interiors* 111 (November 1951): 97.

26. Gio Ponti, *In Praise of Architecture* (New York, 1960), pp. 178–79.

27. Marcello Nizzoli, "Designer e industria," *Stile Industria* 4 (April 1955), reprinted in Germano Celant, *Marcello Nizzoli* (Milan, 1968), p. 141.

28. Palazzo delle Stelline, op. cit., p. 60.

29. Quoted in *Ericsson Review* 33 (1956): 124.

30. Palazzo delle Stelline, op. cit., p. 42.

31. Saarinen, op. cit., p. 66.

32. Hans Gugelot, 1959, quoted in Hans Wichmann, ed., *System-Design Bahnbrecher: Hans Gugelot, 1920–1965* (Munich, 1984), p. 66.

33. Gio Ponti, "Un nuovo televisore," *Domus* 323 (October 1956): 45.

34. Saul Bass, in Mildred Friedman et al., *Graphic Design in America: A Visual Language History* (Minneapolis, 1989), p. 19.

35. Max Bill, "Erfahrung mit Uhren," in *Zeitgemässe Form: Industrial Design International* (Munich, 1967), pp. 65–66.

36. Quoted in Kogei Zaidan, ed., *Nihon no Indasutoriaru: Showa unda Meihin 100 [Japanese Industrial Design: 100 Masterpieces of the Showa Era]* (Tokyo, 1989), p. 26.

37. Ben Shahn, *The Shape of Content* (New York, 1957), pp. 74–75.

38. Gio Ponti, "Senza aggettivi," *Domus* 268 (March 1952): I; translated in Andrea Branzi and Michele De Lucchi, eds., *Il design italiano degli anni '50* (Milan,

39. Bruno Munari, *Design as Art* (Baltimore, 1971), p. 121.

40. Palazzo delle Stelline, op. cit., p. 30.

41. Gillo Dorfles, "Una mostra di mobili a Milano," *Domus* 367 (June 1960): 34.

CHAPTER 7

1. Reyner Banham, "A Throw-Away Esthetic," *Industrial Design* 7 (March 1960): 62–63.

2. Ibid., p. 64.

3. Tom Wolfe, *The Kandy-Kolored Tangerine-Flake Streamline Baby* (New York, 1965), pp. 7–9; Robert Venturi and D. Scott Brown, "A Significance for A & P Parking Lots or Learning from Las Vegas," *Architectural Forum* 128 (March 1968): 38–39.

4. Philip Johnson, "Where Are We At?" *Architectural Review* 128 (Spring 1960): 175.

5. Paul Reilly, "The Challenge of Pop," *Architectural Review* 142 (October 1967): 256–57.

6. Abraham A. Moles, "Functionalism in Crisis," *Ulm* 19–20 (August 1967): 24.

7. Robert Venturi, *Complexity and Contradiction in Architecture* (New York, 1966), p. 22.

8. "Aspen Conference," *Industrial Design* 11 (February 1964): 14.

9. Quoted in Eric Larrabee, "Summary of the Proceedings," in Laurence B. Holland, ed., *Who Designs America?* (Garden City, N. Y., 1966), p. 328.

10. Otl Aicher, "Hochschule für Gestaltung: The Nine Stages of Its Development," in François Burkhardt and Inez Franksen, eds., *Design: Dieter Rams &* (Berlin, 1981), p. 179.

11. Tomás Maldonado and Gui Bonsiepe, "Science and Design," *Ulm* 10–11 (May 1964): 10.

12. Tomás Maldonado, "How to Fight Complacency in Design Education," *Ulm* 17–18 (June 1966): 15.

13. Quoted in "Mostra II, L'Opera di Joe Colombo," in Palazzo dell'Arte al Parco, Milan, *Quindicesima Triennale di Milano, Esposizione Internazionale delle Arti Decorative e Industriali Moderne e dell'Architettura Moderna* (September 20–November 20, 1973), pp. 90–91.

14. Maldonado and Bonsiepe, op. cit., p. 16.

15. Ibid., pp. 22–28.

16. Siegfried Giedion, *Space, Time, and Architecture*, 5th ed. (Cambridge, Mass., 1967), pp. 668–95.

17. No. 2,977,566, patented March 28, 1961 (assigned to Lightolier, Inc.).

18. Marco Zanuso, "Design and Society," in Kathryn B. Hiesinger and George H. Marcus, eds., op. cit., p. 19.

19. Verner Panton, *Form* (May 1969), quoted in Whitechapel Art Gallery, London, *Modern Chairs: 1918–1970* (July 22–August 30, 1970), no. 56.

20. Translated in Pier Carlo Santini, *Roberto Sambonet* (Milan, 1970), jacket flap.

21. Quoted in obituary, *New York Times*, August 1, 1971, p. 52.

22. Olivier Mourgue, "Design, Invention, and Fantasy," in

Kathryn B. Hiesinger and George H. Marcus, op cit., p. 24.

23. Centre de Création Industrielle, Paris, Qu'est-ce que le design? (October 24–December 31, 1969), n.p.

24. Domus 480 (November 1969): 10.

25. Gatti, Paolini, Teodoro, promotional material, 1969, rev. 1981 (typescript).

26. Quoted in "Shapes of Light: Noguchi's New Akari Sculptures," Interiors 128 (January 1969): 12.

27. Ettore Sottsass, Jr., Abitare (1969), translated in Frederick S. Wight Art Gallery, University of California, Los Angeles, Design Process: Olivetti, 1908–1978 (March 27–May 6, 1979), p. 120.

CHAPTER 8

1. Architectural Review 152 (August 1972): 67.

2. Victor Papanek, Design for the Real World (New York, 1972), pp. 252–53.

3. Ibid., p. 309.

4. Ibid., pp. 259–60.

5. Reyner Banham, "Polarization," in Banham, ed., The Aspen Papers: Twenty Years of Design Theory from the International Design Conference in Aspen (New York, 1974), p. 207.

6. Misha Black, "Fitness for What Purpose?" 1972, in Avril Black, ed., The Black Papers on Design: Selected Writings by the Late Sir Misha Black (Oxford, 1983), pp. 53–54.

7. Tim Benton and Geoffrey Baker, Introduction. History of Architecture and Design, 1890–1939 (Milton Keynes, England, 1975), p. 15.

8. "1974 Design Council Awards for Contract and Consumer Goods," Design 304 (April 1974): 35, 37, 68.

9. "Design Review: Consumer Products," Industrial Design 17 (December 1970): 53; John Margolies, ed., Design Review: Industrial Design 22nd Annual (New York, 1976), p. 11; Ann Nydele, ed., Design Review: Industrial Design 23rd Annual (New York, 1977), pp. 60–61.

10. Emilio Ambasz, ed., Italy: The New Domestic Landscape (New York, 1972), p. 141.

11. Victor Papanek and James Hennessey, Nomadic Furniture (New York, 1973), p. 46.

12. Misha Black, "Engineering and Industrial Design," 1972, in Black, ed., op. cit., pp. 177, 195.

13. Arthur Drexler, "The Disappearing Object," Saturday Review, May 23, 1964, pp. 12–15.

14. See "Superstudio," in Ambasz, ed., op. cit., pp. 240–51.

15. Quoted in James Woudhuysen, "Ergonomics: People Aren't as Simple as Machines," Design 340 (April 1977): 54.

16. Tomás Maldonado, Design, Nature, and Revolution: Toward a Critical Ecology (New York, 1972), p. 10.

17. [Tomás Maldonado], "Commentary on the Situation of the HfG," Ulm 21 (April 1968): 12.

18. Maldonado, Design, Nature, and Revolution, op. cit., p. 5.

19. Quoted in Gianni Pettena, ed., Superstudio, 1966–1982: Storie, figure, architettura (Florence, 1982), p. 50.

20. Quoted in "Superstudio: Dal catalogo degli istogrammi alla serie 'Misura,'" Domus, no. 517 (December 1972): 36.

21. Frank O. Gehry, quoted in Joseph Giovannini, "Edges, Easy and Experimental," in Walker Art Center, Minneapolis, The Architecture of Frank Gehry (1985), p. 71.

22. Jack Lenor Larsen and Jeanne Weeks, Fabrics for Interiors (New York, 1975), p. 100.

23. "AEO," Casabella 382 (October 1973): 54.

24. Maria Benktzon, publicity release, Ergonomi Design Gruppen, 1983.

25. "Domus Interviews: Shiro Kuramata," Domus 649 (April 1984): 60.

26. Suzanne Slesin, "Design in Barcelona: New Energy and Resourcefulness," New York Times, October 16, 1980, p. C6.

27. 1ª Colección de muebles especiales de Carlos Riart (Barcelona, n.d.), p. 49.

28. Aldo van den Nieuwelaar, quoted in Visual Arts Office for Abroad, Amsterdam, Design from the Netherlands (1981), p. 39.

29. Bang & Olufsen, Beogram 4002: Design Story (Elk Grove Village, Illinois, 1975), p. 3.

30. Reyner Banham, "Radio Machismo," 1974, in Design by Choice (New York, 1981), p. 117.

31. J. C. Penney Company, Incorporated, 1973 Annual Report, p. 6.

32. Akio Morita with Edwin M. Reingold and Mitsuko Shimomura, Made in Japan: Akio Morita and Sony (New York, 1986), pp. 79–82.

33. Banham, "Radio Machismo," op cit., pp. 117–18.

34. Kazumasa Nagai, in Best 100 Japanese Posters, 1945–1989 (Tokyo, 1990), p. 166.

35. No. 4,210,182, patented July 1, 1980.

36. T. M. Grimsrud, "Humans Were Not Created to Sit—and Why You Have to Refurnish Your Life," Ergonomics 33 (1990): 292.

37. Morison S. Cousins, quoted in Nada Westerman and Joan Wessel, American Design Classics (New York, 1985), p. 115.

38. No. 3,845,986, patented November 5, 1974.

CHAPTER 9

1. See Charles A. Jencks, The Language of Post-Modern Architecture, 3d ed. (New York, 1981), Appendix, p. 8.

2. Charles A. Jencks, The Language of Post-Modern Architecture (New York, 1977), p. 92.

3. Alessandro Mendini, "The Alchimia Manifesto," 1985, in Guia Sambonet, Alchimia 1977–1987 (Turin, 1986), p. 15.

4. Quoted in Suzanne Slesin, "In Milan, the Bizarre Becomes Respectable," New York Times, September

24, 1981, p. C6.

5. Barbara Radice, *Memphis: The New International Style* (Milan, 1981), p. 6.

6. Including Paolo Portoghesi, *Postmodern: The Architecture of the Post-Industrial Society* (New York, 1983).

7. Manfredo Tafuri, *History of Italian Architecture, 1944–1985* (Cambridge, Mass., 1988), p. 192.

8. E. M. Farrelly, "The New Spirit," *Architectural Review* 180 (August 1986): 7–10.

9. "Botta" [interview], *Architectural Review* 170 (July 1981): 23.

10. Quoted in Suzanne Slesin, "The New Bold Furniture Shapes at the Milan Fair," *New York Times*, September 27, 1984, p. C6.

11. See Steelcase Design Partnership, New York, "Gàetano Pesce: Modern Times Again" (November 10–December 8, 1988), exhibition brochure, n.p.

12. Hans Hollein, quoted in Ulrich Conrads, *Programs and Manifestoes on 20th-Century Architecture* (Cambridge, Mass., 1971), p. 181.

13. Radice, op. cit.

14. No. 4,571,456, patented February 18, 1986.

15. Alberto Fraser, unpublished statement, October 9, 1990.

16. Slesin, "In Milan, the Bizarre Becomes Respectable," op. cit.

17. Mendini, op. cit.

18. Rob Gemmell of Apple's design team, quoted in *Industrial Design* 32 (July–August 1985): 75.

19. Quoted in Nonie Niesewand, "The Art of Starckness," *Vogue* (U.K.) 153 (April 1989): 231.

20. Quoted in Ikko Tanaka and Kazuko Koike, eds., *Japan Design: The Four Seasons in Design* (San Francisco, 1984), p. 119.

21. Quoted in Steelcase Design Partnership, op. cit.

22. Perry King, quoted in John Thackara, "Lighting: Inspired by Dodgem Cars," *Design* 421 (January 1984): 38.

23. Quoted in "Botta on Botta's Chair," *Progressive Architecture* 64 (May 1983): 37.

24. Shiro Kuramata, Itsuko Hasegawa, and Minoru Ueda, "A Talk on Materials," *Axis* 23 (Spring 1987): 6–7.

25. Quoted in Suzanne Slesin, "2 Design Innovators, Forging a New Metal Age in Furniture," *New York Times*, November 9, 1989, p. C10.

26. Maggie Malone with Ruth Marshall and Elizabeth Jones, "Barbarians at the Gates of Art," *Newsweek*, May 7, 1990, p. 66.

27. Reiko Sudo, "Junichi Arai: High-Tech Craftsman," in Yurakucho Asahi Gallery, Tokyo, *Hand and Technology: Textile by Junichi Arai '92* (March 7–25, 1992), n.p.

28. Quoted in the Montreal Museum of Decorative Arts, *Frank Gehry: New Bentwood Furniture Designs* (1992), pp. 42–43.

29. Kiyoshi Sakashita, "Toward Designing for the 21st Century," *Design Quarterly Japan* 3 (1988): 8.

DESIGNER BIOGRAPHIES

1. Ron Arad, "The City and Some Thing," in Alexander von Vegesack, ed., *Sticks & Stones, One Offs & Short Runs: Ron Arad, 1980–1990* (Weil am Rhein, Germany, 1990), p. 15.

2. Reiko Sudo, "Junichi-Arai: High-Tech Craftsman," in Yurakucho Asahi Gallery, Tokyo, *Hand and Technology: Textile by Junichi Arai '92* (March 7–25, 1992), n.p.

3. *King of Fashion: The Autobiography of Paul Poiret* (Philadelphia, 1931), pp. 161–62.

4. Julius Meier-Graefe, "Peter Behrens," *Dekorative Kunst* 5 (1900): 3.

5. Max Bill, *Form* (Basel, 1952), p. 11.

6. Max Bill, "The Bauhaus Idea: From Weimar to Ulm," in *The Architect's Year Book*, vol. 5 (London, 1953): p. 31.

7. Quoted in Augusto Morello and Anna Castelli Ferrieri, *Plastic and Design* (Milan, 1988), p. 242.

8. Achille Castiglioni, "Lighting" [interview with Raffaella Crespi], in Kathryn B. Hiesinger and George H. Marcus, eds., op. cit., p. 142.

9. *Compasso d'Oro: Italian Design* (Milan, 1989), p. 35.

10. *L'Art Vivant* (April 1, 1925), quoted in Musée de l'Impression sur Etoffes, Mulhouse, France, *Sonia Delaunay: Etoffes imprimées des années folles* (1930), n.p.

11. Léon Riotor, *Paul Follot* (Paris, 1923), p. 50.

12. Kaj Franck, "Anonymity," *Craft Horizons* 27 (March 1967): 35.

13. Paul T. Frankl, *New Dimensions: The Decorative Arts of Today* (New York, 1928), p. 57.

14. Hartmut Esslinger, quoted in Stuart I. Frolick, "The World According to Esslinger," *Graphis* 43 (March–April 1987): 41.

15. Edmond Bazire, "Huitième exposition de l'Union Centrale des Arts Décoratifs," *Revue des Arts Décoratifs* 5 (January 1885): 193.

16. Roger Marx, "Les arts à l'Exposition Universelle de 1900. La Décoration et les industries d'art," *Gazette des Beaux-Arts* 24 (November 1900): 397–421, (December 1900): 563–76; 25 (January 1901): 536–83, (February 1901): pp. 136–68.

17. Antoní Gaudí, notebook, August 10, 1878, Museo Municipal, Reus, quoted in Cesar Martinell y Brunet, *Gaudí: su vida, su teoria, su obra* (Barcelona, 1967), p. 474.

18. Roger Fry, *Duncan Grant* (London 1923), quoted in Anthony d'Offay Gallery, London, *The Omega Workshops: Alliance and Enmity in English Art, 1911–1920* (January 18–March 6, 1984), no. 129.

19. Piet Hein, "Of Order and Disorder: Science and Art and the Solving of Problems," *Architectural Forum* 127 (December 1967): 65.

20. *The Pritzker Architecture Prize, 1985, Presented to Hans Hollein* (n.p., c. 1985), n.p.

21. László Moholy-Nagy, "Metal Workshop: From Wine Jugs to Lighting Fixtures," in Herbert Bayer, Walter

Gropius, and Ise Gropius, eds., *Bauhaus, 1919–1928* (New York, 1938), p. 136.

22. Mararu Katsumi, "Pro et Contra," in *The Graphic Design of Yusaku Kamekura* (New York, 1973), pp. 11–12.

23. Frederick Kiesler, *Contemporary Art Applied to the Store and Its Display* (New York, 1930), n.p.

24. "Painter in Yarns," *House and Garden* 79 (April 1941): 67.

25. Raymond Loewy, *Never Leave Well Enough Alone* (New York, 1951), p. 84.

26. Raymond Loewy, *Industrial Design* (Woodstock, N.Y., 1979), p. 13.

27. Walter Gropius, "László Moholy-Nagy (1895–1946)," in Krisztina Passuth, *Moholy-Nagy* (New York, 1985), p. 432.

28. Oliver Mourgue, "Design, Invention, and Fantasy," in Kathryn B. Hiesinger and George H. Marcus, eds., op. cit., pp. 24, 26.

29. Josef Müller-Brockmann, *Grid Systems in Graphic Design* (Niederteufen, Switzerland, 1981), p. 7.

30. Bruno Munari, *Design as Art* (Baltimore, 1971), p. 13.

31. Sam Hunter, *Isamu Noguchi* (New York, 1978), p. 26.

32. "The JCPenney Design System" (1973), p. 9.

33. Gaetano Pesce, quoted in Steelcase Design Partnership, New York, "Gaetano Pesce: Modern Times Again" (November 10–December 8, 1988), exhibition brochure, n.p.

34. Quoted in *Jean Puiforcat, orfèvre sculpteur* (Paris, 1951), p. 22.

35. Dieter Rams, "And That's How Simple It Is to Be a Good Designer," *Designer* (September 1978): 12–13.

36. *1º Colección de muebles especiales de Carlos Riart* (Barcelona, n.d.), pp. 48–49.

37. Leopold Gmelin, "Das Kunsthandwerk im Münchner Glaspalast," *Kunst und Handwerk* 50 (1899–1900): 57.

38. Eero Saarinen, quoted in "Dining on a Stem," *Time*, May 13, 1957, p. 88.

39. Quoted in "The Business of Invention," *Industrial Design* 7 (November 1960): 73.

40. G.J.W., "Zu den Arbeiten aus der Ausstellung 'Raumkunst'," *Kunst* 30 (1914): 329.

41. Quoted in Carl Sandburg, *Steichen: The Photographer* (New York, 1929), pp. 54–55.

42. Walter Dorwin Teague, "Industrial Art and Its Future," lecture, School of Architecture and Allied Arts, New York University, November 18, 1936, p. 6.

43. Giuseppe Terragni, "La costruzione della Casa del Fascio di Como," *Quadrante* 35 (1936): 5, translated in Diane Yvonne Ghirardo, "Italian Architects and Fascist Politics: An Evaluation of the Rationalist's Role in Regime Building," *Journal of the Society of Architectural Historians* 39 (May 1980): 120.

44. Julius Meier-Graefe, "Floral-Linear," *Dekorative Kunst* 4 (1899): 169.

45. Robert Venturi, *Complexity and Contradiction in Architecture* (New York, 1966), p. 22.

46. Henry van de Velde, "Artistic Wall Papers," *Emulation* 10 (October 1893): 151.

47. "*L'Art Nouveau*: What It Is and What Is Thought of It. A Symposium," *Magazine of Art*, n.s., 2 (1904): 212.

48. Wolfgang Weingart, "My Typography Instruction at the Basle School of Design/Switzerland, 1968 to 1985," *Design Quarterly* 130 (1985), n.p.

49. Ibid.

50. "In the Cause of Architecture," 1908, reprinted in Frederick Gutheim, ed., *Frank Lloyd Wright on Architecture: Selected Writings, 1894–1940* (New York, 1941), p. 42.

51. Quoted by Charles Robert Ashbee, in Alan Crawford, "Ten Letters from Frank Lloyd Wright to Charles Robert Ashbee," *Architectural History* 131 (1970), p. 64.

INDEX

Page numbers in *italic* indicate illustrations.

PHOTOGRAPHY CREDITS

The photographers and the sources of photographic material other than those indicated in the captions are as follows (numerals refer to figures unless otherwise indicated):

Kristina Aczél, London: 153; Jay Ahrend: 398; Aleph, Como, Italy: 149; David Arky: 235; Dick Arling: 128; Armen/Copyright © The Newark Museum: 127; Art Resource, New York: 95; Aldo Ballo, Milan: 266, 274, 276, 306–307, 316 (courtesy, Artemide, New York), 317, 324–26, 354, 386, 391; Hans-Joachim Bartsch: 122, 118; Photo Basset: 76; V.d. Bichelaer: 82; Will Brown: 198, 224, 237, 277, 357; Lars Cardell, Malmö, Sweden: 268; Doug Carr: 26; Mario Carrieri, Milan: 304; Christie's, New York: 29, 115; Arthur Coleman Photography: 172; Gary Cumberland/ Southend Museum Service: 196; Mark Darley: 173; Karl F. Deckart: 394; Studio Diametro: 384; Alastair Duncan Ltd.: 14, 129; Copyright © George Ermil: 207; Foto Forum, Corning, New York: 64, 179; Frogdesign, Inc.: 383; Barbara Frommann: 11; Mitsumasa Fujitsuka: 392; Joachim Gaitzsch, Munich: 229; Galerie Metropole,

Inc.: 36; Paul Gatt, London: 77; Glasgow Museums and Art Galleries: 65; Sophie Gnamm, Munich: 51, 97, 133, 136, 138, 144, 147, 178, 253; Richard P. Goodbody, Inc.: 28 (courtesy, Kurland/Zabar Gallery, New York), 114, 192, 245; José Gutierrez: 164; Robert Hashimoto/Copyright © The Art Institute of Chicago: 89, 120, 190, 220; Heal Fabrics, London: 323; Herman Miller, Inc., Zeeland, Michigan: 161, 256, 288; Aimo Hyvärinen: 233; Jason McCoy Gallery: 176; Hermann Kiessling: 94; Howard Kingswort: 393; Stefanie Knapp: 146; Studio Kollar: 254; Schecter Lee, New York: 217; Gunter Lepkowski: 91, 96; Serge Libszesewski, Milan: 290, 336; Masera, Milan: 308; Wit McKay, New York: 197; Sal Merlo: 284; Eric Mitchell/ Philadelphia Museum of Art: 123, 202, 203, 298, 299; Copyright © The Museum of Modern Art, New York: 1, 8–9, 72, page 79, 104, 117, 124–25, 141, 158, 166, 174–75, page 176 top, 183, 186, 193, 201, 204, 210–12, 214–15, pages 219–20, 240, 257, 264, 283, 294, 296 97, 301, 305, 311, 327, 330, 339, 381; Necchi S.p.A., Pavia, Italy: 238; New York Public Library: page 150, 153, 181, G. Dagli Orti,

Paris: 61; Simona Pesarini: 205; Philadelphia Museum of Art: 184, 340–41, 373; Otso Pietinen: 241, 272; Christian Radux: 103; Franco Maria Ricci, Milan: 78; Giles Rivest: 185; Rosenthal AG, Bayern, Germany: 260; Jean-Michel Routhier/Studio Lourmel, Paris: 74–75; Sylvia Samer/Cathers and Dembrosky Gallery, New York: 47; Theo Scherrer: 350; Atelier Schneider: 119; Yoshio Shiratori: 388; Copyright © Sotheby's, Inc., New York: 46, 68; Stendig International, Inc.: 289; Peter Strobel, Cologne: 102; Studio Image, Nancy, France: 39; Laurent Sully-Jaulmes: 83, 107, 112, 126; Arch. Luciano Svegliado: 281, 302; Taideteollisuumuseo, Helinski: 148; Emilio Temolada, Milan: 349; Tom Vack/Thirst Corinne Pfister, Milan: 375; Vitra Design Museum, Weil am Rhein, Germany: 52; Ole Wold-bye/Philadelphia Museum of Art: 20, 25, 35, 79, 137, 167, 251; Graydon Wood/Philadelphia Museum of Art: 80, 99–100, 111, 228, 231, 248, 265, 275, 285, 314, 320, 332, 360, 379; Robert Yarnall/Art Resource, New York: page 113.

ADDITIONAL COLLECTION CREDITS

Supplement to the information given in the collection credits (numerals refer to figures unless otherwise indicated):

Copyright © Peter Aaron/Esto, Mamaroneck, NY: page 280; Archivio Fotografico, Triennale, Milan: page 119; Art Institute of Chicago; Richard T. Crane, Jr., Endowment: 89; Art Institute of Chicago; gift of Angelo Testa and Alexander Demond Fund: 190; AT&T Archives, Warren, New Jersey: page 182 top; Baltimore Museum of Art; purchased by the museum's staff and board in memory of Roger B. Lewis, 1940–1983, architect and friend: 155; Bauhaus Archiv, Berlin: page 54, page 81 (photo by Lucia Moholy); The Bettmann Archive, New York: page 12, page 116; Bibliothèque Forney, Paris: page 49, page 50; Bildarchiv Foto Marburg, Marburg, Germany: page 16; Cátedra Gaudí, Barcelona: page 14; Chrysler Historical Foundation, Highland Park, Michigan: page 114; Cooper-Hewitt, National Museum of Design, Smithsonian Institution, New York; Gift of Henry

Dreyfuss: page 113; Corning Museum of Glass, Corning, New York; gift in part of Benedict Silverman in memory of Gerry L. Silverman: 40; Niels Diffrient: page 253; Francis Bacon Library, Claremont, California; Arensberg Archives: page 53; Dr. Heinz Fuchs, Mannheim: page 149; Grand Rapids Art Museum, Michigan; gift of Dr. and Mrs. John Halick: 129; L'Institut Français d'Architecture, Paris: page 15; Library of Congress, Washington, D.C.: page 176 bottom, page 250; Magnum Photos, Inc., New York: page 249, page 254; Alessandro Mendini, Milan: pages 277–78; Metropolitan Museum of Art, New York: page 115; Metropolitan Museum of Art, New York; gift of Jane and Arnold Adlin, Lawrence B. Kantor, and Paul F. Walter: 173; Musée des Arts Décoratifs, Montreal; gift of Geoffrey N. Bradfield: 185; Musée des Arts Décoratifs, Montreal; gift of Hans Zeisl, the Liliane and David M. Stewart Collection: 192; Musée des Arts Décoratifs, Montreal; gift of Nanette and Eric Brill: 195; Musée des Arts Décoratifs, Montreal; the Liliane and David M. Stewart

Collection: 217; Musée des Arts Décoratifs, Paris: page 78, page 80; Museum of Modern Art, New York: page 176 top; Museum of Modern Art, New York; Alfred H. Barr, Jr., Archive: page 79; Museum of Modern Art, New York; gift of Cassina S.p.A.: 330; Museum of Modern Art, New York; gift of Madame Hector Guimard: 8; Museum of Modern Art, New York; gift of the manufacturer, Rosenthal China Corporation, Thomas Division, Germany: 260; Newark Museum, New Jersey; Purchase: 127; Newberry Library, Chicago; Stone and Kimball Publishing Company Archives: 6; Philadelphia Museum of Art; the Henry P. McIlhenny Collection in memory of Frances P. McIlhenny: 111; Copyright © Marilyn Silverstone/Magnum Photos, Inc., New York: page 182 bottom; Barbara Stauffacher Solomon: page 216; University Art Museum, University of California, Santa Barbara; Architectural Drawings Collection: 142; Victoria & Albert Museum, London: page 148; Virginia Museum of Fine Arts, Richmond; gift of the Sydney and Frances Lewis Foundation: 31.